SOUTH FROM
THE LIMPOPO

'What we are witnessing in South Africa now are the problems that the whole world
is going to face increasingly in the twenty-first century. We are witnessing a rich
white enclave having to deal with the fact that it is actually part of a wide world and
it has to share with that world or die. We are at the forefront of a profound global
transition.'

Francis Wilson, Professor of Economics at the University of Cape Town

DERVLA MURPHY

SOUTH FROM THE LIMPOPO

Travels through South Africa

JOHN MURRAY
Albemarle Street, London

First published in 1997
by John Murray (Publishers) Ltd.,
50 Albemarle Street, London W1X 4BD

A catalogue record for this book is available from the British Library

ISBN 0-7195-5789-5

Typeset by Pure Tech India Ltd, Pondicherry

Printed and bound in Great Britain by The University Press, Cambridge

*For Rose, who did a lot to delay the completion of this book,
and for Rachel and Andrew who collaborated in her production*

Contents

Illustrations

Acknowledgements

Special thanks must go to Margaret Fogarty; without her practical help and unflagging encouragement I might never have finished this book. Her mother Daphne tolerated my erratic arrivals at and departures from their home with limitless patience. And her friend Jennifer Alt became my most valuable South African mentor.

On the Cape Peninsula, Ray and Wally in Retreat and Wendy Woodward and Chris Wildman in Observatory provided me with 'homes from home'. Jane and David Rosenthal would have done likewise but time ran out...

Elsewhere, numerous new friends of all colours offered generous hospitality and precious insights into the new South Africa. However, not everyone would want to be directly associated with this book and some names have been changed in the text.

On the last lap, John Murray VII, Hugh Lewin, Justin Cartwright and a Capetonian friend who wishes to remain anonymous gave shrewd editorial advice. And, as always, Diana Murray saw at a glance what was wrong with the first draft and inspired me – as only she can – to try harder.

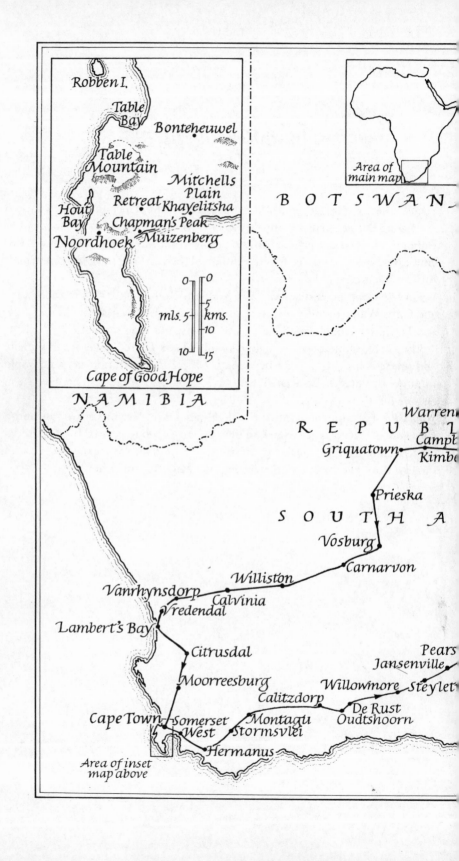

Robben I.

Table Bay

Bonteheuwel

Table Mountain

Mitchells Plain

Retreat   Khayelitsha

Hout Bay

Chapman's Peak

Noordhoek   Muizenberg

mls. 5   kms.

0   0
5
10
10   15

Cape of Good Hope

N A M I B I A

Area of main map

B O T S W A N A

Warren

R E P U B L I

Griquatown   Campb
Kimbe

Prieska

S O U T H A

Vosburg

Carnarvon

Williston

Vanrhynsdorp
Calvinia

Vredendal

Lambert's Bay

Citrusdal

Pears
Jansenville

Moorreesburg

Willowmore   Steylet

Calitzdorp

De Rust
Cape Town   Montagu   Oudtshoorn
Somerset   Stormsvlei
West
Hermanus

Area of inset map above

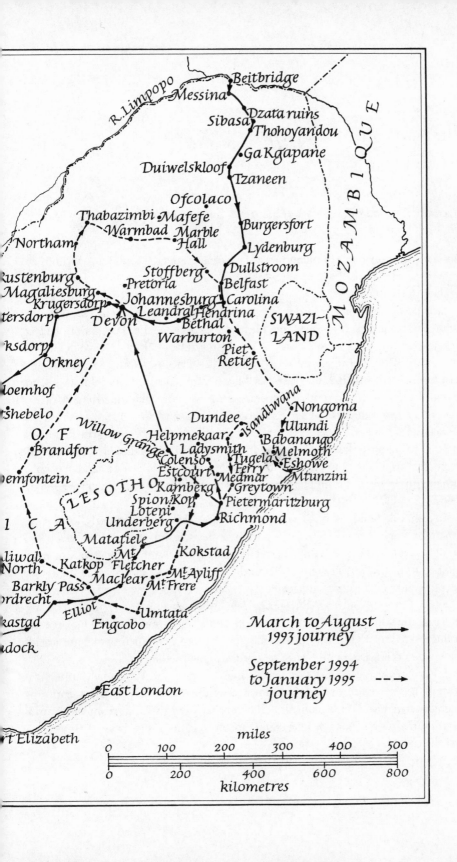

R. Limpopo
Beitbridge
Messina
Dzata ruins
Sibasa
Thohoyandou
Ga Kgapane
Duiwelskloof
Tzaneen
Ofcolaco
Thabazimbi Mafefe
Burgersfort
Warmbad Marble
Hall
Northam
Lydenburg
Dullstroom
Stoffberg
Rustenburg Pretoria Belfast
Magaliesburg Johannesburg Carolina
Krugersdorp Leandra Hendrina SWAZI-
...tersdorp Devon Bethal LAND
...ksdorp Warburton
Orkney Piet
Retief
...loemhof
...shebelo Isandlwana Nongoma
Dundee Ulundi
O F Willow Grange Helpmekaar Babanango
Brandfort Ladysmith Melmoth
Colenso Tugela Eshowe
...emfontein Estcourt Ferry Mtunzini
Kamberg Medmar Greytown
LESOTHO Spion Kop Pietermaritzburg
Loteni Richmond
Underberg
Matatiele
...liwal Mt
North Katkop Fletcher Kokstad
Barkly Pass Maclear Mt Ayliff
...rdrecht Mt Frere
...kastad Elliot Umtata
...dock Engcobo

East London

...t Elizabeth

March to August
1993 journey

September 1994
to January 1995
journey

miles
0   100   200   300   400   500

0   200   400   600   800
kilometres

MOZAMBIQUE

Author's Note

Definition of 'black', 'white', 'Coloured', 'Indian' and other groups as used in the text

In 1993 South Africa's population was guestimated to be 41 million, of whom 76 per cent were black, 13 per cent white, 8.5 per cent Coloured and 2.5 per cent Indian.

It is politically correct to describe as 'black' all South Africans who are not white. This usage is understandable, in reaction to the Population Registration Act and all that went with it, yet for the sake of clarity I have eschewed it. South Africa's Indian citizens are South Africans as the white citizens are South Africans. But they are not blacks. Nor are the Cape Coloureds, to whom I refer as 'Coloureds'. Their ancestry is no more than one-third African, the other components being Asian and European. The Griquas are also mixed, the result of Boer/San or Boer/Khoikhoi interbreeding in centuries past. The copper-skinned San (or Bushmen) and Khoikhoi (or Hottentots) were the original inhabitants of the southern regions of Africa, and the only inhabitants of the Cape and its hinterland when the first Dutch settlers arrived in 1652.

In general, South Africa's whites are either Afrikaners (formerly known as Boers) or English-speakers. Afrikaners are descended from the earliest European settlers: Dutch, French Huguenot, German. Most English-speakers are descended from the British who settled in the Cape Colony and Natal in the nineteenth century. However, this category by now includes Jews from Russia and Central Europe, southern Europeans who were encouraged to migrate – to increase the white population – during the 1950s, and some 150,000 Portuguese 'refugees' from Angola and Mozambique who were welcomed by the apartheid state when their degenerate 'empire' abruptly collapsed in 1974.

I have revived the obsolete term 'Boer' to describe Afrikaner farmers, a dwindling breed for many of whom I developed – much to my surprise – a great affection. The urbanized Afrikaners are very different from their rural cousins; the use of 'Boer' (which simply means 'farmer') is my way of emphasizing the difference.

Another difference in need of emphasizing is that between South Africa's so-called Communists and all other Communists. The apartheid regime, set up at the start of the Cold War, immediately jumped on the West's anti-Communist bandwagon. For the next forty-five years many opponents of apartheid, however impeccable their Christian/liberal/capitalist credentials, were defined as 'Communists' and treated as criminals.

Glossary

Acronyms are usually spelled out in full on first mention. All are listed in the Glossary, as are Afrikaans and other local words.

Foreword

By 1952 I had begun to collect books about South Africa and to realize that apartheid was not in fact a new anti-black weapon forged by the Afrikaners. Since the 1870s British observers – including Anthony Trollope, J. A. Froude, Lord Bryce, Joseph Chamberlain, Lord Milner – had been warning the Colonial Office about the danger of extending the franchise to 'natives'. In 1901 Lionel Curtis – fresh from New College, Oxford, one of Lord Milner's infamous 'kindergarten' of youthful colonial officers – wrote: 'It would be a blessed thing if the negro, like the Red Indian, tended to die out before us.' Two years later John Buchan, Lord Milner's Private Secretary, produced a blueprint for the country's future 'native policy' and noted that:

> Mentally the black man is as crude and naive as a child, with a child's curiosity and ingenuity...His instability of character and intellectual childishness make him politically far more impossible than even the lowest class of Europeans.

Lord Milner then appointed a Commission which recommended segregation policies that shocked his more civilized compatriots. When the South Africa Act was passed in 1909 Keir Hardie protested that MPs 'should not assent to the setting up of the doctrine that because of a man's misfortune in having been born with a coloured skin he is to be barred the possibility of ever rising to a position of trust.' But Lord Balfour argued, 'You cannot give them equal rights without threatening the whole fabric of civilization. The Red Indians are gradually dying out. The Australian Aborigines are even more clearly pre-destined to early extinction. But with the black races of Africa, for the first time we have the problem of races as vigorous in constitution, as capable of increasing in number, in contact with white civilization.' Not only Afrikaners feared the *swart gevaar*: 'the black peril'.

It is no coincidence that several of the designers of Grand Apartheid studied at German universities during the 1930s. Many English-speakers were at first appalled by the Afrikaners' creation of a totalitarian state, yet there is no escaping the fact that apartheid was supported, actively or passively, by the vast majority of South Africa's whites. It was also supported by a minority of

South Africa's blacks who, for personal gain, collaborated in the setting up of the 'independent homelands'.

By 1983 the cracks in the apartheid edifice were visible from Ireland. As an Irish citizen I could then have visited the country for sixty days without a visa, but so brief a visit would have been pointless. Optimistically I applied for a twelve-month work permit ostensibly 'to write a travel book'. After an eight-month delay Pretoria, rightly distrusting my motives, said no. Instead I went to Madagascar.

As the apartheid state disintegrated, amidst increasing, uncontrollable violence, many influential right-wingers – both at home and abroad – rallied round Chief Buthelezi, the Zulu Inkatha leader, still hoping the ANC might be held at bay. Ten months after Nelson Mandela's release, Laurens van der Post dismissed him as someone 'who has nothing more than tired rhetoric to offer' and praised Buthelezi as 'a man of vision, better prepared than any leader in South Africa to lead the way ahead'. Margaret Thatcher, too, drooled over the Inkatha leader and asserted that 'the day the ANC is elected South Africa will be in cloud-cuckoo-land'.

In 1991 the apartheid laws were rescinded. But while all-party negotiations continued spasmodically, a cabal of senior army and police officers – sure of President de Klerk's covert approval – were conspiring with Buthelezi to block the ANC's coming to power. Their ruthless 'Third Force' was responsible for thousands of deaths but could not prevent the inevitable.

By 1993 Afrikanerdom was in such a state of disarray that one could simply ignore its bureaucracy. I entered South africa as a 'tourist' and stayed for six months. During April and May 1994 I was back to witness the birth of the new South Africa. And in September 1994 I returned again to observe the infant's progress. These cycle tours were journeys with a difference. Usually I travel to get as far away as possible from motor cars, advertisement hoardings, fast-food outlets, supermarkets, electricity pylons, television, muzak and that pitiable breed of people afflicted by a bizarre new obsession (they call it 'surfing the Internet'). Plainly no one of my disposition would choose to pedal through South Africa for fun. Yet that country's pull was so powerful that I had felt it all my adult life. So I shouldn't have been so surprised to realize one day that I had come to love the place.

PROLOGUE

Return to Africa

At midnight, on my flight to Johannesburg, an alarming commotion woke us all. A black stowaway had been discovered, a sad mad young man whose history is anybody's guess. At dawn I saw him lying in a narrow space behind the last row of seats, his hands and feet heavily manacled, his expression terrified. When I glanced down at him he began to cry. He had wet himself: they wouldn't, he sobbed, let him go to the toilet. One could scarcely blame them for that; he looked seriously deranged and the midnight struggle had sounded strenuous. Nearby, an Afrikaner steward sat on guard, a tall hulky fellow, his thick sleek hair like a shiny brass helmet, his pale blue eyes close-set, his lips thin in a plump face that was easily rearranged. For me it wore a professional, steward's smile. When I emerged from the loo it wore a snarl of contempt as he addressed some remark, in Afrikaans, to his captive. I asked, 'What's the story?' Discomfited, the steward looked away – this stowaway might, after all, have been a hijacker... Then he muttered, 'Even in the air they make trouble!'

At Jan Smuts airport I changed planes for Lusaka. From there, on the morrow, a bus would take me to Karoi in northern Zimbabwe, where Lear (my dearly beloved bicycle) had been left with friends at the end of last year's ride from Nairobi.

As we took off the extrovert Afrikaner beside me introduced himself as Mr Du Plessis, sales director of a pharmaceutical company. He thoroughly approved of the recent political changes. 'Sure we dodged most sanctions easy enough – Malawi helped a lot. Only our expansion northwards was blocked. The Chinese, Japs, Taiwanese, Koreans – all those yella fellas, they had Africa all sewn up. But since '91 we're right in there, fighting hard.' Mr Du Plessis had no hang-ups about being governed by blacks in the nearish future. 'The ANC know which way to jump, they can smell where money comes from. And their Commie friends don't count any more.'

Gazing wistfully down at Mashonaland, Mr Du Plessis lamented having been born too late to kill an elephant. Hunting was his 'hobby', but now only Arabs and Americans can afford to shoot big game. He didn't seem to notice my failure to make sympathetic noises.

In June 1992 I had left a drought-stricken region, Lusaka's air harsh with dust and despair, starving villagers flocking to the city from hundreds of miles away, the vestigial grass like brown wire, brittle leaves rattling on the trees. Now, eight months later, I stepped out of the airport into warm light rain and a riot of fecundity – all around the brightness of new growth, a gleaming tender green. My impulse was to sing and dance in celebration but that might have alarmed Mr Du Plessis.

Walking to the main road, a pannier-bag in each hand, I passed herds of cattle still bony but now content, grazing avidly. When an archetypal African bus, palsied and hoarse, picked me up at the junction a youth made four inches available at the edge of his seat and asked where my vehicle had broken down. I don't think he believed my story. South Africa beckoned – 'Here are no good jobs' – but he feared capture on the border. 'Down there the police put you working on farms for no wages and the farmers whip you.'

Lusaka is a ramshackle mini-capital, swarming with small highly skilled pick-pockets and large daring muggers. I felt a glow of affection as its few obligatory flourishes of high-risery appeared on the horizon. At a residential centre for AIDS patients, where I stayed on previous visits, ten black South African public-health workers had arrived the day before 'to learn from the Zambian experience'. They were USAID-sponsored and led by a paunchy information co-ordinator from Colombus, Ohio. African countries, he asserted, need teams of Western psychotherapists to enable people to get a handle on all this AIDS trauma. He sounded like a skit on 'the Western helper in Africa'; his protégés made no comment but their body language was eloquent.

In Lusaka's bus terminus – sprawling, thronged at sunrise, the atmosphere cheerful – nothing indicated from where which bus left and the legends over the cabs were best ignored; a bus marked 'Blantyre' might be going to Mbeya. Most of the drivers sitting in empty buses didn't yet know their destinations but hoped soon to find out. Two kind youths noticed mama's problem. When the unmarked Harare bus at last appeared they promptly identified it and trustingly I climbed aboard.

The fare for the 180 miles to Karoi was £3, a the rate commensurate with the vehicle's condition. Only faint traces of cream paint remained on the grey metal of the interior. The red leatherette seats were in shreds. One door handle had long since been replaced by a rusty nail-and-chain contrivance. The other door had been welded to the body after the last crash – so explained our corpulent driver as he heaved himself across the engine to get to his seat. There was no roof-rack, though most passengers were setting off on trading expeditions to Karoi or Harare. They embarked in high spirits, exchanging long complicated greetings and cryptic jokes. Two baby-laden young women had a struggle to enter: their head-loads were a colossal round basket of tomatoes and a bulging sack of maize-cobs. They laughed uproariously at their own predicament, then at last were in, depositing their loads on the floor where other passengers had to surmount them, which they did uncomplainingly.

A green-and-white bus parked nearby looked much smarter than ours but when required to start its engine made resolutely uncooperative noises. At once a dozen men volunteered to push it, resembling a rugby scrum as they bent and shoved, and shoved, and shoved. They were still shoving when we rumbled away, no more than an hour late.

I felt content that morning – and curiously liberated. Without evading the grimness of life in much of modern Africa, one can recognize that this continent is not yet sick as our continent is sick. Most Africans remain plugged into reality. In contrast we have become disconnected from it, reduced to compulsively consuming units, taught to worship 'economic growth' – the ultimate unreality in a finite world.

By noon I was happily reunited with Lear, who had been polished, oiled and pumped in anticipation of my arrival.

It took me eighteen days to cover the 1,270 miles from Karoi to Beitbridge, via Raffingora, Mutorashanga, Mazowe, Harare, Chivhu, Gweru, Zvishavane and a few Communal Areas (ex-Reserves) deep in the bush. Because Zimbabwe's main-road traffic is quite heavy, by African standards, I chose dirt tracks – usually well maintained – wherever possible.

Towards the end of *The Ukimwi Road* I wrote: 'Having sniffed the air south of the Zambezi, I felt Zimbabwe to be not a continuation of Black Africa but – both historically and emotionally – the beginning of South Africa.' This is hardly surprising. Most of the original white settlers, the Rhodes-funded Pioneers, came from South Africa in 1890 and soon apartheid (known as 'parallel development') was flourishing in Southern Rhodesia. The Reserves were the equivalent of South Africa's 'homelands', infertile places of banishment for 'surplus people'. Southern Rhodesia was established not as a new colony ruled from London but as a commercial enterprise run by the British South Africa Company. When the Pioneers failed to find another gold-bearing Rand they turned to farming, with small-scale mining as a secondary interest. In 1897 an official British government report noted that slavery – delicately described as 'compulsory labour' – was widespread, as was the use of the sjambok to make that labour more productive. However, Rhodes' diamond-and-gold-based omnipotence tempted London to ignore his company's ill-treatment of the 'natives'. A century later the residue of that brutal tradition remains obvious enough to shock newcomers.

Most commercial farms are still white-owned though some blacks – whose sources of wealth do not bear scrutiny – have joined the ranks of the landed. A lucky minority of rural blacks own subsistence farms, the soil pale and poor, or have a share in a new and usually inefficiently run co-operative. Many of the landless are seasonal workers who reap tobacco for Z$175 a month, the minimum legal wage, equivalent to £16 at the 1993 rate of exchange. As in South Africa, those workers are allowed to cultivate small plots of their employer's land. In 1948 the Danziger Commission decided that 10 acres (not hectares) was enough for both the cultivating and grazing needs of a black family in Southern Rhodesia. Forty-five years later a tobacco farmer told me that 40 hectares (100 acres) of tobacco could keep a white family in modest comfort – yet farms of up to 80,000 hectares are common. Moreover, in addition to their spacious homes many whites have a holiday bungalow .on the Kariba dam, complete with speedboat. All this under a black government... Peering apprehensively into South Africa's future I wonder if, more than a decade after 'liberation', the needs of the majority will be similarly disregarded.

Zimbabwe, too, had been transformed by the ending of the drought. Everything was thriving: tobacco, maize, sorghum, cotton, sunflowers, pastureland. The clarity of the light, especially after a rain shower, exaggerated each colour: the redness of the soil, the greenness of the forests, the silveriness of the cliffs, the whiteness of high, complicated cloudscapes. Sometimes surreal granite-rock formations towered over the road where erosion had gone mad, creating gravity-defying constructions: piles of house-sized boulders on cliff-edges, looking as though a finger could topple them. Other crazily marvellous geological aberrations were visible in mountain form, thrusting up along distant horizons in a wild disarray of angularity.

Having ascended to Karoi by bus, I had forgotten Mashonaland's altitude: about 5,000 feet. From Zvishavane a spectacular descent, around and around and around precipitous forested mountains, took me into enervating heat. Here stretch many miles of unpeopled rough bush, unused though capable of sustaining cattle. This whole area is extra-securely fenced as the property of Union Carbide – an ominous name, posted on gateways under 'KEEP OUT!' warnings. Throughout Zimbabwe, I found cycling past so much fenced farmland disquieting. Those fences, essential on commercial farms, are profoundly – philosophically – unAfrican.

Next day I was down to the punishing lowveld, sweating towards the Limpopo on a road hideously yellow-carpeted with squashed locusts. The unsquashed compounded the repulsiveness of the scene by eating their dead comrades. All around loomed baobabs, those most improbable of trees, seeming sculptures rather than growths. By sharing their vitality with humans and animals, baobabs – immensely complex organisms – have saved countless lives. In regions otherwise waterless the fibrous wood secretes water, some fruit trees storing up to 5,000 litres. Wherever it grows the baobab's fruit is the locals' main source of vitamin C and women believe it increases their fertility, which may well be true.

I rested under one awesome giant, leaning reverently against a trunk perhaps three or four thousand years old.

My last evening in Zimbabwe was spent in Peter's Motel on the border, beer-drinking with truckers from Malawi, Zambia, Zimbabwe, South Africa, Lesotho, Botswana, Namibia, Swaziland. No one was even remotely interested in the politics of the new South Africa; they had other things on their mind, like feeding their wives and families by fair means or foul. Helpful hints were exchanged about which sort of bribe was most acceptable to which customs officer; everyone seemed to be smuggling something to or from somewhere. An alarming number did not retire alone. One can only hope they used the free condoms found on their bedside tables.

Part I

Pre-elections

March to August 1993

1

In at the Deep End

Messina – Venda – GaKagapane

It was never the bad guys who got into trouble in the townships. It was almost always one of the tiny, tiny minority of whites who were willing to break the unwritten rules that governed everyone else.
Rian Malan, My Traitor's Heart *(1990)*

Messina, Transvaal, 9 March 1993

The wide no man's land between Zimbabwe and South Africa still looks rather sinister. During the 1980s Comrade Mugabe authorized Umkhontu we Sizwe (the ANC's armed wing, MK for short) to open an infiltration route through Zimbabwe from their training camps in Angola. The South African Defence Force (SADF) then devised an 'electrified parapet' – 20,000-volt wires on a high wall – reinforced by dense rolls of razor wire (a South African invention) and a 'living barricade' of aggressive-looking sisal. Now the wires are rusted and sagging but the sisal flourishes, its serrated swords forming a threatening frieze above the road.

From the rail-cum-road Bridge of Beit – a starkly utilitarian construction – I gazed down at the sluggish Limpopo, dully brown, not yet catching the rays of the newly risen sun. At this hour there was no traffic and under a curiously colourless sky all was hushed. For miles on either side of the river lay flat uninhabited veld, green-dotted with thornbushes. To the north-east rose Zimbabwe's Mateke Hills, smooth-crested and powder blue. In the Messina direction towered a high tangle of mine machinery; copper has been mined hereabouts from time immemorial. And to the south (it suddenly seemed improbable, after so many years of waiting) – to the south stretched all of South Africa, a country in transition, Land of Hope and Tension.

The border-post suggests no diminution of white supremacy; it is guarded by well-armed expressionless young Afrikaners in crisp uniforms. Here the AIDS-education posters, so conspicuous on the walls of every border-post between Kenya and Zimbabwe, are replaced by anti-terrorist posters illustrating life-size limpet mines and hand grenades and other such lethal gadgets. A fading legend on a weather-beaten board says WELCOME TO SOUTH AFRICA, a sentiment not

\oed in the voices or eyes of the immigration and customs officers. When a
visa form was thrust towards me I disingenuously declared: 'Purpose of Visit –
TOURISM; Duration of Stay – TWO MONTHS; Profession – RETIRED TEACHER.'
It seemed advisable, even in 1993, not to admit to being a writer on a six-
month visit.

The customs officers ignored Lear's two small dusty pannier-bags, not in a
genial way but contemptuously. My first South African smile came from the
black policeman who opened the gate releasing me on to the highway.

Two Stuttaford Removals pantechnicons were parked nearby – a sign of the
times. In the early 1980s thousands of 'Rhodies' who couldn't take black rule
migrated south. Now, to the sardonic amusement of their friends who stayed
put, many are attempting to re-migrate north. For those who became South
African citizens this is not possible; a fair enough ruling, though they don't think
so. But any who retained Zimbabwean citizenship are welcome back.

The ten miles to Messina, through dreary lowveld, are memorable only for
their litter-strewn verges. Broken beer bottles, plastic milk bottles, fast-food
containers, paper handkerchiefs, disposable nappies, cooldrinks tins, sheets of
newspaper, cigarette packets and plastic bags by the hundred – all proof that
South Africa is a *developed* country... On either side high steel-mesh fences
indicate that this is still military territory. At 8 a.m. it was already too hot.

When Messina's black township appeared on a wide hillside invisible from
the whites' dorp, I turned left and pedalled slowly upwards on a rough track.
Soon I was surrounded by hundreds of little tin-roofed homes in tiny plots –
most gardens neat and flowery, a few slummy, each with an outside latrine.
Many dwellings have brightly painted woodwork and curtained windows,
some have lean-to shacks at the back. Electricity has recently been laid on
for the minority who can afford it. Small supermarkets stock a range of manu-
factured goods and processed foods unseen (outside of the capitals) between
Nairobi and Karoi. I counted seven churches, some hut-sized; South Africa
has approximately 3,500 indigenous Churches, independent of the imported
variety, their memberships varying from hundreds to millions. On the township's
southern edge, upwardly mobile blacks occupy new two-storeyed brick houses
with garages attached. By the standard of black Africa, all this looks like
affluence.

Only one resident, an elderly woman, returned my greeting. The others, of all
ages and both sexes, looked startled, suspicious, occasionally hostile. Mentally I
was prepared for this. Why should – how could – any South African black see
me, inexplicably cycling through their township, as anything other than a
morbidly curious outsider? Yet emotionally the communal rejection hurt, provoking an absurd twinge of self-pity. Why should I be made to feel, within an
hour of crossing the border, personally victimized by apartheid? This journey is

not going to be easy. I can't carry a placard saying I AM NOT A RACIST. As a white, I must accept being identified with the oppressors.

Messina, I had been warned, is a typical Transvaal dorp, its flavour more American than European. My first meal confirmed this: a soggy hamburger and a polystyrene mug of weak tea, ingested under a baobab tree outside a café in the company of a friendly young Venda woman. A few years ago she and I could not have shared a table – or a room. There are no tables, now, inside the café. There used to be but the Afrikaner owner cannot accept a mixed clientele on his premises. These sour little evasions of the new reality, futile in the long term, must (I assumed) irritate blacks. But when I said as much my companion, astonishingly, reproved me. 'Don't blame them,' she said. 'They've just got a bad shock. Leaders can't change people quickly. Give them time.'

I had bought two issues of *The Citizen*, the Afrikaners' English-language newspaper; as a pro-apartheid propaganda weapon, it was originally funded by re-routed tax-payers' money. The 8 March headlines read: THREE HELD FOR SECOND NATAL MASSACRE; RADIOLOGIST KNIFED TO DEATH; THREE ROBBERS SHOT DEAD IN STORE DRAMA. A large colour photograph showed the bullet-riddled naked torso of one robber lying on the pavement. The 9 March headlines read: FOUR DEAD IN NEW NATAL AMBUSH; POLICEMAN ACCUSED OF KILLING COLLEAGUE; DEATH THREAT TO MINISTER OF EDUCATION AND CULTURE. My companion glanced down at the papers, then turned away, her face puckered with distaste. 'We are sick of violence!' she said. 'Madiba [Nelson Mandela] is right, we must *talk* instead of killing.'

I spent the hottest hours writing in Messina's cheapest hotel (£11 for a cramped but air-conditioned room) and then went walkabout – an uninspiring experience. This dorp has a few wide, straight, level streets, several enormous car showrooms, two petrol stations of multinational garishness, three busy banks, a Spar supermarket, a small public library stocking only Afrikaans volumes, a carefully tended public park complete with Voortrekker monument, a few well-kept featureless churches catering for obscure denominations, three sterile ice-cream-parlours-cum-cafés, a police station, another hotel, a small hospital (for whites) and malodorous Wimpy and Kentucky Fried Chicken takeaways. Black hawkers sell oranges, and such European vegetables as cauliflowers and carrots, and buckets of sun-dried dark-grey caterpillars called mopane worms – a nutritious delicacy which I forbore to sample. There is no restaurant or pub; beer is available only from the endearingly named Drankwinkels (off-licences) or in the hotel bars. Each hotel runs a Drankwinkel and has two bars – one an annexe entered from the street, designed to exclude black customers from the hotel proper.

Messina's white natives are not chatty (little English is spoken in the northern Transvaal) and only visual observations were possible. I noted the Afrikaner males' aggressive body-language: how they open or shut vehicle doors, grab goods from a supermarket shelf, fling money on to a counter, silently kick a tyre that needs inflating instead of verbally requesting that service, cuff a dog who is to wait in a bakkie (pick-up truck) instead of using a word of command. The females' body-language is, in its way, equally aggressive – defensive-aggressive, tense, eyes swivelling suspiciously, mouths compressed and down-turned, both hands tightly holding shoulder bags, carriage mincing yet arrogant. Men of all ages wear paramilitary shirts, sharply creased khaki shorts and knee-socks. Most carry handguns openly, thrust into their belts or in under-arm holsters. The older males tend to be pot-bellied; their sons are lean and tanned. Wives are permed, laboriously made-up, fussily dressed; teenaged daughters are lithe and tanned, wearing shorts and sweatshirts. Conformity prevails.

The hardline northern Transvaalers are descended from those Voortrekkers who trekked until they could trek no further. Brave folk they were, ready to take on any number of kaffirs and lions to gain territory where they could be free of all control, whether from Pretoria, Cape Town or London. But by now that bravery and obstinate independence has curdled into a bitter resolve to resist change, to be faithful to the obsolete vision that drove their ancestors north.

By sunset I was sitting with a Long Tom (a mega-tin of Castle beer) under a striped umbrella on the hotel's concrete forecourt. There Dave joined me, full of friendly curiosity – a young fertilizer salesman from Jo'burg, of Welsh–Irish descent, with long wavy fair hair and the uncontrolled effervescence of a large puppy. Proudly he informed me that while with the army in Namibia he began to see blacks as human beings, having been brought up to see them otherwise. Now he lives with Mousie, an Indian woman – 'Very beautiful!' – and so his parents have rejected him. 'Maybe you think there's lots of young whites like me but you're wrong. Mostly my age hate blacks even more than the older people, they're so scared to lose jobs. I don't care. I'm not political. I'm just glad there's no more laws to stop me living with my Mousie and playing in my reggae band in Alex. [Alexandra is one of Jo'burg's biggest townships, soon to be merged with the nearby white suburb of Sandton – a rich rich suburb.] When you come to Jo'burg get in touch and I'll take you into Alex. With my friends there's no hassle, it's all music and dagga. Seeing TV you'd think all township kids are gangsters, but most only want to enjoy themselves.'

Here Dave has been making new black friends and at dusk they appeared, two cheerful young men who work in the supermarket. They thought me quite mad, an old woman planning to *cycle* around South Africa!

'But you'll be safe,' Abe assured me. 'Even APLA [Azanian People's Liberation Army] wouldn't attack a mama on a bike!'

Jo agreed. 'Whites think they're safest driving around locked in a vehicle but they're wrong. That can get people jealous and angry. Most blacks can't buy a car.'

Dave was keen to visit the township's beer hall so we all squeezed into the front of his little van – sacks of fertilizer packed the back – with Abe (small and slight) sitting on my lap. We drove through the copper-miners' hostel compound because Dave decided I should see the men's wretched living conditions. But as we left the van to visit one of the small shacks a police car passed, very slowly, whereupon Joe muttered something to Abe and there was a change of plan. Strolling across the rutted track, we entered a small comfortably furnished bar, empty but for three girls (their profession rather obvious) sitting around a low table eating a wholesome supper of pap, stewed beef and cabbage. They giggled incredulously when Dave explained me.

Here Joe and Abe seemed uneasy. 'Let's go,' said Joe. 'It's Tuesday, the miners have no money left for drink, we'll meet no one.'

'They get R840 [£168] a month,' said Abe. 'That's more than us, we get R650. But I wouldn't be a miner, I wouldn't want all the dangers. And they send most rands home, they only drink weekends. If they didn't send money home their families would die.'

In the township a few very high, very powerful 'security lamps' glared out of the sky – substitutes for street lighting. The huge beer hall has an earthen floor and bare breeze-block walls; dim naked bulbs hang from the disintegrating chipboard ceiling and cheap cigarettes make the air fetid. Scores of young men, standing around in noisy groups, momentarily fell silent as the two whites walked between them. The only seats, in a corner near the bar, were three broken-down sofas. My delight on seeing home-brewed sorghum-beer was genuine, not an affectation to flatter the locals. Good home-brew – and this was excellent – is more palatable than any commercial brew.

While Dave talked to the unresponsive barman Joe fetched my beer (its source lay outside) and the five well-dressed men sitting on the sofas welcomed me courteously. Mr Malchode was elderly, with a neat greying goatee beard. The others were fortyish and all spoke fluent English.

Soon I was regretting Dave's presence. With the fervour of the converted, he set about proving his 'identification' with militant blacks by using the clenched-fist punch instead of the triple handshake and demonstrating how well he can toyi-toyi. Plainly Abe and Joe found all this embarrassing – or maybe more than embarrassing. The motives of unknown white males who behave thus in beer halls are likely to be suspect. However, the seated men listened politely while Dave asserted that only a socialist Azania can solve South Africa's problems. His patronizing tone, his emphatic gestures, his whole demeanour betokened the *baas*. Namibia may have brought him to recognize blacks as human beings; it certainly didn't bring him to recognize them as equals. Inwardly I gave thanks that the local Young Lions were distanced from our corner.

Abe, by now visibly agitated, suggested a *braaivleis*. He, Joe and Dave would go out to get it going, leaving me to finish my beer. Enthusiastically Dave jumped from his bar stool – and a large revolver thudded to the floor. Tactfully, everyone pretended not to notice as he swiftly retrieved it. But anger erupted when he had left.

'If he thinks blacks are his best friends, why come armed? You trust friends. What's he afraid of?'

'He's a fool,' deduced Mr Malchode. 'People who carry guns in beer halls get murdered for them.'

A third man addressed me. 'Whites can get gun licences, we can't. They have six spaces on their IDs for gun licences. Guns were always important for them. They could take our land because they had guns against our assegais.'

'And now again they're very important,' said Mr Malchode. 'We're taking over, in politics, but still they're the ones with the guns. Maybe that helps them feel they can hold out and stay in control...'

There was a silence and they all looked at me.

'Do you carry a gun?' asked Mr Malchode.

'No, in my country not even the police carry guns.'

Mr Malchode moved then to sit beside me. Quietly he said, 'I don't mean to insult, but for your own sake you should know as a white you're intruding here. This is *our* place. It's not a zoo for tourists to see how "natives" live. Even now we can't drink in a Messina hotel bar – the prices are trebled to keep us out. But you take it for granted you can come and drink here – you're white, so you can drink wherever you choose. Do you know enough about South Africa to understand what I say?'

Impulsively I took Mr Malchode's hand and thanked him; on my first evening in South Africa he had taught me a lesson I needed to learn. And he had done so with a grace and dignity that left my own dignity unimpaired. I regretted Abe's reappearing just then, beckoning me out to the braai; surely there was more to be learned from Mr Malchode.

In darkness Abe and I stumbled along a rough, urine-scented track, then saw a rosy glow where the others stood tending our steaks under a sheet of corrugated iron propped up by bluegum trunks. This public grill was for the use of those who brought their own fuel, meat and flavourings. The bottom third of a tar-barrel, balanced on a wooden trestle, held the charcoal over which our meat sizzled on strands of barbed wire. There was nowhere to sit; we stood around gnawing at long thin strips of gristly steak while Joe and Abe intently discussed something in their own Venda language. They sounded rather worried, I thought. And then they fell silent, as we heard voices and footsteps approaching.

An improbable figure loomed out of the darkness, at least six-foot-six and not sober. Several smaller figures tagged along behind. With nervous effusiveness our escorts greeted the giant by name – Louis. He ignored them and advanced on Dave.

'Hey man, you come from where?'

Tiny Abe stepped forward and stood on tiptoe to whisper something to Louis, who immediately swung around and stared at me.

'Hey mama, you know this guy?'

I hesitated. What was the score? I could think only of my own skin: would it be safer to know or not to know Dave? Being unable to see anyone's expression – only their relative sizes – didn't help. Finally I gambled on claiming Dave as an old friend.

Louis grunted and hiccuped. Then: 'OK mama, you shift your old friend outta here and keep him out – see?' Moving to tower over me he added, 'Keep yourself out too, OK whitey?' He turned, swaying slightly, and led his silent followers away.

'Let's go,' said Abe, which seemed a blinding glimpse of the obvious. Clutching our fragments of steak we hastened back to the van. When safely aboard, Dave plaintively demanded, 'What went wrong?' Abe and Joe said nothing. Dave repeated, 'Tell me, what went wrong?'

I said, 'You did.'

Dave's hurt bewilderment was genuine. 'How d'you mean? I *love* these people! I wasn't looking for trouble, I've never had hassle in Alex!'

Wearily I lapsed into triteness. 'So now you know the northern Transvaal isn't Alex.'

Today I have *felt* apartheid, an experience quite unlike reading about it. For more than a decade its official enforcement has been gradually easing and by now most of the laws have been repealed. Yet to me, as a newly arrived white, those reforms seem irrelevant. Which is, of course, ridiculous.

Near Dzata, Venda, 10 March

The 'independent' homeland of Venda, population slightly over half a million, lies east of Messina close to the Zimbabwean border and the Kruger National Park. It is notorious for the widespread practice of witchcraft, sometimes involving *muti*-murders, and for smouldering animosity (occasionally flaring into violence and serious looting) between the Venda people and Indian traders. Since the late 1970s it has been run by a corrupt puppet government, Pretoria-funded as were all the 'Bantustans'. Soon these ten homelands, 'independent' and otherwise, will be reabsorbed into the new South Africa. Naturally this has exacerbated the 'maladministration of funds' as officials compete for the biggest slice of the last annual cake to be sent, gift-wrapped, from Pretoria.

Beyond Messina a narrow road crosses a series of scrubby ridges, the earth drought-cracked. Here baobabs abound, each numbered and preserved. The early traffic consisted of two bakkies. In one a Dobermann sat beside his master while a 'boy' rode in the back, sitting on the bare metal floor. This distribution of passengers is also common in Zimbabwe.

On the final ridge-top one is suddenly facing a misshapen isolated mountain, all lop-sided and deeply fissured, with bulbous boulders growing from its flanks and slim spears of granite pointing skywards from its crest. At the base of this eccentricity winds the little Njelele river, its course marked by irrigated miles of green maize fields.

Our long descent ended at a T-junction; the left turn leads to the 'border', from where a rough dirt track wriggles through a knot of mountains to Venda's 'capital',. Thohoyandou. All these tiresome inverted commas are a matter of principle; the homelands never had internationally recognized borders, capitals or governments.

Near the hamlet of Tshipise, on the 'border', a yellow South African Police (SAP) van overtook me and stopped in the middle of the road. Two thin-lipped Afrikaners emerged and stood there stiffly, watching my approach and not liking what they saw. Neither did I like what I saw: a pair of truculent toughies with burgeoning beer-bellies and a superfluity of weapons.

They signalled me to halt and one asked, without preamble, 'Where are you going?'

'Into Venda.'

'No, not this way! You go back on the main road to the sign for Thohoyandou.'

I hesitated, longing to challenge them – 'Isn't Venda an independent country? What right have you to stop my entering it where I choose?' But prudence prevailed. Repressing my annoyance I obeyed orders.

The next thirty-five miles were pleasantly varied: level cultivated fields, eroded orange-red mountains, ridges scattered with giant cycads, their leaves up to six feet long – and then a surprising remnant of dense subtropical forest. I paused to examine several farm burial plots, sometimes no more than 200 yards from an isolated Boer homestead, their dates giving glimpses of family history. Many farms are now half-abandoned, the houses closed up, the land managed by a black supervisor. During the 1970s more than 10,000 northern Transvaal farmers moved to the cities, leaving 45 per cent of homes in the Messina region unoccupied. The government then invested R32 million in a bid to repopulate the area; farmers were given low-interest loans, subsidized security systems and guarantees of increased military protection. But the MK frustrated this scheme.

By 1985 they were landmining the rural roads, their infiltration helped by sympathetic Vendas, 70,000 of whom live across the Limpopo in Zimbabwe.

The new main road from the 'border' to Thohoyandou is wide and velvet-surfaced. Along it raced the shining motor cars of plump affluent blacks – the apartheid collaborators. On either side rose humpy, greyish, dusty mountains covered with dwellings – a few solid bungalows, some small but sturdy shacks, very many frail tin-and-scrap-wood hovels. People swarmed; at any given moment there were hundreds of children in view, mostly ill-nourished, ill-dressed and either dispirited or, in reaction to me, vocally derisive.

Within moments of entering Venda one sees proclaimed on the gable-end of a small bus-shelter: ONE SETTLER ONE BULLET! YOU DON'T NEGOTIATE FOR FREEDOM, YOU FIGHT FOR IT! PAC (Pan-Africanist Congress). An impressive display of literacy: myself, I have to think twice before spelling 'negotiate'. The PAC's message is not unfamiliar; similar inscriptions greet one on crossing the border into Northern Ireland near Crossmaglen (INFORMERS WILL BE SHOT! – and they are shot). Of course no one could mistake me for a settler – surely they couldn't? Or is 'settler', in PAC usage, a blanket term covering all whites? Every few miles these slogans appear on blank walls. Just now I have been told that the PAC – not generally popular – is quite strongly supported in Venda by angry youths who despise the ANC for having put their MK soldiers on the leash.

I sought advice about lodgings in a large general-store-cum-Drankwinkel standing back from the road beyond a strip of rocky litter-strewn wasteland. This was a startling establishment, more like a high-security jail than a rural shop. Iron grilles from floor to ceiling separated the customers' and sellers' areas with only a few small openings, perhaps eighteen-inches square, to allow the money-for-goods exchange. In Venda the monthly per capita income is R60 (£12) and this evening I was told, 'We've such extreme poverty, and so much corruption in the police, our merchants are all the time under siege. It's amazing we don't have even more crime, maybe some of our kids haven't enough energy to steal!'

The only available accommodation was to be found in a nearby 'tourist complex'. 'It is full of comforts for rich foreigners,' said the squat sardonic woman who sold me a Castle beer. Gloomily I drank it on the wide stoep; I hadn't come to Venda for 'comforts'. Below the stoep, women vendors were selling small hard green oranges, packets of crisps, stale white bread rolls in cellophane and bottles of dreadfully dyed fizzy drinks. When I tried to talk to them they turned away, sniggering. Then four ragged, unfed-looking youths gathered around me, whispering about diamonds. (*Diamonds*, in *Venda*?) Hastily I finished my beer and pedalled on.

Here the landscape became less arid and at dusk the tourist-complex lights could be seen twinkling far off the road on the upper slopes of a wooded ridge.

Unsurprisingly I am the only tourist around and no meals are being served in the spacious restaurant, open on three sides to the cool evening breeze, with simple wooden trestle-tables. Had I booked ahead, the manager remarked reprovingly, a delicious four-course dinner would have been prepared. This I can believe. In my thatched whitewashed rondavel hut the bed linen is immaculate, the plumbing efficient, the armchairs luxurious, the carpet soft. It lacks only the most important of all comforts, a bedside lamp.

My one fellow-guest, Gerald Moremi, was thrilled to meet an Irishwoman. 'It was an Irish priest sponsored me and kept me out of politics after Soweto. I was 12, wanting to be political, but he sent me to school. He was right. "Liberation before Education" – that's crazy! What do you do with liberation if you're illiterate?'

Gerald, a copper-miner's son, had been to an 'open' private day-school in Jo'burg, while living with an uncle in Soweto. These Catholic schools – an innovation started in January 1976, a few months before the Soweto Uprising – were a 'liberal' gesture on the part of a Church until then more submissive than most to Pretoria. In 1989 Gerald graduated from Wits University and his ten years of integrated education convinced him that in the new South Africa schools should be kept separate for at least a generation.

'At first mixed schools won't help poor blacks – that's most of us. We want *equal* education, same budget, same facilities, same teacher training. But separate so our kids aren't put off studying by white intimidation. A lot of our kids show up much brighter than white kids, especially the Afrikaners. They're all cousins – look at their few family names – and that makes them stupid. Then when blacks do well in exams they can't take being beaten by kaffirs and turn aggressive. It's happening already in some mixed schools.'

Gerald is an educational publisher's agent, a job much coveted in the home-lands where millions are spent on school books that somehow never reach the schools. But soon, he is confident, things will change. 'In our new South Africa, when the ANC gives fair shares to everyone, we can all live honestly. Now we can't. Last year Pretoria gave Venda R743 million – for half a million people – but still we have "big financial difficulties"!' Suddenly he fell silent and looked beyond me. Turning, I saw two men and a woman approaching – beaming a welcome to me, eager to hear about my journey. As we shook hands, Gerald slipped away.

Mr and Mrs Makhade and Mr Malatsi – all Vendas – spoke fluent English. Mrs Makhade's diamonds flashed from every possible anatomical angle: ears, throat, bosom, wrists, fingers. Her husband shouted for a round of drinks, then set about interrogating me – smoothly, with expertise. Perhaps my answers failed to satisfy him; all three refused to be drawn on Venda's future within the new South Africa. The majority of the population were dismissed as 'Poor because lazy – look after your possessions, many are criminals and will kill for five rands!'

The Makhades have just returned from New York: 'Now sanctions are being lifted, we must go looking for new business opportunities.' Mr Malatsi, wearing a gold wristwatch the size of a travel clock, believes in Venda's 'great touristical future' (a regional advantage not immediately apparent) and is planning to build a Tribal Theme Park below the Thothe Vondo pass.

'But first,' I said, 'you must do something about all those PAC slogans.'

'They mean nothing!' snapped Mr Makhade. 'Only foolish kids showing off!'

'Are you sure?' I persisted. 'The PAC do occasionally kill people. What about investing in basic necessities before the theme park? Then the PAC might lose support.'

Our party soon broke up.

Sibasa, 11 March

I must see the Dzata ruins, Gerald said over breakfast. They were only a few miles away, Venda's answer to Great Zimbabwe.

Mr Bobodi, Dzata's would-be museum curator, accompanied me – would-be because the museum idea has been abruptly abandoned, for reasons undisclosed, by the infamous Venda Development Corporation Ltd. Skilled local craftsmen have completed an attractive building, inspired by the traditional Venda dwelling, but all the shelves are bare.

An ancient track, lined with giant euphorbia, winds up to the ruins along a grassy mountainside. 'I wish my father spoke English,' said Mr Bobodi. 'He is very old but he remembers well and could make you cry. He remembers when Venda was peaceful – always poor soil, many droughts, no motor roads or towns but the people content. Once our three tribes were all mixed up, in some villages the headman belonged to another tribe but nobody bothered. Vendas and Tsongas and Bapedis lived in peace with intermarriage – one of our chiefs had his Venda wife, his Bapedi wife and his Tsonga wife! But the missionaries came to stop that sort of thing.'

Although Dzata obviously belongs to the same culture as Great Zimbabwe these ruins are diminutive. A layperson might mistake the recently reconstructed waist-high stone walls for a deserted kraal rather than the Significant Remains of something Great. Nevertheless, Mr Bobodi dearly loves his ruins. Standing by a wall, under one of the grotesquely writhing euphorbia, he caressed the long, thin, pinkish stones. 'We must make our young people proud of their past,' he said fervently. 'They are too ignorant because in Africa we had no writing, no history books. They don't understand how the Europeans coming upset our lives. And now they believe the lies in the school history books. It's not true we were always fighting before the whites came to "civilize" us. In Venda our real trouble started in the 1950s, after the Bantu Authorities Act. We never before had fixed borders or quarrels about land. Not until the government made "nations" for blacks and drew borders and forced people from their villages into new "nations" – sometimes only moving a few miles but leaving the ancestors' graves and the land they'd always used. Next came families thrown off white areas – thousands of *surplus* people, trucked in by the army. What sort of minds and hearts did they have, who put such a label on human beings – *surplus!* Most were elders or disabled, or women and children. Healthy men weren't *surplus*, they needed them to work.'

As we returned to the road I asked, 'Is it true the Venda people are closer to the Shona of Zimbabwe than to any South African tribe?'

Mr Bobodi laughed and clapped his hands. 'You are right! You know a lot! We should be part of Zimbabwe! But we are not so cattle-centred as the Shona, this is bad grazing country. Since way back we were iron and copper smelters, trading with Arabs. Have you noticed some of us look a bit different, with light skins and straight noses?'

I had noticed.

By then we were in Mr Bobodi's three-roomed breeze-block bungalow, being served herbal tea by a shy, beautiful teenaged daughter. 'Now you must go to the Mission,' said my host, 'to meet our Irish priest. Things would be even worse in Venda without the missionaries, in these times they make up for past damage. Our little medical care, they give us. In other places they quarrel between themselves, I know. But not here. Here our situation is so bad they all work together, helping us.'

A brutally rough track climbs a stony red hillside to the small Mission compound, its few little brick buildings – chapel, clinic, bungalow – seeming almost luxurious in this setting. My compatriot greeted me with some astonishment. Elderly and understandably weary-looking, he has spent ten years in Venda shepherding a sparse and scattered flock. His most essential task is the supervising of a monthly distribution of dried milk, powdered soup and high-protein biscuits – all provided by Operation Hunger, a private-sector relief organization founded in Jo'burg in 1982 during a major drought.

In the ill-equipped clinic, run single-handedly by a septuagenarian Australian nun, two small AIDS-education posters hang in the darkest corner: one warns against sharing razor blades, the other against using unsterilized needles. Venda has no AIDS problem, according to Sister K—. She opposes AIDS education for schoolchildren because that would 'dirty their minds'. I have met her like before, too often, elsewhere in Africa.

As Fr. McDaid escorted me to the gate – after coffee and biscuits in a bright, simply furnished parlour – he warned me that the temperature was 30°C (86°F).

And it felt like it, over the twenty-five hilly miles to Sibasa. At first the road rose gradually through comparative fertility – feeble patches of maize separating the countless shacks. Then it soared, to cross the Thothe Vondo pass. Resting on the top, I gazed over a deep green valley to low mountains blanketed with commercial timber. Below, ten small children were struggling up a near-precipice bearing firewood on their heads. As they passed me I noticed that three were suffering from kwashiorkor, a protein deficiency which leaves its victims permanently brain-damaged. The descent took us around steep hills monotonously forested for the benefit of the Venda Development Corporation Ltd.

Before the controversial construction of Thohoyandou, a few miles further on, Sibasa was Venda's only commercial centre. Here some of Pretoria's largesse has trickled far enough down to create consumers, and the town has recently expanded into a sprawl of jerry-built supermarkets, grotty boutiques, second-hand car showrooms, electronic-equipment stores and military barracks. I am staying in a truckers' hotel, twenty round thatched huts crowded together behind a collapsing wire fence. My tiny broken window admits swarms of mosquitoes, greedy for the rare treat of European blood. The communal bathroom-cum-wc is waterless but in the Drankwinkel across the road, where lives the uncommunicative proprietor, water can be bought for a rand a bucket. In this area wcs are a planning error.

Having locked Lear to the bed – the keys of all these huts are interchangeable – I went shopping and attracted many unsmiling stares. Soon a surly policeman (black, of course, in Venda) advised me to return to my lodgings. 'White ladies not good here,' he said ambiguously. I assumed he meant 'not safe' and took his advice. Then three crudely made-up young women attached themselves to me and we drank beer in my hut until a truck arrived – whereupon they all rushed out to compete for the driver.

GaKgapane, 12 March

Thohoyandou vividly illustrates how the 'Bantustan' policy worked. The grandiose 'parliament' and administrative buildings are set in elaborately landscaped grounds. The pretentious public fountains are overflowing with litter, not water. American-style shopping malls sell the shoddiest of goods. Soon I sped away.

Seventy level miles took me to Duiwelskloof. For hours the road bordered the non-independent homeland of Gazankulu – population almost a million, the land stony and thornbushy, in contrast to the irrigated farms on my right with their orange-groves and flourishing fields of maize, groundnuts, sunflowers. In South Africa, a naturally arid country, access to water is a privilege in most regions. Since the first settlers arrived major droughts (always described as 'the worst') have been mentioned at irregular but frequent intervals. For the past century, by far the greater share of the water supply has been allocated by law to whites – who in the 1930s received subsidies to encourage private irrigation. Considerable capital is required to install and run the sort of pumps watering those fields I passed this morning.

By 9.30 I was looking forward to a meal at Mooketsi. But Mooketsi is not a dorp, as all the large road signs pointing towards it had led me to expect. It comprises a petrol station and one shop selling the junkiest of junk foods. Luckily the young black saleswoman spoke just enough English to direct me to the farmers' co-op, a mile or so up a steep hill. Halfway up I passed a Boer standing by the roadside instructing his 'boy' about a herd of cattle – all crowding around a gateway, mooing impatiently. The tall hard-faced white was harshly over-bearing; the black, also tall, was sullen, taut with resentment – yet submissive. The chemistry between them put something poisonous into the air. It got to me like a bad smell. After that, it was no surprise to find the huge co-op store heavily guarded, with a barrier-pole at the entrance. Today is Saturday and it was thronged with farmers and their wives. Everyone shunned me but I found a bargain, a kilo of groundnuts for R8 (less than £2).

The foothills of the Drakensberg – high, steep, forested – directly overlook Duiwelskloof, a small dorp described in the tourist literature as 'picturesque'. Its only hotel, long and low, had an ominously expensive aura. On the front stoep, lined with potted shrubs, half a dozen young white women were creating tasteful flower arrangements for a wedding, then loading them into bakkies. They pretended not to notice me; it seems the northern Vaalies consider a grubby foreign cyclist the next worst thing to a kaffir. Around a corner, on the side stoep, several blacks were drinking Cokes or Castles. When I joined them, to their very evident astonishment, one young man beamed delightedly and pulled out a chair.

Two beers later I released my pent-up emotions to this young man – 26-year-old Albanus, a primary-school teacher. He understood. 'Yes, we've many foreign tourists here and I've met others like you – very upset! But I tell them our whites are only privileged in surface ways, in their souls they are poor. In our new South Africa I'd like to have white friends. Real friends who love me as a person, not liberals who think it's their duty to have black friends – or cunning folk who think it will soon be profitable to have black friends! I would like to be able to talk to our whites like I can talk to foreigners. But this won't ever be possible, not even when I'm an old man. Our whites will never be like foreigners. Even the best of them, brave people like the Black Sash women – they're infected too...'

Duiwelskloof was not where I wanted to spend the night and Albanus recommended the hotel in GaKgapane, a black town five miles off the main road. It lies in a shallow valley, semi-encircled to the south by wooded hills, their bluegums drought-killed, brown corpses still bearing leaves. GaKgapane is much bigger than Duiwelskloof. It has three factories (glass, chipboard, furniture), a large hospital in shrub-filled grounds, two schools, several small churches, a few family-run stores and a supermarket, a middle-class suburb of fine bungalows with car-filled garages, an upmarket housing estate under construction, quite a large hotel – even a library. Yet it isn't marked on the map. No black town is, though their populations far exceed those of the nearby dorps. One more dehumanizing device.

Beside the hotel a jolly group of nine men and women sat drinking in the shade of an ancient fig tree. On noticing the white stranger they fell silent, watching me push Lear up a slope riven by erosion channels. Diffidently I asked permission to join them – and immediately everyone relaxed, greeted me warmly, shook hands, asked questions, invited me to help myself from their communal tray of roasted groundnuts. I had fallen among GaKgapane's élite, unwinding on a Saturday afternoon: the supermarket owner and his wife, three teachers, a factory manager, a nurse, a police officer and the librarian who became over-excited when I introduced myself. At once he rushed away to fetch a dog-eared copy of *Muddling Through in Madagascar* for autographing. That boosted my self-esteem: you have to be famous if one of your books is in GaKgapane's public library.

Until sunset we talked, discussing religion, education, different systems (and perceptions) of justice – and of course racism.

'In South Africa it's more than racism,' asserted Kenneth, the youngest teacher. 'It's about keeping the power that makes you rich.'

Moses, the elderly teacher, disagreed. 'No, no! It wasn't money first with the Boers. They started out wanting all the land, to rule and control it all – not sharing. They didn't even use money for generations, they were only interested in land – land and cattle, like us. Europe didn't want them, they were homeless except for here. They became Africans, a white tribe, like they're always saying nowadays – it's true! Then they got obsessed with this Afrikanerdom idea – who else ever made themselves a new language? Think of the Boer War! Only madmen would fight the British Empire! And they hated the British as much as they hated us – maybe more. They've had this mental disease about being "special people", like some nutters think they're elephants or ants! Shame nobody ever gave them medical treatment, not even when they invented their own crazy kind of Christianity! Man, they're sick!'

'But better than the English,' said the policeman. 'Now I'd keep the Afrikaners and throw out the rest. I'd throw out the English, Greeks, Portuguese and all those Jew-boys in Jo'burg – the guys that really run everything.'

The factory manager agreed. 'Afrikaners are straight, no double-talk. Sjambok you in the morning, give you a big food present in the evening if you work hard. Generous, except the real brutes. Most English are polite and smiling but mean and too much pretending.' He looked at me. 'You've heard our joke? The English hate two things: firstly apartheid and secondly blacks!'

Before we dispersed, Gloria, a school principal and ANC Women's League leader, arranged to call for me at 9 a.m. tomorrow. Her husband is in hospital, recovering from a traffic accident, and she wants us to meet: 'He can tell you many details about the Struggle in Soweto and detention and torture. He's been through it all.'

In my room I discovered that something has bitten me on both legs, behind the knees, and those bites are becoming extremely painful. Moreover, I'm feeling very groggy – malaria? The symptoms – lethargy and slight nausea – resemble the prelude to my first attack nine months ago in Zimbabwe. This afternoon I dosed myself with Halfan, hoping an early treatment would work. But now a headache is starting – just a little one, so far.

2

Convalescent in Lebowa

Duiwelskloof – Lebowa – Devon

All the dancing I've done has been alone in the veld, when I've jumped in the
air and thrown up my arms and shouted with the mere joy of living.
Olive Schreiner

Duiwelskloof, 30 March 1993

Within hours of finishing the last entry (more than a fortnight ago) my 'little
headache' had become a road-drill-through-the-skull experience. Until dawn I
sweated hard and couldn't lie still; that strange twitchy restlessness was
uncontrollable and oddly scarey. Then I slept and woke to hear Gloria knocking.
She sat on the edge of the bed and said, 'You'll be fine tomorrow, after so much
sweating. I'll tell them to bring fresh sheets and a bucket of drinking water.'

For the rest of the day I dozed between further bouts of heavy sweating and
violent twitching; the Halfan wasn't working. Malaria apart, my insect bites
were by now things of wonder; each deep suppurating hole had turned purple-
brown and was surrounded by a huge crimson area, all swollen and hard. That
night the fever returned, the sweating stopped, both the hammering headache
and the twitching worsened. It was time to seek medical advice.

On the way to the hospital my legs and thighs throbbed painfully; those sores
would in any case have prevented cycling, so their coinciding with malaria
seemed convenient. In the overcrowded out-patients' department an obviously
exhausted young Indian doctor said malaria is very common in the northern
Transvaal. He advised me to go back to bed and drink water every half-hour. I
didn't mention my bites, regarding them as an occupational hazard.

That evening Gloria pronounced, 'You must see a white doctor, our medical
services are not good. And the Health Department says our malaria cases have
increased *tenfold* this season! We've had warnings about cerebral malaria – you
must be *careful*!'

At sunrise I set off to push Lear to Duiwelskloof; cycling was out of the
question. Dr de Beer, on hearing of the Halfan's failure, looked grave and was
decisive. 'To Jo'burg immediately, by bus. Leave your bicycle here, it will
be safe.'

Enter Margaret – a Capetonian by birth, who became a close friend while working in Ireland. Now she lives in Florida, a far-out Jo'burg suburb, and a telephone call brought her to meet my bus in the city centre at 9 p.m. When I displayed my bites, as a bizarre phenomenon, she rather fiercely condemned my 'occupational hazard' stance and insisted on their being shown to the doctor. She had secured an 8 a.m. appointment.

Dr Eksteen, a congenial Afrikaner, found my case-history puzzling. He felt my pulse, probed my liver, checked my blood-pressure, collected three blood samples. Pending the test results, there was no more to be done. Then I remembered that Margaret, sitting watchdog-like in the waiting room, would be wrathful if I failed to declare the bites. Feeling wimpish, I turned back from the door and said apologetically, 'I don't want to waste your time, but I've got two funny insect bites on my legs – at least I think they must be insect bites...'

When I rolled up my trousers Dr Eksteen looked both relieved and exasperated. 'Why didn't you show them at the start? You've got tick-bite fever – we all get it.' He scribbled a prescription, assured me I'd be fit to cycle in a fortnight and added that my suffering had not been in vain. Tick-bite fever treated on Day One tends to recur. If left to linger in the system for several days an immunity is built up and it rarely recurs. He didn't tell me that untreated encephalitides (the lowveld tick-bite fever: there are many varieties) can, if one's stars are so aligned, cause paralysis and death.

Having finished my antibiotic course I felt as good as new (well, almost) and planned to bus back to Duiwelskloof. Then something improbable happened; on ringing a friend in Pretoria it transpired that he was planning to motor through Duiwelskloof today, en route to an educational conference at the Ofcalaco Mission.

Kevin has been a teacher-priest in South Africa for thirty-five years; more than half a century ago, he and I were schoolmates. As we sped north on the N1, across the flat colourless highveld, he gave me a glimpse of non-racism in action – real non-racism, which has nothing to do with being politically pro-black. He seems to have so transcended race-consciousness that he no longer thinks in black/white terms. If he judges it right to be vigorously anti-black on some particular issue, no guilty inhibitions trouble him. Nor does he talk any nonsense about 'equality' on those levels where the concept is clearly invalid. Unlike many of South Africa's home-grown liberals, he is neither intellectually patronizing towards nor emotionally subservient to blacks. I envy him; I would like to be where he is but I know I'll never get there.

Kevin has invited me to spend tomorrow night at the Ofcolaco Mission, some thirty-five miles south of Duiwelskloof: a suitable distance for my first post-fever cycle. Tonight I'm staying in a tourist 'camp', a pleasant enough place – rondavels on a wooded hillside, each provided with a braai grill. It overlooks the dorp's four-court tennis club, complete with pavilion and bar. In reaction to the segregation laws being abolished in 1991, this club increased its membership fee fivefold. 'What else could we do?' demanded the Afrikaner woman who fed me this unsavoury titbit.

Ofcolaco Mission, 31 March

In the pre-dawn half-light I rejoiced to be back on the road – a narrow hilly road, traversing the base of steep mountains clothed in tea estates or commercial plantations. This area is an esteemed beauty spot and having glimpsed the monotony of the highveld I can see why. As the sun rose the traffic increased, much of it school traffic – mothers (occasionally fathers) transporting their flaxen-haired blazered offspring in large fast cars.

Tzaneen is an attractive dorp; here hilliness defeats the dreary grid-plan. At 7.30 no café was open, but as I paused to read the 'Drakensberg View' menu the Afrikaner proprietress noticed me and immediately unlocked the door. Beckoning me inside, she shouted to the kitchen for a full breakfast to be quickly prepared. Then she sat beside me – her vast bulk so obscuring a little chair that she seemed disconcertingly unsupported – and deplored my travelling alone.

'It's too dangerous these days – why didn't you come before? Then we had a peaceful country, everything under control, everyone happy, running their businesses and farms, doing their jobs quietly, everyone friendly...Now you must get such a bad impression, all crime and cruelty, everyone afraid. I'm cut off from my daughter in Pretoria. I can't drive there any more – all is lawless! This is the end of the world coming soon, as foretold in the Bible – you remember? FW is so weak he'll let the ANC grab all the power. Sometimes in bed I cry to think of our beautiful country falling to bits, given over to Communist terrorists. We can have no hope for the future, we must accept it has to be like the Bible says. Young people can leave but where can I go? And why should I go? I don't want to go, this is my country – but I don't want to see it falling to bits all around me!' She looked directly at me and her red-rimmed brown eyes filled with tears. 'I shouldn't talk about it, that makes it worse. I don't talk much about it since my husband died last year. After a landmine near the border in '86 he never got his full health back. We left the farm then and came here. You know I was never – never once, in my whole life, and God knows this is true – I was never unkind to the Bantu. Why do I have to feel afraid now, seeing them looking at me with hate? Before we were all happy together, everyone knew how to behave...'

When a slim, pretty black waitress brought my giant hamburger with chips and salad, Mrs Stals heaved herself up and patted me on the shoulder. 'Enjoy your meal and then be careful how you go – be *very* careful, remember they hate us now!' She and the waitress disappeared into the kitchen and could be heard chatting animatedly in Afrikaans. Clearly they were good friends.

Cycling on, I found my sympathy-compass veering towards the Afrikaners. It was impossible to imagine Mrs Stals being unkind to 'the Bantu' – to anyone. How could she and her like be held in any way responsible for apartheid? Denied access to information about its dynamics, they must have been blind to the ugliness of the structure in which they lived – the only structure they knew and one ordained, they were persuaded, by the will of God. Surely Mrs Stal's neurotic perceptions – 'everything is falling to bits, all is lawless' – are as much the fruits of total incomprehension as of racial prejudice? If you don't understand the nature of your own society, if all your thoughts and emotions have been distorted by Afrikanerdom's Unholy Trinity – the Dutch Reformed Church (DRC), the National Party and the Broederbond (a Masonic-type, quasi-secret society) – then the imminence of black rule can only be terrifying. To the more sophisticated South African whites and to outsiders this change isn't all that sudden; for years we've seen it coming without knowing exactly how or when it would arrive. But of course the unsophisticated whites have been traumatized by recent developments, perhaps above all by the return from exile of the dreaded MK 'terrorists'. Afrikanerdom's certainties, apparently as solid as the Voortrekker Monument, are now lying in ruins.

'You turn off the main road just beyond Ofcolaco,' Kevin had said. But I almost missed Ofcolaco, another of those much-signposted non-dorps – a general store, petrol station and Drankwinkel set back from the road behind a line of bluegums and pines. While I queued to pay for amasi – fermented milk, one of the few forms of palatable nourishment available in rural South Africa – my fellow-whites did their usual shunning act after a quick sideways look. Outside the store loitered a group of ragged youths, faintly hoping to pick up some casual work from passing farmers. In the shade of a pine tree three elderly women sat behind orange-crate trestles selling home-made buns, small spotty tasteless apples and second-(or third-)hand clothes from Zimbabwe. Their English was adequate, though rusted for lack of use.

The apple-seller offered me a spare crate to sit on and asked, 'Why are you cycling? Where is your vehicle?' My reply attracted the attention of two men waiting nearby for a minibus taxi: an elderly Zionist Christian Church (ZCC) pastor and a young ANC activist from Tzaneen's township. Then we were joined by a truck driver, also drinking amasi, and a Tsonga businessman from Pietersburg who took a picnic basket from the boot of his gleaming Toyota Corolla and sat beside me, having carefully spread a newspaper on the dusty ground. After introductions he offered me an egg sandwich: 'It is clean food, don't be afraid.'

No one seemed to feel any great excitement about the new South Africa. The businessman said, 'Only after Comrade Mandela was released – for a few days then – all went wild with joy. But you see how it is, for most people these changes make no difference – yet. Now there's no law against blacks doing business wherever they want. But still they won't give me a licence to trade in Pietersburg shopping mall. If local bureaucrats choose to keep apartheid, who can stop them?'

'Be patient,' said the activist. 'Our Bill of Rights will take all power from bureaucrats – they won't even have jobs, if affirmative action works well for us. Now is an in-between time, no apartheid laws but no Bill of Rights so whites still running everything. Only zero comma six per cent of senior civil servants are black.' (Using commas thus is one of the South Africans' more harmless foibles.)

When I asked about land redistribution the truck driver – from Mamelodi, a township near Pretoria – proclaimed that all white farms should be seized for the benefit of the homelands' dispossessed. 'They stole our land, now we take it back – that's *justice*.'

The activist was shocked. 'Hey man, no way, man – our policy is not like this! Those guys are on their land for centuries and we pay them – *that's* justice!'

'We can't pay them,' said the businessman. 'It's too much money, our government won't have so much.'

'Around here,' said the pastor, 'some farmers are giving back some land – free, no payment from anyone. God is guiding them, they see injustice was done, they have repentance in their hearts.'

I stared at him, suspecting an hallucinatory state. But this evening I have found his information to be correct. However, I would guess that prudence, rather than God, is the guiding factor. If you have unused land, as many whites do, it is now a sound move to *give* it to the landless who might otherwise (because after all anything could happen in the new South Africa) be tempted to take the lot.

'It's important,' said the businessman, 'not to mess up commercial farming. If too much white land is taken our townships people won't get fed. That's why we hear so little about redistribution.'

'The PAC talk plenty about it,' said the truck driver. 'They want it, that's why APLA kills farmers, trying to drive them all off the land.'

'That is not what God wants,' said the pastor. 'Killing is very sinful.'

'For whites, killing us is OK,' retorted the truck driver.

When the taxi arrived I went on my way, following a red, rough, dusty track. On either side stretched miles of sugar-cane and mango orchards where the trees have been cleverly coppiced. The few people about – ragged farmworkers – gave grovelling responses to my greetings. Tzaneen's activist was wrong about all whites having owned their land for centuries; some of these Ofcolaco estates are owned by English settlers who migrated after the Second World War. Moreover, the elimination of 'Black Spots' continued into the early 1980s, removing thousands from communally owned lands in Natal and the Transvaal. Even those blacks who long ago *bought* their land from the Boers, and had deeds to prove it signed by no less a personage than President Kruger, were forced to move. Village elders who refused to sign title-transfer agreements and lead their people to a homeland were detained without charge or trial for up to six months. Pretoria wanted to make apartheid look legal; hence the manic array of laws, as though injustice could be rendered just, and immorality moral, by the passing of Acts in Parliament. Only when black resistance was uncommonly stubborn did the authorities set about bulldozing schools and churches. If that didn't work, water supplies were destroyed and people threatened with the bulldozing of their homes – containing all their possessions. Then everybody moved.

A mile-long 'private road' – little more than a path, hedged with spiky vegetation – leads to the Mission. Why is it here, this colony of bungalows isolated amidst green-gold savannah and now used only for occasional conferences? Is it a major planning error, or some thwarted ambition? It might be tactless to ask.

One young Irish priest holds the fort between conferences. At sunset he and I sat under an acacia with our Castles, slapping at mosquitoes and lamenting South Africa's laid-back attitude to AIDS. Yesterday, returning from Tzaneen, Declan picked up two teenaged girls hitch-hiking to a nearby farm. They, seeing a well-dressed and with luck temptable young man, eagerly invited him home. Declan, fluent in their language, then did some devious sociological research. 'I have AIDS,' he solemnly declared. 'If you sleep with me you will be infected with the virus, you will become HIV-positive and soon you will die.' The girls giggled and said that was not important. He could have them both, they promised, for the price of one in Tzaneen. 'What do you do,' said Declan, 'when they don't *believe* in AIDS? How to get through to them?'

I remarked that at a time when so many South Africans are murdering each other, and millions don't know where their next meal is coming from, a subtle long-term killer virus must seem unimportant.

Declan is a remarkable man – as he would need to be, living here alone without a postal service or telephone or anything much to do. Luckily he enjoys reading and music and appreciates his surroundings. Only a few miles west of the Mission, beyond a wilderness of thorny woodland and savannah, magnificent mountains rise abruptly from the plain. Old, old mountains, their blue-grey slopes sometimes evenly pleated like an accordion, then becoming a disarray of sharp angles, smooth curves, deep gorges. Such mountains do things to my adrenalin supply. I asked Declan about paths; the map shows nothing. Yes, a rarely used track, said to be one of the original Voortrekker trails, crosses the

Orrie Baragwanath pass. A new motor road goes to the top – this area is being developed as a nature reserve – but on the far side the track is a mere footpath, leading into the homeland of Lebowa. Mentally I licked my lips.

Mafefe, 1 April

A cloudy and blessedly cool morning. Not far from the Mission a red-and-white pole marks the entrance to the Downs Nature Reserve. On seeing me, three black wardens in crisp khaki uniforms registered comical amazement, followed by agitation. Madam must turn back, there is no through road! Madam said she didn't want a through road, only to cross the pass and join the R37 at Zeekoegat. Increased agitation – Madam *must* turn back! The wardens' minimal English precluded a reasoned argument but then their *baas* arrived in a bakkie, a cheerful friendly young Afrikaner – so friendly he seemed out of place hereabouts. I probed and he is out of place; he comes from the Cape, where they breed another sort of Afrikaner. Politely, sympathetically, he told me I'd gone astray: 'There is no way through for cyclists.' But he was amenable to reason and soon the barrier was lifted. His final warning: 'You're into a homeland on the other side, there's no hotel, I don't know where you can sleep.' It's odd how many people imagine travellers must sleep in hotels.

This new tarred road climbs steeply – at times very steeply – for 4,000 feet. First through a magical shadowy forest of ancient contorted indigenous trees, creeper-linked, supporting a multicoloured abundance of mosses, fungi, ferns. Here birds and monkeys were shrieking and chattering, darting and swinging. A swift stream sparkled on the left, then on the right, then on the left again as the road wriggled to and fro. Above the forest, on both sides, rose sheer wooded mountains gashed with bare gullies of carmine rock. From three high escarpments distant waterfalls drew noiseless silver lines through the trees. An avocado orchard (abandoned in 1984 when the reserve was established) filled one long valley. For hours only bird-calls and the petulant quarrelling of baboons broke the silence – hundreds of baboons, teeming on the slopes or sitting on clifftops, abusing me. The final gradient, just below the pass, was so severe that I had to rest at intervals, leaning on Lear, gazing back at all the wild grandeur now below. Then at last I was on level ground where the tar ended.

Ahead lay an immense plateau, distantly bounded – north and south – by irregular ridges of low blue mountains with tenuous cloud fragments drifting over their crests. On the stony and sometimes muddy path cycling was possible for an hour across this wide, bright world of gleaming grassland – the cool breeze varying its shades of green, the sun glittering on granite boulders. But why so many NO ENTRY warnings, engraved on rounds of wood atop pathside poles? No entry to what? Then my binoculars revealed traces of numerous derelict kraals – more forced removals... In pre-reserve times, this must have been superb grazing country.

From the edge of the plateau we plunged into Paradise – a gruelling paradise. The path resembled the dry bed of a rocky stream, the gradient was fit only for baboons. My wrists ached from braking Lear, my thigh muscles ached from braking myself. I thought admiringly of the Voortrekkers who hauled their dismantled ox-wagons and all their worldly goods up and down such mountains – but probably Coloured slaves did most of the hauling. However, the women and children had to *walk* over many such passes. A tough breed; perhaps their present sybaritic lifestyle doesn't suit them. They might be happier – less tense – if still being physically challenged.

These mountains are tightly packed, separated by deep ravines. Escarpments streaked red and grey soar up and up – smooth, sheer, naked, rejecting vegetation. But the path clings to clothed mountains. Extravagantly clothed: elegant yellow orchids, grotesquely writhing cacti, countless varieties of flowering shrubs, richly scented. Around their blossoms – red, blue, orange, white – flitted clouds of brilliant butterflies, from stamp-size to saucer-size. And for hours the silence was unflawed. Something happens to time during such interludes; they are neither long nor short, only intense – and indestructible, forever fortifying.

Then faintly came the sound of an axeman, far away down the valley, signalling my exit from Paradise.

Half an hour later I was on a wide strip of grassland; it felt odd to be so suddenly on level ground. Ahead rose the reserve's high wooden gate, sturdy and firmly locked – an unforeseen contretemps. But not a serious one: neglected wire fencing let us through at the expense of a torn shirt. Then a soft earth path led through woodland smelling of cattle-pads and here were people – many people, though the terrain allowed little cultivation. Three young men, dragging a tree trunk out of the bush, looked at me with something not far from terror; when I dismounted and made friendly noises they cringed. I smiled reassuringly and went on my way.

Soon a 'Surplus People's' settlement appeared, scattered on wide slopes amidst scrub and boulders. The few original inhabitants live in round thatched huts, the many newcomers in tin-roofed concrete cubes. A small store, its Coca-Cola sign faded but still an irritant, was closed and barricaded with iron grilles. Often I had to dismount to negotiate tangles of gnarled tree roots, lying across the path like petrified serpents. The androgynous creature with the bicycle may well enter the local folklore. Small children took one look and fled, adolescents stared with a mixture of alarm and defiance, even the adults registered apprehension. My antennae told me to keep moving.

A homeland 'motorway' – the ruts chasmic, the loose stones large, the dust deep – curved around the base of forested foothills overlooking a vividly green valley some five miles wide; but that marshy land was cultivable only along a narrow strip below the track. Here I met the day's traffic: a windowless bus, loaded beyond credibility, slowly lurching towards me in a cloud of dust. To ford three shallow rivers, from which children and goats were drinking while women washed clothes and pots, I had to roll up my trousers. The consequent two-tone effect – white legs, near-black face and arms – caused the young women to point and smile at me timidly while whimpering toddlers clutched at their skirts.

Beyond that valley, no more greenery – all harsh stony dryness, gaunt cacti, low thornbushes, and on three sides stark jagged mountains, their rock-crests glowing red. At a crossroads I asked the way to Zeekoegat but the two couples sitting on the verge looked away and were silent. Guessing, I turned right and pushed Lear up and up into a wide pale grey valley, its floor fissured by gullies, the arid slopes above strewn with concrete cubes. At 4.45 it was fiercely hot; this sort of terrain acts like a storage-heater. And here it became apparent that I am still convalescent, a fact obscured by my Orrie Baragwanath euphoria. I collapsed on a pile of stones, in the scanty shade of an embankment topped by prickly pear, and ate groundnuts.

How to define Mafefe? Population-wise it is a large town, extending for miles along this dusty valley. Otherwise it is a grievously impoverished village, without running water, electricity, sewage or adequate medical care. Until the nearby asbestos mine was closed in 1974, leaving as its memorial many asbestosis sufferers, Mafefe was used to outsiders. Now whites are a rarity and scores of excited children came racing down to the track to inspect me – from a safe distance. As I nut-munched, they gradually and silently edged closer and closer until I was looking up at a semi-circular wall of malnourished little bodies. Then one of the older boys, aged perhaps 12, summoned his courage and his scraps of English and asked where I was going.

'I don't know,' I admitted. 'I'm looking for somewhere to sleep.' The boy pointed to high white walls a mile away on the next ridge-top – 'Big man, big house.'

Within those walls, beyond a depot for agricultural implements and fertilizers (but where is the land to be fertilized?) Mafefe's 'supermarket' sells salt, soap, Coca-Cola, tinned fish, cigarettes, white bread rolls and bales of cloth. The two young women behind the counter speak no English and made no effort to conceal their distrust of Whitey. As I sat on the high stoep, drinking warm Coca-Cola and longing for a Castle, twenty or so adolescents, male and female, joined my juvenile entourage and stood staring at me. I found their silent scrutiny a trifle unnerving but told myself that if I sat around for long enough something positive was likely to happen; it usually does, in rural Africa.

Soon Doris arrived: a lovely lass, better dressed than the average with large lustrous eyes, unblemished milk-chocolate skin and, I was relieved to notice, a friendly smile. She is aged 17, a member of the Assembly of God and a schoolgirl – 'But no more school, no books last year, this year, why go for school and have no books?'

Doris, the linguist, had been delegated to suss me out. When she reported back to her peers they argued with her, their voices raised in anger. Returning to the stoep she explained cheerfully, 'They don't believe, they say you are thief.'

That took me aback. A police spy, perhaps – but a *thief*? 'Do they say all whites are thieves?'

Doris, for a moment looking solemn, answered, 'Yes.' Well, I thought, one can see their point. Luckily Doris herself had accepted me. 'You wait for my cousin Harry, coming now from Lebowakgomo, he thinks good about foreigners.'

Soon Harry came trotting towards us across the compound, a bouncy excitable little man. Sitting beside me, he declined a Coke: 'It is an impure stimulant.' Heartily I agreed and suggested seeking a beer instead, whereupon he looked utterly scandalized; it seemed his prejudice against Coke was religious rather than scientific. He enthused about the privilege of meeting a lady from overseas, then raged about asbestosis, Mr Nelson Ramodike's vices and Lebowa's consequent underdevelopment. As the sun slid behind a mountain Doris murmured something and he turned to me quickly – 'You need to sleep here? You rest in our home?'

As we set off – back the way I had come – groups of small boys were racing down steep slopes behind wheelbarrows loaded with plastic jerry-cans to be pulled home from a distant unclean stream, using ropes as harnesses. Some adult males also fetch water, Doris said, but only if all their womenfolk and children are dead or very ill.

Last year Harry taught in Mafefe but without textbooks you can't really teach. Anyway, the pay was 'too small to keep alive' and the work too hard, with over forty pupils in each class – and nearly ninety in one classroom. He himself left school at the age of 13, after Standard Five – 'for the other five years, no fees!'

In the six non-'independent' homelands 22 per cent of primary-school teachers are similarly unqualified – and 15 per cent of secondary teachers.

Today Harry was job-hunting in Lebowa's 'capital'. 'A lot of money for that bus fare, then no work! But the Lord will be my shepherd, he will lead me to green pastures and sweet springs!' Harry wore the navy-blue peaked cap and silver-star badge of the zcc, the biggest and most influential of South Africa's indigenous Churches with an estimated membership of 5 million. Its leader, unfortunately, has much in common with certain wealthy American televangelists.

Harry's acceptance of me had transformed the atmosphere. The surly adolescents disappeared and the adults we met along the track greeted me with friendly curiosity. My gold tooth-filling, visible when I smile, was much admired;

one old mama, mistaking it for a movable decoration, begged me to give it to her. The children, their numbers by now trebled, formed a laughing and singing escort, some running up to smile at me and stroke my arms, others helping to push Lear up the gravel-skiddy slope.

As we passed a derelict bungalow where the white mining manager once lived, Harry brooded on the thousands of miners who had come to Mafefe from the Transkei, Natal, Malawi, Mozambique, Zimbabwe. Nineteen years after the mine's closure, no one knows how many have permanently damaged lungs. And anyway, under the Occupational Diseases in Mines and Works Act, black victims are entitled to only 10 per cent of the compensation paid to whites with identical complaints. In Mafefe scores of youngish women, including two of Harry's sisters, suffer from asbestosis; as children they were employed to do 'cobbing' – hammering open those maize-cob-shaped splinters of rock which contain asbestos. Six months' exposure to the fine grey dust is enough to cause asbestosis. This the Mafefe people learned through experience. No wonder they don't much like whites.

An astounding number of decrepit cars passed, coating us in dust before turning off to jolt up hillsides like bucking broncos. Each was packed with workers: Mafefe's envied élite, returning from factories over the 'border'. For black as well as white South Africans the motor car is the ultimate status symbol; even here in Lebowa, the poorest of all the homelands, it is given priority over domestic comforts.

The light was fading as we climbed a barren slope towards long lines of cubes set in minute fenced plots – scarcely big enough, even had the soil been fertile, to produce a family's vegetables. Here a small boy suddenly materialized and handed Doris a 14-month-old baby. 'My son,' she explained proudly, baring a breast. The small boy is her youngest brother; two other brothers and her mother died in a cholera epidemic. She lives in a four-roomed cube with her father, Mr Sevoka, and Phoebe, her older sister, who has three children by an absent miner husband, and Harry and his childless wife, and Harry's brother Tom with his wife Sheba and their four children. As this demographic scene unfolded, I resolved to camp outside. But of course that wasn't allowed; the guest must have the *best* available: a comfortable double-bed which no doubt normally sleeps six to eight persons depending on their size. Doris apologized for the absence of interior doors; money had run out at that stage. Then she pointed me to the earth-closet thirty yards away, shared by three families, and visually clean though olfactorily less so.

Mr Sevoka is a frail 50-year-old who looks 70 and speaks no English. He was completely thrown by my arrival but quickly recovered himself and welcomed me graciously, at first assuming me to be male; correcting this impression took time. Then he disappeared, leaving Harry, Tom and me sitting around the living-room table conversing by candlelight – or in the dark, when the one candle was needed in the kitchen while the eight children were being fed. The only furniture, apart from a Formica table and four camp-chairs, is a huge antique gas refrigerator, retrieved years ago from a Pietersburg dump but no longer used; gas has become too expensive.

'For our future we want a country full of friendship,' said Tom, a secondary-school teacher (unqualified). 'We've had too much hating, it's a bad life when there is hating. We are sad and afraid about our township children, they hate too much. Their world has gone wrong, now they must make their hearts peaceful.'

As we talked, a glory of sound filled the evening – singing at once joyous and plaintive, in sweet flawless harmony. Tom went to the door, then beckoned me. Beyond the wire fence, just visible by moonlight, a massed choir of small children – at least 200 – was staging an impromptu concert. 'To welcome you!' smiled Tom. 'They give you our tribal songs to make you happy!'

I felt a lump in my throat. 'Who suggested this – a teacher?'

'No one suggested it, it comes from their hearts. And they like to sing, they like to have cause for it.'

Before the choir dispersed, half an hour later, I made to go out to thank them. But both Harry and Tom firmly said 'No!' 'It would not be right,' Tom added enigmatically.

Mr Sevoka returned then with bad though not unexpected news. A nephew had just died; six months ago he came home from his miners' hostel with TB, then quickly lost weight, 'grew sore skin on his face' and finally developed chronic diarrhoea.

'In the hostels they have too much TB,' said Harry angrily. 'More and more they die of it – why is this?'

Tactfully I said nothing – perhaps a misplaced tact? The least ineffective AIDS-education is the realization that already one's family and friends are dying of AIDS-related diseases, TB being the commonest in South Africa.

When Doris offered me herbal tea but no food I retired even earlier than usual, leaving the family to eat what little they have, and wrote by torchlight.

A guest house near Buffelsvlei, 2–3 April

My reappearance at dawn caused Mafefe's juveniles riotously to reassemble, singing and cheering as Doris and Phoebe escorted me down to the track. They were going to fetch water from a murky trickle some four miles away in the depths of a steep-sided gully, a punishing twice-daily chore.

'You talk now to the government,' begged Doris, 'to say this people needs water like Soweto have. *Clean* water! This dirty water gives people sick and children die! I listened about Soweto, all peoples there has water near the door.'

Scores were converging on the stream and I marvelled at their personal cleanliness; in such a situation I'd soon give up the washing habit.

In the unpeopled region beyond Mafefe I often had to dismount, so erosion-ravaged was the track. For hours it rose and fell between ochre mountain walls, all knobbly with rounded rocky outcrops, the vegetation a mere stubble of scrub – an austerely beautiful landscape of stern textures, dramatic shapes and strong bold colours glowing under a sky intensely blue. Yet all this beauty is dimmed by one's awareness (throbbing like a wound) of the area's artificial human suffering. 'Artificial' is the keyword. Often I have seen even worse rural deprivation – but as an inescapable fact of local life, not something callously planned.

Towards noon, flat cultivated land replaced the mountains: maize and sugar-cane and miles of desiccated pasture on which skeletal cattle lethargically roamed. Then came another crowded settlement and, startlingly, massive road-works employing hi-tech machinery, all shiny and new and operated by whites.

The little store was milkless. 'Our people have no money for luxuries,' explained the owner – elderly, gentle, with resigned but astute eyes. He surprised me by damning the new road. 'Where no one has work, why use machines? Why spend billions on a two-lane tarred highway? We don't need it, for us a good smooth earth road is enough. That could be made and kept good by the men who live here without jobs or hope. Where is this road going? Over the Orrie Baragwanath pass, for tourists! How much will it cost to put a *road* up there?'

Despair swamped me. A *motor* road through that paradise – that special, hidden, tranquil, inexpressibly lovely place!

'For years it's been planned,' said the store-owner. 'A game park or nature reserve – something like that. They removed everyone living high up – *rich* people, growing potatoes. The soil was so good for potatoes they grew tons and tons and made big money and were happy. Now they are starving in Mafefe and here. How will tourists driving over the pass make them happy again? It's not possible.'

In my rage I scarcely noticed the landscape over the next ten miles. The sheer crassness of it, the double vileness of it – to destroy a prosperous community while exposing such an ecologically precious corner to the physical and spiritual pollutions of motorized mass-tourism. Who, I wonder, is profiting from this? There is of course nothing particularly South African about the immolation of special places on the altar of tourism. Ireland does it too – in fact is among the worst offenders. Witness the desecration of the Burren.

While I was tick-fevered in Jo'burg it was claimed that the Lebowa Tender Board had done a deal with a chemical company, Firechem, which then donated R100,000 to Mr Ramodike's ruling party. The managing director of Firechem, William McNaught, blandly explained that his company has a policy of 'plough-ing something back into the community'. But nobody even attempted to explain why Lebowa needs 2,000 tonnes of cleaning chemicals. The story went that this contract was never put out to tender – though that's irrelevant. Rumour had it as well that Mr Ronald Rasebotsa, a cousin of Mr Ramodike, won a R1.3 million contract to supply meat to the Groothoek Hospital despite his tender being R227,000 above the lowest.

The Lebowakgomo–Lydenburg main road carries an uncomfortable amount of fast traffic through another rural slum on semi-desert hillsides spiky with cacti. The sky was cloudless, the sun fierce, the vehicle fumes queasing. At 4 p.m. I began to look out for a suitable campsite, not very hopefully. The exceptionally high wire fencing puzzled me but that mystery was soon solved by a high arched wooden gateway leading to a privately owned game-reserve-cum-tourist-camp. Tourist camps depress me yet one can't afford to be choosy at a certain stage of heat exhaustion.

My arrival baffled the two middle-aged Pedi wardens sitting outside the reception rondavel. The isolated campsite, one explained, is very far away – *five miles!* Being alone, I should camp on the grassy patch beside the rondavel. Firmly I refused, rejoicing at the prospect of a secluded site. The men muttered to each other, then reluctantly gave in. I paid R15 and signed the register, noting that it had last been signed four months ago by a German couple. As Jack led the way on his ancient bicycle, through tallish trees and thickish bush, we glimpsed giraffe, ostriches, springbok, zebras.

Dwarf acacia hedge the site, a quarter-acre of short grass; the only 'facilities' are a tap over a stone sink, a small bathroom hut and the essential braai grill. Directly behind the hut, on a steep rocky ridge, scores of dassies were giving their bird-like alarm calls. My cup of joy was o'erflowing but Jack's unease remained. 'Too much far away?' he persisted.

'Perfect!' I assured him. 'Very good, no problem!'

'Sure no problem? Not you fear too far away?'

'I *like* being far away, I like to be *alone*.'

Still he hesitated and lingered, seeming more than anxious – almost afraid, as though somehow he himself were threatened. To speed him on his way I gave him a R5 handshake but even that didn't cheer him up. While mounting his bicycle he gave me one last apprehensive sideways look.

An inquisitive giraffe family, including a calf, stood peering at me over the hedge as I devoured an unwholesome supper of stale white bread rolls and tinned fish (species undisclosed) in a sauce with an ominously metallic tang. As I conversed with the giraffes their ears moved to and fro in response to my voice. Only when I stood up did they withdraw, quite quickly; their comical slow-motion lope is deceptive.

Under a crimson western sky I went wandering through the bush, sending a zebra herd trotting before me. Then I was on open savannah, where the gods were kind. Surely the springbok in motion is the most graceful of living creatures. Here eleven of them appeared, no more than thirty yards away, their white 'fans' open, tinted pink by the sunset glow. I watched through my binoculars as they streamed away into the distance, springing ten or twelve feet above the golden grass, clearing fifteen feet with one bound, flowing over the veld like emanations from some other world not limited by the law of gravity. Yet even today many hunters kill springbok for fun...

Back at the site I wrote by candlelight (there was no breeze) while savouring the silence of my solitude. At 8.30 I retired with Thomas Pakenham's *The Boer War* and soon (not Thomas's fault) was sound asleep.

Curiously enough, the headlights – not the engine noise – woke me an hour later. These were powerful lights, shining directly onto the tent. 'Now that's bad luck!' thought I, assuming the arrival of fellow-campers. After some door-banging, footsteps approached and stopped a yard from my ear. A hand slapped the roof of the tent and a voice loudly demanded, 'Come out! I'm here! Get up!' A recognizable voice: Jack's.

I lay motionless and silent, wondering 'What the hell...?' Next the tent frame was shaken and Jack shouted, 'Murphy, come out!' Turning on my stomach I unzipped the entrance flap and stared up angrily. 'How dare you disturb me? I'm tired, I was sleeping!'

Two young Pedi policemen appeared in the headlights' glare, cuddling rifles. 'Come to police cell for night,' said one. Was this an arrest or an invitation?

'Get lost!' I snapped. 'I've shown my passport, signed the register, paid my fee and now I'm staying here!'

The policeman moved closer, made his rifle look more obvious and repeated, 'Come to police cell, this man Jack not trust you, come in van.'

Jack added, 'Come out, Murphy! Come in van!'

I continued to argue – very conscious of being in a disadvantageous position, lying on my stomach – until the second policeman also moved closer. Now there was determination in the air and it occurred to me that were I to continue to resist arrest (if arrest this be) I could be forcibly removed, perhaps without Lear and my possessions. Fuming, I wriggled out of the tiny tent and set about dismantling it.

Ten minutes later Jack lifted Lear into the back of the van and my captors signed me into the front seat. But no one can be expected to leave their luggage exposed to Lebowa's degenerate police force. During the monosyllabic argument that followed my temper shortened by the second. When finally I pushed the policeman aside and climbed in beside Lear, Jack joined me. Our destination was the next big settlement (its name escapes me: I was too enraged to write it down) some ten miles along the road to Lydenburg.

Under pressure, Jack admitted to having telephoned the police, reported the arrival of a suspicious foreigner and urged them to do something about it.

Three armoured vehicles stood outside the long, low police station protected by a steel-mesh fence. The main door led into a brilliantly lit room – a generator growled in the background – where filing cabinets lined two walls and a young lieutenant sat behind a high counter. Only the top of his head was visible when I stormed in, wheeling Lear and followed by Jack, now completely unnerved after our tête-à-tête in the van. When people who rarely lose their temper do get angry, they tend to get very angry. Banging my fist on the counter, I glared at the bemused-looking lieutenant and demanded to see the commander. The lieutenant muttered something about the commander being in his home. 'Then fetch him from his home,' I ordered. 'I want to see him *now*. And then I want to be driven back to the campsite.'

When four more policemen entered from the wings my captors joined them behind the counter. For fifteen minutes I stood silent and scowling while a noisy debate took place – occasionally involving Jack, still cowering by the door. This debate might have continued indefinitely had not Major Nakaphala arrived, wearing a pin-striped royal-blue lounge suit. Affably he shook hands, politely he requested my passport, calmly he asked me to make a statement and diligently he wrote it down – not once but four times, in separate ledgers and copybooks. Then he told one of his men to fetch the commander. Clearly he, too, was angry with my captors; but to have reprimanded them then and there would not have been the African way. He did, however, intimate that they had overreacted to Jack's scare-story.

I couldn't return to the site as the gate was locked and the man with the key 'very far away'. And my R15 couldn't be refunded before morning, those rands being behind the locked gate. I protested that I must be gone by 5.30 a.m. and if the police gave me the money now they could retrieve it later. But allegedly those eight policemen couldn't between them scrape together R15. Instead, the major ordered Jack to deliver my rands not later than 5.25, white time.

Close on midnight the commander appeared: tall, burly, self-satisfied, wearing a crimson and yellow tracksuit and several gold rings. Then things took a new turn. The tacit understanding arrived at between Major Nakaphala and myself (there had been a regrettable mistake) was to him unacceptable. His police force doesn't make mistakes. As a suspicious character I must be searched.

The two policewomen were sympathetic but extremely efficient. In a tiny bare cell (later my bedroom) they stripped me naked – that was a 'first' – and greatly admired my leg muscles. The panniers' contents were also closely scrutinized, even to opening my toothpowder tin and film containers. (Looking for drugs?) We moved into the corridor to unfold the tent, which operation attracted seven mesmerized spectators, all chewing bubble-gum. (Why so many police on night duty in this remote settlement? To earn overtime?) Finally, at 1.10 a.m., the girls pronounced me innocent, Coca-Cola was served and the commander and I improbably settled down to discuss current affairs.

I listened, poker-faced, while being told that the ANC and PAC sell guns to local criminals because they want all Lebowa police officers killed in preparation for the election campaign. The ANC must be prevented from holding election rallies in the homelands, they'd lie to the people. That Mandela fella is a phoney, claims to have a law degree but never went to school. The Nats must stay in control, even if they have to pretend to share power – no one else knows how to run a modern state. Mr Nelson Ramodike must remain Lebowa's leader, he understands very well all the local problems. The ANC are planning to drive the whites out of the country, keeping the mines for themselves and their Commie friends – who now need South Africa's gold more than ever because Russia is going bankrupt.

Studying the commander's face, I wondered if he believes all this. Maybe he does; South Africa's brand of corruption has bred millions who live in whichever fantasy-land best suits their chequebooks.

At 2.15 I retired to my cell. Soon after a policewoman joined me, unrolling her straw mat on the concrete floor beside my flea-bag. Moving over to make room for her, I bruised my brow on one of Lear's pedals. Ten minutes later hymns started, tapes of a ZCC Easter gathering at Moria. Very loud hymns. Very little sleep.

Less than three hours later, Jack was handing me R15. He looked so dejected that – having made my point and feeling guilty about having made it – I gave them back to him. The lieutenant at the desk, bleary-eyed at the end of a long hard night, registered disapproval of this irrational gesture.

Pedalling away – here even the dawn air is warm – I pondered this strange episode. Why had Jack felt compelled to take such drastic action? And why had the police so quickly responded? Did they really suspect me of being a terrorist/drug-smuggler? Or did Jack suspect me of being some malevolent white sangoma wielding dangerous powers and needing restraint? Or did he simply wish to protect me from a night alone in the bush? But no – for whatever reason, he was afraid *of* me, not *for* me. And the atmosphere during the police-station debate prompted by my arrest had been disturbed by powerful psychic cross-currents, baffling to me and evidently distressing to all those present. Hereabouts the belief in witchcraft is so common that hundreds of alleged 'witches' have been murdered within the past ten years.

This evening, reviewing my own behaviour, I rightly feel ashamed. I acted like a white supremacist of the nastiest sort, giving no one time to explain anything (even had they been so inclined) and throwing my weight around as though I were entitled to bully all those stupid blacks. Yet now what shocks me most is not what I said or did but what erupted inside myself. Facing that reality is a chastening experience. As Gramsci said somewhere, 'It is useful to "know thyself" as a product of the historical process to date which has deposited in you an infinity of traces, without leaving an inventory.'

Forty hot miles took me to the Lebowa 'border'. On my right a parched yellow-brown plain extended to the base of low, worn-looking mountains, some mining-scarred. A line of giant pylons bestrides this range, for the benefit of a chrome-mine and industrial estate just over the 'border', while the countless shacks beneath them remain unelectrified. Many families, gallantly determined to brighten their dreary plots, use battered old paint tins as flowerpots. The multitude of vehicles parked around the shacks puzzled me until my binoculars revealed that most have been cannibalized. Among the cacti and thornbushes a few emaciated cattle, donkeys and goats wandered and nibbled. One rarely sees emaciated goats; when they look poorly things are truly desperate. Ragged women and children, equally emaciated, criss-crossed the plain seeking scraps of firewood. Little herdboys sat leaning against boulders, doodling in the dust. My standard Map Studio road map, subservient to apartheid, indicates that this R37 route to Burgersfort crosses uninhabited country – in contrast to the surrounding Transvaal, dotted with dorps.

Here the 'border' is a narrow brown river between high bushy banks. While still in Lebowa one can see white-owned land ahead, the irrigated fields vividly green. Burgersfort, an uphill mile from the river, is a dorplet dominated by big brash white-owned, black-staffed stores where Lebowa folk can buy shoddy goods. On this Saturday morning the streets were thronged and the stores crowded yet the place felt oppressive – sullen, watchful. I bought two litres of amasi and continued, the road rising gradually. Here one family may own 6,000 productive acres, the lush pastures grazed by fat cattle of European ancestry. For ten miles I saw no one, apart from speeding motorists; throughout these 'ethnically cleansed' rural expanses the spirit of Africa is missing. Anywhere else on the continent such fertile regions are busy, colourful, noisy with gossip, laughter, argument, vigorous bartering and bargaining, drunken quarrelling, dancing children.

The next dorp is Lydenburg, thirty-five miles further on and a few thousand feet up beyond a formidable mountain-wall – the sort of challenge I normally enjoy. But today I viewed it without enthusiasm and was relieved to see a simple wooden sign pointing left down a dirt track to a 'Guest House'. This well-maintained track ran downhill past two handsome farmhouses, red-tiled and white-walled, their gardens shrub-filled, their green lawns tree-shaded. I turned left again at a T-junction below an escarpment where swathes of vines drape thin elongated boulders, like organ-pipes. Then, approaching the guest house entrance, alarm bells rang. By the gateway a high, curved mud wall, reminiscent of the Middle East, conceals the servants' quarters – a veritable village. From here the track climbs steeply, through cool indigenous forest, and coming towards us were three blond children in very correct riding attire, mounted on plump glossy ponies and attended by a black syce resplendent in a gold-braided scarlet uniform. Assuredly this track did not lead to a frugal farm guest house.

Soon all was revealed: an enormous two-storey L-shaped hotel, its handsome timbered façade smothered in bougainvillea; an Olympic-sized swimming pool plus a children's pool; two tennis courts with flood-lighting; a bowling green; a miniature golf course; a line of stables; a mountain-bike racetrack; an adventure playground – all surrounded by towering trees and flowering shrubs, and interspersed with succulent rockeries, sparkling fountains, emerald lawns. But it was too late to turn back; I had put another twelve miles between myself and Lydenburg.

In the empty foyer, leopard and lion skins – complete with heads, jaws agape – decorate the shiny stinkwood floor. Other hunters' trophies – a cemetery of antlers – decorate the walls, together with romantic scenes from the heroic Voortrekker days. When the receptionist appeared – a svelte and rather haughty Coloured woman – I haggled spiritedly, pretending to be quite ready to move on, and the charge for my room (without breakfast) came down from R250 to R150 (£30).

I told myself to regard this extravagance as a sound investment, giving me an opportunity to mix with rich Afrikaners at play. There is, however, a snag: these Afrikaners don't seem to be at play and won't mix with an uitlander. The only friendly creature around is a long-haired dachshund named Budser. Obviously the humans share a serious problem, an inability to relax and enjoy themselves. Is this a normal (for them) condition, or a Transvalers' herd reaction to the new South Africa?

Throughout the afternoon young bronzed stern-faced couples swam lengths of the pool swiftly and methodically, as though in training, then sat chain-smoking under a milkwood tree, just occasionally exchanging brief remarks about some evidently gloomy topic. Slightly older couples sat by the adventure playground, stolidly observing their highly competitive and frequently fractious offspring. Elderly couples sat at the long thatched open-air bar, its counter displaying a macabre collection of stuffed monkeys, and glumly sipped vividly coloured cocktails. Weirdly, nobody smiled – not even at each other, never mind at me. Usually I can overcome communication barriers, even in such introverted places as East Belfast and Afro-Caribbean Handsworth. But not here. These are people grimly locked into themselves and uninterested in being released. They remind me of a conversation in Harare with an octogenarian Natal woman who quoted Trollope's 1877 comment: 'The Dutch Boer is what he is not because he is Dutch or because he is a Boer, but because circumstances have isolated him.' In the Natalian's view, 'The Afrikaners are doomed and they know it. Look at their low birth rate! Always a sign, since the decline of the Roman Empire, that the collective unconscious sees the writing on the wall. To survive they must marry out.' At the time I ascribed this to prejudice; the Afrikaner and English-speaking South Africans are not mutually devoted. But now I begin to wonder...

At 5 p.m. I retired to my opulent suite – where Lear's companionship felt positively comforting – and wrote until 7.30. Then everybody gathered around the *braaivleis* to help themselves to a multi-course dinner (R27 extra). My doggedly resumed efforts to communicate prompted a few stiff smiles and many averted eyes – no words. The food and wine were superb by any standards, yet the atmosphere in that open-air restaurant remained resolutely joyless. No buzz of conversation – forget laughter – just people leaning mutely over their plates, shovelling it in, then swigging good wine as though it were beer before going back for another heaped plateful.

While packing in preparation for an early start I pillaged my marble bathroom; its array of mainly unidentifiable (by me) perks will be useful to give as presents en route.

Lydenburg, 4 April

The R37 was traffic-free on this Sunday morning as its many hairpin bends twisted around steep rock-crested mountains wearing dense green-brown bush and populated only by baboons. At the top, on the dramatically definite edge of the highveld, I rested and nut-munched. From here the lowveld seemed all golden grassland, wide and smooth, bounded to the north and east by powder-blue mountains isolated and conical, or forming long jagged ridges towards the Orrie Baragwanath pass. In this region, during the first century AD, Bantu communities were grazing cattle and sheep, cultivating grain and vegetables, carving bone, ivory and soapstone, firing elaborate pottery, forging copper or iron weapons and tools in village furnaces. Yet 'official' Afrikaner history puts the first migration of blacks across the Limpopo in the seventeenth century. According to white mythology, the Transvaal's original goldfield was discovered near Lydenburg in the 1870s. In fact the Bantu had found it some 700 years previously and loaded their women with finely wrought ornaments, to the envious wonder of the early Portuguese explorers.

Even at noon a *cool* breeze was blowing across the highveld and I sprinted thirstily over the last few miles, forgetting that on Sundays bars remain closed until 6 p.m. After three pots of tea in Morgan's Hotel – agreeably old-fashioned – I went walkabout. The only people visible were cheerfully chatting (in Bapedi) churchgoers, the women looking nurse-like in identical white uniforms and blue berets; each indigenous Church has its distinctive Sunday uniform. As no one spoke English I failed to find Lydenburg's most cherished possession, the oldest extant school building in the Transvaal. (This failure was not too frustrating.) I did however pay my respects to an ancient – by South African standards – DRC church built in 1864 and now serving as a Voortrekker museum (closed on Sundays). On the earliest maps of the Transvaal only three towns are marked: Potchefstroom, Pretoria and Lydenburg, the last meaning 'Place of Suffering' – so named by a few grieving Voortrekkers who retreated to these heights from the lowveld after malaria had killed most of their companions and the tsetse fly most of their cattle. In the 1850s this dorp enjoyed a moment of glory as the capital of a short-lived independent Boer Republic. In the 1990s it is hopefully looking forward – so the hotel receptionist told me – to the expansion of South Africa's tourist industry.

Eve and Elizabeth – Natal born – sounded less optimistic as we talked in the ladies bar. Eve now lives in Bristol and is visiting her Jo'burg-based sister. She is tall and stout with dyed raven hair. Elizabeth is also tall but bony and faded: faded blonde hair, faded blue eyes, faded pink cheeks. Eve knows I will be murdered en route, probably before ever I get to Jo'burg, certainly before I get to Cape Town. Returning to South Africa after a thirty-year absence has done her no good. 'Changes I expected, never did I guess the Bantu had taken over! In Jo'burg they've *moved in*! They're swaggering around everywhere, you can't shop safely in the centre – or even walk on the pavements with hawkers spreading their goods, a public nuisance. There's no control any more. It's like – what is it like? It's like *Nairobi*!'

'We don't notice it so much,' said Elizabeth. 'Of course we do, really, but it's not a shock – it's been happening over years, long before they let Mandela out. And it's no good blaming anyone. It had to happen.'

Eve snorted fiercely; I got the impression the new South Africa had driven this sororial relationship onto the rocks. '*Why* did it have to happen?'

'Economic reasons,' Elizabeth replied succinctly.

'Rubbish! I find all our friends poorer – much poorer. Families with three, four servants in the old days are lucky now to have a girl once a week and a garden-boy twice a week. And I see rich blacks all over the place with fine cars and good jobs – while our youngsters must emigrate!'

I asked, 'If the blacks couldn't afford to consume, what would happen to the whites?'

'Exactly!' said Elizabeth. 'That's one reason apartheid couldn't work.'

'It was working perfectly well thirty years ago.'

Elizabeth looked at her sister. 'Remember Boksburg? Just one example. Thirty years ago we'd no well-organized boycotts.'

'I don't remember Boksburg,' said Eve sulkily. 'I don't know anything about it.'

'Tell us,' I urged Elizabeth. (Her surname, Louw, revealed that she was married to an Afrikaner.)

'Well, it taught us a lesson. My husband has a few little business interests there – and did we suffer! In '88 the CP [Conservative Party] promised to bring back segregation and won 70 per cent of the Transvaal town councils. So again Boksburg had full-scale segregation. Next thing, a full-scale boycott for a year – genuine, no intimidation. The CP leader, Clive Derby-Lewis, swore it was only bluff, wouldn't make any difference. He couldn't have been more wrong. All work was suspended on a new R30 million shopping centre and a R110 million hypermarket – that lost who knows how many jobs. The CP mayor had to sell his business for R80,000 though it was valued at quarter of a million in January '88. Nine offices had to close, including my husband's, and eighteen shops – furniture and hardware takings dropped by 30 per cent. It was the Boksburg boycott [of white businesses] pushed the repeal of the Separate Amenities Act in '90. When I joined the UDF [United Democratic Front] in '85 my husband wasn't too pleased – now we've been half-ruined he admits I was right!'

Dullstroom, 5 April

It's uphill all the way to Dullstroom, between round green mountains where fast streams sparkle and sleek cattle browse in wide shallow valleys. All morning the strong tail-wind was cool, the sun warm, the sky cloudless. Soon the altitude became apparent, yet away from the lowveld heat I seemed to have more rather than less energy. At Die Berg – the highest point in the Transvaal, marked by a monolithic boulder inscribed '6,904 feet' – I dismounted to gaze back. Below me only mountains were visible, all smooth-crested, all of the same height, all leaning in the same direction like the immobilized breakers of a stormy sea.

Dullstroom is a holiday resort where rich Vaalies enjoy 'recreational fishing' in the region's well-stocked, privately owned trout streams. As the two hotels charge R400 (£80) for a single room, I turned towards the campsite (£3) on the dam shore. Then suddenly the weather changed; low dark clouds swiftly advanced over Die Berg and it was cold – very cold. For this I was unprepared; on returning to Duiwelskloof I had taken only hot-weather clothes.

A rough track descends to the campsite, ten bumpy acres of coarse short grass cut off from the dam by an eight-foot wire fence. Apart from a taciturn black in a wooden kiosk at the entrance, there was no one – nor any dwelling – in sight. By now a howling gale was sending those dark clouds speeding across the long barren ridge beyond the dam. It wasn't raining, yet the air felt icily moist. I tried to get the tent up but the rock-hard ground rejected the pegs. Shivering, I unfolded my space-blanket at an ill-chosen moment – an extra-strong gust tore it out of my hands and away it sailed, high up into the clouds, never to be seen again.

This site's 'amenity' is a barn-like edifice, open at both ends, with a tin roof that rattles loudly in the wind and a head-high wall of wooden slats on the dam side – through which the gale is now penetrating like cold swords. Here I must sleep, spreading the folded tent on the concrete floor to supplement my hot-weather flea-bag.

At dusk a small caravan parked nearby. Three young men emerged, equipped with braai firewood, and their flames drew me like a moth. But my reception was as cold as the gale. I hesitated, not being a natural gate-crasher, then gave priority to thawing and crouched by the fire with outstretched hands while the men, conversing in Afrikaans, spiced their meat. All were warmly clad, with compact athletic bodies, blunt features, small moustaches and army haircuts. The scene seemed absurdly unreal: me, wrapped in my flea-bag, too desperate for warmth to accept a brush-off while the trio, completely ignoring me, went about their meaty business. They were having a problem; that gusty wind kept the wood flaming and you can't braai over flames. Finally I suggested, 'Why not move the caravan, to shelter the fire?' All three stared, as though noticing me for the first time. But that was the breakthrough. When the caravan had been moved and the meat at last was sizzling they allowed me slowly to dismantle their anti-uitlander barrier, brick by brick.

They are engineering apprentices from Krugersdorp on a fishing holiday – AWB members and proud of it. If Eugene Terre' Blanche can't deliver a Volkstaat they plan to emigrate, though they admit they don't know where to, where jobs can be found... As they condemned the rest of the world for 'misunderstanding' apartheid their voices went hoarse with resentment. 'You people think kaffirs are humans but they're fuckin' not – they're animals! We wasted our taxes giving schools they're too thick to use – they burn them down instead! We're living centuries with these monkeys, we don't need fuckin' sermons from you people!' And much more in the same vein...

It is hard to imagine these young men ever outgrowing their conditioning; for that a certain level of intelligence is required. When I asked what they knew about AIDS in South Africa one said, 'That's a kaffir disease, not our problem.' Another added, 'It could save this country, they say most could be dead in ten or fifteen years.'

'Then who would work in the mines and factories and on the farms?'

They all laughed and one replied, 'We'll get migrant labour from Asia like the Saudis do – that's clever!'

This first encounter with AWB-type hatred has shaken me. Seen from a distance, it can be dismissed as just one more manifestation of fringe fanaticism.

But at close range it has a terrible psychic power; sitting listening to those three, I found myself trembling.

Devon, 8 April

Motoring across the highveld with Kevin had left me resigned to a monotonous few days between Dullstroom and Jo'burg. Instead, I have found beauty. Quiet narrow secondary roads took me over miles of pastureland, golden-brown or copper-tinted. All the verges and many meadows are now gay with cosmos, a tall richly pink flower – South Africa's autumn glory. In the clear air the highveld's horizons induce a heady sense of freedom; no wonder the Voortrekkers, reaching this remote bright spaciousness, decided that here was their Promised Land and came so passionately to love it. Their descendants' red-roofed farmsteads usually lie far back from the road, surrounded by stately spreading trees and dominated by the essential water-pump windmill, whirring against a deep blue sky.

I passed through Belfast, Carolina, Hendrina, Bethal, Leandral, spending nights in Carolina and Bethal. Having escaped from the northern Transvaal, I am meeting some more flexible Afrikaners, still rabidly anti-black but quite pro-uitlander – indeed, often warmly hospitable. Here in Devon's bleak little hotel bar I haven't been allowed to pay for my Castles and concerned locals have made me promise to send the hotel a postcard confirming my safe arrival in Cape Town. But the Afrikaners' thinking (wrong word: their *mindset*) is depressingly uniform. Groups of blacks often disagree in conversation, groups of Afrikaners only rarely. One senses Afrikanerdom's mould holding them together, reducing them to an essential passivity in relation to South Africa's future, even when their response to changing circumstances involves aggressive language. For the blacks, changing circumstances hold a promise and a challenge. For the sort of whites I am meeting in these little dorps, changing circumstances represent defeat – not stimulating argument but encouraging laagerism.

My breakfast companion in Bethal, an obese peroxided travelling saleswoman, shrugged off the repeal of the apartheid laws. 'We know how to protect ourselves, we've doubled the fees for all amenities – and if that doesn't work we'll treble them! I don't mind standing in the same queue in a post office or railway station – I've never been racist, I always thought that was a silly rule. It's when you want to relax, to enjoy yourself, you can't have them around. And no way can you travel with them, because of the smell.'

All the way from Bethal to Devon the Rand's penumbra of pollution was visible across the level treeless veld – an ominous grey-brown haze, 80, 70, 60, 50, 40 miles away. As Jo'burg is a city of macho drivers – a place so inimical to cyclists that the species is never sighted – Margaret had volunteered to drive to the rescue. Near Devon, when a wildly swaying truck tipped Lear and me into the ditch, I judged it was sos time. Margaret will pick us up at 7 a.m. tomorrow – so early because tomorrow is Good Friday and the zcc Easter ceremonies attract millions to Moria in the northern Transvaal, many starting out from the pwv region.

3

A Time to Mourn

Johannesburg

They've shot my daddy, I saw it was a white man...
Nomakhwezi Hani

How do you kill a Communist? You hit him with a Pole.
AWB spokesman

It's time we told the ANC leadership enough is enough and now's the time to hit
back so that Chris Hani will not have died in vain.
MK spokesman

Florida, 10 April 1993

Florida is a trim moribund all-white suburb, a sloping expanse of street after
street of nice houses in nice gardens. It seems to exist in a state of suspended
animation. Silent adults motor to and from work at regular hours; one never sees
or hears neighbours chatting or children playing. During weekends the unnatural silence – unnatural where so many dwell together – is occasionally broken
by the excruciating scream of gadgets used to manicure miniature lawns. When I
go shopping on foot – the characterless commercial centre is a mile or so away –
I meet only a few black servants who, if greeted, go into shock. Here whites don't
walk – and carrying heavy bags too! – nor, it seems, do they acknowledge the
presence of blacks. In these suburbs, as in the dorps' residential areas, apartheid
still hangs in the air like a poisonous cloud left over from chemical warfare.

Later

At 11.30 a.m. I answered the telephone and heard a friend's agitated voice. 'Tell
Margaret Hani's been murdered, just now – an hour ago, in front of his
daughter. A white shot him at close range.'

Margaret was watering the garden. When I had broken the news we sat
drinking tea in the kitchen, listening for hours to frequent special news bulletins.
The first said, 'Former Umkhonto we Sizwe Chief of Staff, member of the
National Executive Committee of the ANC and General Secretary of the SACP

[South African Communist Party], Mr Chris Hani, has been assassinated in the driveway of his house in Dawn Park, Boksburg.'

The assassin's choice of target was shrewd, certain to create another long-drawn-out tension-building crisis, something this already unstable country can ill afford. Next to Mr Mandela, and not far behind, Chris Hani was the most beloved and respected black leader. And how better to provoke the townships' Lost Generation? (So called because they are uneducated, unemployed and increasingly uncontrollable.) Their anger is always smouldering, their impatience mounts as the weeks and the months and the years pass, and *still* there is only talk... Within the Tripartite Alliance – the ANC, the SACP and COSATU (Congress of South African Trade Unions) – Chris's reputation as a courageous and resourceful guerrilla fighter was unrivalled, though rather inflated. Thus the youth idolized him. He was the only leader they fully trusted, seeing him as their special protector, the one Big Man who hadn't been distracted from their miseries and frustrations by the highfalutin rituals of inexplicable constitutional negotiations.

In my Devon hotel, thirty-six hours before his murder, I saw Chris's last television appearance: a Lester Venter interview on the *Agenda* programme. Unlike most politicians, he gave straight answers to straight questions. Asked if the ANC was fully in control of MK he replied, 'People have come back as individuals. They are not in camps, they have gone to their homes. As a movement not yet in government, it's very difficult for the ANC to monitor the activities of each individual. We try our best to control the situation, but there are instances where we admit the Comrades have really gone out of control. Some have been involved in bank robberies.'

As Joe Slovo noted today, this admission 'could have cost Chris popularity but he didn't care two hoots about popularity. He just wanted to get things right.' A week ago Chris suggested the formation of a Peace Brigade, under the aegis of the National Peace Accord, to engage the energies and aspirations of the Lost Generation in a disciplined and constructive way. Throughout yesterday afternoon (only yesterday!) he had been developing his Peace Brigade ideas; on the desk in his spartan office notes were found headed 'Peace Corps'.

By now the townships are in turmoil, which may give the AWB et al. their longed-for excuse to shoot blacks by the hundred, thus ending negotiations for the foreseeable future – the assassin's motive. As one radio commentator put it, 'South Africa is sitting astride a tinderbox.' In consequence, the interregnum is suddenly over – that uncertain, ambiguous three-year 'twilight of the Nats' that began in February 1990. This evening, Mr Mandela flew back from his Transkei home to address the nation (black, white, Coloured, Indian – the *nation*, not just his own ANC following) and all SABC TV and radio channels were made available to him though the SABC remains under government control. Exactly twelve hours after the murder of his close friend, he took over not only the airwaves but the leadership of his country. This is not, after all, just one more tension-building crisis. It marks the *de facto* end of white rule: now President de Klerk is irrelevant and only Nelson Mandela has the moral authority to avert chaos.

11 April

By this morning the details were known. On at least four occasions last week, neighbours saw a red Ford Laser sedan parked outside the Hani home. The driver seemed to be looking for an address; late on Good Friday afternoon he drove past the house more than once. That evening Chris insisted on his body-guard, Sandile Sizani, taking Easter Saturday off to be with his family.

At about 9.30 yesterday morning Chris and his 15-year-old daughter, Nomakhwezi, drove to a nearby supermarket. As they arrived home, half an hour later, an Afrikaner neighbour, 36-year-old Mrs Retha Harmse, on her way to the same supermarket, realized that she had forgotten something. In her own words:

> I turned back and, as I drove towards Mr Hani's home, I saw the red car parked behind his in the driveway. I saw the red car's door open and a tall thin blond man get out. He walked to the front of the open door and I saw him lift a gun. Mr Hani had just gotten out of his car. The blond man pulled the trigger twice. By that time I had just gone a short way past the house. I stopped the car and watched the blond man walk over to Mr Hani as he lay between the garage door and his car. He calmly lifted the gun again and, at almost point-blank range, pulled the trigger twice. I can still hear the shots ringing in my ears. At first I thought it was a security man shooting at a burglar. But as I watched in my rear-view mirror I saw the blond man walk back to his car, get in and begin reversing out of the driveway. I do not know what possessed me, but I reversed my car towards him. I did not even think that the killer might start shooting at me. All I did was look for the registration number. As the car got closer I saw it. I kept repeating it over and over so I wouldn't forget. I sped home. I was so upset. I had just seen a man being shot down in cold blood. It all seemed like a movie that I was somehow caught up in. I ran up my driveway screaming out the registration number. Within seconds I had told the police the make, colour and number of that car.

At 10.35, ten kilometres away, Janus Waluz, a 40-year-old Polish immigrant, was arrested in his car, still in possession of the gun that killed Chris. It had been among a large consignment stolen from the South African Air Force (SAAF) headquarters in Pretoria on 14 April 1990; then Chris himself had foretold that those weapons would be used to murder ANC leaders. No doubt they were 'stolen' in the sense that British Army weapons are 'stolen' by Loyalist paramilitaries in Northern Ireland; there is considerable overlap between AWB, SAP and SADF membership.

South Africa has reason to feel grateful for Mrs Harmse's courage. The instant capture of the white assassin, because of a white woman's 'rapid response', is being used by both Mr Mandela and Tokyo Sexwale in their efforts to calm black rage. Much now depends on the ANC's ability to impose discipline. Will it be able to control the numerous mass rallies and protest marches that must quickly be arranged as safety-valves?

Quotes from today's newspapers:

Archbishop Desmond Tutu has pleaded, 'Please, don't let them manipulate us. Don't let this tragic event trigger reprisals. It is what somebody wants to see happen. I'm devastated.'

From Benoni, one E. Stark wrote to the *Sunday Times*: 'While Chris Hani may have been a popular leader among certain segments of society, he was roundly hated by many others. Many will agree that he merely got what he deserved. He died as he had lived – by violence.'

Dr Antonie Gildenhuys, chairman of the National Peace Secretariat, said, 'Our organization found in Hani a strong ally in our search for peace.'

The Boere Weerstandsbeweging saluted Janus Waluz as: 'A soldier and freedom fighter for the Boer people.'

A white Boksburg woman said, 'It's sad. Chris Hani was a father. He had a family. His neighbour, a white man, is terribly upset by his death.'

Several newspapers have reprinted an autobiographical sketch written by Chris Hani in February 1991:

I was born on 28 June 1942 in Cofimvaba, a small rural town in the Transkei, the fifth child in a family of six. Only three of us are still surviving, the others died in infancy. My mother is completely illiterate and my father semi-literate. He was a migrant worker in the mines and our mother had to supplement the family budget through subsistence farming . . . I walked 20 km to school on weekdays and the same distance to church every Sunday. At the age of eight I was already an altar boy in the Catholic Church and quite devout. After primary school I had a burning desire to become a priest but this was vetoed by my father. In 1954 the apartheid regime introduced Bantu Education designed to indoctrinate black pupils to accept and recognize the supremacy of the white man over blacks in all spheres. This angered and outraged us and paved the way for my involvement in the struggle . . . In 1957 I joined the ANC Youth League, but since politics were proscribed at African schools our activities were clandestine. In 1959 I went to the University of Fort Hare and became openly involved in the struggle as Fort Hare was a liberal campus. Here I was exposed to Marxist ideas and the scope and nature of the racist capitalist system . . . In 1961 I joined the underground SACP as I realised that national liberation, though essential, would not bring about total economic liberation . . . In 1962 I joined the fledgling

MK...and fought with Zipra forces in Zimbabwe in 1967...In 1974 I went to Lesotho, operated underground and contributed to the building of the ANC underground inside our country...In the current political situation, the decision by our organisation to suspend the armed action is correct and an important contribution to maintaining the momentum of the negotiations.

In April 1962, aged only 19, Chris graduated with a degree in Latin and English. He would have liked to be an academic; in retirement he planned to write a history of his own Xhosa people. This leader of the SACP, who admitted to not having read *Das Kapital*, always carried pocket editions of Homer, Shakespeare and Shelley. Liszt was his favourite composer. There was no resemblance between the real Chris Hani and the primitive sadist projected by Pretoria's propaganda.

12 April

Today on television we saw one of the safety-valve protest marches. Some 20,000 township youths, armed with axes, home-made spears, pangas, knobkerries and sharpened wooden staves, converged on the Hani home, chanting and waving placards. A scary sight, it has to be said, and the ANC Youth League president, Peter Mokaba, did nothing to calm the atmosphere. 'Do not let Hani die in vain! Now the Young Lions must not only bark and roar but you must bite!' said he – getting his sound metaphors slightly mixed. He warned that if the police attempt to disrupt planned mass actions 'We will not restrain ourselves.'

Meanwhile, in Natal, Winnie Mandela was addressing a rally and blaming the government for Hani's death, accusing it of attempting a cover-up by arresting Waluz. This contradicts her suggestion, quoted in yesterday's London *Sunday Times*, that a power-struggle within the ANC may have been behind the killing.

This evening a CP (Conservative Party) leader, Dr Ferdi Hartzenburg, quoted from a BBC interview in which Winnie Mandela stated that Hani had definitely been murdered from within the ANC. Why, he demanded, had the two ANC officials implicated by her not been arrested?

Poor Mr Mandela! It astonishes me that even supposedly responsible media folk continue to interview his wife.

13 April

Dr Verwoerd's 1954 justification of the Bantu Education Act and Mr Mandela's 1964 peroration from the dock on being sentenced to life imprisonment must be rivals for the position of South Africa's most-quoted speech. Dr Verwoerd eloquently defended this keystone piece of apartheid legislation, designed by himself.

The school must equip the Bantu to meet the demands which the economic life of South Africa will impose on him ... Until now he has been subject to a school system which drew him away from his own community and misled him by showing him the green pastures of European society in which he is not allowed to graze ... What is the use of teaching a Bantu child mathematics when it cannot use it in practice? That is absurd.

A quarter of a century later, the South African Atomic Energy Board complained that the Republic was short of 17,000 engineering technicians. Only 3,000 were being trained annually, 'widespread efforts to attract suitable technicians from overseas have borne little fruit ... One solution to the shortfall is to train blacks as technicians.'

There followed many more public admissions that South Africa's prosperity was being threatened by a lack of skills; some 100,000 jobs could not be filled. Dr Verwoerd had catastrophically miscalculated 'the demands which the economic life of South Africa will impose on him [the Bantu]' and in 1982 Vista University was hastily founded, under the aegis of the Broederbond, for the educational upliftment of blacks.

Margaret lectures at Vista's Soweto campus (there are five in all) and this morning we set off to attend the students' Hani memorial gathering in the university hall. Several of Margaret's white colleagues had rung her to question the wisdom of entering Soweto just now but she is made of tougher stuff. However, I won't claim either of us felt completely relaxed as we sped down the motorway past the Rand's distinguishing feature: long, high, smooth, symmetrical mine-dumps, dully glowing. These old dumps have an odd, unexpected sort of beauty – shapely monuments to Mammon.

Vista's campus, on the edge of Soweto, is dominated by Orlando's cooling towers just across the road. A nearby wooded ridge provides an illusion of rural calm. Wide green lawns, planted with spindly saplings, provide an illusion of academic calm. (In fact this institution is a snake-pit of racism, suspicion and dissension.) An uninspired Broederbond architect designed the several red-brick, red-roofed buildings, one, two or three storeyed, the interiors bleakly functional.

In the university hall – a new grim, gaunt building, not yet officially open – posters of Comrade Chris covered the walls and tensions criss-crossed the atmosphere like invisible electrified wires. Margaret explained the interacting of the two main factions: ANC Youth League/SACP and PAC. Few other whites were present though the majority of the staff is white. By far the most impressive speaker was a sturdy young woman – ex-MK, wearing jungle fatigues – whose personal distress was obvious as she recalled Chris Hani's commitment to what is now known as 'gender equality'. Not surprisingly, female MKs were expected not only to be good guerrillas but to do traditional things – washing clothes, cleaning tents, cooking... Chris, however, campaigned against this by washing his own uniforms, cleaning his own tent and cooking his own food. While the Hanis lived in Lesotho, his wife Limpho worked as manager of the National Tourism Department and he did more than his fair share of baby-minding and household chores. Many male comrades were puzzled by one of his favourite sayings: 'Anyone who does not respect his own wife cannot be a revolutionary.' Last Saturday morning he wanted to go for an early run but his teenaged daughter would not let him leave the house until he had made his bed. South African women of all colours need more champions like Chris.

The other speeches exposed a comical ignorance of Communism. One attributed 'War is a continuation of politics by other means' to Lenin. Another vehemently asserted that Communists never use or condone violence unless forced to do so by capitalists. A third argued that things went wrong in the Soviet Union only because it never became a true dictatorship of the working class. My eyes wandered to the posters: 'Chris Hani died for Freedom, Justice, Democracy'. It's all very sad: these confused young people represent the 'found' of the Lost Generation, now embarked on an academic career for which their schooling has not prepared them. Last year only a minority of black pupils passed their matric (the South African equivalent to A levels) and, of those, many were later discovered not to be fully literate. This year the matric failure-rate is certain to be even higher. For months there have been student strikes protesting against the payment of exam fees and teacher strikes protesting against retrenchments – and now this upheaval...

Halfway through the last speech – in Xhosa – the PAC contingent began to toyi-toyi and the few other whites hurriedly left. Soon after, the commemoration concluded with the singing of The Internationale in Xhosa and Nkosi Sikelel' iAfrika – the latter sung with much more feeling than the former. Yet The Internationale is peculiarly appropriate to the present situation of South Africa's blacks: 'Tis a better world in birth...'

This evening Mr Mandela again addressed the nation, still seeming close to tears:

This is a watershed moment for all of us... Tomorrow, in many towns and villages there will be memorial services to pay homage to one of the greatest revolutionaries this country has ever known... Chris Hani was a soldier. He believed in iron discipline. He carried out instructions to the letter. He practised what he preached. Any lack of discipline is trampling on the values that Chris Hani stood for. Those who commit such acts serve only the interests of the assassins and desecrate his memory... To the youth of South Africa we have a special message: you have lost a great hero. You have repeatedly shown that your love of freedom is greater than that most precious gift, life itself. But you are the leaders of tomorrow. Your country, your people, your organization need you to act with wisdom. A particular responsibility rests on your shoulders.

Tomorrow much will hinge on the response to Madiba's heartfelt plea. What do the Young Lions make of this courtly, gentle-voiced, reasonable, conciliatory leader who was imprisoned before they were born? As a legend, was the invisible hero-martyr of Robben Island perhaps more powerful than in his present role? Inevitably many youngsters have been brutalized by the violence that was and is part of daily life in most townships. And Madiba is not a communicator in the sense that Chris Hani was. While Chris was in exile, dealing all the time with uprooted and difficult young men and women – often very difficult, in the MK camps – Mr Mandela was cut off from the world. Moreover, he is not 'of the people'. And most township youngsters are too alienated from their own culture to feel the respect for his birth that would otherwise come naturally to them.

I like some of South Africa's idiosyncrasies. Anywhere else the holding of hundreds of church services in memory of the leader of an atheistic political party would seem incongruous; here it seems perfectly normal. Nor does anyone think it odd that the Hanis chose to send their three daughters to a convent school.

Since the assassination, President de Klerk has faded into the background – he might not exist – while Mr Mandela and other ANC leaders broadcast repeatedly. The frightened whites realize that their fate is now in black hands – which may, if things go well, help to resign them to black rule.

14 April

Today my innate urge to participate at worm's-eye level had to be repressed. 'Participating' whites don't help already overstretched ANC marshals, Peace Monitors and the SAP. Colonel Dave Bruce, the Witwatersrand SAP spokesman, broadcast a warning this morning – 'Events are likely to be emotionally charged, so the fewer outsiders the better.' This nationwide Day of Mourning (really more a day of homage) is not government sanctioned. It is ANC sanctioned, which tells all about South Africa's rump parliament.

Like many other whites, I attended the midday ecumenical service at the Central Methodist Church, accompanied by Jennifer – a very un-nunnish Dominican nun who, during my tick-fever interlude, taught me an immense amount about the significance of *ubuntu*. We walked into the city centre through streets Sunday-quiet; all shops and most offices were closed. Jennifer seemed to know everyone in the mainly black throng around the church and as we were queuing to be frisked by ANC marshals only the heavy SAP presence generated unease. A Xhosa beside me muttered, 'Why they come around with all that tear-gas? They're not here to protect us. If the AWB came they could shoot first and be arrested after – like in Vanderbiljpark!' He was referring to the shooting dead last Sunday of two black men, and the serious wounding of two others, by a middle-aged right-winger. Under the noses of the police, this CP member fired into the crowd from his bakkie during an orderly Hani protest march.

We were early enough to get seats close to the altar-podium. Then tension rose, as everyone realized there was no room for half the would-be congregation. A frustrated crowd, either forcing its way in or seething on the street under the eyes – and guns – of the SAP, was not a good idea. At such moments leaders have to think fast. Immediately it was decided to hold a repeat service for the excluded in an adjacent park; each speaker, having said his say to us, would go out and say it again to the overflow.

Senior clergy of all colours and denominations, with a preponderance of magnificently robed Roman Catholic bishops, gave the proceedings an air of solemn respectability far removed from what was going on in the places where I longed to be. Yet I was glad not to miss Dr Frank Chikane's valediction. This distinguished theologian dealt directly with Chris Hani's Communism and showed it for what it was: a passionate commitment to the poor, of which Christ himself would have heartily approved. (Like many others, Dr Chikane refers to apartheid as still operative: 'In pulling the trigger Waluz has released unstoppable energy, which will destroy apartheid.') Other speakers followed: Tokyo Sexwale, Peter Mokaba, and characters whose names were unfamiliar. But Dr Chikane's words had so moved me I hardly took in what else was said.

Then came a stirring of the congregation and, looking around, I saw Mr Mandela beside me on his way up the aisle – walking slowly, seeming physically frail. He hadn't come to speak, just to be there, and as he sat among the bishops, facing us, I saw his sadness and my heart felt sore. It is too easy to forget that after people have become symbols, leaders of profound significance to millions, they remain vulnerable human beings. Now Nelson Mandela, anguished by the death of his close friend, has to handle that private, common-to-us-all kind of grief while the public Comrade Mandela is sending forth his extraordinary psychic energies to protect South Africans of every sort. Here is a man, unjustly imprisoned for twenty-seven years, striving today to protect the people whose regime imprisoned him and many of whom continue to mistrust and hate him. That is greatness. That is the finest flowering of *ubuntu*.

Later today, Mr Mandela addressed some 30,000 – mostly young people – in Soweto's Jabulani stadium. A tolerant mention of the Nats, now the ANC's negotiating partners, provoked loud, prolonged and very angry booing. When Mr Mandela urged the youth to go out and make friends of their former enemies there was a sullen silence – then considerable numbers could be seen leaving the stadium. (We were watching on television.) The most enthusiastic cheering was reserved for the PAC leader, Clarence Makwetu. Today he modified his war-talk ('One settler, one bullet!') but everyone knows what he believes in and the crowd responded accordingly.

Meanwhile, in Cape Town, the ANC marshals had lost control and a serious misjudgement by Tony Yengeni, the radical ANC Western Cape leader, led to frenzied rioting and massive looting – R4 millions' worth of damage, acres of broken glass but 'only' three killed, including a policeman shot in the head. It seems the mood in the Cape townships is at present extra-angry: on 9 April the police murdered a local MK hero.

Durban and Port Elizabeth also had their share of rioting and looting, on a small scale. And in Pietersburg Mr Nelson Ramodike was terrorized out of the stadium by an infuriated 5,000 whom the marshals couldn't calm. However, once he had left the memorial service proceeded serenely.

When it was announced tonight that 26,000 security personnel are now being deployed to maintain law and order we wondered why the government hadn't long ago assigned a few security men to guard Chris Hani. Despite three earlier attempts on his life, the authorities had repeatedly refused Mr Mandela's and Mr Sisulu's pleas for a police bodyguard for one of the country's foremost political figures. And the police had repeatedly refused his MK bodyguards firearm licences. Yet his assassin legally held four weapons.

15 April

The tension will continue high until after Monday's funeral. The emotion in the air is almost tangible; one can feel it plucking at one's own nerves and sympathies.

After yesterday's Jabulani rally an estimated 12,000 marched three miles to Soweto's heavily fortified Protea police station, where a memorandum was handed to Major-General Braam Strauss. Moments later violence started; some Peace Monitors blame the police for driving fast through the crowd with provocative irresponsibility. The police claim they had to open fire because the mob was petrol-bombing the station. They shot four people dead. Five were critically wounded, 245 suffered lesser injuries including a BBC soundman, Lee Edwards, who was peppered with bird-shot and is now in hospital. According to him, the shooting took place after the ANC marshals had called for restraint and the marchers were dispersing. But obviously some Young Lions had planned an attack; people don't carry petrol bombs around like handkerchiefs, just in case they might come in handy.

In this torrid political climate some disquieting plants are appearing above ground. We've had the ANC Youth League demanding that Waluz be delivered to 'the people's justice', while the Congress of South African Students (COSAS) is specific about the form this justice should take. They favour – quoting biblical precedents – stoning to death in the street. A predilection not calculated to diminish white fear of black rule.

Amidst all the marching and praying, the rallying and chanting and toyi-toying, the fevered media speculation about what may or may not happen, personal grieving has impinged on South Africa's public as I don't think it ever could in the West. Those to whom Chris was close, those who have lost a beloved friend – Nelson Mandela, Desmond Tutu, Sam Shilowa, Tokyo Sexwale, Joe Slovo, the Sisulu and Tambo families – all are openly shattered, to be glimpsed in tears on TV or in press photographs. This gives a major political crisis, to which the whole world is paying attention, an intimate human quality that is strangely comforting. Here leaders are not required to be detached manipulators of mass emotion, but can share with us all their real feelings.

16 April

Illogical howls of complaint are now coming from some sections of the media. Wednesday's violence, they predict, will drastically reduce tourist earnings. If this is so, the media's own exaggerations, national and international, are largely to blame. One of the more pernicious TV devices is the repeated showing of the same violent scene; in many viewers' minds this creates the illusion that there have been multiple incidents of looting, arson or whatever. In fact, as today's responsible *Star* leader pointed out, 'Nelson Mandela did not lose control over his followers ... For every ten or a hundred thugs who behaved criminally there were tens of thousands who were disciplined – at more than ninety memorial services and rallies held all over the country on Wednesday.'

This point needs emphasizing because most whites, looking ahead to the weekend, are jellified. On Saturday thousands will be converging on Jo'burg for Sunday's lying-in-state at Soweto's FNB stadium and Monday's funeral – in all but name a State funeral. The elaborate arrangements for these events require the ANC and the authorities to co-operate as never before. In reality we have here an involuntary dress rehearsal for the new South Africa – which in fact this whole week has been. Wednesday's stayaway, described as the largest in the country's history (92 per cent), was the new South Africa in action. The workers, this time, will not be punished for staying away. Nobody, this time, would dare to punish them.

Between pre-colonial Africa and Ireland's ancient Gaelic society there are certain mysterious links, baffling to historians, concerning land tenure and cattle ownership. A contemporary link is the funeral – as a public display of solidarity with the bereaved, a social occasion far removed from the furtiveness with which the British bury (or cremate) their dead. In modern Ireland, long after wakes have been abandoned, hundreds of mourners may be observed thronging to small rural graveyards, some from other counties, other countries, even – in the jet-age – other continents. As a development of this, Northern

Ireland's 'political' funerals draw thousands of marchers, the mourning occasion transmuted into funeral-as-demo. In a parallel evolution here, township funeral rallies in the local stadium may be attended by fifty or sixty thousand. ANC marshals control crowds waving ANC and SACP banners, proclaiming loyalty to Nelson Mandela and singing the praises of the MK. Even when these rallies were illegal, the security forces couldn't arrest so many 'subversives' simultaneously breaking the law. However, they could intervene and during the last phase of the Struggle much of the violence was provoked by police attacks on funerals – leading to more deaths, more funerals, more attacks, more deaths...A bloody spiral, the blacks now unconquerably defiant, the security forces increasingly ruthless.

In February 1986 a celebrated four-day battle took place in Alexandra between militant youths and the army and police. Thirty-one Young Lions were killed, yet their side won. Both the Pretoria-imposed black councillors and the resident black police fled from Alex, never to return. But without a formal military structure you cannot switch violence on and off. Having tasted victory, not all the Young Lions were amenable to being caged when Ringmaster Mandela gave the signal. After February 1990 they were much praised for their contribution to the Struggle. Then, intoxicated by the success of violence, some groups set up ANC Self-Defence Units, ostensibly to protect their communities. Quickly those SDUs degenerated into gangs involved in protection racketeering, car theft as a business (usually in collusion with white SAP officers) and kangaroo courts that inflicted floggings and necklacings. In July 1992 an alarmed ANC asked Chris Hani to investigate the SDUs. They were running wild, he reported, committing appalling atrocities and 'simply had no conception of democratic tolerance'. He concluded, 'We can no longer keep quiet about this...We must take action, not only speak out. Whether we like it or not, these SDUs are associated with the ANC.' One can fairly assume that the booing of Mr Mandela in Jabulani stadium was led by SDUs.

17 April

Many people are now recalling examples of Chris Hani's efforts to foster racial harmony. He worked hard at this, attempting to establish one-to-one relationships with right-wingers and to persuade them that the new government would not be hostile to any whites. Recently he addressed right-wing students in Pretoria and, incredibly, was well received by them, such was his sincerity and the power of his oratory. In his role as champion of the poor he could move everybody who met him personally. To Chris 'the poor' were not an anonymous mass, an underclass, a 'political problem' for the new South Africa. They were suffering individuals.

Making a home in hardline CP-controlled Boksburg, and encouraging other blacks to do the same, was part of Chris's anti-racism campaign. His aged parents, still living in the Transkei, disapproved. They had feared for his safety ever since he returned to South Africa in August 1990 after twenty-seven years in exile (apart from clandestine visits). They begged him to settle in a black township – and they were right. It is certain that neither Janus Waluz nor any of his allies would have driven into Soweto or Alex, shot a black man and driven out again. Not, that is, unless they had police protection – as many white assassins have had over the years. However, Chris insisted that blacks and whites could live happily together, 'even when the black is me, MK and SACP, bad news!' He had proved his point before he died. Already Dawn Park is seen as a wholesome foretaste of how things can be in the new South Africa. As blacks moved in, the hardliners showed suspicion and fear. Then tolerance began to blossom. 'Block parties' were instituted, some black and white neighbours enjoying their braais and beers together – a scene I like to picture as a prototype. But the blacks will have to take the initiative, as they did in Boksburg.

18 April

Since yesterday, and all through the night, thousands have been arriving in Jo'burg from all over South Africa – from the Limpopo to the Cape – in buses, kombi taxis and special trains. At 11 a.m. Margaret dropped Jennifer and me at a junction on the Soweto Highway, about a mile from the FNB stadium. There was little 'normal' traffic; today the SAP limited it throughout the PWV area. Many other pedestrians coming from Soweto were crossing the dusty littered veld and the two elderly white females – arriving *on foot*! – were regarded with much curiosity, some friendliness, no hostility. Turning left onto a dirt road, we passed a grove of ancient plane trees – stately giants – and between them glimpsed the Rand's oldest 'residential area', a short nameless street of seven little red-brick houses belonging to Crown Mines. This isolated (perhaps forgotten?) hamlet remained 'mixed' – Coloured and white – throughout the apartheid era.

Hawkers swarmed outside the stadium; for R15 I bought a red SACP Hani T-shirt. At every entrance uniformed ANC marshals stood guard; thousands are on duty today and have been given powers of arrest. Only MK cadres are 'unofficially allowed' to bring guns into the stadium – a phrase with an Irish flavour! At once we got lost in a labyrinth of ill-lit concrete stairways; the bowels of all big stadia are intricate. But eventually Jennifer met black nun friends who guided us out into brilliant sunshine. As yet the stadium was scarcely half-full. We sat low down, close to the ramp entrance through which the hearse would arrive, behind an enormous stage where frowning, shouting men were frantically struggling with miles of tangled electric flexes. Beside us a group of youngsters, who had travelled overnight by bus from the Transkei, were not too exhausted to sing melancholy songs – slow waves of a Xhosa funeral chant.

Quickly the seats filled and below us privileged people – richly robed clergy, choristers in black and green, altar boys in scarlet and white, primary-school musicians in yellow and blue – went to their appointed places on stage or pitch. By 1 p.m. some 70,000 had assembled – singing, talking, laughing, toyi-toying.

'Now we will be silent,' said the MC. And we were silent. All 70,000 of us were silent, immediately. Then the ivory-coloured hearse emerged from the underground ramp and drove very slowly onto the grassy pitch. An MK detachment bore the coffin to its stand under a yellow and black awning on the halfway line, followed by a solitary Comrade, carrying Chris's camouflage cap on a white satin cushion. The MK, in olive-green uniforms, formed a guard of honour behind the coffin. (This was their first public parade in South Africa.) Then the family filed past: three beautiful daughters, a dignified widow, frail parents. At this point several of the MK – veteran guerrilla fighters, tough as they come – began to weep without restraint. And the silence continued unbroken, a silence I shall never forget. There is something altogether overwhelming about an absence of sound in such a vast crowd; within that silence is the concentrated essence of mourning.

For several hours an orderly line filed past the open coffin – VIPs by the hundred, from every continent, and blacks by the thousand, mostly young people. I thought, 'What an appalling ordeal for the family, sitting there on the stage for so long, the focus of everybody's attention!' But Jennifer assured me this ceremony would comfort them.

We left in time to get home before dark and were wandering rather vaguely outside the stadium, unsure how to find transport back to Jo'burg, when three Sowetan women hurried to overtake us and advised not *that* way, which could be dicey, but *this* way... For us, 'that way or this way' was a one-off problem. For them, it is a daily concern – they live with the threat of random violence. Not only whites are at risk in the anarchic townships.

19 April

Last evening, as I sat writing the above, nineteen people were murdered, including two little children sleeping in their beds, by unknown black gunmen cruising around the Vaal township of Sebokeng. The SAP have offered a quarter-of-a-million-rand reward for information leading to the arrest and conviction of the killers. Also, a mother was found shot dead on the veld with her baby still asleep on her back. Some say the Sebokeng massacre was a right-wing plot to destabilize the situation further and cause the funeral crowd to erupt. Happily it didn't have this effect, though there has been tragedy enough today.

From 9 a.m. to 3.30 p.m. most of South Africa again came to a halt while television showed us the funeral service in the stadium and the burial in South Park cemetery (until recently 'Whites Only') near Boksburg. At least 100,000 were present in a stadium built to hold 85,000; daring youths had perched on every roof and wall, however apparently inaccessible. Soon after the opening ceremony we could detect trouble outside. Despite being safe in cosy Florida, I felt twinges of fear as menacing clouds of dark smoke billowed high above the stands. Then occasional shots could be heard through the speeches and, even on television, the rising crowd-tension was palpable. Moments later, Cyril Rama-phosa requested all doctors present to go to the first-aid tents and ordered the crowd to stay put until 'the emergency' was over. Everyone obeyed this order. The mourners inside were just that; the mob beyond were criminals. This contrast was a comforting reminder that South Africa's ghastly violence is minority-generated. Well, of course, like violence everywhere. Yet here it is more taken for granted; newspapers casually report, in a brief paragraph, the sort of bloody mayhem that would be headline news in Europe.

Then came another comforting contrast: between the crowd's welcomes for Nelson Mandela and Peter Mokaba, the ANC Youth League leader, whose current favourite slogan is 'Kill the farmer! Kill the Boer!' The stadium's fabric seemed threatened by the crowd's ecstatic stomping reception of Comrade Mandela. Mokaba was received warmly enough, but not with delir-ium. Wisely he had been muzzled at the last moment. On the programme he headed the list of six speakers but – 'No time for a speech,' he explained, starting a toyi-toyi.

Mr Mandela's address was mainly directed to the youth. 'Be part of the reconstruction of our country,' he urged them. 'Black lives are cheap and will remain so as long as apartheid continues to exist. And let there be no mistake, there have been many changes and negotiations have started, but for the ordinary black person apartheid is alive and well!' Loud cheers.

The core of this speech went a long way to explain South Africa's present state of instability:

No effort has been spared to criminalize both MK and Chris Hani. This has created a climate of acceptance when an MK cadre is assassinated, as dozens have been over the past few months . . . the hunting down of an outlaw is regarded as legitimate . . . Those who have deliberately created this climate . . . are as much responsible for the death of Chris Hani as the man who pulled the trigger and the conspirators who plotted his murder. In this regard, the Minister of Law and Order and the Chief of the Army both have a great deal to answer for.

Quite soon after my arrival in South Africa I realized that the government's two-timing on this issue has been (apart from anything else) unfair to ordinary whites. Like it or not, they are eventually going to find themselves with SACP and ex-MK cabinet ministers, and it is now their leaders' responsibility to calm their fears. Instead, even while negotiating with the ANC/SACP, many Nats continue to present them as threatening Commie terrorists.

The funeral programme stated: 'The burial service at the cemetry [*sic*] is limited to family members only.' Inevitably, this wish for privacy was disregarded. An estimated 30,000 bussed from the stadium to Boksburg, some youths dancing on the roofs of speeding vehicles. Astonishingly, only one fell off and was killed. Near the cemetery heavily armed AWB contingents were lined up to defend Boksburg from the *swart gevaar*. The more nervous whites had taken refuge elsewhere, the new black residents stood by their gates to let the crowd know whose homes are these. Despite the AWB 'defenders', five Dawn Park homes were robbed during the burial service, a supermarket was looted then burned and a maize-field was set alight though several ANC marshals tried to save it. No white was attacked but the SAP killed one looter. Most whites (even quite civilized specimens) take for granted the SAP's regular killing of robbers and looters, as though death were an appropriate punishment for stealing.

On the East Rand three ANC members on their way to the funeral were killed by shots from the Inkatha Thokozani Hostel and in Katlehong Inkatha gunned down three others.

This evening 'the emergency' outside the FNB stadium was explained. A mob of a few hundred attacked, looted and eventually burned those seven Crown Mine houses we passed yesterday. Two white men and four dogs were cornered inside one house and roasted to death. A fifth dog was tied to a tree, petrol-soaked and set alight. The besieged men's ordeal was prolonged; they made repeated frantic telephone calls to the police, explaining that more and more youngsters were trying to break into their home to kill them. But the police arrived only after the murderous arson had started.

The SAP knows it has an image problem. Last January a Community Relations Division was established and equipped with a Police Creativity Section Officer (whatever that may be) who said, in February, 'Already 15,000 policemen have received awareness lessons. We teach them to realize that things are changing and they must handle it. But they must not only cope with change, they must become part of the change.'

20 April

In Washington, the South African Embassy flew the national flag at half-mast until today; not only blacks were shocked by the government's failure to do likewise here. Even more distressing was its refusal to suspend yesterday's sitting of Parliament. Miss Dene Smuts of the Democratic Party (DP) requested this 'as a gesture of sympathy and solidarity'. The rejection of this request was an insult, at the end of the white era, in tune with all that has gone before.

22 April

On 17 April Clive Derby-Lewis, a member of the President's Council and a senior CP leader, was arrested in connection with the assassination. Yesterday evening his wife Gabriella ('Gaye') was also taken into custody. An Australian ex-nun, it was said she ran a gay bar in Hillbrow, central Jo'burg, for several years before marrying Derby-Lewis; her first husband was an SADF officer. While the male of the species was trying to retain segregation in Boksburg, the female was running a vigorous and notably unsuccessful campaign to 'Keep Hillbrow White'. Now people are remembering the obliquely named Western Goals Institute, led by Clive Derby-Lewis, which announced in June 1992 that it was offering 'self-defence training' to South Africa's whites to equip them to protect themselves from the 'ANC terrorist onslaught'. This training, explained Derby-Lewis, would be conducted under his supervision by professional ex-soldiers from the SADF, the old Rhodie army and the British SAS. The Institute, he added, was founded 'to protect the Western way of life', and had offices in Krugersdorp and London. He is also a director of the Stallard Foundation which looks after the interests of English-speaking CP members and recruits from among the thousands of right-wing European émigrés who found their spiritual home in the old South Africa. Like Janus Waluz and his brother, many of these are Eastern Europeans consumed by a pathological hatred of Communism. Oddly, no one is commenting on the double coincidence that all three charged with Hani's murder are non-Afrikaners – a Pole, an English-speaker and an Australian – and all were brought up as Roman Catholics.*

24 April

The leaderships of the ANC, the SACP and COSATU overlap bewilderingly. Many whites, seeing the ANC clinging with one hand to the SACP, while the other beckons foreign capitalists, continue to cling with both hands to the Commie bogey they were brought up on.

'Workers Unite for a White South Africa!' was an early slogan of the SACP, founded in 1921. Although Moscow soon put a stop to that, the SACP leadership

---

* On 15 October 1993, Janus Waluz and Clive Derby-Lewis were sentenced to death for the murder of Chris Hani. Gaye Derby-Lewis was released for lack of evidence.

long remained white and its influence limited. Most politically active blacks were then committed to liberal democracy as defined by their Christian middle-class leaders.

When the 1950 Suppression of Communism Act outlawed the SACP, Nelson Mandela and Oliver Tambo suggested expelling the few Communists in their new organization, the ANC Youth League. Only when Western governments refused to oppose apartheid were they driven to seek allies of any ideological hue. (Not long before, white South Africans had been Stalin's allies.)

In the late 1950s the SACP leadership suggested sharing expertise and resources with the not yet banned ANC. A Kremlin-approved collaboration began in 1962 and within months the SACP's Arthur Goldreich had persuaded Moscow to donate US$2.8 million to the new-born MK. Among the 13,000 (approximately) exiles who were eventually being fed, housed, clothed, doctored, taught, employed and armed in the 'sanctuary states' – Tanzania, Zambia, Angola – there was grateful support for Communists-as-generous-comrades. And the SACP officially condoned the Soviet invasions of Hungary, Czechoslovakia and Afghanistan. But among the exiled ANC leadership, the increasing closeness of the ANC/SACP relationship and the compromising dependence on Soviet funding was causing much friction and many defections.

Yesterday, in Soweto, I met a returned exile whose parents encouraged him to leave in 1980, when he was 17, and at some risk to themselves organized the first stage of his journey, into Botswana. After five years at the ANC college (SOMAFCO: the Solomon Mahlangu Freedom College) near Mazimbu in Tanzania, Musa worked in one of the ANC's Lusaka offices: 'My mother made me promise never to join MK, she wanted to think of me safe in Lusaka.' (MK was then based in Angola, linked to the ANC's government-in-exile in Lusaka but acting almost autonomously and, at times, with a barbarity that mirrored the behaviour of the SADF.) 'My parents did well to send me away. In '76 I was out there in front, enjoying the excitement, getting to feel it would be fun to kill a policeman. That was OK, when policemen were killing us, but by '86 I could have been necklacing and that was bad – not justice. If some of the necklaced were real informers, others were only suspected. And beating up is enough – not *necklacing!*'

I asked how it was, being a student at SOMAFCO.

'Lonely at first, wanting my family. And hard work! Most of us needed remedial courses. Primary-school kids were aged up to 19, high school up to 25. Our teachers were all ANC supporters, some from Europe and America and Australia, but most had no qualifications. The older exiles ran the place, they'd left after the banning and been living in London and all over. They worried we'd get too violent and every week we'd get lectures about ANC ideology, getting ready to work with whites after the Struggle was won. They said fighting a guerrilla war with commercial sabotage was good, killing white farmers and bombing shops and cafés was bad. Those old people were away too long, they didn't know how things had changed since they left. Now it's all changed again and Comrade Chris was right – more violence will only slow things up, delay the election.'

Musa's parents want him to be a teacher, he wants to be a journalist. 'I have a lot inside my head to say and soon we'll have ANC papers to write in. But now I'm 30 – getting old and no qualification! In Tanzania we'd only technical training, no university chance. They said technical skills make it easier to get jobs, so now I work on vehicle repairs. Some went to Soviet universities, they gave 400 scholarships a year for ANC students. I didn't want to go there, my parents frightened me about Communism, they knew about it. But in exile I couldn't say that, the Soviets were helping us so much. They sent food, clothes, trucks – and to Angola weapons instructors from East Germany. Most kids didn't understand Communists are against Christians. I had to watch it – talking against Communism is agreeing with Pretoria and they'd suspect me. Only another boy thought like me and we'd whisper together. We wished other countries like America would help but we knew they only *said* they were against apartheid.'

And in Lusaka's ANC colony, how was it?

'Very tense! We feared informers sliding in, so no mixing with others, no jolling with Zambians! But everyone said it was better than Angola, that was real heavy, all going crazy suspecting informers. Some leaders tortured – even killed – too many cadres. About 8,000 Comrades were there, armed and trained to fight but not many sent on missions so the others got restless. Now we've thousands of them home again but Comrade Mandela tells them, "No more fighting!" They ask why, when we're still getting shit in the townships. The Nats have two mouths, one for negotiating, one for telling Inkatha to kill us!'

25 April

On today's *Sunday Times* letters page, one Ralph Pentecost, Oranjezicht, demonstrated his incomprehension of the nature of apartheid: 'If ten separate, independent and self-governing homelands – encompassing 16,7 million inhabitants, ideally situated within the South Africa market area and provided with an annual golden egg of R6 billion from South Africa's tax-payers – have proved a failure even after so many years of probation, what hope for the ANC or a black-controlled homeland called South Africa?' It is safe to assert that Mr Pentecost has never visited a homeland though he must have driven through several.

A few evenings ago on TV, Carl Niehaus of the ANC conveyed sympathy to the CP on the death of its leader, Dr Treurnicht, and invited the party to join the ANC in the negotiating process, for South Africa's sake. Pretty remarkable, in view of three leading CP members having been charged with Chris Hani's murder. 'A gesture of unusual magnanimity,' the press noted today. They also noted Eugene Terre' Blanche's boast that Janus Waluz has been an AWB member since 1986.

27 April

My Hani T-shirt, incorporating a large picture of Comrade Chris on the bosom, is proving an invaluable research instrument. This morning as I walked along Smit Street in central Jo'burg, nine male motorists slowed down to abuse the white woman flaunting her SACP sympathies. The vibes thus generated reminded me of my evening with the Dullstroom trio.

A week ago, in Florida station, the tall thin AWB-faced railway clerk stared at me savagely (no other word for it) and asked, 'Are you proud of your shirt?'

'Yes, very,' said I, whereupon he snarled at my request for a third-class ticket ('None left!') and flicked me a first class.

When I appeared again this morning with Comrade Chris on my bosom he sneered, 'First or third?'

'Third,' said I, causing him to lose his cool completely. Pushing the ticket towards me he shouted, 'That's where you belong! Yes, that's where *you* belong!'

When I told Jennifer about this duel she went into a dangerous spasm of laughter – we were motoring and the humour of the situation so overcame her we might have gone off the road. Mopping up tears of mirth she chortled, 'In *Florida* station! A *white* woman in a *Hani* T-shirt travelling *third*! Poor man, the *shock*! For years he'll be having nightmares about it, you don't know what you've *done* to him! This will become an obsession, proof of the Apocalypse, he'll not be able to talk about anything else in his Roodepoort bar!' Thus did Jennifer make my earnest indignation look silly: South Africa needs more of her sort. This country quite quickly defuses the traveller's sense of humour, until someone who can keep everything in perspective comes along to reactivate it.

29 April

Given its origins, one can't reasonably criticize Jo'burg's charmlessness. They came, they dug, they spent. And that's how Jo'burg looks and feels, at least to the casual visitor. There is only one surprise – the many destitute whites, always unkempt and malnourished, often drunk and/or stoned, who sit on kerbs in the downmarket areas or beg at corners, grateful for the small change of affluent blacks.

Visitors are supposed to feel a thrill because three miles down, below their feet, tens of thousands of miners are scrabbling for gold in temperatures which the Chamber of Mines coyly declines to specify. This visitor failed to feel that thrill. Nor did I kneel to worship the Carlton Centre (Africa's highest building) or Jo'burg's other corporate excesses – horrors belonging to a nightmare set in the twenty-second century, when genetic engineers are designing architects. This whole unlovely metropolis (population 3.5 million) is unmistakably alien; it hangs on Africa like a crude fake jewel on a beautiful woman.

If one could forget the surrounding suffering townships, it might be mildly enjoyable to ramble through Tycoonville where wide silent streets are lined with majestic trees, between which may be glimpsed the mansions of the fabulously rich – including, now, Mr Mandela. Here each electrified gateway has its warning plaque: the legend says 'ARMED RESPONSE!', the illustration is a cocked gun. (It is generally assumed that most criminals are illiterate.) In theory, 'Armed Response' is provided by your expensive security firm whose officers arrive within moments of a button being pressed. But many are the tales of buttons being pressed in vain. This living under siege has nothing to do with the new South Africa; thirty-five years ago it startled Jan (then James) Morris.

Like most Florida folk, Margaret eschews 'Armed Response' and relies on heavy metal gates, with complicated locks, to reinforce all doors and french windows. From her high stoep on a ridge-top the view is quite pleasing, over-looking miles of wooded suburbs. A century ago there wasn't a tree to be seen on the dusty veld, now Jo'burg is reputed to be the most treeful city in all the world – gold talks! Yet it has never talked loudly enough to furnish Jo'burg with a public-transport system, apart from the countless trains, kombi taxis and buses that ferry black workers from and to the townships. Florida's railway link has enabled me to reach the city centre independently – otherwise, my social life has been limited. As the residential suburbs sprawl all over the ex-veld, your dinner host may have to drive sixty miles or more between fetching and delivering. Few guests are worth this effort so not everyone on my Jo'burg list has been contacted.

Tomorrow Lear and I are being driven to Krugersdorp, some fifteen miles from Florida, where the lethal-to-cyclists metropolis ends. In this notoriously right-wing Derby-Lewis home town, feelings are now inflamed on both sides. The ANC have announced a consumer boycott by the residents of Kagiso, Krugersdorp's township, and their demands are not calculated to lower the temperature: 1) the resignation of all Krugersdorp's white town councillors and their replacement by a mixed-race interim administration accountable to every-body in the area; 2) the removal of all white policemen from Kagiso until South Africa's security forces have been put under multi-party control; 3) government financing of Kagiso's SDUs(!). This is just one of many consumer boycotts being planned countrywide.

On 26 April negotiations were resumed at the World Trade Centre. This time they must succeed – and quickly.

4

The Platteland Volk

Orkney – Kimberley – Griquatown

The Afrikaners are decent people who have been misled by their leaders.
Nelson Mandela

From far away you can recognize us as the bearers of God's light in Africa.
Eugene Terre' Blanche, AWB leader

I don't think our roots as Afrikaners are planted in the soil of justice.
Wilhelm Verwoerd, grandson of Hendrik Verwoerd and ANC member

Orkney, 7 May 1993

I have enjoyed the past week. None of my three guidebooks (1897, 1939, 1993) mentions the region between Jo'burg and Kimberley. 'It's boring, very boring,' Jo'burg friends had warned me. (I'm sure no pun intended, though English-speakers lack affection for their Boer fellow-citizens.) However, any rural landscape must seem enchanting after three weeks on the Rand and this season provides perfect cycling weather: the sun warm, the light sharply brilliant, fleets of white cloudlets sailing high. Regularly each morning, between 8 and 9 a.m., a cool tailwind rises, enabling me to make good time on narrow smooth secondary roads where the few cars and bakkies now travel in convoy for security reasons. Usually I cover seventy or eighty miles by mid-afternoon, leaving ample time for conversation in dorps or on farms.

The well-named platteland seems unnaturally level: not a hint of a rise or fall, mile after mile, day after day. Only colossal silvery grain-silos punctuate this treeless expanse – often several visible at once, in the far distance. Vast maize-fields alternate with what here passes for pasture: wiry sparse brown grass and the ubiquitous khaki plant, its peppery aroma scenting the early mornings. During the Anglo-Boer War, khaki-plant seeds travelled from India in the cavalry's fodder and it has spread all over South Africa – and beyond. The winter colouring is sombre: cinnamon, fawn, grey-green – more grey than green. Those tints somehow emphasize the sense of boundless space: immeasurably remote horizons, the sky dominant, its deep blue immensity drawing the gaze upwards in awe, diminishing the ego.

Afrikaner hospitality is legendary (though uitlanders may not notice it in the northern Transvaal) and since leaving Jo'burg it has overwhelmed me – a hospitality spontaneous, generous, taking the stranger to the family's heart. The Boers' endearingly old-fashioned homes recall rural Ireland in my childhood when 'appearances' mattered – keeping them up by getting out the best china for the visitor, sitting in the parlour, baking special cakes. English is spoken haltingly, in many families not at all. Throughout the western Transvaal the Boers have few English-speakers with whom to practise.

One of my hosts, George, went to some trouble to organize a visit to new schools in the nearest township. First a call to the police – yes, all was quiet at present, whites could safely enter Mphebana. Then by Mercedes to the dorp, ten miles away, driving between George's maize-fields: withered brown leaves on tall stalks, cobs still drying out – to be harvested, George explained, when the moisture content is down to 16 per cent. He worries more about the Transvaal's future water supply than about the Republic's future government. In his boyhood, fifty-odd years ago, several now-vanished springs and streams blessed this region; lines of dead or dying bushes still mark the streams' stony courses. In the decades ahead, George foresees water becoming more precious than oil – or gold, or diamonds, or uranium.

In Voortrekker Street we picked up the Afrikaner butcher who was to be our 'liaison officer', introducing us to Eric, an ANC community leader who would show us around the schools. In Koster, a month ago, this precautionary chain of contacts would not have been necessary. Now everyone is aware that the post-assassination anger, though so remarkably well-controlled, has not evaporated.

Eric is a young Tswana, short and neatly built, intelligent, realistic, energetic and with a self-confidence, in relation to whites, not common among South Africa's blacks. He works for the township's Civic Association; its most recent achievement has been electrification, at last the poles and wires are going up. Not for the first time, I wondered why so many whites feel pride rather than shame when they see their local township being electrified in 1993.

From afar, one can see Mphebana's long, three-storey, red-brick high school blending into its background of red-brown veld. A splendid building; rural Ireland doesn't have many such fine schools. As we arrived pupils were streaming towards their classrooms, a considerable number young adults whose scholastic careers were fractured by the Struggle. An encouraging sight, *but...* The usual 'buts': poor equipment, teachers themselves uneducated, overcrowded classrooms. However, truancy lessens that last problem; often half a class is missing for reasons unspecified. Teachers also go AWOL quite often, to supplement their miserly salaries. Yet in the junior classrooms one could only exult, looking at those friendly, eager, happy faces – the first liberated generation, for whose right to grow up free so many have suffered so much.

'The problems are very big,' said Eric. 'For us education was never compulsory, our kids will take time to settle to it. First we need keen well-trained teachers to get them interested – and good equipment. The easy bit is a smart building, the hard bit is making right what happens inside it. Last year we got 48 per cent of the education budget, twenty years ago we got only 16 per cent – but 48 per cent won't do for 76 per cent of the population!'

The new primary school, another 'smart building', is slightly better equipped and much better staffed by dedicated, articulate, elegantly dressed young women. Classes had just ended and each room was being swept and tidied by small pupils with big smiles. The boys, I noted approvingly, were doing the sweeping while the girls tidied.

'Here they don't truant,' said Eric. 'This age group is getting the habit of regular schooling. They will become ambitious, seeking top exam marks and university. And they must learn not to expect university only because they're black. Affirmative action like that is not good.'

Education for adult whites is also needed. Back on the farm, George chanced to switch on the TV as Oliver Tambo's funeral began. He frowned and wondered, 'Who's this fellow?' Censorship has left most whites ignorant about the evolution of their own country's destiny. For thirty years Oliver Tambo, as leader-in-exile of the ANC, was a respected international figure, someone of a stature unmatched by any contemporary white South African leader. Yet while he was influencing the future – bringing about the present – of his (and George's) country, whites were not allowed to be aware of his existence. He was a 'terrorist', a Commie, deleted from their lives. No wonder so many ordinary whites are now in such a mental and emotional muddle.

Ventersdorp, at first sight, seems just one more dorp with the standard features. In fact it has a significant extra feature: the headquarters of the AWB. Even if one didn't know that on arrival, the vibes would soon impinge. Since the Hani assassination groups of men wearing black AWB uniforms and wielding rifles have thrice invaded Tshing, Ventersdorp's township, swearing and jeering at the residents and threatening them with 'What we did to Hani.' In reaction, the Tshing folk erected barriers and armed themselves. Those barriers remain up – and so does the tension. Ventersdorp struck me as a dark place despite the cloudless sky, wide tree-lined streets, brightly painted shops, flowery front gardens. Men in khaki uniforms, with guns on hips, strode around looking angrily purposeful. Women with suspicious eyes, tight perms and thin lips were short-tempered with their small children. No English-language newspapers, not even *The Citizen*, were on sale. No blacks were visible. Every lamp-post displayed a notice summoning farmers to an anti-new South Africa rally in Potchefstroom. The hotel admitted the sweaty, dusty uitlander only after some hesitation.

The AWB headquarters is a modest, surprisingly unfortified bungalow at the end of van Riebeeck Street. At the entrance loomed a scowling hulk of a security officer. Beyond him a thin elderly peroxide blonde sat at her desk under the AWB's adaptation of the swastika. Having glanced at her watch she said, 'You must be the Irishwoman – you know Dr Paisley?' My disclaiming that honour obviously disappointed her. 'He is a fearless man of God,' she pronounced. 'He will save Ireland.' I could see her logic : Terre' Blanche saves South Africa, Paisley saves Ireland.

The dominee (DRC minister) who had agreed to meet me is reputedly the AWB's second-in-command. However, the right wing is so fractured and fractious one can't be sure about these finer points. Now Dominee Snyman suddenly appeared by my side, a towering figure with a corpulence problem and bright, very blue eyes. His slouch hat and long bushy grey beard replicate those of the Boer War leaders, several of whom stare sternly from the walls of his office. This room is half-filled by a Voortrekker ox-wagon, superbly crafted; in 1988 it was drawn to Pretoria's Voortrekker Monument during the 150th anniversary celebrations of the Great Trek. As Freda Troup noted, 'The Great Trek was to become so central an event in South African affairs as almost to institute a new calendar...'.

My host welcomed me with old-world courtesy, called for coffee and biscuits, lit his long-stemmed clay pipe (another Boer accessory) and opened his bible. It was a much-annotated tome of great age, recalling the Landman family bible in André Brink's *An Act of Terror*. Strips of parchment marked the passages justifying – nay, exhorting – apartheid. Having been cursed by the Lord, explained Dominee Snyman, the sons of Ham turned black and became irredeemably degenerate – subhuman. The Afrikaans language, as it evolved, took care of the distinction between *mense* (meaning people, who are white) and *skepsels* (meaning creatures, who are non-white). Every right-wing thought, word and deed is inspired from On High; the AWB are only doing what they have to do, as men and women who heed the word of the Lord.

The oddest thing about this encounter was its time-warp quality. From a 1993 perspective, Dominee Snyman seemed unreal, epitomizing the extremity of mad Verwoerdianism, standing so far from where South Africa is now that I wanted to laugh. Yet he is also completely authentic – uncannily so, as though in Madame Tussaud's President Kruger came to life and offered coffee. He is a vigorous, eloquent anachronism, his fanaticism off the scale; yet he didn't repel and scare me as the Dullstroom trio, the Florida railway clerk and many others have done. His focus seemed different. Theologically he has it all sorted out; the

Bible tells him how to handle blacks, and it may well be that he is consistently kind to those who remember they are *skepsels*.

Fringe fanaticism is intellectually boring, however politically exciting at times. Little groups stuck in historical grooves, denying the validity of changing ideas and circumstances, induce yawns. Yet not all their members are to be despised. As individuals, some fanatics have an integrity lacking in many mainstream moderate politicians. There is nothing to be gained in the new South Africa by dedicating yourself to the cause of an Afrikaner volkstaat. The materially ambitious now support the winning black team and queue up for the perks of political power. If you sit in a bungalow headquarters in Ventersdorp, raving and ranting about your God-given right to rule over the *skepsels*, you're mad but disarmingly other-worldly.

To fill in time before my next appointment, with a CP leader, I toured the trim, prim suburbs where garden-'boys' were sweeping up the autumn leaves and Rottweilers in fenced dog-runs became hysterically xenophobic on seeing/smelling the uitlander. The only other signs of life were a few housewives motoring back from the shops – scarcely half a mile away.

Beyond Ventersdorp's staid DRC church – narrow-fronted, tall-steepled, whitewashed – I turned back, averting my eyes from yet another quartet of jolly gnomes prancing around a plastic grotto on a sun-bleached lawn. (Nowadays not all whites can afford to keep their lawns sprinkled.) How much, I wondered, has the loosening of the DRC's grip to do with the Afrikaners' acceptance of change? Those upwardly mobile, semi-Anglicized Afrikaners one meets in Jo'burg are by now a numerous breed, proof of the economic effectiveness of ruthless 'affirmative action'. And they have long since escaped from Christian Nationalism's straitjacket.

Seeing the present level of white prosperity, it's easy to forget that during the Great Depression tens of thousands of tenant farmers (bywoners) were urbanized, willy-nilly, and became a homeless and hungry proletariat. Their plight stimulated the development of Grand Apartheid and some argue that Verwoerd's social engineering should be described as Afrikaner tribalism rather than white racism. He might equally have discriminated ruthlessly against English-speakers had that been possible. But it wasn't. Most English-speakers (then 40 per cent of the whites) were rich, educated, influential and in control of the economy.

Their 'evolution in isolation' is what distinguishes the Afrikaners from all other settler populations of European descent. The pioneering Boers, once beyond reach of the Cape Peninsula, were for generations cut off from 'outside', untouched by any current of new European thinking. For 150 years they fought, enslaved, co-operated with (sometimes mated with) the 'natives' – Hottentots, Bushmen, Bantus. They became another cattle-centred tribe, living frugally, sustained by Calvinism at its most rigid, using the Bible (reinterpreted) to 'prove' their racial superiority and being literally lawless because there was no one around to administer laws. The European mindset changed radically between 1652 and 1948; the average Afrikaner mindset changed remarkably little.

During the 1940s the Broederbond planned to create an Afrikaner middle class powerful enough to stand up to the English-speakers. J. H. P. Serfontein, an Afrikaner liberal, described the plan in action.

> The Broederbond represents the vast majority of Nationalist cabinet ministers and parliamentarians as well as leaders in the Church, education, cultural movements, newspapers, labour, police, government services, universities. It links leaders to Church councils and local village communities in the smallest centres. They are tightly knit together, each cell receiving regular directives. Study materials and instructions are intensively discussed, so forging the members into a cohesive, nation-wide unit. A common approach to issues and problems is created so that public opinion can be masterminded.

The 'new South Africa' envisaged in 1948 looked like this: 'A free, independent, republican, Christian-National state, based on the word of God, eschewing all foreign models... with a Christian-National educational system... and the strongest emphasis upon the effective disciplining of the people.' A committee of Nat politicians and Potchefstroom professors had devised the new educational system. Parents had to appoint and closely supervise teachers, 'unless the teacher is a Christian he is a deadly danger to us'. The most important secular subject had to be the mother-tongue – henceforth the official language, with English grudgingly tolerated for reasons of expediency. Geography had to give children a detailed knowledge of the country allotted to them by God – to inspire them to die, if necessary, in its defence. The history of the Fatherland had to include all the facts (*sic*) about the Creation, the Fall, the Incarnation, the Life and Death of Christ, the Second Coming and the End of the World. The franchise, a precious privilege, could not be given to 'undeveloped' people, or to humanists, Communists or other factions upholding anti-Christian philosophies. Off-the-wall – yes? Yet this nonsense skewed South Africa's governance for forty years.

Back in van Riebeeck Street, I sat waiting for Mr Hoogendyk in the cp's regional head office, next door to the awb headquarters – so 'next door' ideologically that the two buildings beat as one, and I had already met Mr Hoogendyk outside Dominee Snyman's office. Opposite me hung a life-size photograph of the new cp leader, Dr Ferdi Hartenberg, who has been described as 'so *verkramp* you could plough with him'. The useful words *verkramp* and *verligte* scarcely need translating: hardliners have cramped minds, moderates have enlightened minds.

Mr Hoogendyk is youngish, tall, handsome, clean-shaven, with a friendly open face and a firm welcoming handshake. His humdrum lounge-suit made him seem out of place in militaristic Ventersdorp. It would be pointless to record his various febrile fantasies – for example, 'God gave us this land so we know nobody human can take it from us.' When I expressed some doubts about divine intervention in the 1990s he said calmly, 'But I believe in *miracles*, don't you? The Bible is full of them. A miracle can save South Africa if we manage to defuse this situation with minimal loss of life, according to God's will.' I refrained from mentioning the Derby-Lewises but my tact was superfluous. According to Mr Hoogendyk, a few more precisely timed 'selective assassinations' could save many lives, both black and white. The Derby-Lewises and Janus Waluz are God's instruments.

I may be giving the impression that Mr Hoogendyk is not nice to know. On the contrary, he's a decent upright fellow, efficiently processed by the Christian-National educational machine and truly believing that enfranchising blacks must lead to civil war. To avert catastrophe certain key figures must be eliminated, mentioning no names – but those names have already been mentioned on the hit list found in the Derby-Lewises' flat. Ruled by such convictions, his pro-assassin-ation stance makes sense. I rather liked him, even after his assertion: 'Blacks are animals with no brain power, they know they need us. It's only Commies with degrees from places like Yale and Cambridge come home to make trouble.' I forbore to ask what *muti* enabled *skepsels* with no brain power to graduate from places like Yale and Cambridge.

As I returned to the hotel, people eyed me speculatively. In all dorps, and especially in Ventersdorp, strangers' movements are monitored. I had arrived on a bicycle so I wasn't a journalist. I had spent the forenoon with the AWB and the afternoon with the CP. I am aged and shabby – what could the story be? Had anyone even half-smiled, or wished me the time of day, I would gladly have stopped and told them. But the Ventersdorp volk don't unbend.

The hotel bar is male territory; everyone was loaded with weapons and looked impatient to use them. Then I noticed a slim unarmed fortyish man standing alone at the far end of the counter, looking the way I felt. His gloom lifted on my approach. 'What,' he asked, 'brings you to this museum?'

A mining engineer from Orkney, on the Free State border, Gerrit was stuck in Ventersdorp because his car had broken down. 'Look at them!' he muttered. 'You see them on telly but you don't believe it – you have to see them live... Hey! It's too heavy in here, let's move to the lounge.' As we left, the barman was showing off his pump-action shotgun, kept under the counter in a locked metal case.

The empty lounge smelled of spilled brandy and decades of cigarette smoke. Debilitated pot-plants trailed tangled tendrils. The SABC was providing an

American TV comedy geared to the mentally subnormal which Gerrit assassin-ated before pouring our beers. 'Those dinosaurs in there,' he said, keeping his voice down, 'they're looking back to the Boer War! I'm just as Afrikaner but looking forwards. Afrikanerdom – hell! You can't make a nation out of a fragment of the population. In America and Australia they killed their natives, then made their nations. I'm glad we didn't do that, now we're going to show the world a multiracial state *can* work. We've been learning the hard way how to play our piano using black and white keys together.'

'What about the dinosaurs: will they be a long-term problem?'

Gerrit flicked his fingers dismissively. 'That lot don't feature, politically. They're our criminal element, like the tsotsies in the townships. It's all stupid bluff, fooling around in uniforms like kids pretending to be cowboys!'

'But some of their leaders are clever men, distinguished academics like Hartzenberg. And it's not all bluff – Chris Hani was killed. And they could kill... other people.' Some superstition prevented my saying 'Mandela', a pos-sibility too awful to be voiced.

'OK, so they killed Hani – and it didn't work. Now Mandela looks good as a leader, and they look like idiots – couldn't even organize a getaway car for Waluz!'

A meal had been reluctantly thrown together for the unexpected guests: tough steaks, pallid chips, tinned peas. In between strenuous bouts of mastication I remarked on how well most Afrikaners seem to be coping with their trauma – taking the Apocalypse on the chin.

'And so we should,' said Gerrit. 'If we say we're Africans – white Africans – then we must muck in with other Africans. Right? And we must admit it's their country, too. I'm not a crazy liberal, though my Dad thinks I am! I'm not saying I'd like my daughter to marry a black – I'd fight that... But we can co-operate without copulating – you with me? Have you heard about the Broederbond? They're thinking of letting *blacks* in! But only males, rich males. What d'you make of that? My wife isn't surprised, she figures our sexism is worse than our racism. She can easily imagine black and white Broeders in a huddle, being male-chauvinist-piggy together!'

Mealie fields, mealie silos, mealie prices, mealie porridge, mealie biscuits – mealie and Boers go together. Ninety-five per cent of commercial maize-farmers are Boers, now looking back on the 1970s as the good old days, remembering the drought-stricken 1980s with horror and living fearfully through the 1990s. They themselves are partly to blame for their present economic difficulties; many Boers, having raked in lavish government subsidies, dodged taxes by buying superfluous machinery now rusting in the background. They still receive much larger subsidies than other farmers, though even their fellow-Afrikaners agree that racket must soon stop. It has surprised me to find the Boers more like Ireland's pre-EEC farmers, in terms of untidiness and inefficiency, than like the Dutch.

The van Niftrik homestead is invisible from the road, at the end of a red rutted track running straight through miles of brown mealie. Yet it was easily found; farmers hang signs by their entrances, usually giving the surname or sometimes simply the couple's first names. During the afternoon I had declined Willem van Niftrik's offer of a lift, whereupon he offered hospitality.

Four dogs rushed out noisily to defend the homestead: a fluffy Maltese poodle, a golden cocker spaniel, a Border collie and a ridgeback/Rottweiler cross. I stood still – white-owned South African dogs associate bicycles with blacks whom they are often bred to hate. But this pack was unthreatening; the van Niftriks are too kindly to keep efficient guard-dogs.

Willem and Ella, when looking ahead to a black government, don't panic. Recognizing the inevitability of the new South Africa, they hope it will all settle down soon, and bring peace and prosperity to everyone. However, they distrust Mr Mandela.

'But they had to let him out,' said Ella. 'The way things were going, he'd have made more trouble from inside.'

The fact that Nelson Mandela should never have been in prison escapes all my Boer friends. Trying to see the new South Africa through their eyes, I fail – perhaps because they themselves can't see it, in the sense of comprehending it. It is happening as droughts and plagues happen. There's nothing to be done about such disasters; you can only grit your teeth and resolve to survive.

Meanwhile, life is uncertain. As in many new bungalow farmhouses, french windows in the long sitting room make this home seem vulnerable; but the sleeping quarters are secure beyond a heavy iron gate, floor to ceiling, and strong iron grilles protect the bedroom windows – a sadly necessary 1990s version of the laager. During the past fifteen months, 369 farmers have been attacked.

On my first evening the dogs barked furiously during supper and Willem quietly asked a teenaged daughter to fetch his gun from the bedroom. Otherwise the conversation flowed on – tension perceptible but under control. Stiff-upper-lip, Boer-style. Next evening the telephone rang during supper and the police reported a PAC threat to the white school bus. Would Willem and a neighbour (both officers of the local commando) please escort it at 6.30 a.m.? Of course, no problem, such crises are now part of everyday life in rural areas.

Willem farms 700 hectares: mostly mealie, a herd of sixty cattle, a few sheep for domestic consumption. If COSATU finally obtains a minimum-wage settlement, he will have to sack three of his seven labourers. Pre-mechanization, his father employed fifty men; now the other forty-three – as it were – are living in some township, unemployed or at best underemployed.

The prospect of having to dismiss three men genuinely upsets Willem. 'I can't turn them out of their homes, they must stay on as squatters, their families have been with our family for generations. I'll still give them mealie, milk, firewood – that's all I can do. It's bad, *they* don't ask for more money, we've always looked after them well and they're grateful. Our problem is the ANC's Commie agitators. I won't let those gangsters onto my land – not nowhere near my people! And anyone going to their rallies will be sacked and they know it!'

In Jo'burg I heard white liberals, engaged in voter education programmes, debating how best to deal with the average black's inability to understand the democratic process: freedom of assembly, freedom of speech and so on. This same inability handicaps all the Boers I've met this past week – admittedly an unnerving week, for them. On 1 May new laws came into force dealing with farm labourers' hours of work, days off, sick leave. (But not wages; that most contentious issue needs 'further consultation'.)

In Willem's view, labour relations are being used 'as a political card, played to suit the ANC, not the workers'. This may be half-true. In a few recent cases, when COSATU 'activists' became hyperactive and tried to burn the farm buildings of Boers deemed recalcitrant (or intolerably brutal), 'boys' risked their lives in defence of their employers' property. But does this tell us more about loyalty and/or the fear of unemployment than about working conditions?

This new protective legislation was urgently needed. However, I do share Willem's doubts about the practicality of a forty-eight-hour week. The customary system required X number of jobs to be done between sunrise and sunset, and whether a 'boy' takes six or twelve hours to complete them doesn't bother his *baas*. But in future, said Willem, a farmer paying a fixed wage for fixed hours will have to supervise his workers non-stop, something likely to generate a whole new set of frictions. Is this one more example of an imported institution not suiting Africa?

Ella and Willem took me to visit the labourers' spacious compound, a mile or so from the homestead. The substantial mud dwellings have flat tin roofs, everyone looked adequately fed and clothed, an affectionate relationship was apparent between these Boers and 'their people' – within that rigid framework which excludes any relaxed human-to-human contact. One retired house-servant lives here with her 12-year-old grandson whose congenitally deformed right leg was treated eleven years ago in Soweto's Baragwanath hospital at a cost of R9 for a three-month stay. Now the charge is R20 (£4). This fee covered regular physiotherapy and special shoes for the right foot as the boy grew up. In most African countries he would have been a cripple for life, dragging himself around in the dust.

'Viva feudalism!' you might be tempted to say, contrasting these families' advantages with township living conditions. But not all Boers are like the van

Niftriks and feudalism puts no brakes on cruelty and injustice – nor does it provide an escape hatch. Farm schools cater for the workers' children up to Standard Six (aged 12 or so). The Boers donate the buildings (no big deal); the government pays the black (occasionally white) teacher; the parents, out of their wages of R8 to R15 a day, must pay for the textbooks. Pupils may then go on to the nearest high school, if they can afford the fees and the distance is not too great to be walked. Only white pupils have buses laid on though the van Niftriks' farm is typical in being twelve miles from the nearest high school.

Visiting with the *baas* and the *nooi* – therefore being perceived as part of the apartheid world – is discomfiting and inhibiting. 'I'd like you to have seen inside the huts,' said Ella, 'but they never ask you in.' She looked incredulous on hearing that in black Africa hospitality is often extended to the passing white. Here are so many stark contrasts: a boy saved by the white regime from a life in the dust, but the inter-racial gulf unbridgeable.

Klerksdorp has recently been elevated to city status and is geared to the needs and tastes of rich farmers. Agriculture-related businesses abound. So do enormous furniture stores where indoor plants writhe amidst expensive but hideous suites and carpets, mirrors and oil-paintings, lamps and brassware, plus garden ornaments of a vulgarity matched only by their variety.

At 10.30 I had an appointment at the South African Agricultural Union (SAAU) office where I was coldly received by a grey-haired, florid-faced Afrikaner with a pendulous belly who sat behind a wide tidy desk under a photograph of ex-President Botha. The SAAU is allergic to foreign journalists or writers – indeed, to any journalists, in this dangerously uncensored New Age. Only persistent pressure, applied by one of my Boer hosts, had got me this appointment.

I began by asking innocent questions to which I already knew the answers and Mr de Vos thawed slightly while explaining why it simply won't be *possible* to raise wages. Life is too hard for farmers now, what with severe drought losses last year, maize prices down this year, interest rates up, the EC dumping beef, government subsidies drastically reduced, the rand devalued. Tractor sales are down from 15,000 a year in the mid-'70s to less than 2,000 in '92, and many farmers are unable even to afford spare parts because of new import tariffs...Mr de Vos spoke in despairing tones that were almost convincing; he and those he represents *believe* they are verging on destitution. Yet most farmers own a Mercedes (you see them parked by the dozen outside dorp kerks on the Sabbath), plus a Golf or Corolla for the wife and kids to run around in, plus a bakkie for farm work. But of course whites live in *this* style and blacks live in *that* style, and the need to lower white standards by way of raising black standards cannot be faced. Yet on this readjustment will depend the new South Africa's long-term stability.

Mr de Vos's Afrikaner accent became more pronounced – almost unintelligible – as he denounced COSATU. Only last year less than 1 per cent of farmworkers belonged to a union and most of those were employed by companies. Now COSATU is recruiting on the farms – 'coming onto our *land*!' – through bribery and intimidation.

When I asked how SAAU is dealing with illegal child-labour, one of COSATU's main concerns, Mr de Vos turned puce. 'It's not true!' he shouted. 'Child labour is a Commie lie! We run schools for our children with our own money – in your country do the farmers have to run schools *and* pay taxes?'

Mildly I pointed out that neither Unicef nor the National Children's Rights Committee (NCRC) is a Commie organization. Before I could say more, Mr de Vos remembered that he had another appointment, elsewhere.

In Jo'burg last month I was invited to a discussion to mark the publication of a Unicef/NCRC report which records that in 1991 more than 780,000 black and Coloured children between the ages of 5 and 14 were being illegally employed. Many were – and still are – being trucked in from the 'homelands' on contract to white farmers. They are paid R3 a day for twelve hours' work; sjamboking and sexual abuse are common. Other unpaid children, who live on farms, work under duress. If they don't work, their parents lose jobs and perks: a monthly sack of mealie flour, a daily litre of milk on dairy farms, occasionally the ribs and shanks of a slaughtered ox. 'Free firewood and water' are also described as perks although the notion of whites *giving* blacks firewood and water, and expecting this to be seen as a benevolent gesture, seems more than grotesque.

The discussion group had also invited a representative of the Department of Agriculture who failed to turn up. It might have shaken him to see slides showing many of these children and their living conditions in gruesome detail – photographs taken over a long period by a brave black photographer who would probably have been murdered if detected. Although 780,000 is such a horrifying figure this scandal is rarely mentioned, even by the liberal media.

The eight miles from Klerksdorp to Orkney were on a dual carriageway bedevilled by fast heavy traffic. It took time to find Dickens Avenue; there was no one around of whom to ask the way as I wandered through other avenues commemorating Shakespeare, Fletcher, Milton, Addison, Byron, Brontë, Peacock, Wells... A bookish gentleman from the Orkney Isles founded this mining dorp – now an Afrikaner stronghold, its founder's name forgotten. The total absence of pedestrians in white suburbs is one of South Africa's oddest features. It makes the foreigner on foot (or awheel) feel strangely excluded, marginalized, deprived of all those casual encounters that, in normal societies, can lead to interesting conversations, perhaps an invitation to meet the family – even, occasionally, to long-term friendships. In this country the lone traveller needs to be genuinely self-sufficient.

Here I am staying with Sheila and Wayne Blignaut, parents of Shayne Dalkin who rescued me in Karoi in June 1992, when I was miserably malarial. Their hospitality is as boundless as the Transvaal horizons and today they arranged for me to be given a tour of the mines.

Despite my ethical objections to the activities of AAC et al., I found myself being caught up in the romance of the dramatic final act of gold-mining – when liquid gold pours out of a furnace to form a brick. An awesome moment: the fierce purifying flames, the stream of molten gold – then the small brick. Small, but so heavy that anyone able to pick it up with one hand can keep it. Nobody is able to pick it up with one hand. Even to hold it for a moment, with both hands, strains the biceps. The riveting associated statistics should be noted down here but have by now been drowned in Castle beer.

Bloemhof, 8 May

Today's eighty-five miles offered only one minuscule dorp a little way off the road. This is a seriously desiccated region: few farms, several dried-up river courses, many barren miles of hard red earth, colourless scrub, low flat-topped acacia and dwarf cacti.

Bloemhof is visible from afar, its mealie silo and churches rising above the municipal trees. South Africa's modern DRC churches are remarkable for their very thin metal spires: ugly, aggressive, spear-like, suggesting conflict rather than neighbourly love. And in Bloemhof, just now, there is much conflict, as I discovered when buying amasi. The Indian store-owner explained – white business people are refusing to sell to blacks and have cut off all supplies to Boitumelong, the township, including petrol supplies and medical aid. Even calls to the ambulance service are being ignored. This is their response to a black consumer boycott launched when the Boitumelong Civics' demands were spurned last month. Boitumelong wants a unified town council, improved working conditions and desegregated 'recreational facilities' – all reasonable demands, consistent with the new South Africa. However, Bloemhof's black workers have now been dismissed and won't get their jobs back until the consumer boycott ends. So this wee dorp, tranquil as it looks on a sunny Saturday afternoon, is seething beneath the surface. Mr Ranchod advised me to avoid Boitumelong – where I have a contact, the brother of a Sowetan friend. 'There are too many people around in a bad mood,' said he. 'And we see intimidation on all sides. The blacks intimidate their own to support a boycott – not always, but often enough. And here the whites have been trying to intimidate us. It's not a nice situation for the Indian community, we're at risk whatever we do. Here we've refused to sign a solidarity pledge with the white business committee, we're still selling to blacks. Now we'll be punished, whites boycotting us! But isn't all this better than fighting with guns?'

I agreed. Seen from afar, there is something pouty and playgroundish about these tit-for-tat boycotts and counter-boycotts and mass-dismissals and road blockades. But consumer boycotts are extremely effective when a township is dealing with hardline dorps whose councils insist on retaining segregation and allocating funds unequally. Small businesses can soon be driven to the edge of bankruptcy and then the whites give in. Moreover, though the raised tension can be dangerous, 'rolling mass action' does serve as a safety-valve for black communities enraged by white intransigence. Despite some peripheral violence, it is essentially a campaign of peaceful protest. Certain Civic Associations make unreasonable demands through ignorance of how the system works – they tend to exaggerate the power of local councils – but in general they are merely seeing to it that down on the ground, in their everyday lives, *things change*, however tardy the negotiators may be up there in the remote fastnesses of the World Trade Centre.

Bloemhof deserves its hardline reputation. Yet the further south one goes the less dour are the Boers and I have found this a friendly little place – very little, though looking large and important on the map. In the hotel bar everyone greeted me warmly – especially Hans, Leon and Andries, three patriarchal sheep-farmers. Hans is very tall and slightly rheumaticky, with a wispy ginger beard, and he bought me a Long Tom before unburdening himself.

'I was born the same year as the Union of South Africa. I was middle-aged when we got our Republic; now I'm old and watching my country die. That is a sad thing, I hope it never happens to you. A man's country is a part of *himself*. Maybe you don't think like that because you don't have to, your country is always there, the same, safe. Now try seeing it our way – it's frightening, feeling you won't have a country any more. No way to defend yourself or your property, Communists ruling who can take your land in the morning – or make you fight for it, until all your family is dead.'

Leon is small and wiry with a bad limp. Many years ago, when a berserk ox tried to kill him, two of his 'boys' saved his life. 'You see, lady, they don't hate us, they love us, we provide all they have.' Suddenly he produced a leather key-wallet and said, 'Lady, I want you to have this – look, it says "Bloemhof". Keep it and don't forget us! Soon we may be shot in our beds, remember we were good people!'

At the far side of the small circular bar, five young men from Welkom in the Free State (Bloemhof is on the provincial border) were tanking up before going to a right-wing rally. Their anti-AWB faction has one of those improbably long Afrikaans names not readily assimilated. Their spotty pallor suggested a diet of fast food and Coke. They wore crew-cuts and black leather jackets, and their jeans were stuffed into jackboots a few sizes too big. They grinned at me quite amiably but couldn't speak English. Many hardliners refuse to speak it on principle, but I think these young men genuinely couldn't; they looked as though learning even one language might present problems. Yet they were eager to communicate – Lear, leaning against the wall behind me, aroused their curiosity – and used the patriarchs as interpreters. Why wasn't I afraid of the kaffirs? What sort of gun did I carry? Where is Ireland? How much does it cost to fly from there? Why no vehicle? Then someone shouted from the stoep and they gulped their Castles, picked up their six-packs and tramped out.

'Troublemakers!' Andries muttered in my ear. 'Looking for violence, be as happy killing you or me as killing kaffirs! Still you get fools taking them seriously – why?'

Two men had thus far kept out of the conversation, for different reasons. The plump young man beside me was head and shoulders on the counter, gently snoring; I had noticed him mixing cane-spirit with his Castles. The other character – middle-aged, heavily bearded, ostentatiously armed – now suddenly leaned across the stupefied one to shake hands. 'Name's Jan. Your name's Murphy? My wife's a Murphy, Maura Murphy she was – father from Cork. Any relation?'

Murphys in Ireland, I explained, are like van der Merwes in South Africa.

'But you must be a cousin,' said Jan. 'All the van der Merwes are cousins – did you know? You'll stay with us tonight, we're near, edge of town – I want to talk to you. Those guys will show you where to find me.' Abruptly he stood up and left.

I looked questioningly at 'those guys'. 'He's OK,' said Leon. 'He's AWB and we need them around here. If we're attacked, Jan can't defend us, nobody can, we're all way out on the veld. But he can organize revenge. He'd take his men into the location, they'd get ten dead kaffirs for every dead Boer.'

Jan's four-roomed bungalow was easy to find; his security guards are seven ferocious ganders who converged on me with wings flapping, necks extended, eyes glaring, hisses gurgling. Opening the door, Jan dismissed them. 'Cheaper than dogs, and better – makes the kaffirs wet themselves.'

Maura sat in a cramped, untidy, grubby kitchen trying to mend an ancient sewing-machine. This is my first 'Poor White' household; Jan does odd jobs – a bit of plumbing, a bit of tractor maintenance, a bit of carpentry. When I invited them to a meal at the hotel Maura said no, she had nothing to wear for an evening out. She is thin and sallow, of indeterminate age with dyed hair and bad teeth. She has no links with Ireland; her father emigrated as a young man. As Jan moved a stack of dirty saucepans from one of the three chairs she said, 'We have to fight, we can't just give in – de Klerk's a fuckin' traitor! Would you give in? Would you lie down and let them walk all over you?'

'She wouldn't!' said Jan. 'The Irish are fighters, like us.' He leaned forward and stared at me across the table. 'If we had car bombs Waluz wouldn't be caught. *You* know about car bombs. We need help, the IRA can help. You tell them, we want to learn. We want to get like them – smart, fuck the Brits, they win! If we learn from them, there's no new South Africa, we can fuck it up – right? You tell them we want to learn, especially about bombs. We helped you – your Paisley guy, we gave him weapons a few years back when he was desperate. Now you help us, right?'

Greasy soup boiled over on the gas stove and there was a conflagration, which crisis gave me time to compose myself. In fact the AWB already have Irish help; their élite force, the Ystergarde (Iron Guard), is being trained by an Irish immigrant who may or may not be ex-IRA. But Jan would not be up to Ystergarde standards: they tend to be ex-SADF or ex-SAP Special Forces – though not all may be 'ex'.

When the crisis had been dealt with, and the window opened to release fatty fumes, I asked, 'Jan, d'you think Paisley represents the IRA?'

He looked puzzled. 'Why you're asking? You're the one from Ireland! You know the line-out, all those guys work together.'

The ganders hissed and flapped and Maura's right hand darted to her left armpit.

'Shit!' said Jan. 'I'm around, stuff your gun!'

Maura looked at me. 'Is it like this in Ireland? How much do these British soldiers attack you? Have you ever had to shoot one?'

Spontaneously I laughed at Maura's image of me crouching behind the barricades in my Co. Waterford home, aiming at my British oppressors.

'What's the joke?' snapped Maura.

As I tried to explain my companions looked increasingly suspicious; evidently I am some sort of fuckin' traitor, like de Klerk. In an uncomfortable silence we ate what remained of the soup, then retired.

Today's *Citizen* carried a report of yesterday's farmers' protest rally at Potch-efstroom – rough stuff, organized by the Transvaal and Free State Agricultural Unions:

About 15,000 farmers, some from the distant Cape and northern Natal, vented their fury with fiery speeches calling for Afrikaner unity, mobilisation and, if necessary, armed conflict. They loudly voiced their rejection of the 'new South Africa'. They vowed to fight back and take up arms in the event of one more murder of a farmer, which they would regard as a declaration of war against them . . . Other matters which aroused the feelings of the emotionally charged crowd were the extension of labour legislation to agriculture and the recently announced maize price . . . Many placards contained messages such as: 'The White Race is the Master Race' and 'Farmers, it is time to grab your guns'. Neither the Deputy Minister for Agriculture nor the President of the SAAU was able to address the crowd. Both had to sit down amidst loud jeers and catcalls.

Warrenton, 9 May

This morning a smudge of distant ridges to west and south – long, low ridges – signalled the end of the platteland. At noon a small faded sign proclaimed CAPE PROVINCE and I crossed a border that is where it is for only one reason: diamonds.

In 1867 nobody cared a hoot about the ownership of this semi-desert region inhabited by a scattering of mixed-race Griquas and a few impoverished Voortrekkers settled along the river banks. Then one day Daniel Jacob's children collected a handful of glittering stones by the Orange River and brought them home as playthings. The prettiest pebble soon passed to a travelling trader, John O'Reilly, who could find no one to buy it, even for a penny, in the little dorps along his route. In Cape Town he had it identified; it weighed twenty and a quarter carats and was sold to the Governor of the Cape Colony for £500. Not long after, the first diamond diggers arrived and the ownership of Griqualand West became desperately important. Devious dealings followed. As the Boers' Orange Free State could not prove their claim to the region, the diggers invited the British to annex it – which they did, in 1871. But the Free State continued to grumble, until soothed by a compensatory lump sum of £90,000. Eighteen years later, Rhodes paid £5 million for the Kimberley Mine.

On this Sunday afternoon, Warrenton – only slightly bigger than Bloemhof – seemed sound asleep. I now plan ahead for Sabbaths and Lear was laden with Long Toms; in my bedroom I became a secret drinker until the dining room opened at 6.30.

It is a typical dorp hotel dining room: red cotton tablecloths, blue plastic condiment trays, bouquets of paper flowers, a large tapestry featuring a tiger about to spring, a cabinet displaying mass-produced 'native handicrafts' and many souvenirs from the Kruger National Park, the Victoria Falls, Mauritius – the last being the whites' favourite holiday resort when they had little choice.

This setting suited the conversation. By request of the management (there is a lighting problem) six of us shared a table – the only occupied table, dorp hotels being mainly dependent on their bar trade. Alf and Muriel, a middle-aged Wenwe couple, now live in Jo'burg. ('Wenwes' are a new tribe: 'refugees' who irritate South Africans by harping on the 'good old days wenwe lived in Rhodesia'.) The other couple, Duncan and Doris, youngish English-speakers, vied with each other in telling repulsive 'kaffir jokes'. Only the Afrikaner, Danile, was congenial.

Alf and Muriel read *The Citizen*; all other English-language newspapers have become 'too Communist'. Their four sons being AWB members worries Muriel, not because she disapproves of the AWB ('at heart most of us support the right wing') but because she fears for their future safety. Duncan and Doris believe it will 'all blow up', either before or after the elections, and those four fed each other's fears, swapping the standard scare-stories about anti-white plots.

'They're so treacherous!' exclaimed Muriel. 'I should know all about that, I'm a third-generation Rhodie. I *hate* the munts! I could go out with my gun and shoot more than Strydom did! But I'd never be unkind to servants. My father was too harsh, he'd leave them waiting hours when they needed driving to hospital. I wouldn't do that when they're suffering.'

Alf laughed. 'Your dad was right, they don't really feel pain, not the way we do.' He looked at me. 'You know something – I can put up with the black *gentlemen* but I can't stand the women, won't have them in the house.'

Later, when Muriel and I were tête-à-tête over coffee in the lounge, she confirmed that this is literally true: her two maids must arrive after Alf has left for his office and be gone before he gets back. Does she see the implications of that? Probably not. She also confided that she daren't tell Alf she pays R20 a year towards a maid's son's school fees and buys medicines for the 'boy's' bad stomach.

Between the tinned tomato soup and the mixed grill, Duncan recalled a recent business trip to Malawi. Doris glowed at the memory. 'Shame Banda's so old – Africa's best leader. Now we'll see Malawi going phut like the rest!'

'Mangope's OK too [leader of the Bophuthatswana 'homeland'],' said Duncan. 'He's someone we could work with – let's have him instead of Mandela! Then the blacks would be happy with a black President and we'd feel more secure.'

Danile, hitherto almost silent, raised an eyebrow. '*Blacks* happy with Mangope? They'd prefer de Klerk!'

Alf nodded. 'They wouldn't buy Mangope, they want a Commie. Mangope knows how to run an economy, he won't have any shit in Bop – no strikes, marches, rallies, boycotts, stayaways! He must be laughing at us now!'

'Why are you all so negative?' demanded Danile. 'Let's make the best of change. For starters we could get rid of all this hypocrisy about "corrupt black governments" – the Nats are as bad as the rest together! And most Immorality Act offenders were dominees or white cops arresting black women to rape them.'

Alf retrieved a chip from amidst his Voortrekker beard and stared accusingly at Danile. 'You're a *kaffirboetie*!'

Danile shrugged. 'I look at facts. I've a Xhosa colleague who's a lot brighter than most of us – my computer analyst. A brilliant guy, can take his own decisions, dresses better than I do – and doesn't smell!'

Alf sneered. 'You mean you could have him in for a meal?'

'Right! And his brother and sister too – all at Wits, not some crappy bush-college. Hey, man – I couldn't keep up with that lot in an argument – and *none* of them smell!'

The cherished fallacy that blacks smell more than whites must be rooted in the circumstance that most South African whites never meet fellow-whites poor enough to be smelly. When I pointed out that unwashed blacks merely smell *different*, not *more*, everyone – even Danile – looked at me with blank astonishment.

Kimberley, 10 May

From ten miles away, across slightly undulating semi-desert, Kimberly's sky-scrapers are visible and the heart sinks. Is this going to be a mini-Jo'burg? But no, there are only two skyscrapers. One is an extraordinary isolated monolith – apparently windowless, severe in shape but tinted a warm pinkish-gold. In fact it has hundreds of concealed windows, specially designed to ease the task of the diamond-sorters who sit within. Emeralds are precious because of their rarity; diamonds are precious only because De Beers controls most of the world's supply. Were tourists allowed to wander along Namibia's Diamond Coast, gem diamonds would soon lose their monetary worth – though a few odd bods might still value them for their intrinsic beauty, their mysterious storing of colour and the unpredictable vitality with which they release those shafts of light.

On arrival I strolled around, pushing Lear, to get the feel of the place. Cheerful blacks shouted friendly greetings, something unthinkable in the Trans-vaal. Several gave laughing advice like 'Get a motor-bike!' or 'Try the train!' In a CNA store (South Africa's W.H. Smith) the Afrikaner and Coloured staff delayed me for forty minutes, curious about my journey, my family life, my views on South Africa – and nearby customers eagerly joined the party. I seem to have landed on another planet.

The Grand Hotel offers the cheapest accommodation, its servants' wing being now open to poor whites. I'm enjoying this hostelry after all those dull dorp hotels. In the scruffy foyer a Coloured girl booked me in for two nights by computer. (Why by computer, in a hotel obviously down on its luck?) Then a gigantic noisy lift, imported from the US in 1890, took us to the second floor where a startled-looking part-Griqua woman wordlessly pointed to the un-grand wing, its corridors uncarpeted. Each door displays a warning notice: 'This room does not form part of the registered and graded premises'. Most doors have been damaged in an interesting way, either kicked in or attacked with some heavy sharp instrument. Their handles and locks also bear the marks of violence – has there been a police raid? I peered into several rooms. All were like my own, with filthy walls (one prefers not to analyse the source of the filth), radios and light-fixtures long since torn from the walls above the twin beds, frayed towels wrapped around the pillows in lieu of pillow-slips, the only furniture splintered plywood dressing-tables, their mirrors forcibly removed. The hand-basin taps and communal lavatories at the end of the corridor are waterless. My small window won't open and, after dark, unfamiliar very small insects race around the floor – to and fro, in a demented sort of way. But the bed, surprisingly enough, seems free of wildlife.*

The same, 11 May

Modern South Africa was born in Kimberley when a trio of ruthless youngsters (Cecil Rhodes, Alfred Beit and Joseph Robinson – two 18-year-olds and a 21-year-old) gained control of the diamond output. De Beers Consolidated Mines Ltd. made millionaires of all three before they were 30 and provided them with the capital to develop the Rand's gold mines.

The pioneer diggers were independent, self-funding, self-governing, paying no taxes. Their dusty camps stood seven miles from the nearest spring and more than 400 miles from the nearest port town. There was no railway, food was scarce and vile, sanitation was non-existent, diseases were rife. Town planning was the last thing on the diggers' minds and Kimberley's central maze – short streets, all higgledy-piggledy, at odd angles to one another – reflects the frenetic atmosphere of this pioneering era.

Although celebrated as 'the Diamond City' it remains a town – quite a small town, with an air of contentedly belonging to the past rather than ambitiously eyeing the future. Its most attractive building is De Beers' Head Office, in constant use since Rhodes was chairman and occupying the whole length of Stockdale Street, just around the corner from the Grand Hotel. This solidly elegant two-storey building of mellow brick has eight arched dormer windows and many slender pillars supporting a balcony of lacy wrought-iron. It appears to have no security of any sort, though I daresay appearances are deceptive.

The Big Hole failed to excite me. Yes, it is a very big hole – over 3,600 feet deep – and an impressive monument to the efficacy of picks, shovels and buckets. To create it, men dug for ten years and shifted some $22\frac{1}{2}$ million tons of diamond-bearing rock which yielded three tons of diamonds – give or take a few carats. By 1914 the Big Hole had been abandoned. Now it holds a

---

* A few weeks later, when the *Cape Times* reported that Kimberley's Grand Hotel had been burned to the ground, it was described as 'the city's most historic hostelry'!

small, black, rather sinister-looking lake, shadowed by purplish cliffs, and visitors are frustratingly restricted to a 'tourist observation platform'.

At the Bultfontein Mine I longed to 'go down' but underground tours must be booked in advance by groups. The surface tour would have been tedious but for my guide, Janet, an Afrikaner liberal who divined that the new South Africa interests me much more than mining machinery. Diamond miners, she re-assured me, now earn R1,400 a month, exactly the same as her intern doctor daughter. 'Which is fair – my daughter is paid for her knowledge, the men here are paid for their endurance.'

This afternoon I tentatively pedalled towards the township across a grievously littered no man's land – tentatively because, post-Hani, there is a new tension in the air. One can't explain how or why one senses it, but unmistakably it exists, even in friendly Kimberley. And when I was confronted by a group of surly youths loitering on the township's edge, my antennae told me to turn back.

I then sought compatriots in St Patrick's College, originally a Christian Brothers day school founded in 1897 to cater for the sons of the many Irish diamond-seekers. (One was a grand-uncle of mine who stopped seeking dia-monds to assist the Boers during the Siege of Kimberley and then disappeared from view. Family rumour has it that he ended up in Cape Town, contributing Murphy genes to the Coloured community.) St Patrick's developed rapidly, acquiring an imposing neo-classical façade, spacious sports grounds and a fine academic reputation; pupils came from all over South Africa, the Rhodesias and Nyasaland. But its fortunes declined with the end of colonialism and its numbers are now down to 350, although (or because?) it has been 'mixed' since 1976. I could find only one surviving compatriot, 80-year-old Brother Malachi, who entertained me to tea while reminiscing about his least reputable pupil: Clive Derby-Lewis. He relishes the piquant detail that the accused's first wife, a teacher in Cape Town, is an active ANC supporter.

A few days ago, COSAS called for a nationwide school stayaway in protest against (among other things) increased examination fees. St Patrick's staff, who also run a day school in the township, rashly ignored this call and last night youths set fire to it – destroying computer equipment worth R90,000, recently donated by white well-wishers. And the headmaster of a Bloemfontein Roman Catholic college, who also defied this diktat, was awakened by the police at 3 a.m. last night – the school bakkie had been stolen from its garage, pushed a mile down the street and set alight.

This sort of intimidation is now so common, all over the country, that it has ceased to be 'news' and often goes unreported. Brother Malachi shares the general view that, post-Hani, all political leaders – black and white – are losing control of their extremists.

Campbell, 12 May

Griqualand West is so sparsely populated that for lack of anything else to put on the map farms are sometimes marked. Today's seventy miles were flat and arid – few farms, no visible people of any colour, no trees, no traffic, brown bush, the depressingly named Asbestos Mountains away to the west, low and smooth. From the beginning of human time, this was part of the San people's territory. Then gradually the Griquas – so named in 1812 by the Revd John Campbell of the London Missionary Society (LMS) – migrated north. And these semi-nomadic cattle-herders of mixed ancestry were mainly responsible for exterminating the San in this region. Incinerating live children was one of their ploys. But more usually they captured the children of slain parents for sale as slaves in the Cape Colony. Now Griqualand West is a misnomer; in the mid-nineteenth century most Griquas were forced to move to Griqualand East on the Transkei–Natal border, where a few small communities remain intact.

Approaching Campbell the terrain becomes slightly hilly and from a ridge-top one sees mission-planted trees in a hollow to the left of the road. Although officially a dorp, Campbell has no hotel. The only edifice on the main road is the new Livingstone Drankwinkel, a small neat brick building with a petrol pump to one side. I drank my Long Tom sitting on the ground beside Lear. Nine Coloureds of both sexes and all ages were hanging about: ragged, hungry-looking, apathetic, uncommunicative. *Sad* people . . . The Drankwinkel owner advised me to camp near the ex-mission, now a farmhouse with good watchdogs who would guard my tent.

'Livingstone's Mission' said a faded little signpost pointing down a stony track. In a stake-fenced compound strewn with scrap-iron two spreading fig trees shade a derelict bungalow. Here the track ends but tractor-tyre marks led me on across an expanse of baked earth. There was no one in sight, no sound. Beyond this hollow rises a long grey rocky ridge where game abounded in Livingstone's day; now only snakes, lizards and spiders remain. Then I came upon a tiny church and a Historic Monuments Commission notice:

CAMPBELL MISSION STATION

This site was one of the earliest centres of Christianity north of the Orange River and was the out-span of such early travellers as William Burchell, John Campbell, George Thompson, Dr Andrew Smith and Dr David Livingstone. The church was built by John Bartlett and opened in January 1831.

Nearby, four gnarled dead pine trees are reverently fenced because – said another notice – under them Livingstone preached to the Griquas and proposed to Mary Moffat. Several local sites claim to be 'the actual spot' where this unromantic alliance began. Griqualand West is short of tourist attractions, you've got to make the most of the Livingstone connection. In fact the marriage was arranged in Kuruman, some hundred miles to the north.

The church was open – and curiously touching, in the way of old unchanged places. It is a simple stone and mud building, with crude wooden pews and a stark stone altar. If Livingstone returned today he would find only one innovation: a glass-topped display case containing a few trivial mementos and a copy of *Missionary Travels and Researches in South Africa*, open at the title page. It was published in 1857 by John Murray, 50 Albemarle Street, London. I felt a sentimental glow; in the middle of Griqualand West, this tangible link with 50 Albemarle Street was absurdly pleasing.

The track led on to Livingstone's house – a solid bungalow, only minimally refurbished, with a deep stoep and a small green lawn. Three brindled Boxers were chained by the door and 'Pieter de Beer' was chalked on a square of cardboard nailed to the gate. As the Boxers' barking brought no one to investigate I explored further – and terrified a skinny little Afrikaner woman stoking an outside wood-furnace to heat bath water. Mevrou de Beer, I presumed. She really was terrified; her eyes widened and she shrank back against the wall as though expecting me to shoot her on the spot. Reassurance was difficult as she spoke not a word of English and my publisher's 'To Whom It May Concern' letter failed to have the desired effect. I pointed to the church and beckoned Mevrou to follow me, waving the letter and saying 'Livingstone!' Slowly, still looking apprehensive and utterly bewildered, she moved forward. In the church I laid my letter on the display case and indicated the link. Only then did my companion relax; the precise nature of this link certainly escaped her, but in some unfathomable way I became authentically associated with Livingstone and therefore acceptable.

Back at the house, Pieter de Beer – tall, well-built, dark-skinned – was jumping off his decrepit tractor. Perhaps he (or his father) had 'passed for white'? With an unmistakably thoroughbred Afrikaner wife, he can't be officially Coloured. He viewed me with alarm and suspicion but his scraps of English made some explaining possible. The couple then discussed my campsite request at length, worriedly, before reluctantly offering hospitality. Reluctantly because they have no idea how to cope with a guest. They lack the social graces to an extent unimaginable among Africans, even in remote villages where whites are a novelty and the language barrier is insurmountable. They couldn't convey a welcome; their essential kindness is evident yet can't be expressed. Unavoidably the word 'boorish' springs to pen. Having walked back to the Drankwinkel to fetch a dozen beers as a 'thank-you' gift, I settled down to write at the kitchen table while Marie prepared supper and Piet bathed. It occurred to neither that I might have washing or peeing needs. The door of the small kitchen, leading directly off the stoep, is kept double-locked – even when Marie goes out for only a few moments. But the de Beers can afford none of the elaborate security systems seen on larger farms.

Supper was served in the small, square dining room: boerewors (one each), boiled maize cobs (one each), tomatoes (one each), fried potatoes, a stack of sliced pan and a cup of black lukewarm ersatz coffee. Conversation was difficult and seems a skill not much practised between husband and wife. Strenuous efforts on my part prised out the information that four daughters are married elsewhere, that Piet farms sixty hectares (subsistence farming, given the quality of his land) and employs two men. Marie does all the domestic chores and tends the four sows and their litters. After that I gave up and, as we ate in Cistercian silence, tried to imagine this room in Livingstone's day. It is much more pleasing than the opulent living rooms of rich Boers. Nineteenth-century craftsmen rather than modern factories produced the dining table and chairs – their tapestry upholstery woven by a great-grandmother. Inherited copperware fills a tall handsome dresser and two enormous Voortrekker chests, fancifully carved, hold spare bedding. Six portrait photographs of formidable ancestors – austere unsmiling faces with visionaries' eyes, the women looking even tougher than the men – help to explain why it took the British three years to win the Anglo-Boer War.

This is being written in quite a large bedroom; two double beds occupy most of the floor space and rather beautiful tapestries, depicting Voortrekker battles, decorate the walls. What do Marie and Piet make of their guest? Probably they don't even try to understand the phenomenon.

Griquatown, 13 May

Unusually, I slept badly; maybe Livingstone's ghost disapproved of me. During the small hours hyperactive rats, above the ceiling and behind the walls, sounded like a furniture-removal team. Occasionally the Boxers, now loose on the stoep, barked loudly – then at once a window opened. Living in Campbell, is it necessary to be so twitchy? Maybe it is, just at the moment...

By 5.30 Marie was cooking mealie porridge, a simple process – fistfuls of flour thrown into boiling water quickly form little lumps. A soup-plate of lumps was placed before me: delicious with milk and sugar. When I conveyed my appreciation, Marie smiled for the first and last time – a small timid smile.

The dawn sky was a chilly pale green, soon streaked with crimson. Here on the edge of the Great Karoo the early cold has the steely quality of desert winters – hand-numbing. Our narrow road rose and fell over a series of monotone ridges: grey-brown grass, grey-brown earth, grey-brown stones. Soon after 8 a.m. the sun suddenly felt pleasantly warm and I stopped to remove my jacket.

Then a gusty gale-force crosswind sprang up, blowing fine stinging sand from the Kalahari; without goggles, cycling would have been impossible. Beyond the next ridge sheep were sprinkled across an expanse of flatness, nibbling at a sage-green plant that is highly nutritious for both sheep and goats – but not for cattle. Copses of spindly sweetpepper trees marked the entrances to two farms, ten miles apart; their clusters of tall windpumps were whizzing so fast the noisy blades formed a blur. This harsh metallic music, its rhythms obedient to air currents, is the Karoo's signature tune.

Griquatown dozes in a hollow between arid ridges. When I arrived dust-devils were dancing at each street junction and the noon sun glowed copper behind its veil of sand. The small, spread-out white suburb looks surprisingly prosperous; the blacks and Coloureds look demoralized-poor. The Hotel Louis – long and substantial on a high stoep – seems superfluous; it was built during the diamond-rush, now this region experiences no rush of any kind. In the large foyer an elderly grumpy Afrikaner emerged from a sombre jungle of tall pot-plants. He could not or would not speak English. Having booked me in he watched, silently disapproving, as I wheeled Lear across a frayed dingy carpet towards a wide, dark, high-ceilinged corridor.

Today my five-litre water bottle is leaking and a semi-desert lies ahead. Anxiously I toured the local stores – all three of them – but could find neither a replacement nor anyone who took the slightest interest in my problem. So now I'm dependent on a roll of sticking-plaster and a tube of glue.

The Mary Moffat Museum is Griquatown's tourist attraction; the future Mrs Livingstone happened to be born here when her parents were waiting to start the Kuruman Mission. On my way to the museum two young Tswana men greeted me, introducing themselves as ANC Civics workers. They wished to discuss their work and 'to learn about democracy'. When I suggested meeting in the hotel bar they hesitated, looked doubtfully at each other, then asked if they could come to my room. They wouldn't feel good in the bar – for them it is 'a bad hotel'. Did I understand? Yes, I did, and we arranged to meet in my room soon after five.

Formerly the museum was the Griqua Mission house, a four-roomed thatched dwelling built in 1828, fifty-one years before the town grew up around it. I always enjoy South Africa's dorp museums where one can be alone with the past – completely alone, in this case, as no curator was visible. Facing the entrance, Mary Moffat looks down on her rare visitors with an air of stoical resignation. If only she could be summoned back from that grave by the Zambezi to give us her honest opinion of her spouse!

One has to admire Queen Victoria's attention to detail. The British Empire was very big and the Griqua Mission very small – five mud huts in the middle of nowhere – yet here stands an organ presented by the Queen to 'her' Griqua converts. As I was examining an old ship's bell – brought from Cape Town on the back of an ox for the first church – the curator arrived. An erudite middle-aged Afrikaner woman, she told me no pure Griquas remain here and their language – an archaic Dutch dialect – has long since died. We talked for nearly two hours, about the future as well as the past.

The Tswanas' failure to turn up at five did not surprise me; life's like that in Africa. Then, as I was about to go to bed, someone tapped on my door. It was the hotel security officer, an elderly man whose flat nose and fairish skin indicate San or Khoikhoi genes not too far back. He slipped in, closed the door and whispered, 'Lady, you say nothing to *baas* if I tell? At five come two men, say you told them go to room – *baas* say you change plan, gone away, not here. He don't like them talk in his hotel with white people. Men very angry, don't believe him but *afraid*, go away.'

5

From the Centre to the Sea

Prieska – Lambert's Bay – Cape Town

Even before the days of water-boring, men and beasts could live wherever springs
welled up in the hollows of the hills. But on the Great Karoo such favoured spots
were so rare that this vast high plain was to all intents and purposes
a gap in the centre of the Colony.
Eric A. Walker, The Great Trek *(1948)*

Prieska, 14 May 1993

The further south the darker the mornings and I left Griquatown by Venus-light;
never have I seen that planet so large and luminous. After a night of heavy rain
the cold air was rich with the aromas of refreshed herbs and earth unaccustomed
to moisture. Here for the first time since leaving Jo'burg was mountainous
country – mildly mountainous – and the slow pastel dawn revealed a surprising
landscape: Scottish moors in midwinter rather than African semi-desert. As the
light strengthened, a strange blueness suffused this 'moorland'; grey-blue brakbos blankets miles of shallow valleys between long low ridges. Where the terrain
becomes more broken – the valleys deeper, the hills steeper – huge holes mark
the spots where impatient diamond-seekers, on their way to what was not yet
Kimberley, paused to dig hopefully. A few miles away is the river bank on which
those children found such pretty playthings in 1867.

This miniature mountain range is the gateway to the Great Karoo; soon after
8 a.m. I was freewheeling fast towards a plain that extends almost to the Atlantic
coast. All day I met only three vehicles (bakkies) and passed only five invisible
farms, their names gloomy – like Modderfontein, Brakfontein, Bitterfontein. It
remained invigoratingly cold, the cloudless sky cobalt blue, the clarity of the light
deceptive. Isolated koppies forty miles ahead, rising abruptly from the plain,
looked close.

It is misleading to refer to the Karoo's 'mountains': that suggests peaks
and valleys, a road rising and falling, a confining of the horizons. These koppies
are lowish hills, made dramatic by the unconfined immensity of space in which
each stands alone, emphasizing the surrounding flatness. Some are great
piles of loose, rough-hewn, red-brown rock, precariously piled – their jutting
slabs outlined preposterously, irrationally, against that cobalt sky. Erosion has

also produced some masterpieces of precision. Two pointed, breast-like hills, identical in size and shape, rise on either side of a flat-topped koppie – a carefully arranged tableau, formal, dignified, in contrast to the chaos of piled boulders. Other hills are crowned by serrated grey-brown rock, the symmetry of each crown quite perfect. And sometimes by the wayside lie jumbles of jagged boulders, angular and multicoloured – ochre, silver-grey, toffee-brown, brick-red, black, fawn – with an occasional mighty, many-sided solitary rock combining all these colours on its various facets. Like the rest of South Africa, the Great Karoo has been tampered with: fenced, telegraph-poled, boreholed. Yet amidst its limitless grandeur such interventions are scarcely noticeable.

The township's supper-fires were beginning to smoke when Prieska appeared, still four miles away, its giant mealie silo burnished by the setting sun. This sizeable dorp stands on the south bank of the Orange River where my gravel track crosses the R32 highway. Apartheid's statutory gap between dorp and township is now being closed by new buildings: small bungalows for the black bourgeoisie, a clinic, a supermarket.

Groups of young blacks had gathered on Voortrekker Street and there was tension in the air. As so often, my first informant was an Indian store-owner. There has been yet another school stayaway, with pupils and teachers marching together in protest against teacher retrenchment. South Africa's educational scene is daily becoming more shambolic. Why *retrenchment*, when there is such a desperate shortage of teachers?

In the hotel's public (black) bar – large, crowded, very noisy – the barman gave me a friendly smile but hesitated before serving me, glancing towards the entrance to the ladies (white) bar. Other customers responded briefly to my greetings with downcast eyes – or turned away, embarrassed. The foreigner had made a mistake, didn't know her way around . . . It was inconceivable that she might simply want to talk to blacks. Then Ronnie appeared at my side: well dressed, welcoming, a high-school teacher – one of the organizers of today's demo.

'You are not a common person,' said he, 'coming on a bicycle. Are you a male or a female? Looking at you hard, I can't decide.'

'I am a female, an Irish female.'

'And you have come on that bicycle from where?'

'Today, from Griquatown.'

Ronnie laughed. 'You lie! Griquatown is from here 128 km – impossible! Impossible for a young male and you are a female not young.'

Impaired hearing is a disadvantage of being not young and in that noisy crowd Ronnie's pronunciation was hard to follow. He agreed that we should move into the ladies bar, then disappeared as I was manoeuvring Lear through the narrow doorway. Ten minutes later he was back. 'Excuse my long absence, to sit here I must find the manager, for permission.'

'*Permission?* But those laws have been repealed!'

Ronnie leaned forward to whisper: 'Be patient, I must live in this town. I ask permission, it's OK. I walk in here casually, like a white, some people could get angry.'

As he spoke the manager strode past, glancing contemptuously at the *kaffir-boetie*. A tall, lean, blond Afrikaner, he sold his northern Transvaal farm six years ago after a landmine killed a neighbour.

Poor Ronnie is painfully mixed-up. 'From the villages we learn only stupid ways, we need a full European education to turn us into gentlemen. We are not gentlemen, but now we meet foreign businessmen and politicians and we must know how to be like them.' (Steve Biko come back!) 'Colour is not important – am I right? It is silly to think of it, we are all human beings together.'

Moments later two whites entered the bar and greeted me before ordering their brandy and Cokes: a brief greeting to which I replied briefly.

Ronnie turned huffy. 'You want to go and be with those people? OK, you go! I don't need our talk if you want to be with them – why should you talk to me? But my father married Seretse Khama's wife's niece and my son is as fair as you!'

Soon after I made my excuses and set about hauling Lear up two long flights of stairs. Ronnie, watching from the hallway, felt no impulse to help.

Vosburg, 15 May

Over today's sixty miles I met no vehicle and, apart from birds, only one fellow-creature – a tortoise, some three feet in diameter, crossing the road. When I stopped to photograph, s/he prudently withdrew and was still, becoming a marvel of protective colouration. That mottled reddish-grey shell merged into the red earth and grey grass, while its circular fawn spots uncannily resembled nearby stones.

Grey grass is another unique Karoo feature; it hibernates, as it were, surviving until the next rainfall. A semi-desert stimulates nature's ingenuity and the Karoo supports numerous small plants dependent on long tap roots and water-storing leaves. In springtime – late August, September – an explosion of colour draws people from every continent to witness this botanical wonder of the world. More mundane are the wait-a-bit bushes, bearing six-inch thorns as strong and sharp as steel needles; Lear has to be kept well away from the verges.

The first weaver-bird nest on a telegraph pole bewildered me from afar; briefly I mistook it for a human construction. These nests, up to four yards in diameter, comically resemble the traditional Zulu hut; they house 200 or more birds who remain permanently in residence but breed only after good rains. Sometimes a pair of pygmy falcons – Africa's smallest bird of prey – is allowed to lodge in one of the many chambers. These diverse species get on splendidly and should perhaps replace the springbok as the emblem of the new South Africa. Nests can last for years, if not damaged by honey badgers or snakes, and their weight does nothing for the operational efficiency of telegraph poles. Therefore officialdom has provided other poles, specifically for the use of weaver-birds – an endearing gesture on the part of officialdom. But, perversely, the birds prefer telegraph poles (maybe they get a buzz?) and most provided poles remain bare.

During the dinosaurs' era the Karoo was one enormous fresh-water swamp. (That era lasted much longer than *Homo sapiens'* is likely to, at our present polluting rate of progress.) Now there is virtually no surface water and the rainfall (an annual average of four inches) too often comes violently in flooding thunderstorms that do more harm than good. Most South African farmers depend on their dams; here they must depend on boreholes 150, 170, even 200 feet deep. No one in the Karoo disputes the water-diviners' power; without them, one-third of South Africa would be uninhabitable.

Some Karoo farms are the size of Co. Cork and the region's succulents and herbs sustain millions of sheep. Thirty-five million or so are merinos, descended from four ewes and two rams presented by the Spanish royal family to the Dutch royal family and shipped to Cape Town in 1789. Karoo mutton has a distinctive flavour, celebrated throughout South Africa, and many Karoo farmers are reputed to be extremely rich – though fleeces are now fetching little. It is not uncommon to run 5,000 sheep on 30,000 acres yet few shepherds are employed. Predators have long since become extinct, apart from the black-backed jackal, and meticulously secure fencing prevents straying. All this information I gathered this evening from Koos, a sheep-farmer who owns Vosburg's hotel.

On the outskirts of Vosburg a notice says: WELCOME! ENJOY OUR SHADE TREES! In these parts all you need to attract tourists is a small grove of trees maintained through irrigation. As most Karoo plants are dwarfs, these few pines, bluegums and willows make Vosburg look like a rainforest. On this Saturday afternoon the three shops were closed, as was the petrol station, and there was no one in sight. Yet finding the hotel was not difficult; it takes four minutes to cycle all around Vosburg.

The Hunters Home Hotel is a splendid building – long, two-storeyed, well proportioned, elegantly balconied, over a century old and therefore preserved as an historic monument. During a few months, in 1871, more than 30,000 optimists rushed from Cape Town to Kimberley, prompting a frenzy of inn-building where water was available. So now the Karoo is dotted with such monuments.

This weekend every room is booked but Marlene promised to find space for me – one of the family could sleep in the lounge, something like that... The ladies bar is full of hunters and their wives, from Durban and Pretoria, assembled to have fun tomorrow killing springbok. Over the doorway a large 'PRIVATE' notice reinforces 'The management reserves the right...'

At 4.30 the management exercised its right when a new Corolla parked outside and three well-dressed, well-spoken black men thirstily approached. On being refused admission they protested, vehemently, and a khaki-clad youth standing beside me began to strain at the leash, making neck-wringing gestures. His mother held him firmly by the arm – 'Remember, you can't touch them now!' Collective resentment of the whites' diminishing power was palpable; a few years ago no black would have dared to argue thus – but you can still rely on the SAP. Someone rang them and within moments two toughies had arrived in a patrol car. If the blacks didn't move on they would be arrested and charged with causing a disturbance. The blacks did move on and everyone looked gratified.

During this unpleasantness Syd, a Wenwe, had settled beside me – a balding, wheezing, garrulous character who wanted to make sure I understood why the police had to be summoned.

'You can't let them in, they can't afford to buy drink, they just ask for a box of matches and sit around crowding us out making the place stink.' A typical contradiction soon followed. 'They're all lazy swine, only fit for beer-swilling!'

I escaped to the stoep where Gabriel introduced himself – a spade-bearded Afrikaner from Pretoria, youngish but pot-bellied. 'I like the Irish, I've an Irish colleague, arrived last year. A great lass, game for anything. Says she was anti-apartheid back home, going to student demos, holding "Free Mandela" vigils – all that shit! Now she admits she got it wrong – no way can you treat them like equals. She figures the outside world doesn't know what we're up against, misjudges us.' Gabriel put down his glass, wiped his beard, stood up and beckoned me to follow him. 'Come and look and tell me whether these are humans or animals!' Around the corner we gazed into the public bar, not long opened but already crowded. Rhetorically Gabriel asked, 'How could we share a premises with *them*? No way!'

Back in the ladies bar, Mr Mandela appeared on television looking deeply distressed about yet another East Rand horror. Hennie, a local Afrikaner, said, 'See him, in prison twenty-seven years, what do you expect if he gets power? We'll be massacred!'

Later, Hennie volunteered to show me the township's new school tomorrow. 'You'll see, helluva lot better than what our kids have!'

Afrikaners all along my route have been keen to show me 'the new township school' (if the township in question was calm enough to be visited) or at least to describe it: how many classrooms, how many millions of rands it cost ('from *our* taxes!'). Everyone expects me to be impressed; surely this 1980s building programme *proves* the government's concern for the blacks' welfare – not to mention proving their magnanimity. 'Remember '76? Remember all those schools and universities burned down and vandalized?' The illusion that white tax-payers have been discriminated against, by being forced to contribute to the welfare of 'lazy' non-tax-paying blacks, has become an obsession.

The same, 16 May

Last evening, as I was reading in bed, a crowd of a few hundred went toyi-toying and ululating past the hotel, shouting threats to kill whites – or so Hennie reported this morning. Undoubtedly they were aggressive-drunk and a white who got in their way might well have been killed. The cause of the unrest, according to a Coloured teacher, was an abortive funeral. Following the death near Cape Town of a 40-year-old local black woman, many Vosburgers now living in Nyanga returned for the burial – which didn't happen. The corpse was missing, the family couldn't pay the fee for ten days in a deep-freeze mortuary. As family members may be hard to contact, and then need time to collect fare-money, high 'cold storage' fees are common. If these go unpaid, the authorities cremate the unclaimed body and the spirit never rests – or not until some reliable sangoma has calmed it, which also costs money. A grim example, this, of blacks on Third World incomes being trapped by a First World society able expensively to freeze corpses.

En route to the township Hennie stopped between Vosburg's cemeteries. On our left, crude little wooden crosses – mostly nameless – marked low stony mounds. On our right, railed and gravelled graves were furnished with long-robed angels, chubby cherubs, massive marble slabs and gaudy plastic-flower arrangements.

'See?' said Hennie. 'No respect for their dead, just shove 'em in the ground like they were dogs!'

Recently several white graves have been vandalized: wreaths scattered, cherubs mutilated, angels' wings clipped. Copy-cat crime, perhaps, following the publicity given to gravestones damaged during the Hani funeral. A new way to taunt whites...

'If we catch 'em,' said Hennie, 'they'll never stand up again.'

In the 'yellow' location (Vosburg's Coloureds are known locally as 'yellows') insubstantial shacks occupy a shadeless expanse of pale, cracked, rock-hard earth. Friendly smiles and waves welcomed the bakkie. Hennie waved back, without smiling. 'They seem easy-going, they grin at you all the time – next minute they'd shoot you in your bed!'

The boarding-cum-day-school, opened in 1987, is a pleasantly designed complex of red-brick single-storey buildings, securely fenced. It caters for 200 pupils, mostly Coloured though last year some blacks were admitted. The four-bed dormitories, in separate buildings for boys and girls, are roomy, tidy, cheerful. The dining hall is more agreeable than many dorp restaurants and both laundry and kitchen boast the latest equipment. At noon, two Coloured women in starched white uniforms were dishing out large helpings of tinned fruit salad and custard for forty pupils; the rest go home at weekends. None of the teaching staff was available and the locked classrooms frustrated me. How does their equipment compare with the other amenities?

For Hennie, our tour was a masochistic exercise. 'See how things will be? Our kids are still stuck in that old building near the church! Gimme the fare and I'll be gone to Australia!'

'But soon,' I said blandly, 'all schools will be mixed, everyone having fair shares of what's new.' And I described my visit to the recently desegregated Western Reefs primary school in Orkney, where most parents have accepted amalgamation. When a minority tried violently to oppose it they were bravely dealt with by the Afrikaner principal, Mr Labuschagne, whose calm leadership persuaded those families to resign themselves to the inevitable.

Hennie scowled. 'What are the AWB doing up there? That area's their home-base – have they lost their guns?'

We stopped outside the police station. 'Take a photo!' urged Hennie. This is Vosburg's pride and joy, winner of the first prize as 'South Africa's best-kept police station'. Wide green lawns surround a tree-embowered bungalow, painted cream with a pale blue tin roof. It has no security fencing, no bars on the prettily curtained windows. But for the two flags (RSA, Cape Province) it could be mistaken for the cosy home of a good gardener.

'Lovely, hey?' said Hennie. 'We've so little crime round here they don't need all those fortifications you see other places.'

I spent the afternoon among Vosburg's San rock-paintings, too faded to be tourist bait therefore hard to find. On my way back Syd's wife beckoned me in for coffee. Do I realize the world is doomed because politicians no longer heed the word of the Lord? Mina believes in the death sentence for rape and child abuse. She recalled that 'wenwe' she personally supervised the cutting off of the ear lobes of any 'boy' who stole stock – even one calf, even a hen. 'That way they're marked for life, can't ever again get a job.' Mina looks an amiable, motherly soul.

Back in the bar, Syd advised me to buy a gun without delay. Gabriel added, 'And shoot to kill, it's you or them!'

When the hunters and their wives invited me to join them for dinner I declined. This invitation – and the genuine disappointment when it was refused – touched me. But I couldn't take any more shot-by-shot accounts of killing springbok. And the tedium of South African racism is getting to me. In Northern Ireland, and certain multiracial parts of Britain, the prejudices can be as extreme (among extremists!) but the monotony is less. Individuals make more of an effort to explain or excuse their prejudices and one can be surprised into thinking about a centuries-old bias or conflict from some new perspective. However, the South Africans' mind-numbing uniformity of attitudes may prove healthy in the long term. Their prejudice often seems impersonal, something inherited, imposed, carefully fostered by the Unholy Trinity. When white supremacy collapses completely, all these programmed volk may be jolted into thinking for themselves. And then, just as plants have adapted to the Karoo, even the worst racists may mutate quite quickly if racism is seen to be hindering instead of promoting the well-being of individuals, families, businesses. Or is this my optimism running wild?

Carnarvon, 17 May

At dawn, a flock of Karoo sandgrouse – another of the region's unique species – was settling to drink by Vosburg's dam. The males carry water in their sponge-like belly feathers and, having stood for some time in the shallows, hasten back to their chicks who suck from the feathers.

The Karoo's abundance of birds is unexpected. So far I have spotted bush-shrikes, larks, Karoo robins, long-tailed widow birds, the Karoo korhaan, geese, cranes, storks, secretary birds and (I think) a pair of Maccoa duck – but perhaps not, as my bird book says these are 'everywhere uncommon'. Often I hear the scolding-cock – security officer for all the veld – very loudly calling 'krak-krak-krak'; a tantalizing bird, always sounding close yet never seen.

For abstruse geological reasons, the Karoo's colours and contours are also unique. As is the silence. It is a rich, alive silence. It feels like a blessing. It is awesome, a religious experience – somehow utterly different from the equally flawless silence of never-inhabited mountain regions. Here is an underlying melancholy; the Karoo stirs emotions more opaque than the joyous liberation felt amidst the high Andes or Karakoram. Although so desolate, this silent place is companionable. Mysteriously, one never feels alone. Is it too fanciful to think back to the San, whose ghostly paintings smudge many rocks? The Karoo was not always so underpopulated and San stone tools still litter the ground; yesterday I collected several, to adorn my desk.

This may well be the only territory continuously inhabited by us and our direct ancestors for three million years, since the advent of *Australopithecus*. The Karoo has yielded evidence for the earliest controlled use of fire; one and a half million years ago *Homo habilis*, a species of our own genus, was already into the braai culture. Certainly modern man (anatomically modern man, *Homo sapiens*) has been roaming the Karoo for at least 100,000 years. Ten thousand years ago the San were *in situ* and for some 8,000 years remained Southern Africa's only human inhabitants. When the pastoral Khoikhoi moved down from what is now northern Botswana there was space enough for both tribes. But then a white tribe arrived and, although the Khoikhoi at first showed willing to share grazing lands, Whitey wasn't interested in sharing. He wanted to possess.

If the Great Karoo feels mysterious to travellers, to scientists it *is* mysterious. Between 200 and 300 million years ago – they guesstimate – layers of sandstone-forming sediment were deposited one upon another, layer after layer after layer. Then came the Big Melt, causing an ocean to cover the region. Time passed. A lot of time, like 70 million years, during which the ocean was reduced to a swamp. There followed the event that baffles scientists, an unimaginable cata-clysmic convulsion of our planet; the basalt lava then spewed forth covered thousands of square miles. Next, erosion set to work on the sandstone lower layers, leaving the volcanic dolerite to form the Karoo's hauntingly beautiful koppies.

Today's stage was only fifty-seven miles so I dawdled: much bird-watching, long intervals of simply sitting and looking and feeling the silence.

It bothers me that the importance of silence now goes generally unrecognized. Surely this must be one of humanity's not-so-minor problems at the end of the twentieth century. Why, during our endless inconclusive debates about juvenile delinquency, does no one ever mention the loss of silence? It seems so obvious that not to know silence – never to have known it – is to be dangerously deprived at that deep inner level where human beings, as they mature, get themselves sorted out. Yet most contemporary youngsters rarely encounter true silence and are frightened of it if they do. Are they frightened because their noisy subculture leaves them too disorientated to cope if ever they find themselves alone with their own thoughts? Or is our world so intrinsically frightening that they prefer *not* to think about it – and about their own role within it? The provision of incessant background noise – an immensely profitable industry, now reaching into the remotest corners of Asia and Africa – is one more example of Western exploitation and pollution.

Miles of prickly pear plantations mark the approach to Carnarvon, a biggish dorp with a large treeful triangle at its centre, surrounded by three quite imposing churches.

In mid-afternoon there was little life on the streets – a few white sourpusses doing their shopping, a few stocious Coloured men slumped senseless on the pavement outside the Drankwinkel. The only visible black, a hawker, spoke excellent English and looked so downcast at the end of an unprofitable day that I bought silly quantities of his inferior tomatoes and carrots. The palatial Astoria Hotel has an air of Edwardian complacency; the Wenwe-owned Hotel Carnar-von is almost as large but comfortably shabby. Eileen welcomed me to the bar where beer cans from all over the world decorate walls and ceiling. My fellow-drinkers, a bunch of tall tanned sinewy young sheep-farmers, ignored the uitlander. 'Their English is poor,' Eileen apologized. 'And they could be shy, we're not on the tourist route.' Then Marie arrived, an attractive young woman who was automatically served with a gin and tonic – a sign she does not belong to the dorp scene, where everyone drinks beer or brandy and Coke. Eileen introduced her as an SADF officer from Stellenbosch.

Post-Vosburg, Marie seemed like a being from another galaxy. We talked for hours: about the Afrikaans language, its past and future, about reforming the SAP and then about the SADF/MK merger.

'Myself, I've no problem with it,' said Marie. 'I mean, no psychological problem – the practical problems will be endless. Remember, I grew up expecting the new South Africa – it's been on the way, for those who had eyes to see, ever since I was a kid. But most guys do have a big problem. All their heavy brainwashing – really heavy – presented the MK as the arch-enemy, hellbent on destroying *their* country. Then, hey presto! they're told they must accept them as mates! But you can't program toughies one way, then do a political U-turn and expect them to match it with an emotional U-turn. Yes, fine, let's have a united army – but only after a cooling-down time. Our guys aren't robots to be switched on and off, they're human beings with limitations. Dangerous limitations, you could say. Then what about the limitations on the other side? What do the MK know about the sort of formal discipline we impose? And how will they react to it?'

Williston, 18 May

Beyond Carnarvon, horizontal sun rays touched towering piles of shiny red-black rock, creating a momentary theatrical effect as though the piles were lit from within. Then I saw a lone springbok – a sad sight. The early boertrekkers sometimes had to camp for two days while migrating herds of tens of thousands crossed these plains. Throughout the Karoo dassies and meerkats – both enchanting – are common and every day I have seen several small silver jackals (no threat to sheep) and occasionally a killer black-back. These are swift yet rather ungainly animals and much more timid, for obvious reasons, than their harmless cousins.

Today I was back on a tarred road – the first since Griquatown – and the traffic seemed heavy at two vehicles an hour. Hereabouts miles of raw red earth have been dramatically riven by erosion, farms are very far apart and the vegetation consists mainly of a small wiry grey plant known simply as 'Karoo bush'. I crossed one wide river-bed – dry, unmarked on my map, paved with smooth amber rock slabs, lustrous as marble. When the diamond-diggers were riding fast from Cape Town to Kimberley, covering on average fifty miles a day with a halfway change of horses, they dreaded this eighty-mile stage from Williston to Carnarvon – the toughest and most waterless, needing two changes of horse. The diggers' luggage, if they had any, followed in a wagon dragged by sixteen oxen and covering five miles a day.

Williston sleeps on the right bank of the narrow Sak river at the foot of a sheer, flat-topped koppie with the dignity of a mountain. This is the dopiest dorp of them all – delightfully dopey. As crime of any sort is unknown, the hotel bed-rooms lack keys. The telephones are wind-the-handle models, the TV sets offer only frenzied blizzards with Afrikaans cackles in the background and the shops have never even heard of such a thing as an English-language newspaper. No one is interested in the new South Africa – if, indeed, they are aware of its imminence.

The elderly, courtly proprietor, who describes himself as 'half-Afrikaner', inherited this hotel from a cousin and seems not to take it seriously as a source of income. It was built in 1903 to replace a corrugated-iron inn. In the foyer old photographs recall the hectic excitement of the 1870s when it was well worth riding day and night because, on arrival at Kimberley, you could keep what you found. Pride of place is given to a hand-coloured photograph of the eighty-three carat Star of South Africa, picked up on the banks of the Orange River and sold to the Earl of Dudley for £25,000 – the gem that spurred so many to race across the Karoo.

Calvinia, 19 May

From early morning I could see a rugged dark-blue wall extending all along the southern horizon, sixty miles away – the Hantamsberg, rising to 5,000 feet and therefore impressive, as mountains, in the Karoo. When still thirty miles away I correctly guessed exactly where the road would penetrate them to reach Calvinia.

Most Karoo Boers speak little or no English and the few bakkie-drivers who pass me stare curiously but never stop. I met no one walking on the road nor have I seen anyone off the road through my binoculars. The four homesteads visited – ostensibly to fill my water bottles, really to be inquisitive – seemed considerably less prosperous than the average Transvaal home but this may have more to do with sophistication than economics. Some farmers' bungalows are not that much bigger than their Coloured workers' mud-brick or breeze-block dwellings. Each has its protective semi-circle of bluegums and firs and, usually, a hard-won flower patch: bougainvillea, petunias, cannas. The nearby groves of windpumps fill huge ugly tanks of concrete and galvanized iron; from these, water is piped many miles to countless sheep troughs.

Paranoia briefly afflicted me in Calvinia's hotel bar when I found myself talking to Jacobus, another young SADF officer. Could MI be keeping me under surveillance? Could Marie have been an *agent provocateur*? But no, those days are over. In 1993 Military Intelligence concentrates on fomenting conflict in the townships and homelands.

Jacobus, a Cape Afrikaner, is what I have come to think of as a 'liberal racist': he regards blacks not as animals but as children. And he deplored the Lost Generation's being used as 'political pawns'. His total ignorance of the mechanics of Grand Apartheid explains his impatient contempt for the current turmoil on the educational scene. In ex-Communist countries it is easy to remember past constraints. In this country, which displayed all the trappings of a parliamentary democracy (albeit for whites only), one can forget that the Unholy Trinity were rather better at thought control than most Communist regimes.

Vanrhynsdorp, 20 May

Just outside Calvinia I paused on a humpy little bridge over a dry river-bed, transfixed by the dawn. All about me the land lay dusky, indistinct, its hollows full of darkness, the sun not yet risen. But already long veils of diaphanous cloud had caught the light and I watched the whole north-eastern sky, to the meridian, become a palette of the most delicate merging shades: the palest yellow, the faintest pink, a tinge of green, a hint of mauve, a trace of gold. When the sun rose from behind the surreal formations of the Hantamsberg the colours flared, then faded – and I went on my way.

Those clouds signalled the Atlantic's nearness; we were only forty-five miles from Vanrhyns Pass and soon the implacable Karoo dryness was being softened by a touch of moisture. Here the Hantamsberg and the Bokke-veldberg replace koppies and the whole Karoo plateau tilts perceptibly towards the coast. Within an hour the vegetation had changed; short green grass was growing on the verges – lush grass, hard-to-believe-in grass. I found myself looking at it reverently, realizing how fortunate are we who live in lands forever green. This region has been experiencing freakishly heavy and early rains, hence my preview of the spring flowers near Calvinia. On the rocky ground lay a wondrous quilt of purple and bronze, white and red, blue and yellow, pink and orange.

Another ten miles – and abruptly all was populated fertility: green sloping pastures, bushy hedges supplementing fences, brimming dams sparkling near Cape Dutch farmhouses half-hidden by old orchards or giant pines, resinously aromatic. During a long descent, the dorplet of Nieuwoudtville (it seems smaller than its name) is visible in a hollow from which the road ascends a steep ridge of the Bokkeveldberg – climbing straight up, as is the way of old roads, without benefit of hairpin bends.

Over that ridge lies a pleasant, lightly wooded, almost level landscape. Then, turning a corner, I found myself on the very edge of a sheer escarpment. Directly below – 2,460 feet below – lay the coastal plain's pinkish-brown expanse. Never before, in a long lifetime of travelling, has the terrain so taken me by surprise.

Quite close, to the south, this plain is bounded by a stepped series of lavender-blue table-topped mountains advancing to meet the ocean – which should have been visible some twenty miles away. But an extraordinary phenomenon intervened. Along the coast, for as far as the eye could see, stretched a grey-brown wall of solid-seeming motionless cloud – beneath a cloudless sky.

I lingered, sitting on a pile of silvery boulders inhabited by plump chestnut dassies who popped out to stare at me, then gave their ridiculous bird-like alarm call and vanished – only to reappear moments later, eyes agleam, whiskers aquiver, evidently enjoying this hide-and-seek. When a petrol-tanker could be heard, grinding very slowly and noisily upwards, disturbing the peace, I reluctantly remounted. During that sensationally steep four-mile descent – the road is cut into black and silver cliffs – aching wrists twice forced me to stop.

The coastal cloud-wall did not long remain motionless. As I pedalled across the plain, reduced almost to walking-speed by an icy headwind, it moved inland to meet me. Soon I was soaked through and numb – feet numb, hands numb, face numb, teeth chattering. People who choose to cycle through the Western Cape in midwinter should be prepared for this sort of thing but I am not. In South Africa, I had assumed, a cycling-cape could be bought in any sports shop. Not so, however – no South African has ever heard of such a thing. Luckily my circulation was stimulated by some stiff climbs – a strange landscape, this, of steep grey sandy hills wearing thin cloaks of grey heather. All rather dismal today, under a low grey sky.

At the best of times, it is safe to say, Vanrhynsdorp would not be lively. On 20 May, a national holiday, it is tomb-like – all shops shut, including the Drank-winkel, and the only sound the howling of the gale through winter-bare trees. Beside the hotel, long since closed and boarded up, a signpost says 'Tourist Camp: 2 km'. I pushed Lear up a rough track to a bare muddy compound on an eroded hillside. The shy Afrikaner youth in charge of a row of prefab huts (bedroom and bathroom, £6 per night) has a friendly smile but little English. All these camps are self-catering; for supper I dolefully munched the last of that abundance of carrots bought from the young man in Carnarvon. And this evening has been teetotal, when I so desperately need a free flow of Castle to drown my sorrow at having left the Karoo.

Lambert's Bay, 21 May

This morning, during the fifteen downhill miles to Vredendal, I enjoyed a blue sky, warm sun, emerald pastures, variegated wild flowers, birds nesting, ewes lambing – to Irish eyes, a springtime scene. Vredendal is an ugly dorp surrounded by vineyards irrigated from the Clanwilliam dam through a network of canals. While sitting by the roadside eating breakfast – takeaway snoek (barracuda, fresh and delicious) and chips (soggy and revolting) – I read a disarmingly honest tourist brochure: 'Vredendal is a very "modern" town, therefore there isn't much of historical interest to be seen. The average annual rainfall is only 140 mm and the town is less than 100 feet above sea-level. If possible, avoid the gravel road between Spruitdrift and Lambert's Bay.'

That warning eased my post-Karoo depression. At once I turned towards Spruitdrift and during the forty-five miles to the coast met only one vehicle, a beat-up bakkie loaded with cow-hides and slowly lurching from chasm to chasm. This track climbs steadily into a range of sparsely inhabited hills. The fynbos vegetation is wholly unfamiliar: heathy and shrubby, with occasional coppices of stunted shapeless trees. Merino sheep graze on newly green slopes – greened by herbs, not grass – and around isolated Coloured homesteads small vegetable plots battle with the aridity.

This lonely range, feeling half-forgotten, will remain in my memory as a place of great beauty. A few eagles slowly circled over the broad slopes and deep narrow gullies – almost ravines. A flock of bustards – gigantic birds, now protected – bumbled through the protea scrub keeping their distinctive crested heads low. Small, copper-tinged kestrels perched on tree-tops, guinea-fowl abounded and a secretary bird strutted across grassland looking pompous. All day the sun shone warm and a cold breeze sent high thin white clouds drifting in from the sea. Often I had to walk a few miles at a stretch, even downhill, so dire was the surface.

Then at last I could hear the Atlantic, its roaring and booming uncannily familiar, the same on the southern extremity of Africa as on the western extremity of Europe – my own Irish coast. Quite an emotional moment, perhaps because I am an islander. Soon I could smell the Atlantic: the same smell, too, of saltiness and sandiness and pop-pod seaweed. Another ten minutes and I could *see* the Atlantic, an even more emotional moment for now I have crossed South Africa from the Limpopo to the sea.

Lambert's Bay (Admiral Sir Robert Lambert charted this coastline between 1826 and 1840) is a pretty little dorp overlooking a sheltered harbour where small fishing boats, all freshly painted white and red, are reflected in translucent green water. Miles of smooth beach and pale sand dunes curve around the bay to the rocky point of a distant headland. The crayfish canning factory, built in

1918 – the rest of Lambert's Bay followed – is not unduly obtrusive. Tourism aside, it is the only source of jobs and provides not nearly enough; many impoverished blacks and Coloureds aimlessly wander the streets. Lambert's Bay, famous for its Bird Island, has long been popular with both (white) native and foreign tourists. The latter, rightly regarding it as 'safe', come in droves for the Flower Season.

Ida van Wyk's 'Luxury Guest House' offers the least expensive accommodation (R120). Three years ago the van Wyks came from 'South-West', as most whites still call Namibia; a succession of droughts had forced them to give up farming. Ida is a nervy, loquacious character, immensely kind and now frantically worried. Post-Hani, all the local hotels and guest houses have suffered a staggering 80 to 90 per cent cancellation rate for this year's Flower Season.

'People overseas,' said Ida, 'imagined Cape Town's looters were some terrorist army taking over the whole country! And now people like us are in deep trouble. We had to borrow to set this place up, we can't afford even one bad season. Don't journalists ever think of the *results* of sensationalism? Those rioters weren't political – thanks to Mr Mandela, I've a lot of time for him. They were thugs, criminals like you get anywhere. But they were running amok in Cape Town and all our foreign guests fly into Cape Town. Why don't the media tell the world most South Africans are moderates? White, Coloured or black, most of us want peace.'

My only fellow-guests are Mr and Mrs de Necker from Paarl, a couple in their late seventies who regularly visit Lambert's Bay. This evening they have invited me to accompany them to a renowned open-air restaurant, the Bosduifklip: 'Not expensive, but the best food in the Western Cape.'

The same, 22 May

This morning I woke feeling slightly queasy. One's digestive system becomes used to a certain workload and it is a very, very long time since last I glutted myself on so much rich food.

The Bosduifklip restaurant, family-run on the Albina farm, is as memorable for its setting as for its cuisine. By torchlight we followed a narrow path, between head-high contorted rock formations, to a crescent-shaped ledge below a sheer cliff. The dozen wooden trestle-tables were only dimly lit by storm lanterns, most illumination came from cooking-fires. A whole sheep was being slowly roasted on a spit while vegetables and puddings simmered on huge mud wood stoves overlooking an apparently bottomless ravine.

We helped ourselves to four courses and for the same price could have progressed to six or even eight. The de Neckers advised me to choose crayfish and an elaborate Russian salad, followed by Karoo mutton with roast potatoes and herb-stuffed tomatoes, then shellfish and onion kebab – finally delicious Afrikaner dumplings, cinnamon-flavoured in a tangy fruit syrup. Alas! there was no beer (too plebeian?), only sherry and a strong muscat, both over-sweet. Our fellow-diners were pairs or parties of vivacious Capetonians whose laughter, echoing back from the cliff, grew louder as the muscat flowed faster.

Over coffee and brandies, my companions recalled their childhood days in the 1920s. Both grew up as poor whites in the Eastern Cape, their families bywoners. They walked barefooted to school, in winter carrying heated stones to thaw their feet on arrival. When the mealie crop failed – the '20s were drought-stricken – they went hungry for months on end. New clothes were unknown, they bathed in tin tubs in the kitchen and used an outside earth-closet.

Potent memories of the Anglo-Boer War were passed on. Mr de Necker's father had been a *bittereinder* who fought all the way; his maternal grandmother and two of her children died of typhoid in the Bloemfontein concentration camp.

Viewing the Nats' 1948 victory through de Necker eyes, it can be seen as the long-delayed, hard-earned liberation of a downtrodden white tribe. At last Afrikaners were free to elevate their own hitherto scorned language above English, to compete academically and economically with the imperialists and, most important of all, to govern 'their' country for their own benefit. Only then, said Mr de Necker, were they given 'a fair chance' to climb the prosperity ladder – in his case some considerable way up, through a civil-service sinecure.

'Our only mistake,' said Mrs de Necker, 'was to give apartheid a name. Every country has segregation, nobody would have noticed ours if we'd kept quiet.'

This morning at 5.30 I made my queasy way to Bird Island – alas! no longer an island. In 1959 a concrete breakwater was built and one walks along this unsightly construction to a high wooden watchtower. Here, to my incredulous delight, I was alone, apart from some 14,000 birds performing their preening rituals before dispersing for the day. (Their sunset convergence on the island is even more dramatic.) This was a subdued dawn, the sky lightly clouded, the sun rising as a silver disc from the steel-grey ocean, spume flying high as waves broke against a nearby islet.

Cape cormorants and Cape gannets form the bulk of the colony. The cormorants feed in flocks of several thousand – an awesome sight – and pursue their prey underwater, disappearing for what seems an impossible length of time. The gannets mate for life and lay one egg only each season – in a guana nest, always on the same site. I spotted an ibis breakfasting off a rotten gannet carcass, enthusiastically sinking its long beak into the putrid flesh. Until recently jackass penguins were numerous, now they have been reduced – by oil pollution, pilchard over-fishing and stealthy egg collecting – to fewer than fifty pairs.

One sad solitary specimen was standing still among the cormorants, looking from side to side as though wondering where everyone else had gone.

Each dorp has its public library, clearly signposted, which impressed me until I discovered that these were set up as part of the Christian-National education campaign. Originally every book was hand-picked to reinforce that ideology and the present stock remains heavily contaminated. Here a young Afrikaner woman librarian apologized for the half-empty shelves. 'These new cutbacks are shaming – downright irresponsible just now, when we should be encouraging black kids to get the reading habit.' (Not many Transvaal Afrikaners worry about black kids.) She admitted that she herself prefers imported English books – 'Afrikaans literature is so limited!' At which point my mind's ear heard a grinding noise: Verwoerd's skeleton revolving.

A farm in the mountains, 23 May

For some twenty miles south of Lambert's Bay the landscape looks quite Irish: small green hedged fields. Then I turned onto a rough gravel road, traffic-free but for a tractor and trailer overloaded with farmworkers returning from a shed-church. When addressed they were uncomprehending and the women giggled derisively. Several of the men seemed more than half-drunk; passing the church, I noticed an adjacent shebeen.

Another perfect cycling day: cloudless sky, warm sun, cold breeze. On either side rose low mountains, fancifully shaped; at this season a flowering heather-purple bush covers their lower slopes. Large lake-like dams irrigate expansive orange-groves – the main commercial crop hereabouts – and fields of mealie. The few homesteads, standing close to the road, are unprotected.

Most South African signposts fail to specify distances, an exasperating failure from the cyclist's point of view. At 4.30, as I was wondering 'How far to Citrusdal?', a youth approached wearing the farmworkers' uniform, a dark blue boiler-suit. My question baffled him but in Afrikaans he warned me to beware of the shooting.

I had already heard shots and assumed them to be recreational. In fact they were educational; peering through a shadowy plantation of cluster-pines I glimpsed two small boys enjoying a Sabbath revolver practice under parental supervision. When I shouted 'How far to Citrusdal?' the boys were so fascinated by Lear and me (in that order) that they lost all interest in revolver practice. And then their father shyly invited me to drink coffee.

Jan represents one of the standard models of the Afrikaner male: of medium height, blond, burly, his eyes close-set, his heavy moustache matching heavy jowls. Amy is raven-haired, pale, obese – almost ugly – but warm-hearted and outgoing and clearly thrilled to have a foreign visitor. The boys are Hendrik (aged 9) and Jan junior (aged 7). The toddler, equipped with a grimly realistic toy rifle, is Reubens. The two dogs – muscular mastiff–ridgeback crosses – look lethal but are slobberingly sentimental; each is big enough for the boys to ride with their feet off the ground.

Jan carried Lear through orange trees for 200 yards, lest he might be punctured. Then I was left sitting alone on the lawn under a Cape chestnut while Amy made coffee and Jan, evading conversation with the foreigner, attended to a broken tricycle. Afrikaners tend to be sensitive about limited English though equally limited Afrikaans would swell my head.

The Beylevelds' small bungalow is newish and lies in a slight hollow surrounded by orange-groves and overlooked by a shapely mountain – a perfect cone, royal blue in the evening light. The nearest neighbours live six miles away; the workers' families, in their nearby invisible shacks, do not of course count as neighbours.

Amy's English became more fluent as we talked. 'It's three years since I last spoke English – would you believe that, living so near Cape Town?' She hails from 'South-West', where her Voortrekker family settled in the 1850s. 'Some of those trekkers went all the way to Angola – hey, they were tough folk! But so few reached Angola they had to go for incest up there, marrying first cousins, sometimes even half-brothers and sisters. Who knows what's happened them now?'

The Beylevelds moved here in 1986 when a childless uncle left 2,500 unculti-vated hectares to Jan. 'The government gave no help,' complained Amy, 'we had to borrow from the bank and now we're paying R58,000 annual interest. Is that fair, when Bantustan blacks get free implements and seeds? Paid for by us!'

On nearby mountains Jan runs a flock of some 120 sheep 'as a hobby and to feed us and our workers'. Here shepherds are needed; this is the only (non-game-park) region of South Africa where leopards survive. Instead of a wage, Jan pays his shepherd with ear-marked lambs. But Coloureds dislike being alone on mountainsides – 'They must always be in a crowd' – so reliable shepherds are hard to find.

When Jan went to rescue the boys' rugger ball from a gutter Amy remarked uneasily, 'You can't get to Citrusdal by daylight – I'll ask my husband if you can stay.'

The sun had slid behind the mountain and suddenly it was cold. We moved inside, to a small kitchen furnished with the minimum of mod cons: a gas cooker and refrigerator. Amy apologized for the untidiness; they can't afford an indoor servant. Times have changed; in 'South-West' her mother employed four maids.

All food is kept in a locked pantry off the kitchen. 'They're so feckless, you can't trust them. They never think of saving for emergencies. It's like having an extended family and there's no choice, we have to look after them when the kids go sick or have no clothes in cold weather. The fathers drink their wages. But we must count our blessings, the Western Cape has always been trouble-free, never any friction between us and the Coloureds. They used to fight with us against the Hottentots and the blacks – not many remember that now. But my family were never allowed to forget it – in the Siege of Kimberley a coon saved my great-grandfather's life.'

While the children were being fed (white bread and margarine with fried eggs) Jan opened an unlabelled bottle of wine from the neighbour's vineyard, a glorious dry white that in Ireland would cost an arm and two legs. Amy sipped while ironing Hendrik's shirts for the morrow; he is a weekly boarder at a Clanwilliam school where Jan junior will be starting next term. His mother grumbles that he is learning no English ('That teacher doesn't try!') but his father seems quite happy for him to remain untainted. Jan foresees a black government obliterating the Afrikaans language and culture – 'That's why we need a volkstaat.' But Amy regards fluent English as essential for survival in the new South Africa. 'Do you want your sons to end up in the gutter?' she challenged. 'They'll be discriminated against anyway because they're white, if they can't speak good English they'll be *finished*!'

Amy met Jan during her five years in the SADF. 'He was sympathetic when he saw I hated having to do what the men did, like the leopard crawl – that's going through the bush for 5 km on your stomach. And if you ease up one little bit and raise your body you get a sjamboking. But after two years I was promoted to MI. So I know how real the Commie threat was – still is. Only fools think the defeat of Europe's Communism makes us safe, you can't beat the devil so easily!'

Sooner or later, in most Afrikaner homes, the conversation turns to religion. As Amy recalled this morning's sermon in Clanwilliam, her face was transformed. The dominee had exhorted his flock to trust in God who knows the Afrikaners' cause to be just and the Lord loves just men. 'He warned about all the forces of darkness gathering against us and the Devil tempting us to despair – but we must not give way, despair is the worst sin! I know he's right, I feel the Lord protecting us, I can see his strength being given to us now that we have another hour of need. I can see it coming towards us like a big golden cloud with beams shining down on us – I know if I trust in the Lord my boys will be safe and get good jobs and we won't be thrown off the farm. But when I don't keep my mind fixed on the Lord it's so easy to despair! You'd like our dominee, he's a just man. He says we must admit some mistakes. Flogging workers was wrong – well, I always thought that.'

This was not just 'women's stuff'; Jan seems no less dependent on DRC support. Such interweavings of semi-hysterical religious fervour and political fanaticism I do not like. But I suppose when humans have made a mess of their country, and now feel threatened by that mess, it helps to pass the buck to the Almighty – who by definition can sort out any mess. At times I feel almost as sorry for the whites as for the blacks. It's certainly unfair to censure them for their fear and loathing of the ANC, a phobia implanted and nurtured over decades. No wonder people like Amy and Jan feel so betrayed, scared and confused; when de Klerk did his 1990 volte-face he never confessed on behalf of the government that the 'Total Onslaught' was a Nat invention. A 1985 poll of white voters showed 85 per cent resigned to some degree of change and in favour of 'negotiating with blacks'. Yet less than 4 per cent approved of negotiating with the ANC. The whites had not been allowed to realize that the ANC leaders were the only blacks with whom the Nats *could* negotiate.

Citrusdal, 24 May

During breakfast the police rang; today COSAS is organizing a sit-in at Hendrik's all-white school – Coloured would-be pupils plan to take over the building. Jan laughed. 'No problem, I'll be there!' His vigorous sjamboking gestures were immediately understood by the boys who gazed up worshipfully at their role model – then grinned at each other, imitating the gestures. Amy looked uneasy but said nothing.

Jan, once a famous rugger star, spends time on his sons' physical development; already the older boys have bulging biceps and calf muscles. After breakfast Jan junior asked if he might jog along for a few miles and his speed did not slow me, so steep and rough was the track. Before we parted he insisted on climbing a high wire fence and going far up the mountain to fetch me a farewell gift, a pink-flowered herb of some special significance he couldn't explain. A natural charmer, he hugged me tightly as we said goodbye.

This is an unsignposted region of vaguely wandering tracks – none marked on my map – with crossroads and T-junctions where there is no particular reason to turn left or right. I proceeded according to whim and soon was happily lost. (In a country usually so well signposted that even I can't go astray, journeys lack an important ingredient – unpredictability.) Here the red-rock mountains are too sheer and arid for sheep, the fynbos-filled valleys too narrow for cultivation. The unfamiliar vegetation gave off a rich complexity of scents and towards noon I saw – far below the track, leaping and singing through a steep ravine – the first full stream on my route since leaving Jo'burg. Will dehydration be the new South Africa's main problem?

In mid-afternoon this idyll ended abruptly. Turning the shoulder of a gleaming silver rock mountain I heard traffic noises and saw our track plunging down to the N7 highway. Far below lay the Olifant River valley, wide and green and sunny. And beyond rose the Cedarberg, a long, rough-hewn, grey-blue range.

Cycling on the comparatively narrow N7 is perilous – especially now, during the orange-harvesting season, when countless trucks are travelling at speed in both directions. Mercifully a bridge soon allowed me to escape across the river onto a parallel gravel road.

Pre-agribusiness, the Olifant valley must have been very lovely with its wide strips of pure white riverside sand, its neat vineyards and orange-groves, its merino flocks scattered over gently sloping pastures. Several old Cape Dutch farmhouses, dignified in a manorial way, are half-hidden by oaks, poplars and walnut trees. Even the light seems Mediterranean rather than African – no wonder the first 'free burgers' felt at home here when they and their slaves moved out from Cape Town to grow wheat for the Dutch East India Company. Before those settlers took it over, this valley provided the local Khoikhoi with some of their best grazing land.

The Cape and the Transvaal might be on different continents – and not only in terms of climate and topography. Here in Citrusdal – a pleasant little town between river and mountains – people smile at you in the street and, given the slightest encouragement, stop for a long chat. The elderly Afrikaner in the Drankwinkel told me why he thinks the new South Africa will be better than the old. The young woman in the small store told me why she thinks it will be worse for young whites – she's keen to emigrate to Australia if her fiancé can find work there. Everyone advised me to stay in Louis' farm guest house – 'He can tell you all about the area, his family are here 250 years.'

Low black clouds were obscuring the Cedarberg as I bumped down an atrocious track, past the family graveyard, to a handsome farmhouse (1736) with a discreetly modern guest-wing extension. Seven Heinz dogs welcomed me, including a minute puppy who at once set about untying my shoelaces. There were no humans in sight but the house is innocent of locks or bars. I could have stuffed my panniers with the family silver – a lot of it lies around – and quietly pedalled away. As this orange farm covers 4,000 hectares it seemed pointless to look for Louis so I sat on the stoep drinking a Long Tom until a co-op truck arrived – the signal for him to appear, driving a mini-tractor loaded with crated and graded oranges. Grade One: perfect, for export. Grade Two: very slightly imperfect, for sale in urban South Africa. Grade Three: obviously imperfect, for sale to a juice factory. Louis, a kindly and gracious young man, happily boasted that this year his crop is 70 per cent perfect.

As Louis showed me to my four-room self-catering flatlet (excellent value at £6 per night) the rain started: torrential rain, like a theatre curtain coming down.

'This sort of weather continues for at least thirty-six hours,' said Louis. 'So we'll talk more in the morning – no harvesting for me, no cycling for you!'

The same, 25 May

As predicted, it rained heavily all day. The leading item on the news: Janus Waluz and the Derby-Lewises have been charged with conspiracy to murder nine people including Mr Mandela, Joe Slovo and Pik Botha. Also, in Venda the PAC national organizer has told a mass rally of many thousands that white farmers are legitimate APLA targets: 'We will always be after the farmers who have so illegally occupied our land.'

'Down here,' said Louis, 'we've another sort of relationship with our Coloured workers. Not quite as good as before, but better than anything possible between the Vaalies and their blacks. Some call the Coloureds "brown Afrikaners" and that's not far off the truth.'

According to Louis, sanctions were only a minor problem; oranges could always be exported via Malawi, President Banda being broad-minded. Granted, that reduced profits – transport costs were higher and Banda had to have his reward. 'For people like us,' said Louis, 'sanctions worked psychologically rather than economically. They upset my father terribly. He hated having to export furtively, disguising the crop he'd worked so hard to make perfect – that was a bad feeling. It hurt to think millions would throw your oranges in the gutter if they knew where they came from. The campaigners were right to persist, they became like water dropping on stone. We had to have change, so the sooner it came the better. I belong to the Nats, but right now I'm sitting on the fence. I could vote for the ANC, they've an amazing number of able men in the leadership – the Nats have none!'

This evening the other flatlet is occupied by Retha, a fortyish Afrikaner woman lawyer: tall, blonde, elegant even in a tracksuit, hoping to hill-walk tomorrow. She looks as though she might hold strong views – and she does.

'I was ready to vote ANC when Mandela was released, when I saw black rule coming. Now I couldn't vote for them, my conscience wouldn't let me. I cannot go along with this disruption of schooling, it's criminal. Isn't one Lost Generation enough? How are the townships ever to be stabilized with another coming up? In Nyanga and Guguletu I do voluntary legal advice work, I see how worried parents are – especially the mothers. They want their children at school, if they're lucky enough to have the fees – not roaming the streets getting a taste for gang warfare and risking their lives baiting the security forces. Mandela pleads with them on the media to go back to school and they ignore him. If the ANC can't control COSAS and their own Youth League, how can they govern South Africa?'

It seems here I've escaped from that uniformity of thinking which so got me down further north.

Cape Town, 27 May

Yesterday morning, soon after I left Citrusdal, the deluge resumed, forcing me to abandon a dirt road through the Swartruggens – impassable in such weather – and return to the N7. After a night in Moorreesburg (where I arrived sodden, having seen nothing of a famously beautiful area), the N7's multiple horrors had to be endured again: many fast trucks, a treacherous gusty gale-force crosswind, extreme cold, ceaseless rain, visibility almost nil.

Freewheeling for miles from the high land around Malmesbury, I looked in vain for the Mother City; she was shrouded in a burkah of dark cloud. Down at last to sea-level, I was immediately engulfed by an enormous industrial estate and a newish Coloured township of tiny identical dwellings behind a high concrete wall; one glimpsed the houses only where this grim barrier allowed vehicle access. Here the urban traffic was quite terrifying. Intent on self-preservation, I missed the Muizenberg turn-off and was appalled to find myself on the N1, pedalling towards Messina via Johannesburg – so said the overhead sign. Walking back, against the traffic, I shrank from the noise and vibration of vehicles speeding past, very close. The gale whipped my face with icy horizontal rain, diesel fumes nauseated me and powerful jets of oily black water repeatedly struck my left side. This, I thought, would serve as a perfect model for hell: all the senses being simultaneously tormented.

On one side stretched a desolation of colossal warehouses, engineering workshops, second-hand-car showrooms – all beyond a metal barrier, cutting me off from the 'normal' road. Then a battered kombi pulled up ahead and out jumped a tubby, elderly Coloured man, braving the deluge to rescue me. Wordlessly he manoeuvred Lear into the back – with difficulty, kombis not being designed to accommodate bicycles. In response to my expressions of gratitude he observed, 'Cyclists are forbidden on the motorway so no one cares if they kill you – they won't be blamed. And we must always help one another, that is how the good Lord likes it. But if I'd seen you are a woman I wouldn't have stopped, I would have feared to frighten you.'

Fifteen minutes later I was put down on Route 4, at Mowbray, an agreeable place of shabby two-storey buildings and small shops, some arcaded. This was once a mixed area where Coloureds and the less-well-off whites happily shared territory. Most of the businesses – explained my rescuer – are still Coloured but now their owners have to travel daily from Mitchells Plain or some other distant new township on the Cape Flats.

Cape Town has to be long and narrow, stretching at the base of its mountains from Table Bay down to Muizenberg on False Bay. Route 4 took us through several suburbs, each with rather a villagey feel and, usually, an English name: Observatory, Rosebank, Claremont, Kenilworth, Plumstead, Newlands. Close as were the mountains, only their lower slopes could be glimpsed through the rain. I was impressed by the number of white cyclists beside me at each robot stop, the ecologically correct sort who pedal to and from work in all weathers. Their existence inspires Capetonian motorists to behave themselves; here one doesn't feel at risk.

From Malmesbury I had tried, unsuccessfully, to ring a friend. At 5.45 her office was closed and I have lost her home address so this gruelling day has ended in a Coloured hotel undeserving of even one star. Simple doss-houses please me; sleazy hotels tend to depress. The bar and restaurant are closed because Cape Town is now without electricity – storm damage. My room smells unclean in an indefinable sort of way and, as the management could provide neither lamp nor candle, this has been written by torchlight on a saggy, grubby and chillingly damp bed.

6

A Worried Mother

The Cape Peninsula

The object of the Dutch East India Company in establishing a station at the Cape of Good Hope in 1652 was but a means to an end. It desired a place where its ships, sailing to and from the East Indies, could obtain refreshments, and where the seamen could recuperate after a long voyage. There was no idea at first of making the place a colony where men and women from Holland could settle and build up a strong colonial possession.

C. Graham Botha (1926)

2 June 1993

In the Kirstenbosch Botanic Gardens, on the eastern slopes of Table Mountain, you can touch the past and find it still alive. Today I did just that, sitting in the deep shade of a hedge planted 333 years ago. For long the imaginations of South African writers have been stirred by the symbolism of these bitter-almond trees, their low tangled branches contorted but their foliage still vigorous. Jan van Riebeeck planted this hedge to exclude the Khoikhoi and their cattle from the first white settlement in southern Africa. Once it extended for miles along the mountainsides, now only fragments remain. I stole a leaf as a souvenir.

When van Riebeeck landed on 6 April 1652 there were no blacks around, only the pastoral Khoikhoi – and the San, hunting and gathering in the least accessible regions. Three hundred and forty-one years later things are very different and the Mother City is worried. Involuntarily, since 1982, she has acquired an additional 700,000 black children, making 900,000 in all. (The majority are 'refugees' from the intolerable poverty of the Xhosa 'homelands'.) Understandably, the Peninsula's one and a half million Coloureds and whites have been made uneasy by this mass migration. Their Mother is undergoing a personality change about which nothing can be done. Daily 'they' travel in from their ever-expanding townships and squatter camps (to be politically correct I should call the latter 'informal settlements') on the sandy Cape Flats. All over the city centre and throughout the suburban 'villages' they are to be seen hawking and loitering and desperately job-seeking and to most Capetonians they seem ominously omnipresent. Yet it surprises me, given their nearby numbers, that so comparatively few appear on 'white' territory. The younger generation speak little English;

their elders, often fluent English-speakers, are always polite but maintain a dignified reserve.

Since 28 May I have been based in Retreat, some ten miles south of the city centre on Route 4, overlooked by the sheer silver rock-walls of nearby Constantiaberg and Steenberg. Here Margaret's friends live in a large bungalow facing level grassland with the Rondevlei Bird Sanctuary beyond. They gave me the sort of welcome that dissolves inhibitions about staying indefinitely. I have been made to feel *not* like a guest, surely the greatest compliment one can pay one's host and hostess.

5 June

Here I delight in travelling by taxi, usually a battered old kombi driven at death-defying speed and overcrowded with jolly Coloureds. (The darker skinned the jollier, it seems; those who could pass-for-white – a considerable minority – tend to be rather more buttoned-up.) For my benefit some fellow-passengers speak English among themselves and even when they don't I can relish their enjoyment of repartee, their laconic, quick-on-the-draw wit. The politically progressive say 'we' meaning blacks and Coloureds; the rest say 'we' meaning whites and Coloureds. For generations their language-bond with the Afrikaners, implying a shared culture, reinforced Coloured self-esteem. But then came rejection, Grand Apartheid's demotion of all non-whites. Since that time, in urban communities, many Coloureds have pointedly tried to learn English. (The prosperous middle class, not usually encountered in taxis, are bilingual, speaking perfect English.)

In June 1971 the Afrikaanse Studentebond Congress in Pretoria sought to repudiate their distant cousins by passing a resolution affirming that the Colour-eds' only ancestors were the Khoisan and Asian and black slaves. Ten months later they got a nasty shock. In the *South African Medical Journal* Dr M. C. Botha, an internationally acclaimed immunologist, reported that genetically Afrikaners are 7 per cent non-white. After all that effort to segregate, no such thing existed as a racially pure Afrikaner society. And soon Dr Botha's horrible findings were confirmed by independent research of an entirely different sort. Dr J. A. Heese, of the DRC Archives, had studied the Cape's early marriage records and calcu-lated that Afrikaners are 6.9 per cent non-white.

According to Dr Botha, the Cape Coloureds are the only authentic Cape-tonians, the only community to have evolved on the tip of Africa. And by now they form, in his words, 'an anthropologically distinct population'. They also form, visually, a genetic jigsaw puzzle. Looking around any group of Coloureds, each face seems a tantalizing enigma, the possible combinations endless. Here are genes from all over Europe, from West Africa, Mozambique, Madagascar,

India, China, Malaya, Indonesia, Arabia, the Philippines... Most of the European genes were contributed a long time ago: first when there was a serious shortage of white women and the original Dutch settlers took Khoikhoi brides, then while it was acceptable for a Boer farmer to lie with his nubile slaves, who might be African or Asian. Van Riebeeck soon realized that the Khoisan were resolutely uninterested in cultivating land for the settlers' benefit; instead, slaves were imported and a slave-state existed for 182 years.

I gleaned much information yesterday during a nine-hour session in the magnificent and well-ordered South Africa Library, founded in 1818 with funds obtained through the imposition of a special wine tax. A translation of van Riebeeck's detailed *Journal* revealed that by the time he left for home, in 1662, many familiar nastinesses were already firmly rooted. The Khoisan had been put in their place, Robben Island chosen as an ideal place of banishment and the deadly 'tot' system instituted – the origin of the Coloureds' notorious drink problem. Instead of cash, farmworkers – from the age of 13 or so – were given a quart of rough wine at intervals throughout the day. Despite increasing criticism over the past twenty years, this system has not yet been completely eradicated. In Lambert's Bay one farmer told me 'They're never late, being late means missing your morning tot! And they're never off work without a genuine excuse, they work much harder for wine than for cash.'

7 June

Bo-Kaap begins at the interesting end of Longmarket Street, where it leaves the fumes and speeding traffic of white Cape Town and is reincarnated as a steep cobbled laneway climbing straight up Signal Hill. Allegedly the Group Areas Act spared this Muslim district because the authorities recognized its potential as a 'picturesque' tourist attraction. But Bo-Kaap is not merely picturesque; it has that indefinable quality usually defined as 'character'. The district covers less than a square mile. Some streets run level along the side of Signal Hill, intersecting with other vertical streets which climb and climb until one is level with the sheer, gaunt, upper slopes of Table Mountain – from here Cape Town's city centre 'developments' look like Lego constructions. All these narrow cobbled streets are lined with one-storey, narrow-fronted, flat-roofed terraced houses on high stoeps, painted in contrasting colours. Many date from the 1780s and have family names engraved over the main entrance. Some are in a sad state of disrepair, others have recently been restored.

Quite a number of the present residents' ancestors were political prisoners, exiled rebels from the Dutch East India colonies, learned and once-wealthy gentlemen who provided spiritual and intellectual leadership for their enslaved fellow-Muslims. In 1694 the pioneers arrived: a Bantamise resistance leader,

Sheikh Yussuf of Macassar, and forty-nine of his followers. All were dispatched to labour on a farm far from Cape Town, up the Olifant Valley. A Tidore prince from the Moluccas, Imam Abdullah Kadi Abdus Salaan (Tuan Guru, for short), was the most illustrious 'criminal'; while imprisoned on Robben Island he transcribed the Koran from memory and without error. The richness and complexity of an Islamic East Indian background enabled these exiles and their descendants to maintain their own identity and escape the worst horrors of slavery. The Cape was then critically short of craftsmen and women (most early European settlers came from the least gifted strata of their societies) and soon the talented newcomers – joiners, stonemasons, plasterers, metalworkers, seamstresses, tailors – gained tacit acceptance as an élite; the design and decoration of the distinctive Cape Dutch farmhouses are their most conspicuous legacy. Being in such demand, they could evade the standard oppressions of slavery and charge commissions for their work and thus eventually achieve manumission. As *vryezwarten* (free blacks) they took over the lower slopes of Signal Hill and created Bo-Kaap.

Achmat Davids and his wife Karima Davids-Jacobs live halfway up Signal Hill, directly opposite the miniature Boorhaanol Mosque, built in 1884 and now a national monument, lovingly described by Achmat in *The Mosques of Bo-Kaap*. I was lucky to find this remarkable couple at home. Only yesterday they returned from six months in the USA, where Achmat – an authority on the evolution of the Afrikaans language – had been a visiting professor in Yale's Linguistics School. He is also a pioneer social worker – the first produced by the Bo-Kaap community – as is his poet wife. Karima's being quarter-Irish nicely proves Achmat's point that 'Cape Malay' is a misnomer, resented by the people so called. They should be described as 'Cape Muslims' since it is religion, not race, that binds this little society together. Most slave names, Achmat explained, indicate places of origin and less than 1 per cent of 'Cape Malays' came from what we now call Malaysia. The confusion probably arose because the East Indian slaves' common language was Malayu, for centuries the main trading language from Madagascar to China – now extinct, though traces remain in Afrikaans.

Only sixty years ago many educated Afrikaners habitually spoke English, their Dutch having lapsed. In contrast, uneducated Afrikaners spoke neither English (still regarded as the enemy's language) nor Dutch – only Afrikaans, scorned by their superiors as *kombuistaal*, a kitchen-language. Yet it had been named 'Afrikaans' in 1875 by a group of intellectuals who had just named themselves 'Afrikaners'. These men were determined to forge a new national identity for the Boers, too long suspended in a vacuum – neither European nor African – and now threatened with absorption into the loathed British Empire. (In 1877 the Transvaal Republic was annexed by Britain.) At that point it became expedient to fudge the origins of Afrikaans. Much was denied and then forgotten, like the fact that the Cape Muslims were the first to write the language, using the Arabic script. The first book published in Afrikaans, in 1856 – a homily on the Islamic faith – was written by a Cape Muslim when most Boers were only semi-literate, if that.

Achmat's researches into the origins of Afrikaans have aroused the rightwingers' ire. How dare this cheeky 'Malay' analyse their language's component parts and assert that it is far from being a thoroughbred descendant of High Dutch? Smiling tolerantly, Achmat pointed out that his academic work is the reverse of treasonous; he has merely reinforced the cultural bond between Coloureds and Afrikaners.

In 1925 Afrikaans was at last included in the constitutional definition of 'Dutch' and soon High Dutch vanished from the South African scene leaving Afrikaans to develop, astonishingly quickly, into a coherent modern language. This marked a significant turning-point in the fortunes of poor whites, hitherto barred from public service by their ignorance of both English and Dutch. But then – as Karima dryly recalled – a mere fifty years later the attempt to impose Afrikaans on black pupils provoked the '76 Soweto uprising, an event now identifiable as the beginning of the end for white supremacy.

Like many Bo-Kaap houses, the Davids' is much bigger than it looks from the street; several large rooms open off a long hallway. As we talked, much laughter and a merger of delicious aromas came from the kitchen where three generations of the extended family were preparing a 'welcome home' feast. (The Malay cuisine – so called – is universally acknowledged to be South Africa's best.) This Cape Muslim community is exceptionally tight-knit; even now, many parents encourage their married children to live nearby. Monogamy is the custom (*pace* the Koran) and because Muslim marriages were not recognized in the old South Africa most couples also went through a civil ceremony.

Karima is the main inspiration of a pioneering organization called Streets. Cape Town's street children, who prefer to be known as 'strollers', are heartbreakingly numerous and she spoke with passion of the need to deal with the emotional/psychological reasons for each child's transformation into a stroller. 'Sometimes you find that poverty is not the main reason. The best way to help is to make contact with the children's local community – persuade them to identify individual problems, then set up neighbourhood support groups for both parents and children.' Karima deplores the dependency culture fostered by do-gooders who concentrate on effects while ignoring causes. She sees little hope for the Cape's impoverished Coloureds unless they are encouraged to take some responsibility for their own advancement. Before going to Yale she saw one of her projects completed: the publication of a substantial anthology of strollers' poems. This indeed is social work with a difference.

From Longmarket Street I rambled on through Bo-Kaap where many men wear kufias and many women and girls are veiled. The city centre being so close, Bo-Kaap has a predictable post-apartheid problem: whites see it as a desirable residential area. What to do? According to one agitated old gentleman, who invited me to drink tea on his stoep, market forces will destroy what the Group Areas Act left untouched. Bill Rawson Estates is now busily distributing leaflets (I was shown several) to let householders know their property is 'worth a lot of money', a message often reinforced by repeated telephone calls.

'This is cultural genocide!' exclaimed my host, whose family have occupied the same elegant little house since the 1840s, when most Boers were still living in mud huts. Strong language, yet I see what he means. Bo-Kaap's nine mosques, to which muezzins successfully summon males to prayer five times a day, are central to both the religious and social life of these Sunnis – a devout and quite orthodox community though not at all fanatical.

Some white newcomers cause offence by drinking alcohol on their stoeps while listening to very loud pop music 'with lewd lyrics'. A few communes have been set up 'where boys and girls share bedrooms and if they are married or not married is all the same'. Still worse, these communes are attracting the much-feared Cape Flats drug dealers. In desperation, a campaign has been started to have Bo-Kaap protected as 'a cultural heritage site' where only Muslims can buy property. However, this demand for a new sort of exclusion order uncomfortably recalls the bad old days, as estate agents are quick to point out. Most of the residents to whom I spoke have already accepted, with varying mixtures of grief and rage, the fact that Bo-Kaap as a cultural entity is doomed.

10 June

A Coloured middle class has existed for generations in Cape Town, many now living in Retreat and Grassy Park, across the railway line from my base camp in white Retreat. Were one to walk through without seeing anybody, this resident-ial area might be mistaken for a dorp. The same solid well-maintained bunga-lows (though on average a trifle smaller); the same tidy gardens populated by gnomes and Bambis; the same well-polished cars and children's swings and litter-free verges. Only when the residents appear does one notice a difference: the Coloureds, of both sexes, dress with a flair and good taste rarely seen among dorp whites.

Two days ago, in the middle of Grassy Park, on my way back from the Rondevlei Bird Sanctuary, I met Jimmie: a 20-year-old Arts student, stocky and fair-skinned and crinkly-haired, wearing an ANC T-shirt and also riding a mountain bike. He appreciated Lear's special qualities, we discussed my journey, then he invited me to supper. 'Come tomorrow evening, I must warn my mother and give her time. She's uptight about whites, she'll want to impress you, she doesn't understand the new South Africa!'

Mr and Mrs Currey and Granny Currey, wearing their best bibs and tuckers, were I fear rather taken aback by my slacks and Chris Hani T-shirt. (I had thought, correctly, the latter would please Jimmie.) A slight conversational logjam was deftly shifted by Jimmie's remarking that I was the first white ever to visit the family socially, as distinct from whites calling on business.

I asked, 'But why? Why now only on business?'

Jimmie chuckled; his narrow eyes, above chubby cheeks, almost disappeared when he smiled. 'Dad is rich and influential, wrong colour, right bank balance. Not fit to jol [relax] with but still worth knowing.' Dad looked embarrassed, Mom beamed fondly at her one-and-only. I had the impression she would approve of almost anything he said or did.

Then Mr and Mrs Leonard arrived: he tall and lumbering-obese, she scarcely five feet and wispy, both argumentative. He is Dad's business partner and brother-in-law, she runs a privately funded remedial school for strollers and greatly admires Karima. Within moments the Leonards had plunged us all into a stormy ocean of debate about the election, the ANC's role in the new South Africa, Bishop Tutu's role at the Hani funeral (both families are devout Anglicans), how to rehabilitate the Lost Generation, how to reduce the Cape's black population by setting up industries in the Transkei – and whether or not it would be safe for me to cycle through the Transkei on my way back to Jo'burg.

During a superb five-course 'Malay' meal Mrs Currey recalled her student days at the University of the Western Cape (UWC) in the early 1970s when enthusiasm for Black Consciousness swept the campus, causing much turmoil and once prompting the Afrikaner rector to close the university for six weeks. 'For us educated Coloureds,' said Mrs Currey, 'those years were a turning-point. Ever since, our best political leaders have seen we must struggle *with* the blacks, not separately, looking for privileges for ourselves.'

'We should never forget Steve Biko,' agreed Mr Leonard, accepting a third helping of pudding – a luscious concoction of fruits and whipped cream and brandy and something strange but wonderful.

'How would he have fitted in now?' wondered Mrs Leonard. 'What would he have thought about the negotiations? He was against the Freedom Charter.'

Her husband said, 'Steve would have fitted in fine. BC [Black Consciousness] wasn't a racist philosophy, that's Nat propaganda. It was what we all needed *then*, Coloureds and blacks and Indians. We needed to be kicked out of our torpor, made proud and assertive and self-reliant. That's what BC was all about – not hating whites but loving ourselves.'

'I knew him,' said Mr Currey. 'We were exactly the same age. He was a great man – I mean *great*. Losing him was like losing Hani.' He glanced at my shirt.

'Biko taught us Coloureds that our ancestors backed the wrong horse. Why did we ever imagine if we stuck with the whites, one day they'd love us? Instead they tricked us out of our voting rights and threw us out of our homes!'

'Twenty years ago,' remembered Mrs Currey, 'I called myself "black". Mostly we did, on campus. Now the struggle's won it upsets me when our kids call themselves black. In the new South Africa we can all be proud of what we are!'

'Those kids are chameleons!' said Mrs Leonard. 'They call themselves black to get in with the Young Lions and go rioting and looting, saying that's "political activism". Give them jobs and they'll change back to what they were born.'

'You're wrong!' said her husband. 'It's the old wanting-to-identify mistake the other way round.' Having paused to light a fat cigar, he turned to address me. 'Look, let's face it – you won't meet many admitting this but we're going to have an identity problem for a while yet. Grand Apartheid detached us from the whites – and wow! that hurt! Next there has to be an interim – you've noticed "interim" is our buzz-word? An interim government, an interim constitution ... And another interim for us to get a grip on our identity and learn to feel secure with it.'

'I feel perfectly secure!' protested Mrs Leonard. 'You do talk nonsense!'

'I'm not referring to you,' retorted her husband. 'Or to anyone here. I'm thinking of the uneducated poor – that's most of us.'

'Identity is why I'm going to uwc,' said Jimmie. 'I got a place at uct [University of Cape Town] just to prove I could but the other is our university. And it won't ever be any good if all the brains go to uct.'

'You'll regret that,' pronounced Mr Leonard. 'I told you so at the time – a uwc degree is like a used postage stamp. People throw them out. And now it's swamped with illiterate blacks it can only get worse.'

Mom rose to her son's defence. 'Jimmie's an idealist and we need those around.'

'Ideals butter no parsnips,' said Mr Leonard conclusively.

Later, as Jimmie drove me home, I asked why he still thinks of uwc as 'our university'. 'Aren't those days over? You've got me confused.'

Jimmie was silent for moments. Then: 'I guess we're all still thinking apartheid, know what I mean? I'm thinking as a Coloured, what to do for *my* people. At uwc I can try to up standards in all sorts of ways. For me, choosing uct wouldn't be like you see it, meaning I'm thinking non-racist strictly as an academic. I guess all South Africans have a long way to go. Maybe for generations we'll be thinking racist – no, I mean thinking *separate*.'

When I asked about his career plans Jimmie laughed. 'I've big plans, I want to be something new, an honest politician – or d'you reckon that's impossible?'

Briefly I hesitated before replying, 'In Madiba's South Africa anything may be possible.'

'OK,' said Jimmie, 'so you think I'm crazy – and weren't you, aged 20?'

12 June

Between Cape Town and Jo'burg there can be no genuine rivalry: when everything is immeasurably unequal, competition doesn't arise. This city is quite small, easy to cycle around and old enough to have a heart, a soul and layers of history. Often I walk through the Company Gardens in the centre where the very first vegetables were grown for those scurvy-riddled Dutch sailors. (How strange that such an innocent need, for fresh fruit and veg, should have brought such misery to all the indigenous peoples of South Africa!) Since the eighteenth century the Gardens have been an arboreal paradise where mighty trees – wondrously exotic, from every continent – shade smooth green lawns and vivid flower-beds. In this haven of coolness and calm doves coo, grey squirrels beg cheekily, feral cats and kittens live happily in the shrubberies – being fed by friends among the open-air restaurant's customers – and tall fountains splash and sparkle, their source the underground springs that watered those first vegetables.

Cape Town's finest colonial buildings surround the Gardens. Most are gravely imposing British legacies: the Houses of Parliament, the South African Museum, the South African Library. Vigilant policemen guard the more modest and very elegant Cape Dutch Tuynhuys, residence and office of the State President – soon to be occupied, if all goes well, by a black ex-convict. Not far away is the Cathedral of St George, its exterior heavily dull, its neo-Gothic interior pleasing enough, all the trappings mainstream Anglican. The Groote Kerk on Adderley Street is the country's oldest church where eight Dutch Governors rest in peace; whenever I pass by it is locked. On the Grand Parade King Edward VII still reigns monumentally, facing the vaguely baroque City Hall – once pre-eminent, now dwarfed by commercial 'developments' of breathtaking ugliness. Nearby crouches South Africa's oldest building, the pentagonal Castle of Good Hope (style: Renaissance Military) completed in 1697. Since 1666 it has served as a fortress, official Residence, torture chamber, military barracks, prison, bank, museum, administrative centre, warehouse, hospital and church. Just now it is closed for renovation – good timing, pre-election South Africa not being a tourist magnet.

Too many of the visible links with Cape Town's past have recently been obliterated and, when viewed from street level, the city centre's architectural excesses seem higher than Table Mountain. Also, the whole peninsula has suffered grievously at the wheels of the internal combustion engine. In times past this must have been among the most dramatically magnificent places on our planet, now tiers of motorways scar the flanks of its noble mountains. And yesterday I found the famous Steenberg Pass defaced by two vast litter-strewn car parks. I could have wept: the violation of such splendour hurts me, deep down inside.

13 June

On Sunday mornings the trains from Retreat to the city centre are packed with well-dressed, well-spoken, prayer-book-laden Coloured families faithfully return-ing from their 'exile' on the Cape Flats to those churches in the 'white' suburbs where their forebears worshipped for generations. Now some are optimistic – perhaps they can move back? The more realistic see little hope of this. Why should whites who have invested in the improvement of their properties be willing to sell? And anyway, how could the average Coloured afford the price demanded?

These are the sort of people – models of respectability, temperamentally introspective and sensitive – who felt branded in a peculiarly hurtful way when sexual relations between whites and 'others' became a crime punishable by seven years in jail. This morning, in the train on my way to a lunch appointment in the Gardens, I sat beside a middle-aged lady resplendent in an old-gold and jade-green ensemble, topped by a flower-laden panama hat. First she recalled her childhood in Wynberg, then she declared, with unexpected bluntness, 'It's not pleasant for a whole community to feel labelled as the fruits of past *criminal* unions.'

Time has given Cape Town a subtly complex persona. Starting as an *ad hoc* settlement of Dutch market-gardeners, it soon became the inefficient and cor-rupt administrative capital of a slave-state. Then it acquired gravitas as the governmental seat of a remote British colony, before degenerating into the apartheid state's parliamentary headquarters. And now it is waiting to clasp to its maternal bosom South Africa's first multiracial Assembly.

Many Vaalies condemn Capetonians as lazy and frivolous and snobby. I however find them agreeably laid-back and their superiority complex, in relation to other white South Africans, seems amply justified.

Some people, even now, regard the Mother City as essentially *English*. Since 1805, they assert, its dominant ethos has been 'English liberal' rather than 'British imperial'. Hence the Cape Afrikaners had a chance to absorb civilized attitudes, unlike those rebellious Boers who eventually became the Vaalies and Free Staters. Not all history books reinforce this perception of the English role. Yet it persists, giving many English-speaking Capetonians a certain innocent – almost comical – smugness.

The educated Cape Afrikaners, sometimes described as Anglo-Boers, have been likened to the Anglo-Irish. By 1805 they had lost any sense of loyalty to or affinity with their ancestral lands (Holland, France, Germany) and had suffered much under the decaying and enfeebled Dutch East India Company administration. When the British built schools for their children, engineered roads over formidable mountain passes and opened up a new lucrative market for Cape wines, it seemed sensible to accept British rule. But on the remote eastern border of the Cape Province, where for generations the boertrekkers had been living beyond reach of anyone's rule, feelings were otherwise. Therefore many of those boertrekkers became the Voortrekkers.

My platteland Boer friends were wont to refer to the Cape Afrikaners as wimps who had got stuck into gracious living on the fertile Peninsula and wouldn't risk the unknown even if staying put meant being forced by the British to give up their slaves and learn English – while the *real* Afrikaners were hauling ox-wagons over the Drakensberg and boldly confronting the savages met en route... The Anglo-Boers, in turn, see the platteland volk as unfortunates who spent so long isolated in the wilds that they mutated into a subspecies with limited brainpower, no taste and far too many guns.

I notice here another interesting contrast, in the whites' attitudes to the Coloureds. English-speakers tend to emphasize their infamous murderous street gangs, their long-established reputation for drug addiction, alcoholism and every sort of domestic violence, their rape and homicide rates – both higher than among either blacks or whites and rising annually. Afrikaners are more likely to tell you about their musical and literary talents, their religious fervour, their outstanding bravery in battle and – if given opportunities, as not many were in the past – their high academic achievement rate. Blood is thicker than water, even if it's only 7 per cent.

Tomorrow I move to Khayelitsha for eight days, a plan frowned upon by the overprotective among my white friends. Khayelitsha, meaning 'new home' in Xhosa, is allegedly the most lawless and violent of the Cape townships. In retrospect, its controversial creation looks like apartheid's last stand – a final effort to escape the *swart gevaar*, at least to the extent of keeping *them* as far away as possible from the city centre. In the mid-'70s the whole world was shocked by the brutal destruction of the Crossroads squatter camp and global protests did bring about a reprieve of sorts. But when the squatters were offered a barren windswept site on the False Bay coast they resolutely refused to move; to have any hope of earning a living, they needed to be much nearer Cape Town. Then their own leaders, bribed by officialdom, betrayed them. With overt police support, those leaders organized a terror campaign of killings, maimings and shack-burnings. In 1986, when the migrants reluctantly gave in, Khayelitsha was founded. Since that date many thousands more have moved south – because for the first time in a century blacks now have a legal right to live permanently on the Cape Peninsula.

7

One Corner of Khayelitsha

The Cape Peninsula

The 'homelands' into which blacks were packed...are bursting at the seams,
ecologically devastated and in economic despair. The result is that when the
government relaxed its influx regulations in the mid-1980s, this dammed-up rural
poverty flooded out to the cities.
Allister Sparks, The Mind of South Africa *(1991)*

June 1993

Khayelitsha covers I don't know how many acres of the sandy Cape Flats –
enough acres to make square miles. You see its edges from the N2 motorway: a
classic shanty city, pullulating with people, the frail dwellings cobbled together
out of bits of this and that, litter-strewn beyond one's worst nightmare,
apparently an instant monument to desperation, destitution and despair. The
population is said to be at least half a million – perhaps closer to a million? No
one knows and not that many care. All the time the numbers increase. The
unemployment rate is around 80 per cent, though job-seeking prompted the
migration – you don't create a shanty city for fun or to oblige the ANC. (Many
Capetonians accuse the ANC of enticing their Xhosa followers to the Western
Cape to counterbalance the unreliable Coloured vote.) Most white and
Coloured Capetonians speak of Khayelitsha with fear and disdain, as do many
blacks from the older townships. It is supposed to be, and probably is, a
dangerous place for whites.

One of my new friends, a young English-speaking woman doctor, works on
Mondays in Khayelitsha's day hospital on the township's periphery. (There is, of
course, no 'real' hospital.) Not everyone approves of Mary's continuing to work
there post-Hani, given the palpable heightening of tension. But in a hospital
staffed only by overworked nurses a doctor's attention is, in Mary's view, 'a
human right'. She agreed to take me with her one Monday morning and having
seen the facilities (an improvement on many African countries' state hospitals,
but that's not saying much), I wandered into Khayelitsha.

I had done some forward planning. In such places it is best not to seem a
curious sightseer, gawping at local miseries, but to have a purpose. So I was

carrying my jungle-trousers – after more than 5,000 miles of saddle-friction, between Nairobi and Cape Town, major repairs were needed. Ostensibly I was visiting Khayelitsha in search of a seamstress.

Where narrow sandy alleyways wriggle between shacks the vibes conveyed a guarded neutrality rather than hostility. My initial enquiries were thwarted because no one spoke English. Then Phineas approached me, a small sad youngish man with a broken camera who wondered if I could mend it. I confessed that I'm pushed to change a light bulb – someone emphatically not in the camera-mending league. He nevertheless invited me into his two-roomed tin shack, the living room furnished with a couple of camp chairs and a small table holding a Primus stove, three saucepans and a few plates.

The chipboard walls had been carefully papered, floor to ceiling, with bright magazine pictures. The other room held only two single beds: one for the four children, one the marital couch. Phineas's wife was away in Cape Town trying to sell the shopping bags she weaves from unpicked fertilizer sacks.

Phineas admitted to being an ex-policeman. After six years in the force his nerve broke – 'everyone wants to kill you' – and he joined the ANC and moved to Khayelitsha as an 'organizer'. Joining the ANC was for him, I gathered, an 'insurance-policy' move rather than a conversion. However, it is no protection against the PAC, who particularly dislike black policemen (or even ex-policemen) so Phineas confines himself to MK-controlled sections. He advised me to do the same. 'The PAC keep away from this side, here is safe. Khayelitsha is a very big place – so big! But without amenities, very bad for children. Toilet dirt comes onto the roads, in summer you can smell it from the N2 and people say we live like animals. How would they live, without amenities?'

Phineas had found an expensive camera (in Khayelitsha, read 'stolen' for 'found') and hoped to be able to earn something as a photographer: 'I am good at that and people like photographs.' He showed me the broken camera with tears in his eyes. 'Maybe I should have stayed with the police, there I had a little money, now we have nothing. But I was afraid. Things have got very bad. There is too much killing. Lately two constables were necklaced here. My wife liked me to leave. She was afraid, day and night. She said it is better to be alive, with no money.'

Phineas couldn't direct me to a seamstress. 'But you ask, people will tell you. Here are many women with Singers, liking to sew for money.'

I crossed a dusty, rubble-rough wasteland on which youths were kicking a football. They paused and stared and laughed mockingly; a few shouted something that wasn't a greeting. The sky was cloudless, the sun brilliant, the air clear – Peninsular pollution is spasmodic, wind-controlled. A superb mountain range overlooks the Cape Flats, its jagged grandeur accentuating the immediate squalor. A few miles away, beyond bushy dunes, are the long sandy beaches of False Bay. Khayelitsha could be (maybe one day will be) a desirable residential area.

A few boys and girls, aged tennish, approached and smiled uncertainly as we passed. Then I turned and asked about a seamstress. They giggled and said nothing. Unfolding my holey trousers, I used extravagant sign-language. They shrieked with laughter, the holes being in an amusing area, then beckoned me to follow them and led me into a maze of laneways beyond the wasteland. There I was delivered to a group of young men and women, the latter queuing for water by a standpipe, one of the former laundering clothes in a plastic baby-bath. It is always surprising to find African males attending to domestic chores; but these, it emerged later, were ANC activists.

All these young people spoke English more or less fluently. I was warmly welcomed, offered a drink of water, closely questioned about my identity and reasons for visiting Khayelitsha. I told the truth: a travel writer from Ireland, frustrated by being so cut off from blacks in a mainly black country – reason enough for visiting Khayelitsha. It was at once apparent that they believed me.

One handsome young man, tall and well built with dreadlocks (unusual here) remarked, 'You've come to a safe area, other parts could be dangerous for you – don't walk far alone, one of us can go with you.' He was holding his youngest brother by the hand, a subdued-looking 5-year-old. Later I learned that nine months ago their mother was shot dead by the SAP during a night raid (an arms search) on their shack. The little fellow, with his 9-year-old sister and 12-year-old brother, were sleeping in the adjoining bed and saw their mother die.

Mrs Mgidlana was the nearest seamstress, in M948 Site D. (All but the newest shacks are numbered.) The Mgidlanas' compound is upmarket: three shacks of two rooms each, the façades painted in green and white stripes. And their bigger-than-average plot allows them to grow a few vegetables and a papaya tree. However, given an extended family of twenty-seven, three shacks hardly represent luxury.

Mr and Mrs Mgidlana are elderly, he half-crippled by rheumatism, she by childhood polio. Being fervent Jehovah's Witnesses, they spent some time trying to save my soul, very gently and compassionately. Then they gave up on that and offered me lunch: pap and a stew made of something's (a goat's?) intestines. Evidently they are prosperous: not many Khayelitsha folk eat at lunchtime. In Umtata they had owned a textile factory employing forty women. Sanctions killed it – unlike white fruit exporters, blacks were unable to organize sanctions-busting. Then they and most of the staff, whose families had been largely dependent on their wages, moved to Khayelitsha.

'So were sanctions wrong, a mistake?'

Emphatically and in unison they said, 'No!' – and Mrs Mgidlana laughed. 'You expected us to say yes because in your world money comes first! Here we have learned this is not so. Freedom comes first. But you people have always had it so you can't understand... It was good, the world joining us in our struggle. For us and our workers sanctions were bad – yoh-yoh, *very* bad! But necessary, to frighten the government. And now Madiba is free and soon we'll have the vote!'

Mr Mgidlana was considering me thoughtfully. Then he said, 'Writing this book, you need to live here for a little time. Looking for a few hours is no good. You need to share our days, so you can write how it *feels*.'

My heart bounded with joyful hope. 'But is that possible?'

'It can be arranged,' said Mr Mgidlana. 'I'll call people.' Stiffly he stood up, with the aid of a crutch, and limped away.

The people he called were formidable: ten MK heavies whose AK-47s, one intuited, lay not far away. Politely they all shook hands while viewing me with extreme disfavour. Once in a while I have encountered as tough a bunch of men, but nothing tougher. They crowded the small room, six of them sharing with me a sofa made for four. Suspiciously and aggressively they grilled me, scrutinizing my passport page by page, discussing in Xhosa my publisher's 'To Whom It May Concern' letter, demanding to see my notebook and passing it round. Who was paying me? That seemed of major importance. The freelance writer's way of life baffled them. Ditto the desire of a white to live, however briefly, in Khayelitsha. 'Here's no hotel,' said the leader – a tall, broad, scowling character. 'Here's no bathrooms or restaurants or swimming-pools or tennis courts – all those things you need.'

At that I flipped. Thus far I had been ingratiating, on the defensive. Now I went into the attack, forcefully pointing out that the needs of South African whites are not the needs of all whites, that my main need at the moment was to be with blacks.

An uneasy pause followed. Then the heavies withdrew to the yard, led by Mr Mgidlana. A twenty-minute *indaba* ensued. Watching through the doorway, I noted that Mr Mgidlana's status is high. Finally the heavies gave in. Four of them returned to say that we were going, now, to head office in Cape Town (the ANC head office). There was none of the usual sauntering to and fro, arguing about transport, then hanging around waiting for it. With military briskness I was escorted to the tarred road where a battered kombi-taxi was requisitioned and away we rattled – having been joined by Georgina, a remarkable 19-year-old who was soon to become an important person in my life. She speaks fluent English but on this journey didn't use it: the MK aren't into small talk.

The Western Cape head office is a rambling old three-storey building on Victoria Street with medium-level security in the big drab entrance hall. Normally, though not when escorted by the MK, one signs a grubby visitors' book before being handed a pin-on permit-to-enter label. Upstairs, a labyrinth of corridors connects countless cramped offices created by the partitioning of large high-ceilinged rooms. There is an aura – not misleading – of earnest endeavour and serious disorganization.

I felt slightly like a captive as the heavies ushered me into an enormous conference room, its only furniture a very long table and rows of metal chairs. Posters covered the walls, most depicting either Comrade Mandela or Comrade Hani with quotations from their speeches. Like the rest of the building, this chamber is functional to the point of asceticism. Here no money has been wasted; among a certain section of the ANC such asceticism is a point of honour, a mark of their ideological distance from the capitalist consumer society.

Three senior officials were summoned: charming gentlemen, courteous, tactful, kindly. Their grilling didn't feel like a grilling though it was no less thorough than the MK's. Under a regime whose Dirty Tricks Brigade is endlessly innovative and extremely ruthless, no chances can be taken. When asked about previous links with the ANC I mentioned subscribing annually to the London office and receiving their newsletter. And of course, I added as an afterthought, I'd met Kader Asmal when he lived in Dublin. (He now lives in Cape Town.)

All expressions changed and one man bounced to his feet. 'Come, we'll ring Kader!' Which we did, from an adjacent office, and five minutes later the MK had been told I could spend eight days in Khayelitsha, as their protégé, starting a week hence – a delay needed to spread the word that I had been guaranteed trustworthy. Among a population lacking newspapers, telephones or a regular postal service, it takes time to circulate information.

On the way back to Khayelitsha the heavies loosened up, becoming almost chatty. Although 'chatty' doesn't quite suit either their conversational style or their subject matter in this case – SAP excesses. Before leaving them I received my orders. On the following Monday at 9 a.m. I was to wait outside the hospital for my two-Comrade female bodyguard – Georgina would be one. Under no circumstances was I to go roaming alone around any part of Khayelitsha. Should misfortune befall me, they would have to take the unpleasant consequences. Being a friend of a friend of Comrade Mandela, I was now seen as a valuable commodity.

At the appointed hour I stood waiting, as instructed. When Georgina and Lucretia arrived at 10.20 they made no reference to the eighty-minute hiatus and I knew I was back in African territory, mentally as well as geographically.

During the next week I was never alone, day or night, except when on the loo and even then someone guarded the door. My main minders were Georgina and Lucretia, relieved briefly at intervals by another pair of equally vigilant, affectionate and intelligent young women.

Georgina and Lucretia have a problem in common: their MK partners, who returned from exile in 1991, are in Pollsmoor prison awaiting trial for the possession of illegal weapons. Georgina is philosophical about Albany's misfortune. 'He isn't being tortured, that's what would really upset me. And my revolutionary fervour keeps me going!' I half-suspect her of glorying in this situation; certainly having a hero-lover enhances her status among the Comrades.

Lucretia, however, is inconsolable. She doesn't lack would-be Tony-substitutes (uninhibited in their pursuit by my presence) but firmly tells them all she wants to go to bed only with Tony. One night she confided, 'I love him too much to enjoy anyone else. He loves me the same way. We trust each other. How would he feel, when he comes out, if he heard I'd enjoyed someone else?'

Tony and Albany could be out on bail were R800 (R400 each) available. There seemed to be a role here for me but my hand was stayed by the young men's lawyer. Some people are safer in than out.

From the station we walked some two miles to Blossom's shack, my progress through the maze of alleyways causing quite a sensation. Often we stopped for me to be explained (in Xhosa) and to be introduced (in English) to various significant local personalities. After heavy rain during the night many stretches of track were completely under water – stinking water, where sewage visibly bubbled up from defective pipes through defective manholes. ('Personholes,' corrected Georgina – she is at that stage.) When we met three toddlers happily splashing, there was a delay. My minders shooed them back to their respective shacks and delivered punchy lectures on the hazards of playing in sewage. These ANC Youth League leaders have a well-developed sense of civic responsibility.

Some laneways are road-width, their verges patchily green now the rains have come, and occasional small trees and shrubs alleviate the grimness of the dwellings. Everywhere laundry billows in the breeze, its abundance outside minute shacks telling of the overcrowding within. The universal African devotion to personal cleanliness is unconquerable, which is why South Africa's shanty cities never seem like slums. The word 'slum' implies dirt, slovenly disorder and bad smells – not features of black homes, however littered and sewage-scented their external environment may be.

Twenty-one-year-old Blossom was chosen as my hostess because most of her family had returned to the Transkei for a funeral, leaving a double bed available for my minders and me. (Nine of us slept in the two-roomed shack and eight had gone to the funeral, so normally this dwelling sleeps fourteen – somehow.)

We found Blossom in her doorway, sweeping sand out of the living room. Khayelitsha is built on fine silvery sand, the incursion of which into dwellings requires them to be swept out every few hours. This corrugated-iron shack is painted bright green and Blossom made a pretty picture in the doorway, wearing scarlet pants and a canary-yellow shirt-blouse. She welcomed me with hugs and kisses as though I were some long-lost friend. In the living-room-cum-kitchen three small beat-up sofas (beds at night) occupy most of the floor space. Behind the sofa facing the door is the kitchen area, four-feet wide with crockery neatly arranged on a miniature dresser and everything else (not that there is much else) stored in the cupboard below. The cooker is a reeking home-made oil stove – a two-gallon paint tin, which also serves as a space heater when the temperature drops at sunset. The fumes from this hazardously flaming contraption give all who huddle around it sore eyes and throats – and thus was solved my main Khayelitsha problem. The Xhosa are a proud people; it is offensive for a guest to supply food even if that means the guest must go hungry for a week. But I knew a farewell gift of a super-de-luxe oil stove would not be offensive.

It seemed my arrival had been eagerly awaited and soon Blossom's shack was packed. Little welcoming gifts were brought: a strangely shaped stone from the Transkei – a model bicycle made of wire, perfect in every detail – a model Xhosa stool, carved from driftwood. Comrades set about teaching me essential Xhosa phrases and how to toyi-toyi. The latter lesson I found easier than the former though it does test one's stamina. These Comrades take their toyi-toying very seriously; there must be no cheating with only one hop and that double hop is what wears out the novice. Then it was decided I should be given a Xhosa name. After some debate (in Xhosa) I became Comrade Noxolo, meaning 'Peace', which touched me deeply. As did the conferring of the Comrade title, marking my acceptance as a reliable friend, a person with the right attitude. But there were admonitions, too. I must be disciplined, stay close to my minders, obey them. Regrettable things happen in Khayelitsha. Only two months ago a young Englishman, a volunteer social worker, had been shot in the back and head while playing soccer in the Community Church Centre. No one knew by whom or why. 'Except we can guess,' said Blossom. 'By the PAC, because he was white.'

Part of me couldn't take these warnings too seriously; people are murdered in their beds in rural Ireland. Granted, a current of anti-white feeling is now running through the townships but traditionally, in South Africa, anti-white-ism has been strictly political – not racist. Since the ANC was founded in 1912 it has been consistently non-racist, apart from a half-hearted flirtation with Gar-veyism in the 1920s. This is its greatest moral (and now political) strength. Consistently, ANC leaders have stressed the crucial difference between black Africa, comparatively recently colonized, and South Africa where the White Tribe took root in 1652. Zimbabwe, for instance, was colonized a mere twenty years before the founding of the ANC.

On that first evening, sitting back in one corner of a sagging sofa, I knew an extraordinary sense of relief and release. I felt it physically as well as emotionally and mentally; my body relaxed as though after a Turkish bath and massage; I was on every level at ease. But from what had I been released? I thought about that later, lying between my sleeping minders. Released from unreality, I decided. The artificiality of white South Africa, to which the habitual pattern of living institutionalized by apartheid has been largely confining me, sets up a tension both hard to describe and hard to tolerate. Logically, in Khayelitsha, the white guest should have been feeling more tense. Instead, I felt liberated and soothed. Amidst the poverty, the suspicion, the fear – of police raids, rival black factions, hunger, disease – the blacks relate to their friends with a vitality, a spontaneity, a warmth and humour not often found among South Africa's whites. Have those whites self-destructed, by choosing to live as they do? Their materially comfortable (though no longer emotionally comfortable) world rests on such morally rotten foundations that one often senses a corrosive shame somewhere deep down inside them. Hence those endless, compulsive, synthetic 'justifications' of apartheid. By now the majority must know that their affluence depends on blacks being ruthlessly exploited. 'Exploited' can seem a stale, weary word, so often angrily shouted in absurd contexts that its repetition irritates. Yet in South Africa it would be an affectation to look for a fresher equivalent. Here exploitation was, and remains, the central issue.

Next morning I felt integration had gone a stage too far when Happy, a local ANC Youth League leader, sprang it on me that a rally had been arranged for that afternoon – to be addressed by Comrade Noxolo, who has always been phobia-afraid of speaking in public. But somehow this occasion was different. Throughout the morning butterflies gyrated within, yet when the time came concern for the new South Africa overcame my phobia and I spoke from the heart for thirty minutes.

Not everything I said went down well with the rank and file. Commending political tolerance, as one of democracy's vital organs, does not bring a standing ovation from Youth Leaguers. To most of them 'democracy' means, quite simply, getting the SAP off your back and doing what you feel like doing. Among this segment of the population, the new government will be celebrated not because it guarantees Freedom of Speech, Freedom of Assembly and so on but because it will secure power for the ANC – albeit shared power, until 1999. Given this mindset, anyone seeking to reduce the ANC vote by normal pre-election campaigning can only be seen as an enemy. I don't envy any Nat speakers who may venture to hold election rallies in Khayelitsha.

'Middle-class' shacks like Blossom's have flush lavatories some six yards away in double 'sentry-boxes', each serving two households. A tap on the outside wall provides clean, drinkable water, no problem there. Given the massive influx to the Cape Flats during the past decade, it could be argued the authorities haven't done too badly. Not a PC comment, but inevitably I contrasted Khayelitsha with the so-called compounds around Lusaka where a drought-driven influx took place in 1991/92 and the authorities couldn't begin to cope. However, my flicker of 'let's be fair to the whites' was speedily quenched by Lucretia. 'This is a *rich* country, Zambia is a poor country! Now you're being silly!' I relish the Youth Leaguers' directness. They are awed neither by my age nor my tenuous Madiba connection; they say what they think, never arrogantly but always decisively.

Early on my first morning I committed a grievous *faux pas* by quietly slipping out to wash my face and hands at the tap. Those few neighbours lucky enough to have jobs were on the move and I exchanged greetings with several women filling buckets at their own taps. Later, Blossom was appalled: the neighbours would think her too mean to heat my washing water. In vain I protested that at home I always wash in cold water – that I *prefer* it. Obviously Blossom and my minders didn't believe me and anyway that wasn't the point. Blossom's reputation as a hostess had been blemished. (Even in hot regions of black Africa, I then recalled, one's village hostess insists on providing a basin of steaming washing water.) Moreover, I had been insubordinate, I had left the shack on my own. Meekly I apologized for both offences and promised not to repeat them.

Blossom is a qualified hairdresser; her framed certificate hangs on a wall beside a poster of some famous Afro-American rock star whose name escapes me. However, being a qualified hairdresser in Khayelitsha doesn't get you very far; not many can afford hairdos. Five customers per week is Blossom's average, at R4 for a three-hour session – three hours because water heats slowly on a paint-tin stove. Then a plastic tub is put on a tin chair, in that small space between the three sofas, and the process is under way. At the final stage Blossom's younger sister, 15-year-old Beauty, assists, holding a pot of sticky stuff with which the *coiffure* is completed. (Only reckless parents name a baby 'Beauty' but in this case the gamble came off.)

To outsiders, Khayelitsha can seem an undifferentiated mass of jobless, hopeless, feckless poor – a threatening mass, with strong criminal leanings. Yet like any other human community it contains all sorts. No doubt having a writer-in-residence quickened the pace of Blossom's social life: each evening, activist groups of both sexes and all ages gathered to meet Comrade Noxolo. It exhilarated me to hear them spiritedly arguing about the new South Africa in terms that would take the average white way out of their intellectual depth. But it distressed me to find people like Aki, Muriel, Eddie, Antonia, Pius, Sam, William, living in Khayelitsha. This is illogical, even snobbish; I should be equally distressed to find *anyone* living in Khayelitsha. However, those individuals – if one must be snobbish – were people on (or above) my own educational level and of my own middle-class sort. When Antonia and I were tête-à-tête in her shack, my minders having left her in charge for an hour, I discussed this illogical distress. She laughed. 'Yes, we should be living at ease in Claremont or Obs – and we would be if we could choose! But for Khayelitsha that would be bad, I hope we help to keep up standards. Maybe not standards of honesty, in your terms – to survive we all have to be dishonest, one way or another. I mean standards to do with our social life, with human relations, what we call *ubuntu*. We can't do much, Khayelitsha has to be anarchic, given its problems – especially those parts you're not allowed to visit. But it might be even worse if we weren't around.'

Khayelitsha's élite are critical of the Western Cape ANC leadership for not keeping their faithful township followers in touch with the progress of the current all-party (well, almost all-party) negotiations. Of necessity these are slow, opaque and tortuous, liable to being delayed by petty disputes or bouts of sulkiness on one side or the other. 'But also they're heroic,' said Pius, a retired teacher from the Ciskei. He was referring to a general determination, among all the participants, not to let the legacy of apartheid poison the future. And something truly remarkable is happening, as representatives of all colours and most ideologies debate and manoeuvre, month after month, seeking workable compromises. Said Pius, 'Their honourable task should be explained to everyone, particularly the young. It should be held up to them as a model of conflict resolution without violence. Instead, we have lawlessness and suspicions growing in the townships because this delay is not understood.'

William, a fully qualified electrician able to find only occasional odd jobs, voiced some (widespread) doubts about the final outcome of the negotiations. Is this carefully organized transfer of power, blessed by the capitalist West, likely to lead to rich whites sharing their wealth with poor blacks? Is it not much more likely that the new multicoloured rulers will go into a mutually profitable huddle and tailor a new South Africa to fit their own ambitions? A South Africa only ostensibly 'democratic', paying only lip-service to the poor, yet pleasing to a West that feigns concern for 'human rights' – unless, of course, their protection impedes 'commercial interests'.

'Is the Struggle really over?' wondered William, 'The star of democracy has risen above the horizon – but what next? Will exploitation stop because apartheid has been outlawed? I don't believe it! Exploitation started long before apartheid was invented and you'll see it going on long after apartheid is smashed.'

Within forty-eight hours, because I felt so at home in one corner, Khayelitsha no longer felt like a shanty city. Even my perception of 'shacks as wretched dwellings' had changed – though during heavy rain on my second night multiple roof leaks forced Blossom, my minders and me to join the five in the less leaky living room. But one soon comes to appreciate the countless small but strenuous efforts made to enhance people's homes and immediate surroundings. At sunrise a man down the laneway could be seen deftly rearranging the white pebbles with which he creates an astonishing variety of elaborate geometrical designs on the sand of his plot. Wallpapers are ingeniously devised using printers' discards (sheets of obsolete advertisements) or factories' discards (defective cigarette packets, soup-tin labels, soap wrappings). Bits of delicately carved driftwood hang on either side of a rotting entrance door under rusty eaves. Several poinsettia cuttings are being cherished outside the windowless shack of a widow whose six children, aged 2 to 13, are always neat and clean. Eight months ago, during one of those numerous night raids, the SAP murdered her husband. I photographed the bullet holes in the door; the police offered her R10 (£2) in compensation for the damaged door.

This is not a broken-spirited community, demoralized by poverty and brutality. Khayelitsha is no monument to despair, as it seems from the N2, but a monument to resilience, creativity and courage.

That is the positive side; inevitably Khayelitsha induces mood-swings. Moving out from 'my' corner, we visited areas of utter misery where the one-room shacks could be demolished with a bare fist and are so closely huddled together there is scarcely space to walk between. The interiors are unfurnished, the children puny and listless, the adult faces set in lines of hopelessness, the future – no matter what colour the government – seen only as a threat. These are the truly destitute and there are many thousands of them. In Blossom's less deprived area, migrants arrived with a little capital and it makes a difference that many are young ANC activists who have faith in the new world that Madiba is preparing for them.

One afternoon at a crossroads we came upon a throng of young women excitedly trying on fashionable garments each bearing a city-centre dry-cleaner's label. The kombi to which they had been transferred, after the hijacking of the dry-cleaner's van, stood nearby. The three hijackers were content to collect a few rands for garments worth a few hundred. There were dozens of coats, jackets, skirts, slacks; by local standards these entrepreneurs are now rich and their customers are smartly dressed at prices they can afford. Viewing this enterprise from within Khayelitsha, I failed to see it as either criminal or immoral. I've always been a Robin Hood fan.

Those young men are, of course, exceptionally daring. More usually, people sustain their families through small-scale shoplifting. A common late-afternoon sight is a trestle-table going up outside a shack. Home is the hunter with, for example, two small bottles of shampoo, a tube of toothpaste, three bars of soap, a small packet of biscuits, a small jar of jam. Everything is small: when shoplifting, you don't go for bulk. These goods, sold at 25 per cent of the supermarket prices, enable the 'thief' to buy basic foodstuffs for the family's supper at one of Khayelitsha's numerous spaza shops (tiny shops in people's shacks, illegal until 1989).

However, shoplifting is not regarded as a desirable way of subsistence. One young husband, standing behind his trestle at sunset, put it like this: 'If I could get a job in the bakery [where two of his friends work] I'd be so happy. With regular money every week and no fear. This way of work, you live all day in fear of prison. The white people call us lazy thieves. It makes me sad. I'm not lazy, I want work and to have no worry. Do these people want us to let our families starve? How do they expect us to live *without money*. In the past we lived without it, growing food, keeping cattle. Now we're without land and must come here, hoping to work. When there's no work we must still feed our families.'

Day after day – almost hour after hour – people begged me to find them a job. They pleaded with the sort of urgency that makes one feel guilty about one's inability to help. Don't I know someone in Cape Town who needs a maid, a gardener? Or someone who could employ an electrician, a hairdresser, a plumber, a tailor, a bricklayer, a tinsmith, a weaver, a shoemaker, a carpenter, a baker, a seamstress? In Khayelitsha live many who are skilled yet hungry; where little cash circulates, local jobs are few. A favourite white theme – 'most blacks only pretend to look for work, they wouldn't stick with a job if they found it' – has been infuriating me for months past. Now it makes me gibber with rage.

Some old people have reluctantly moved from the Transkei or Ciskei to help support children and grandchildren with their meagre government pensions. One old man caused me a pang every time I passed him. All day he sat in the sun on a Coca-Cola crate and his gaze was fixed on the past, on the mountainous spaces of home. That is not my fancy. When I asked, 'Why does he look so terribly sad?' Georgina suggested, 'Talk to him, he went to a mission school, he speaks nice English.'

He spoke very nice English, slow through disuse but carefully correct. 'I am sad because I love my home. It is peaceful there. The land is wide. My ancestors are there. Here is a foreign land and no peace. But my family need me. I can pay some money for my grandsons' schooling. They are clever, but without my pension they have no fees. If they get a good education they can do well in our new future. So I left the mountains behind.'

Wednesday 16 June was Soweto Day, the anniversary of the 1976 student uprising. That event may be described as the conception of the new South Africa and during the protracted parturition there has been too much haemorrhaging. But surely the negotiating obstetricians must soon safely deliver the infant, despite that vicious alliance of black and white right-wingers still hoping for – and threatening – a stillbirth.

A fleet of ANC-hired buses took us for free to the ANC Youth League rally at Guguletu's rugby stadium. Instead of driving straight up the N2 we took a roundabout route, via Mitchells Plain and Nyanga; the buses' collective health was poorly and they preferred to avoid traffic-cop attention. On the way we passed a district from which whites were moved under the Group Areas Act; an abandoned DRC church, derelict and vandalized, marked the spot. Comrade Noxolo was honoured by being put in the front seat and entrusted with our group's huge SACP flag to be flown from the window. A trivial task, you might think, but considerable muscular effort is required to hold a large flag steady in a fast-moving vehicle. My companions sang loudly and the mood was euphoric on this last Soweto Day to be celebrated under white rule. A year hence, if all goes well, 16 June will be an official national holiday – not, as now, unofficial, with whites still trying to run the country normally in defiance of the fact that most blacks take the day off.

One song made me feel slightly queasy: a rollicking MK chant in praise of the AK-47, sung with gusto. While struggling to control the flag, I also struggled to understand the emotions inspiring this chant. If, for centuries, you have been forced to accept the domination of well-armed whites, then there is indeed a horrible inexorable logic about the possession of arms being glorified. And about the particular weapon you can most easily get hold of (from Mozambique: US$40 each) being seen both as a liberation symbol and a guarantee that Whitey won't ever again have all the arms. A depressing development, to those of the ahimsa persuasion. But violence does breed violence.

In an already crowded stadium the ANC flag flew at half-mast from a goal post above a flat-bed truck equipped with a temperamental public-address system. The pitch had been turned to mud by a night's rain but the sun shone brightly, the massed youth in their most colourful garments looked like a mobile patchwork quilt and the atmosphere was effervescent – revolutionary in a cheerful way. I saw only one other white, an exuberantly charming young American woman named Amy Biehl* with whom I talked briefly; for almost a year she has been working in Guguletu on a voter education programme. She speaks fluent Xhosa (how I envy her!) and is obviously loved by her black friends. We made an appointment to meet in the Heidelberg on my return to Cape Town.

My minders thought it fitting that I should join the geriatrics, a few score elderly men and women occupying the only available seats – the stadium's 'stand', an unsteady wooden contraption singularly unsuitable for those whose bones take a long time to mend. Having deposited me between Mr and Mrs Mdolela – they live near Blossom and understood about 'minding' me – Georgina and Lucretia romped away onto the pitch to salute an MK detachment in camouflage battledress who were marching from the entrance, being loudly cheered. The SAP helicopter, all the time circling overhead, flew much lower

* Two months later, the day before her flight home, Amy Biehl was hacked to death in Guguletu by a gang of PAC youths inanely described by the media as 'radicals'. I can think of other, less bland descriptions. They killed her because she was white. When they noticed her car they were returning from a rabble-rousing APLA rally.

when they appeared. This guard of honour was for the main speaker, the Revd Allan Boesak, a Coloured theologian trained in Holland and now one of the ANC's most prominent Western Cape leaders.

Other speakers included a poet who had been on death row in Pretoria's notorious Central Prison, so memorably described (including its gallows facilities) by Hugh Lewin in *Bandiet*. An MK senior officer claimed, wrongly, that MK and the SADF are about to be merged. A young white man, not long returned from exile in Zambia, recalled in lurid detail two MI assassination attempts on his life. An SACP praise-poet wearing tribal dress was traditionally histrionic. An ANC Youth League leader drew loud applause and many 'Vivas!' when he spoke of 'rejecting gutter education and demanding free and compulsory schooling for all'. Many more 'Vivas!' greeted his call to the youth to 'rededicate themselves for the final offensive' (i.e., the elections). Then Allan Boesak spoke – in English, but using African oratorical devices. Listening to him, I remembered the comment of a white friend who lectures in UWC's English department. In her view, black students writing in English are at a peculiar disadvantage. Often their tutors criticize them for being repetitive and beating about the bush, not realizing that, in African languages, such 'flaws' are cultivated as component parts of an art much admired throughout Africa.

In between speeches, music was provided by Phambili, Chorimba and the Black Sufferers – esteemed musicians, all, but the sound system did not do them justice. A Xhosa dance group drew frenzied applause though they must have been invisible to 90 per cent of the crowd. When Mr Mdolela complained about the lack of political education at such rallies I saw his point. Several Comrades have asked me, 'What party does de Klerk lead?' and 'What does a government do with a cabinet?' and (perhaps not as naive as it sounds) 'Do the mines pay the government's wages?' Most township youngsters have been involved only in their local politics of protest, akin to warfare. The staid world of conventional national politics, to which they are about to gain access, is *terra incognita*.

As we all streamed from the stadium, my minders again by my side, a rumour went around that some of our buses had been driven off by the PAC, who were holding a rival rally in Khayelitsha – better attended than ours, we learned later. Many of our buses had indeed vanished, for whatever reason, and the consequent mêlée was soon out of the marshals' control – a wild struggle to board each vehicle, with little consideration given to geriatrics. Yet there was no ill-temper involved, just impatience – which is odd, given the black attitude to time. Everyone shouted and sang and laughed while pulling and shoving and elbowing each other out of the way. Several slim youths climbed in through windows, grinning triumphantly, and many swarmed onto the roofs. There was no room, on the way home, to unfurl our flag.

At breakfast next morning my minders seemed abstracted. (As usual, breakfast was one slice of bread and marge and a cup of herbal tea.) Then abruptly Lucretia told me that I must move to another shack, some distance away. When I registered reluctance, being so very happy *chez* Blossom, Georgina said, 'They know you're here, they say they'll torch the place if you stay.'

My heart lurched. After a short shocked silence I asked, 'Who are *they*?'

'Pack your things,' said Lucretia, 'and we'll move.'

'But wait! If my being here is putting people at risk I'd better leave. I don't want to be responsible for burned homes – or worse...'

'No!' said Georgina. 'We never give in to intimidation. We promised to protect you and we will – don't be afraid! There's no problem, we're in charge, we know how to manage it. We want you to stay. They can't intimidate us – *ever!*'

I assumed 'they' were the PAC. Of course I may have been wrong; but I lack the courage of investigative journalists and when questions are unwelcome keep my mouth shut.

My new hostess, Ika, a middle-aged physiotherapist, is relatively rich. She worked in Umtata, the Transkei's capital, until her husband was murdered in Durban by (it is generally believed) an Inkatha hit squad. She then moved to Khayelitsha for the sake of her three beautiful daughters, now aged 17, 19 and 21. 'I hoped here they could get better schooling and so better jobs. And better schooling was possible, in Cape Town – but so far no jobs.' The 19-year-old has an adorable and adored 10-month-old son. 'They get up to mischief when they've no work,' said Ika with a twinkle, cuddling the infant.

In Khayelitsha, as in every artificially constrained and desperately impoverished community, one hears of abused and neglected children. Yet I myself saw no unloved child, however dire a family's circumstances, and the joy children bring to people's lives seems like a comforting glow, warming and illuminating shackland. When we visited Lucretia's home her younger sister's infant was having his nappy changed by a 15-year-old uncle who dotes extravagantly on his nephew. That lad is very much a Young Lion; but here it seems carrying a baby around, and playing with it in public, does not mar one's leonine image.

Ika now works in a Mitchells Plain hospital. Externally her four-roomed shack looks 'average', with unsteady walls constructed from various substances. Internally it is affluent, with real wallpaper, pretty floor tiles, luxurious armchairs, lace curtains. The living room is dominated by a menagerie of china figures imported from Taiwan. These lions, dogs, zebras, cats, fish and several species of bird are an inexplicable black addiction; hawkers sell them by the roadside and they don't cost very much – nor should they. Given pride of place in the plywood china cabinet was a small TV set, souvenir of the good old days in Umtata. When/if Khayelitsha is electrified, it will again serve its purpose – and there will be fewer stimulating conversations when the sun sets and oil lamps are lit. Inevitably Ika's poorer family members have followed her south and the shack sleeps twelve. A niece was ousted from Ika's bed to make room for me; my minders (now augmented, during nights, by two male MKS) slept in the living room.

Before sleeping, I unloaded my anxiety: did Ika know about the threat to Blossom's shack? She chuckled. 'You don't understand, we all know about everything – we have to. And no one is going to attack *my* home. We've organized things that couldn't be organized on Blossom's Site. Don't worry your head about it. Go peacefully to sleep.' Which I did. Mine not to reason why, or how or what or where...

Friday is a Pollsmoor prison visiting day and my minders invited me to join their ANC-funded party. I was reminded of expeditions to Northern Ireland's Maze prison in minibuses provided for relatives by IRA or UDA 'Prisoners' Welfare Organizations'. The crucial difference here is the ANC's role as government-in-waiting, sure of the votes of at least 60 per cent of the population. The ANC was never comparable to the IRA, a paramilitary group without popular support on either side of the border.

Georgina remarked, 'Soon blacks will no longer be refused gun licences and then jailed for not having them! Hey, man – doesn't that just sum up the whole apartheid regime!'

When our kombi stopped at a Wynberg supermarket to buy 'comforts' I was at last allowed to spend. The most appreciated comforts are cigarettes, Coca-Cola, tea, bread, milk, cornflakes, sticky buns, packet soups and a hideous polony that looks as if it had died of apoplexy.

That was a strange journey; humans adapt rapidly and after my brief immersion in Khayelitsha I found myself looking at the whites' world through black eyes. Having adjusted to the shacks' scale and drabness, the brightly painted little bungalows of Wynberg and Retreat seemed like mansions and their modest little gardens like estates. Tokai's ostentatiously affluent Blue Route shopping mall seemed both morally offensive and a vulgar indicator of where South Africa went politically astray. Georgina, who quite often read my thoughts, said, 'Now you're seeing it all the way we see it?'

'Yes,' I replied. 'Yes, that's exactly how I'm seeing it.'

'And it's upsetting you, you can feel now why we need a revolution.'

'Definitely you need a revolution, but not a violent one – what would that solve?'

'You think? You could be right. I don't want violence – but without justice, soon, how to avoid it? More and more of it. We're not going to hang around waiting for things to improve slowly, slowly – we've been patient too long. We'll have a revolution that looks like crime getting worse, outsiders won't see it as a revolution. Do you read Engels? No? But you should – I like him so much! In 1844 he wrote something that fits us now. "Crime is the earliest, crudest, least fruitful form of revolt against degrading poverty and social oppression." Our new government should hang that on their walls to remind them to hurry up with wealth redistribution. Trotting along on the capitalists' lead, still saying "Yes *baas*, no *baas*" – that won't work.'

The Pollsmoor barrier lifted casually to admit our familiar vehicle. We parked, then went to sit in the huge, bare, white-walled waiting room with its long rows of hard seats. At one end were lavatories, at the other a kiosk selling cigarettes, crisps, biscuits, sweets, soft drinks known as 'cooldrinks' in South Africa. 'Buy nothing here,' instructed Lucretia, 'or you're supporting the System!'

For forty years the South African government's survival depended on violent state repression, both overt and covert. Yet security is strangely lax. When I went to the loo, carrying a large bag of comforts, I could have planted a bomb; thus far there had been no security check. But perhaps this isn't as odd as it seems to an Irishwoman. In 1990 Allister Sparks wrote:

Although the ANC has been the target of several assassinations and assassination attempts, it has never sought to retaliate in this way. It has no hit squad and no hit list. No black person has ever made an attempt on the life of a white South African leader, and President de Klerk and members of his cabinet move about with less security protection than just about any other political leaders in the Western world.

An hour later our group of twelve was summoned by a brown-uniformed Coloured warder shouting Georgina's name. We were led to the remand wing around the main building: a long high fortress, its red-brown walls blank. The acres of grounds are pleasant enough in an unimaginative municipal way: smooth green lawns, evenly spaced-out shrubs, bright orderly flower-beds. A nearby glory of mountains semi-encircles Pollsmoor – some forested, some stark and sheer, of silver-grey rock. This must be the world's most magnificently situated prison; anywhere else it would be a five-star hotel.

From a wide flight of steps we entered a cavernous hall through a narrow doorway where the heavily armed warder ignored my extended passport. Nor did anyone check our numerous bags and boxes before we climbed three flights of concrete stairs to another waiting room, small and windowless and reeking of stale cigarette smoke. (Why is that smell not merely repellent but positively depressing?) In this cramped gloom one could empathize with the prisoners' longing for the sunny spacious beauty beyond these walls.

I drew my minders' attention to four excellent AIDS-education posters, something too rarely seen in South Africa. Even they – both relatively well informed, Georgina with literary ambitions – were shockingly uninformed about the virus. Yes, they had heard of it – recently the ANC Youth League magazine ran a couple of warning articles – but they tended to dismiss it as more Nat propaganda to demoralize blacks.

At 11.30 precisely we were admitted to a long hall bisected by a glass-and-steel partition, with speaking-holes at two-yard intervals, above a wooden counter – the general effect not unlike a security-conscious bank. Allegedly every conversation is bugged but this didn't deter Tony from denouncing the remand prisoners' ill-treatment, especially their being allowed exercise only on Mondays, for one hour. However, the cells are not too crowded, leaving room to do press-ups. He and Albany have been inside for seven months; in three weeks' time their case will come up at Mitchells Plain magistrates' court. Having been arrested for illegal possession of firearms, they are now being charged with arson, robbery and assault. A cooked-up charge, they insist, and I met no one in Khayelitsha who disbelieves them. The police commonly bribe false witnesses: not difficult in a destitute community where perjurers may be hired for R200 plus their bus fares to somewhere else. Meanwhile Tony's and Albany's families are having to borrow legal fees: R2,180 (£436) to date. Luckily Tony's secretary mother has a regular salary and Albany's parents are both in jobs, his father a factory nightwatchman, his mother a domestic worker with a generous madam. The nature of the charges precludes any financial assistance from the ANC which, reasonably enough, distances itself from members accused of criminal offences.

As visitor numbers are unrestricted for remand prisoners, relatives and friends thronged the hall. Everyone seemed to know everyone else and a jolly time was being had by all. Later, Georgina told me the atmosphere was quite different a few years ago. To political or even quasi-political prisoners, the new South Africa promises justice, something hitherto unknown if you happened to be black or a 'dissident'. Listening to the confusion of voices and languages, and marking the decibel level – always high on black social occasions – I felt sceptical about the effectiveness of that bugging system. At noon a bell clanged and two warders – one white, one black, both brutal-looking – hustled us out. Lucretia's eyes were brimming as we joined the queue at the food-parcel checkpoint.

Immediately in front of me stood a small, thin, threadbare woman with baby on back and toddler at foot. I wondered why she was queuing; she carried no comforts. The queue was long and slow. Two nasty young warders with blond mini-moustaches and thick necks squeezed every loaf of bread, opened every packet of biscuits, felt every soup sachet, stirred every pot of jam, smelled every bottle of Coca-Cola. Behind their counter rose high strong iron bars through which the prisoners could be seen eagerly crowding forward, thrusting a hand between the bars when their turn came. At last the woman in front of me stepped forward, reached into a blouse pocket and handed over one cigarette. Then she and her husband exchanged quick smiles – smiles of love and reassurance. A lump came to my throat. That was a vignette I shall never forget. Later, as we drove away, she was walking along the verge, carrying the toddler, and I suggested giving her a lift. Georgina, however, said we had no room. Which was almost – but not quite – true.

I had an invitation to Khayelitsha's Hampstead-equivalent (Site K) where lives Maria, the twice-a-week cleaning-lady ('house girl') of a Cape Town friend. This opulent corner is far from my corner and none of the Comrades has ever been there. So complications arose – as they usually do, in Khayelitsha, if you need to *organize* something. And Georgina and Lucretia being off duty that morning didn't help; their replacements spoke no English.

Site K homes have electricity, running water and telephones and Maria had asked me to ring, confirming time of arrival. But our nearest telephone was a long taxi-ride away, in a supermarket recently built by a Mitchells Plain tycoon to service Khayelitsha. This vast, oddly Stalinist building stands isolated on an expanse of muddy wasteland, guarded by a glowering black police officer who suspiciously followed us to the telephone – which, rather to my surprise, was unvandalized. When I remarked to Georgina that most Irish inner-city telephones don't work she laughed and said, 'You're lucky, you've many – our kids know their families depend on this one so it's safe!'

Maria would be home by noon, her daughter Clare said, and then told my minders how to find Site K, two long taxi-rides away. Between taxis we had a twenty-minute wait in cold rain on a stretch of main road lined with some of Khayelitsha's newest and frailest shacks, made of woven twigs, cardboard, driftwood, plastic sacks. Nearby stood hundreds of lavatory sentry-boxes – row after row among the bushy fynbos on the sand dunes, awaiting the next influx. I found this pre-planning quite chilling in its acceptance of the fate of newcomers. Yet it is also an essential public-health precaution. And in one sense it is an advance; less than a decade ago new arrivals were being beaten up by the police, then forced back to the Transkei or the Ciskei.

As time passed and no kombi stopped my minders registered increasing unease – possibly we were in PAC territory. Then came a driver who recognized us and allowed us to overload his vehicle; uncomplainingly, three passengers made their laps available despite our being rain-sodden.

In the pre-Hani era Khayelitsha was a tourist attraction and the tour ended in Site K 'to let foreigners see how things are improving'. It is almost beyond belief that tourists could not imagine how people must feel, living on a crust in a shack, when sightseers from luxury hotels cruise past in luxury coaches staring at 'the influx' as though at animals in a game park. Some white liberals argue that these tours 'helped to stir the conscience of the world' – which argument doesn't go down well with any Khayelitsha resident of my acquaintance.

Site K consists of some 16,000 identical houses, each in a minute fenced garden, lining narrow tarred roads. The verges are piled high with reeking garbage and no attempt has been made to remove the builders' rubble. This lies about in heaps, disfiguring sand dunes that might otherwise have been pleasantly landscaped. Yet at least the houses are well spaced out; there is no sense of overcrowding.

I despaired of ever finding No. 2983A; the illogic of the numbering induced a Rubic-cube-type frustration. As in a white suburb, few people were visible; if you can afford to live here you have a job, or several jobs. But my minders remained undaunted. Diligently they sought guidance, time and again, and within an hour we had arrived.

Alas! Clare had got in a muddle: her mother wouldn't be home until the late afternoon. Well, that was just another of those African things – possibly my minders had mistranslated? Clare, newly arrived from the Transkei, speaks no recognizable English. But she made us very welcome, suggested we await Maria's return and looked disappointed about my having an important meeting fixed for 3.30. Again I marked the difference between black and white social interactions. Clare and my minders were at once relaxed together, chatting and laughing like old friends, then trying on each other's scarves and shoes. Meanwhile I sat back on the smart-but-shoddy two-person sofa, relishing the Castle which teetotal Maria, with typical black generosity and tolerance, had laid on for the decadent visitor. She and her husband are paying R20,000 (approximately £4,000) in monthly instalments and will own their home before reaching retirement age. Peter is a 'garden boy'; he and Maria are among the fortunate minority, both having a variety of steady jobs.

The outer door opens directly into this eight-foot-square parlour with white-washed breeze-block walls – very cold in winter, complained Clare, lighting an oil heater under the neatly curtained window. A black-and-white portable TV set, long since discarded by a 'madam', occupied a shelf on my right amidst a profusion of thriving potted plants, some ceiling-high. It was showing a fuzzy documentary about Alaska. Between the sofa and two easy chairs, covered in the ANC colours, stood a coffee table draped in a skilfully woven red-and-gold Transkei cloth.

Proudly, Clare showed me around her home. From the parlour one enters a tiny hallway leading to two bedrooms smaller than the parlour, a bathroom and a kitchen dominated by a giant antique refrigerator – shades of Mafefe! A dwarf electric cooker, a folded card-table and two stools furnish the dining corner where an electric kettle had been plugged in to make coffee. Apart from the tiled bathroom and kitchen, the floors were wall-to-wall red-carpeted with some soft but sturdy synthetic material. Everywhere was neat and Swiss-clean. Later my minders told Lucretia that Comrade Noxolo's friend lived in a house 'like you'd died and gone to Heaven!' Well, yes – but suppose a couple had six children and four dependants? These houses are barely adequate for a family of five. And the average black family is rather larger.

Were I to become a permanent resident of Khayelitsha – and I can think of worse fates, like becoming a permanent resident of London or Dublin – I would choose to live in 'my corner' rather than Site K. The juxtaposition of all those thousands of identical houses with the reeking piles of garbage beside the tarred roads adds up to a dismal sort of squalor with which I could not live. In shackland every DIY shack is *different*, you know you are among a community of individuals. Also, my corner is not litter-strewn. No one can afford to generate much litter and they dump what there is on the motor-road verges, beyond those prefab concrete walls erected to deter lawless youths from stoning passing vehicles. (That was a naive plan; at convenient intervals the youths knocked holes in the walls, then decorated them with bright graffiti – the texts in Xhosa and, I believe, bloodthirsty.) This method of garbage disposal gives passing motorists the impression that shackland dwellers are filthy savages. In fact it proves the reverse. For all its vastness and against all the odds, Khayelitsha proper upholds rural Africa's traditional standards of cleanliness and tidiness. Yet in Site K that sense of communal pride seems to be lacking, as though comparative affluence – lessening dependence upon neighbours – had cut it off at the roots.

Some South African whites assume that blacks can afford to migrate from the homelands so impulsively and fecklessly, by the hundred thousand, because shacks come free. But in fact they come dear, appearances notwithstanding, because of black-on-black exploitation.

'But what else would you expect?' said Ika. 'You complain about cut-throat profiteering in your world and this is our version of it. It's human nature's the problem.'

We were standing outside the depot of Messrs Matolengwe and Ndou, viewing their wares spread on the sand. They beamingly posed for my camera under a skewed little notice, balanced on the roof of their storage shed: 'WE SELL Second Hand Doors, Poles, Windows, Zincs, Nails. WE ALSO CUT GLASS.' These entrepreneurs drive around in their third-hand kombi scavenging from dumps and derelict buildings. 'It's hard work,' said Mr Matolengwe. 'They grumble we charge too much but we earn it! And petrol is a big cost.' Typically, he spoke good English and Mr Ndou, some twenty-five years younger, spoke none.

I noted down a few prices. Short sheets of corrugated iron with few holes: R18 each. Others, longer but very rusted and holey: R23 to R28, depending on the number of holes. New (doubtless 'found') long roof beams: R20, shorter ditto, R14.50. Metal window frames four feet by six, R65 to R120 depending on condition. Flimsy inside doors, R48 to R70. More solid hall doors, R290. Sections of wooden crates, for inside walls, R10. Cardboard 'panels', four feet by three, also for inside walls, R4.

Ika remarked, 'They do overcharge but I like them, they work hard. And they spend their profits sensibly. Young Jack is saving for a kombi, then he'll be independent. Mr Matolengwe is sending his children to Cape Town schools and we need a well-educated new generation.'

On the way home we received our daily dose of provocation. An SAP chopper circled low overhead while two menacing Hippos, bristling with weapons, slowly toured the wider laneways, accompanying a ten-man foot-patrol. On either side of the track five troopies moved like automatons, rifles at the ready, eyes fixed ahead avoiding hostile stares. I remembered superficially similar scenes in Northern Ireland. But there the soldiers' eyes are darting, afraid; and the IRA's campaign is some justification for patrolling residential areas. Here is no such justification. When I asked friends 'Why?' they replied, 'Intimidation and provocation!'

'They want to be stoned or petrol-bombed,' observed Georgina. 'Then they've an excuse to fire at us. In Angola too many of them got a taste for killing kaffirs. But this isn't the East Rand, here we won't play their game.'

'All the same,' said Ika, 'they tighten the tension. This sort of needling, day after day, keeps the kids' anger boiling. One young fool could start something – it's all waiting to happen again, like in the '80s. I pray to God to help me to forgive these patrols! They're planned to undermine law and order. Khayelitsha is our home place where most of us try to live decent lives. Why should we have to put up with this insult? We're not traitors or subversives, why should our place be invaded every day? Did these people not notice what happened in February 1990?'

'Worst is the night raiding,' said Lucretia – and involuntarily she shuddered. 'When you hear the Mello-Yellos coming in the darkness. And you don't know who are they after, who'll be shot up next. When they came for Tony they half-killed him to make him say where [his AK-47] was. But he wouldn't say, not even when they had him on the floor twisting his private parts. They never found it, that's why there's this terrible charge against him. They hate people stronger than them.'

Georgina recalled a statement made in May 1991 by Adriaan Vlok, Minister of Law and Order (!). He said, 'Just as the SAP in the past successfully hunted down terrorists, so now the SAP will hunt AK-47s and those who smuggle them into the country.'*

We were sitting around Ika's table, tea-drinking. Lucretia banged her fists on her thighs and said, 'The boere can't face it, that we're not terrorists! They can't accept us as "the armed wing of the ANC", entitled to become part of the SADF.'

Georgina smiled sourly and said, 'I suppose Vlok felt sorry for the SAP, deprived of their natural prey, so he was offering AK-47s as substitute.'

Six weeks ago the last white Parliament debated a new Bill setting a minimum five-year sentence for the possession of an AK-47 – maximum: twenty-five years. Again the ANC insisted on the MK's right to retain its firearms, arguing that whites own more than 3.5 million licensed weapons – truly a frightening figure, in a population of just over 5 million. 'We're in a time of confusion all round,' observed Ika. 'Have you heard about the latest poll, all-race? Eighty-six per cent of South Africans don't know the apartheid laws have been repealed!'

Apart from the overt tension caused by day patrols, and the terror caused by night raids, another, more insidious, covert tension is associated with informers and collaborators. Without anything being said in English, I could sense a deep distrust of certain casual callers; although welcomed politely, their presence impeded the free flow of conversation. Incidentally, I noticed that adults never knock before entering a shack but children always do, even if closely related.

Saturday morning brought high drama. Someone had paid those R800 and Tony and Albany were being released on bail and would at any moment appear among us. My minders and their contemporaries went wild with joy. Lucretia wept on her mother's shoulder, then apologized: 'Those are all the tears I've not been crying.'

Ika and others of her generation, including the young men's parents, were less joyful. They don't trust the unknown benefactor's motive. Is it just a coincidence that these releases follow on the rumour that a well-known anti-SAP English-speaking magistrate will be hearing the case three weeks hence?

My Jo'burg research into SAP malpractices yielded abundant evidence from a reliable source (Peace Action, which thoroughly investigates each case it reports) that the police really do go, extra-viciously, for MK returnees and their families. Tony and Albany returned in August 1991 and, until their arrest fifteen months later, suffered constant low-key police harassment. Yet apart from having kept their AK-47s, as advised by the ANC leadership, they were blameless citizens, both studying for matric. Whites in this country see the possession of firearms as a human right; Tony and Albany share that view. (I have another view but that is

* In 1996, Adriaan Vlok applied to the Truth Commission for amnesty.

beside the present point.) False charges against MK returnees are two-a-penny and these cases look very like more of the same.

Both sets of parents fear that rumours of an anti-SAP magistrate may inspire the elimination of their sons to avoid the SAP being exposed yet again as a force too incompetent to get away with corruption when seriously challenged. Does this sound neurotic? But a third young man, charged with the same offences, was murdered a fortnight ago within twenty-four hours of his parents bailing him out.

'Robot murderers' are easily hired: average fee, R800. South Africa's traffic lights are quaintly known as 'robots' and the jobless stand by them at certain crossroads – informal employment bureaux – hoping for a few hours' casual labour which might earn them R10. If offered R800 for an assassination, you think not of your victim but of your family – or so I was told in Langa, by a middle-aged man with a tubercular wife and nine children. He was chillingly uninhibited about this way of earning money, the main theme of our conversation. He knew nothing about his victim. The SAP fingered the man and lent him a weapon; he used it, returned it and collected his R800. As he was working for the police he couldn't be breaking the law.

My minders swept me off to greet Tony and Albany. Hundreds of Comrades were awaiting them and both looked dazed with happiness as they scrambled out of the taxi. Lucretia and Georgina hung back at that point; their hour would come. This was the moment for male solidarity: hugs and kisses, the MK warriors not being afraid to express affection physically. In a jubilant noisy procession we all moved off to Tony's home where a feast was being prepared. But that was not to be. Orders soon came from On High: neither young man is to spend any time in his home and for the next three weeks they must sleep each night in different – and separate – shacks. (Georgina and Lucretia were badly shaken, their rejoicing turned to apprehension.) The welcoming crowd was ordered to disperse; Tony and Albany must become inconspicuous. They then went to a specified – from On High – shack, where my minders and I joined them fifteen minutes later. In due course the 'welcome home' feast followed us, as did half a dozen Comrades, close friends of the released heroes.

It astounded me that these young men could so quickly adjust to being free (if their peculiar situation may be so described) after seven months in Pollsmoor. Observing the scene over the heads of the two toddlers who had settled in my lap (small children abounded in this shack) I felt again the power with which Africans reinforce each other. Our individualism, our *self*-consciousness, cuts us off from that sort of reinforcement. We have developed other resources, other coping mechanisms – but have we become too isolated, one from another, too proudly self-reliant? Why do we need professional help – counsellors and 'support groups' – to see us through divorce, bereavement, rape, bankruptcy, car-accident trauma, life after prison? Tony and Albany were getting all the help they needed from their friends.

The liking I took to these young men, in Pollsmoor, grew by the hour during my time in their company. Both are hearteningly clear-thinking about the new South Africa but otherwise unalike: Tony the more sensitive, now seriously upset by his parents' anxiety, Albany the more extrovert and resilient. Although equally enraged, they seem extraordinarily (to me mysteriously) unembittered by their imprisonment. They are, however, very, very frightened. I had to repress my own anger (negative energies unhelpful) when I considered the outrageousness of their situation in a supposedly 'liberated' South Africa. If I qualified for the role – obviously I don't – I would willingly be their compurgator.

My substitute minders came on duty at sunset.

Even when all allowances have been made for poor communications, the Comrades are not very good organizers. On Sunday 20 June an ANC Youth League rally was planned for Nyanga – a long-established township some eight miles away – to be addressed by the Young Lions' favourite idols, Comrades Winnie Mandela and Peter Mokaba. On Saturday afternoon word went around that 10 a.m. was the hour. Next morning – CORRECTION! Noon was the hour and by 11 o'clock hundreds were wandering around, seeking the usual ANC-hired buses. But they didn't come – and didn't come – and didn't come ... Someone said 3 p.m. was the hour; someone else said the rally had been postponed for a week because of the weather forecast; finally, word came that the venue had been changed from the soccer stadium to the community hall. My minders then decided to put me in a 'taxi for the privileged' (a limousine taxi, not a kombi) with Tony and Albany, who at present dare not travel in ANC vehicles. We drove to Nyanga by a circuitous route – part of the 'special protection strategy' – and I wondered why riding in a taxi that might at any moment be shot up, by a person or persons unknown, was supposed to be a privilege.

At 2.30 we found Nyanga's huge community hall jam-packed and the first speaker in full flow. The door marshals didn't want to admit us; there was no room for even five more, they argued. I tended to agree as Georgina and Lucretia, clutching my hands, bulldozed a few yards through the compact mass of sweating bodies to secure me a view of the platform. Outside, thousands of Winnie/Peter fans were milling about, vociferously disappointed. Although enormous, this hall was an unwise substitute for a soccer stadium. Soon the excluded began to shout angrily and try to force their way in. The few marshals on duty had no hope of restraining them and as we were pushed forward I resigned myself to broken ribs yet again (for the ninth time). The speaker faltered and stopped, the dozen ANC officials on the platform went into an emergency huddle. Five alarming minutes followed. There is something unsoothing about being trapped in an already overcrowded space which enraged thousands are trying to invade – especially when those thousands are young, mostly male and very frustrated. At last the MC announced that the 'event' would be transferred to a vast car park immediately outside. Everyone was to leave at once, in an orderly way, the seated élite taking their chairs with them.

The car park was, naturally enough, full of cars and the scene took on a surreal quality as more and more people – scores carrying chairs above their heads – streamed into an area through which frantic drivers were trying to nose their vehicles while Young Lions banged impatiently on the roofs and went toyi-toying between the cars to celebrate their victory over the elderly Lionesses. (The ANC Women's League were responsible for the crazy decision to move the rally indoors.) Then came a reinforcement of marshals, not before time. One moun-tainous man, tall and grossly fat, wielded a long iron-tipped stick with which he drove the youths out of the way of cars; his uncontrolled ferocity drew loud protests from the Women's Leaguers in whose care I had been left. The SAP would be proud of him; his expression may fairly be described as 'depraved' and one could imagine him committing any sort of atrocity. Eventually he was checked by an elderly distinguished-looking man who had the authority to order moderation. Then things settled down, the élite arranged their chairs close to the improvised speakers' platform – and I found myself upgraded and seated.

Banners are important on these occasions. So important that there followed a ninety-minute delay while three (ANC, ANC Women's League, ANC Youth League) were removed, with difficulty, from above the platform in the hall and rehung, with even more difficulty, high on the outside wall. This enterprise required builders' ladders which looked capable of treachery, and daring feats of balance, agility and co-ordination. All three banners were large and unwieldy. Why are they considered so important that, for their sake, everyone accepts a long delay and the risking of lives and limbs? Is it because for so long such statements of allegiance were illegal?

The Winnie/Peter double-act always attracts media attention: in this case an SABC TV team, several black journalists, a few whites. Peter Mokaba, President of the ANC Youth League, has been keeping himself in the limelight for months past through his defiant repetition of the MK chant 'Kill the farmer, kill the Boer!': '*Bulala Amabhunu.*' In fact those Xhosa words, when accurately translated, are a degree more sinister. *Amabhunu* means Afrikaners in general, rather than farmers. And *Bulala* means 'execute' as a punishment for crime. Ever since the ANC's unbanning, at rallies all over the country, crowds have been singing a Xhosa war-chant that includes this phrase. But only post-Hani has it been used in English, thus sparking controversy. In mid-April the SAP announced

an investigation into inflammatory statements by both Mokaba and Terre'
Blanche, who has often roared in public: 'I myself would like to have killed
Chris Hani!' In response to the SAP, Mokaba told a Northern Transvaal Tech-
nikon rally,

> Whether they like it or not, this is our chant. This is our song. This is our tradition.
> This is our culture, whether they like it or not. We will chant. And I want to tell them
> today, whether or not they are going to charge us, myself and Comrade Winnie, we
> are telling them today they can go to hell. Let them tell de Klerk he can go and jump
> in the river. We don't care about him. We will sing our song. We will fight on. I repeat:
> *Kill* the Farmer! *Kill* the Boer! Shoot to kill the prey!'

Since then Mokaba has been all over the place, usually with Comrade
Winnie, leading tens of thousands of youngsters in this chant – often before TV
cameras, to his evident delight. Neither the SAP nor the distressed Mr Mandela
dare muzzle him, not with all those Young Lions longing for an excuse to spring.
But the ANC leadership recently persuaded him to mumble a half-hearted
retraction, something about killing Boers being his 'personal view, not policy,
not to be taken seriously'. It is, however, taken very seriously. Many South
Africans, black as well as white, feel it proves their country is, in practice,
leaderless – speeding towards anarchy. And the SABC is co-operating in the use
of this chant as a form of psychological terrorism. Whites can't dismiss it as
demagoguery; farmers are being killed, quite regularly, and a considerable
number have moved to dorps or cities. In fact few such murders have any
political flavour; most are the results of armed robberies. Yet the failure to
restrain Mokaba means that a minority of militant young blacks have the sort
of power they could not have in a stable society, hence the whiff of anarchy in
the air. For me, it's easy to appreciate the dilemma of Madiba and his Comrades
when confronted by Mokaba and his Comrades. But, to many whites, the
Mokaba chant expresses the ANC's true feelings which the leadership is cleverly
concealing while manoeuvring itself into government.

In every way, Mokaba is the wrong sort of role model for the township youth.
In a *Horizon* interview (the ANC Youth League magazine) he recently described as
his 'greatest extravagance, designer clothes and a good time socially', and
referred to his need for two cars, a BMW and a Jetta. He reminds me of those
odious Young Conservatives one hears being interviewed around Tory Party
Conference time. They come in all colours.

Mrs Sosikela, sitting tight-lipped on my right, announced, 'This is make or
break day. To chant or not to chant, that is the question!'

When Mokaba's famous BMW was spotted nearby excitement tingled in the air
and a pack of Young Lions climbed recklessly onto the unstable roof of a

community hall annexe. In response to the marshals' ordering them down they shouted abuse and another pack swarmed up to join them.

'Like animals!' exclaimed Mrs Sosikela. 'So many of our young behave like they've lost their souls.' She gestured towards the roof. 'Look at them! All ignorant, violent, thinking they won the Liberation Struggle single-handed, wanting to dictate to the rest of us! Madiba's too civilized for them, they can't understand him. Mrs Tambo says it's wrong to call them the Lost Generation – but they are! She can try teaching in Nyanga, then she'll see for herself.'

Grey-haired Mr Msilana, sitting on my left, demurred. 'Through jobs they can be rescued. Any kind of job. Uneducated they can only get small jobs, but a job's the answer. With work and wages they're back into ordinary life – not outside it like now, angry and fighting.'

Mrs Sosikela smiled sardonically, 'Those up on the roof, they've never lived an ordinary life. And they're not interested in small jobs, they expect big jobs in offices with fine cars like Comrade Mokaba's.'

I thought back to 1987 when Oliver Tambo, then exiled President of the ANC, named the rioting students 'Young Lions'. 'Hail to the Young Lions!' he proclaimed. 'They have united in combat groups and confronted the enemy.' Soon after, the ANC realized that international sanctions, boycotts and COSATU-organized strikes could achieve more than combat groups of schoolchildren and ill-trained MK guerrillas. That was hard on the Young Lions; until 1989, power achieved through negotiations was never on any agenda they could read. This sudden switching of the Struggle onto new tracks left them without a role, or with only a negative role as an embarrassment to the ANC negotiators. Can one blame them for having readjustment problems now?

Mr Msilana introduced himself, with a twinkle, as 'a retired collaborator'. He had been a minor civil servant – very minor, of course. Demographic pressures, he explained, had compelled Pretoria to employ thousands of blacks; without them the Republic's gigantic, unwieldy bureaucracy could not possibly have functioned. The notion of blacks helping to run the apartheid state – in effect, making it possible – always discomfited anti-apartheid campaigners far away in the West. They didn't want to hear about all the Mr Msilanas who felt they had no choice but to do the best they could for themselves and their families within the apartheid structure. Most of the millions who consistently defied it, deviously and in desperation, were bottom-of-the-pilers who had to be defiant to survive. Now, among the Young Lions, it is cool to despise the docile oldies. The post-Soweto generation has grown up in an atmosphere of revolution, change, hope. They were ready to risk – and thousands endured – detention, torture and death. They cannot remember how it was under Verwoerd and Vorster, when the apparently immutable *status quo* made Mr Msilana and his educated ilk grateful for even the most minor post.

On Mokaba's appearance the marshals had trouble protecting our 'elders' space' from being overrun. All around us clenched fists punched the sky and the 'Vivas!' sounded semi-hysterical as Comrade Mokaba ascended the platform – designer clothed, slightly swaggering, pausing to make sure the TV team was being given every assistance. Interestingly, there was no visible SAP presence.

As the English section of Mokaba's speech made clear, the Youth League leadership is seeking to reinforce its own position, and stem leakage to the PAC, by publicly defying those ANC leaders who are now living it up in Jo'burg and – it was insinuated – in the process of selling out to the Nats. Forbidden chanting affords Youth Leaguers a marvellous opportunity to show their mettle. Yet when 'Kill the Boer!' time came Mokaba repeated the slogan only twice – hurriedly and almost uneasily. The TV crew looked cheated.

Disapproval was coming off my companions in waves. Loudly Mrs Sosikela declared, 'Shame! He has no respect or consideration for Comrade Mandela!'

Then – consternation! We were told Comrade Winnie had been 'unavoidably detained', would not be speaking. Rumours spread fast. There had been a car crash . . . An assassination attempt . . . She had been poisoned – or arrested again – or kidnapped . . . Her house was burning down – her daughter had been shot . . .

The disappointment was acute; Mrs Mandela is worshipped by most of the township youth and many of their elders. They have their own perception of the Mother of the Nation and are indifferent to (more likely, unaware of) other estimates of Comrade Winnie. Her long years of house arrest in a remote Free State township are remembered, her subsequent sordid career is disregarded. I heard several implied criticisms of Mr Mandela, in Khayelitsha and elsewhere, for his insistence on a legal separation. He didn't have much choice, I suggested, as his wife plunged from one scandalous morass to the next. But my point was not taken. Comrade Winnie continues to be admired for her persistent challenging of the authorities on practical matters immediately affecting the lives of the poorest, like housing and sewage and clinics. Such matters cannot receive the attention of her husband and his lieutenants while they are engaged in arcane negotiations about constitutional issues. Few in Khayelitsha could tell you what 'constitution' means – a limitation they doubtless share with many European citizens.

The limousine taxi had already slid away with Tony and Albany. As we struggled through the crowd (everyone seemed to be trying to go in a different direction) a young black woman rushed up to me, embraced me, burst into tears and said, 'I'm sorry, sorry! It's not right, it's not how we feel about white people! Don't be afraid, we don't want to kill you – this is a bad man.' My minders reassured her. 'This is a Comrade from Ireland, she is not afraid of black people.'

Our haggard bus was spectacularly overloaded with two passengers to each seat – the lighter sitting on the heavier – and the gangway crammed. The driver seemed either drunk or high on ANC Youth League rhetoric – maybe both. At each corner we keeled over and our not crashing seemed impossible: yet the impossible repeatedly happened. Meanwhile the inflamed cargo was chanting non-stop, 'Kill the farmer, kill the Boer! Kill, kill kill!' The standing passengers were simultaneously stamping on the already decrepit floor and thumping the roof with their fists. Many more Comrades rode *on* the roof, also stamping and thumping. When we passed another bus, overturned on the verge with a huge angry crowd seething around prone bodies, I felt glad that I had left my affairs in order.

I was sitting at the back with a young man on my lap – a kindly young man who often stopped chanting and twisted round to beam down at me and shout above the din, 'But we don't mean *you!*' I assured him that I felt threatened only by the driver's dementia. Predictably, Mokaba's slogan has quite a different flavour when tasted on the Cape Flats. Sitting on that bus, I could only regard it as a joke in very poor taste – a black joke, if I may be forgiven the irresistible – a macabre teasing, a taking the Mickey out of Whitey. I doubt if any of those present, all chanting and stamping and punching the roof, with big grins and twinkles in their eyes, would ever have gone out to kill a Boer – other than in their capacity as MK guerrillas ordered to do so.

I felt sad, going from shack to shack, saying goodbye. As usual Sisi was busy outside her door, having that morning loaded a supermarket trolley (the commonest township vehicle) with sheeps' hoofs and shanks discarded by a Mitchells Plain butcher. These she grills slowly over a tin of charcoal until they themselves become like charcoal – crunchy and (Georgina affirms) nutritious. Sisi scrapes off the outer layer of burned skin and hair before selling them for ten cents each. Ndima was shoe-mending outside his one-roomed shack, a handmade shoe hanging over the door to advertise his craft. Blossom was boiling water for a client on her new oil stove; she expects to have an exceptionally busy week because of an approaching wedding. Mrs Mgidlana and her fellow-seamstresses were busy making attractive children's garments from offcuts. Mrs Sekgonyane was washing bullocks' guts in a baby bath and hanging them out to dry on the clothes line; they brightened the scene, glistening pink and ivory and purple. When dry these too are grilled, in strips, and bought for a few cents each as a special treat. In the ANC Women's League-run crèche, donated food was being cooked for twenty-six toddlers whose parents are too ill to cope with them. The crèche is an unfurnished and seriously leaky shack, its floor always damp. Outside, Women's Leaguers sat in the sun teaching a few small girls how to weave village-style. Spaza shops were selling minute quantities of essentials. A carpenter was converting three broken tables, retrieved from a dump, into one sound table. A tinsmith was converting dog-food tins, also retrieved from a dump, into trays for domestic use – price: fifty cents. When you look closely at a corner of Khayelitsha, many people are hard at work. Unemployment statistics belie the industry and inventiveness of the 'informal sector'.

At 5 p.m. Georgina and Lucretia delivered me to the hospital to be transported back to Unreality Land. 'Don't forget us!' they urged. I won't.

8

Back to Mother

The Cape Peninsula

> Boers are much easier to mislead than lead.
> *Andries Botha, an Anglo-Boer War Commando Leader*

24 June 1993

Since yesterday I have been house-sitting for friends in Observatory, known to
its residents as 'Obs'. This is my favourite corner of Cape Town, built quite close
to the city centre at the turn of the century to house artisans and workers, white
and Coloured. Now it houses many young academics and students, with enough
of its original families remaining to preserve an air of continuity. The streets are
short and narrow, the small dwellings – mostly one-storeyed, no two alike –
stand in tiny gardens, often tree-shaded, and display a variety of ornamental
detail that blends Coloured creativity with imported fashions. Residents sit on
their little stoeps and greet passers-by, children are seen and heard, dogs are
taken for walks and traffic is light – people go shopping *on foot*. This afternoon
the postman met me walking back from the pub and asked, 'Have you lost your
bike?' – he had noticed me arriving on Lear. That's very Obs, heart-warmingly
non-urban *and* non-dorpy.

On Lower Main Road a welcoming bookshop offers bargains to the persistent
burrower. A 'Malay' health-food shop sells delicious home-made titbits and
excellent cheeses. In the congenial Heidelberg Tavern, not yet Americanized,
all races and mixes of races relax together – or sit outside at long trestle-tables
beneath trellised vines.*

Observatory's recent gentrification bothers some older residents. A cobbler
who has been cobbling here for forty-five years – and his father before him since
1903 – grumbled much about the chic new boutiques, the picture-gallery-cum-
ceramics shop, the antiques shop where five obese cats sleep rolled up on velvet
chairs (at first I mistook them for cushions), the AIDS Advice Centre and, worst of

---

* I worried about my Obs drinking-companions on the morning of 31 December 1993 when the
World Service reported four young people shot dead, and seven seriously wounded, in a PAC
machine-gun and hand-grenade attack on the Heidelberg Tavern.

all, the Artists' Co-op where 'young women sit around all day in front of men with no clothes on'.

Directly above Obs rises the 3,000-foot Devil's Peak, wide and sheer and sharp, displaying various shades of silvery grey in the changing light. Seen against this season's flaring sunsets the mountain turns purple, then black, and seems to grow bulkier and come closer. Often in the early morning fragments of cloud wander around it, wisping over rocky shelves or lingering scarf-like on the summit when elsewhere dispersed. Obs is fortunate to be thus dominated.

26 June

Yesterday morning, at the ANC head office, I sat in a little windowless room talking with a new Xhosa friend. Peter spent ten years on Robben Island (1980–90) and is now Peace Co-ordinator for the Western Cape. This oddly named job involves him in the worst township crises and requires patience, tact and extraordinary courage. Just now his main worry is a renewal of taxi warfare. Most Cape taxis wear a large blue-and-white sticker depicting a flying dove. (You avoid any that don't.) This means the association concerned signed the truce ending the 1989–92 taxi war between Lagunya and Webta, a war that began as fierce competition for the most profitable routes but soon came to be manipulated by criminal factions from Crossroads and Khayelitsha. Within six months, in 1991, it led to sixty-seven murders, the burning of countless shacks and more than a million rands' worth of damage to vehicles. The Rand, too, has its taxi wars; one such caused the murders of more than fifty people in 1990.

'Of course the police don't help,' said Peter, 'because often they get a cut. But suppose taxi wars killed whites? All concerned would be in detention! Tell me, why do sentimental foreigners try to make excuses, saying it's all apartheid's fault for creating such poverty? Taxi warriors are not poor or how could they own taxis? An owner makes at least R5,000 a month clear profit – nearly ten times a worker's wage!'

All the ex-prisoners I have met are remarkable men. After ten, twenty or more years in jail – their only crime opposition to apartheid – they remain not only unembittered but serene. Many prisoners were highly intelligent and well educated; Robben Island became known as 'the University of the Struggle', a university in which the warders were also, involuntarily, educated. These officers had to be replaced frequently, as daily association with their courteous, articulate captives weakened their allegiance to the apartheid state. The removal from black society of so many of its natural leaders, through imprisonment, exile or death, recalls Ireland's Flight of the Wild Geese. But South Africa has been luckier: most of its wild geese have now flown home.

The ex-prisoners' magnanimity is genuine; they are not coping with years of suffering by repressing memories. In Guguletu I met a gentle elderly man who recalled how some warders repeatedly smashed the delicate figures certain prisoners liked to carve out of flotsam. 'Those carvings showed the survival of our spirit. We weren't really imprisoned, the most important part of us was beyond reach of the system. We thought that form of cruelty very significant. It exposed the vulgarity of apartheid.'

A striking phrase, 'the vulgarity of apartheid' – more stinging than any condemnation of physical ill-treatment. And it helps to explain the survival of the prisoners' spirit. If vulgarity is seen as a system's defining characteristic, brutality and injustice can be withstood from an unassailable vantage point.

Many prison friendships, Peter said, developed a supportive quality unlike anything experienced 'outside'. Also, prisoners learned the importance of affectionate – as distinct from erotic – touching and soon discarded the inhibitions instilled by white mission-school regimes. 'It was *better* than university!' laughed Peter.

At that moment we heard a commotion outside – people racing along the corridors, jumping down the stairs, doors banging, anxious voices shouting questions.

Peter vanished, then reappeared to tell me I must leave at once. The AWB had just invaded the World Trade Centre in Jo'burg where the negotiations are taking place, and this could be the start of something serious. All ANC offices had been put on Red Alert.

In fact the invasion proved to be a mini-drama, though terrifying at the time for the twenty-six senior members of the negotiating council trapped within the building. The previous evening, when warned about an AWB demo, they had contacted the SAP and vainly expressed concern for their own safety. The TV cameras recorded a shocking sight: 630 armed police officers passively watching as a Viper armoured vehicle, with ET riding on the back, smashed through the plate-glass frontage and was followed by a howling armed mob of between two and three hundred, all khaki-clad. These went swarming through the building – accompanied by an AWB band, defiantly drumming – and assaulted negotiators while yelling insults. Television cameras were encouraged to film their activities: good publicity, by the skewed standards of the right wing, if an organization doesn't have to worry about incriminating evidence. Having beaten up any delegate who couldn't hide in time, including women, the mob withdrew in triumph, their quasi-swastika flags held high. On the way out they paused to slash thirty tyres in the delegates' car park, under the eyes of that 'protective' ring of 630 police. Then off they marched, behind their kettle-drummers and buglers. Today's newspapers carry outraged reports of their next move. On a nearby grassy patch the conquering heroes celebrated, having brought *braaivlei* grills, picnic hampers and six-packs. Police were photographed chatting and laughing with them.

Imagine SAP's reaction had that private army been black! Not long ago a PAC demo, of course unarmed, was sjamboked and tear-gassed outside the Trade Centre. On hearing SAP's excuse – 'But the AWB were armed!' – Tony Yengeni ordered all Western Cape ANC members to ignore the government's call to hand in their arms under an amnesty arrangement.

As destabilization was the motive for the invasion, its organizers see it as a great success. It has heightened the feeling that now South Africa has no effective government, is poised on the brink of chaos; President de Klerk's feeble response has stoked black anger and aroused white contempt. The dodging of tough decisions is giving too much space to extremists both black and white, all of them cunning enough to use that space destructively.

Since visiting the AWB's headquarters I've regarded its antics as more amusing than frightening, though I do notice how few South Africans are able to see the funny side. Maybe I have been under-reacting.

27 June

Again, seething black rage requires a safety-value and the ANC have responded swiftly and wisely. Yesterday posters went up all over Cape Town naming 1 July as a nationwide Day of Action to protest against AWB aggression and show support for interracial harmony. Mindful of the Hani riots, the City Council and the ANC are limiting Tripartite Alliance participation to 3,000 and the demo is to last only one hour – the lunch hour, when SAP have agreed to close Adderley Street to traffic.

Another wise response, on a different level, has come from Wilhelm Verwoerd, lecturer in political philosophy at Stellenbosch University. This 30-year-old grandson of Hendrik Verwoerd – 'the architect of Grand Apartheid' – is hopeful for the future.

> Once Mandela is President and people see there won't be any violent destruction of those things they hold dear, they will become more moderate. But the Trade Centre incident is a terrible tragedy. It is a tiny minority reinforcing the old stereotype of the Afrikaner while many Afrikaners are trying to break loose from this historical bondage. What we saw at the Trade Centre was a bunch of people who have been impoverished emotionally and intellectually by the success of apartheid propaganda. They are trying to stop the wheel of history. One hopes there will be strong enough action to marginalize the dangerous ones, while at the same time efforts should be made to draw into the process the more moderate right-wing Afrikaners. We must not write off all of them. We must find ways, for example within the ANC, of build-

ing relations with them, and showing them that their fears are built on sand, on disinformation.

1 July

By 11 o'clock the Day of Action crowd was assembling around St George's Cathedral, as yet mainly whites and Coloureds – mostly middle class. Several whites admitted that this was their first demo; only extreme concern about the implications of the AWB's confident defiance of the police had compelled them to venture forth. Then the chanting township contingents began to arrive, spilling out of their buses waving SACP flags while prim-looking women from the affluent suburbs eyed them nervously. But soon these ladies were to be soothed by the ANC marshals' efficiency and the theological content of the speeches delivered by Revd Allan Boesak of the Dutch Reformed Mission Church, a black Roman Catholic bishop, a Muslim imam and a Xhosa-speaking Afrikaner *predikant* with a bald pate but shoulder-length grey ringlets. This mesmeric character wore a long black robe and a plain wooden cross; I spoke to him afterwards, but was so overcome by his aura I forgot to ask his name.

Never, anywhere, have I attended such a moving demo. As it gained spiritual momentum, that against which we were protesting seemed to fade into insignificance. Looking to the future, what mattered was this novel coming together of staid Coloured business folk and professionals, ebullient Comrades from the turbulent township, Afrikaner bank clerks and secretaries, timid English-speaking housewives – all united in a longing for peace. One could sense their longing overcoming diversity and generating optimism about the new South Africa. At least in Cape Town, the AWB spectacular has backfired on its organizers in a glorious way.

Why did the media fail to reflect this? Why focus on half a dozen jolly Coloured and black teenagers burning an AWB flag? Or on a minor post-demo scuffle with SAP outside the railway station? Neither incident was typical of the occasion. Why not have a description of those thousands of blacks, mostly young and deprived, sitting quietly on the ground listening attentively to an Afrikaner clergyman? And why did the TV cameraman not zoom in on the Xhosa youth, wearing a black leather jacket and peaked cap, who stood on the plinth of Smuts' statue holding aloft a placard that read: 'NOT ALL AFRIKANERS ARE AWB'? Although the media habitually seek drama they don't always recognize it when they see it.

Yesterday twenty-one of the AWB invaders were arrested – four days after the event, giving them ample time to get rid of incriminating evidence. ET is not among them. The police claim to be 'unable to establish what role he played'. It seems they need help from the millions of TV viewers who watched him riding the Viper as it smashed through the plate-glass frontage.

2 July

The Coloureds are frank about their own colour snobbery, a characteristic of most 'mixed-blood' communities. Unless constrained by political correctness, most admit to valuing fair skin, straight hair, European features – sometimes even to the extent of one child being favoured over another on this account.

Four weeks ago I met Sylvia (endowed with all these genetic 'advantages') outside a ramshackle, overcrowded primary school in Bonteheuwel, one of the dreariest Coloured townships. She was waiting to collect her youngest son, aged 8, and immediately invited me home for coffee; she and her three older children speak excellent English.

Among this family's problems the latest – and one of the worst – is Sylvia's youngest sister. In May 1990 Marigold emigrated to the USA and within months had married a black man. Seriously black, ebony black: a photograph was shown. Shock! Horror! Disgrace! And now Marigold plans to return home with this creature and what will the neighbours think? It would be best if the couple settled elsewhere, kept away from Bonteheuwel. They are moving because Marigold hates the USA, misses the Cape unbearably. Jeff, her lamentable mate, is a computer analyst and will have no trouble getting a good job in the new South Africa. Given the extreme poverty of this damp, cramped, sparsely furnished home, it surprises me that Jeff's prospects fail to compensate for his colour. But so it is.

Two years ago Sylvia's husband lost his job in an Epping Industria textile factory, closed as a result of sanctions. ('It was a cruel thing the outside world did – why punish *us*? We didn't invent apartheid!') Eric had worked there for twenty-two years, since the factory was built. After eighteen months of enforced idleness he took to his bed where he has been lying ever since – eating little, never talking, not wanting to meet anyone, feeling humiliated and worthless. 'But some say I'm lucky. So many took to the bottle – and then to crime, to pay for all the bottles!'

Sylvia's main worry is universal: will her two jobless teenage sons get onto the drug-dealing scene? During that first visit they talked with me for half an hour – intelligent, handsome lads, polite to the visitor but showing to their mother and older sister the hopeless sullenness of unemployed youths everywhere. When they had slouched aimlessly away Sylvia said, 'They're bright boys – too bright! It's the brightest get into drug-dealing – not only for the money, it's a way of using their brains. Then they'd be into our gang wars, we have that all the time on our streets like an American movie. It's nothing new. When I was a kid in District Six whole areas were ruled by gangs.'

Lilian, the 22-year-old daughter, did well enough in her matric to get into UCT but she can neither afford the fees nor find work. To pass the time she writes reams of poetry, directly descended from Wordsworth whose *Collected Works* is this home's only visible book. She showed me the pile of jotters and wondered if someone in Ireland would publish a selection? I fielded that one as tactfully as possible and hastily moved on to the job crisis. Jeff is willing to pay Lilian's fare to New York where he could guarantee her a secretarial job in a friend's office. But she feels her mother – with a husband in a depression and sons in temptation – needs her support. Unease about Mom would prevent her from settling down to a new life.

Sylvia looked at me then and asked, 'Should I be encouraging her to go? No, no! I do need her, really I do. She's my only daughter! And my closest friend – Marigold used to be that but not now…'

This chance meeting led to my forming a little circle of Bonteheuwel friends – many jobless, a few tubercular, all living in 'sub-economic' housing, a bureaucratic euphemism for thousands upon thousands of cut-price council hovels thrown up in a hurry during the '60s and '70s. Here are numerous Nat supporters, as fearful as any whites of the *swart gevaar* – indeed, more fearful, since they can see that word made flesh all around them on the Cape Flats. But Lilian, my self-appointed interpreter, is an active ANC member, much to her mother's disapproval.

Coloured/black tension is most noticeable in bustling Mitchells Plain, a new city of 400,000 Coloureds and the nearest business district for the surrounding black shanty towns and squatter camps. I have spent several days there but seen no fraternization; blacks seem outsiders, just as they do in Cape Town's city centre. Yet when one surveys a busy street or crowded store, a bank or hospital queue, they often outnumber Coloureds.

On Mitchells Plain's periphery, a 'house war' is now provoking sporadic violence. Truculent and very determined blacks are squatting in empty new council houses for which Coloureds have already paid rent to secure tenure. ANC pleas for 'peaceable behaviour' are being ignored and rumour has it that Comrade Winnie is encouraging the squatters to hang in there. When I approached one area of conflict five Young Lions appeared from behind a barricade of builders' scrap, mistook me for a journalist and told me to get lost. No media attention is tolerated.

Today, at last, the Negotiating Forum announced the election date: 27 April 1994. Immediately I decided to return to South Africa on 1 April.

3 July

At weekends the early cyclist escapes the traffic and before dawn I set off for Hout Bay. But alas! the Peninsula's air pollution is today more than twice the World Health Organization's 'recommended level' and a thick brownish pall veiled the view from the Steenberg Pass. Whites tend to associate this problem with the cooking-fires of the black 'influx'. Scientists who spend their days analysing the smog put most of the blame on unregulated industrial emissions and motor fumes.

From the pass a gradual descent, through heathery moorland, is followed by an easy climb into terrain befouled by another sort of pollution. Apart from a nature reserve, even the remotest corners of the Peninsula – all silent wild beauty not long ago – are now being built over by 'Secure Estates'. These clusters of luxury homes, behind high walls with sophisticated electronic gates and lights, have proliferated as refuges from 'them'. Many élitist extras are offered on hoardings, including 'bridal paths' – which I assume are bait for horsey types rather than honeymooners.

At Noordhoek, on the Peninsula's west coast, everything suddenly looks English to the point of caricature: acres of seaside caravan parks, oaks shading 'Tudor' farmhouses and dozing over-fed labradors, small green paddocks with neat white fences where Thelwell-type ponies graze when not being galloped along sandy beaches by rosy-cheeked children.

Then, for seven miles, a narrow corniche road climbs around Chapman's Peak, its cliffs of glowing sandstone soaring up to the 2,300-foot summit – vertical, layered cliffs, geological antiques. Below glitters the jade-green Atlantic, so very far below that its waves break silently at the base of erosion-distorted precipices. Deep gullies hold a chaos of spherical granite boulders – and strewn among them a gruesome number of rusted car-corpses. At this distance the waters of Hout Bay, on three sides mountain-sheltered, are sapphire blue, bordered by a silver sandy crescent. In midwinter, if you are lucky (I wasn't) calving whales may be seen here, close inshore. Some gross entrepreneur recently put forward a plan to take tourists out in *motor* boats to view the mother whales in labour. Presumably there are enough humane people on the Peninsula to stymie this.

At first sight Hout Bay also seems quite English. Originally a Coloured fishing village, motor transport brought it within reach of wealthy Cape Town commuters and retired folk; then it was developed as an upmarket tourist resort. But now 'they' have arrived – an overflow from the Cape Flats and elsewhere – and below Hout Bay's tranquil surface dissension simmers. Pedalling along the discreetly affluent main street, I was taken aback by my own gut reaction on first seeing groups of disconsolate, down-at-heel blacks. They looked utterly out of place, they even looked (the word did flash through my mind) like intruders. Severely I reminded myself that they are South Africans who have very sensibly moved from some intolerably overcrowded region of their country to another region where there is plenty of room for them – if the whites push over...

So discreet is Hout Bay's affluence that the best hotels are undefiled by lettering; only one small wayside notice told me that an old (1800) Cape Dutch farmhouse is now a hotel, with bar. Into this sort of establishment one does not wheel a bicycle, so I pushed Lear around to the back where a pleasant patio is overhung by winter-bare trees. Sitting alone with his beer was a tall, bony, middle-aged man. His rugged features, bushy grey hair and dark-blue eyes looked disconcertingly familiar; soon it transpired that I had lunched with his sister a fortnight ago. The Peninsula's small white world is like that.

At present the professor – of Anglo-Boer stock – is working on a book about eighteenth-century agriculture in the Cape Province. Having grown up in Hout Bay, he feels uneasy about the area's immediate future. Naturally blacks have moved in – that's what the new South Africa is all about – yet he doesn't condemn whites for foaming at the mouth when noisy, unsightly squatter camps arise at the end of their gardens. I had to admit that neither would I want squatters, of any pigmentation, as neighbours. Recently, to avoid a much lesser calamity, I bought a next-door garden, though the large garden I already own is a shaming wilderness of weeds.

'What does upset me,' said the professor, 'is the denial of the newcomers' humanity, seeing them as encroaching vermin who lower property values. It's not helping that the rates are about to go up. We must pay to turn the camps into a town so we lose every way round. Not before time, you might say. But somehow the historical perspective gets lost when your own patch is being sacrificed to justice.'

We talked for hours; Afrikaner liberals make exhilarating company. The genus is unmistakable; some special quality comes across be the individual an ancient dame, an adolescent boy, a young mother, a middle-aged academic. Such people must be scattered all over this country (except perhaps in the northern Transvaal) but so far I have found specimens only around Jo'burg (a few) and on the Peninsula (quite a number). Unlike most Afrikaners, they understand where they have come from – and why where they have come from was as it was. And now they know where they want to go: into a new South Africa of mutual respect. 'But it must be genuine respect,' said the professor, 'not only polite speeches and expedient gestures in public.' With luck, given a change of climate, this genus will spread.

Here I am the weekend guest of classic Capetonian liberals, their links with the ANC close and long term. Sue is a first-generation English settler; Cecil, though of Russian extraction, also counts as 'English'. Their home, on a steep forested mountain, combines gracious living with comfortable informality. To my delight Cecil has suggested a mountain walk tomorrow, a serious day-long hike.

4 July

The sun rose as we set off, well provisioned and laden with water bottles. At the foot of Constantiaberg (2,800 feet) Cecil's hiking-club awaited us: open-air types wearing shorts and knapsacks and looking, I thought, unduly purposeful. Two were octogenarian ladies, snowy-haired, weather-beaten, short, compact – both eminent botanists. A few eager dogs – one a bull-terrier, the other indeterminate – completed the party.

As we ascended on an easy zigzag path the talk was all of plants, referred to by their Latin names. The region around Cape Town – known as the Cape Plant Kingdom and equal in area to the Republic of Ireland – offers some 8,600 types of flowering plant. On the Peninsula alone, more than 2,600 indigenous species have been identified, plus 600-odd species of heather, and all these hikers live in hope of attaining immortality by spotting a new species.

The path ended at the base of a towering cliff. Having become absorbed in a political conversation with Ann, a young UCT French lecturer, I had been paying no attention to our companions. Now I looked around, puzzled; half the party seemed to be missing. And where did we go from here? Where *could* we go? Then Ann moved towards the cliff and I glanced up to see the octogenarians ascending it effortlessly, like lizards running up a boulder. 'We go up here,' said Ann casually, over her shoulder. I stared at the cliff, wide-eyed with horror. I have never been a mountaineer, I thought we were going for a *walk*.

Ann took off (another lizard) as Cecil appeared by my side. 'It's easy,' he assured me. 'You just find handholds and footholds.'

I scrutinized that almost sheer grey wall but could discern nothing even remotely resembling a handhold or a foothold. However, there seemed to be no alternative to self-destruction. So I also took off, sweating with terror. On my right the dogs were swiftly ascending – this was unreal, dogs aren't baboons. From the top Ann shouted guidance. 'There's an easy handhold just to your right – now stretch your left leg and you'll reach that solid foothold. No! Don't use your knees – *never*! Now let your left arm take all the weight – that's it! You're doing fine!'

Doing fine? I knew that at any moment the law of gravity would claim me. The whole enterprise was preposterous. When normal people climb cliff-faces they wear ropes and things. No wonder this lot had been looking purposeful. As I dragged myself onto level ground, pale and trembling, everyone made kind congratulatory noises. 'You'll soon get the knack,' they encouraged me. 'It's easy, really – it's just a knack.' But I had no interest in getting this knack; you can't teach an old bitch new tricks.

Onwards and upwards: no zigzag path here but straight up on a severe gradient. My thigh muscles are at present out of order (too much toyi-toying in Khayelitsha) and now they felt inflamed. I was lagging far behind the rest as we approached the next sheer (in my terms) cliff-face, even higher and smoother than the last. I paused to gaze up, in a misery of fear. The octogenarians – both well into their eighties, I'm not exaggerating – were almost at the top, biceps and calf-muscles bulging efficiently. Capetonians are *very* abnormal, I decided at that stage. On I crawled, to the base of the cliff, where Cecil eyed me solicitously – then proved himself a perfect host. 'Should we go home?' he asked.

Selfishly but emphatically I said 'Yes!' thereby wrecking his day. On the way down he explained that a sizeable proportion of the Cape's population, human and canine, is trained to this sort of thing from childhood and puppyhood. In their view, walks aren't worthwhile without a series of these death-defying obstacles. They don't call it 'climbing', they call it 'scrambling'. For non-Capetonians, it is the stuff of nightmares.

While recovering from my ordeal I read the *Sunday Times* which today dwells complacently on 'the extraordinary success of South Africa's political parties in crafting a constitution that faithfully follows the mainstream Western liberal-democratic models . . . The constitutional principles take us closer to the American and German models than to any of the calamitous socialist models that were once held as examples for South Africa to follow.'

This sounds like white supremacy doing a phoenix. Is a 'Western liberal-democratic model' really suited to this mainly black country where almost half the population is illiterate and poverty and crime are rampant? And where, among all race groups and most political parties, there is a marked shortage of the raw materials from which democracies are fashioned. The recognition of one-(wo)man-one-vote as the definitive action ending white supremacy – each individual contributing to end it, tasting triumph – is not at all the same thing as knowing how to, or wanting to operate within a democracy day by day. However, these elections must happen; there is no acceptable alternative route to a new South Africa.

6 July

My last day on the Peninsula: but next year I'll be back. Tomorrow I leave for Jo'burg, taking as motor-free a route as possible through the Klein Karoo and the Transkei.

9

The Klein Karoo

Hermanus – De Rust – Elliot

British Kaffraria, in which a new model for relations between the Cape Colony
and the Xhosa was so rapidly being forced into existence, was the only military colony
in the British Empire. The martial law at Colonel George Mackinnon's disposal meant
that he and his assistant commissioners could be as arbitrary as they wished on civil
Xhosa matters and they were when it suited them.
Noel Mostert, Frontiers *(1992)*

Hermanus, 9 July 1993

I left Obs at the seventh hour on the seventh day of the seventh month which
should have been auspicious timing but wasn't. The Mother City chose to send
me on my way as she had greeted me – only more so. By the ninth hour a strong
tailwind had become a gale, its gusts up to 150 m.p.h. Dismounting, I walked the
last five miles to the home of an Irish friend on the outskirts of Somerset West.
Often I had to stand still, leaning hard on Lear, forcing my feet to stay on the
ground. Branches were being ripped off wayside bluegums – some thirty feet
long yet whirling high in the sky like autumn leaves. All day the storm continued,
killing eleven people and doing millions of rands' worth of damage.

Next morning a normal tailwind helped me on my way. But soon it was
raining again – heavy cold persistent rain – and upon the famous Sir Lowry Pass
sat a cheating cloud, hiding the view across False Bay to the Peninsular mountains. Then the gale resumed, forcing me to walk almost twenty miles on an
exposed road undulating between low mountains, heathery and uninhabited.
There was no traffic; those gusts could overturn a vehicle.

At dusk a Coloured township appeared below the road. I looked down
speculatively at its little houses and biggish hotel. Outside the bar door drunks
were singing and shouting and quarrelling and I decided against ... Had they
been black, that same rowdiness would not have deterred me. Even now, after
six weeks on the Cape, I cannot feel quite at ease with Coloureds. Going on my
wet and weary way, I thought about this. Why, despite so many instances of
impetuous hospitality ('Come now to my home!') do I find them, in general,
more difficult to get on with than blacks? Some unforeseen and baffling barrier
exists. On the whole it is easy – much easier than with blacks – to establish a

superficial, chatty relationship. Then suddenly one realizes just how superficial it is, how much higher stands this barrier which at first seemed lower. All the exceptions I can recall have been chip-free academics: so is the barrier in fact built of Coloured chips? Not even the most deprived blacks seem as insecure as this community.

In Hermanus, a favourite seaside resort of the rich, most hotels are several-starred. The exception, the Astoria, is closed for the winter, apart from its grotty bar where all the men were AWB types with foot-long bushy beards, collar-length hair, narrow eyes, aggressive voices and guns in their belts. Then Dan arrived, an extrovert young Capetonian who soon decided I must stay with friends of his, an 82-year-old New Zealander and his English-speaking wife. Both are good company and seem to enjoy having a guest. Life must lack variety in midwinter Hermanus; many of the permanent residents are retired couples or lonely widows and widowers.

Today the gale continued relentlessly. Venturing out at noon, I found that no one else was being so rash. In the Victoria Hotel bar sat a young Afrikaner couple from Jo'burg, also storm-bound. Hendrik runs a textile-printing business and is equally happy to take orders from the ANC, the AWB, APLA, the Nats. 'I work fourteen hours a day, average,' said he. 'Now we gotta get off our back-sides, face up to the new competition. I say Mandela's right about affirmative action – why not? Those poor bastards, they're waiting long enough for jobs. I'm no liberal, just a realist. We're living already in the new South Africa. It's not in the future and maybe something we can avoid. Plenty of my age think the same but you don't hear about us, we're not news.'

Montagu, 11 July

Yesterday's long climb from Hermanus, on a quiet narrow road, took me inland. Here were chunky mountains, their summits half-clouded, and deep woody glens, and small steep green fields hedged or stone-walled. A brown flooded river raced noisily to the Indian Ocean, carrying vegetable debris and a few dead sheep, swirling and churning between rocks, often overflowing bluegum-lined banks. The occasional isolated farmhouse had its date over the main door or on a gable: 1709, 1726, 1748.

Then comes a transmogrification; beyond the chunky mountains I might have been back in central Transylvania. All around rose high smooth emerald ridges grazed by enormous flocks of merinos or sown with new wheat – a brilliant green dusted over the red-brown richness of the soil. In three hours I saw only one person, a farmer checking his flock, driving a motor-buggy such as American golfers use. I fumed at this idyllic scene being polluted visually, aurally and olfactorily by the latest walk-avoidance gadget. Then I tried to be reasonable.

Without a buggy it would be necessary to ride a horse across these vast pastures. And by now most Boers have lost that skill, once central to their way of life.

Last night was spent in Stormsvlei, an aptly named dorplet; as I arrived another storm suddenly blew up, after a calm sunny seventy-mile ride.

This morning, outside the Sabbath-dead dorp of Bonnievale, I paused to view a river wildly in flood: a pinkish-brown torrent, quarter of a mile wide, loud and fast, dotted with the tops of bushy green trees. As I watched, two trees were uprooted and several nearby bungalows were being inundated, the water higher than window-level and still rising.

Pedalling on through a magnificence of mountains – all naked jagged red-brown rock – I wondered why predictions of civil war are becoming so much more frequent. Between now and the elections increasing violence is to be expected – but that is something else. South Africa's political scene is too incoherent for civil war which, like any other war, needs organization. And the economic scene is too coherent; those senior officers now organizing a covert dirty war against the ANC will never attempt a military coup post-elections. That would require the go-ahead from South Africa's corporate mentors. In this context, the dominant materialistic ethos has its short-term uses. Everyone knows on which side their bread is buttered and civil wars butter no loaves. The various ideologies, ideals and principles – paraded as precious, sacred and immutable, with much talk of dying in their defence – are in reality less important than staying within reach of the butter dish.

Montagu, an attractive little town on the edge of the Klein Karoo, is a popular summer-holiday resort but this evening there are only two other guests in its enormous Edwardian hotel. Wayne and Betty, English-speakers about my own age, are born-again Christians heavily into evangelizing. When I at last succeeded in turning the conversation from my own rebirth, Wayne told a story to illustrate how well whites understand blacks. In the 1950s, as a junk-jewellery salesman, he employed a Xhosa youth to carry boxes of samples, polish the van, make morning tea and so on. Once the youth overslept and Wayne gave him 'a sound beating'. When he spilled tea over the bedclothes he got an even sounder beating. And when he forgot to load a box 'I stopped the car, dragged him out on a verge and gave him a hiding so he was stiff for a week. Result? He's a fat cat now, with a Mercedes! You with me? It's like training puppies. You got to thrash 'em some to get any good of 'em.'

Calitzdorp, 13 July

Although the Klein Karoo is topographically more conventional than the Great Karoo, its vibes are no less eerie, its light is no less brilliant, its ancient silence no less solemn. During yesterday's mountainous sixty-five miles I met no one;

beyond the highish and very steep Ouberg Pass the extreme ruggedness of the terrain precludes even sheep-farming.

This year's early rains have brought out an abundance of flowers in mid-July. Often I stopped to climb steep slopes, marvelling at the strangeness of these plants; many, before they flower, imitate the surrounding rocks and stones in shape and colour. Usually the petals are tiny and close-set, glowing in patches of magenta, mauve, burgundy, purple, pale yellow, dark blue. At the base of a low ridge, on a level expanse of cinnamon earth, I was lucky enough to see one of the rarest plants in the world, the many-headed euphorbia. From a little distance I mistook it for a rounded boulder. It was some six feet by four and perhaps three feet high, the solid rubbery surface olive-green, faintly pink-tinged. When of these proportions the many-headed euphorbia – a succulent – is likely to be hundreds of years old.

In mid-afternoon, turning the shoulder of a mountain, I saw the first dwellings since leaving Montagu. The Coloured hamlet of Anyberg, a dozen mimosa-shaded cottages, lay in a spectacularly deep gorge made noisy by a flooded river.

That long descent took me into an area well wooded by local standards. Here were trees as strange as the flowering plants – some not true trees (what *is* the definition of a 'true tree'?) but giant succulents, their thick silver leaves also serving as seeds. Anything is possible in the Karoo...Now the karee trees are fragrantly in flower, minute yellow-green blooms clustering densely on the tip of each branchlet. Here too were many witgats, the benign 'shepherds' trees', standing about twenty feet tall with very thick and silky smooth off-white bark. These have countless uses, as a source of both sustenance and medicines for humans and animals. Traditionally, all the peoples of the Karoo so valued witgats that their felling was forbidden and happily they remained protected by a colonial law.

Another climb followed, onto a plateau from which the mountains stood back, allowing pasture-space for sheep. Here were two farm entrances, ten miles apart, both homesteads invisible from the track.

After a perfect day – cloudless sky, warm sun, cold breeze – suddenly at 5.30 a gale sprang up, driving inky clouds from the west. Camping on the veld no longer seemed a good idea. At this altitude, during winter, Karoo storms often bring lethal hail, capable of killing not only humans but oxen. A normally severe hailstorm (not freakish) produces stones the size of cricket balls with jagged needle-sharp protuberances which shatter car windows and wreck the rest of the vehicle. In olden times travellers used their saddles to protect their heads and, if they were lucky, could afterwards crawl home – frequently leaving a dead horse behind. The unlucky were badly concussed and died hours later, where they had fallen, of hypothermia.

I scanned the plateau through my binoculars, hoping to see a grove of windpumps and trees. None was visible, nor was there any natural shelter of any kind. My anxiety level rose as I hurried on, the gale behind me, the sun setting. Then deliverance came – a rather grand farm entrance, with two crescent walls on which were painted, in letters large enough to be read by twilight, WILLEM ERASMUS. Elated, I turned left towards Mr Erasmus but soon had to dismount; the track's surface failed to match the grandeur of the entrance.

As I walked into the darkening bush just one long streak of red remained in the western sky and, ahead of me, black clouds were piled over low hills. How far to the homestead? Hereabouts it could be eight or ten miles.

Forty minutes later – by then it was pitch dark, starless dark – a distant golden glimmer deceived me. Alas! this was only the workers' compound, a line of cinder-block shacks. My shouted greeting brought a Coloured man to a door-way; he stood silhouetted against the lamplight within, excited small children clustering around his legs. Our conversation was inconclusive but his gestures told me to continue along the track. Here one cannot suggest staying with workers – which anywhere else in the world would be the natural thing to do, after dark in the middle of nowhere.

A mile or so further on I arrived unexpectedly at the homestead – unexpect-edly because it was unlit, deserted but for a Rottweiler bitch. Instead of enhan-cing the reputation of her breed by savaging the intruder she fell in love with me at first sight. (Or is it first smell in the case of dogs?) In a huge barn/shed – its side door was open – I spread my flea-bag on the diesel-scented concrete floor. The bitch snuggled down beside me as I ravenously chewed biltong, remember-ing all those commandos who lived on it for months at a stretch during the Anglo-Boer War. I was almost asleep when my companion uttered a joyous yelp and raced away to meet her master.

The workers had warned Willem that a man with a bicycle had gone towards the homestead. 'But I think you're a woman!' he exclaimed, peering at me by torchlight. He is a burly young man with crinkly brown hair, kind brown eyes and a big happy smile. He apologized for not asking me to stay, he himself had to spend the night with friends nearby – that is, an hour's drive away. This was a momentous night. His land must be irrigated when the flood came down at about 4 a.m. – or maybe 3 a.m. – a 'boy' would be on guard all night watching the river. However, Retha and Tertius could give me a bed, not only for the night but for a week – or a month, should I wish to make an in-depth study of the Klein Karoo. As the nearest dorplet (offering no entertainment) is twenty-five miles away, and there are on average twenty miles between farms, this boundless hospitality is understandable.

When Willem heard where the flood had got to by 3.30 p.m. – I had to remove the panniers and take off my trousers to wade through it – he was able to calculate, almost exactly, its time of arrival on his land. Yet he described himself as a novice farmer, brought up in Pretoria. His father, a heart surgeon, never showed any interest in farming though the family had been settled on these 30,000 hectares since the 1870s. Willem moved here three years ago and relishes every aspect of his new life; he hopes his city-bred wife will soon come to do likewise. Their first child, a son, has just been born in Pretoria and will in due course inherit the farm, or so Willem plans. It seems he doesn't feel threatened by the new South Africa's land-redistribution policy.

Retha and Tertius have recently retired to their family farm; in Stellenbosch Retha was a librarian and Tertius a civil servant in the Native Affairs Department. While glorious wine flowed copiously, three handsome and lordly cats sat together on my lap. Retha's meal was one of the best I have eaten in South Africa and the party continued until 1.30 a.m.

This morning I was tempted to rob a bank in Ladismith – not to be confused with the more famous Ladysmith further north. It is my practice to collect cash in dorplets where there are no queues. In Ladismith there was no staff either, just a wide-open bank and much hammering overhead. Eventually I found the staff (all two of them) in a café across the street. The roof had been blown off during last night's gale and, irritated by the noise consequent upon its replacement, they moved to the café.

While pushing Lear up the long steep slope beyond Ladismith I passed a lone ragged Xhosa, a young man carrying a cattle-stick over his shoulder. He civilly returned my greeting but could speak no English. Moments later an elderly Afrikaner couple in a Mercedes overtook me, then stopped to offer a lift – though loading Lear would have been troublesome for them. 'It's dangerous', said the husband, 'to be on a lonely road with that black fella.' I should have denounced their assumption that black men are more likely than not to be criminal. But that would have seemed ungracious.

The next twenty-eight miles wound through mountains whose like is to be found in only two other locations, somewhere in South America and on a South Sea Island. They are known scientifically as the Enon conglomerate and locally as the Red Hills, a prosaic name for one of the wonders of South Africa. From profound inaccessible ravines rise sheer red cliffs – mighty walls, miles long, of glowing rough sandstone and glittering quartz. Their vegetation (what one can see of it by the roadside) is sparse but fascinating: improbably shaped succulents, many of them unique to this tiny area. On the long descent from the pass I stopped at each hairpin bend to sit and gaze. Once a hawk came into view, circling above a ravine – quite close, at eye-level. It was Africa's only polyandrous bird of prey, the pale chanting goshawk who shares his mate with another male. I could clearly see the grey back, pure white rump, bright orange legs – and soon a second appeared, further down the ravine. Perhaps his co-husband?

Calitzdorp is a pleasant little town, intent on luring tourists away from the famed Garden Route but, so far, not having much success.

Tourist camp in Grootswartberg, 14 July

Seven miles beyond Calitzdorp I was tempted by another gravel road and went off on a fifty-mile detour through the Swartberg. This bone-shaking track carries little traffic as it rises and falls, always steeply, going from valley to valley – small fertile valleys, irrigated from rivers filled by the rainfall of other areas. The long-established irrigation system looks Asian but these valleys' overall pattern is oddly European: rich ploughland, trim vineyards, lush meadows, verges green enough to recall Ireland in May. Then come many ostrich farms as the track rises – leaving fertility behind – onto expanses of stony veld overlooked by the dark blue precipices of the Swartberg. Several giant bluegums were uprooted the other night; one fell on a farmhouse, smashing the roof and seriously injuring the sleeping farmer and his wife. The rains rarely reach here but gales blow regularly.

Ostriches roamed over most of South Africa when van Riebeeck arrived and he sent several supposedly tamed specimens as gifts to Oriental rulers. Otherwise the Europeans paid scant attention to these bizarre birds, apart from using their plumes as fly-whisks, wielded by slaves while the family ate. Then, in the 1860s, a Karoo Boer named Booysen began to breed ostriches and sell their plumes to Europe's richest ladies. As the Klein Karoo was then about as far as you could get from the world of *haute couture* (it's not much nearer now) this inspiration is one of life's minor mysteries. Within a decade ostrich feathers were fetching £100 per pound, a lush sum in those days. By the 1880s one pair of young adults cost £200 and all Mr Booysen's neighbours were frenziedly hatching ostrich chicks. Rapidly the market expanded; plumes were *in*, globally. Spacious manor houses – I passed a few today – replaced more humble dwellings and the region's economy was transformed. Calitzdorp and Oudtshoorn's prosperity was founded on ostrich plumes; the latter town's imposing Victorian mansions are still known as 'feather palaces'. But fashion is fickle: the liberated, cloche-hatted young ladies of the Roaring Twenties spurned ostrich plumes and suddenly the boom was over. As suddenly, some seventy-five years later, ostriches again became Big Biz – bred for their meat and their skins which are used to make purses, wallets, belts, handbags, shoes and (if you've inherited an oil well) tunics. Most plumes are now sold as cheap feather-duster souvenirs but have retained their 'special' value for one piquant purpose – to dust the most delicate bits of electronic equipment made in such places as Silicon Valley. It pleases me to think of our high-powered boffins depending on those plumes – as the Khoikhoi did to control vast cattle herds, using a technique even more baffling than microchips. The cattle were trained to graze and then lie ruminating around a bunch of plumes set upright in the earth, representing the herdsman. This left him free to take time off knowing his animals would not stray. So many feathers went into the making of each bunch that it was equivalent in value to a young ox.

Hereabouts the ostrich population marks this as the industry's birthplace. Some flocks, living a more or less natural life on ample expanses of veld, look healthy and happy – insofar as ostriches are capable of looking happy. Others, owned by the greedier farmers and crowded into bare smelly little paddocks, look wretched – their plumage bedraggled, their demeanour dispirited, their interpersonal relationships very obviously embittered.

Today I enjoyed several long wayside discussions; the friendliness of the local Boers makes up for their hesitant English. It seems the casualty rate among ostrich-minders is quite high. One farmer has lost two 'boys' within the past three years, both killed by the same cock – disembowelled with one swift kick. (They kick forwards, not backwards.) Your average cock is eight feet tall and weighs several hundredweight; being armed on each foot with two long claws, resembling thick curved steel nails, he is much more likely to kill than to maim. Some birds – hens as well as cocks – complete the job by kneeling on the prone body, splintering their victim's bones. Their own bones are virtually indestructible. Eve Palmer records one instance of an 18-month-old chick breaking a gap through a two-foot-thick stone wall by charging it; the chick suffered no ill effects. And without difficulty an adult can snap a thick pole of sneezewood – one of Africa's toughest woods – by running into it.

Recently a local farm was put up for sale, something almost unknown hereabouts. The asking price is R5.5 million and now rumour has it that an American bought the place a few days ago, intending to stock it with 8,000 ostriches – though my informant asserts it should carry only 4,000. The thought of an American (or any uitlander) farming *their* land outrages the locals. But what else can you expect with the blacks taking over?

By 5.15, when I came to a T-junction and a tarred road, habitations and farms had been left far behind and all around rose the austere, sublimely beautiful Swartberg. It was piercingly cold and the familiar evening phenomenon of heavy dark clouds obscured the Swartberg Pass. My plan to cross it and sleep in Prince Albert no longer seemed feasible. Reluctantly I turned and freewheeled down to this nasty 'Mountain Retreat' where the artificial lake is empty, the shop is almost empty, there is no bar, there are no other guests and the staff are sullen. But my self-catering chalet costs only R30.

De Rust, 15 July

This morning's long descent took me past the famous Cango Caves into an area reeking of tourism. I paused only to admire Oudtshoorn's fine public and domestic architecture – the 'feather palaces' – then pedalled on to this endearingly dopey little dorp. At 4 p.m I found the hotel empty, like the bank in Ladismith. I could have helped myself to whatever I fancied from the bar and sped away. It's soothing to come upon these relaxed corners of South Africa where political troubles are but items on the TV news and the attitude to security is normally rural.

Here my only fellow-guest is Mr Pelotti, a middle-aged man whose family migrated from Calabria in the 1950s. (At first I mistook him for a Coloured.) He lives in Germiston but is negotiating to buy De Rust's takeaway, the PWV violence having broken his nerve.

Over supper Mr Pelotti told me that in the 1950s the *verkramptes* opposed the Nats' indiscriminate encouragement of white immigrants, seeing an influx of Papists as a source of moral corruption. The DRC then organized not very successful evangelizing missions among the white heathen and my companion recalled with entertaining irreverence being pursued as a child by those zealots.

All immigrants, unless settled in dorps exclusively Afrikaans-speaking, eventually joined the English-speakers. Socially, however, merging was limited, apart from those who made their way into the academic, artistic or corporate worlds. The original English-speakers regarded the southern Europeans as lower class (a term still used freely here, PC being optional) though few English settlers were themselves escutcheoned. Also, many of the newcomers preferred to remain within their own close-knit communities.

Post-war immigrants (Greeks, Italians, Spaniards, Cypriots) own many of the small stores and takeaways where I pause for sustenance and we often talk while I drink my amasi or eat my fish-cake. Most oldies claim to have been not at all 'colour-sensitive' (!) when they arrived, to the great alarm of the ruling class. But they soon became so – and, as is the convert way, often extremely so. One meets few ANC supporters among them: Mr Pelotti is an exception.

Pearson, 16–18 July

On the Meirings Pass, not far from De Rust, the weather turned vicious. Over sixty-five miles to Willowmore I had to battle with a gusty crosswind while it rained from a low sky restricting visibility to a hundred yards. Such conditions – recalling brown bogs, gorse, heather – make the Klein Karoo's aloes and karees, dwarf acacia and euphorbia look quite wrong.

In Willowmore's scruffy hotel bar several Coloureds and whites, listlessly playing cards together, seemed to regard my arrival as a welcome diversion. According to Mr van Imhoff – old and stiff but mentally vigorous – this region's race relations have always been good. Even Verwoerd didn't spoil them; as the Coloureds already lived in their own locations, forced removals never became an issue. And in that well-regulated era there were few blacks around though now they are moving in 'like locusts'. The Coloured card-players then tried to outdo their Afrikaner friends in expressions of contempt for the newcomers, an easy way to boost self-esteem and emphasize cousinhood.

Mr van Imhoff's card partner, a 33-year-old ex-train-driver from Graaff-Reinet, was sacked last year because of a drink problem. He now mends blades in the local sawmills, perhaps not the most appropriate job; horrendously scarred hands suggest that he still has his problem. The future fills him with foreboding: 'My kids will never find work.'

Yesterday's ninety-five miles from Willowmore to Jansenville were covered in seven and a half sunny hours, yet on arrival I felt as though I had been loitering along the way. Viva tailwinds Viva!

Beyond Willowmore stretches a level grey-brown plain with unbroken mountain-walls, low and dusky blue, quite close on either side. Here I saw jackals at dawn, several troops of vervets and a herd of wild springbok. As usual, a few jackal corpses – and numerous other motor-victims, small unidentifiable mammals – lay on the road providing breakfast for large black-and-white crows. One lost springbok kid – panic-stricken – got caught in a fence and his little heart was hammering so fast when I lifted him free that I wonder he didn't die of fright.

The only dorp on my route was Steyletville where I failed to find fresh milk, amasi or biltong. In all such places the Coloureds look miserably down-at-heel and the few stores are poorly stocked. Here I turned west and for forty miles a good gravel road took me over or between low, round, parched mountains – no hint of spring green – and across wide tracts of semi-desert sprinkled with sheep and Angora goats. I passed scarcely half a dozen farms and not many more vehicles.

In contrast, today's forty miles presented another endurance test as a strong headwind drove fine, icy rain across uninhabited uplands. On arriving here at noon my hands were too numb to sign the register.

Since crossing the Limpopo, I have been regularly warned to 'avoid the Transkei'. Now these warnings are becoming more frequent and, given the rising tension, it's hard to decide what to do. The Transkei's APLA activists are reputed to be seriously into killing whites – indiscriminately, not hand-picking their targets. At the end of March the security forces sealed off the boundaries 'to protect South African citizens from cross-border attacks'. In April four whites, including two German tourists, were badly injured in ambushes as they motored through. There have since been nine more 'incidents', with three whites killed – a casualty list not long enough to justify the hysterical public reaction. As most attacks have taken place on the N2 motorway, I decided this evening on a compromise: the Maclear to Matatiele gravel road, which crosses the Transkei at its narrowest.

Cradock, 19 July

This is D-Day: Defeat Day for Dervla who, in difficult circumstances, took a thirteen-mile lift. Seemingly an insignificant aberration, during the 3,120-mile (to date) cycle from Karoi. Yet, absurdly, it worries me. Cyclists of my generation have a superstition about taking lifts and this break in the rhythm of our journey feels like a bad omen.

Between Pearson and Cradock the map shows two passes but when I set out at 7 a.m. I imagined arriving in mid-afternoon – it's only fifty-five miles. However, I'd reckoned without 'exceptional conditions'. Most Karoo tracks are really private roads, servicing a few farms, and today's specimen was not gravel but deep sand, converted by yesterday's downpour into a sticky sludge. Pedalling or pushing, against yet another icy gale, was literally nightmarish – that feeling of uselessly exerting oneself to the utmost. The first climb begins at Pearson and those eleven miles to the pass took three and a half hours. But almost always the Karoo provides compensations. Like this morning's sombre dawn of heart-stopping beauty above infinitely varied mountain crests – flat-topped or sharply peaked, smoothly curved or serrated. In a sky of low torn clouds Light and Darkness battled as the rising sun thrust pale-golden spears into the gloom – briefly dispelling it, creating a luminous lake of pearly cloud – then being defeated by heavy masses of blackness.

As I struggled slowly upwards an old red-roofed homestead was visible in the sheer-sided valley on my left, below a wall of naked wrinkled grey-brown rock. Long white clouds went drifting and coiling through that valley and between the complex of ridges on my right. Those clouds seemed substantial and animated, each separate, going its own way – at first level with the track, then below it as I approached the pass.

In fact this is not a true pass: there is no matching descent. Ahead lay many miles of chaotically broken terrain, uninhabited and overlooked from both sides by long sheer ridges, their lower slopes olive green, their crowns of fluted silver granite. Vast expanses of coarse grassland were separated by narrow shallow valleys where strange dwarf trees lined stony watercourses. The sun never shone yet under a metallic sky the light was clear, the colours vivid. And the air was very cold, too cold for me to sit while chewing my lunch of spicy ostrich biltong.

The thickness and stickiness of the sludge compelled me to walk for hours down a gradual descent to the wide valley of the Little Fish River, which rises nearby and was in flood. Here the track turned west and the full force of the headwind gave me that irrationally self-pitying feeling of being *personally* attacked. Crossing a lowish though steep pass at 3.30, I assumed it to be the second marked on the map. Not so. By 4.30 our track could be seen soaring straight up a massive mountain that from my exhausted perspective looked like Everest. And I mean soaring straight up – these farmers' tracks eschew wimpish hairpin bends. Fervently I hoped for a farm entrance, then rejoiced to see a herd of Angoras.

Not long after, their owner drove onto the track and rescued me. The notion that human beings have guardian angels perhaps arose, over the centuries, because of such coincidences; had I been five minutes later, I would have missed Mr Hofmeyr. And his entrance is unmarked and his homestead invisible.

At once I warmed to Mr Hofmeyr; unlike most South Africans, he didn't see my form of transport as a symptom of mental illness. In his distant youth he and his brother, when boarders at a Cradock school, cycled home on Saturday evenings and back to town on Monday mornings – 'Unless it was snowing, we often get snow here, it's coming tonight.'

As we crawled up the perpendicular mountainside Mr Hofmeyr remarked, 'A bakkie couldn't do this, we have to run a Land Cruiser.' He calculates that when opposed by the local gales a vehicle uses 25 per cent more fuel than normal. Therefore, he deduced, I must have used 25 per cent more energy today. Allowing for the sludge, I would have reckoned 50 per cent more . . .

Mr Hofmeyr – 'We're fourth generation here' – loves his region as I love West Waterford. His Coloured workers are 'loyal and dependable, not infected by Communism' and whatever the future may hold he feels he can continue to trust them. In Cradock, however, life is not so simple any more. There 'the blacks are intimidating our people and offering phantom bribes' – promises of land after the elections if they vote ANC. 'And you must understand,' said Mr Hofmeyr, 'they couldn't use land productively, they need someone to give them orders.'

By Karoo standards Cradock is quite large, occupying high ground above the gorge of the Great Fish River. Like so many South African towns, it began as a military post and was still a village when Paul Kruger lived here before taking off, aged 12, on the Great Trek. As we approached the centre I seemed to be hallucinating: St Martin-in-the-Fields stood ahead. Mr Hofmeyr explained – this replica was built to cheer up the homesick wife of a British governor. He then pointed out the carefully restored tuinhuisies, Cradock's main tourist attraction, and advised me to stay in one. These were used when Boers converged on a dorp from faraway farms, for the quarterly Holy Communion service, arriving in ox-wagons laden with goodies for parties – this being a great social as well as religious event. By the beginning of the nineteenth century many Boers owned enormous cattle-herds and contemporary travellers noted the towers of dung in front of each farmhouse door – a boastful display, indicating the size of their scattered herds.

The smallest and cheapest town house (self-catering) is excellent value at R50. All the living-room and bedroom furniture is 'authentic' and several ancestors keep me under surveillance: sour female faces with compressed lips, unyielding bearded male faces with watchful eyes. Can they really have been as humourless as they look? I fear the answer is yes. Similar faces are not uncommon among their descendants.

The same, 20 July

Here I am appreciating how apolitically relaxed were all those little Klein Karoo dorplets. It seems Cradock has been unrelaxed since June '85 when Matthew Goniwe, aged 38, and three other ANC activists disappeared. Eventually their mutilated and charred bodies were found in the bush near Port Elizabeth. Last March, documentary evidence from police files confirmed what every black already believed: SAP officers had ordered the 'permanent removal from society' of those four young men. This crime, like the killings of Steve Biko and Chris Hani, deprived the new South Africa of a gifted political leader. And it left Cradock's black community doubly devastated, grieving over their loss of an inspired school principal whose matric pupils habitually achieved As and Bs in maths and science.

Early this morning I set out to visit the graves of the four in the Lingelihle township cemetery. But an ANC community leader, met on the way, turned me back. 'Mama, take care! Anger is too hot here after Hani. This township is big, 13,000, impossible for us to control – and with many factions! Two weeks ago PAC kids burned a bread-van, though their own families need bread! Why? A white owns the bakery! Last week a good friend of ours was attacked, a white guy detained and tortured in the '80s for helping us. He often visits and drove in to look for his plumber. They stoned his car to bits, all the windows smashed, sixteen gashes on his face. Before Hani, I would have introduced you to Matthew's family – and maybe in the future? Come back after the election!'

In 1775 the Great Fish River was proclaimed the eastern border of the Dutch East India Company's territory. Beyond lay 'Kaffirland' and it took the whites, reinforced by Coloured and Khoikhoi recruits, another century to vanquish the Xhosa and totally destroy their well-regulated society. Yet none of the nine Kaffir Wars (1779–1878) damaged the Xhosa as much as their self-inflicted Cattle-Killing Movement (1856–7) and the resultant famine. This extraordinary phenomenon was for long attributed to 'native ignorance, superstition, and hysteria'. Now we know, thanks to J. B. Peires's researches, that it emerged from the complex responses of a war-demoralized population to infectious cattle lung sickness.

One of the saddest chapters in Africa's colonial history was written here in the Eastern Cape though few South Africans know the true story. While nosing through Cradock's library this morning I came upon a typical South African history book, *The Story of the British Settlers of 1820*, published in Cape Town in 1957. The author, Harold Hockly – a Settler's great-grandson – gives the Authorized Version:

> The most formidable native tribes to oppose the onward march of the Europeans were the Kaffirs, a branch of the mighty Bantu race which was slowly advancing south-wards down the eastern side of Africa. These people were barbarous savages whose lives were ruled by ignorance, cruelty and superstition, the stock-in-trade of clever witch-doctors.

Even now many believe that as whites were moving up from the Cape, blacks were moving down and the two groups met hereabouts. This is an important white myth – both groups on the move, each equally entitled to whatever could be conquered by force of arms. However, pottery used by the Bantu in the seventh and eighth centuries has been found near East London. And by the end of the sixteenth century the ancestors of the present-day Xhosa-speaking peoples, with their vast cattle-herds, were long established in 'Kaffirland' – from where, around 1700, they began to expand into territory later coveted by the trekboers. Incidentally, the 'barbarous savages' killed only men, despite white families being often at their mercy, and despite the provocation of both Boers and British regularly slaughtering Xhosa women and children.

Cradock's Great Fish River museum is strong on local history, social, military and political. A caption under a portrait of Lieutenant-General Sir John Cra-dock, Governor of the Cape Colony, noted his popularity among both white communities. We can only guess how he was viewed by the Khoikhoi when he decreed, in 1812, that all Khoi children maintained to the age of 8 by their parents' masters must be 'apprenticed' to those masters for the next ten years. Whole families were thus reduced to serfdom for long periods while successive children grew up. Already the Khoikhoi had been deprived of their land and their right to possess land. And the first Pass Laws, promulgated by the Earl of Caledon in 1809, tied them to a 'fixed place of abode' – their masters' farms.

The museum's curator, a middle-aged Afrikaner woman, needed no prod-ding. 'You're the first overseas visitor this year and I don't blame them. Our country is doomed. Cradock's been suffering for years past, we know what to expect. In '85 they burned down the Family Planning Clinic, wanted more "soldiers for the freedom struggle", wouldn't let their women use contraceptives. Then they burned our garden-huts in our veg plots by the river. And now all our store managers must hire ANC blacks or they'll be boycotted. A Coloured working for the council had his store burned in May. Even my husband's been threatened. He runs the petrol station, stops people on foot using the toilets – they make such a mess, they're not used to our toilets, the place must be clean for motorists. So in April they petrol-bombed it and if the pumps blew up everyone would be dead.' Neither the '86 murders nor the Hani assassination were linked by the curator to any of this violence. An uninformed tourist would be left with the impression that 'they' are prone to mindless eruptions of anti-white hatred.

Then for the umpteenth time I heard about the legendary ANC leaders who are collecting R10 monthly from their followers, this payment guaranteeing possession of a white's house, fully furnished, the day after the elections. An elaboration on this theme describes 'madam' finding her maid measuring the windows for the curtains she plans to hang after the change of ownership. Other legendary creatures are the countless maids who ask their madams, 'When did the government give you that TV?' Indignantly, madam explains that whites have to work hard to earn money to buy their TVs. Whereupon her maid insists an ANC leader has revealed that whites get free TV sets, a privilege soon to be transferred to blacks.

While the curator made coffee in a back room I studied a wall-map of the Zuurveld (1820–35), naming the various Settler families and showing the exact positions of their allocated farms. (They have awarded themselves a capital S.) The year 1820 saw the planting along this border of some 5,000 British Settlers whose emigration had been officially encouraged to stiffen white resistance to the 'Kaffirs'. This scheme, half-baked in a Whitehall oven by civil servants ignorant of local conditions, soon fell apart. Most of those innocent pawns – from every social class, many immigrating en famille – were ill-equipped, both mentally and materially, to survive in untamed bush infested with wild animals. At first they suffered much hardship. Families were given 100-acre quit-rent farms (the average Boer farm was then 4,000 acres) though the majority knew nothing about farming. And slavery, the secret of the Boers' economic success, was forbidden. Within three years most had moved to the embryonic towns, including Cradock, where they prospered as artisans and traders – and, in later generations, as professionals. The rest extended their acreage, set about breeding merinos and founded a woollen industry that still flourishes, merinos now augmented by Angora goats. Would a cross-section of contemporary British society, confronted with an equivalent of the virgin Zuurveld, cope as successfully as the Settlers did? I doubt it. No wonder their descendants are so keen to let one know 'We came in 1820'.

A significant gulf existed between the barely literate Boers and the Settlers – fresh from a country where a new political breed had recently emerged, resonating to America's Declaration of Rights. British demands for administrative reforms upset the Boers and provided one of several motives for the Great Trek. Yet the Settlers' liberal campaigning was never on behalf of non-whites – with the exception of a few derided individuals. Similarly, seventy years later, Gandhi campaigned exclusively for the benefit of his fellow-Indians, urging them to fight with the British against the Zulus in a shameful punishment exercise – too unequal to be called a 'war' – that left 3,500 Zulus dead. This image-denting fact has now been discreetly forgotten as new statues of the Mahatma pop up all over the country commemorating him as a champion of 'human rights'.

To the white stranger, Cradock is warmly welcoming and outside the Olive Schreiner House Mrs S—, an Afrikaner high-school teacher in her forties, spontaneously invited me to supper. She lives in what was the family tuinhuis, built in 1845 and furnished from the farmhouse, now sold. The small sitting room is made to seem even smaller by two tallboys, three long carved chests and a burnished copper vat for distilling home-made spirits – alas! no longer in use. We sat sipping sherry by a window overlooking an avocado-shaded lawn, across which strutted several rare-breed bantams – red, green and gold – wearing pantaloons and ankle socks. Then Mrs S—'s second sherry undammed a flood of 'urban legends'.

After the elections mobs will surge out of the townships, looting and killing and burning homes. Blacks are being told that once Mandela is in power they will be entitled to steal white property; no one will oppose them. All guns and vehicles will be stolen, leaving whites unable either to defend themselves or escape. Maids are being incited by ANC leaders to kill each other's madams, but not their own. (Whoever is conducting this campaign must realize that no madam could believe in her own maid's capacity for homicide, whereas an unknown black is believed to be capable of anything.) When I queried the source of these legends Mrs S— admitted there might be some *slight* exaggeration – 'But there's no smoke without fire!' Whatever else may happen, she is convinced rampaging blacks will reduce Cradock to a smouldering ruin. Yet, in all other respects, she seems a perfectly sensible, intelligent woman. It is impossible to imagine her equivalent, in any European country, being so destabilized by such scaremongering. And destabilized she is, her fear real enough to be almost infectious.

Today I have directly benefited from another urban legend, one of the few to produce a measurable result. Oranges are being sold in all Cradock's shops at R1 (20p) for bags of forty. Why? Because of a countrywide rumour that many oranges have been injected or sprayed with HIV-positive blood. Either an AWB member has injected oranges with his labourers' infected blood, or a right-wing Natal farmer has sprayed his orange crop with his own infected blood. (Anyone who imagines that South Africa is not a lunatic asylum writ large is quite wrong.) Since mid-June this belief has been sweeping the county, reducing orange-farmers to tears. It is said to have emanated from around Port Elizabeth, where someone chanced to buy a bag of blood oranges. By now it has so seriously damaged the nation's citrus industry that an emergency press conference was called yesterday in Jo'burg to explain that blood oranges occur naturally, though they amount to less than 1 per cent of South Africa's annual crop. Said Jasper Coetzee, Outspan International's marketing manager, 'Now we hope the story will die a natural death.' Perhaps it will, but how soon before some other equally preposterous belief replaces it?

An Angora farm on the Veld, 21 July

This morning my departure was delayed by Lear's need for a new back tyre.

Cradock's large cycle shop stocks scores of sturdy no-frills bicycles imported from Taiwan for the farmworker market; given the extent of Karoo holdings, it pays a farmer to use mounted labour. The young cycle merchant is one of four graduate brothers who have failed to find 'degree jobs' but are doing quite well as traders in their hometown. However, being mainly dependent on non-white custom they are vulnerable to the increasingly frequent ANC boycotts which have made the nearby dorp of Hofmeyr a 'ghost town'. My informant, though reticent about the root cause of Hofmeyr's conflict, gave graphic details to illustrate 'how intimidation works'. One poor lady who defied the boycott was set upon by 'township savages' and forced to drink a bottle of detergent which killed her. These 'savages' are marvellously mobile; I have heard about them in dorps all over South Africa. Invariably they do their dastardly deeds in another dorp, never where you happen to be, within reach of the poor lady's grieving family.

This region is enduring its third drought-stricken year – the dams shrunken to muddy pools, the stream-beds baked hard, even the bore-hole supplies threatened and many of the stock moved elsewhere if their owners have suitable contacts.

I was halfway to Tarkastad, freewheeling between high cliffs, layered red-brown, when Bernie overtook me. I had noticed his farm entrance (only the second since leaving Cradock) a mile back: 'Bernard & Virginia Viddicombe in their Villa-on-the-Veld'. Bernard is an impulsive, outgoing character; soon he had deflected me from Tarkastad to the villa. He was going to fetch a bakkie-load of shearers but would soon be back. Virry is visiting the children in their Port Elizabeth school but the maid would provide beer.

A five-mile 'private road' – thick dust, big loose stones, deep ruts – crosses undulating pale brown veld, now supporting only thornbush and karee trees. On either side, in the middle distance, stretch rocky ridges. Far ahead, lavender blue against a cloudless sky, rise rounded, smooth-crested mountains. Once, the track dipped to cross a narrow river-bed paved with long slabs of light grey rock, flood-polished. Occasionally I glimpsed Angoras, standing on their hind-legs to reach the few remaining leaves.

The villa looks incongruously urban. In 1950 Bernie's father demolished a dignified old farmhouse and replaced it with this high-roofed bungalow, the size of a small factory, overlooking a fifty-metre swimming pool glinting between a tennis court and a bowling green. 'We came in 1820', from Yorkshire. In the 1860s great-grandfather, starting as a magistrate in Grahamstown, gradually accumulated vast tracts of land. Bernie and his four brothers now farm about 8,000 hectares each, in various parts of Natal and the north-eastern Cape.

Nearby – nearer than is usual, within sight of the villa – are six workers' cottages, small but solid, of whitewashed breeze-block. Father started a farm school for the Xhosa workers' children, now attended by children from two other farms. 'But why do I keep it going?' wondered Bernie. 'It's a farce, pretending they can learn like white kids.'

At present Bernie feels he has his economic back to the wall. In 1989 the Angora-wool price dropped from R22 to R8 per kilo. And now the drought... Most of his stock are with a brother in comparatively lush Natal, the remaining few hundred were being sheared this afternoon, in a huge shed, by Pondos who have 'got stroppy about pay since that fella was let loose'. Never have I witnessed such bloody shearing; those Pondos wouldn't be allowed near an Irish sheep. Yet Bernie took all the nasty nicks for granted.

Tarkastad, 22 July

Decadence set in last evening, as I was about to retire. The villa's long, over-furnished drawing room is redeemed by a handsome manorial stone fireplace where the Coloured maid lit a log fire while the Xhosa 'boy' was stocking the refrigerator at the bar end of the room, complete with counter, stools and spirit-laden shelves. Evidently Bernie expected me to tell Travellers' Tales for my supper.

On South African beer inebriation is not easily achieved but at 2 a.m. – or so – I wobbled en route to my room.

Three hours later was compulsory getting-up time; before leaving for Port Elizabeth at 5 a.m., Bernie had to co-ordinate the villa's ingenious security systems. Aroused from a drunken stupor, I was shattered by my first South African hangover. While walking to the road, in dissipating darkness, each stumble over a stone or rut sent another set of white-hot needles through my head. I reached the entrance as the first glimmer of dawn, touching the long white thorns on the leafless bushes, created an illusion of hoar frost.

Every mile of the twenty-five to Tarkastad felt like one hundred. Each slight incline felt like an Andean pass. The wages of sin is debility... Arriving in this congenial hotel at 9.30 a.m. I fell onto my bed and slept for six hours.

Tarkastad has the usual wide streets – some untarred – a few stores currently badly hit by ANC boycotts, an English-village-style war memorial and, decorating one corner, a battered little cannon captured in East Africa by some local heroes during the First World War. The white natives number less than 900; many are retired urban couples or elderly Wenwes drawn by low house prices. A 'nice home' may still be bought for R10,000–15,000.

The Royal Hotel (c. 1890) is long and low, freshly painted white and grass-green, its many windows flanked by outside shutters in the Cape Dutch style, its deep pillared stoep a mini-museum of obsolete agricultural implements. Last year it was taken over by English-speaking Jill and Hugh (Jo'burg-bred) who describe themselves as 'refugees from the rat-race and pollution and violence'. Said Jill, 'We liked Tarkastad's clear air and tranquillity – nobody warned us about the local farmers! You'd think they owned the town *and* the hotel! They know they underpin the local economy, there's nothing else. Some weekends they get mad drunk, breaking the place up, shooting at the ceilings, throwing wads of money on the floor to pay for the damage – then reeling off shouting for their wives to drive them home. They're like naughty nasty children – not normal. Cheap labour and subsidies spoiled them long ago. I'll not weep if the blacks get bits of their farms.'

The same, 23 July

On impulse, this morning, I decided to visit Zola, Tarkastad's township (population about 7,000) and en route I passed the Coloured location (population about 700) where the two-storeyed homes of affluent traders are conspicuous among a cluster of tiny red-brick cottages. It is extraordinarily difficult to imagine a spatially desegregated South Africa.

In 1962 Tarkastad's blacks were moved from a site close to the dorp, where they had been allowed free grazing near their shacks. Since then they have had to lease grazing for which, by now, they are paying R10 per animal monthly to a white farmer. I observed that the several groups of Zola folk walking into town looked not particularly well disposed towards Whitey.

A long steep ridge – its flanks of naked brown earth, its crest of fluted grey rock – hides hundreds of shacks and quite a few small bungalows, scattered over the stony dusty veld. In summer Zola must be hellish; even today I sweated under a cloudless sky.

At the end of the two-mile rough-track approach road stands one of those outwardly impressive new secondary schools – securely fenced, its high metal gate kept locked after school hours. The security guard, his weapon discreetly holstered under a padded anorak, advised me to seek out Mr M—, a retired plumber and community leader who knows all about Zola's needs and woes.

Mr M— lives in a modestly comfortable little bungalow, complete with bathroom and wc in expectation of piped water arriving one day – perhaps soon after the elections? He despairs of Zola's youngsters. 'If they attend church it's only to smash up the place, they've vandalized two churches here.' His wife, a retired nurse, added that stock theft flourishes, mainly sheep and goats for lack of the means to organize cattle-rustling.

Recently Mr M— endured 'just the most terrifying ordeal'. A Port Elizabeth NGO, funded from overseas, set up a food programme for Zola's poorest families and R43,000 were banked in Queenstown to be administered by Mr M— in his capacity as a community leader. A fortnight later 'four thugs' threatened to torch his bungalow unless he immediately handed over this money to be divided between all Zola's residents. They forced him to drive to the bank and deliver the cash in ten-rand notes. 'And if I'd resisted I'd be homeless now. The police don't care what happens out here, we're left at the mercy of tsotsies!'

An hour later, in a shack on the far side of Zola, I was hearing a startlingly different version of this story from Hamlet, a youngish unemployed car mechanic. Mr M—, he was convinced, had staged this 'terrifying ordeal', paying the 'four thugs' some small sum and transferring the rest to his own account. Those youths were not Zola residents and no one knows where they came from.

Hamlet appointed himself my minder – 'It's not good for you to walk around alone' – and introduced me to an ANC Youth League leader who observed that Mr M— was an excellent plumber in his day but has now 'gone odd'. Since 1984, the M—s have been running Zola's taxi service and allegedly Mr M— promotes local boycotts for personal gain. When Tarkastad's shops are out of bounds, taxis must be used for the eighty-mile round trip to Queenstown, the ANC paying the fares of the boycotters who themselves could not possibly afford this journey. The latest boycott, to force the town council to provide Zola with a post office and improved services (electricity, water, sewerage), came to nothing because the ANC Youth League, as part of their feud with Mr M—, called it off.

I asked Hamlet and his wife Becca, an unqualified teacher, what would happen now if black families could afford to move into 'white' Tarkastad. Becca laughed and replied that she for one wouldn't want to move because there would be no neighbourly feeling, only silent nods – if that – when she emerged from her home. 'We live in different ways. White people like to rest in the afternoon and they say our kids playing and singing and shouting disturb them. We only want our own areas improved, brought up to white standards, we don't want to live among them.'

Zola's nursery school, subsidized by an overseas NGO, is adequately housed but inadequately staffed; two untrained women look after forty 3- to 6-year-olds, warmly clad in donated garments. Western swings, climbing frames and round-abouts amply furnish its spacious playground. (At least space is not lacking in Zola.) As usual, the foreign visitor triggered pleas for 'more funding from your country'. South Africa's 'dependency culture' has put down deep roots; in Cape Town I noticed how much this worries responsible ANC leaders.

At the secondary school surprisingly few pupils were dispersing as I arrived. The principal, from Lingelihe, is a youngish Wits graduate – tall, handsome, elegantly dressed, eloquent. 'I'm battling here,' said Mr K—. 'Battling with frustration, almost despair. How can I motivate my staff when the kids are unmotivated? We've rarely more than a 50 per cent attendance. On Monday this lot don't turn up, on Tuesday another lot is missing, on Wednesday maybe only one-third appear. They don't believe in learning. But they do believe in "education" ' – his forefingers supplied the quotes. 'They expect to pass matric as a human right and then get degrees and good jobs. I can't go on much longer, we're not earning our salaries, we're only pretending to run a school. I'm not picking on Zola, it's only average nowadays. OK, black education was always underfunded. But even on our poor resources, look what Matthew Goniwe achieved. He taught me for a year, then became my model. Coming here two years ago I thought I could revive the culture of learning, I was all enthusiasm – or was it conceit? Many parents support me but they're scared of their own kids. What's going to turn it round? The elections, Mandela for President? I don't believe so. Mrs Tambo says we mustn't talk about the Lost Generation, we mustn't give up on them. In principle I agree, that's why I'm here. But they've given up on themselves – though we've talent in Zola, no shortage of degree material. But too many kids are too destabilized to use their brains. My mother says I should make more allowances, they're victims of the Struggle. Is she right? She's a wise woman – and teaching herself since before I was born! Only now something tells me to be hard on them. We're into a new struggle. But of course the old Freedom Struggle appealed more – defiance, aggro, justifiable law-breaking. Marches, rallies, funerals – all action and suspense and excitement. The new struggle needs discipline, routine, hard work – boring! So now we must concentrate on the little ones, make sure they don't get infected...'

As Mr K— unlocked the gate he said, 'Thanks for listening' – and suddenly there were tears in his eyes. I walked away loaded with his distress.

Tarkastad's residental area has flower-beds in mid-road and handsome Cape Dutch bungalows and one gracious colonial two-storeyed house – Irish Geor-gian but for a long porch, its white trellis-work of delicate wrought iron. Here I passed a score of black youngsters wearing the Zola school uniform and noisily having fun – recalling Becca's comments. Their game would have puzzled any onlooker unaware of the 'AIDS infection' legend; oranges were being thrown, juggled with, kicked to and fro.

The new South Africa allows the destitute to see how the rich live, a privilege previously enjoyed only by those in Whitey's employ. All day, blacks of all ages hang about Tarkastad's streets: strolling to and fro, standing around corners, sitting on kerbs and steps – for whites a disconcerting phenomenon. When the jobless were invisible you could forget about them; now, as they wander all over the place, impatiently awaiting a black government, the sense of expectation is palpable. And the whites react as to an invasion by hostile forces, a feeling heightened in boycott-afflicted dorps like Tarkastad where white livelihoods are already at risk.

Dordrecht, 24 July

Normally hotels are deserted at dawn. This morning, however, the Royal Hotel was all bustle as I wheeled Lear from my room. People hurried to and fro bearing jugs of coffee, plates of sandwiches, six-packs, bottles of brandy. From the kitchen came the smell and sound of sizzling boerewors. TV sets blared in every corner. The lounge was crowded, mostly with men and boys – the latter waving small South African flags. Obtusely I asked, 'What's going on?' Everyone stared incredulously at the zombie. How come I didn't know the Springboks were playing in Australia at 6.30? Didn't I want to watch? Quickly I thought of a plausible excuse for not watching; it had to be plausible, the Afrikaners are sensitive about their rugger team – about rugger as a quasi-religious rite.

During the forenoon a traffic-free gravel road took me past three distant farmsteads, their dams glinting beside small patches of green, their cattle and sheep grazing level miles of golden-brown grassland. On low but steep koppies, round red boulders were set amidst euphorbia, aloes and thornbush. Many aloes are in bloom, looking from afar like motionless flames burning in grotesque candelabra of long pointed leaves – leaves grey-green and fleshy, their edges spiked. Like so many Karoo plants, aloes are multi-purpose. By retaining both soil and water they deter erosion. Their dried sap is used as a purgative, and to alleviate toothache and rheumatism. Their burned leaves, added to snuff, give it that little extra. The nectar held in abundance by the flowers is a narcotic to which both children and baboons become addicted, sometimes to their detriment: an overdose can cause paralysis.

By noon uninhabited mountains surrounded me, their shapes fantastical, their colours – under a cloudless sky – varying from violet to powder blue to pinkish-grey to royal blue. Higher and higher I climbed, the silence broken only by bird-calls, through the Stormberg's ranges of flat-topped or 'pudding' mountains, sometimes overlooking deep brown valleys below long silver-crested ridges.

Coming to a crossroads, unmarked on the map, ancient signposts set at indeterminate angles confused me. Then, as I sat undecidedly chewing biltong, the day's only vehicle approached. It was driven by a lone woman who, when I tried to stop her, smiled nervously and accelerated. At 6,000 feet the wind felt icy and I could sit around no longer. Luckily my guess was right; soon we had joined a tarred road five miles from here. Freewheeling through the dusk I could see the township's supper-fires scattered like rubies on a wide mountainside opposite the dorp.

Dordrecht's enormous Highveld Hotel – a superb balconied building (1892) – proves this dorp's past prosperity. Now its location on the Transkei 'border' has made it a backwater and the hotel's interior is agreeably shabby. Less agreeable this evening was the bar, smelling of vomit and overcrowded with young men who had been drinking non-stop for twelve hours, drowning their sorrow. (The Springboks lost by one point.) At first these louts mistook me for a man and shouted remarks like, 'We don't want fuckin' beggars on bikes!' When this misapprehension had been corrected they tried to maul me: 'So it's a woman, find her tits!' I bought two six-packs (tomorrow is the Sabbath) and retreated to my room.

Elliot, 25 July

Today's gravel road, along the Transkei 'border', often overlooked the 'independent homeland's' densely populated, arid hillsides – while all around me the land was populated only by sheep. These flocks occupy a magically beautiful region: miles and miles of tall grass, shimmering in the wind, some expanses a rich auburn, others pinkish-gold or purple-tinged. And beyond the nearby low ridges rise high mountains, range after range, their slopes and peaks tinted an improbable variety of pastel shades.

Midway a bakkie stopped beside me, with three 'boys' in the back. The driver got out to express his concern – was I going into the Transkei? If so, I shouldn't. My plans must be changed, whatever the inconvenience. We talked for some fifteen minutes, then he drove on.

As the bakkie disappeared, I realized something deeply disturbing. I hadn't reacted to the three men in the back though they had reacted to me – leaning curiously over the side, trying to follow the conversation. Talking to my fellow-white, I had ignored them. They weren't there, or only there as the bakkie was. I had behaved like a white South African. Have I picked up the apartheid virus? Now I'm trying to analyse that incident, transposing it to Europe. If a vehicle stops in Ireland and the driver engages me in conversation, do I interact with his unknown passengers who are not directly involved? Maybe I don't, if I'm concentrating on the topic under discussion. But were the Irish passengers interested in what was being said, is it conceivable that I *wouldn't register* their presence? No, that is not conceivable. South Africa is corrupting me; during that conversation I was the driver's accomplice in excluding fellow-humans with a natural interest in what was going on. How has this happened? This is not *me* – yet it was me, then and there. Are there excuses, if one digs deep enough? Not really. Only the feeble excuse of adapting to the local mores out of supine politeness; had I drawn the 'boys' into our argument, their *baas* would have been both outraged and bewildered. He was that sort ('those Transkei kaffirs are treacherous') though his stopping to advise me had been prompted by genuine kindness. But too often such kindness is labelled 'Whites Only'.

Elliot stands at 4,500 feet in the as yet 'undeveloped' foothills of the Drakensberg. On the outskirts I saw two gigantic SADF armoured vehicles slowly rumbling towards the 'border' a few miles away. In this apparently tranquil and sedately attractive dorp they looked both sinister and absurd.

When the Hurters, from Pretoria, bought the Stanford Hotel (Jim had just retired from 'the Bantu Department') they seemingly got a bargain. Traditionally commercial travellers used to base themselves here, then go into the Transkei on day trips. (Whites were forbidden to stay overnight in black areas.) But now both tourists and 'reps' keep well clear of Elliot. As so often happens in these dorps, I am the only guest and was invited to share (no charge) the Hurters' evening meal, eaten around the TV set in a large dismal lounge. This hospitality is touching; one could forgive these hard-hit hoteliers for overcharging their rare guests. But then, most of them are not 'professionals'. It's odd, how many elderly couples have recently bought rural hotels on retiring from urban jobs. Perhaps it shows faith in the new South Africa's tourist appeal, post-elections.

10

Surplus People

Maclear – Matatiele – Pietermaritzburg – Johannesburg – Home

Some people plead that the right to own land should be granted to Bantu living in White areas...If these concessions are granted such a population will not be satisfied with social rights only, but will certainly insist on the franchise and make further demands...My department would view the alienation of White land as a nail in the coffin of the White nation and of the fundamental principle of apartheid. We shall therefore be only too glad to assist those Bantu who are interested in buying land in towns in their respective homelands.

I. P. van Onselen, Secretary for Bantu Administration and Development (1972)

Maclear, 26 July 1993

When Jim switched on the TV news this morning we saw a bloodstained church floor strewn with blanket-covered bodies. It is assumed APLA killed those eleven people, and grievously maimed many more, in last evening's gun and grenade attack on Kenilworth church in Cape Town. The Hurters exclaimed that only blacks would slaughter people at prayer, within a church building, but I had to contradict them. Northern Ireland has endured an identical atrocity in a rural church in Armagh.

Over the forty-five mountainous miles from Elliot to Maclear a formidable gale blew either against or across me. Here all the telephone lines being down has closed both banks – most improbably there are two – and I must live on credit in this friendly no-star hotel where the last guest checked out sixteen days ago.

Maclear is a dispirited little place. One can't buy cheese, butter, yoghurt, amasi, even sardines – or a daily newspaper in any language. The Jo'burg *Sunday Times* arrives on Wednesdays, the bread is stale and black/white relations are extremely uneasy. In part, this has to do with the township's grazing land having been seized only a few years ago for yet another commercial forestry plantation. (Approaching Maclear, one sees a landscape devastated by this development.) However, some local blacks supported the seizure; South African Paper and Pulp Industries (SAPPI) gave much desperately needed employment while the land was being cleared and planted. But now fewer jobs are available and the grazing is gone for ever – or until such time as there is a revolution more radical than anything envisaged by the ANC.

Tonight the hotel business is booming; I have three fellow-guests – two Xhosas and an Afrikaner – all employees of a cane-spirit company. (One of the favourite township drinks: cheap and nasty.) Here is affirmative action in practice, the white rep training blacks in a dorp ladies bar. An interesting tableau, the English-speaking regulars being carefully polite, the blacks ill-at-ease behind an over-jolly façade. One farmer has just returned from his first journey overseas, a visit to cousins in Wales. South Africans, he assured us, don't know what *real* apartheid is – they should see how things are between the English and the Welsh! He saw it for himself when an Englishman entered a pub and everyone spoke Welsh to exclude him – how's that for racism? The blacks registered shock/horror and agreed no such thing could ever happen in South Africa.

The same, 27 July

Sheer 1,000-foot table-tops almost completely surround Maclear and on one is concealed the township. When I climbed up this morning, invited by Mrs Ntloko who runs the clinic, I found an extremity of destitution that makes Zola seem affluent. Mrs Ntloko introduced me to several men who, having found their first job on the forestry project and become accustomed to earning, are now again unwaged and seething with anger; recently they had to sell their cattle for lack of grazing. Equally angry are the hundreds of ex-miners, sacked during the past few years from worked-out Rand gold mines. This community, like countless others, was dependent for generations on miners' wages. But South Africa never ceases to surprise. Even the angriest of the men apologized to me, as a white, for the Kenilworth slaughter. 'We are very sorry, that was bad, we don't like it.'

At noon the bank opened but no cash was available until 3.30. The manager tried hard to put me off the Transkei. 'They'll steal your bike in Mount Fletcher! And that track is so rough you'll be days getting there. Why not let me give you a lift back to Elliot? You could go on to Jo'burg through the Free State.'

Tomorrow I mean to take the sort of precautions that always make me feel silly. Normally my journal travels in a pannier-bag, my camera around my waist and the binoculars over a shoulder. While in the Transkei I'll carry my journal over a shoulder (under my shirt) and the camera and binoculars in a pannier-bag. This apprehension is uncharacteristic but Maclear's blacks are – it has to be admitted – slightly unsettling.

In the bar this evening a young man put on the Mandela turn, a popular entertainment. From under the counter came one of those shockingly realistic rubber masks that cover the whole head, not just the face. These are repulsively clever caricatures, the unmistakable Mandela features modified to present a monkey-man. The wearers mockingly mimic Mr Mandela's voice, making Winnie-related speeches which provoke guffaws of ribald laughter, or putting PAC and APLA slogans into the mouth of their President-to-be. Among the white hoi polloi no distinction is drawn between the ANC and the PAC, a symptom of their uninterest in their own country's political evolution.

Mount Fletcher, 28 July

This is being written under the influence of drink. A lot of drink, consequent upon the locals' determination fittingly to celebrate the arrival of a *white tourist*! It's unlikely they'll shoot me hereabouts: alcohol poisoning is the main hazard. I can't imagine what the potation is (not any form of beer) – it comes out of a ginormous tin kettle and my liver will take weeks to recover. When I arrived, free-wheeling down the steep main street, the whole town came to a halt. Stopping at the bottle-store, I was at once surrounded by ten or twelve grim-faced young Comrades. (By now I can tell a Comrade at a glance; they have a persona all their own.) But quarter of an hour later everyone was smiling and I had been persuaded to spend two nights here.

The same, 29 July

The above entry was curtailed by the contents of that kettle.

Yesterday's thirty-seven miles were the most exhausting – and among the most beautiful – of this whole journey. First, a very steep two-mile climb from Maclear to a wide plateau where the sun rose over a distant range of strangely peaked mountains, the peaks all leaning sideways as though pushed out of shape. In that slanting light and clear air each colour was vibrant: the red-gold of grassy slopes, the dark yet glowing green of trees marking watercourses, the brown-gold of maize fields.

Over the next eight miles I met no one. Then from the plateau's edge appeared the Transkei beyond a deep valley: countless tiny dwellings on barren hillsides. The Halcyon Drift 'border' post was manned by two white soldiers, three black police officers and an Alsatian tethered to an armoured vehicle. The white cyclist enraged this creature; he literally foamed at the mouth and almost broke his chain in a frenzied effort to get at me. One soldier glanced at my passport, handed it back, then asked my nationality. His mate described as 'suicidal' my entering the Transkei unarmed.

Slowly I pushed Lear out of the valley on one of the worst roads I have ever endured. Here a truckload of Mount Fletcher folk, who had stopped to pee, gave me a heart-warming welcome, counteracting the recent build-up of 'Transkei tension'. Immediately I knew this was going to be a happy experience, a feeling reinforced when Joel joined me, full of curiosity and chat. Elsewhere in Africa such encounters occur daily, here they are very rare.

Joel, a 23-year-old road worker, wants to be a teacher but has had to take a menial job to feed the family: parents in poor health, an elder sister crippled by polio, plus a wife and two children. As we walked to the ridge-top he told me about his three cows whose calves were stillborn because of the drought. Drought-stricken white farmers receive government aid – more than R3 *billion* last year – but blacks must suffer their losses unaided.

As we passed a gigantic new earth-mover abandoned by the wayside, Joel mentioned a plan to tar this Maclear–Mount Fletcher road. When work began some months ago he was one of the team breaking rocks and scattering them on the surface as a foundation. But the money ran out; under Transkei's grotesquely corrupt puppet regime such crises are common. I had to walk the next twenty-five miles, dragging Lear over these large, loose, sharp fragments of mountain.

Although in white terminology Katkop is a 'village' it extends over several square miles (or rather, long miles) and here live uncounted thousands, far from water, without electricity, chronically short of firewood and grazing. About one-third of the dwellings are round thatched huts – the most skilful thatching I've seen since Cameroon – the rest are tiny oblong shacks, their tin roofs stone-anchored. Many are brightly painted – duck-egg green the favourite shade, but also lemon, pale pink, buff, sky blue. Some external walls are decorated with elaborate traditional designs in red, black, brown, white. Some minuscule windows wear incongruous suburban lace curtains tied back with pretty bows. Every few miles a tiny 'café' or huxter shop offers basic sustenance. The local litter consists almost entirely of plastic bags fluttering in the breeze on rusty wire fencing, itself a form of litter left over from the days when this land was white-owned.

Here the heights and depths are truly awesome. This is a red-rock landscape, deeply riven by irregular gorges below 2,000-foot precipices – a topographical chaos of visual splendour leaving little space for human habitation or cultivation. Yet in an emotionally muddled way I rejoiced to be in an area where some traces of 'normal' African life remain. Little herd-boys sat on high boulders guarding their pitifully small herds of cattle, others walked behind a flock of goats on a contour footpath, coloured blanket draped gracefully over a shoulder. Women were laundering blankets in scanty streams, then children carefully spread them to dry on tennis-court widths of smooth polished rock. Blanket-wrapped men rode small sturdy Basuto ponies up and down precipitous slopes – sitting straight-backed, their feet almost touching the ground. White South Africa's landscapes, however beautiful, remain memorials to apartheid – their unpeopled spaces cruel, black activity channelled towards the *baas*'s enrichment.

Beyond Katkop came a mysterious region of crumpled dark-grey rocks, uncannily resembling giant crocodiles or prehistoric monsters. Then we crossed a high pass, the gradient making my struggle to drag Lear over that surface like some medieval penance for the most heinous of sins. But my reward was a scene of the wildest splendour – the opposite mountain walls golden in the noon light, against an intensely blue sky. I half-regretted getting to the top, from where could be seen the next 'village', Lalangubo, very far below.

Four (mostly downhill) hours later Mount Fletcher appeared in a wide valley, bounded to east and west by long low ridges.

As the Comrades escorted me from the bottle-store to the Castle Rocks Hotel we were followed by excited children and adolescents, some exclaiming at my achievement (as well they might!) and shouting friendly questions. Unsurprisingly, no washing water was available until morning. Then Mr Nxesi – a one-eyed raggedly dressed elder who speaks near-perfect English – swept me off to his kraal of thatched huts on a distant hillside. There that potent kettle was produced and an impromptu party laid on for the 'brave lady from Ireland'. (Xhosa songs and dances – shades of Mafefe!)

Before the contents of the kettle took effect (a brief period: my tummy was very empty) we discussed regional politics. Said Mr Nxesi, 'Comrade Mandela isn't tough enough, he'll never control our robbers in Umtata [Transkei's capital]. Money is power. And our Mafia is numerous, thousands will fight to keep jobs and perks. Poverty isn't the worst thing the Bantustans did to us. The worst is corruption – *so* much money from Pretoria! Our leaders and their hangers-on are destroyed. Destroyed in their souls.'

I refrained from questioning Mr Nxesi about his fluent English, a question with the implied corollary, 'How come an educated man lives in such poverty?' But I had my suspicions confirmed today. He lost an eye, and his job, in a drunken brawl; not so long ago he was head of the English department in a black university. The kraal is his ancestral home; last year he had to sell a bungalow built in happier times. And his wife has left him. Sad...

The Castle Rocks Hotel – and Mount Fletcher in general – could be said to prove a white point. Once this was a typical small-town hotel, its two rows of bedrooms overlooking a wide lawn. Now everything is ramshackle. And the lavatory is inaccessible; one has to find the person with the key – and who is that? At any given moment, where is s/he to be found? When those questions prove unanswerable I use my mug as a jerry and tip it out the window, as did many London citizens in the seventeenth century to Pepys's distress. Here no distress is caused, only astonishment on the part of adjacent livestock: hens, geese, goats and a pathetically lean cow. I'm writing this with my room door open and a hen and ten fluffy chicks have just wandered in to hoover the floor – expecting, and finding, numerous crumbs left by the last occupant. In Mount

Fletcher, with fowl busily pecking around my bedroom floor and that cow scratching her neck against my windowsill, I feel more at ease than I ever could in a dorp hotel. Also, R30 covers the cost of supper, room and breakfast, for which one pays at least R130 in 'South Africa'.

In contrast to the dorps' crowded hotel bars, neither bar here is much used. Both are dingy, ill-lit, stale-smelling, their shelves almost bare, equipped only with three unsteady stools and two glasses (one each!). Most customers sit on the stoep's parapet, high above the main street where noisy geese, minute black piglets and another bony cow nibble and root in the short brown grass. The pavement slabs have long since been removed to serve some other purpose.

At present Mount Fletcher is sorely afflicted by political dissension, its ANC activists disunited. The Mafia of whom Mr Nxesi spoke may be encountered in government offices overmanned by incompetent officials. In the ANC office – which, rather confusingly, doubles as a doctor's private clinic – Dr P— pointedly ignored my arrival while continuing to operate his computer, the screen showing a list of expensive drugs. Then, having put Whitey in her place, he delegated Mrs Sokhupa, who describes herself as a 'social worker', to show me round the hospital founded in 1934 by a philanthropic Englishman. The original single-storey dark-brick building is pleasant enough, the jerry-built addition less so. The nursing staff impress more by their kindness to patients than by their knowledge. They complain, with good reason, about shortages: of medicines, bandages, oxygen, bedpans, wheelchairs. The wards and corridors were cleanish – but only *ish*. Nobody seemed sufficiently AIDS-aware to take seriously the need for unwavering vigilance. Yes, it's a bad disease. But Transkei people don't get it. The main worry is an increase in TB deaths.

The hospital's director is a Kampala doctor, amiable and courteous – much taller and darker skinned than the average Xhosa. He invited us to drink tea in his roomy, comfortably furnished bungalow on the edge of the compound, with a fine view of the town below and the hills beyond. On the way we passed through a colony of flimsy rusting caravans parked close together: the nurses' quarters, each small caravan accommodating two.

The doctor had felt no scruples about taking this job in 1985 when State repression was at its worst – the Last Stand. In Uganda he couldn't earn such a salary and he had to think of his family: four motherless children to be educated, a dependent father and aunt...Remembering how implacably much of the white world boycotted South Africa – cutting its citizens off from the BBC and isolating academics from the latest research – it is ironic that so many blacks were then hurrying south to support apartheid directly by availing of good job offers in the 'Bantustans'.

Today the secondary school is closed; either the teachers or the pupils are on strike – maybe both. 'The teachers are so ignorant it doesn't matter,' said Mrs

Sokhupa. 'They can't even keep the kids sitting down. This year I'm sending my two sons to Elliot, to a good white school. The other kids treat them badly but I say it doesn't matter. There they can learn – if I pay big money!'

According to Mr Nxesi, the under-30 generation hereabouts is largely illiterate. Many children don't start school until they are 8 or 9; only then can they walk the necessary distances, up to sixteen miles daily. Even more detrimental, most boys drop out after circumcision at the age of 16. It would be too humiliating for *men* to have to accept the authority of their own age-group – any teacher under 40.

There was much rejoicing today when light rain fell for an hour; this morning the hotel dishes were rinsed in my washing water – *after* I had washed. Out of a similar water shortage came my (and my daughter's) Madagascan hepatitis-A.

This is a soothingly silent town; most people are too poor to afford ghetto blasters.

Matatiele, 30 July

I had just commented on Mount Fletcher's tranquillity when the party started. A newly arrived army platoon was celebrating its last night of freedom before barrack life closed in. End of tranquillity.

Yesterday morning a bucket of steaming water and a teapot of coffee (no tea available) were brought to my room by a buxom young maid with a smile like the sunrise. Later, I enjoyed a substantial breakfast of fried eggs and liver. But this morning – nothing. The dining room was shambolic, the entire staff AWOL. As I packed, several hungover teenaged soldiers, clad only in underpants, came wandering in and out of my room – fascinated by Lear's panniers – and deplored no water, no breakfast...The lack of water seemed to bother them most. Soon they had to report for duty and how could they be expected to don uniforms before washing?

On the road to Matatiele – new and velvet-smooth – the taxi traffic was heavy and the concomitant litter repulsive. For South Africa's prodigiously littered countryside all races are to blame. James Bryce, visiting 'white' Beaufort West in 1897, noted, 'Most of its houses are stuck down irregularly over a surface covered with broken bottles and empty sardine and preserved meat tins.' A century later, cyclists are seriously at risk when speeding motorists open windows to dispose of bottles.

This small market town is just over the 'border' in Natal. During my afternoon's dander I saw only two whites, apart from busy storekeepers. Xhosas throng the streets, many wrapped in colourful blankets, and the pavements are piled with hawkers' goods. The whole scene – noisy, bright, animated, scruffy – is the very antithesis of your average dorp.

Matatiele is reputed to be an APLA/PAC stronghold and by sunset a dozen young APLA warriors had occupied the ladies bar. Already they knew all about me (slightly disconcerting if not surprising) and were keen to publicize their Africanist ideology. The most articulate and forceful favoured anonymity, so let's call them Tom, Dick and Harry.

'We don't believe in killing foreigners,' explained Tom. 'Not in the Transkei or anywhere else. It's the boere does those murders, then blames us.'

'But we do believe in "One Settler, One Bullet",' said Dick. 'Why not? Settlers have a legal right to our land, they tell us, through "armed conquest". OK, to get it back we use violence – right?'

Harry boasted, 'We've more and more township kids joining our struggle.' (This is untrue.) 'They don't trust the ANC, they know the capitalists have bought them. A new South Africa – what's new? Without armed action there's nothing in it for the exploited. Who's negotiating for them? We're only violent because the whites won't back down, not really, unless we fight.'

Underberg, 31 July

Today I broke a rule, arriving here an hour after sunset. Reason: a strong relentless headwind over the eighty-five hilly miles from Matatiele.

For hours commercial forestry frustrated me, completely concealing one of Africa's most splendid mountain ranges. These pines and bluegums, covering the lower slopes of the Drakensberg like some disfiguring disease, retain the water that previously filled rivers and are an ecological and social disaster. Each tree's roots reach down some sixty feet to groundwater level and each absorbs more than 100 litres a day. Largely because of the activities of SAPPI and MONDI, South Africa's dwindling rivers have become an international problem, threatening the survival of countless peasant farmers in southern Mozambique.

In Underberg's hotel bar a party of transplanted Rhodies gave me a heroine's welcome.

'From Matatiele today on that bike? Hey, you're some woman!' Wenwes like action and physical stamina and what they imagine to be daring deeds – like cycling through a very small area of the Transkei.

Ixopo, 1 August

More plantations today, including miles of nurseries – proof that SAPPI and MONDI are planning ahead, confident of being unhampered in the new South Africa. To escape, I took a narrow dirt track along the edge of a small separate segment of the Transkei which the APLA warriors had warned me to avoid. (Hence my Underberg detour, instead of the direct route through Kokstad and

Umzimkulu.) This track overlooks a series of deep, wide, winter-brown valleys – far below, densely populated, with bulky blue-hazy ranges beyond. Then suddenly, high among superb unplanted mountains, I found myself over the 'border'; there was no roadblock, perhaps because this area is so remote. Here shacks crowded the steep slopes and the atmosphere was distinctly unwelcoming, as predicted by APLA. Pushing Lear up one long hill I felt quite vulnerable as young men scowled speculatively at the panniers. In this sort of terrain a cyclist does not have the advantage of speed; turning to freewheel away from any difficulty would simply take me back to the base of an equally steep hill. I was halfway up when three youths began to shout at me aggressively – a nasty moment. But then an elder with an air of authority emerged from his neat little bungalow and silently shook hands (he spoke no English) before escorting me to the edge of the settlement. From there the track dived into a boulder-strewn, uninhabited valley.

The Eastern Cape is hilly enough but Natal is outrageously hilly; here is no such thing as a short climb or a gentle slope. On the main roads wayside notices warn that the next hill is five or six miles long with a gradient requiring trucks to take Special Precautions.

What must the first British settlers have made of this terrain when they arrived by the boatload between 1849 and 1851? But soon they were flourishing and marvelling at Natal's fertility: lush grass growing five feet high, an abundance of free building timber in the kloofs, soil suitable for growing sugar-cane, cotton, tobacco, indigo and yielding two crops a year. All that plus a climate they incredulously described as 'perpetual summer' – and thousands of dispossessed 'Kaffirs' reduced to working for a pittance. (In 1848 five 'native locations' had been demarcated on land 'unsuitable for European occupation'.) By 1853, families who had been starving in Britain a few years earlier were living in relative comfort, many killing their own mutton – the ultimate criterion of prosperity.

On this Sunday afternoon Ixopo (to pronounce it correctly you must make a choking sound) was moribund. A pleasant little town, its suburbs are even leafier than the norm, its homes and gardens spacious and English-looking. The bigger hotel is closed. The other, also big, has recently been bought by a cheerful Indian with no hang-ups about selling alcohol at 4 p.m. on the Sabbath. Yet again I'm the only guest and in Ixopo even the bar-trade is feeble. But Mr Moosa (Billy to his friends) remains resolutely optimistic.

'This time next year things will be better. By then we'll all feel we're simply *South African*. A historic change is coming, a psychological change. Even Natal will be better, even kwaZulu.'

I wonder... This province is blood-soaked like no other. Last weekend saw sixteen murders: a 'normal' statistic. Men, women, children and babies are routinely butchered, by the dozen. Weapons abound and intimidation is general. Fear, hate, suspicion, bitterness, grief and wild demoralizing rumours have corroded the black communities and to some extent infected everyone.

Later, Billy and I were joined by Rudi, a middle-aged Coloured friend of the Moosa family. Ixopo, he informed me, is the Zulu word for the sound cattle make when withdrawing hooves from mud. Rudi has white skin, grey-green eyes and crinkly light-brown hair. 'Wearing a wig' – he grinned – 'I could've passed for white if I'd wanted to. But the way things were as I grew up, you'd be ashamed to be white.'

Billy then took charge of an elfin 3-year-old daughter while her mother Seetha, a primary-school teacher, made scrumptious samoosas in the kitchen from where she shouted comments at intervals.

As a building contractor, Rudi worries about the immediate future. 'Everything is at a standstill, I've no work for my men. Hey, it's tough! They can't live on sunshine, I have them on half-pay. But after the elections business will improve all round. The ANC won't be having any more scary revolutionary ideas. There's no risk here of a mess like up north.'

'We're solid behind the ANC,' called Seetha from the kitchen, 'us and all our families – though living here we don't say so. Only to foreigners!'

Billy nodded. 'Now no one else can run the show – politically, I mean. And we have our white tribe to run the economy.'

Seetha brought us a mountain of samoosas and a packet of paper napkins. 'As I see it,' she said, 'our only danger now is too many whites hating and distrusting Mr Mandela. We don't, we can respect him.'

'But let's talk straight,' said Rudi. 'Most Indians and Coloureds are anti-black. It's a gut thing. All the same, it's not like white racism. We're only anti-black in bulk – see what I mean? Doesn't stop most of us having some good black friends – real friends. How many whites can honestly say they've a black friend, a real friend? Maybe a few up in the university world, but damn few!'

Richmond, 2 August

Miles of swift freewheeling took me down to the Josephine Bridge (who was Josephine?) across the Umkomaas, altitude 1,800 feet. The river is low, yet this lush narrow valley yields an abundance of fruits and vegetables all the year round.

Between there and Richmond (4,500 feet) my sweat-loss was sensational and on the outskirts of the town, in Websters Garden Stall, I drank two litres of amasi while a garrulous Anglo-Irishman chose his flowers, fruits and herbs. Long ago he left a mouldering Big House in Co. Cork and he has done well for himself in Natal. He excoriated the media. They report local black-on-black violence as

1. A late-nineteenth-century homestead in western Transvaal

2. The author and friend beside a traditional Boer open-air bread-oven

3. Koppies in the Great Karoo

4. Lear in Griqualand West

5. Sunday braai in Vosburg

6. Lear in the middle of a dry river-bed in the Klein Karoo

7. Weaver-birds' nest on telephone pole

8. A corner of Khayelitsha

9. A Khayelitsha track flooded with sewage

10. The author with a Khayelitsha Xhosa friend

11. A Khayelitsha shoemaker

12. A Khayelitsha
shack – upmarket

13. A Tswana helper in Kimberley

14. A Boer family graveyard in Western Cape

15. Lear with a young Boer admirer

16. Local enterprise in Khayelitsha

17. Khayelitsha crossroads

18. The end of an era, 16 December 1994: the last Day of the Vow

19. Lear in the Great Karoo

20. Chris in the Transkei

21. Gable-end in Umtata, December 1994

22. A bar attendant in Eastern Transvaal

23. Chris on the battlefield

24. A Zulu kraal between Melmoth and the coast

25. Isandlwana

26. A friend in her family graveyard

27. A church serving the Anglican community in Griqualand East

28. Khayelitsha in midsummer

29. Waiting for a taxi on Christmas Eve

happening in Richmond. It's not happening in *Richmond*, it's happening in Richmond's townships. But the media can't spell those names so they say 'Richmond'. Consequently, property prices have halved and the two hotels have closed. Then there's the drought. When they can't cultivate, farmers find it's best to go on long holidays to cheap Mauritius instead of staying in expensive South Africa. Many have sold their livestock and are giving all their water to the orange orchards. But the '93 crop is dwarfed – unsellable. This victim of drought has just returned from a three-month holiday on Mauritius.

Beyond Websters I noticed a signpost to Byrne, a nearby village named after J. C. Byrne who in his lifetime was loathed by the hapless emigrants he cheated with such ease. Mr Byrne, operating from a smart London office, was among the many con-men who planned large-scale emigrations to Natal for their own profit.

During 1850 Natal – hitherto virtually unknown in Britain – suddenly became the fashionable colony. Some 'independent' emigrants, travelling cabin class, brought agricultural implements and a few farm animals. But most early settlers were destitute labourers who eagerly took advantage of such schemes as the Earl of Egremont's Petworth Emigration Society. When the Duke of Buccleuch dispatched a shipload of surplus tenants they settled around Richmond. Numerous noble lords were only too pleased to get rid of their 'distressed tenantry' by paying £10 per head for fares and outfits consisting of clothing for two years. Also, as Britain was then in a panic about overpopulation causing 'unrest', the Poor Law allowed parishes to assist emigrants from the rates. Quite often, assistance became compulsion. Imprisoned felons' families being dependent on the rates, many thieves and foot-pads were offered a choice: conviction or emigration.

Richmond's tree-lined main street (Shepstone Street – no Voortrekkers here please!) proves how quickly the settlers recreated England. Natal's first Anglican church was built here in 1856 and its rectory stands on the site of Natal's first girls' school (1869). Country crafts are now on sale where James Hacklands was making wagons by 1862. The court house began to dispense British justice in 1865. The Freemasons Lodge opened in 1884 (it seems the apostrophe had already fallen into disuse locally) and in 1897 came the railway station, at the end of a branch line from Pietermaritzburg.

Along Chilley Street you can smell the chillis. The Indian colony took root in the late 1860s and has been quietly flourishing ever since; Billy and Seetha were both born here. Can there really – I wondered, looking at the shops – be so many Patels in South Africa? Or has 'Patel' been adopted in lieu of names too long and unwieldy for settler tongues? I was seeking a *Weekly Mail*, nowhere to be found since I left Cape Town. By now the national media's morbid navel-gazing has completely cut me off from the rest of the world; the only widely available global news concerns either sport – chiefly rugby and cricket, soccer is the blacks' game – or the British Royal Family. The latter fixation defeats me; why should South Africans – including Afrikaners – be so riveted by the minutiae of royal deeds and misdeeds?

Mr A. P. Patel sells the *Weekly Mail* and Mrs Patel, remarking that I looked tired – I felt humidity exhausted – invited me into a back room for cinnamon tea and home-made sweetmeats. She had heard all about me from Seetha; one doesn't travel quite anonymously through rural South Africa.

Richmond's motel is closed but was bought a few weeks ago by a young English-speaking couple who have just reopened the bar and offered me a free bed in a garden shed. At the bar sat four Afrikaner SAP officers, unwinding after a stressful foray into a township. They competed to stand me beers and for my entertainment swapped the latest jokes – for example, 'How many poles does it take to kill a Hani?' Then they recalled various horrors in which they or their friends have been involved. Like the slaughter of eighteen Inkatha Freedom Party (IFP) supporters in nearby kwaShange. And the night an important Zulu chief was assassinated outside his Pietermaritzburg home – the very same night an equally important chief and two of his followers were shot dead in northern Natal. On one of the worst nights, twenty-three were killed in Richmond. Soon after, two women were hacked to death with pangas in a local IFP leader's house. This led to nineteen being arrested, including a member of the SADF. When an IFP member talked aloud about having proof of heavy white involvement in all this violence, he was shot dead next day – the very day Chief Ndlovu, known to be working hard for peace in the Richmond area, was assassinated near Ixopo. By now hundreds – no, thousands! – have joined both the ANC and the IFP in an effort to protect themselves.

The truth's elusiveness compounds the terror aroused by the present crisis. It is impossible to establish the facts about any crime or to distinguish information from disinformation. Even in those rare cases when impartial Peace Monitor witnesses are present, they can observe only a fragment of the action and have little hope of obtaining reliable evidence from either side about motives, provocations, methods, consequences. This opacity is unnerving for the mass of politically uninvolved township dwellers – helpless victims of divisive rumours, accusations, denials and reprisals.

My kind hostess brought me, unasked, a large plate of boerewors and chips. As I ate, a fifth SAP officer joined us, an English-speaker in his early twenties. Soon Charlie was explaining, 'My background is liberal – DP parents – and at school I used to stand up for blacks when that was risky. I'd notions about helping to reform the police. Now I hate blacks. After seeing how they treat each other, I hate them all. Last week only a few hundred came to an ANC demo in the town centre so the bully-boys toured the townships. Three hours later we'd 3,000 to control! Richmond's two townships, Magoda and Pateni, had 30,000 blacks. Now there's less than 15,000, most ANC have fled to the Rand or the Cape.'

George arrived next, in a Mercedes, the 24-year-old son of one of those hard-hit local farmers. Three years ago he was appointed manager of a large sawmill and he reported a recent 'sensible' SAPPI directive to all managers: 'Employ only whites in the important jobs to keep production up.' He reckons he's sorted out all that subversive trade-union nonsense. 'I told them, "If you put your trade-union subscription into the bank instead, you'll soon have something to show for it. Why should you pay for a fine car for some trade-union dictator? Soon the bank will give you more money than you'll ever get fighting with your employ-ers." It's like always with blacks, you've got to think for them...'

Last year George heard the shots when his uncle was being murdered in his garage after 'they' had pillaged the house. 'He wasn't even trying to catch the bastards, he'd just driven in, they killed him for fun – or spite or something...'

It is hard to cope with South Africa's relentless daily death-toll. Yet an extraordinary feature of this transition period is the overall normality of every-day life from the traveller's point of view – while for the majority of citizens law and order is rapidly breaking down.

Pietermaritzburg, 3 August

Leaving Richmond at dawn, I wondered how the new South Africa will change the town. Surely it cannot continue to look as though neatly excised from Victorian England, carefully packaged and shipped to Natal.

Soon I had the Sugar Hill Racing Stable on my right and the Baynesfield Estate on my left. This estate was established in 1863 by Joseph Baynes, on 24,000 of the region's most fertile acres; Mr Baynes, we gather, travelled cabin class. Next came miles of canefields and dairy pastures and then, near Pieter-maritzburg, I passed thousands of shacks crowded on a wide mountainside which may or may not be fertile – there is no space left for cultivation. Speeding down the final slope – Natal's capital lies in a hollow surrounded by high wooded hills – I noted a penumbra of pollution. Yet cities do have their compensations, like the Africana second-hand bookshop, my first halt. There I lost all self-control and a large parcel of rare vols is now on its way to Ireland.

I'm staying here with Glynis and Steve Bach, first met in Vosburg – staying only two nights because my return flight is booked for 17 August and I plan to return to Natal next April.

The same, 9 August

The fourth of August 1993 is a date I shall never forget. Early that morning I heard deeply distressing news from home and for the first time – being in a state of shock – neglected adequately to guard Lear. Two hours later he was stolen from my friends' back garden.

Two black workmen in an adjacent garden witnessed the theft. When they questioned the intruder he claimed Steve owed him money but had refused to pay so he was taking Lear instead. The workmen must have known this was nonsense but they said no more. Were they afraid lest the thief might pull a gun? Or did they feel some sympathy for his enterprise?

Everything possible has been done to retrieve Lear but I never had any hope. At Steve's insistence, a dim-witted Coloured police officer came that evening to take a statement. However, it would at present be unreasonable to expect the SAP to exert themselves in pursuit of a cycle thief. I offered a R500 reward – NO QUESTIONS ASKED – on the front page of the *Natal Witness*, this being the local price of a new mountain-bike. To publicize my loss the *Witness* also ran a half-page interview complete with a pathetic photograph; I didn't have to feign looking stricken. The SABC did a long radio interview, broadcast countrywide. The local Zulu-language radio station gave a detailed description of Lear (but how easy it is to change a bicycle's appearance!) with a passionate plea for his return and much emphasis on the reward. The local ANC offices displayed enlarged photographs of Lear accompanied by further passionate pleas. All, predictably, to no avail.

It is ironical that after months of dodging the sort of publicity likely to attend a female sexagenarian's bicycle tour of South Africa in 1993, that journey has had to end under the spotlight. In consequence, some of my readers have surfaced and a new friend has nobly offered to lend me her bicycle – a precious machine, so I am touched and flattered. But now I lack heart (and time) for the last lap to Jo'burg. Tomorrow, Margaret and Jennifer are driving down to collect me; Margaret had already planned this trip to visit an aunt in Greys Hospital.

I am absurdly upset. On the practical level a bicycle is just a machine, an inanimate object easily replaced. But not so on the emotional level. To me Lear was a friend, my only companion on quite a long journey that started in Nairobi. I feel utterly desolate without him. (What would a shrink make of this admission?) One could argue – I have to try to make excuses – that a bicycle is not, after all, 'just a machine' as is a motor car. The cyclist and the bicycle form a team; they work together as the motorist and motor car do not. Perhaps other cyclists exist, somewhere out there, who can understand this. Or perhaps not. Maybe I'm uniquely dotty.

Now I must count my blessings. In fact only one is visible at the moment: that this journal was not stolen. It might have been, as it lives in a pannier-bag. But having rummaged through both panniers and found nothing of value to him, the thief ripped them off, no doubt fearing they might arouse suspicion (obvious 'tourist property') as he sped away. The only balm on my wound is the certainty that he needs Lear, in material terms, more than I do. A similar theft at home would have enraged me: you can't feel enraged in South Africa when a black steals from a white.

In the air over the Transvaal, 17 August

However little they may deserve it, the whites do at present arouse sympathy – emotional earthquake victims, their whole world collapsing, fear of bloody chaos a dark shadow, incomprehension of blacks distorting their view of the future. An incomprehension nonetheless heartbreaking for being inevitable, in South Africa – and of course vehemently denied. How often I've had to listen to both Afrikaners and English-speakers explaining why they understand blacks so very well – because as children they had no other playmates and went off to boarding school speaking better Sotho/Xhosa/Zulu than Afrikaans or English. The implied insult to African culture is breathtaking. Imagine a Chinese child growing up to the age of 10 on some remote nineteenth-century European farm, playing only with the children of illiterate, impoverished labourers and on the basis of that experience claiming as an adult that he understood Europeans very well. People would laugh at his stupid arrogance.

Why am I already eagerly looking forward to my return on 1 April '94? I seem to be entangled in a love-hate relationship with South Africa, a baffling emotional involvement with its variegated tribes and their tragic problems. Now I care about what happens to them – all of them – to an extent I would not have believed possible six months ago.

PART II

Elections

April to May 1994

11

States of Emergency

Johannesburg – Durban – Pietermaritzburg

I have a huge constituency, so how could I not have confidence?
We are entering a period of resistance politics.
Chief Mangosuthu Buthelezi (March 1994)

In the air over Central Africa, 1 April 1994

Until discovering the cost of a bullet-proof vest (hundreds of pounds) I had dutifully sought one in London – by way of calming friends rather than avoiding death. Foreigners are unlikely to be at risk during the election period unless they choose to enter zones of maximum violence. But perhaps some friendly fussing is forgivable; seen from afar, pre-election South Africa looks quite bloody.

A fortnight ago three of the AWB invaders of Bophuthatswana were shot dead by a black policeman in front of the world's TV cameras – after the invaders had murdered seventy Tswanas while driving around firing at random. Then there was last Monday's IFP-organized Zulu march through Jo'burg's Central Business District, an area traditionally sacred to white money-makers, during which at least fifty-nine were killed. And people forget that the chances of being involved in such exceptional tumults are a million to one.

At Heathrow I talked with two distressed young Zulu couples, all law students in their final year at Wits. They come from kwaMakthutha, in the Natal Midlands, and a few hours previously had heard of the murders of three ANC activist friends by an Inkatha gunman. They too are ANC members – 'Most urbanized Zulus, even the uneducated, follow Mandela' – yet they admitted certain local ANC leaders must accept 'a share of the blame for our crazy war'. All four raged against foreign journalists' misinterpretations of this conflict as 'Zulu versus Xhosa'.

Some see the Inkatha/white-right-wing alliance as a sinister hybrid, genetically engineered by America's New Right and Europe's more fanatical free marketeers, with support coming from shadowy neo-Nazi organizations. For this hypothesis there is considerable evidence. It is not in the interests of the American mainstream right wing to rock the new South Africa's boat; they can profit more by steering its course. But throughout southern Africa New Right fundamentalists have long been at work – in collaboration with the CIA, here as elsewhere, during the Cold War. In the mid-'80s they launched a lavishly funded anti-ANC campaign, applauded by Laurens van der Post among others. In 1990 Sir Laurens asserted, 'For the West to help the Communist ANC to gain power would be suicidal. Only Buthelezi truly cares about the blacks and understands their needs. Inkatha's warriors and the kwaZulu police should be armed and trained to fight the terrorists...' And so they were being, at that date, by senior officers of the SADF and SAP, in collusion with the Department of Military Intelligence – and therefore with I'm told President de Klerk's knowledge. Since 1987 Third Force operations have caused many thousands of deaths – more than 5,300 in kwaZulu/Natal alone, during 1992. Last year's statistics have not yet been published.

Florida, 4 April

Tomorrow Jennifer is motoring to Natal and will drop me off in Ladysmith. But my plan to buy a bicycle in Pietermaritzburg, and resume my journey where it ended last year, may be thwarted by recent developments.

During the past week 123 blacks have been murdered in kwaZulu/Natal and two days ago the Transitional Executive Council (TEC, the interim government) declared a State of Emergency throughout the province. Troops are being dispatched to the area in an attempt to create conditions allowing 'substantially free and fair elections', regardless of Buthelezi's whims. ('Substantially'? In the context a fudge word.) This TEC decision was made under pressure from Judge Kriegler, head of the Independent Electoral Commission (IEC), who insisted that otherwise no voting would be possible in kwaZulu. But here we're into cloud-cuckoo-land, where I suspect we're going to remain for some time to come. A State of Emergency imposed by an Inkatha-scorned TEC, and enforced by a mere 2,000 troops, will encourage no one to go to the polls in defiance of kwaZulu Police (KZP) hit squads – the IFP's allies. Recently Buthelezi has been using phrases like 'ethnic cleansing', 'obliteration of opponents' and 'a fight to the finish with the ANC' – phrases not easily dismissed as bombast in a province already blood-soaked.

Meanwhile, throughout South Africa, thousands (millions?) of whites are frantically stock-piling tinned and dried foods, brandy and Coke and beer, cooldrinks, candles, kerosene, bottled gas, chlorine pills, loo paper, soap, tampons, antibiotics, dog biscuits, cat munchies and etc., etc., etc. A CP 'List of Emergency Provisions' includes 'arms and ammunition, a small Bible, and a panga or small axe'. All this in preparation for some post-election cataclysm (the sabotaging of electricity and water services? blacks slaughtering whites? whites slaughtering blacks?) – some cataclysm that will confine people to their fortified homes for weeks on end. Already the hyper-jittery have fled to Zimbabwe's tourist resorts in overloaded camper-vans and plan to remain there (the IEC will provide voting facilities) 'until things are calmer'.

Foreigners are both amused and bemused by this panic buying. However, it seems semi-hysteria has marked the white response to political crises since 1838. And the elections have been defined, in numerous widely disseminated right-wing pamphlets, as a major crisis. The whites' proneness to irrational fears is understandable enough; at some level they must know they deserve punishment, even if none is threatened.

Ladysmith, Natal, 5 April

Jennifer, by now familiar with my priorities, dropped me off outside a Drank-winkel. The Afrikaner owner – tall, balding, big-bellied, red-faced, with a short curly golden beard – was not into reconciliation. 'Here in Natal,' said he, 'we see those lefties who encouraged all this running away now to Granny Britain. But we've nowhere else to go – right? If blacks can run a bottle-store like this and buy a big house and a Merc – fine, fine! Only I'm not paying for it, no way! They want it all without the hard work. Now that monkey's promising them heaven – and what next, when he can't deliver? Would *you* believe me if I told you diamonds would grow on trees next month? Course not! But they believe it – see what I mean? Me and you, we can meet and talk and understand one another. With them it's like talking to a dog!'

In the bank, an English-speaking farmer's wife and a well-tailored Zulu gentleman were united in their resentment of TEC interference – the State of Emergency. A long, slow queue allowed me to be investigated and the young woman soon recalled last year's Lear-theft publicity. 'It must have been you – shame! For it to happen in Natal, after safely crossing Africa!' She advised me to stay at the Breedts' guest house and directed me to Andy Breedt's office at the end of the street; soon he'd be driving home for lunch. Ladysmith is the sort of place where personal routines are common knowledge.

When Andy came ambling amiably towards me he at once seemed like a friend. An Afrikaner, born forty years ago in Zimbabwe, he is tall, blond, well built, slow-moving, quick-thinking – his smile kind, his eyes shrewd. Yes, he'd soon be driving home.

His young Indian receptionist, graceful and charming, admitted to feeling on edge – worried about her family in Durban. 'There things are very bad, not like here. Ladysmith never has problems, except now we're doing no business. The whole country is paralysed, waiting for the elections – and not knowing what next...'

Andy remains relaxed. 'My optimism is genuine. Most South Africans – all sorts – are sensible. Give them a chance to live peaceably and they will.' But he admitted that his eight Zulu employees are at present living in a state of terror, juggling with membership cards, claiming allegiance to both the ANC and the IFP. Secretly all long to vote for Mandela, but unless things change dramatically they won't dare.

We drove steeply up, through the standard leafy suburbs, to a narrow ridge-top strewn with Boer War fortifications. The Breedts' new house – large, thatched, open plan, with steep wooden stairs and low roof-beams – is poised on a cliff-edge and blessedly cool within. Andy's wife Sheila was also born in Zimbabwe, of 'Rhodie' parents; she is small, slim, energetic, witty, warm-hearted – another 'instant friend'. Immediately she invited me to join this evening's dinner party as a guest.

I am writing this in a short sloping garden under a regal fir tree that witnessed the Siege of Ladysmith. Far below lies the little town, backed by a scrubby ridge, and all along the southern horizon the distant mighty Drakensberg form a pale blue wall.

Later

At sunset we assembled in the bar – no ordinary bar, this, for Andy is a Boer War buff. His collection of souvenirs covers every inch of the little room's walls and ceiling and overflows onto the bar shelves and counter – guns, tools, posters, newspapers, hats, uniforms, bullets, flags, medals, saddles, bridles, snuff boxes, cigarette tins, biscuit tins, mugs, plates, water bottles, billy cans, haversacks, badges and buttons. In the sitting room is a library to match.

A convivial time was had by all and the rapid drowning of inhibitions exposed some raw emotions among my fellow-guests. Hereabouts the Commie bogie thrives, among Afrikaners and English-speakers alike. Christianity also thrives. One man, a doctor, was completely thrown by my being an unbeliever. 'But you seem like a good person!' he protested naively, to my considerable embarrass-ment. This equating of goodness with Christianity depresses me. South Africans, mentally ghettoized for generations, have a lot of catching up to do. As one of their own academics, Geoff Durant, observed recently, referring to his native land – 'It's an intellectual dorp.'

Pietermaritzburg, 6 April

Last night, as I slept soundly, another sleeping woman was shot dead in the nearby township of Ezhakeni. As were five residents of Ekuvukeni, also nearby. That Indian lass ('Ladysmith never has problems') is seriously disconnected from her black fellow-citizens.

At 7 a.m. Andy drove me to the taxi station, around the corner from his office, and for an hour I sat in the back of a kombi while it filled. Unless at the centre of a taxi war, most such stations are noisy, bustling and quite jolly. This one wasn't. The few people about looked tense and unhappy.

Pietermaritzburg's taxi station is in a district reputedly afflicted by pick-pockets, muggers, drug dealers, rapists, murderers. In other words, a district not white – and perhaps moderately dangerous though the atmosphere is friendly. A nearby beer hall – up a short alleyway, prettily overhung with bougainvillea – tempted me. Long metal tables and benches were screwed to the floor of the huge gloomy hall and iron grilles protected the bar from predators. The arrival of a white female startled everyone. For several moments I was silently eyed, with sheer incredulity, by a dozen young men, two teenage girls, three homeless old women with their worldly goods in plastic bags at their feet and four elderly men playing cards – playing very slowly, so worn and sticky was their pack. Cardboard cartons of maize-beer were being shared. Then a tall, thin, grey-haired man emerged from behind the bar, demanding to see my passport. When he had guaranteed me as a genuine foreigner the begging started. Two young men held out their polystyrene mugs, pointing to my beer bottle. One girl boldly asked for a Castle. An elderly man asked for a packet of cigarettes. Another asked for R5 'to buy stomach medicine'. The second girl leaned over my shoulder, helped herself to one of my mini-cigars, lit it – then coughed, laughed and threw it onto the stoep. From there it was retrieved by a young man who smoked it with relish and winked at me and grinned and said, 'Better than dagga!'

That was an odd interlude. No one showed any hostility but to people so desperately poor I naturally seemed like fair game. My battered and dusty pannier-bags do not suggest goodies within but when one youth began to contemplate my leather binoculars case I judged it time to move on.

In a large shabby Indian hotel on the next street there was more fall-out from last year's publicity. The owner, Tommy Naidoo, at once recognized both my face and my voice. He beckoned me into his tiny office (also Reception) and offered, 'G and T? Or brandy and Coke?' Were his wife not in Durban he would have invited me home; but I could have a room in the hotel as his guest.

On the floor behind my chair a life-sized photograph of Mr Mandela leaned against the wall. 'I've just demoted him!' chuckled Tommy. 'He's failing badly, not controlling ANC violence, not talking enough to our man [Buthelezi]. When we look back apartheid seems not so bad, then we'd no such violence and crime and uncertainty. And most people want to live with their own sort, that's a fact of life worldwide.'

Tommy foresees my not being allowed to cycle through kwaZulu. 'It's wild there now, they'd think you were on about voter education and they'd kill you.'

On my remarking that voter educationalists don't cycle Tommy shrugged. 'Do they know that? They know nothing! You look the type – friendly old white lady with a do-gooder face. You wouldn't be the first *kaffirboetie* to be carved up – remember Amy Biehl? You'd be lucky if you were shot nice and quick!'

Tommy is a shrewdly benevolent Mr Fix-it whose office is never empty. For a few hours I sat in a corner observing rich and poor, of all colours, seeking help and advice – and getting it, unless Tommy smelled exploitation. Casual disputes and comments swirled around me, confusingly.

'In Empangeni yesterday the KZP couldn't stop ten thousand Zulus carrying traditional weapons. [These are banned under the State of Emergency.] Police interference would have started the civil war.'

'Didn't the TEC know that ban couldn't be enforced? Being televised defying it only raises Inkatha's morale.'

'It must've been the *army* in Empangeni, Mandela said on Thursday the police were to be confined to barracks. And our security legislation is suspended. Who does he think he is?'

'He knows he'll soon be President, he's giving us a trailer of phoney ANC democracy.'

'Mac Maharaj contradicted him then, said if the KZP co-operate they won't be chained up.'

'Is this how to make a democracy? Putting quarter of South Africa's population under military rule!'

'All the same, thousands feel safer since the army moved in.'

'How safe? In six days of the Emergency we've had ninety-two murders – not counting today's that we haven't heard about yet...'

'That's less than before. And we've not got a civil war, only gangs.'

'The nine Mzelemus weren't a gang. A grandmother, mother and seven daughters – not forgetting a five-months-old baby with her head sliced in two by a machete.'

'Seems the father was an ANC supporter, when the killers asked for his Inkatha card he couldn't show it.'

'And the Nats are bribing with food and money. They give a rand for every poster put up in a township.'

'*One rand*? Would you put up a Nat poster in a black township for less than ten thousand? Plus all funeral expenses paid!'

'NEON [National Elections Observer Network] is desperate for volunteers here – needs 800, can only recruit 300. And how reliable will those be? They'll be tough down-and-outs, ready to risk their lives for free meals!'

'They can't be down-and-outs. They must be able to speak, read and write English.'

'You mean we've a shortage of starving graduates?'

'Kriegler said yesterday polling might be postponed here, if voting can't be free and fair.'

'It should be postponed everywhere, it's a nonsense. How can it be free and fair with the ANC running it?'

'Are they running it? The IEC's just fined them R100,000 for intimidation in the northern Transvaal – blocking Nat rallies.'

'A suspended fine – window dressing!'

The foyer outside Tommy's office serves as an informal club for minor Indian businessmen – a close-knit community, their first language English. They invited me to a snack lunch: a sliced pan laid on the table in its wrapper, a big dish of delectable tomato, onion and chilli mush. A black lawyer joined us, self-important and evidently influential; most of those present deferred to him. Although a member of the IEC, and as such supposed to be neutral, his ANC allegiance was plain to be heard.

As I walked to a bicycle shop recommended by Tommy the most obvious thing was *normality* – here in Natal, in the eye of the storm. Shoppers shopping, beggars begging, taxis loading and unloading, traffic racing, teenagers stuffing their faces with fast foods, hawkers trading, Muslim schoolchildren streaming home from their academy beside an imposing mosque, the dainty little girls wearing long stockings and tight headscarves despite the heat. Perhaps at that very moment unspeakable atrocities were being committed nearby. Yet I find myself unable to believe that South Africa now – even kwaZulu/Natal – is a country about to implode into civil war. Am I being an obtuse outsider, unaware of all the nuances? Or as an outsider am I sensing something the South Africans themselves have lost sight of under the pressure of day-by-day destabilizations? I am very conscious of a nationwide *longing* for peace and calm, a force that feels stronger than the destabilizers.

Buying a bicycle is a momentous event, akin to marriage: you are acquiring a partner. Now I have acquired Chris (in memory of Chris Hani) and it remains to be seen how our relationship will develop. Lear was a thoroughbred, Chris is a mongrel – bits and pieces from Singapore, Taiwan and Korea, assembled in South Africa. Riding him feels like riding a carthorse after a Derby winner. But I daresay shared experiences will eventually make that invidious comparison seem irrelevant.

Durban, 7 April

Our first shared experience took us over South Africa's most televised road, the hilly fifty-five-mile route of the annual (31 May) Comrades' Marathon. A confusing name, in contemporary South Africa; these Comrades are not ANC/SACP members but hundreds of men and women of all ages and types whose whole lives seem geared, both physically and psychologically, to this yearly challenge.

Looking down from Durban's densely wooded suburbs, high above the city, I could see navigation problems ahead. Durbanites are inexplicably proud of their 'modern infrastructure', some of which now lay below me: six motorways, on three separate levels, turning and twisting and twining around one another like a pit of demented snakes. I had to walk the last few miles to the centre, past serried blocks of commercial high-risery. This port city is almost as uncongenial as Jo'burg, without the highveld compensation of a pleasant climate; Durban's humid heat is hellish. The friends with whom I am staying, in the most affluent Indian 'location', tell me I'm seeing the place at its worst. During the Easter holidays multitudes of Vaalies descend on this 'Fun Capital of South Africa' to enjoy the Golden Mile – in fact three and a half miles of beach where everything in sight is the very quintessence of vulgarity – and to romp amidst the gaudy plastic and concrete delights of Funworld and Waterland: go-karts, boat rides, motor chutes, aerial cableways. The Vaalies' unpopularity may be gauged from a remarkable advertisement in today's *Natal Mercury*:

> On average, 11 tourists create one job. Multiply that by a million or more and that's a lot of jobs. But a booking from the Transvaal will become a special event if we don't make our visitors feel really welcome. We need our tourists. For goodness sake let's be nice to them.

The same, 8 April

Before the fun merchants and infrastructuralists took over, Durban must have been quite attractive. Remnants of dignity and calm survive: the City Hall, several lush public parks, the occasional untouched nineteenth-century street where history echoes.

This morning I had to choose between touring Durban's 'violence-torn townships' (the favourite cliché) with a member of the National Peace Secretariat – who would lend me a bullet-proof vest – or visiting Professor Azikiwe in his tenth-floor flat overlooking the port. I chose Professor Azikiwe. The idea of touring any black township with a group of whites makes me uncomfortable. And the townships in question being violence-torn compounds that discomfort. To the unhappy residents, it must seem that writers, journalists and TV crews are there only to exploit their distress.

Professor Azikiwe is a Nigerian anthropologist; he and I have been communicating since he wrote to me after the publication of my Cameroon book, in which I referred to the activities of an internationally famous sangoma. In 1990 he spent three months in Namibia during its first 'free and fair' election campaign. There the main parties agreed to hire – at vast expense – foreign, neutral inyangas (witchcraft practitioners) whose public rituals in the polling stations freed them from malignant spells and made them safe for all voters.

'In South Africa,' said the professor, 'there's also quite a widespread fear of the opposition enspelling polling booths. Some believe spirits will see to whom their vote goes. Others are convinced a spirit will take over their minds and force them to vote for "the enemy". But can you see Mr Justice Kriegler hiring inyangas?'

Having learned Venda and Zulu, Professor Azikiwe turned his attention to witchcraft in Venda, Northern Natal and the northern Transvaal. 'In some areas traditional beliefs are stronger than in many other parts of Africa, but distorted now. It didn't help when tribal courts were forbidden to try accused witches. Banishing them was more usual in the old days, instead of killing them. These days hundreds are being killed. I've met young men who think it's their duty to protect the community by killing them – having first bullied people to give money to pay a sangoma to "sniff out" their victim. Over the past few years there's been much more action. Witches are blamed for all sorts of things – political hounding, family quarrels, personal illness, lightning deaths, drought. It's believed they can create zombies by reviving corpses which they then control. And there's an expanding market for protective battle *muti*. The Boipatong killers smeared themselves with this before attacking. Most of the 10,000 Zulu marchers in Jo'burg on 28 March were smeared – and that's a lot of *muti*! Since 1990, 15,000 or so have been killed in political violence – how many died because they trusted *muti* to deflect bullets? This delusion you find all over Africa and it's centuries old. Here the *muti* murder rate is soaring – killing people for body parts. The brain makes the most potent *muti*, that's why so many violence victims have their skulls cracked open. But whole skulls are needed to put into the foundations of a new business premises to bring prosperity. The genitals and breasts are obviously for fertility rites. Like with everything nowadays, it's all over-commercialized. So you get too many traditional healers corrupted by the big profits. I've witnessed one sangoma paying R3,000 for a liver. Some whites here are very naive, imagining the Christian blacks – that's most South Africans – are uninfluenced by old beliefs. As though a century of European prosletyzing could cancel out millennia! I doubt you'd find 20 per cent without a belief in some elements of their own traditions. Sure, they'll tell whites they don't believe in any of this mumbo-jumbo, it's the work of the devil, they only believe in what the Bible says. But those denials are part of their being broken by their treatment in this country.'

When I left Professor Azikiwe Durban's main thoroughfare was thronged with sun-reddened Vaalies returning from the beachfront, for once on foot.

Occasionally people ask me why, in books about Africa, I avoid 'witchcraft'. I do so because the whole area of African spirituality is closed to outsiders.

Non-Africans – however sympathetic their attitude and whatever their academic qualifications – can only peer over the fence, glimpsing fragments of a mystery beyond our comprehension. It's easy to deride and condemn witchcraft. But there are many genuinely compassionate and wise sangomas who play constructive roles in their communities. I've met several, here in South Africa and elsewhere.

Today's most exciting rumour: the IFP is splintering! One Zulu-led faction favours a climb-down, another white-led faction is urging Buthelezi to stand firm. Good news, if true.

The same, 9 April

Overnight, Durban has broken out in a colourful rash of IFP election posters. These show the party logo, a large photograph of Chief Buthelezi at his most benign (followed by an 'X') and the slogan: 'Make our Country Free, Support the IFP!' This proof of a split is doing nothing to lessen public bemusement. 'But I thought Buthelezi was against the elections!' said one astounded young Zulu as we stood together viewing a vertical line of posters on a lamp-standard.

Yesterday, in a remote tourist camp in the Kruger Park, Mr Mandela, President de Klerk, Chief Buthelezi and King Zwelithini met to make yet another effort to avert the disaster of an election minus the IFP. For hours the four talked, apart from their courtiers and advisers. What a novel situation for the Afrikaner State President of the Republic of South Africa, to be sitting powerless out in the veld with three black leaders whose decisions now matter more than his! Mr Mandela offered to entrench the King's status, to make him the constitutional monarch of kwaZulu in the new South Africa. How the King may feel about that is irrelevant – Buthelezi rejected the idea, the meeting was a total failure, more troops are to be sent into the province and public despondency and anxiety is increasing. But what about those posters? Not referred to by the media yet surely immensely significant.

Durban's Poor Whites are numerous, wandering around in rags, their placards pathetic. 'I will work honestley for a small wage.' 'I can make good furnisher.' All day a young mother sat on the pavement outside Adams bookshop with an apathetic toddler by her side, a whimpering baby on her lap and downcast eyes. Her placard said: HOMELESS AND HUNGRY. She made no other attempt to attract attention and I wondered about her feelings as prosperous blacks strode past, many pausing to toss coins into her tin.

My Indian hostess, the vivacious widow of a wealthy businessman, lives with her octogenarian mother and three graduate daughters, all swiftly climbing their respective professional ladders. These independent-minded young women wear the latest Western styles and are determined to marry whom they will. Here, too, in this community of sophisticated Indians, election jitters are perceptible. Particularly post-election jitters, though not on the panic-stricken white scale.

'Let's face it,' said my hostess, 'there's no love lost between the Indian and the Zulu. Never was and never will be. We had our time of unity – expedient unity – when apartheid was at its worst. But once those laws were gone things soon went back to normal. I guess most of us will vote Nat. And in Natal we count, we're nearly a million – we could make possible a Nat/IFP coalition.'

Grandma observed, 'As a community we started from nothing, got ourselves organized, outdid the British as traders, built our own temples and mosques and schools. Why didn't the Zulus do the same? Because they were too lazy! They wouldn't work on the sugar plantations, so Indian labour was imported. And now they're jealous of us.'

Stanger, 10 April

My escape from Durban took two hours. I knew an alternative to the N2 existed but every attempt to find it led back to the motorway. Finally, in despair, I dragged Chris across fields of cane towards the sea – an inspired move. But even on that old road traffic was heavy, servicing countless caravan parks and luxurious resorts with names like Westbrook Beach and Willard's Beach. Between these excrescences the coast was very beautiful, the dazzling blue sea scarcely fifty yards away, its wavelets curling whitely onto golden sand. The dense subtropical vegetation on my left included mangroves and in the wayside grass a vivid abundance of wild flowers bravely bloomed amidst an equal abundance of tins, bottles and cartons. The strong headwind was welcome to temper the sun's ferocity. Near here miles of road are being widened by the sadistically named Savage & Lovemore construction company. When will such funding be redirected towards the ex-'homelands' and townships?

Stanger, an old colonial town near the Zululand border, was built on the site of King Shaka's capital where he was assassinated in 1828. It has long since lost the importance gained during the Zulu Wars. This hotel is grubby, the loos malodorously out of order, the mosquito netting on my bedroom window in tatters and the light switch broken. At Third World prices such details don't bother me but here the charge is R80, plus R12.50 for breakfast, and the black waiters are sullen and slothful.

Above the door to the Private Bar a faded notice reads: STRICTLY SMART. Within, three scruffy Afrikaners in dusty dungarees were quarrelling loudly, banging their beer bottles on the bar. My arrival prompted a slim, neatly suited Indian to try to quieten them. 'Lower your decibels!' he shouted. When they ignored him he hesitated, scowling – then grabbed one man by the arm and yelled, 'Get out and fight someplace else!' Pop-eyed with rage, the Afrikaner struck him across the face. At that the Indian barman vaulted over the counter – and I withdrew to enjoy my Long Tom in the warm dusk under a fragrant tree.

Five minutes later the Afrikaners came stumbling out – two with bleeding noses – pursued by the barman, the Indian customer and three black waiters. One of the Zulus with whom I was sitting grinned and said, 'See? Already we have our new South Africa!'

Those three young Zulus were neither ANC nor IFP but PAC, aching to vote and angrily scornful of Buthelezi's manoeuvrings. Sipho, an assistant teacher (i.e., unqualified), means to leave his ill-paid job after the elections and 'go into commerce' because 'then we'll have opportunities'. At the age of 32 he claims to have eleven children to support, seven of them born out of wedlock by four different mothers. He believes AIDS is 'propaganda from Pretoria to keep our numbers down'.

Tomorrow I hope to follow the tarred road to Kranskop and from there take dirt tracks to Ulundi, kwaZulu's capital. This plan has engendered much conflicting advice. An Afrikaner road-construction foreman says I'm suicidal, all Zulus are in murderous mood. My PAC friends say I'll be fine, much safer than in the Transkei because Zulus *like* whites and are only interested in killing each other. A white farmer agrees with them; his wife drives weekly to Tugela Ferry and never has a problem. An Indian high-school principal says I should return to Durban; too many are being given battle *muti*, in preparation for attacks on white farms after the elections, and they might like to test, as it were, the *muti*'s efficacy on me. Here my survival technique (Take Local Advice) isn't working, all such advice being politically and/or emotionally skewed.

Krankskop Police Post, 11 April

No, I haven't been arrested, though I am being confined here. My cell (unfurnished but clean) is not locked – yet were I to try to escape I would probably be captured.

The forty-eight miles to Kranskop are all uphill, rising from the coast into the mountains of kwaZulu. A memorable ride/walk (as much walking as pedalling) with little traffic, few settlements, much beauty – lushness being exchanged for austerity and the heat decreasing as I gained altitude. But then, frustration...

At 4 p.m., soon after turning onto the dirt road, kwaZulu's unwelcome 'invading force' – an SADF roadblock – confronted me. 'Where are you going?' demanded a stressed-looking young Afrikaner captain.

'To Ulundi,' said I cheerfully.

'No!' said he. 'There's an emergency here – have you been asleep? Who are you? Why are you here? We have big problems, get off this road!'

Two Indian KZP lieutenants strolled onto the scene. 'Come,' said one, 'come and rest with us and tomorrow continue to Greytown. This is a bad place now, we must protect you.'

New Hanover, 12 April

Near Greytown I again turned off the main road, Ulundi still my destination – via Tugela Ferry. This time I was prepared for the army roadblock and they, it seemed, were prepared for me. Kranskop must have warned them to beware of the crazed foreign female on a bicycle. Understandably, their tolerance level was low.

'Get lost!' said the captain crisply. 'Get out of kwaZulu and stay out! We've hassle enough without a dead tourist – right?'

'Right,' I meekly replied, turning away from a Paradise of mountain ranges.

Half an hour later, in Greytown – an inconsequential little place, only just in Natal – I admitted to myself that the SADF knew the score. On the main street I was momentarily touched by a fear that is hard to explain because nothing happened. But throngs of Zulu youths were eddying to and fro – not purposefully, as though about to march somewhere or do something, yet angrily. The atmosphere felt oddly ominous and I attracted many quick suspicious glances. When I stopped to buy amasi and a newspaper the Indian storekeeper said, 'Don't hang around, we could have trouble soon.'

'Why? What goes on?'

He half-smiled and replied, 'We don't ask, it's *their* problem. We only try to survive. Now move on and good luck!'

Moving on meant moving back to Pietermaritzburg via New Hanover. And then to where, kwaZulu being verboten? Cape Town, I decided, for two reasons. In the Western Cape the electoral contest has a unique flavour; nowhere else, if Buthelezi refuses to play, is an ANC victory in doubt. And last year I made many friends of all colours on the Peninsula. So Chris and I will go by overnight train to Jo'burg and there take the Transkaroo Express.

One of the most curious features of this election is that all the tension associated with it is divorced from the result. The *result* – with or without intimidation, with or without IFP participation – is already known. Nelson Mandela will be the next President of South Africa and the ANC will have an overwhelming majority of MPs in the new national parliament (the Constituent Assembly).

On a high, commercially forested ridge, facing the distant Drakensberg across the Valley of a Thousand Hills, I ate repellent sandwiches: shocking pink slimy polony between slices of gluey white bread, thoughtfully provided by the KZP.

Although that force has an even viler reputation than the SAP, my Kranskop hosts seemed decent young men – too decent to be happy with their present leadership.

From nearby foresters' shacks a dozen children, ragged and vitamin-deficient, came racing to inspect me. Their grandfather followed slowly and, unlike them, spoke English. He earnestly begged me to pray to God every hour that de Klerk and Buthelezi would be made the new leaders because Mandela as President would certainly cause civil war. He himself won't vote, he doesn't believe the ballot will be secret, he plans to remain indoors between 25 and 29 April. Having no comprehension of the political processes through which the new South Africa is being born, he is fazed by kwaZulu's electoral crisis. It's easy to forget that in a country with a huge illiteracy rate, and many homes too poor to own radios, millions don't know what the hell is going on.

Near New Hanover the SADF came rumbling towards me: three tanks with horrible protruding weapons. More than once in the mid-nineteenth century, up these same steep hills, struggled columns of redcoats accompanied by cavalry and countless ox-wagons, their mission to subdue the Zulus. Since this region first became the border area between Zululand and the Colony of Natal, its history has been grimly consistent. Hereabouts the Bambatha uprising of 1906 was put down by Natal's settlers with a savagery that shocked not only the Colonial Office in London but whites elsewhere in South Africa. Here, too, there was extreme unrest among farmworkers during the late 1920s and at intervals thereafter – unrest that is being replicated as I write.

New Hanover is a prosperous little town occupying a well-wooded slope above the main road and surrounded by large fertile farms. In the small hotel's ladies bar I was shown a smudgy, much-photocopied leaflet which I had already seen in Durban.

A terrible conflict is inevitable. Our crisis is only a microcosm for the macrocosmic racial assault taking place worldwide on everything the white man has built. The assault is driven by a no-name communism that is far from dead and involves Western collusion on a scale largely unsuspected. The forces behind it are such that black rioters and terrorists can break thousands of windows and kill thousands of innocent whites, but the international media will blast the world over the breaking of a single window by the AWB, who have killed no one. The AWB is preparing for a war involving firepower and firearm training must be given.

Signed Dr van Rensburg, Vereeniging

Said an English-speaker, 'Now they're trying to call up the commandos for security duties around the election. Do they think we're going to leave our places unguarded, for the kaffirs to grab? Bloody fools!'

Said an Afrikaner, 'Any kaffir coming near my land, I shoot him dead on the spot!'

This is not bombast; recently an Afrikaner shot dead five unarmed youths trying to raid his henhouse.

Pietermaritzburg, 13 April

The State of Emergency is coinciding with the closing down of Pietermaritzburg's 2,000-bed Edenvale Hospital because of an indefinite nurses' strike. More than 700 patients have been moved to other hospitals, already overstretched, and the sixty-three abandoned babies in the children's ward have been temporarily adopted by the non-striking white staff: doctors, social workers, administrators. (The number of abandoned babies is one more symptom of black demoralization.) Eight months ago strike action was brewing and perhaps it's no coincidence that it has happened now, during this time of general turmoil. In turn, it is aggravating white jitteriness. A strike-closed hospital rings alarm bells; in stable societies this sort of thing is not allowed to happen. And today the kwaZulu/Natal ambulance and emergency services have also gone on strike because they are paid only half the wages of their colleagues in other provinces.

Since last weekend twenty-three people have been murdered in nearby townships. When a joint SAP/SADF patrol intervened in a kwaMancinza battle the factions stopped fighting for just long enough to fire more than 300 shots at the security forces.

These days, few whites are seen in town centres. My English-speaking friends admit, 'We are in retreat' – shopping hurriedly, not strolling around the pleasant parks or meeting friends for leisurely sessions in Pietermaritzburg's cosy little coffee shops. However, many more blacks are visible; hawkers trade everywhere, including on the wide steps of the municipal offices and court house, where they assert 'equality' by spreading woven blankets and crocheted tablecloths on the ornamental shrubs.

Early this morning, as I pushed Chris along one-way Church Street, an oldish thin woman, coughing painfully, was spreading her wares on the pavement: red and green apples, oranges, pears and small bottles labelled 'whisky' or 'gin' or 'vodka' and containing God-knows-what home-distilled hooch. Young women were settling their babies into cardboard cartons for the day; many speak good English (hawkers tend to be among the better educated) but none is at present disposed to discuss politics. When I overtook a well-dressed woman, carrying an expensive leather handbag over one arm and a huge wooden box on her head, she called after me – 'Are you the Irish lady?' Six filthy little street boys were tying ANC posters to every other lamp-standard. They looked depraved, with old cruel faces, and their leader wielded a sharpened bicycle spoke; only these juvenile desperadoes are unafraid to perform this task in kwaZulu/Natal. What does the new South Africa hold for them?

Towards noon, at the junction of Boshoff and Bulwer streets, roads were being blocked off by yellow SAP armoured vehicles while eight well-armed soldiers on motorbikes cruised up and down. A pair of girl hawkers on a corner fumbled nervously as they packed up their few boxes of fruit and the packets from which cigarettes are sold singly. They hastened away as I heard cheerful chanting and saw an ANC Women's League march approaching, led by three youngish women bearing an enormous white banner with the legend: ONE CHICKEN IN EVERY POT, ONE HOUSE FOR EVERY FAMILY, ONE CAR IN EVERY DRIVEWAY. (Is a car really more important than education and medical care? Or was this a deliberate tease, playing on current white fears?) The 150 or so women and a dozen men were escorted by almost as many troops and police. Joining the march, I noticed that a remarkable number of low-ranking, poorly paid KZP officers wear costly gold watches.

The women welcomed me jovially and we walked in hot sun for an hour, past the railway station, up a long hill to the rallying point on an open grassy space in a not very affluent 'white' area. From their neat gardens, residents with blank expressions watched our passing. Their more nervous neighbours peered through windows protected by newly installed security grilles.

What my companions told me came as no surprise. That shorthand phrase 'political violence' veils the terrible complexity of the townships' present bloodiness. Those communities live all the time on the edge of anarchy, tormented by faction feuds, taxi wars, drug wars, land wars. A political crisis merely takes off all the brakes; then conflicts with multiple roots are labelled 'political violence'. An overweight woman on my right, gallantly panting her way uphill, said, 'It's not the elections have brought us to this. It's forty-five years of overcrowding and poverty. But now things will be better. Buthelezi can't stop destiny.'

Other marchers had come by other routes and this was quite a large rally; unfortunately all the long, impassioned speeches were in Zulu.

Today a team of seven international mediators, led by Lord Carrington and Mr Henry Kissinger, arrived in Jo'burg to tackle the ANC/IFP impasse. Their appearance on the scene has occasioned much hilarity. A planeload of foreigners imagining they can solve this peculiarly South African problem – hey man, that's crazy!

The same, 14 April

This afternoon the international mediators departed, having had not a single meeting with anyone. (I'd like to be a fly on the wall of their aeroplane.) Neither the ANC nor the Nats were prepared even to consider postponing the elections and without postponement high on the agenda the IFP refused to negotiate. End of silly story.

Last Monday seven young black men, distributing voter-education pamphlets from a minibus in rural kwaZulu, were murdered. None had any link with a political party; Natal Pamphlet Distributors had hired them for that reason. A local Inkatha chief told them no voting would be allowed in kwaZulu and ordered their deaths – after some two hours of torture. One 19-year-old, aptly named Lucky Mkhwanazi, escaped by feigning death after his head had been hacked with a panga and two of his fingers shot off. It took him forty-eight hours to walk the fifty miles back to Durban; no one would stop to give him a lift. When Natal Pamphlet Distributors reported the team's disappearance on Monday evening the KZP refused to investigate. The bodies were found only at noon on Tuesday, by a special Pretoria-based SAP unit. Thanks to Lucky's evidence, the chief and five other men are now in jail. Had he not survived, no one would have been arrested. It's easy to get away with murder in kwaZulu/Natal.

It was odd to read in the *Natal Witness*, amidst various accounts of undetected or unpunished murders, a paragraph headed 'Man Fined for Hitting Lamb at Auction' – in Arkansas, USA.

This evening, in the large crowded bar of Tommy's hotel, at least half the customers didn't bother to watch the vigorously hyped TV debate between President de Klerk and Mr Mandela. This imported stunt seemed meaningless – a Government of National Unity (GNU) has already been accepted as the way forward. It put both men in a false position, performing live in a TV duel that flatly contradicted GNU's reconciliatory objective. President de Klerk, an experienced professional politician, was of course the more polished performer though his English is less fluent than Mr Mandela's. (Both were using their second language.) The latter, aware that his hardline followers rage against this demeaning debate with a man they despise, too often attacked the President personally in an un-Mandela-like way. Much dirty linen was dragged out of both laundry baskets, a tactic not calculated to lower tension. But this is all part of the present muddle – seeing a TV confrontation as mandatory during a 'democratic' election campaign, however inappropriate it may be.

I'm aware of a growing sense of unreality; we seem to be living in a world of sheer make-believe. One day the IEC announces that elections cannot be held in kwaZulu/Natal, the next day that they can. Meanwhile it has become clear that the elections, nationwide, cannot possibly be 'free and fair'. Yet the IEC, the main parties and the thousands of international monitors and observers will not dare to declare them unfree and unfair; the repercussions would be, literally, unimaginable. So everyone must pretend that the new South Africa will be a stable, investor-friendly 'democracy'. And the world's media, well trained to walk to heel, will not question what really goes on here.

Sadly, Gilbert Hani died yesterday in a Durban hospital at the age of 83. If only he could have lived one more fortnight!

12

The Miracle

The Cape Peninsula

Ubuntu says I am human only because you are human. If I undermine your humanity,
I dehumanize myself. You must do what you can, in the new South Africa, to maintain
this great harmony, which is perpetually threatened by resentment, anger, desire for
vengeance. That's why African jurisprudence is restorative rather than retributive.
Archbishop Desmond Tutu

Observatory, 24 April 1994

Since my return to the Peninsula a week ago life has been stimulating, bewilder-
ing, exasperating and just occasionally alarming. (As yesterday, when a mob of
Coloured Nat supporters ran out of control at President de Klerk's final election
rally in the Good Hope Centre.) My notebook is full of comments on various
ANC, Nat and DP rallies, some cerebral and decorous, others emotional and
rowdy.

At no rally was there any sense of the speakers having the power to influence
their listeners' voting intentions. These were gatherings of the faithful, people
who had turned out not to weigh up the politicians' policies or promises but to
support them with uncritical enthusiasm. Being well aware of this, party leaders
regard the printed word as the most valuable electioneering tool – one that has
been shamefully abused by the Nats. Here in the Western Cape their virulently
racist *'swart gevaar'* campaign makes nonsense of their claim to be 'the New Nats'.
One brochure warns: 'Under an ANC government, this could easily become the
slogan – KILL A COLOURED! KILL A FARMER!' Another brochure depicts a snarling
Communist wolf inadequately disguised by an ANC sheepskin and the bilingual
text asks,

> What lies beneath the ANC? Communist lies! The Communists, with their own agenda,
> have infiltrated the ANC to its core. How can they be trusted? Their policies have failed
> everywhere. If they are not stopped, they will ruin South Africa as well. Only the NP
> can stop the ANC!

Repeatedly the Nats insist that an ANC/Communist government will oppress
the Churches. Outsiders may find such a recycling of the Total Onslaught myth

merely ridiculous but to the ill-informed it is spine-chilling stuff, as Saatchi and Saatchi well know.

At the end of March the Nats went too far by distributing 70,000 glossy, reprehensible, comic-type booklets. These show a black youth named Mike Sibasa beating up with his rifle-butt an elderly Coloured lady – carrying prayer books – while he shouts, 'There is no God! The government is your God!' On the next page Mike is shooting dead a gentle young Coloured man as he plays his guitar. 'Now we're finished with you!' taunts Mike. 'You were *useful idiots*!'

The IEC, responding to ANC and other protests, quickly banned this publication and confiscated the unused copies. President de Klerk and Hernus Kriel, the Nats' candidate for the Cape premiership, of course knew nothing about it – just as they know nothing about Third Force operations.

Saatchi and Saatchi are being helped to run the Nats' campaign by Sir Tim Bell of Lowe-Bell Communications who is credited in the local media with 'Margaret Thatcher's transformation from Lincs. grocer's daughter to Iron Lady'. He may find the transformation of the Nats' image rather more difficult; in that Lincs. grocery store the iron was already there.

As for the ANC, they steadfastly preach their 82-year-old non-racist gospel and both their literature and their leaders' speeches are above reproach. But some of their rank-and-file supporters, ignoring Madiba's pleas, are behaving abominably – and some of their local organizers not too well.

However, the Western Cape – an Inkatha-free zone – remains comparatively peaceful. Unlike the PWV where last weekend an ANC-versus-Inkatha gunbattle left nineteen dead. The victims included the young photographer Ken Oosterbroek, thrice South Africa's News Photographer of the Year; two of his colleagues were badly wounded. On the edge of Tokoza an army officer had warned journalists, 'Our situation is very bad. You may enter but you do so at your own risk.'

Subsequently Themba Khoza, the PWV Inkatha leader, threatened to spread the violence throughout his region. Recently Judge Goldstone's Commission revealed that Mr Khoza has been in the pay of the SAP secret terror unit since 1989.

Yesterday, in Ulundi, two ANC canvassers were shot dead in the KZP station while another was being burned to death outside, in his car. Several IEC monitors were also attacked and imprisoned in the police station; white KZP officers protected them until Buthelezi arrived from Bloemfontein by air and ordered his loyal Inkatha Youth Brigade to disperse. Mr Mandela then requested him – as kwaZulu Minister of Police – to confine the KZP to barracks until after the elections.

Throughout South Africa hearts have been lighter since 19 April when Buthelezi at last gave in, accepting far less than was previously offered. It seems the country has reasons to be grateful to an elderly Kenyan, Professor Washington Jalang'o Okumu, a member of the 'damp-squib' mediation team who lingered when the rest left and quietly set about making the Inkatha leader see sense. The *Cape Times* quoted him: 'Western mindsets clouded an essentially African problem. You give deadlines and say you must do such and such by this date. In Africa that does not work. You must address sensitivities and deeply felt prejudices.' Doubtless the professor helped Buthelezi to realize that having failed to delay the elections or secure more power for provincial governments he would soon find himself in a cul-de-sac with the AWB and the Afrikaner Volksfront. Not a prestigious – or lucrative – place to be under GNU. Now he is sure of a cabinet post.

According to Judge Kriegler of the IEC, Buthelezi's brinkmanship will add millions of rands to the election bill. Eighty million IFP stickers have had to be hurriedly printed and stuck to the end of the ballot papers where there is barely room for them. And in kwaZulu/Natal 700 polling stations must be set up within six days. Many are smirking because the Nats have lost their place at the foot of the ballot papers only hours after a new rash of posters urged the populace: 'To be tops, vote at the bottom!'

On 21 April came more reassuring news: another right-wing split, providing a safety-valve for those who might otherwise favour the bullet over the ballot. General Viljoen's new Freedom Front party has rejected a 'Boycott the Elections' pact with the CP and instead made a pact with GNU-to-be. At once most CP-controlled councils deserted their leadership and urged whites to vote Freedom Front. In this context 'freedom' means freedom for the Afrikaners to set up their own volkstaat, an ambition few take seriously – least of all, I suspect, General Viljoen. An intelligent man, he is much respected by right-wingers as a general who led from the front during South Africa's covert war in Angola. But of course his pact with GNU has enraged the CP leadership. In reaction, Mr Kobus Beyers, MP, warned that his followers will disrupt the elections and 'it might be dangerous to vote in certain areas'. That evening we also had an AWB announcement: 'Thousands of members of the AWB are already moving into the Transvaal and Free State to secure a base against a future Communist government.'

Three days ago all this fantasizing seemed to me a giggling matter. But this morning a colossal car bomb, planted in Jo'burg between the ANC and PAC headquarters, killed nine people and wounded more than a hundred. One woman lost her three small children when a ceiling collapsed. Another victim was an Irish-born ANC election candidate, Susan Keane, who happened to be waiting in her car for traffic lights to change. The police have offered half a million rands reward for information.

Unsurprisingly, the IEC have advised me not to visit Khayelitsha at present. Nat and DP canvassers 'have no access' – as the IEC delicately puts it – to any of the black townships or squatter camps. (To balance this, ANC canvassers 'have no access' to that one-fifth of the black electorate who live, countrywide, on white farms.) However, in a brave attempt to demonstrate how democracy should work the IEC, a few days ago, organized 'Operation Access'. Nat, ANC and DP speakers were escorted to four Khayelitsha venues where they gave bland speeches in each other's presence. There was no threat of violence. Nor was there any heckling because nobody gathered to listen. The politicians found this quite an eerie experience – addressing large empty spaces through a megaphone.

Another of these elections' eccentricities is the population mystery. How many South Africans are there? No one knows; when people are surplus you don't bother to count them. Officially, in the Western Cape, blacks make up 18 per cent of the population; unofficial estimates range from 20 to 45 per cent. It is impossible to guess how many have recently arrived.

A local idiosyncrasy is the invisibility of Hernus Kriel, the Nat candidate for the provincial premiership and a known ally of the Third Force. Throughout his career, but especially as Minister of Law and Order (!) in the present government, he has shown a dangerous and sometimes ludicrous lack of judgement. Last week an emergency meeting of 1,000 policemen and women of all races passed a unanimous vote of no confidence in their minister, something unprecedented in SAP history. So far I haven't seen the hated Kriel face on a single poster, lapel badge or leaflet. Instead, President de Klerk beams fondly on the populace. Nor does Kriel often share a platform with his leader as de Klerk energetically tours the Western Cape, the only province where a Nat victory is possible because of the Coloured vote.

Both contenders for this provincial premiership are flawed in the public's perception. The ANC's Revd Allan Boesak, though a powerful orator, didn't much appeal to me at last year's Sowetan Day rally. And he seemed no more appealing when I listened to him a few days ago at a UWC-organized debate with the DP's Hennie Bester. Many ANC activists deplore Mr Mandela's choice of this Coloured clergyman with an unorthodox (by clerical standards) view of matrimony, a man who not long ago was a source of bitter dissension within his Dutch Reformed Mission Church. Madiba does have one serious handicap as leader, an allergy to unwelcome advice however sound it may be.

Two days ago a small blurred black-and-white handbill – 'Unite Against Racism' – was stuck to Cape Town's lamp-posts, scarcely noticeable amidst the profusion of garish election posters. It invited people to a Cape Against Racism (CAR) ecumenical gathering in the Concert Hall (part of the City Hall) at

3 p.m. today. CAR is a tiny organization, newly formed to counter the Nats' irresponsible electioneering.

The Concert Hall boasts a famously sonorous organ behind a vast stage and, as a setting for CAR's meeting, there was something piquantly incongruous about the baroque décor, the ornate brass chandeliers, the four gilded boxes on either side of the high-ceilinged auditorium. We were only 250 or so (mostly black) when the celebrated Langa Adult Choir filed onto the stage, the women wearing crimson and white, the men crimson and black.

This was indeed an ecumenical occasion, chaired by a black Anglican theologian, Barney Pityana, one of the founders with Steve Biko of the Black Consciousness Movement. Other speakers included a white Buddhist monk, a Coloured Baha'i preacher, a black Methodist minister, an Afrikaner Unitarian and a Muslim imam – Faried Essak, who yesterday was badly beaten up by Nat marshals during the Good Hope Centre fracas. From their exhilarating variety of theological/philosophical perspectives these remarkable men – the majority youngish – considered South Africa's most urgent problems without any soggy piety or platitudinous reassurances. It was therapeutic to be transported from a world of political rhetoric and scheming into their world of genuine compassion and intellectual integrity.

25 April

I woke this morning longing for physical exercise in a motor-free zone and soon was pushing Chris up cobbled Longmarket Street towards Signal Hill above Bo-Kaap. Near the summit, rich Muslims have recently built a colony of two- and three-storey mansions and here the road becomes concrete. Dismal piles of builders' rubble still stand around and the verges are sordidly littered – blemishes unthinkable in rich white areas.

Beyond the colony two kind Eksom workers lifted Chris over a wire fence and showed me where to wriggle underneath. Then, as we bumped along a rough track, smoke began to rise from the far side of the hill. Astonishingly quickly the puffs became a towering cloud – black, flecked with crimson morsels. Soon the urgent sirens of speeding fire engines could be heard on the roads below; I had chosen the wrong hill on which to exercise.

From a high shoulder I watched the drama, feeling an oddly pleasurable frisson of primitive fear. Starting low, above Ocean View Drive, the flames swept up a steep slope with a crackling roar, devouring the dry grasses and indigenous vegetation. Scores of firemen, helped by Forestry Department workers, struggled to drag hosepipes uphill while others led them downwards from tankers parked on the summit viewing-point. One could see their plan: to contain the flames by a pincer movement. Then, as it seemed they were succeeding, the strengthening wind swung from north-west to south-east and the flames jumped Signal Road – a truly scary sight – and raced away towards Green Point along a sheer inaccessible 1,200-foot mountain flank.

Back in Cape Town's centre I chanced to notice a small crowd – mostly media folk – gathered as close to the House of Assembly as the police would permit. A friendly Coloured SAP officer told me that South Africa's white parliament was sitting for the last time – a special one-day sitting to secure the position of King Zwelithini, as recently agreed with Buthelezi, by amending the new Constitution. Soon the King's emissary, Prince Gideon Zulu, appeared on the steps surrounded by five Paramount Chiefs – naked torsos gleaming, pot-bellies protruding, each carrying his shield and sporting a leopard-skin cloak, leopard-skin wristbands, armbands woven from the tail-hairs of white oxen, belts of jackals' tails and a lion-claw necklace. This was the moment the cameramen had been waiting for. But before posing the chiefs demanded the return of their spears and knobkerries, confiscated as they entered Parliament. I looked in vain for President de Klerk; perhaps he sensibly chose to make his last exit as President through a side door.

Today Cape Town is SAP-saturated, with good reason. Less than twenty-four hours after yesterday's Jo'burg bomb, another killed ten and seriously injured forty-one at a black taxi-rank on the East Rand. The police have doubled their information reward to R1 million but no arrests have been made.

This evening, in Pretoria, two were killed and twenty-nine injured when white motorists threw a bomb into a black restaurant while driving past. Within the last three days ten other major bombings have caused immense damage but no casualties, though one exploded in the 'Ladies' of the Randfontein taxi-rank during the morning rush-hour. Others wrecked a Wonderfontein electricity pylon and several polling stations in right-wing areas. At noon yesterday three empty taxis parked below a bridge near Pochefstroom were demolished when white motorists tossed a bomb over the parapet.

The Deputy Law and Order Minister guarantees that more than 100,000 police, supported by tens of thousands of soldiers, will be protecting all polling stations. There has been the biggest call-up of reserve forces in the peace-time history of South Africa. From tomorrow until 29 April, the sale or public consumption of alcohol has been forbidden.

26 April

Wondrously, the right-wingers' violence seems to be having little or no effect on public morale; one senses it being dismissed as the last convulsive spasm of a doomed monster.

This morning polling stations opened for the elderly, the disabled, the pregnant, hospital patients and South African citizens abroad. Nobody can accuse Judge Kriegler's team of laziness; on the 23rd, a charter flight carried 140 whites to a beachfront hotel on the Comoros Islands where, by special arrangement with the IEC, a polling booth has been installed.

As I toured the Peninsula this afternoon a joyous calm prevailed. Perhaps the orderly functioning of those 'special' polling stations has turned a key releasing all races from their cage of pre-election tension. My Mandela badges and Chris's ANC stickers prompted many beaming blacks to greet me by punching the air and shouting, 'Viva President Mandela Viva!' Forget 'irregularities at the polls'! Already the whole world knows who the majority of South Africans want to lead their country.

It is now 11.30 p.m. In half an hour the Interim Constitution will come into force marking the birth of the new South Africa. At 11.59 the old *baasskap* flag will be lowered, to the strains of Die Stem, in the nine capitals of the new provincial legislatures. At 12.01 the new flag will be raised and both anthems played (Die Stem and Nkosi Sikelel' iAfrica). All speeches have been banned during these ceremonies. Given this country's history, the two-anthem symbolism is moving beyond words. Who but Madiba could have inspired it?

As I write I feel curiously numb, sitting alone in my little room in Obs while the last minutes of the old South Africa tick away. Evidently the sheer improbability of the new South Africa is paralysing my emotions; some occasions are so awesomely significant that one fails to react to them. But I find myself questioning the current buzz-phrases: 'democracy for all', 'gender equality', 'a new constitutional order'. What is happening here and now is something peculiarly African: *ubuntu* in action. (Or, cynics might say, the exploitation of *ubuntu*.) My watch lies on the desk in front of me. It is 11.57 and I am about to open a Long Tom to drink to the new South Africa.

27 April

A still grey morning, clouds low, a hush over the city as I cycled to the nearest polling station at 6 a.m. Already the queue was in place and lengthening by the minute. Hundreds of Coloureds, blacks, whites: not talking, looking rather solemn. As yet there were no Monitors or Observers on duty and only one of those 100,000 police officers. Strangely, unchecked cars were allowed to park within easy bomb-reach of the queue.

Sitting on a bollard I thought, tritely but accurately, 'This is the day – the hour – for which so many have suffered so much.' And then my mind roved over all those places I know, between Cape Town and Messina – everywhere everyone queuing together, in a ritual discarding of the past.

Many steps lead up to the entrance to Woodstock's polling station. At the head of the queue, on the top step, stood an elderly black couple. Precisely at 7 a.m the door opened and they entered to cast their vote. That was the trigger. A wave of emotion rippled through the crowd. Still no one spoke but people turned to look at one another, whites and blacks and Coloureds communicating without words. Tears flowed, including mine. Ostensibly this was a political event, the election of a government. In reality it was – what was it? It felt then, and all day, like a sacrament of healing.

Near the exit behind the building only one journalist was visible, defying the 600-metre exclusion zone – a young Dutchman, diligently seeking 'reactions' as the voters emerged. But seemingly he was a sensitive character and he soon gave up. For the world's journalists, today was a major media event. For most South Africans it was a profound, private experience, something to be happily celebrated yet in its essence beyond the reach of words.

At a Bo-Kaap polling station, a new school on a hillside, two police officers had just arrived in an armoured vehicle drawing a kennel-trailer full of snarling Alsatians. Many in the queue objected to this. 'We've no problems here,' shouted one young man. 'Why bring those dogs to start trouble?'

I could see his point; police dogs reek of *baasskap* terrorism. Yet the police have been ordered to make their protective presence felt everywhere and right-wingers on the rampage might fancy a soft target like Bo-Kaap. As three International Observers remonstrated with the officers everyone intently watched while the dogs continued to scrabble at their wire mesh and bare their teeth. Those Australians were exceeding their brief by intervening and the police might justifiably have told them so. Instead, they removed their provocative canine back-up. 'Off to make trouble someplace else!' muttered the young woman beside me, adjusting her headscarf. Happily she was wrong.

Countrywide, 11,000 South African Monitors and 5,000 International Observers were on duty today. The latter are just that – passive observers, supposed merely to report their observations to the IEC. They have been drifting around the country for weeks and by now are generally viewed as freeloaders enjoying an extended holiday in sunny South Africa. Said one Monitor this afternoon, 'Most are too ignorant to know the meaning of what they observe. Only foreigners who've lived here in the past are useful.'

The Monitors themselves come in three colourful varieties: IEC Monitors (white bibs and pale green baseball caps), Peace Committee Monitors (bright orange bibs and armbands) and the Network of Independent Monitors (pale blue jackets and baseball caps) – known as NIMS.

Today only the weather was unkind. As I cycled to Retreat and Grassy Park, stopping at various polling stations en route, a strong wind drove sheets of cold rain along the Peninsula. But this did nothing to shorten queues or dampen spirits. Instead, it emphasized the prevailing harmony as umbrellas or plastic sacks were shared, and whites who lived near the queues made thermos flasks of tea for shivering blacks and Coloureds.

At Newlands I heard about this morning's 7.15 car bomb at Jan Smuts airport – a mega-bomb, its timing significant. Inexplicably no one was killed though three were seriously injured and much structural damage done.

Near Claremont's polling station I sheltered under an arcade beside three 'information tables' presided over by several ebullient young blacks and Coloureds. They were handing out ANC literature – until an electoral officer arrived, following a DP complaint about breaking IEC regulations. An argument then started with the Claremont presiding officer – why had he reduced the 600-metre control area? When I returned three hours later negotiations had just ended peacefully. At most stations similar mini-squabbles were arising but even incidents with the potential to turn nasty never did so. Everyone finally accepted IEC decisions – despite the increasingly apparent muddle within the commission itself – even if it took them three hours to climb down.

Outside Mowbray's station a policeman moved me on when I inadvertently entered the control area; the ANC sticker running along Chris's crossbar broke IEC rules. Then, as I stood just beyond the line of white tape, a nervous NIM told me that reports were coming in of crises (no ballot papers!) in Khayelitsha and other black townships. As she spoke a solitary troublemaker appeared, a small, slight, goatee-bearded Xhosa, elderly and well dressed. Loudly he ranted against the Third Force saboteurs who were now depriving blacks of their democratic rights. Everyone ignored him – except the police, who conferred by radio with IEC headquarters and were advised to take no action.

Moments later, the various species of Monitor and the Coloured ANC marshals became perceptibly agitated. According to their radios, the ANC Youth League had hired one hundred buses to transport township voters to white suburbs not short of ballot papers.

Soon the first convoy arrived from Khayelitsha and parked on the main road. Again tears came to my eyes as I watched those Xhosas toyi-toying and dancing down a side-street to the polling station, cheering and singing and laughing and clapping, waving South Africa's new flag and radiating joy. Many habitually wear ANC T-shirts or baseball caps or badges; today, all respected the rule forbidding 'party favours or colours'. On reaching the end of the queue – more than half a mile long, stretching around two blocks – they joined it in as orderly a fashion as any citizens from Constantia or Green Point. And for hours they stood there, patiently, happily, singing and laughing and being drenched at intervals when another squall of rain came riding on the wind. Many young women carried babies and did a brisk trade by renting them to those who could afford to expedite their exercise of the franchise. (Baby-laden mothers were given special treatment and infants were not invisibly inked.)

But where were all the thugs, the tsotsies, the hooligans, the extremists of every colour? Nowhere to be seen today, in any region of South Africa. Yet this influx of township voters was the very stuff of pre-election white nightmares – the invasion of 'our' areas by thousands of hyped-up young blacks who would certainly run amok. Those fears proved how little whites understood the significance for blacks of 27 April 1994. Why should they, on today of all days, run destructively out of control? Now the new flag of liberated South Africa – *their* flag! – is to be seen flying high, outstretched in the wind, above every police station, army post and public building. Moreover, all saps officers have a tiny patch of sticky tape at the end of their name-badges obliterating the old flag. To people who have suffered so much at their hands (and their batons, guns and dogs) this is the most potent symbol of all.

Outside Green Point's station I happened upon a Peace Committee Monitor friend. She offered me a mug of coffee from her flask and wondered, 'How many ballot papers will be spoiled?' I, too, had been wondering that. The TEC's reverence for democracy led them to over-indulge dotty minuscule parties like KISS (Keep It Straight and Simple) and SOCCER (Sports Organization for Collective Contributions and Equal Rights). Not to mention the Ximoko Progressive Party, which has never let the public glimpse its policy. And the Dikwankwetla Party, led by T.K. Mopeli of whom no one has ever heard – but surely anyone swayed solely by euphony would vote for the Dikwankwetlas. All this works against South Africa's novice voters who must cope with a foot-long national ballot paper listing the names, logos and leaders' photographs of eighteen parties, the greater number completely irrelevant. And some of the provincial ballot papers list twenty-eight parties.

This evening's TV Election Special revealed that eight of Khayelitsha's sixteen polling stations opened seven hours late and thirteen closed early for lack of ballot papers, invisible ink and infra-red lamps. Miles of voters queued for up to ten hours, until the IEC and army got their acts together and dropped papers by helicopter. An IEC spokesman admitted to 'major systems failures' which I suppose is computerese for a cock-up. The problems, he assured a throng of infuriated presiding officers, would be given 'top priority' overnight, with more helicopter drops at dawn.

For many, a busy night lies ahead. The army will be printing an extra 9.3 million ballot papers to supplement the 80 million already printed in Britain. But how are the IEC going to deliver them to remote areas all over the country by 7 a.m. tomorrow? It seems there are many more South Africans than anyone ever suspected. And virtually all of them over the age of 17 are determined to vote. Some IEC officials are privately confessing that thousands in kwaZulu/Natal will be frustrated, Buthelezi's brinkmanship having caused insuperable logistical problems. And now he is being tiresome again, threatening to pull out of the elections because some papers were minus their IFP stickers. Peevishly he rejected an IEC concession allowing individual voters to write in the IFP – some 60 per cent of 'his' people are illiterate and already unnerved at the prospect of having to handle a pen...

To the fury of employers and the delight of everyone else, tomorrow has been hastily declared another paid public holiday; and, if necessary, the voting period will be extended to 29 April.

28 April

Something mysterious has happened within South Africa during the past forty-eight hours. Extreme tension has been replaced by an extraordinary calm, a deep calm that can be felt as though it were a climatic change – physically felt, in the body as well as the soul. And this phenomenon is nationwide.

Since 25 April there has been an eerie lack of crime. My favourite explanation was hinted at by Colonel Henriette Bester of the West Rand police: 'I've visited all the polling stations and there's so much goodwill going around you can feel it.' Even in kwaZulu/Natal and on the East Rand, the security forces have been able to relax. And in the Free State, during the past three days, the police have recorded no crime of any kind – not even one stolen chicken. Cartoonists and columnists are beginning to mock those whites who crammed their cellars, garages and garden sheds with every sort of durable but unappetizing comestible. How soon will the divorce rate go up as husbands rebel against tinned beans and frankfurters five times a week?

Meanwhile the electoral shambles has fallen over the edge into comedy and the count will take longer than expected – much longer. Computers are playing up or being fed the wrong diet. (Everyone is astonished to hear that the Irish run all their elections with flawless efficiency sans computers.) Ballot papers beyond reckoning have not been delivered to the 800 counting centres because their armed escorts failed to turn up. Accusations and denials of intimidation, muddle, rigging and conspiracy are flying in every direction. Here we wonder who secreted 900,000 ballot papers in a merchant's warehouse near Cape Town's airport on the 26th? On discovering the contents of the boxes the merchant called the police, then received an anonymous death-threat. Allegedly the boxes were moved to a security company's store but no one knows what happened next. Does their fate explain the Khayelitsha crisis? A flustered IEC spokeswoman explained, 'We are now reorganizing the distribution of ballot papers. Serious misplacement [sic] has taken place and we are asking the police to investigate.'

Today SAPS announced that thirty-one men, including a policeman and a police reservist, have been arrested in connection with the recent car-bombings. Among them are ET's son-in-law, Leon van der Merwe, and the AWB's executive secretary and Chief of Staff. Unusually, none is being granted bail. That million-rand reward, the largest in South Africa's history, was money well spent.

The first three new South Africans were named Freedom and Happiness (boys) and Thankful (a girl) – all born within five minutes of midnight on the 27th.

29 April

This has been the fourth day of voting, though only in kwaZulu/Natal where Buthelezi insisted on 'his' people being given time to use the newly printed ballot papers.

During the past fortnight or so more than 3,000 foreign media folk have been swarming all over South Africa, the majority endearing themselves only to hoteliers and restaurant owners. Their pesterings reached 'public-nuisance' level in some black areas, especially kwaZulu/Natal where the search for grue-some details sickened bereaved locals. It was also noted that while themselves wearing bullet-proof vests, they expected their interpreters to enter danger zones unprotected. And their lack of interest in an area's everyday problems did not impress. Now most have moved on to genocidal Rwanda.

'And yet' – commented my host – 'our present peacefulness is surely among the "stories" of the century!'

'But they're vampires,' said his wife, 'can't survive without a blood diet!'

30 April

Passing through Simonstown at noon, I stopped off at the Navy pub where a 17-year-old English-speaking midshipman – a beardless youth, pink-cheeked and blue-eyed with curly blond hair – was sad to have missed voting by ten months. 'I would have liked to help make history. But you know, it wasn't a mystery or a miracle, like people are saying. It only seemed that way because whites got so panicky beforehand.'

Out of the mouths of babes and teenagers... 'Go on,' I urged, 'say more.'

'Isn't it obvious? I've nothing clever to say. It's just that most South Africans want peace. The elections were to set things up so we could have it. So why should they have caused trouble? When things change people go along with it. My dad was a racist five years ago, now he's not. Well, what I mean is he can take a black president now, I don't mean he'd ever have black *friends*. Maybe he couldn't take every black president but Mandela made it easy. Even people who go on about him being a Commie really *trust* him. You have to, you'd be screwed up yourself if you couldn't see he's a good guy.'

A good guy... Yes, indeed. While pedalling across the Peninsula to Scarborough, I reflected that Madiba is no mere politician; that's what distinguishes him from other national leaders. He has the dignity and confidence of someone who has inherited authority rather than striven to acquire it. Truly he has become the Father of the Nation and he talks like a kind but firm Victorian papa – his vocabulary democratic, his tone more often benignly authoritarian. This paternalism has been especially noticeable recently as he addressed mass-rallies that in spirit were celebrations of his imminent election as President. Even here on Nat territory he made no effort to avoid unpopular home-truths and, as the responsibilities of the Presidency drew closer, I noted his speeches becoming increasingly didactic and explicit. (During these past weeks I have watched more television than in all my previous 62 years.) Consistently he has impressed upon his followers the need to wait for change. And he has urged them to support the security forces – no longer the 'enemy' but *their* security forces. And to respect the chiefs, even those on the side of 'reactionary elements'. And to remember that, under GNU, most white civil servants will retain their jobs 'because we need them for a future government'.

1 May

All the election results were supposed to be in by midnight tonight; none will be. Some counters have failed to turn up, others have been accused of innumeracy, others are on strike for more pay. The ballot boxes from Mitchells Plain, this province's most populous district, arrived at the counting station only yesterday afternoon. On 28 April Mitchells Plain's chief electoral officer, Mr K. Mqamqo, strode off the scene, having quarrelled with colleagues, and hasn't been seen since. As no replacement was appointed the collection of boxes simply didn't happen.

The Free State has discovered that 115 per cent of its voters turned out – 200,000 more than expected. In parts of the Northern Transvaal, Northern Natal and the Transkei, thousands were disenfranchised by the failure of ballot papers ever to turn up. Hundreds of thousands of unused papers were found in warehouses in the East and West Rand, a matter now under investigation by the IEC and SAPS. All over the country boxes are missing, or have been found unsealed, or in kwaZulu have been tightly packed with neat piles of papers marked in favour of the IFP.

At Nasrec, near Jo'burg, security has broken down in the main counting centre and ballot papers have been photographed strewn all over the floor. Outside Nasrec, Nat and ANC agents exchanged blows when twelve boxes of

unused papers were found in the back of an unguarded unofficial car. An IFP
agent provoked the fight by citing this irregularity as evidence of collusion
between the IEC and ANC. Soldiers had to be called in to control the crowd.

Long delays in the 'reconciliation' of papers have forced the IEC to declare
that this process, previously described as 'essential', is not really necessary. ANC,
Nat and DP officials have criticized the IEC's 'breathtaking inefficiency and
outrageously lax security', then hastened to assure everyone that these flaws
cannot affect the result. Judge Kriegler, who two days ago pronounced the
elections 'substantially free and fair', is being reviled by many – though still
defended by a few – and looks like a man who won't ever again run an election.

Hout Bay, 2 May

Strangely, only today have I myself *felt* the new South Africa, in the sense of fully
realizing the glory and the wonder of it. That appreciation came to me like a
vision as I sat beside Chris on Chapman's Peak Drive. Below me, a calm Atlantic
sparkled blue – or turquoise, where the water broke on grey-brown boulders, the
dissipating foam making map-shapes. I was looking down high sheer cliffs,
supporting numerous varieties of aromatic fynbos. Above me towered the
reddish and fawn precipices of layered Chapman's Peak – sandstone and
mudstone, deposited near the shore of a shallow sea 450 million years ago. (So
said a nearby notice.) The waves were rhythmically languid and peaceful. Hout
Bay's sentinel peak leaned out towards the ocean in a listening position. Three
little fishing-boats were drifting towards me – and suddenly I was filled with a
pure uncomplicated joy. All the anxious pre-election debates (how to loosen the
corporate grip, how to reform the educational system, how to salvage the Lost
Generation and so on) – all those concerns were temporarily dissolved in the
realization that the new South Africa *exists*, as a *fact*, a dream become a
constitutional entity, a State led by President Mandela. I have been so immersed
in other people's powerful and complex emotions that all my energies were
going into trying to understand 'the miracle'. Hence my own emotions had not
crystallized – until this magic moment, alone on a silent clifftop, with brightness
and beauty all about me.

Freewheeling down to Hout Bay, it seemed joy instead of blood was coursing
through my veins. And I remembered Archbishop Tutu's characteristic excla-
mation on Election Day: 'It's like falling in love!' Now I know what he meant.

After the Chapman's Peak climb, sweat-replacement is indicated. Sitting with
a Long Tom outside Pitchers Bar I watched one of those meteorological dramas
typical of the Cape. A cloud swiftly advanced from the sea, a silver mist against
which autumn-sombre trees, still sunlit, stood out glowingly – briefly golden.
Then the sun was obscured and a damp chill replaced pleasant heat. The

Peninsula is a playground for clouds; they move among the mountains like live things, pouring and coiling over the Lion's Head, Devils' Peak, Table Mountain, Sentinel Hill, the Twelve Apostles – changing the light, meeting each other along the shore of Table Bay, then separating and rising – fickle, graceful vapours.

Late this evening President-elect Mandela came live on TV and radio to make his 'Victory Speech' and, as I write, millions all over the contry will be staging impromptu street parties. On the Grand Parade jubilant blacks from the townships are gathering and I have been caught in the wrong place, staying with white friends in Hout Bay. Naively I expected these celebrations to take place a few days hence when all – rather than half – the votes had been counted. But South Africa is not as other countries are; it is running this show in its own zany way. A headline in today's *Argus* perfectly conveyed the flavour: 'Provisional Final Results Out Today, Says IEC.'

This evening we also know that the thuggish Hernus Kriel will be Premier of the Western Cape – an expected Nat victory, not as yet unduly depressing ANC supporters.

3 May

An IEC Commissioner has warned the organizers of the 10 May Inauguration celebrations that they should make contingency plans; the counting may not be completed in time. As almost every Head of State in the world has been invited, this warning spread panic. One organizer yelped, 'You just don't tell Prince Philip to come next week instead!' But the constitutional process is cumbersome: nine provincial legislatures must meet to elect senators to the Upper House before Parliament can meet to elect the President who, reasonably enough, must be elected before being inaugurated. Almost certainly his election, planned for 6 May, will have to be postponed.

By last evening, in kwaZulu/Natal, counters had got through less than 1 million of some 9 million votes. An infuriated IEC officer has accused them of 'taking their time'. Unwisely, they are being paid by the hour and most are jobless so naturally they are taking their time. A moment's thought would have avoided this source of delay.

Sadly, violence has been resumed in kwaZulu/Natal; thirty political murders marred the weekend. Elsewhere, South Africa remains at peace.

4 May

At 7 a.m., on the way to Khayelitsha, most of my fellow-passengers were singing and sharing bottles of cane-spirit and two youths hung out of the taxi windows waving sheet-sized ANC flags. At intervals these were blown across the windscreen – while the general celebratory mood inspired each driver to try even harder than usual to overtake all others.

For a time I avoided Blocks L and M, savouring my freedom to wander alone and unguarded where eleven months ago I was at risk. The shebeens were full of swaying customers who had been drinking all night – or maybe ever since Madiba's Victory Speech? Young faces that last year were surly and closed – eyes averted when Whitey appeared – today were laughing and open and direct welcoming looks came from bright eyes. Older faces, previously tense and worn, today looked relaxed and jolly. Everyone seemed to be walking – when they weren't dancing – with a spring in their step. Yet daily life is no easier now than then. Economic equality remains invisible, away over the horizon: whites will continue to enjoy lives of luxury, joined by more and more successful blacks, but the average shack-dweller does not expect soon to have adequate schooling and medical care, four-bedroomed houses, good jobs, Toyota Corollas. (Only in the Macassar squatter camp did I meet a few recent arrivals from a remote Transkei village who cherished such illusions.) Those 'unrealistic black expectations', so often pinpointed as 'the main threat to future stability', are yet another urban legend.

To me, the change in atmosphere felt like a spiritual regeneration, a liberation from something even more destructive than extreme poverty. Last year the new South Africa was *in utero*, yet people could still be beaten up, tortured, killed, jeered at, stolen from – with no possibility of redress. Now the new constitution guarantees *legal* equality: no longer are blacks defenceless non-citizens counting for nothing in their own country. No wonder Khayelitsha is so jubilant today!

Most of my Xhosa friends, apart from senior community leaders, have only the vaguest notion – or no notion – of the structures of government in their new South Africa. And they are not much interested – Madiba is President! Viva President Mandela Viva! Some of those who crowded into Blossom's shack displayed a certain puzzled unease about the Nats' local victory but were easily reassured. Of course all will be well, the *country* is to be run from now on by President Mandela and as a mere provincial premier Kriel must obey Madiba – which prospect gave the most exquisite pleasure to all present.

It is emerging that in some regions good luck contributed to the miracle of peaceful elections. According to my reliable community leader friends, an ANC Youth League activist single-handedly defused a ballot-paper time-bomb in Khayelitsha by decisively taking the initiative and organizing transport to 'white' polling stations. But five days later, when the Nats' local victory was confirmed, this same 23-year-old at once began to organize a pride of Young Lions to invade Mitchells Plain that night *to kill Coloureds*. Madiba's Victory Speech came just in time. Then it was realized that Kriel's election did not mean a nationwide defeat for the ANC.

5 May

On 30 April someone calculated that vote-counting, at the rate it was then going, would take eight and a half years. Things have since speeded up, but not enough from my point of view. Madiba's election by Parliament has been postponed to 9 May, which kills my plan to take the Transkaroo Express on 7 May and revel with the Inauguration crowds in Pretoria. Now what do I do? In fact this choice is not too difficult. The Inauguration – an immensely elaborate and formal event, a global TV Spectacular – appeals to me less than that moment when Nelson Mandela will first address his people as President of the Republic of South Africa.

Some of Cape Town's architectural juxtapositions can be eloquent. Like the arrogant domination of the Houses of Parliament by the Hendrik Verwoerd Building, a Stalinesque block of skyscraping government offices. (Afrikanerdom's fondness for the Stalinesque is not surprising, when you think about it.) Today black workmen were enthusiastically painting the Parliament's dignified façade; from the scaffolding one looked down at me with a big grin and shouted, 'Now this belongs to us!'

I felt elated with him, yet his words induced a muddled sort of sadness. Neither the Houses of Parliament nor what goes on within them is part of the black tradition. Had Africa been left undisturbed (a fantasy concept) its peoples would never have constructed such a building or designed the system of government that will henceforth (we hope) operate within its walls. Why can't one utter this important truth aloud without being accused of racism?

The friendly Afrikaner SAPS officer on duty at the gate wanted to know why *ouma* (granny) was using a bicycle. We talked for quarter of an hour. 'Us police' – said this young lieutenant – 'we don't have problems with our new South Africa... We're only ordinary South Africans, we're not devils. OK, some of us had to do tough things in the old days – but now same as everyone else we want peace.'

Sitting in the Gardens, I watched a feral kitten stalking a grey squirrel. A Coloured couple, aged fiftyish, chose the same bench and were also curious about Chris. Soon the new South Africa was again under consideration.

'What upsets me,' said the husband, 'is how this election was supposed to unite us all but now on the Cape we're more divided than ever.'

His wife deplored the Nats' bribing of black squatters to take over houses newly built for Coloureds. 'There's no quicker way to set us at each other's throats! But still we knew we had to vote Nat – our only defence against affirmative action. We haven't forgotten the past but now we must think of the future. Politics is about survival.'

Later, in the Heidelberg, a Coloured student wearing three finger rings and a gaudy cravat offered the opinion that bloodshed has merely been postponed. 'Mandela's lekker but the rest of that lot are only shit. Day he dies the ANC falls apart, they'll kill each other, fighting for top jobs. And the township tsotsies will have Winnie to lead them, she's going mad not being First Lady. She's a greedy racist bitch. You heard she wants UWC for blacks only? Says if we're so fond of Whitey we should clear out to UCT. I'm UWC and those illiterate black fuckers have no place there – it's primary schooling they need. You know Mandela's a Coloured but he won't admit? He's no Xhosa, he's *Coloured*. That's why he's so cosy with whites. De Klerk knows he's *Coloured*, that's why he can talk to him. He couldn't talk that same way with a black.'

6 May

At 2 p.m. today the final election results came through because the parties had agreed to 'fix it'. Judge Kriegler admitted as much. 'Let's not get overly squeamish,' said he. 'I expected the election results to be manipulated to resolve political disputes and election irregularities. They're in a power game with one another, and if they want to settle on the basis that they withdraw objections there's nothing wrong with it, ethically or legally. We've never been asked to certify this particular political process is substantially free and fair. *Verneukery* [crookery] was expected, but what mattered was its effect on the outcome of the elections. You can't work in a brothel and remain chaste.'

We have all thoroughly enjoyed the electoral shambles, chuckling as the comedy of errors unfolded. On 3 May the Jo'burg Stock Exchange reeled when the IEC announced that 744,039 spoiled papers had been recorded in the PWV district; shares were about to plummet when someone discovered a typing mistake. It seems the IEC and ANC did indeed have a special relationship. Most of the 300,000 comparatively well-paid IEC employees were unskilled ANC supporters, beneficiaries of Affirmative Action. Few of these tyros exerted themselves to thwart the many underage voters, equipped with forged ID cards, who contrived to outwit (or intimidate?) the Monitors. Moreover, the prevailing chaos has facilitated the disappearance of 45 per cent of all IEC computers, including 80 per cent of laptops. If this is a 'negotiated revolution', who needs the other sort?

7 May

Listening to Madiba today, I wondered if he needs to rein in his reconciliation campaign. While addressing an emotional crowd in Cape Town's oldest mosque – the Owal Mosque in Bo-Kaap – he stressed the need for GNU to be seen as South Africa's first corruption-free government. Then he talked about 'all religions supporting morality'. Well, yes – but who is to define 'morality' in the new South Africa? My anthology of election literature includes a half-page newspaper advertisement explaining:

WHY NON-MUSLIMS SHOULD VOTE FOR THE ISLAMIC PARTY

- The Party sets the highest moral standards known to man.
- The Party will call for the death penalty for murderers, rapists and drug peddlers. This will discourage would-be criminals of this nature.
- The Party will support the ANC government but will lobby against them on moral issues like legalised prostitution, abortion, gambling, gay rights, alcohol, etc.

Madiba continued, 'It is our task to find a role for the churches, to keep moral standards very high. We would like the Muslims' high moral values to penetrate into government structures.' But ANC and Islamic Party policies are fundamentally irreconcilable as Madiba must be aware. This listener feels uncomfortable when logic and honesty are sacrificed to reconciliation – which then becomes tainted by hypocrisy.

8 May

During the past two days King Edward VII has been gradually disappearing amidst the Grand Parade's soaring tiers of seats; but he remains unscathed, having two Xhosa workmen specially delegated to protect him.

This afternoon, to one side of the City Hall balcony, a high wide stage was being erected for the dance groups, singers and acrobats who will entertain tomorrow's waiting crowd. Manholes were being checked, then given a permanent guard. I spoke to several Coloureds whose nearby stalls were burned and/or looted during the Hani riots, now referred to as 'Cape Town's Day of Shame'. In the changed atmosphere they are unworried about tomorrow when 2,000 police officers, 800 ANC marshals and 400 Peace Committee Monitors will be on duty.

This evening one of the new MPs (an old friend) invited me to watch the President's election from the Distinguished Strangers' Gallery and I hesitated – but only briefly. Within Parliament I could watch history being made, as an observer. On the Grand Parade I will be able to *feel* history being made, as a participant.

9 May

On an early commuter train to Central Station I marvelled at my fellow-passengers' stolidity. Surely, on 9 May 1994, they should have been waving little flags and clapping and singing, instead of reading fat romantic novels, or doing crosswords, or knitting, or exchanging office gossip in the English-sounding accent shared by educated Coloureds and suburban English-speakers. However, the sky was celebrating. Above the Hottentot Hollands floated a wide archipelago of pastel cloudlets – suddenly all golden, as the first sunrays slid over the mountain tops.

In that early light the City Hall's sandstone façade glowed warmly and the urban crest and motto (SPES BONA: appropriate at last) glistened after yesterday's scrubbing. Banners in the national colours, fifty feet long, were being draped on either side of the balcony; otherwise the scene was set. On an open space between the street and the grandstand – now completely concealing His Majesty – 300 red plastic chairs had been neatly arranged, no one seemed to know for whom. Both grandstand and chairs were surrounded by strong seven-foot-high wire-mesh fencing. And the public were forbidden to set foot on the street below the City Hall balcony.

It was a warm windless morning with a fringe of cloud draped over Table Mountain – not its heavy tablecloth, just translucent shreds. As yet only lines of alert police occupied the Grand Parade. But soon the first trainful arrived from the Cape Flats, led by a group of cheering elderly women waving large ANC flags and wearing Madiba gowns and scarves and headdresses. As the crowd swelled, black, green and gold predominated. An old Guguletu woman on crutches came to sit beside me on a kerb and observed that really the ANC had won in the Western Cape but no black votes were counted. First the boere tried to withhold ballot papers and when that didn't work they discarded them. One more urban legend. Ironically, many township folk perceive the Kriegler-led IEC as a *baasskap* institution.

Sauntering towards Parliament, I paused to view the international-press corps congregating in the ground-floor auditorium of the Verwoerd Building to watch the ceremonies on big-screen TV. Hyperbolically they complained about 'disorganization like nowhere else' and several showed symptoms of incipient panic. Delays had been forecast, so how could they meet their deadlines? This was a small corps; most of their colleagues, I gathered, were relaxing in Pretoria.

Rambling around the colossal Verwoerd Building, I was startled to find myself alone on a low balcony opposite one entrance to Parliament – an entrance in use. An exuberant colourful throng of MPs and their families was slowly flowing through a narrow pedestrian way; from my unsought vantage point I could lean over and shake hands with passing friends. Why had no security officer prevented me from taking up such an ideal assassination position? I might have been a neo-Nazi from Poland or Bosnia... But then, no security system is perfect.

For half an hour I stood there, elated by the fairy-tale-come-true atmosphere, savouring the joyousness of a conquest without violence. This was the moment when the orderly defeat of white supremacy could be celebrated – was being celebrated – without rancour or vengefulness, when the miracle of the election days became visible. History incarnate was passing before me, individuals whose presence there and then personified the new South Africa.

Some faces were recognizable. Joe Slovo looked pallid but very happy; without his logjam-breaking 'sunset clause' we might still be waiting for the elections. Hernus Kriel, in a bright blue suit, for once was attempting to seem amiable. Thabo Mbeki – animated, eyes twinkling – went into exile as a teenager and is now, aged 51, First Deputy President of South Africa. Joe Modise, looking as crafty and tough as he is, commanded the MK from 1965 and, as Defence Minister, is already ominously close to Pretoria's military establishment and European arms manufacturers. Derek Hanekom, the new Land Affairs Minister, also looks what he is, an Afrikaner farmer – but a Boer with a difference, an ANC member who served three years in jail for passing information to the MK about the SADF's illegal activities in Mozambique. Bantu Holomisa, the youngish ex-military dictator of the Transkei, was laughing loudly; his qualifications for being Deputy Minister for Environmental Affairs are obscure. Kader Asmal, the Natal-born founder of the Irish Anti-Apartheid Movement, I think of possessively if illogically as Ireland's contribution to the new Cabinet. For many years he lived happily in Dublin as a Trinity College law lecturer; now he is Water and Forestry Minister. Chief Buthelezi came striding along with his head held high but looking grumpy despite being Home Affairs Minister. Terror Lekota, ex-convict with Mandela, has been elected Premier of the most conservative province, the Boers' beloved Orange Free State. Kobie Coetsee, previously Justice Minister, is now President of the Senate; this is – they say – his reward for having been a key figure in the initial top-secret negotiations between his most distinguished prisoner and P. W. Botha's government. His ruggedly handsome successor, Dullah Omar, was twice detained while a member of the Cape Bar. Next came Pik Botha, one of the staunchest defenders of apartheid, a vigorous and powerful ally of Renamo in the Mozambican war and, until last week, the world's longest-serving Foreign Affairs Minister. He has been demoted to Mineral and Energy Affairs and replaced by Alfred Nzo – awarded the USSR Order of Friendship a mere nine years ago. Then, as I was turning away, I glimpsed the most 'symbolic' figure of all: Melanie Verwoerd, the 28-year-old granddaughter-in-law of Hendrik Verwoerd, now an ANC MP.

This is indeed a Government of National Unity: heroes and villains, the honest and the dishonest, the brilliant and the dim-witted, idealists and schemers, rabid racists and fervent liberals – all on their way, as I watched them, to vote unanimously for a black President of the Republic of South Africa.

Back on the Grand Parade I positioned myself beside the wire fence near the grandstand, from where I had a clear view of the balcony. By then a Mpondo dance group was bounding all over the enormous stage wearing ersatz 'native dress', mostly glitzy nylon and plastic with tall dyed ostrich plumes. Then came a famous Cape Flats band, the Sexy Boys, followed by a white pop group who were rapturously received and cheered semi-hysterically as they sang of 'unity'. While watching them dance, a young woman in front of me exclaimed to no one in particular, 'And you think whites can't jump!' Halfway up a tall palm tree, a Coloured youth and two blacks were clinging to the trunk while jiving – a more memorable achievement than anything happening on the stage. Beside me a Xhosa elder with cataract-blurred eyes, sunken cheeks, tidy shoddy clothes and a homburg hat stood leaning on two sticks, his expression serene. He was born, he told me, in 1907. 'Soon I will die, happily, as a free man.' One of the ANC marshals was his great-grandson. Today many marshals were unarmed MK, wearing smart new beige uniforms instead of jungle camouflage battledress. As the crowd grew denser, they advised that all small children should be lifted onto shoulders – where thousands already were, impatiently bouncing and brandishing miniature ANC flags.

Time passed. Everyone sang and clapped or ululated. The sun shone from a cloudless autumn sky and the air trembled with joy. But meanwhile many packed trains and buses were continuing to arrive from the townships, from rural areas, from nearby towns. Today the authorities provided free transport – an admirable ploy, were it not that the organizers of this event lack imagination. When some 150,000 Madiba-worshippers are expected to converge on an open space to see their idol it is worse than tactless to exclude them from the best vantage point by erecting a grandstand that blocks their view – apparently for the benefit of foreign media people who failed to attend. In the bad old days this crassness might have provoked a full-scale riot. In euphoric, Madiba-guided South Africa it at first seemed to be causing only a good-humoured crush. Inexplicably, the 300 red chairs, occupying a large space in front of me beyond the wire fence, remained empty.

At 12.20 – twenty minutes after the Presidential party was due to appear – the two marshals standing closest to me, on the other side of the wire, began anxiously to confer. Normally I am not crowd-allergic; I enjoy the casual intimacy of close physical contact with my fellow-beings. But now I began to sense danger. A new sound was mingling with the singing and clapping and saxophone-playing – angry shouting, coming from the railway station's direction. Moments later we all realized that some of the thousands trapped behind the grandstand were trying to push their way around that irritating obstacle. This was mob madness; only a mouse could have moved among the throng already assembled.

As the surge of bodies became more urgent, an odd sort of muted panic gripped most of those around me. Beyond us, in that baffling and tantalizing open space, the ANC marshals reacted – as SAPS did not – to the incipient crisis. Swiftly they instructed those of us by the fence (mostly women) to grip the wire mesh, put one foot on the solid metal frame in which it was set, bend low as if in a rugger scrum and pull the fence towards us without a moment's let-up.

'This way our ribs won't be broken,' explained a cool young Khayelitsha woman on my right. Evidently she was a seasoned campaigner, accustomed to such life-threatening situations. On their side, the marshals were also keeping one foot on the frame and pushing the fence towards us. I remembered the recent Athlone stampede, at Madiba's final election rally, in which three unfortunates were trampled to death and scores badly injured. Why hadn't I opted to become a Distinguished Stranger?

'Hey! We're lucky!' said the seasoned campaigner. 'This is a strong fence – you get a weak fence, you have problems. Don't worry, we're fine while everyone pulls and pushes.'

Worry? I wasn't *worried*, my guts were twisted with terror as time and again the surge behind us pressed on my buttocks and I strained harder to pull the wire towards us and push on the metal bar. This was grotesque, to be so frightened during the happiest event I have ever attended – frightened as rarely before in a long lifetime of travel.

Peace Monitors reinforced the marshals as the angry shouting grew louder and the surges more frequent. Then, at the very moment of President Mandela's appearance, youths broke through from behind the grandstand, having demolished the fence, and swarmed onto the chair space yelling 'Viva Madiba Viva!' At once the marshals – the majority teenagers, a few mere children – fled from the scene and it seemed the fence would collapse. But quickly more Monitors replaced them as the police at last arrived.

Order was rapidly and roughly restored within the chair space, but throughout Nelson Mandela's first public address as President that terrifying pressure was maintained behind us. In our scared and tumultuous corner Madiba was inaudible and those of us in the frontline – heads down, buttocks up – could only glimpse him out of the corners of our eyes. (So much for participation...) To most of the crowd what their new President *said* was unimportant – in fact unintelligible, to the non-English-speaking younger generations. Therefore the loudspeakers relaying his words did nothing to calm those behind the grandstand who yearned to *see* their idol taking precedence on the balcony over Mr de Klerk and various other white ex-supremacists.

Mercifully this historic event was not too prolonged. When we were freed from our duty as Upholders of the Fence, I found myself trembling all over.

As the crowd dispersed, long lines of police officers – seeming needlessly twitchy – moved to guard the city centre's main shopping streets. On Adderley Street a stray police dog caused understandable panic among the blacks; these creatures are no better trained than their handlers. This morning, behind the City Hall, a loose dog approached me aggressively, ignored H.M.V. and would certainly have attacked me had I not stood still. He had to be dragged away by the collar, his handler having lost his chain. However, this stray's only concern was to find his officer; looking pathetically anxious he ran to and fro, nose to ground, then heard a familiar whistle and raced around a corner.

Within an hour the contented township dwellers were making their way back to the railway station, showing off their most advanced toyi-toying skills or holding aloft huge banners: A BETTER LIFE FOR ALL, MANDELA FOR PRESIDENT, GOD BLESS AFRICA. Today Mandela *is* President, joy is unconfined, the time for looting is over.

I took a bus back to Obs. Several passengers, hanging from the windows, displayed life-sized placard photographs of President Mandela. En route the Coloured driver, wearing an ANC stocking-cap, played a triumphant tune on his hooter.

Now I am stiff and aching, my hands lacerated by the wire fence. Yet on TV the central drama of my day seemed no more than a blip. According to police estimates, at least 150,000 had assembled on the Grand Parade by 1 p.m. I can believe this. During the chaos in our corner, other sections of the crowd sang the Peace Song led by Archbishop Tutu. He faltered only for a moment when the fracas looked nasty a few yards from where an Irish citizen was contributing her mite to the new South Africa's stability-image. So after all I did participate.

13

What Next?

Johannesburg – Home

We place our vision of a new constitutional order for South Africa on the table not as
conquerors, prescribing to the conquered. We speak as fellow citizens to heal the wounds
of the past with the intent of constructing a new order based on justice for all.
President Nelson Mandela (10 May 1994)

On the Transkaroo to Jo'burg, 10 May 1994

In Central Station an elderly Afrikaner Spoornet clerk, tall, thin and bald,
helped me to lock Chris to a window bar in the luggage van. The recent
lessening of violence has impressed him. 'This is what Mandela promised. Let
him go on keeping his promises and I'll have nothing against a black government. There's a new feeling now in this country. If blacks can govern, why
shouldn't they? If our kids have to work harder to compete, that's how life's
meant to be!'

I have a six-berth compartment to myself; few chose to be away from their TV
on Inauguration Day. Spoornet's second-class carriages are luxurious. A shelf-
table covers the wash-basin (running H & C), the heater is controllable, the
window spotless. Each coach has its shower-cubicle and drinking water is
available from drums on the walls between coaches. The air-conditioned
restaurant serves good food at reasonable prices, beer is no dearer than in a
Drankwinkel and at sunrise a waiter brings coffee around – or what passes for
coffee in South Africa.

Slow trains are my favourite conveyances and this 'express' takes twenty-five
hours to cover approximately 900 miles. Beyond Cape Town lies flat farmland
where sheep were grazing on old-gold stubble fields and distant irregular hazy
mountains rise sheer from the plain. The beginning of the long climb is marked
by a gigantic outcrop of jagged red-grey rock sporting patches of orange and
green lichen. Here the mountainside is so close one can lean out and pick
souvenir leaves. (I favour free souvenirs: leaves, stones, oddly shaped bits of
wood.) As we climbed the blueness of the sky deepened and on both sides
mountains crowded in – before receding to the left, making space for green
pastures and small farmhouses snuggled among fir trees. Beyond Worcester

stretched miles of autumn-red vineyards, then we were crawling around the base of strange slab-like mountains, all leaning one way as though carefully stacked.

Up on the Karoo, in the tiny dorp of Touwsrivier, groves of willows shone pale gold against a steep olive-green mountain flank; near this summit, white letters painted on flat boulders spell out JESUS REG. In the elegant little dorp of Matjiesfontein, the Anglo-Boer War headquarters of the Cape Western Command, it seems memories are long and attitudes not flexible. Above the Lord Milner Hotel the *baasskap* flag still flew between two Union Jacks – on Inauguration Day! Near Laingsburg I recognized the Swartberg, looming massively magnificent along the horizon. A fertile region surrounds Leeu-Gamka: three fine dams, clusters of windpumps, fields of bright green alfalfa, huge expanses of new-ploughed land, many overcrowded ostrich enclosures. Here the lambing season has begun – some newborns so minute they look like toys.

All day blacks from the third-class coaches sauntered up and down the corridors looking happily arrogant; now none can dispute their right to use the restaurant car. Not many could afford a meal, mostly they bought sandwiches at the bar.

'They've no culture,' observed a young Afrikaner mining foreman with whom I shared a table. If his ancestors could see the Inauguration 'they would drop dead again'. Then rhetorically he demanded, 'How can I accept being ruled by kaffirs and coons and coolies?' Yet plainly he does accept it; he was merely saying what he felt obliged to say, what all his mates will be saying this evening in the bars – not meaning it either. His fear of the right-wingers' destabilizing potential was palpable, his priority is *peace*. When he concluded, 'We're finished now, there's no hope for us' his tone conveyed neither resentment nor anger.

I stood by a corridor window watching the sun decline in a cloudless sky while a dusky pink tinged the long low ridges to the west. Soon the distended blood-orange globe had dropped behind a koppie, leaving a golden haze lingering over an arrangement of navy-blue sculpted summits. Then I was distracted from the matchless beauty of the Karoo by a smirking Afrikaner, aged fortyish, who suggested that I might like to find space for him in my compartment. He was not at all abashed when I scoffed at him for lusting after someone who could be his mother. Some South African white males are incomprehensibly indiscriminate; not for twenty years have I had as many 'suitors' as since crossing the Limpopo.

This has been a soothing day, slowly traversing vast silent spaces with few people visible at the infrequent stations and little traffic flowing where the N1 can be seen – while in Pretoria multitudes were making merry. An emotional day, too – especially for those who can remember Nelson Mandela's 1964 trial and his speech from the dock.

Still on the Transkaroo, 11 May

It was a leisurely, complex dawn: solid towers of dark cloud being lit first from their base, then the light slowly seeping up, purple merging into pale yellow and russet – then an explosion of crimson filling the whole sky, briefly dyeing the Karoo's sombre expanses of grey scrub and brown earth.

Behind me in the restaurant car four elderly English-speakers (first class) bewailed their uncomfortable night. The train, they complained, swayed as it never used to in the old days. At a nearby table two Afrikaner Spoornet officials were mocking their new President, imitating his voice and sniggering. One of the English-speakers quoted a calculation that the amount spent on the elections (R1 billion, R300 million more than expected) would have built 40,000 three-roomed houses. 'And don't they need houses more than democracy?'

Last week it was revealed that President Mandela will be one of the three most highly paid Heads of State in the world, earning R734,350 per annum including expenses and allowances. All parliamentary salaries and allowances have been set, by the TEC-appointed Melamet Committee, at private-sector levels. This is rumoured to have been part of the 'deal' with the Nats. South Africa however is not a profit-making corporation run to benefit shareholders. Most of its citizens lucky enough to have jobs earn about R10,000 per annum while millions of jobless go permanently hungry. Nor is this a naturally rich country; the whites' lifestyle gives a false impression. South Africa's gold is dwindling fast and has always been harder to mine than other countries' deposits. Its manufacturing industry has a poor reputation for both productivity and quality. Its black population rapidly increased during the period when modern farming methods were throwing thousands out of work. Much of the land is arid and becoming more so by the decade. In Cape Town I heard several veteran observers of the Struggle attributing its 'happy ending' – the much-admired negotiated revolution – to Nat shrewdness. When a country's problems reach a critical mass, it makes sense to let someone else try to stop the explosion.

Florida, 12 May

Watching the Inauguration video, provided by Margaret, I much preferred the clumsy SABC camerawork, and Madiba's late arrival, to the slick perfection of Western filming and ceremonial timing. Today the commentators' failure to identify all VIPs is being rather unfairly criticized – not long ago most VIPs had South Africa on their boycott list. Yet I did slightly take umbrage at the over-looking of President Mary Robinson who was probably assumed to be some-body's wife.

Throughout the formal rituals, followed by the informal jollifications, President Mandela (writing those two words still thrills me) looked happy and relaxed. Physical stamina is not the least of his leadership assets. Three of his ex-warders were among the VIPs and to them he paid a generous tribute.

My favourite participant was the praise-poet. His contribution had an ancient significance – was no mere 'romantic colourful tribal custom' – and this gave his functioning within the precincts of the Union Buildings an extra piquancy. My least favourite participant was the SAAF, but it seems this puts me in a minority of one.

According to commentators both black and white, the highlight of the day's events was the helicopter fly-past, trailing the new national colours and thus proclaiming that now the armed forces belong to 'everyone'. The crowd responded rapturously to this imaginative display and I might have done like-wise had I been present. But perhaps not; both the SAAF fly-pasts (fighter planes and helicopters) and the twenty-one-gun salute seemed more appropriate to the old militaristic South Africa than to the new peace-seeking regime. And they suggested the armed forces' determination to remain in the forefront of national life when logically their status should be radically changed. Nor is it irrelevant that fly-pasts are costly gestures.

Even the poorest blacks approve of extravagance when a chief is being installed; it is seen to be honouring them as well as their leader. But does this justify the new South Africa's stepping onto the world stage disguised as a rich man? Could not the extraordinary celebrations demanded by President Mandela's inauguration have been organized otherwise, nationwide, with street parties and village parties on a simple scale? The TV Spectacular may be seen as a unique extravagance. But it is more likely to be taken as a tone-setter for the new South Africa, sending the wrong subliminal message to the general public.

Pretoria's 'party to end all parties', designed to be viewed by billions, has certainly contributed to misleading the outside world. By now the mass media set the agenda in every sphere – sport, war, politics, financial crises, natural disasters. And they encourage the homogenization of public reactions, the thought-stopping glamorization of complicated events. The birth of the new South Africa is a very complicated event. The phrase 'Successful Democratic Multi-Racial Elections' does not sum it up. Nor does 'Mandela's Victory!' In Madiba the media have an ideal hero, someone whose image needs no touching up. Yet every leader deserves some criticism and may be rendered less effective by a media canonization that stifles it.

Nelson Mandela's dedication to reconciliation – that supremely civilized concept – is often seen as the keystone of the new South Africa. His reconciliation campaign began years before his release and by the mid-'80s was having an effect within Afrikanerdom. Since 1990 he has been tirelessly preaching: 'Let everybody start from the premise that we are one country, one nation, whether we are white, Coloured, Indian or black.' From most politicians this might sound like an expedient exhortation, from Madiba it sounds like the expression of a passionate, personal longing for harmony. His sincerity seems to have touched all but the most fanatical right-wingers; even those who continue to revile him verbally have been reassured, within themselves. They know they are not going to be victimized in the new South Africa. But – is Madiba attempting the impossible? It takes two to reconcile. If only one is dancing to that tune, does 'reconciliation' become a euphemism for 'appeasement'?

Yesterday President Mandela spoke of the need to 'heal the wounds of the past' and construct 'a new order based on justice for all'. Those wounds were inflicted by whites in pursuit of wealth. And in 1994 the fragile national 'prosperity' remains dependent on the exploitation of black labour. An increasing number of blacks will now have access to wealth but rich blacks are no more (sometimes less) sensitive to the needs of the poor than rich whites. Constructing a new order must involve wealth-sharing and that would sink the reconciliation boat. In the real world, 'justice for all' and Madiba's noble ideal of reconciliation are incompatible. And because this incompatibility is built into the foundations of the new South Africa no political construction engineer would certify it as a sound edifice.

Here and now, these may seem inappropriate – even heretical – reflections. But South Africa is like that. It spawns inappropriate reflections and irrational mood-swings and intellectual culs-de-sac. It is the most confusing country I have ever travelled through – not surprisingly, given its past, present and future.

Recalling last year's atmosphere, the Afrikaners' placid acceptance of change astonishes me. Among them one now senses an immense relief and many have said to me, wonderingly, 'The tension is gone.' They might be referring to that neurotic pre-election fear of blacks running amok, which is how some do interpret their new calm. But obviously a greater tension was involved, a guilty tension.

Yesterday, on the telephone, one of my Boer friends summed it up: 'Now everything's different, we needn't hate each other any more.'

Those ten words, from a man who in May 1993 admitted to AWB sympathies, prove that the elections generated more than a transient euphoria. Yes, the country is at present on Cloud Nine – but there have also been deep psychological shifts. The implications of 'We needn't hate each other any more' are staggering. Apartheid did indeed make it necessary to hate blacks; only hatred could have fuelled such a machine. But Afrikaners are 'decent people who have been misled by their leaders' (Madiba's words), and decent people cannot live at ease within a system based on hatred. For all South Africans, 27 April 1994 was Liberation Day.

During the Anglo-Boer War Lord Wolseley dismissed the enemy as 'The only white race that has been steadily going backwards into barbarism.' Ever since,

Afrikaners have had a bad press. Latterly their loud-mouthed right-wingers, staging camera-attracting melodramas, have compounded that. Yet, as Fergal Keane has recently observed, 'Hidden by the simplifications of the mass media are the stoic majority who work hard and obey their God.'

For that stoic majority I have come to feel a genuine affection. Behind their now demolished façade of Christian Nationalism they are less implacably racist than the British settlers' descendants, the tribe we have always been led to believe are the more liberal – or the less illiberal. In general those English-speakers, handicapped by colonial snobbery, are likely to find it harder to accept the new South Africa. They never needed to hate, they simply despised the natives here as elsewhere. This was part of their cultural conditioning, whereas the Afrikaners' hatred was nurtured for political reasons. Turn the political scene upside down and 'We needn't hate each other any more.' Cultural conditioning is less easily reversed.

During this visit, at a few mixed parties in Pietermaritzburg and Cape Town, I have noticed English-speakers and blacks being politely on edge with each other – the former straining to be nice to the latter (influential people, now!) while the blacks eyed them with cynical amusement, well aware of the effort being made. In contrast, most blacks and Afrikaners seemed genuinely relaxed together.

The same, 13 May

In 1971 scaffolding went up around the Voortrekker Monument near Pretoria and rumours of its imminent collapse sent shock waves throughout Afrikaner-dom. The Chairman of the Monument Control Board hastened to reassure – 'There's no need to panic. The structure is being made safe for the future.' However, what it represented could not be 'made safe' and this morning I approached it feeling merely curious about Christian Nationalism's 'cathedral'.

Margaret dropped me off at the base of that low bare hill on which the Monument was built between 1937 and 1949. Although Afrikanerdom's exclus-ive property, tax-payers of all colours and opinions paid most of the costs (R719,202 – what did the last two buy?). The DRC described it as 'a sacred shrine where God is thanked each year for the maintenance of white civilisa-tion'. In 1974 a man was ejected for not removing his hat inside the sacred portals and until recently only those attired as though for attendance at DRC services were admitted. The Monument has been variously likened to an elaborately moulded jelly, a pop-up toaster and a 1940s wireless. It is 120 feet high, built of greyish-brown granite and supremely ugly – almost comically ugly, I thought, light-heartedly climbing the many wide steps.

I did not long remain light-hearted. Even now, three days after Madiba's Inauguration, the psychic impact of this sinister edifice is deeply disturbing.

Within those oppressive walls, beneath that high dome, one feels – like a Presence – a concentrated essence of evil.

The Hall of Heroes is vast and circular, its floor of sombre mottled marble. Heavy webs of concrete trellis-work embellish four giant arched windows of dirty-yellow glass. In the centre one leans over a waist-high wall, also circular, to look far down into a dim cellar-like space surrounded by grey pillars, squat and square. There a granite cenotaph commemorates all who died during the Great Trek. At noon on 16 December, through an aperture in the remote dome, a sunray falls on an Afrikaans inscription. (Translation – 'We for thee, South Africa.') According to Riana Heyman's 1986 booklet, this ray 'symbolises God's blessing on the work and aspirations of the Voortrekkers...The Monument was built as a tribute to those who brought civilisation to the interior. Order, geometrical precision and symmetry are therefore basic to its design.' One page contains seven references to this 'bringing of civilisation'. And we are informed that 'the black wildebeest symbolises both the barbarism that yielded to civilisation and Dingane's warriors'.

Before those warriors were defeated at the Battle of Blood River, on 16 December 1838, the Voortrekkers had made a covenant with the Lord. If victorious, they and their descendants would always commemorate that date with prayerful gratitude. However, this covenant was not generally observed until 1886 when the British threat inspired its use as a device to unite squabbling Boer factions. Subsequently the actual events of December 1838 were 're-adjusted' by certain historians and 16 December acquired a sacred aura. In 1952 it officially became a 'Sabbath', within the terms of the Sabbath Act, and had to be observed by the whole population – Zulus included. (Hark to an echo of the Orangemen's Twalfth.) Eventually the 'readjustments' came to be questioned by a brave minority of historians, among them Professor Floris van Jaarsveld who in 1979 gave a lecture in the University of South Africa entitled 'A Historical Mirror of Blood River'. That lecture was never finished. ET led an AWB gang into the Senate Hall, the unfortunate professor was tarred and feathered on the spot, an outsize Vierkleur was flown high and ET thundered that such blasphemy would always and everywhere be punished.

I had the monument to myself, apart from an elderly Afrikaner gentleman behind the reception desk. Feeling both physically and spiritually chilled, I dutifully examined 'the largest existing marble frieze in the world' – 92 by 2.3 metres, carved in Italy. Twenty-seven panels depict the hardships endured and battles fought during the Great Trek, with much emphasis on the 'barbarians'' treachery and cruelty.

Last year, a consortium of Afrikaner cultural organizations formed a private company to run the Monument. Explained Christo Kuun, its chairman, 'We realize the Voortrekker Monument will be a very sensitive issue in the future. We want to keep it out of politics.' His words caused some amusement, this 'issue' being South Africa's loudest political statement in granite. At once the ANC protested against a private company's appropriation of State property 'just before a democratic government takes over'. Said André Odendaal, 'The intention is not to demolish it but there is a need to contextualize it'. (ANC spokespersons are woefully addicted to such jargon.) Someone is going to have fun 'contextualizing' that frieze.

From the Hall of Heroes 169 steps lead to the roof. It seems the architect, at this point, couldn't think what to do next, how to present the desired external effect without the whole monstrosity collapsing inward on itself. So he contrived all manner of grotesque reinforcements – crude protuberances and sweeps of barren concrete, awkward curves and angles which have grievously wounded the aesthetic sensibilities of thousands of foreign visitors.

On the roof, four corner viewpoints overlooked the mid-Rand, its flatness criss-crossed by freeways and humming with engine noises beneath a hazy yellow-brown industrial smog. A nearby army base provides the appropriately aggressive sound of gunfire. Long gloomy walkways connect the corners; one paces between quasi-medieval arches and here, within aimless embrasures, the less reverent visitors are – it is very apparent – wont to pee.

Sitting on a parapet in the sunshine, I probed my unexpected reaction to the Monument – why, in the new South Africa, should its atmosphere have so shaken me? Is it because the evil spirit informing apartheid has not yet been exorcized? Afrikaners raised the Monument and it has always been associated with their traditions. Yet its perversion of religion to justify frenzied racism and its sick glorification of cruelty have never been resolutely repudiated by your average English-speaker. The extremism of the Monument's message is no longer lekker. But the sediment remains, after the extremism has been poured away. A noxious sediment, feeding the universal human reluctance to admit 'I did wrong...'

Too many whites still find it impossible to acknowledge that apartheid *was* evil – as evil as the Holocaust. Others are already in denial mode – 'Of course we never liked apartheid...' Obviously some did not. But very few disliked it enough to join in the struggle against it. And the majority so relished their apartheid-generated prosperity that they repeatedly voted for the Nats – or, at best, for parties offering only timid modifications, changes essentially unthreatening to white supremacy. Within the past year, some details illustrating the system's most vicious excesses have been revealed and many are claiming to be shocked and distressed about 'what was going on and we never knew!' Granted, the media were muzzled in a variety of ways and the government's worst crimes either hidden from the general public or presented as 'necessary to defend the State'. Yet there was no legitimate State – legitimate in international law – to be defended. And the legitimacy of the Struggle was repeatedly affirmed: e.g., in

1979 by Resolution 183L of the UN General Assembly which confirmed that the liberation movement was entitled to use 'all available and appropriate means, including armed struggle' to overthrow the apartheid regime. The concealed barbarities sustaining that regime were not the aberrations of a few psychopaths but the hideously logical consequences of a government policy which had been clearly spelled out, decade after decade, by a succession of the whites' chosen political leaders. Moreover, the routine enforcing of the apartheid laws took place in broad daylight, hidden from no one. Hence the whites' heavy burden of collective guilt. Only their support, consistently given in election after election, enabled apartheid to survive for so long. Even Pretoria's formidable resources, military and otherwise, could not have prevailed against an anti-apartheid white electorate. Yet even I find it hard by now to keep in mind this collective guilt. Having acquired so many white friends, there is a temptation for me to slide into forgetfulness of the old South Africa in which all whites benefited directly from the merciless, institutionalized oppression of the majority. If the oppressors themselves persist in cultivating this soothing amnesia – encouraged by their First World 'constructive engagement' allies – true reconciliation cannot be achieved. That requires more than smooth speeches, cordial handshakes and cosmetic festivities.

What I wrote a few days ago, about the elections having liberated all South Africans, was perhaps too facile – though an understandable (certainly a widely felt) emotional response to the peaceful transition. To liberate themselves fully, the whites must do more than quietly accept the inevitable. They must contribute to reconciliation by confessing their collective guilt, both to themselves and publicly. They must abandon their favourite fudge, their pretence that anti-apartheid violence justified pro-apartheid violence; and this will involve recognizing that those criminalized by an illegitimate government (including their new President) never were criminals. But – are these demands unreasonable? Is such an exorcizing of the evil enshrined in the Monument beyond the average white's capacity? Yet what is the alternative? A new South Africa debilitated by the Monument's miasma can never grow up healthy.

Descending to the Monument's shrub-bright grounds, I strolled beside the laager-wall of sixty-four ox-wagons; above them flew the new flag and the Transvaal flag. A Tswana gardener had two large 'Mandela for President' badges pinned to his dungarees. He chuckled when I muttered – glancing up at the Monument – 'What a vile place!' Said he, 'Now it doesn't matter. Our President says no thinking about the past, only all working together for our new South Africa. No hating or having revenge, no more racism!'

Elsewhere, during this season of euphoria, his beaming face and cheerful words would have elated me. In the shadow of the Monument, they increased my unease about the gloss being put on the new South Africa. Glossing began in

1990 when the release of Madiba and his comrades, and the initiation of all-party negotiations, prompted much of the world to applaud F. W. de Klerk. This was bizarre. Would Hitler have been applauded, had he at some point decided to halt the Holocaust?

While the long-drawn-out negotiations were taking place the Nats continued desperately to hope that they could divide and discredit the ANC and so 'manage' the transition to give themselves an undemocratic share of post-election power. Between July 1990 and December 1993 more than 12,000 civilians were killed and at least 20,000 injured in countless incidents engineered by the Third Force. In the 1991/92 financial year operations designed to sabotage the ANC cost tax-payers over R21 million. This State-organized violence against black civilians exceeded even the ferocity of the '80s and horrors previously unknown appalled the nation – drive-by shootings, frequent murders on commuter trains, well-organized attacks by armed hostel-dwellers on township folk. Last year I travelled through a country unnerved and bewildered by what was then tendentiously described as 'mindless black-on-black violence'. Now the motive for this elaborate destabilization campaign is clear. Yet while the State was thus occupied, the naive Nobel Peace Prize committee – deluded as so often before by media hype – chose the State President, F. W. de Klerk, as a man worthy to share their annual award with Nelson Mandela. Many saw this equating of the ANC leader and the Nats' leader as an insult to the former. In an essay on the assassination of Chris Hani, André Brink succinctly summed up the then State President: 'Nothing has exposed this man so mercilessly for the petty and vicious little securocrat he is at heart than the events that have shaken South Africa since 10 April [1993].'

As I walked away, down that slope where those still loyal to Afrikanerdom gather on the Day of the Vow, a few families were arriving: young silent couples, impassive, with wide-eyed small children likely to be excited by the sheer scale of the Monument, the detailed frieze, the climb to the roof. But if they learn their history here they'll not be happy citizens of the new South Africa.

Looking back from a little distance, one is struck by the Monument's darkness. At noon today, in brilliant sunshine, there was no hint of brightness, no glittering reflection from those huge windows. It seemed to be repelling and rejecting light – and that I found even spookier than all the rest.

The same, 14 May

Tomorrow I fly home, wondering how the liberated of all races will use their freedom. And what will happen in kwaZulu/Natal? On my return in September I plan to tour that problem province, see more of the Transkei and at last visit the Free State. Meanwhile Chris can relax, hanging from the ceiling of Margaret's garage.

INTERLUDE

Ireland – Mozambique

June to September 1994

Serious injuries should happen in appropriate settings: during a war in Central America, an election in Angola, an earthquake in Armenia or on some daring journey through trackless wastes. Merely to have tripped over the cat outside the kitchen door adds indignity to injury and I could hear my friends involuntarily giggling at the other end of the telephone. Huffily I protested that this was no giggling matter, that for the first three of my five days in hospital I had been on a morphine drip, that numerous shattered bones (originally my left elbow and forearm) were now being held together by eight pins and a strip of metal. Penitently, the friends sympathized. Too late! To punish them I pressed on, explaining that now, back home, the vibrations of a door banging in the distance – never mind *any* movement of the body – caused exquisite pain. That lowered my friends' telephone bills: they couldn't ring again because they wouldn't want to occasion bodily movements...

It happened at 9.15 p.m. on 2 June when Sebastian – a frail elderly feline gentleman – was mugged by the neighbours' ginger tom, a notorious hooligan. Hearing an agonized wail I raced from my study, rounded a corner of the cobbled courtyard at speed and tripped over the fleeing victim. Luckily, I fell to the left. Had I fallen to the right, my head would have struck the sharp edge of a stone step and I might well have been moved not to a casualty department but to a mortuary.

It pleases me to live in the Irish equivalent of a dorplet, remote from urban influences. But remoteness has certain disadvantages and, while lying motionless on the ground, I considered one of those. Undoubtedly I had broken something. It was too soon to diagnose precisely what but I am familiar with the body's response to broken bones. The nearest hospital is forty-five miles away and at 9.30 p.m. one cannot expect friends to drop every-thing and drive ninety miles. I decided to put myself to bed and send out an sos in the morning.

By then Sebastian and Mingmar, my dog, were standing by looking anxious, as animals do when their human is in any kind of distress, mental or physical. They watched me slowly pick myself up, during which ordeal the nature of the damage became apparent. 'Think positive!' said I to Sebastian and Mingmar.

'At least it's not the right arm.' As usual they followed me to bed, looking puzzled when the undressing routine was omitted.

The chemistry of shock/pain is interesting. No painkillers were to hand but having gently arranged my bent arm on my chest I lay all night in an odd sort of semi-coma, unaware of pain though trembling violently. It seems the shock of shattered bones stimulates within the body some temporary analgesic device.

At 8 a.m. my sensible doctor refrained from examining the injured limb; by then I had realized that the elbow was also dislocated. He gave me a horse-sized shot of painkiller, scribbled a letter to the casualty department and soon I was in a friend's car on the road to Cork. I used to think this was a smooth road; that morning I thought otherwise.

The term 'casualty department' suggests a unit where efficient professionals deal swiftly with emergencies. It is a misleading term – or was I an emergency only in my own egocentric estimation? For four pain-bemused hours I sat in a bath chair, at intervals being pushed from queue to queue through hundreds of maimed men, women and children. The men were mainly young, victims of industrial or sporting accidents. The women were mainly elderly. Most of the children whimpered quietly. The queues tended to be bureaucratic rather than medical. The exact sequence of events is a blur but I vividly recall the radiologist's expression when she looked at the X-rays, then at me. 'You've done a thorough job!' said she, almost admiringly. The plates seemed to show a pile of kindling thrown in a grate; here was a thrilling challenge for an orthopaedic surgeon.

My operation was scheduled for 6 p.m. I longed to see that pile of kindling being reassembled into an arm and pleaded for a local anaesthetic. (If born without a compulsion to write, I would have been a surgeon.) But my plea was spurned, perhaps wisely: the operation took over an hour.

After a blissfully happy night on a morphine DIY drip (how easy to become addicted!) an ambulance moved me to another hospital, maybe because one-third of the X-ray machines at Cork's Regional Hospital were out of order, as they had been for five months.

On 8 June I was sent home with instructions to keep the plastered arm in 'an elevated position'. At once a local carpenter made a mobile stand from which The Arm was suspended, day and night, for three weeks. (It had, by this stage, acquired capital letters.) During those weeks sleep was scarce; not since adolescence have I read so many novels. Then came a riveting phenomenon: for the next month or so, Nature dictated that out of every twenty-four hours I should spend approximately fourteen deeply asleep.

In due course I found an inspired physiotherapist in Dublin; Mary Pender's name should be written up somewhere in letters of gold. Within three days of the plaster's coming off on 30 June she had me swimming, a week later she had me cycling. Broken elbows are notoriously intractable, not to be pandered to or you may be crippled for life. Hence Mary's relentlessly sadistic approach: 'Never mind the pain, just get on with it.' At each session her treatment was fourfold: acupuncture, laser ray, electrical massage and (ouch!) manipulation. Yet even she failed to get me typing. However hard I tried, The Arm *could not* function at the typing angle until 27 July.

On Sunday 28 August my daughter Rachel, then working in Mozambique, met me at Harare airport. She had a week's leave; on 4 September her partner, Andrew, would drive up to Mutare to collect us. I planned to fly onto Jo'burg ten days later, by which time The Arm would be fit for a full day's cycling. However, I had calculated without Mozambican bureaucracy. At the Harare Consulate tourism was not at the top of anyone's agenda. My visa would of course be granted, within two or three weeks...

'Never mind,' said Rachel briskly. 'There's a smugglers' path over the mountains on the border. If you sneak in that way, before dawn, we'll pick you up on the far side. But remember the landmines, don't ever leave the path. If you need to pee, pee *on* the path.'

We took the Wednesday night train to Mutare and next day spent several strenuous hours in rough terrain sussing out exactly where this path began. Viewing its continuation through binoculars, I felt some misgivings. This route involved more than walking: it ascended an escarpment that might require *two* sound arms. But by then it was much too late to 'think sensible', I was completely hooked on the smugglers' path.

Late on the Saturday afternoon Andrew arrived from Beira, to be informed by Rachel that at four o'clock next morning he must deposit Mamma a mile from the start of the path. For security (noise) reasons a vehicle could go no closer. Quickly Andrew adjusted to the situation, at which point I recognized a kindred spirit.

In pitch darkness I was deposited on a ridge-top; we had driven up a rough track from the main road and the invisible Zimbabwean border-post lay some three miles away. As the vehicle disappeared I stood still, allowing my eyes to become accustomed to starlight – a magical moment, the silence broken only by tiny mysterious noises in the bush. During our recce I had imprinted on my mind exactly where the path branched off from this track; a convenient solitary tree served as landmark. Soon after finding it the dawn came: a quiet pastel dawn, light slowly seeping through the surrounding dense tangles of dwarf acacia and euphorbia. From afar, through binoculars, this had looked like a fairly direct path across a wide valley. But it was no such thing. For a variety of topographical reasons it wandered to and fro, up and down, this way and that, often meeting other paths. Twice I near-panicked: I have no sense of direction and a wrong turning might expose me to the full fury of the Zimbabwean and/ or Mozambican immigration officers, who presumably also use binoculars. Rachel had of course foreseen such a disaster; a lifetime of gruelling experiences has left her with no illusions about the maternal sense of direction. So I was carrying only a walking-stick – no camera, no binoculars, no passport, no notebook, no food or water. If apprehended by officialdom, I would seem an eccentric geriatric who enjoyed walking in the cool of the morning and had innocently strayed into the border area.

Tension built up as I hesitated at these numerous junctions – then, at the base of the mountain, my spirits soared. Confronting me was an eight-foot-high wire fence marking the Zimbabwean border. The smugglers had long since cut the two bottom strands and wriggling through was easy. Some fifty yards further on came the Mozambican wire fence and another easy wriggle. For the next half-hour the path climbed steeply through comfortingly dense forest – and then came the escarpment, some 400 feet high. With two arms it would have been difficult enough, with one and a half arms it was quite terrifying. The technique of ascending this near-precipice involved hanging onto strong, ancient tree roots, polished by the hands and feet of countless smugglers. My problem here was not pain, which under pressure can be dealt with – mind-over-matter. My problem was The Arm being physically incapable of supporting my weight. But desperation is the mother of innovation and I discovered that hanging onto tree roots can also be done – though less securely – with a *knee*, improbable though that may sound. Halfway up I almost lost my nerve as the soil became looser and the roots seemed less dependable. However, any attempt to descend would have been even more risky. Having paused for a few moments to recover my nerve, I continued very slowly – and felt weak with relief when I got to the top.

It was a flattish top, some 150 yards by 100, with huge boulders lying between tall trees. And obviously it was mine-free: beer and Coca-Cola cans and cigarette packets and condoms littered the short brown grass. (Are smugglers an unusually sophisticated, AIDS-aware segment of local society?) As I rested, leaning against a boulder, I heard voices which drew me back to the edge of the precipice. At the bottom, five men were unloading. Then one swiftly ascended, let down a rope and drew up the enormous head-loads: square and oblong boxes, wrapped in blankets. When his friends had followed they all greeted me politely, tactfully registering no surprise at finding an elderly white female on their path. 'You have lost your passport?' suggested one, in sympathetic tones. 'Yes,' said I.

What were they smuggling? I longed to ask but tact must be two-way so instead we talked about the weather. In Europe weather-talk is trivial chit-chat, in Africa it's often a life-or-death issue. They told me all about their losses during the cruel drought of 1992 and shared with me their Coca-Cola – a swig from each tin. Then they moved on, having earnestly warned me not to put a foot off the path.

Cautiously I followed, down and down and down, very steeply, through thin forest or scrubby bush, the two border-posts now visible in the distance on my left. But where the path eventually joined the motor road (the notorious Beira Corridor) those hazards were far behind me.

No one took any notice of the illegal immigrant as I walked the ten miles to Manika, the first little town in Mozambique. That was an exhilarating walk through superb mountains, quite densely populated; here, round straw huts replaced the more Westernized dwellings favoured by the Zimbabweans. On the verandah of Manika's ramshackle hotel I drank many beers while waiting to be collected. When the young arrived at noon Rachel looked unsurprised to find me where I was supposed to be. Andrew, I gathered, had been preparing to bail me out of Mutare's police station.

Re-entering South Africa proved equally stressful in a much less enjoyable way. But that was all my own fault, as several Jo'burg friends scornfully pointed out. During the hour-long flight from Maputo we were required to fill in immigration forms and, this being the new South Africa, I uninhibitedly ticked 'work' as purpose of visit. But at Jan Smuts airport, in September 1994, honesty was the worst policy. A small pot-bellied Afrikaner immigration officer, with thin sandy hair and angry pale blue eyes, demanded my work permit. Then I made mistake no. 2 by firmly asserting that in the new South Africa I didn't need a work permit. Resentment of the new South Africa is strongest among exactly this category of Afrikaner: minor civil servant, immediately threatened by affirmative action. Moreover, I was, technically, wrong. GNU hasn't yet had time to deal with all the laws scheduled to be changed.

The immigration Commander-in-Chief now came on the scene – a tall, thin, megalomaniacal bureaucrat who seized on me as a glorious opportunity for the full exercise of his powers. Yes, I could get a work permit but it would take time – all day, in fact, because my application must be processed in Pretoria. (It was then 9.30 a.m.) Meanwhile I was forbidden to make any attempt to contact the outside world, where the long-suffering Margaret was standing by to collect me.

Off, then, to an office where a conspicuously armed policeman supervised my form-filling. Bizarre forms these were, demanding the name of the corporation for which I worked, its global headquarters (Tokyo? London? New York? Hong Kong?), the South African addresses of all its agents, the period of my employment with it, the precise nature of that employment, the address of my South African bank and my account number, my health-insurance details, my destination(s) in South Africa with addresses, telephone and fax numbers – and more besides, which I left unanswered because I couldn't understand the questions.

Karel Schoeman, an Afrikaner author, has commented: 'Afrikaners hardly read books, never mind showing admiration for people who write them.' You could widen that comment: South Africans in general lack any understanding of the literary way of life. Yet now, when presented with a fourth form, I attempted in desperation to explain that freelance authors are just that – free spirits, not even remotely associated with any corporation. The C-in-C's eyes glazed over when I outlined my 'work' in South Africa: cycling from Jo'burg to Bloemfontein, via Bop, kwaZulu/Natal and the Transkei. In South Africa even *blacks* don't cycle; they use communal taxis.

At that crucial moment the telephone rang; Margaret had detected the crisis and was forcefully rallying round. I'll never know what she said but her intervention unnerved my captor, already badly shaken by all this talk about cycling and writing; for me, he had no bureaucratic pigeon-hole. Somehow Margaret's spiel completed his demoralization. Grabbing my passport, he stuck in a form ordering me to report to the Home Office in Central Jo'burg seven days hence to collect my work permit. And then I was released into the not-so-new South Africa.

A week later I obediently queued at the Home Office for one hour and forty minutes. But alas! nobody knew anything about Dervla Murphy's work permit. End of story. Dervla Murphy spent the next four months happily working in South Africa, then departed with no questions asked.

PART III

Post-elections

September 1994 to January 1995

14

Post-euphoria

Rustenburg – Warmbad – Piet Retief

How real a concept is freedom? You start to function when coming to terms
with a set of limitations.
Athol Fugard

Freedom of association also implies freedom of disassociation.
Johan Heyns

Florida, 24 September 1994

Welcoming me back, several friends have remarked, 'You'll find everything
changed and nothing changed.' They didn't need to expatiate; the paradox is
tangible, powerful, the keynote of the new South Africa. And though unsurpris-
ing it disconcerts.

In Sandton an elderly English-speaking couple were honest about how much
they value 'freedom of disassociation'. Recently, driving back from their Knysna
holiday home, they stopped as usual at a Willowmore café.

'But it was full of blacks!' said George. 'Crowded with them!'

'So we drove on,' said Mary, 'though we were dying for a pot of tea.'

'We should have stayed,' said George – genuinely contrite.

'But at our age it doesn't matter,' said Mary. 'Our children would have stayed
– I think. Certainly our teenage grandchildren would. And that's what matters.'

Next morning, beside Florida Lake, I met an atypical Rhodie sorting out his
fishing-tackle. He has been running a business in Krugersdorp since 1982 and
was full of cheer. 'One day,' said he, 'this will be a great country. Don't listen to
the pessimists. I'm surrounded by right-wingers, they're my customers and my
friends and I tell you I'm stunned by their climb-down. It's like they're fed up of
posing as Boer War heroes. Two have asked well-heeled blacks to join them in
business – as equal partners! I'm not kidding! OK, the headcase killers are still
around. But every country has those, they're not a *political* problem.'

Among blacks, the 'infant' simile is in frequent use. Returning by train from
my Home Office expedition, I sat opposite a Xhosa pastor (Anglican) who asked
with a twinkle, 'You want to hear my favourite sermon? It's like this. When your
baby is born you feel very happy and have a big party. A baby is all good news.

You don't think about problems, how will you feed and clothe and educate it. But maybe twenty years later you are sad because it is not a good person, or not healthy. Now we are content, having our baby democracy. But we mustn't forget we're all its parents – everyone, every race. This new baby depends on us. Foreign investors won't rear it. They want nothing but more money, they don't *care* about us. So we must care for one another – am I right?'

This afternoon I saw a hard-faced white woman and her daughter, aged sixish, leaving a Florida shop, the child clutching two bars of chocolate. As Mom dealt with the car's security system a well-dressed young black woman passed, followed by her son, also aged sixish. Suddenly the little girl turned, ran after them – and presented one bar of chocolate to the boy. Although both mothers looked astonished they didn't communicate, didn't acknowledge each other's existence. The boy, wide-eyed, solemnly said, 'Thank you.' The little girl gave him a quick hug before running back to Mom. Walking on I felt I had witnessed Florida's very own mini-miracle.

Rustenburg, 25 September

The Arm has passed its first serious cycling test; today's sixty miles have caused only the mildest discomfort.

Our first stage, to Magaliesburg, was familiar. Lear and I followed this road seventeen months ago when South Africa was in a very different mood – the post-Hani tension high enough to be menacing. Pedalling across unexciting farmland – most pastures burned black to encourage growth – I reflected on euphoria as a phenomenon. Its impermanence does not have to mean its inspiration was illusory. It seems the elections interlude, that period when a healing calm came upon the country, really did lay the foundations for long-term reconciliation. Not instant reconciliation, an absurd goal though so popular among sentimentalists during the euphoric phase. (In fact, more than absurd – an oblique insult to those who have suffered so much for so long.) But there is no need to feel embarrassed, in retrospect, about the nation's mass-excursion to Cloud Nine in April/May 1994.

The noon heat forced me to lie reading for two hours, in the shade of a wayside shed, and all day on this narrow road a constant stream of two-way Sunday traffic plagued me – families in long fast cars, a child or two plus a dog or two in the rear seats.

Near here, four curious white police officers stopped their van to offer me a lift – and, when that was declined, a long cooldrink from their ice-box. They commended GNU – 'So far it's an OK government' – and proudly explained that they are community police. 'That's a new sort of work,' said the captain. 'We're learning how to make everyone love us! Everyone except the criminals and tsotsies. It's easier for us now, we're not puzzled who's a criminal and who's an *activist*. Now they've got a black President, everyone who does bad is criminal.'

Rustenburg's run-down motel is owned by a disagreeable Indian who overcharges (R100 minus breakfast) for a room in which the TV set works but the bedside lamp doesn't. The adjacent store offers only gluey white bread, that revolting shocking-pink polony and sour milk – sour because the fridge broke down yesterday. The bar and restaurant are permanently closed.

On a grassy expanse, behind the long row of rooms, several rondavels are occupied by Afrikaner families. When I arrived, trios and quartets of large women with coarse features were sitting silently in white plastic chairs around a small swimming-pool reeking of chlorine. Meanwhile their husbands drank beer under a distant tree, their male offspring kicked a rugger ball and their female offspring bickered over the dressing of dolls. Then the women were stimulated to converse (muttered remarks, certainly rude) by the arrival of six Tswanas from Gaborone in a luxurious camper-van. Botswana's rich are very rich and these youngsters displayed the latest gaudy Outdoor Life fashions and state-of-the-art music-making machines. Having unloaded a giant ice-box of booze they set up their braai, laughing and arguing and singing. This is how the new South Africa hits your average Vaalie. The invasion of hitherto 'white' space is the measure of change.

For The Arm's sake I did thirty minutes' side-stroking in that cramped, warm pool – not my idea of fun. Then a bouncy young Tswana woman asked, 'D'you have some salt to spare?' I gave her half my supply but when the tourists discovered that I am travelling by bicycle they tittered behind their beringed hands and thereafter ignored me.

Northam, 26/27 September

Last night's lodgings were not conducive to diary-writing.

Yesterday, as dawn broke, I was again circling that small smelly pool, watching the sky turn from dove-grey to the faintest pink, tinged with primrose and violet – then streaked with crimson. Already the air was warm. And this is only springtime...

Two hours later I had escaped from a hellish region of platinum mines and miners' hostels, articulated trucks and strange mobile mining monsters forced me onto rough verges strewn with broken glass. Then an unsignposted road, tarred but unmarked on my map, took me into one of former Bophuthatswana's many segments – at first a vastness of undulating, waterless, uninhabitable bushveld. Next came square miles covered by thousands of shacks and hundreds of mini-bungalows and scores of two-storey villas. As I was filling my water bottle at a windpump standpipe it became apparent that these 'surplus people' are used to being tourist-fodder.

'You've come to see how blacks live?' shouted one woman, standing outside her cacti-hedge.

I turned and hesitated; her tone was sardonic, yet not aggressive. Slowly I pushed Chris across the space between us, a littered patch of grey dust and sharp little stones. She laughed when we came face to face. 'But you're a *madam*! I thought you were a man!'

A dozen adults and a pack of begging children ('Give money! Give sweets!') were already converging on me. The woman extended her hand and said, 'You call me Pleasure, my other name you couldn't say or remember. From where do you come?'

'From a country called Ireland, very small and far away.'

'You have little money,' observed Pleasure, eyeing Chris. 'Why so little? Your country has bad droughts?' Suddenly she raised a fist and yelled at the pestering children who, by now, were trying to pick my pockets. They fled, then re-assembled in a fascinated huddle some thirty yards away.

A rheumaticky grey-haired elder stepped forward to shake my hand. 'I know about Ireland, at the mission school we had Irish teachers. Ireland is a poor country, people eating only potatoes. Comes a drought and no potatoes they die.'

Pleasure looked at me sympathetically. 'Put your bicycle inside,' she directed, 'or it will be stolen. Now I will give you tea.'

Cheap and cheerful furniture – the sort sold by the wayside in the bigger townships – overcrowded Pleasure's three-roomed shack. She is a retired nurse, a shrewd self-confident woman who now does voluntary work in a primary-health-care centre funded by a Scandinavian NGO. 'My children say it's crazy to work for nothing. But why sit idle when I have knowledge to help? That is not the Lord's plan!'

As friends and relatives arrived, a large tin of biscuits was taken from a cupboard top, thoroughly dusted and opened in my honour. Many invitations were issued and during the noon hours I drank herbal tea in four other shacks. Pleasure, bearing the biscuit tin, escorted me along rutted laneways and – despite her friends' hospitality – sullenness marked the general attitude to the visitor. The traffic consisted of numerous water-carts drawn by two, three or four miniature donkeys with spindly legs and sore backs. Pleasure informed me that only 20 per cent of Bop's rural population (which comprises 84 per cent of the total population) have access to what is officially described as 'adequate sanita-tion' – 'adequate' including pit-latrines.

We sat outside the shacks, our torsos in the eaves' sparse shade, our legs exposed to the sun: a lesser evil than the intolerable heat within, under tin roofs.

Local expectations of the new South Africa are low. Recently the platinum mines laid off 1,500 workers – what can GNU do about *that*? Despairing faces surrounded me. We pity blacks who must endure a working life spent underground. Those blacks pity themselves when they cannot find such work.

The tales then told of Mangope's misdeeds sounded like urban legends, but from other sources I know them to be true. Few of the billions of rands poured into his coffers by Pretoria benefited the 'common people'. Bop was reputed to be the best-run and most prosperous Bantustan, yet its rulers' corruption makes the mind reel. I am told Mangope and his twenty-three ministers collected luxury properties in London and Paris and fleets of expensive cars. Mangope himself had twenty-nine; now he has only two, a BMW and a Mercedes-Benz, both bullet-proof. Judging by my friends' comments, bulletproofing is an essential extra.

Posters of President Mandela – and other ANC election flotsam – decorated the walls of each shack but some doubts were expressed about the effects of 'victory' on the ANC.

One of my hosts, a redundant miner, asked, 'What happens in their heads when they get big jobs in government?'

His wife said, 'No – what happens in their *hearts*?'

Pleasure said, 'Give them time. Now they're all excited with their big houses and cars and salaries and forgetting us. But if they go on forgetting us they can't keep power. They've given us democracy – right? So *we* have the real power. When enough people understand that, we'll be OK.'

On the way back to Chris I asked, 'Who owns these grand bungalows?'

Silence for moments. Then Pleasure said, 'Good businessmen. Smart operators. Now they can move out and live with whites. We won't miss them.'

As this Bop road is a cul-de-sac, I had no choice but to return to the nearest main road, struggling against a strong, hot headwind. Pleasure's illusion – 'we have the real power' – saddens me. Possessing a violin is not the same thing as being able to play it.

At a junction, five non-English-speaking Tswanas conveyed that the nearest hotel was at Pilanesburg, a dorp unmarked on my map but if it had a hotel it must exist. As I sped across flat drab veld the low summits of the Pilanesberg drew closer on either side – then loomed directly ahead, beneath a swollen crimson sun. And still there was no dorp in sight. Then, rounding a corner, I was confronted by a series of gigantic illuminated roadside signs, forty feet high, their disco-type lights flashing on and off, synthetic colours glaring through the dusk. I stopped and stared. These signs were all to do with money – unimaginable amounts, nine-figure sums. I shuddered as the ghastly truth overwhelmed me: Pilanesburg's hotel is SUN CITY. No dorp exists, only the four most luxurious hotels on the African continent. Because the Unholy Trinity forbade gambling, casino/hotels proliferated in the 'homelands'. But none could compete with Bop's 'international playground', created in 1979 by Sol Kerzner, the Midas son of penniless Russian-Jewish immigrants.

So, what to do? On my right a ten-foot steel-mesh fence bounded the Pilanesberg National Park with its recently imported populations of kudu, rhinoceros, elephant and leopards. On my left smoke rose from an invisible valley to which hundreds of factory workers were now being returned in a fleet of orange coaches speeding downhill from the direction of Mogwase. This was not camping territory, unless I could find a corner within the Midas kingdom.

Pedalling on between those illuminated mega-signs, I soon saw Sun City's castellated entrance, a hyped-up version of a motorway toll gate. Armed security guards hovered and two pretty white girls peered at me from their IN and OUT booths. It is possible (even probable) that for them Chris was a first. Smiling frostily they left their booths, beckoned the guards and held an emergency meeting. A guard then requested my passport, studied it closely and made a telephone call. In his absence one girl asked, 'You have money?' 'Of course,' I replied loftily. '*Lots* of money.' The guard returned and waved me on as a coach arrived from Bloemfontein.

For two miles I pushed Chris uphill, at first parallel to an elevated monorail that conveys day-trippers to the casinos from the acres-wide car park by the entrance. Beyond a crocodile-enclosure-cum-restaurant I turned right and climbed a steep mountain. Anxiously I looked for a camping corner but none appeared. Where the ground levelled out, ponds ('picturesque') were surrounded by tropical vegetation. Their visible residents – black swans and pink flamingoes – showed symptoms of disorientation: all about them was bright as day. Here stands the hideous Cascades Hotel (1984), a clone of all those other multi-storey hotels now defacing every continent.

Morbid curiosity propelled me into a long, low-ceilinged foyer where mobile multicoloured spotlights induced giddiness and every sort of gambling-machine lined the walls, whining and clattering and squeaking. Ladies in voluminous West African robes sat cross-legged on triangular purple sofas drinking champagne and eating potato-crisps out of cut-glass bowls, while their menfolk tried to get richer quickly. When I pushed Chris to Reception he left snakes of grey dust on the gleaming black marble floor.

Something odd was going on at Reception's immense semi-circular counter. An elegant Afrikaner couple, both tall and slim and wielding calculators, were angrily arguing with the Tswana receptionists. Then a battered cardboard carton was drawn from beneath the counter and placed on top. It contained bundles of R50 notes; outside of a bank, I have never seen such an accumulation of cash. The Afrikaners, tense and narrow-eyed, followed the count while each bundle was checked and rechecked. No one even glanced at me as I stood nearby, leaning on Chris, streaming sweat after that climb. Finally the Afrika-ners admitted defeat; they had not, after all, been cheated. But what was all that loot doing in a carton on the floor? When the couple had moved away, I asked. A woman receptionist giggled and explained: 'Someone's lost the key of our safe, but don't tell!'

The cheapest room costs R460. Sympathetically the receptionist observed, 'It's much when you are poor on a bicycle.'

While investigating the outdoor possibilities I moved furtively, trying to keep in the shadows. On one side, the monorail on its high concrete pillars imitates a motorway flyover – would you pay £92 for a view of a flyover from your bedroom window? Skirting another car park of cosmic proportions – this one for coaches – I came at last upon a secluded, tree-surrounded grassy slope behind another of those 'four most luxurious' hotels. The gradient required me to lie against the tree to which Chris was chained, lest I might gradually slide onto the concrete path.

Soon after I had settled down, if you can call it that, a Tswana security guard appeared.

For a long moment he stood over me, saying nothing; I felt he didn't believe I was real. Then he asked, 'Why?' I explained.

'You are not afraid?' marvelled the guard. When reassured on that score he said, 'You like it this way, OK! Goodnight, lady. Have deep sleep!'

Sun City's security system explains why the receptionist could afford to giggle about that lost key. Throughout the night an armed guard regularly toured the complex in a silently rolling little tin box (electrically powered?) and shone a dazzling lamp into every corner, including mine. But that was the least of my nocturnal worries. I needn't have bothered locking Chris – it was impossible even to catnap.

Our tree chanced to belong to a peacock who came home to roost at about 9 p.m. and whose piercing resentment of the intruder was articulated, continu-ously, until dawn. 'May-O! May-O! May-O!' he screeched from amidst the foliage. 'May-O! May-O! May-O!'

Then there were the mosquitoes, unaccustomed in this area of five-star hotels to easy pickings (or stabbings) and eager to make the most of me. And there were numerous coaches, arriving with blaring tapes and ill-tempered, argumentative passengers. Also there was a cat – one of the larger models: a leopard? – confined somewhere nearby. From midnight onwards his growls and snarls, added to 'May-O!', formed a contrapuntal jungle chorus. Many people regard Sun City as 'an exotic experience'. And I suppose, in its way, it is.

This morning I decamped at 4.45, very hungry (only groundnuts for supper) and cross-eyed with exhaustion. While Chris was being unchained the peacock shat on my head; perhaps he felt better after that. At the exit a security guard wanted to search the panniers but I was in no mood to be trifled with; making a noise like that large cat I sped on my way. Inevitably, guilt followed; I am after all a suspicious character, in the Sun City context, and the poor fellow was only trying to do his duty.

I arrived at Northam in tar-melting heat. This dorplet is the commercial centre for workers in three nearby platinum mines and blacks thronged its two short streets. It is – or used to be – proud of its Afrikaner 'purity'; there are no resident English-speakers. A single-track railway has to be crossed en route to the hotel, though not at any particular point; the mile-long goods trains chug to and fro at walking-speed.

Within the hotel compound eight whitewashed rondavels are shaded by fig trees, their leaves floating on a long-neglected mini-swimming-pool. The elderly Afrikaner at Reception was sympathetic when I described my Sun City night; she disapproves of gambling and was pleased that I had refused to subsidize the vice.

I shared a table in the homely little dining room with a youthful bank clerk, in Northam on his first posting. Usually Jan drives home after work to his parents' farm near Thabazimbi, but today his third-hand car broke down. Cheerfully he remarked, 'Now more whites will have old cars and more blacks Mercedes and BMWs. But I don't mind. Our changes let us into the free market and that's good for everyone. Last month rich blacks from Mmbatho bought the farm next ours but my folk don't mind. Dad says they're good neighbours, they go to church and have polite children.'

Conversation with Jan required slow speech and a restricted vocabulary. The standard of English teaching in most Afrikaner schools has ill-equipped his generation for the new South Africa where English will soon become the main language, however 'equal' in status the other ten official languages.

The same, 28 September

Mr Uys, a supermarket manager and chairman of the town council, invited me to lunch in his eyrie-office overlooking the supermarket's length and breadth. Without pretending that he could ever regard blacks as equals, he is now prepared to work with them for the mutual benefit of both communities.

I warmed to Mr Uys (bred on a Free State farm) when he confided his main current worry. Northam's whites are all set to oppose the admission of blacks to *their* school – built for 400 pupils but now down to 208, a measure of the rapidly declining white birth rate.

'It's the town parents who are angry,' said Mr Uys. 'The farmers are adjusting better. OK, so they hate the notion of an integrated school – that's natural. But they've got the message – we've lost power and making trouble won't help. The town parents – well, too many still listen to ET!'

(A pretty frog has just hopped into my room: russet flanks and legs, a pale grey back with four symmetrical black spots.)

This evening in the bar a mining engineer pulled a wad of leaflets from his pocket and handed me one – 'Your souvenir from Northam!' I read:

> MANDELA IS MY SHEPHERD
> Mandela is my Shepherd
> I shall not work
> He maketh me to lie on park benches
> He leadeth me beside the still factories
> He restores my faith in the Conservative Party
> He guideth me in the path of unemployment
> Yea though I walk through the Valley of the Soup Kitchen
>   I shall still be hungry
> For I feel they are evil against me
> They have anointed [sic] my income with tax
>   My expenses runneth over my salary
>   Surely poverty and hard living shall follow me
> All the days of the commie administration.

Warmbad, Northern Transvaal, 29/30 September

Poor Chris is doomed to be compared unfavourably with Lear – punctured only once between Kenya and Zimbabwe despite carrying me over some of Africa's roughest tracks. At dawn yesterday the back tyre went flat a mile from Northam. But then, all of Chris cost £100 and each of Lear's tyres cost £150.

The two Tswanas on petrol-station night duty spoke no English but were coping effortlessly with their office computer; the rapid spread of computer literacy makes me feel obsolescent. While one young man tended to Chris the other put on a rap tape and offered me chewing-gum which I gallantly masticated in the interests of good race relations. In this country no one thinks it odd that I can't mend a puncture; 'madams' are expected to rely on the nearest 'boy'.

For thirty-five miles a not-too-busy road descended gradually through grey-green thornbush veld. Then, near Thabazimbi, it seemed a shawl of sky had fallen on the nearby mountainsides: all their jacaranda trees are in full blue bloom. This little dorp exudes civic pride; richly glowing flower beds bisect the streets, an orderly jungle of tropical trees and shrubs shades the pedestrian shopping mall and each lavishly sprinkled lawn shines like an emerald – despite this being one of South Africa's most parched regions.

Leaving Chris in my room I dandered around the dorp for a few hours and felt sorry for Thabazimbi's whites – buttoned-up folk, at first uneasy with the uitlander. But it was not too difficult to unbutton them and then they exposed sheer bewilderment. Not fear of the *swart gevaar* – that was left behind on 27 April 1994 – but an incomprehension of Afrikanerdom's apparently sudden collapse. And varying degrees of uneasiness when they looked ahead, based on a not entirely unfounded scepticism about GNU's capacity to govern.

Today I discovered what The Arm does not like: fifty-five jolting miles on a severely corrugated dirt track. But the beauty of this route more than compensated for The Arm's complaints.

I was on my way before sunrise, the dawn air cool, the dawn scents fragrant in a herbish way, the dawn chorus loud but staccato or harsh, not melodious like ours. Beyond Thabazimbi I turned off the R510 and soon low mountains surrounded me – steep, rocky, thinly forested – and for hours the landscape was dominated by a shapely, conical 6,000-footer slightly to the north. Sometimes the track was squeezed between high cliffs, creeper-draped. Sometimes the mountains drew back, leaving grazing-space for herds of glossy red-brown Afrikaner cattle who thrive on the matching red-brown bush as imported breeds do not. A few farm entrances appeared but no farmstead – or any other building. We met only two bakkies; both farmers were nonplussed when I declined their kind offers of a lift. As I brunched on a bridge, high above a wide, dry, rocky river-bed, hundreds of baboons entertained me – the babies playful, the adolescents daring, the mothers anxious, the fathers abusive. All day it remained overcast, the breeze cool: perfect cycling weather.

This hotel in the centre of Warmbad was bought only three weeks ago by Judith and Piet, a young Afrikaner couple (smallholders ruined by the '92 drought) who have no notion how to run the place and no cash left to pay staff. Judith, aged 22, almost wept with relief when I explained that my flea-bag renders sheets superfluous. Her four children – she married at 17 – look like Botticelli angels but behave otherwise. This is being written by lamplight because the local authorities have pronounced the wiring unsafe and Piet must somehow raise a loan before rewiring.

The same, 1 October

Warmbad was once a quiet spa town. Then the developers moved in and around its natural hot spring created the Aventura Leisure Centre: many acres of prefab chalets and caravan parks, with their attendant horrors. When the turnstiles opened at 7 a.m. I paid R15 and the date was stamped in invisible ink on my right hand – allowing me leave and re-enter at will throughout the day. Walking to the main pool, I winced. From amplifiers on all the many tall lampstands pop music blared. To break me quickly and extract a false confession, that's all the police would need.

Caravanners and chalet-dwellers were already disporting themselves in the strangely shaped hot pool – all inlets and coves, as it were, dominated by a central metal tower from which artificially heated water gushes. (This bizarre pool is far from the original hot spring.) Most people stood around the edges, shoulder-deep, splashing each other's faces. For The Arm's sake I plunged in and spent a penitential thirty minutes enduring a truly horrible experience – who wants to *swim* in hot water? Moving onto the allegedly cold pool, I found it lukewarm. An hour later I retreated to my room with the *WM&G*, reluctantly returning at noon to give The Arm more therapy.

Aventura's black employees provided today's silver lining. Enos, one of the garbage collectors, spent his lunch-break hour with me. We sat on a shaded bench overlooking one of the children's pools. In 1990 Warmbad grudgingly desegregated its 'public amenities' and simultaneously Aventura raised the adult entrance fee from R5 to R15. As under-12s have to be admitted free, many more juvenile than adult blacks were visible on this hot Saturday afternoon. We watched several white mothers beckoning their young out of the water when blacks joined them.

'They think we have diseases,' said Enos, smiling indulgently, as at the error of a child too young to understand.

Enos earns R700 (£140) a month and his wife R600 as a maid in Pretoria. Out of that she must spend R120 on taxi fares; his monthly fares come to R60. He longs to buy a bicycle but can't afford the R25 deposit. 'We've three children to feed – three's enough! After feeding comes education, let them wear old clothes but have enough school books. This new government is no good for our young people if they can't get education.'

Looking at Enos – courteous, dignified, intelligent – I thought, 'In no other country with South Africa's resources would this man be a garbage collector.' And then I thought, 'For one hotel night I pay four times what he needs for a bicycle deposit.'

However, Enos and his wife are lucky – employed. An estimated 32 per cent of urban blacks live below what is known to sociologists as 'the minimum living level'. In plain English, they are permanently hungry. And in rural areas the figure is approximately twice that.

Blessing replaced Enos. She washes floors in the Steak House and has six children, aged 8 to 18. 'Morning and evening I thank God for He has given me good children, always to church on Sundays, no dagga, no fighting, no politics. They try to study well but that school is *bad* with stupid teachers.' She wore a ZCC cap and badge. 'How is it with blacks in your country? They have good schools?'

'Ireland has no black communities, only a few students from Africa.'

'*No* blacks? You have Coloureds and Indians? No? All white people? Aah – that is a funny country!' She reflected for long moments. Then, 'So that's why you sit talking with us, not same like our white people talk to us? You have a curiosity about blacks?'

'More than a curiosity. I like the peoples of Africa. I've been to other countries where there are few whites, as there are few blacks in Ireland.'

Blessing chuckled. 'Aah – you are funny! Our white people say they like blacks only if we do things their way. Then we're *good* blacks, we say, "Yes, *baas*," they like us. Now we all have a black *baas* and they hate him!'

Left alone, I gazed at the whites (mostly obese) lounging under beach umbrellas above the children's pool. An unlovely sight, many with lobster-red backs, their chief occupation applying lotions to each other. They had no aura of enjoyment (I recalled that day in the 'guest house' near Lydenburg) but presumably being herded together in this horrendous place gave them some satisfaction. Between blacks and whites I saw not one social exchange. Each behaved as though the other did not exist.

To restore my flagged spirits I bought a bottle of homemade 'lemon wyn' from a pathetic-looking Afrikaner woman of advanced years; like several other poorish whites she had set up her little stall – selling home produce both edible and wearable – outside Aventura's entrance.

Marble Hall, 2 October

Pre-dawn exits from security-conscious hotels can be complicated but Warmbad's hostelry has a broken side door. By 1 p.m. I had crossed seventy-five miles of drab, flat maize-farms interspersed with stretches of dusty, dehydrated bush. Our narrow, almost traffic-free road was entirely dorpless and only on arrival here did I remember that this is the Sabbath. Everywhere was closed – including, it seemed, the hotel bar.

At Reception I was sourly received by the owner's elderly wife who has dyed black hair and a jutting nose like the prow of a ship. She also has a pure white bulldog with azure-blue eyes, by name Pretty. This creature is the centre of her universe and when I made much of him, and he in response licked my sweat-salty arms with slobbering relish, Mrs de Beer admitted that the bar, though not *open*, could be – was being – used by friends. Pretty, evidently suffering from salt-deficiency, showed me the way to this irreligious scene, then scrambled onto the counter via a stool and resumed licking my arms.

The friends were two jolly early-middle-aged couples from Germiston, still at the 'kaffir' stage and not worried by the new South Africa because they believe

FW will win the '99 elections after everyone has realized that Mandela remains a
Commie at heart.

Mr de Beer – tall, fat and florid, with a haystack of white hair – drew my
attention to a poster hanging beside a blonde almost-nude calendar woman
posing on a beach. I read:

The Americans have	We have
Bill Clinton	Mandela
Stevie Wonder	No Wonder
Bob Hope	No Hope
Johnny Cash	No Cash

'How's that?' grinned Mr de Beer. 'Hey, man – that says it all!'

A farm near Stoffberg, 3 October

Today: more maize-farms in shallow valleys and cattle crowded near dams; they
will be moved, after the rains, to the wide bare slopes across which our road
switchbacked for fifty-five miles. From 9 a.m. onwards the heat was punishing
and I needed four rest-stops.

Stoffberg consists of a grain-silo and a petrol-station-cum-general-store. There
Nettie overheard me asking about accommodation and at once offered hospitality; the nearest hotel is in Belfast, twenty-five miles on. Nettie's husband is
descended from a famous Voortrekker leader whose son, in 1860, demarcated
their farm in the customary Boer way: the new settler was entitled to as much
land as he could ride around in a given time. For 134 years this land has been
passed from father to son but now there are only three daughters, aged 16, 14
and 12. Comely lasses, who shyly welcomed me into their Landcruiser.

For fifteen miles a vividly red track took us up and up and ever up into a
region where the new South Africa seemed unreal. The R—s' nearest neighbours are ten miles away – 'We can't see their smoke', the old Boer ideal. Here is
a world apart, high and silent and very beautiful. Subtract motor vehicles and
this could be 1894, yet the PWV is only an hour's drive away. Not that the R—s
ever go to Pretoria or Jo'burg; they venture as far as Middelburg only when
compelled by some exceptional necessity.

We had turned onto a five-mile private track when the weather changed with
theatrical abruptness. As the sun dropped behind a nearby range a gale-force
wind swept across the maize-fields. Instead of a sunset glow, black clouds filled
the sky, racing over and then obscuring the mountains. 'Rain!' exclaimed Nettie
and the girls in unison, their faces radiant. All evening thunder rumbled and the
gale raged coldly around the farmstead, depriving us of electricity, bringing
down the party telephone line and frightening the dogs by sending zinc buckets

rattling across the yard. But the rain came only an hour ago (at 10.30: I'm up late tonight) and was no more than a brief deluge.

The R—s' hospitality is bountiful though a trifle awkward. Father (Jan) speaks no English, and Nettie and the girls only a little. However, *Oupa* (grandpa) saved the situation. He lives in a 'dower-bungalow' and, having been schooled in the Smuts era, speaks 'the imperial language' fluently and correctly – though with long pauses to recall forgotten words.

On 10,000 hectares (25,000 acres) the R—s run more than 1,000 cattle, 5,000 sheep, hundreds of pigs and fowl, and a herd of wild horses descended from Voortrekker stock and cherished for sentimental reasons. Their thirty farmworkers, plus large extended families, live in round thatched huts with Ndebele designs on the exterior walls.

Those South Africans didn't vote in the elections because – *Oupa* asserts – 'they don't want anything to change'. They are so cut off they probably don't realize change is *possible*. And without help from the *baas*, how could they have got to the nearest polling station at Stoffberg? Suggestions that the farm-school should be used as a polling station – the arrangement in most areas – were rejected by Jan, who forbade both voter-education teams and ANC canvassers to set foot on the property.

Helen, the eldest daughter, invited me into her room to admire a litter of newborn kittens and then confided that she wants to leave her Belfast school *now*. Mother quite approves of this idea but father won't hear of it; you don't leave any endeavour unfinished – faint-heartedness didn't get the Voortrekkers into the Stoffberg mountains. Poor Helen finds school boring and meaningless – apart from bookkeeping, a skill needed by farmers' wives. She is radiantly in love with and unofficially engaged to the 22-year-old son and heir of their nearest neighbours, who must relish the prospect of uniting the R—s' 10,000 hectares with their own 8,000. By our standards this romance seems almost unnaturally neat. Yet one can understand its flourishing in an isolated community where, even now, the young rarely challenge their traditional codes of discipline and decorum. This farm feels like a leftover from the pre-Grand Apartheid era, an authentic remnant of that Boer feudalism I encountered last year on a few Western Transvaal farms.

Jan's plans for his farm's future indicate that he feels unthreatened by the new South Africa; nothing has happened to alarm this little colony. Nettie remarked that President Mandela comes across on TV as 'a good man' and everyone concurred. The numerous potentially destabilizing problems facing GNU are of no concern (as yet) to people whose own prosperous world is peaceful and under control.

However, without generous state subsidies this world will be much less prosperous. In March 1993 Dr Japie Jacobs, then adviser to the Ministry of

Finance, announced that the Land Bank's government-backed selective lending policy, favouring white commercial farmers, was no longer serving any useful purpose. Two months later the Land Bank, glowing with political correctness, publicized its decision to grant loans to part-time farmers by way of helping blacks. But *Oupa* refused to see the significance of this move. 'It's not important,' said he. 'It's only crazy political talk. Blacks can't run farms.'

Belfast, 4 October

The dawn sky was overcast as I loaded Chris outside Stoffberg's store (his lodging house) while the girls boarded their school bus. Half an hour later another gale rose, forcing me to walk most of the mainly uphill miles to Belfast. It is hard to credit that yesterday I suffered from heat exhaustion. Why did no one warn me that in springtime the highveld can be Siberian? All morning visibility was restricted to a few hundred yards and at 1 a.m. a freezing cloud sat firmly on Belfast. Reputedly this is the coldest place in the Transvaal and all the blacks wore thick blankets, woolly caps and long scarves. Clutching a bottle of cane-spirit, I retired to bed in a refrigerated room, supplementing the skimpy bedding with my flea-bag. It took me three hours to thaw.

This hotel's design is perverse. Around the corner from the main entrance, on another street, stand its jerry-built bedrooms to which the gale finds easy access through ill-fitting windows opposite ill-fitting doors leading directly onto the pavement. Poor value for R90, especially as my bath is non-functioning – an inconvenience soon to be rectified, the manager claimed, but the depth of dust on its enamel belies him.

Venturing out to the bar at dusk, I hurried through an opaque cloud of ice particles. At least the bar was warm – as was my welcome. The only other customer, a lean elderly English-speaker from Natal, had passed me on the road and was congratulatory. 'Well done! I never thought you'd make it – and at your age, too, if I may say so! What's your poison?'

Having been poisoning myself all afternoon with cane-spirit, I chose more of the same. Mr Rowland looked shocked. 'But that's a shebeen drink! You going a bit native?'

Soon he was telling me that during the previous weekend he had visited a township for the first time in all his sixty years. Driving his thatcher to fetch a load of grass, he was astounded to see 'the rotten shack' where dwells this well-dressed, well-mannered, well-spoken Zulu. 'You know, he's such a decent respectable fellow I'd pictured him living in some neat little bungalow. That shack, I couldn't believe it! No running water, no electricity – but his wife and kids clean and well turned out! How do they do it? All those shacks and squatter camps you see on TV – I'd got it wrong. Took it that's where gangsters and agitators live – and lazy scroungers.' Mr Rowland beckoned the barman, ordered another round, then continued. 'To talk truth, I'd not have dared set foot in a township before the elections. Not even in my youth when things were quiet. Hey, it's strange to look back! In those days we didn't *think* about blacks. They were off the scene, except when we needed them. Not that I'm complaining, as long as we have Mandela I'm happy. Even after him the ANC have some good chaps, clever fellows we never heard of before. *And* they've some bad chaps, but no worse than the old guard – we're used to corruption in high places. It can't get worse and it could get better.' He looked at his watch and finished his whisky. 'Must go, I won't stay in this stable. Carolina's hotel is better.'

'I know,' I said, 'last year I stayed there. Give my regards to the fat corgi and the tortoiseshell cat.'

Mr Rowland's township shock helps to explain white resentment of the blacks' failure to pay income tax. Seeing so many 'respectable well-dressed' blacks around the place, they cannot conceive of their living in untaxable poverty.

Discovering that the hotel restaurant has been closed for two years, I rushed out to buy food. But all the shops and takeaways were closed and the foggy streets deserted, save for a youth with a bloody gashed skull lying unconscious in a gutter. I reported his life-threatening situation to SAPS, then nut-munched.

The same, 5 October

Today the weather is even worse – and what a place to be weather-bound! Last year I paused here on a sunny morning to breakfast after my gruelling Dullstroom night. Now Belfast is in the new province of Eastern Transvaal, but what else is new hereabouts? One can't expect many tangible changes, five months after the elections. However, my fear is that five *years* hence there still won't be many, from the majority's point of view. Particularly worrying is the World Bank's meddling. Its goal is to create a small but prosperous class of black commercial farmers on freehold land, a comparatively rich peasantry whose interests will coincide with the white farmers' – leaving the rural masses in Square One. This policy has already increased the misery of millions throughout the Third World. And the countries of southern Africa have been hardest hit. To see the damage done by World Bank/IMF manipulations, GNU need not look far.

Warburton, 6 October

All day a cloudless sky but the icy wind blew hard as I covered sixty hillyish miles, mostly through commercial forestry, every slope in sight wearing a dark green uniform.

Approaching Carolina I was startled to see a new bright sign, high and wide, depicting the flag of the old Transvaal (Kruger's) Republic and proclaiming in red-and-blue lettering: CAROLINA VOLKSTAAT. A feeble gesture of defiance; whatever the design defects of the new South Africa, it is secure enough for Volkstaat nonsense to be discounted.

Halfway along Voortrekker Street, a tall slender young Muslim woman – her black gown ankle-length, her black headscarf theologically correct – called a greeting from a shop entrance and offered a 'cooldrink'. When first we met, in April '93, Nazeem had been a member of the DP. After that party's election obliteration she joined the ANC: 'My husband didn't approve, he thought we should remain loyal to the DP, try to revive it – he's still mistrustful of all those black ministers! But though I dress like this I keep my independence of mind. And it helps people like me, knowing our new regime stands up for women's rights.'

Nazeem does indeed think independently. 'Too many in our community are scared of blacks, the Nats always tried to make us feel just privileged enough to give us something to defend from the *swart gevaar*. It's time to resist that conditioning, otherwise Tutu's rainbow nation won't work. Because we have been a bit privileged we should give a lead. It's true most blacks dislike us even more than they dislike whites. They see whites having some sort of "natural" right to be superior and richer, but when we do well they're jealous. It's also true some of us exploit and cheat them, especially small traders and travelling hawkers. I don't want to deny our own faults, now everyone must look at the whole picture. We all have a chance to start again, that's the President's message. And he's right. Shame he can't talk more directly to the young. Those black kids adore him but laugh at his old-fashioned way of talking. Only Hani could have got the Mandela message across to kids with no schooling. I'm glad you called your new bike Chris!'

After the conversational aridity of the past fortnight I needed the refreshment provided by an educated Indian.

This country's cartographers baffle me: why give Warburton the status of a town? No such place exists. Not even a petrol station or grain-silo marks the spot, only a minimalist store opposite a large wayside notice saying WARBURTON. Usually groups of blacks hang around rural stores, but not here. The young Rhodie woman sitting behind the counter, knitting a tiny garment, looked momentarily scared when I arrived. Then, collecting herself, she tentatively suggested my seeking food and shelter from her aunt and uncle, to be found in a log-cabin in the Mundi forestry workers' compound a few miles further on.

The Johnsons – effusively kind – have amply fed and are cosily sheltering me. In 1980 Don gave up managing a lowveld cattle ranch in 'Rhodesia'; as someone 'prominent' in the Bush War his life was threatened. The whole family – husband, wife, granny, niece – have been Born Again to the point of semi-hysteria. It was obligatory to pray, all tightly holding hands, not only before and after supper but before and after watching TV, that the Lord might guide our reactions to what we saw and heard. By great good fortune what we did see and hear was an excellent BBC documentary about Ruth and Seretse Khama. It took me back to my adolescence, when that long-drawn-out drama first drew my attention to the race problems of southern Africa.

A farm near Piet Retief, 7 October

Around Marble Hall one enters a region where the new South Africa is suffering from post-natal stress. This has to do with the farmworkers' rejection of feudalism; human-rights lawyers describe labour tenants' living conditions as 'the closest we have to slavery in South Africa'. A labour tenant provides free labour in exchange for the right to cultivate a small patch of land; the R—s' thirty tenants have ten hectares between them. In the 1960s the Nats outlawed this system, not because they had anything against slave labour *per se* but because they foresaw a 'blackening of the countryside', given the size of each tenant's extended family. (The R—s' 'village' has a population of 227, including infants and octogenarians.) Over 1 million blacks were then banished to the 'Bantustans'. But in this south-eastern corner of the Transvaal, and in much of Natal, farmers resisted the outrageous notion of paying wages to blacks and dodged the new law by giving each tenant a nominal R10 per month. Now those hardliners are up against a less accommodating government. A proposed Bill (part of a scheme designed to give the rural poor 30 per cent of South Africa's arable land within five years) would entitle quarter of a million labour tenants to live on white farms, without fear of eviction, and to purchase land (with state subsidies) from farmers who refuse to pay a fair wage. This has prompted many farmers to evict tenants *now*. Families are being compelled, by the use of physical force, to leave their homes and growing crops at a few hours' notice. In retaliation, the evicted are burning maize- and canefields, stealing or hamstringing cattle and cutting fences. That last ploy, if stock are involved, endangers both animals and passing motorists.

From the invisible Warburton a little-used road undulates through more miles of forestry, then between gentle slopes of yellowed grassland, desperate for rain. All day the Kingdom of Swaziland lay on my left: chunky blue mountains in the distance, brown foothills nearby. Not far from Piet Retief I came upon a stretch of dismantled fencing, presumably cut last night.

Where the de-fencing ended, at a farm entrance, five infuriated Boers stood beside three parked bakkies, loudly arguing. I dismounted and feigned bewildered concern: 'What happened the fence?'

The five stared as though I had dropped out of a UFO. Four were youngish, the fifth a patriarchal type complete with white beard – a mighty man, no less than six foot four and broad in proportion. (They breed them like that around here.) Suddenly he laughed and extended a hand. 'I know about you, Jan R— told me. You're that crazy woman from overseas. Hey man! Those kaffirs will get you! Here and now they're running wild – what you reckon happened my fence? I'd a visit from Mandela's Commie friends. Gone rabid they have, think now they can intimidate us, grab our land – this government is telling them to do it. Yesterday they burned a milking-shed, on the next farm. Day before they lamed ten cows. But we know where to find them – they want another war, they can have it.' He pointed to the gateway. 'Up there, you'll find my wife. Tell her I say you're to drink coffee.'

A two-mile dusty track ended at a 1970s bungalow. On the way I paused to walk around the original four-roomed homestead: of mud and stone, thatched, now used as a fertilizer store. Later, my host reminisced about his youth in that typical Boer home, without electricity or running water – never mind wall-to-wall carpeting and microwave ovens. He spoke nostalgically of those more robust days when men weren't afraid to wash in cold water or women to slaughter sheep.

My arrival did not surprise Mrs Van der Walt; Jan, it transpired, is her nephew.

'Tonight you stay here,' she said. 'It's good for us to talk with overseas people. I have lived seventy-two years but you will be my first overseas guest.'

Mrs Van der Walt is small and round and rosy-cheeked and disagrees with her husband (though never in his presence) about almost everything. 'My thinking is more like the younger people's. The change has happened. War-talk is no good now. We must trust Derek Hanekom [the Minister for Land Affairs]. Even if he's ANC, he's also an Afrikaner farmer. He promises we'll be paid when blacks get some of our land and he wouldn't break a promise. It's true we don't need so much land. I say that to Jan but he won't listen. Is it easier for women to see things the way they are? Jan doesn't live *now*, he's lost in the past. You saw for yourself. Up there on that mountain they think they can go on like that for ever – but they can't.'

Over supper Mrs Van der Walt made no reference to the de-fencing but her husband did. 'They destroy my property because I look ahead. The more tenants you have the more land you'll lose. I only got rid of five families and that's crazy – I'm too soft, should've got rid of ten. The Commies are organizing all this. In July we'd 7,000 or more marching in Piet Retief, handing demands to that Phosa fella.'

Mr Mathews Phosa is the Eastern Transvaal's provincial premier. I already knew about those demands: an end to evictions, the immediate return of all the labour tenants' impounded livestock, the rebuilding of homes demolished by farmers or police.

The Van der Walts could produce only one daughter. Her second son, Willem, now aged 24, is their live-in heir. After supper he and I talked while *Oupa* and three Rottweilers went kaffir-hunting and *Ouma* loaded the dishwasher. Willem's father is a wealthy Natalian (English-speaking) cane-farmer and his parents had to elope, so strongly did *Oupa* disapprove of the alliance. 'It was a secret marriage,' chuckled Willem, 'though my Dad's family is so rich. *Oupa* would have preferred his daughter to marry a poor Afrikaner, which is good – that's having principles. Now he's out with his gun and if he finds blacks making more trouble he'll shoot them dead. But that's OK, blacks understand violence. They don't understand my father's sly way of exploiting them without violence. I went to an English school near Maritzburg but I'm happier here – I *feel* Afrikaner.'

This labour-tenant trouble is not new; it has been recurring, at irregular intervals, for a century. What's new is blacks having the law on their side, the most positive aspect of the reborn South Africa – at present causing turbulence hereabouts, yet allowing people to see 'liberation' functioning, not merely being proclaimed from on high.

Piet Retief, 8 October

Piet Retief is as expected only more so: a dull, tight-lipped and now uneasy dorp. Unusually, the township is visible from afar, covering a few high hills. For two hours I wandered up and down its very steep, dusty, stony tracks beside stinking open drains. The burgeoning middle class have built some fine new bungalows – even a few two-storey 'villas' – and many of these have lavatory bowls propped outside the front door, awaiting the arrival of piped water, as promised by GNU. But the majority occupy mud-brick shacks or flimsy hovels, the latter known as 'informal housing' in bureaucratese. Several outwardly imposing schools dwarf all other buildings. The abundance of litter must be deeply demoralizing – or do township residents accept it, as city dwellers everywhere accept air pollution?

My tour caused general amazement but communication was limited. Most local blacks speak only Afrikaans as their 'white' language – or, if they come from Swaziland, as thousands do, minimal English which they seem reluctant to use. However, the barrier between us was not mainly linguistic. This corner of the Eastern Transvaal and the adjacent north of Natal are so notoriously right-wing that no white stranger could reasonably expect to be made welcome in a township.

Back on Voortrekker Street, I saw yet another example of that gratuitous violence towards children so disturbingly common among Afrikaners. Outside a pharmacy a small boy and an even smaller girl were sitting on a step, licking ice-creams. When the boy dropped his cone they began to squabble and a florid thick-set young man – presumably father – rushed from the shop, angrily shouting. He struck both simultaneously and, as they screamed with pain, picked them up by an arm and flung them through the doorway. We hear a lot about child abuse in Europe but only in South Africa have I repeatedly *seen* such examples. And the public nature of these incidents points to uncontrolled aggression being tolerated behaviour, associated with no feelings of guilt or shame.

In Jo'burg last month a Cape Afrikaner educational psychologist assured me that the many horror stories related about South African schools are not exaggerated. Every male state-school pupil and many females (of all colours) retain memories of regular and severe beatings for trivial misdemeanours – or simply for failing to achieve academically. This institutionalized brutality matched the militaristic flavour of the old regime and something similar was to be found in Ireland when the authoritarian Roman Catholic Church controlled most schools.

On the rugby field, foul play – especially the sort that draws blood – always gratifies a large section of a South African crowd. This afternoon the Springboks were playing Argentina and I withdrew to the hotel's empty lounge to watch. The men gathered in the bar were too awful, their testosterone seriously over-stimulated by the occasion. Among Afrikaners, the role of rugger is akin to that of hurling and Gaelic football in Ireland; it has been co-opted as the athletic expression of a people intent on asserting their nationalistic distinctiveness. Another South African irony – that the Afrikaners should have adopted, as one of their most cherished tribal totems, a game invented by 'the imperialists'.

15

The Problem Province

Pongola – Ulundi – Isandlwana

You white men have encircled us; but perhaps the day may come when you will
allow us to pass through your country, and remind those nobody's people that the
Zulus are still on the face of the earth.

Anon., after the Battle of Ulundi (1879)

Pongola, Natal, 10 October 1994

For many miles this morning I was pedalling through dorpless mountain territory, parallel to the Swazi border. Beyond the high wire frontier fence, only a few
yards away, ragged Swazi emerged from tin-roofed shacks and thatched huts –
alerted by their bicycle-allergic dogs – to stare at me. Behind the dwellings lay
golden-brown hilly land, too rough and dry to be cultivable, rising soon to meet
low brown round mountains, their straggly indigenous forests much depleted by
firewood-seekers.

Halfway to Pongola I crossed the provincial border, marked by a population
explosion: more 'surplus people' overcrowding steep slopes and deep valleys.
Here my welcome was warm; children came rushing down to the road, waving
and smiling and shouting greetings. On several long uphill walks barefooted
groups escorted me, full of chat and local gossip. One small boy pointed to a
large new bungalow and identified it as the home of a taxi tycoon who owns
eight kombis. 'Eight!' the child repeated, in awed tones. At present the local hens
are dying of Newcastle disease, their loss no mere misfortune but a tragedy
amidst such desperate poverty. Last year I heard about this disease when it
started in an enormous battery-hen 'factory' near Pietermaritzburg.

One 12-year-old girl wondered, 'Why don't you ask people of your own sort
to give you help with transport?' (An interesting turn of phrase: 'people of your
own sort'.) The children then struggled to come to terms with a concept both
novel and absurd: that Mama *prefers* to cycle, *chooses* to cycle . . . 'In your homeland are no vehicles?' suggested one little girl with the brown-tinged hair of the
malnourished.

In local schools the smallest classes have forty-five to fifty pupils, the largest
eighty-five to ninety. School hours are 7.15 a.m. to 3.45 p.m., with two short

breaks and an hour for lunch. 'We work hard,' said a 10-year-old boy. 'We all want to get to the university.'

'To study what?' I asked, correctly guessing the answer: 'To be a lawyer.'

'But many days,' said an older girl, 'teachers don't come to us. They go away doing other jobs, they say the government doesn't give them enough money.'

Hereabouts the adults were no less relaxed and thrice I was invited into huts (stone and wattle walls, thatched) and offered maize-beer or herbal tea or home-distilled pineapple spirit – reputedly good for the digestion but with an aroma like stale urine. It shames me to remember that last year I became irrationally anti-Zulu in reaction to these blacks being the favourites of so many whites.

Throughout the forenoon – this being the last day of a long holiday weekend – Vaalies were streaming home from the coast, many vehicles towing large boats with comic names: Waves Galore, Dad's Delight, Rough Riders, Sun of Jamaica, Hearty Folk Here, Going for the Big One. All were travelling in convoy, four or five together. Coming upon one lot picnicking – their side-arms conspicuous – I paused to converse. Even now they consider Zululand a 'high-risk zone'. And maybe it is, when the ostentatiously rich are driving through a region without health care, easy access to water, sewerage, electricity or land enough to feed the population. But I suspect they are merely being paranoid.

Abruptly the weather changed. Low black clouds created an eclipse-like twilight and a cold gusty crosswind blew choking, blinding, stinging dust from eroded mountainsides and precipitous paths. When the wind became a gale, carrying occasional spatters of large raindrops, my juvenile escort deserted; blacks are unstoical about getting wet. Luckily the clouds hesitated for an hour before delivering their deluge and by then Pongola was near, a dismal dorplet surrounded by cane-farms.

Pongola's hotel was built in British colonial style; its rooms lead off deep verandahs overlooking wide lawns, ornamental ponds, tall palms and a gay variety of flowering shrubs. Now the owner is black and – I was informed in Piet Retief – whites boycott the place because of its 'filth'. I can detect no filth and my room supplies the usual modest comforts. But the young Zulu woman receptionist was almost insolently unhelpful, doubtless aware of the boycott.

Finding the ladies bar closed (until 5 p.m.) I intruded on the windowless public bar. Its high unsteady metal stools seem to have been designed to torture customers, old sardine tins serve as ashtrays and a lone twenty-five-watt bulb illuminates the dingy scene. Four male Zulus, drinking cane-spirit, stared at me blankly. The one female – a teenage prostitute, her complexion ruined by skin-lighteners – tittered when I ordered a pint of draught. Looking baffled, the barman suggested that I should retreat to my room, ring the bell and order a drink from the waiter – in short, behave like a madam. But I still resent South

Africa's compulsion to segregate. Stubbornly I held my ground, unfolded the map, pretended to study it, then asked advice about tomorrow's route – an ice-breaking device that usually works. Here, it didn't.

At last, the tall, handsome, slightly greying man on my left addressed me. 'Your room number is what?' he asked. When I feigned not to remember he guffawed and said, 'OK, I'll find! I like you in bed.' The prostitute tittered again, unable to take seriously, as a rival, this aged odd bod.

Then the man on my right, sporting a dense beard and a de Klerk election badge, leaned towards me and tapped FW's chubby face. 'You like this man? This good man, fighting Mandela for our Chief, our Gatsha Buthelezi.' When I had cravenly expressed my devotion to Mr de Klerk, silence fell again. Punctually at 5 p.m. I moved on to the 'ladies'.

There the Afrikaner barmaid – small and thin, a blonde haggard 43-year-old – had given me her life story within ten minutes. Married at 19; husband beat her up; divorced at 26; daughter gone to the bad ('ran off with a *Coloured*'); son a SAPS officer who divorced last year and is now on sick leave with a nervous breakdown.

As we brooded over Fate's unfairness four other customers arrived, three local cane-farmers and an Afrikaner truck driver already slightly drunk, very depressed and also in autobiographical mode. Slowly his tale of woe reached its climax: six months ago his second wife (by then we had heard all about the first 'bitch') absconded with their two small children. 'I miss my kids, I want them back but I can't find them!' Piteously he looked at the barmaid whose bulging pale blue eyes filled with tears. As their hands met on the counter I tactfully transferred my attention to the farmers.

Their talk was all of sugar prices and rugby. Something in the Pongola air prompted me to avoid the new South Africa but I did seek their views on world affairs. As conversational gambits go, this was not a great success. They mistook all of Ireland for a province of the UK, didn't know where Rwanda is and had never heard of Bosnia.

One young giant had shoulders like a bulldozer, curly yellow hair and a coppery tan. He offered me a lift to Nongoma tomorrow. 'If you go on your bike you'll be hacked to death – slowly. There's big trouble these days around the King's palace.' My declining to be protected upset his companions. One said, 'We've trouble enough here without more bad publicity. We're trying to put Pongola on the tourist map, we don't need foreigners getting killed. It was in all the papers last year when a Swiss woman on a bike got murdered.'

I promised to work hard at not being killed and said goodnight. As I write, the deluge continues. Having crossed so much thirsty land since leaving Jo'burg, the sound and sight and smell of rain give me an odd feeling of personal physical gratification.

Nongoma, kwaZulu, 11 October

At dawn the air was moist and cool; high dove-grey clouds covered the sky, tinted pink and primrose to the east. Overnight the wind had swept the streets, decorating petrol pumps with shreds of plastic bags, piling sodden litter against the walls of the KFC takeaway and the new Plaza shopping-mall.

After a gradual fifteen-mile climb, through sugar-cane and rough pasture, the end of the tarred road marked my re-entry into kwaZulu. From here a bone-shaking track ran level across unpopulated acacia savannah, then climbed into bare mountains. Soon I dismounted; on a surface so ravaged, walking is faster than pedalling. I met only three vehicles over today's fifty miles.

Where the track curved around the base of a sheer precipice something bizarre appeared on a distant clifftop: a gleaming white edifice. My binoculars revealed an architectural mongrel, a cross between the Regent's Park mosque, a modern Irish Catholic church and an environmentally friendly German factory. It took me a few moments to diagnose King Goodwill Zwelithini's main palace – he has several others. Amidst such wild uninhabited country, it was quite a shock suddenly to come upon this symptom of royal lunacy.

Twenty minutes later I was being suspiciously scrutinized by the two police on sentry duty at the palace entrance. Cheerfully I greeted them, sullenly they scowled. I averted my gaze from the building and quickened my pace. On this high plateau hovels cluster densely around the King's extravaganza and beyond sight of the sentries I paused to talk to three friendly elders, sitting on low stools outside a kraal. They are very proud of the palace – had I taken photographs to show to people overseas? No, I said – the sentries seemed hostile.

One man stood up and beckoned me. 'Come, I will talk to these police, they are *fools* – they are like an ancestral curse on our land!'

'But I don't have a camera,' I lied.

My would-be liaison-officer – tall and thin, his ragged blanket detracting nothing from his dignity – frowned and looked puzzled. 'You are a tourist without a camera? No camera, no vehicle? You are poor?' The question was rhetorical; obviously I am poor.

Another man, looking at Chris's panniers, asked, 'You have goods to sell? You are trading? You have medicines?'

'No, that is my luggage – books, clothes, a tent.'

The third man stood up, hurried to his hut and returned with a wodge of maize dumpling in a plastic bag. 'For your food tonight,' he said. 'I think you will be hungry.'

Not long before I had eaten my fill of nuts, a luxury food in the villages. Thanking my benefactor profusely, I secured the dumpling in a pannier and shook hands all round.

This plateau overlooks a wide, long, shallow valley, its countless kraals holding round thatched huts or oblong tin-roofed hovels. A few cattle and many goats browsed on meagre scrub. Near the track stood the newish bungalows of the local quislings now intent on obstructing GNU's reforms.

Nuts have their limitations and the elder's donation of carbohydrate was appreciated an hour later, after I had pushed Chris up another few hills. From my boulder-seat was visible a vast turbulence of smooth or rugged mountains, dusky blue under a pale grey sky. In this heartland of the Zulu kingdom there once roamed herds of thousands of cattle, inexorably impoverishing the soil as both human and animal populations increased throughout the seventeenth and eighteenth centuries. Already, European influences were seeping in from Delgao Bay (now Maputo) not far to the north-east. The first whites to disrupt this region were neither Voortrekkers nor English colonizers but Portuguese traders who introduced the gun to the Zulu and other tribes, then encouraged them to compete for access to the new power-enhancing commerce in slaves and ivory.

As I continued the gradients became even more severe and the surface so rough that Chris felt like a recalcitrant pack-animal who has to be dragged along. Nongoma appeared an hour before we reached it, standing high above a complex of deep narrow valleys, their floors packed with huts, bungalows and shacks. From a distance, Nongoma resembles a Basilicatan hill-town.

The teacher who accompanied me over the last lap had been walking since dawn to have his ulcer treated in the three-storey Benedictine Hospital, once run by Catholic missionary nuns but long since taken over by the State. My companion, though obviously exhausted, remained cheerful. 'Tomorrow I'll feel better,' he assured himself. 'This is a good hospital.' Later, I heard otherwise. Before we parted, I asked the way to the hotel. 'Hotel? Here is no hotel, you must go to the police – up there.'

The steepness of this final hill required me to walk on tip-toe, leaning far forward. On my right was a new suburb of neat, pastel-painted prefab bungalows set in tiny gardens. Here live government employees whose housing subsidies and other perks partly explain Buthelezi's popularity.

Nongoma covers the slopes and flat summit of a high, wedge-shaped mountain commanding an awesome expanse of Zululand – austere beauty extending for scores of miles in every direction. The KZP District Headquarters, surprisingly unguarded, dominates the summit. I entered the forecourt as an importantly uniformed but thuggish-looking senior officer was driving out. He stopped, listened impatiently, then brusquely dismissed me. 'This is not South Africa, we have no lodgings here.' (In the old South Africa the SAP were obliged to provide shelter for stranded white travellers.) He accelerated onto the main road without stopping and almost struck a woman carrying a baby on her back and a sack on her head. As she gazed after the long sleek car, her expression conveyed hate mingled with fear.

Slowly I pedalled past a row of shoddy shops, attracting many stares but no smiles – until a kindly young man approached to ask, 'Are you lost?'

'Not lost, but without shelter. Can I rent a room here?'

'A room, to sleep in? You are tired? Mr Ford maybe can help you, no other white person lives in this town. He owns the big store and a big house.'

'It doesn't have to be a white person,' said I, a trifle irritably.

The young man looked away. 'We black people, we have no nice spaces for white people.' He indicated a long steep hill, tarred but pot-holed. 'Down there, on the big street, you can find Mr Ford.'

I sped past a small police-post, a cinema and yet another new Plaza shopping-mall. Mr Ford's cavernous emporium sells blankets and biscuits, ladies' under-wear and insecticides, toothpaste and builders' materials, leather belts and saucepans, plastic toys and tinned milk. Inexplicably, four heavily armed soldiers were guarding its entrance and a small but excited crowd had gathered nearby.

Behind the counter stood a fat friendly Zulu woman who explained, 'You must wait a little, Mr Ford is still with the King.'

I blinked and repeated, 'With the *King?*'

'Yes, but soon they'll be finished their talking.'

I leaned Chris against the counter and sat on a pile of blankets conveniently to hand – or to bum. There was tension in the air. I noted the soldiers' alertness: faces taut, eyes darting, rifles at the ready. This was no boring routine job.

Meanwhile customers were wandering in and out: women comparing the prices of knickers, men looking for six-inch nails or purple paint, children buying one sweet each. In between customers the staff questioned me, wonderingly. Then we were joined by a member of the royal entourage, dressed like a City gent and carrying a mega-briefcase, gold-embossed. We discussed the weather. This year, there is a 'bumper sugar crop'. Yet the farmers cannot quickly recover from four years of drought. And some cattle-farmers lost so many animals they will never recover. Just now, in kwaZulu/Natal, one doesn't discuss the political climate with those who are creating it.

Eventually a counter-flap was lifted and His Majesty emerged from some back room. Noticing a foreigner on the premises, he nodded regally in my direction, then sat into a small, dusty, non-regal motor car – followed by two soldiers – and was driven off to his palace. When he appeared on the street the crowd stood still and was silent, devotion shining in their eyes.

Mr Ford – an octogenarian with a pasty, sagging, bad-tempered face – was unhelpful. 'You must go on to Ulundi, to the Holiday Inn. Here we've nowhere for tourists. My home is full of these people' – he indicated his staff – 'and their families and friends. Every room is packed with them. I've only one room left for myself. They just *squat* on my property, they won't leave unless I give more wages. How can I? What profits can I make with all these blacks embezzling money to build themselves supermarkets?' He glared at me, his eyes red-rimmed and angry, as though I were an embezzling black. Then he gestured towards Chris and added, 'You'd better hurry, to get to Ulundi before dark.' (Ulundi is fifty miles away and sunset was two hours away.)

At the small Nongoma police station my luck turned. No, I couldn't camp on the grassy space in front – 'too dangerous' – but when the day's work was done an office floor would be available.

Despite the KZP's evil reputation, Nongoma's underworked officers seem to have a good relationship with the locals. As I relaxed on the stoep several passers-by sauntered in to investigate me. A group of secondary-school pupils sought to improve their execrable English – 'We has teached English into six years with teachers so bad! This teachers know nothing!' And one rheumaticky elder, wearing a threadbare army greatcoat, sat on the bench beside me to bare his political soul – a refreshing deviation from the norm.

A few weeks ago the annual Shaka Day celebrations were boycotted by the Zulu Royal House in retaliation for the stoning of the King's Enyokeni palace, while President Mandela was visiting, by an IFP gang. (My companion pointed out that to call these gangs 'impis', as journalists often do, is to dishonour the Zulu military tradition.) Then the IFP Deputy Secretary-General delivered two head of cattle to the King, on Buthelezi's behalf, as 'a self-imposed penalty'. Here the elder's voice quavered with indignation. This was an insult, a most grievous insult. Only the King – not Buthelezi, a mere subject however blue-blooded – should decide on the penalty for any offence committed against the Royal House. Therefore an affronted Royal House rejected the cattle. It is inappropriate to laugh at the apparent pettiness of Zulu squabbles; these can be life-and-death matters.

My companion could remember Zwelithini versus Buthelezi dissension twenty and thirty years ago, when the Nats were using the young King as a pawn. They planned to make him ruler of an 'independent' Zulu homeland, which idea greatly appealed to him. But Buthelezi, his uncle and self-appointed 'Prime Minister', was determined to spoil the overall Grand Apartheid design by keeping this most populous province within the Republic of South Africa. Thus the Zulu never became legally 'surplus people', deprived of their South African citizenship. And the King's political ambitions were easily atrophied by Uncle's threat drastically to reduce his stipend if he continued to make trouble. According to my informant, those ambitions have only recently been revived by blandishments 'from outside our place'. (Code for the ANC.)

The King was aged 22 when installed as the eighth Zulu monarch in 1971. He makes an ideal pawn, being not very bright and fond of money. By

European standards the Zulu monarchy is very new. Yet its power enabled King Zwelithini's canny relatives – the Royal House – to legitimize Buthelezi's rule over kwaZulu as an autocratic Chief Minister. That remained his status from 1976 until he became GNU's Minister for Home Affairs.

At sunset my companion rose stiffly, leaning on his stick, and pulled a woolly cap from his coat pocket. 'Our big Zulu weakness is faction fighting,' he pronounced sombrely. 'You know why Chief Zwide of the Ndwandwe chose this hilltop as his Great Place? He chose it because it stood between the lands of two factions, the uSuthu and the Mandlakazi. But his peace-keeping failed. In 1888 the uSuthu burned Nongoma and the British Colonial Police moved in and built Fort Ivuna, where that Plaza place is now. The contractor's bulldozers uncovered the fort and we should have kept it for tourists. People came from Ulundi to protect it – then what? When nobody watched the contractors destroyed it! How could I watch? I'm an old man, I can't spend all my time on a building-site!'

Later the commander joined me and said, 'You have been honoured! You were talking to Chief M—, a wise and clever man. But he's not IFP so he gets none of the perks.'

If the KZP has many more officers like this commander, there is hope for it yet. He has a conscience much troubled by the conduct of his Nat-corrupted colleagues. 'Also it concerns me that our people have been so upset by this feuding between the King and Chief Buthelezi. They want to be loyal to both, that is their tradition. How can they understand what's going on in Pretoria or Cape Town? They are fearful because their traditions seem at risk. Then fear makes anger and anger makes bloodshed. Ours is an unhappy province. I look out over the rest of the country and feel envy.'

Anywhere else in Africa the commander's equivalent would have invited me to his own home for the night. When will South Africa have healed sufficiently for such gestures to be psychologically possible?

This is being written in a bleak little office with a concrete floor, unpainted breeze-block walls and a door that doesn't shut properly. I'm sitting at a long rickety table laden with bulging files marked STRICKLY CONFEDNSIAL (*sic*). What a wealth of raw material, if only one hadn't been nicely brought up!

Ulundi, kwaZulu, 12 October

For much of the way to Ulundi Nongoma remained visible, sometimes hidden by a nearer mountain, then reappearing – white against a cloudless sky – seeming to float above the earth. Rural slums alternated with undulating savannah or desolately beautiful hills haunted (in my imagination) by the ghosts of the wildlife that once roamed these ranges.

From the early sixteenth to the early nineteenth century all of this area – the Eastern Transvaal, kwaZulu/Natal, Swaziland – was quite densely populated by the Northern Nguni, who include the Zulu. Fertile soil and a benign climate (on the whole: there were always periods of drought) allowed the development of many well-organized chiefdoms and subchiefdoms, their wealth measured in cattle, each family responsible for growing its own food. But by 1800 over-population had set the scene for a series of conflicts that culminated in Shaka's manic wars which left much of the Free State and Transvaal temporarily unpopulated at the time of the Voortrekkers' arrival.

My map, of old South Africa provenance, marks Ulundi as a village though it is the capital of kwaZulu. Seen from a distance, scattered over the Mahlabathini valley, its recent expansion is obvious: white dots represent thousands of new houses. This valley – the centre of Shaka's kingdom – is overlooked by the aloof heights of Mthonjaneni, traversed by the White Mfolozi river and bounded on the south-west by the escarpment of the distant Babanango plateau.

Now Ulundi is the Inkatha/Buthelezi stronghold and it seems white strangers are assumed to be ANC spies. The first person I met was faintly alarming; he stopped his Merc to shout across the road, 'Where do you come from? Why are you here?' He wore a silk shirt, a Rolex watch, several gold rings and an expensive after-shave lotion too liberally applied.

Standing by the car window I explained myself honestly.

'So – you're looking for problems here? You want to make trouble for us overseas? We have no trouble in kwaZulu, except what the ANC makes. That's our only problem. Any ANC person coming here interfering will be dead in two hours. Two hours maximum – right? You go and tell that in your book – it's *fact*!'

The provincial murder rate gives substance to this rhetoric and I could easily imagine my interrogator organizing the killing of an ANC supporter and boasting about it afterwards, perhaps to a policeman friend. I watched him drive on, then turn into the car park beside the 'legislative complex'. Evidently he is a kwaZulu lawmaker. Poor kwaZulu!

In Piet Retief I removed a long ANC election sticker from Chris's crossbar and, while doing so, accused myself of being melodramatic. Today that precaution seems justified.

Ulundi feels unlike either a town or a city. In the small commercial centre it apes a dorp, with its harshly coloured shopping-malls and transnational offices, most as yet unoccupied. Some entrepreneur has recently built a covered market opposite the only hotel, the Holiday Inn. But the local hawkers (cheerful rural folk, warmly welcoming) cannot afford to rent stalls and continue to spread their wares on dusty patches of wasteland while cattle and goats wander through the enormous empty market. Unrestrained livestock are Ulundi's most agreeable feature; all developers had to guarantee animal freedom of movement when doing a deal with the villagers who previously dwelt here. Entering the bank, I was followed by a kid (four-legged) with whom I had already established a meaningful relationship in the Spar supermarket. Both staff and customers took our relationship for granted; when I tried to imagine reactions to his presence in Florida's branch of the same bank my imagination failed me.

The Holiday Inn's park-like grounds are protected by a wide cattle-grid of awkward design, suggesting that walkers and cyclists are not expected. However, the young woman receptionist proved sympathetic. She condoned my wheeling Chris into the plushly carpeted foyer – 'Yes, take care!' – then noted my reaction to the list of tariffs and offered to ring the Ondini tourist camp. But, unusually, every hut is booked for tonight. Painfully I parted from R214 and took Chris to my room between tall palms where thousands of weavers are noisily nesting. For that outrageous sum (breakfast extra) the Holiday Inn offers no more than your average dorp hotel.

Back in the almost empty foyer, I wondered why its dazzling white walls display only blown-up photographs of King Zwelithini and Chief Buthelezi in tribal dress: would pictorial competition constitute *lèse-majesté*? On one side of a long back-to-back zebra-skin sofa (typical Holiday Inn furniture) sat a quartet of white corporate-types playing with the electronic tools of their trade and loudly conversing in corp-speak. Morbidly fascinated, I eavesdropped.

It seems Durban is experiencing a project-driven development renaissance that was kick-started by public-sector commitment, but there is a need to relook at potential linear development opportunities along the northern beaches. And all role players must be up and running by December to create spin-offs into the private sector. An international convention centre is being planned and Durban must prioritize this to ensure hotel-bed occupancy on a twelve-month cycle.

Inwardly I wept for the new South Africa. An international convention centre being built within a few miles of Durban's myriad homeless ... These international conventions have become an integral part of the UN/EU/World Bank/IMF (etc.) flight from reality. Instead of taking action about urgent problems, you 'read papers' and simultaneously give your partner and several of your staff a free luxury holiday. So the conventions become part of the problem, soothing consciences (where such exist) while circulating resources among the Haves.

Corp-speak scares me. As the language of those who wield the only power that seems to count in the 1990s, it reveals their disconnectedness from the needs of the mass of humankind – their victims. 'When words lose their meaning,' said Confucius, 'people lose their freedom.'

This year R4 million is being spent on luring tourists to kwaZulu/Natal and in the bar I studied a stack of newly published tourist literature – glossy magazines, no mere brochures. Evidently, political correctness now requires some grotesque distortions of history. The official British and Afrikaner versions have been equally tendentious but in the new South Africa why not attempt 'transparent' history? This buzz-word is now used in every context, as though there were something discomfiting or naive about the word 'honesty'. But I must stop. My present environment has put me in a cranky mood.

Ondini, 13 October

For once I slept badly – perhaps those R214 were bothering my subconscious. On the concrete floor of Nongoma's police station I slept soundly.

This morning's weather was Irish summery: warm gentle rain. Going walk-about, I soon passed the KZP Headquarters, its innocuous appearance belying its reputation. Within those walls were identified many Third Force hit-squad targets. Associated in many people's minds with the Third Force were some who now hold top jobs, including Chief Buthelezi himself, then also Minister for Police; Prince Gideon Zulu, now kwaZulu/Natal's Minister for Justice; Celani Mtetwa, rumoured to be a professional smuggler of AK-47s from Mozambique and now kwaZulu/Natal's Minister for Safety and Security; Captain Leonard Langeni, Commander of the kwaZulu Legislative Assembly guard; Zakhele Khumalo,* Buthelezi's 'personal assistant'; Lindiwe Mbuyaze, the IFP Women's Brigade Deputy Chairwoman, now a National Assembly MP, and Major-General Sipho Mathe, now Acting Commissioner of the KZP, who has just been advised by GNU's Minister of Safety and Security that he faces suspension for 'alleged involvement in hit-squad activities'.

A government commission is now investigating those activities and late last Friday evening death threats were received by a couple due soon to give evidence. They sought KZP protection and were driven to Newark police station in a plain van. En route a following car, driving without lights, overtook them and ten shots were fired into the van. Luckily the couple escaped – this time. The commission has since promised to set up a witness-protection unit; without it, no one can expect non-suicidal witnesses to come forward.

At noon I took off for Ondini, some four miles away. The tarred road ends at Ulundi's airport and nearby stands a squat stone monument, its metal dome sporting a cross by way of maintaining that cherished European military fiction – 'God was on our side'. This marks the site of the Battle of Ulundi (4 July 1879), one of the British Army's least glorious victories.

Now this battlefield is covered by the shacks of the destitute, spread over hilly expanses of unproductive veld. Yet two miles away R281 million have been

---

* In 1995 Khumalo was brought to trial for the mass-murder of thirteen ANC supporters.

spent on Buthelezi's pet prestige project, the 'legislative and administrative complex'.

Why do Africans, all over the continent, allow themselves to be victimized by a tiny minority? Why should these Zulus have to live in such misery when *money is available* to improve their lot? According to the tourist literature, 'Huge development potential remains untapped in Ulundi, with only 23 of 461 business sites developed.' But what would the development of those sites do for the poor, apart from providing temporary work at slave wages? And not much of that, since construction firms make bigger bucks faster by using machinery.

Near the tourist camp stands King Zwelithini's latest palace, built for his fifth (or is it sixth?) wife; traditionally each must have her own Royal Residence. This one is a sprawling characterless 'suburban' house, its garden still rubble-strewn. A young woman, carrying a crate of cheeping chicks on her head, stopped beside me. 'You like this palace?' she asked eagerly. 'Is a pretty palace?'

'Very pretty,' I agreed – then added subversively, 'but it cost much money, too much money when you have no money.'

The young woman was not subvertible. She laughed and boasted, 'Our King has *much* money!'

Ondini's ancient acacia woods conceal authentic-looking Zulu huts 'with modern catering and ablution facilities' which provide 'tourist accommodation within the precincts of King Cetshwayo's Royal Residence'. A tetchy receptionist said my booking for tonight had been a mistake, no hut is free. Then a young man suggested my talking to Mr Barry Marshall, Director of the kwaZulu Monument Council, who lives within these Royal Precincts. He could be found in the restaurant hut, entertaining colleagues from all over the province. To avoid gate-crashing on a luncheon party I lurked in the acacia until spotted by one guest, whereupon the rest welcomed me with a warmth that made my lurking seem silly. Suddenly I was surrounded by archaeologists, anthropologists, sociologists, historians, librarians – a very pleasant culture shock.

When his guests had dispersed Barry took me on a dual journey: through the acacia to King Cetshwayo's kraal, back in time to the Battle of Ulundi. There is no longer, he said, any dispute about the origins of the six-month Anglo-Zulu War. Although Cetshwayo was threatening neither the British to the south nor the Boers to the west 'a conflict was engineered which had to lead to war'. The British aim was a militarily emasculated Zululand which could never destabilize their planned confederation of white-settled southern African states. Six times prior to the invasion of Zululand, and eighteen times during the war, King Cetshwayo dispatched messengers to negotiate with the British. Some were delayed by a series of tricks, some were given a list of demands blatantly impossible to fulfil, some were insultingly imprisoned. Then, on 4 July 1879, revenge was taken for Isandlwana by the mass-slaughter of Cetshwayo's warriors. Shell and rocket fire and Martini bullets opposed assegais and shields. The impis did have 800 or so Martini rifles captured at Isandlwana, but for lack of training in how to use them these were more ornamental than lethal. The British lost ten men and three officers killed; sixty-nine men were wounded. The official estimate of Zulu killed was 'not less than 1,500'. Captain Shepstone admitted that the pursuit of the fleeing Zulu 'had become butchery, rather, at last'. Another officer (Buller?) reckoned that his pursuing irregular cavalry killed at least 450. The regular cavalry claimed 150 'kills'.

Some retreating warriors attempted to set fire to their *amakhanda* (Zulu military homesteads) but the day was windless and they failed. Then the British did the job for them, burning eight *amakhanda* on the plain of Mahlabathini, including Ondini, the royal homestead, which smouldered for four days. On 28 August Cetshwayo was captured and eventually imprisoned in Cape Town's Castle. Sir Garnet Wolseley's 'pacification' of Zululand was complete and on 1 September the chiefs formally accepted his settlement. It abolished the independent kingdom, reducing it to thirteen fragments whose chiefs would in future be nominated by the British. Subsequently, the relentless exploitation of Natalian farmworkers gave rise to various embryonic political movements, some with militant tendencies. But most chiefs remained loyal to the whites.

'Cetshwayo was a great leader,' said Barry, 'no way resembling the tyrant in our history books. Of all the Zulu kings he was the most loved. When we thought about honouring his memory, rebuilding his homestead seemed the best way.'

I tend to shy away from such re-creations but Ondini is different; under Barry's knowledgeable and sensitive direction its ghosts have not been exorcized. The plan of the original *amakhanda*, built in 1872 and covering some three acres, has been precisely followed. Excavations revealed many earthen hut floors – preserved, through baking, by the fire – and in every detail the high, wide, skilfully woven beehive huts replicate the originals. Sections of the outer fencing were also discovered and those charred branches, incorporated into the restored fence, give one quite an eerie feeling. A wooden watchtower, by the main entrance gap, overlooks the battlefield. On a nearby slope a herd of pure white Nguni cattle – the colour favoured by Zulu kings – usually grazes but has now been drought-driven to Natal.

I'm glad I've seen Ondini now. Its 'potential' is being discussed by tourist-hungry officials and probably not even Barry will be able to defend his beloved site – so moving in the simplicity and reverence of its restoration – from becoming an electronic theme park with fast-food outlets among the acacia.

Tonight I'm staying with Maggie and Barry in their thatched cottage, built fourteen years ago by local labour using only local materials. Maggie has persuaded me (it wasn't difficult) to stay on tomorrow. She wants to show me the Legislative Assembly building to which she has privileged access, having worked as Chief Buthelezi's translator for nine years.

The Marshalls speak fluent Zulu and are very much 'of Zululand'. It is impossible to imagine them happily based in Cape Town, Jo'burg or Port Elizabeth. South Africa is like that: its various regions put their own stamps on the white natives.

The same, 14 October

Ulundi's aspiration to became the capital of the new province of kwaZulu/Natal arouses angry ridicule among all white and Indian (and many black) Natalians. A booklet produced by the kwaZulu Heritage Foundation claims that 'Ulundi has all the infrastructure necessary to qualify it as a seat of government. The Legislative Assembly offers seating capacity for 760, a sophisticated public address system for each MP, catering facilities, and modern parliamentary library facilities for members' use. Well-appointed accommodation is available for MPs, also fully-furnished Ministerial dwellings. A further 1,256 departmental houses/ flats are presently occupied by more junior officials. Subsidized private housing consists of 1,370 units.'

What do all these officials actually *do*? Since they obviously have no interest in the welfare of the majority, how do they while away their time?

Outside the Assembly, Maggie and I paused to gaze up dutifully at King Shaka's statue on its massive marble plinth. Despite his spear and shield, and his tribal warrior's ensemble, he looks oddly European. His body-language is wrong, suggesting some defiant Nordic hero.

Ulundi's white elephant would look at home in Brussels, as an EU extravagance. Inside, one wanders through a circular vastness of artificially lit wasted space – lavishly carpeted, furnished with groups of deep armchairs, decorated along one wall by many yards of a kitschy tapestry depicting the conquest and gradual Westernization of Zululand. To get anywhere one must go round and round and round, seemingly for miles, or up and up and up in state-of-the-art lifts. Briefly we sat just inside the main portal to the windowless parliament chamber, its mock-daylight derived from countless spotlights set in the gold-painted ceiling. Opposite us, suspended above the former Chief Minister's dais, hung an ornate gilded metal representation of the kwaZulu coat of arms. This, and the kwaZulu mace, depressed me. Such imitations of the Mother of Parliaments speak of a people conquered spiritually as well as territorially, their notion of 'progress' the adoption of the external symbols of their conqueror's culture – symbols arcane and ancient and incomprehensible, rooted in a past as unlike the Zulu's as you could get.

Earlier, Maggie had remarked on unusual activity around the complex: many cars arriving, many security officers scuttling about, many serious-looking, brief-case-laden *amakhosi* (chiefs) greeting each other on the forecourt. These were the Iso leSizwe (Eye of the Nation), a new association of members of the former kwaZulu government, gathering for an *indaba* (consultation) with Chief Buthe-lezi. Officially its purpose was a State Secret but in Ulundi there are few such; although little is admitted, almost everything is known. Soon we heard that today's *indaba* was summoned to secure the chiefs' support for the establishment of a new provincial House of Traditional Leaders, an innovation unlikely to incur their disapproval. Both the ANC and the King oppose this Assembly. It is designed to boost the IFP by securing the loyalty of stipend-conscious chiefs who might otherwise desert to the ANC, the party certain to control the national purse-strings for the foreseeable future.

Out of 360 Zulu *amakhosi*, 292 attended this *indaba*. We watched them filing into the parliament chamber, all soberly attired, Western-style, like any gather-ing of European politicians. Many were grey-haired, most had an air of author-ity and *gravitas* – whether chiefs of a community of 15,000 or 500. What do they really make of Ulundi's white elephant? Do they all feel good because this Assembly has 'the most modern facilities in southern Africa'?

When Buthelezi arrived Maggie and I (the only whites present) had to leave, together with a few other commoners – local journalists and elected representat-ives of the people. Traditional Zulu *indabas* must be held in camera, or so Buthelezi says. Historians deny this.

When an Inkatha spokesman insisted recently that 'Chiefs were created by God', the riposte came swiftly from Mike Sutcliffe of the ANC: 'The only God who creates chiefs in kwaZulu is Buthelezi.' Yet the IFP leader's power has dwindled since the elections; his party received only 10 per cent of the national vote. And now it lacks its former paramilitary strength, based on Third Force training and arming.

Melmoth, Natal, 15 October

At dawn the sky hung low and grey and soon I was not only rain-soaked but mud-covered; Chris lacks mudguards. One of kwaZulu's finest views remained invis-ible during a tough climb out of the valley and on the cloud-wrapped pass cars needed their headlamps. In wet weather Chris's brakes are unreliable and twice on the long descent I found myself unable to slow down approaching sharp bends.

Perversely, the sun came out as we ascended steeply to Melmoth, once a 'white' town but at noon the centre was crowded with not very friendly blacks. In a small Greek takeaway (from which I took away a nauseating fish-cake) the owner commended Melmoth's peacefulness. 'We don't have many murders, all the blacks are IFP and the ANC leave us alone. Even last year we didn't have many murders. Everyone is for Buthelezi. They want him to stop fooling around with this new government and come back to lead kwaZulu/Natal.'

'And do you want that?'

The Greek shrugged. 'I want whatever keeps us peaceful. South African politics is not my business. I came here twenty years ago to make an honest living – not to get into trouble!'

Rottweilers and Dobermanns protested at my passing through the jacaranda-shaded residential area where many gates bear large bilingual (and surely superfluous?) notices: BEWARE DOGS BITE/QAPHELA IZINJA ZI YALUMA. Here, spruce pink-tiled bungalows stand in gardens all aglow with purple, orange and crimson shrubs.

In the Indian-owned Melmoth Inn I'm paying R90 for a small, stale-smelling room with a kloof-like bed, no table, chair or towel and a badly cracked handbasin yielding only cold water. But my fellow-guests provided compensation: three generations of a lively Indian family, from Durban.

The grandparents are Nat supporters, but the young couple – Harry and Sita, their son and daughter-in-law, both attorneys – are optimistic ANC activists. The grandchildren, aged 6 and 2, confined their comments to our meal, an inferior curry.

Most Indians seem to feel a need to emphasize their South African identity. Said Harry, 'You must understand, though we're a small bit of the mosaic we're disproportionately important. It's annoying that outsiders often see us as not *quite* South African.'

'But it's understandable,' said Sita. 'Our culture is so *visibly* Asian.'

Harry continued, 'By now we're more like Afrikaners than English. They're decoupled from Europe, we're decoupled from India.'

When the temperature dropped dramatically at sunset Grandma asked Sita to fetch her overcoat and slipped it over a shimmering sari. Sita herself was wearing designer jeans and an expensive flame-red sweater. The elders were drinking tea while Harry and Sita shared a bottle of wine.

Looking ahead, Sita predicted, 'Our community will see big changes, now we're all constitutionally equal. Indian kids may feel it's less important to seem *different*. Before, we had to prove something – that we weren't like blacks, could build our own schools and temples and mosques, generally fend for ourselves. And all that in spite of so much hostility from all sides.'

Harry, bouncing his son on his knee, agreed. But the elders looked uneasy.

Sita went on, 'Everywhere old rules are going. No way will our kids accept nineteenth-century customs brought from India – why should they? We'll keep our temples and festivals and all the fun bits – I hope. Otherwise we'll see our kids doing their own thing.'

Harry smiled at her lovingly and agreed again.

Grandad cleared his throat, hesitated, then wondered, 'Will our young people be *happier* without rules and customs? See how it is already with this new government – no decency left! Everything to be legal – gambling, abortion, prostitution, filthy magazines, shameful shops you couldn't walk past with your wife and daughter... Don't young people still need protection?'

It seemed this conversation was covering old contentious ground. Anyway it was my bedtime. We exchanged addresses and said goodnight.

Eshowe, Natal, 16 October

I had planned to remain in the cool uplands, but at Barry's luncheon party invitations to Eshowe and Mtunzini proved irresistible. As there are not many roads hereabouts, this deviation means a return to Melmoth next week.

Not far from Melmoth I was back in kwaZulu which like the former Bop is all bits and pieces. Its borders were based, roughly, on the 'reserves' delimited after the Anglo-Zulu War. The road runs level while crossing a long narrow saddle overlooking deep green valleys on either side. All around, mountains are piled against the sky: lavender ranges in the distance, their flanks creased with gullies, their crests wavy lines traced against pale blueness. On the nearer slopes stand wattle coppices between groups of beautifully thatched huts, some washed white or blue, others natural red-mud. Here is no rural slum; each compound – scrutinized through my binoculars – was litter-free and meticulously swept.

Beyond a mighty mountain-wall of bare rock I was freewheeling for miles to flat fertile greenness bounded by low hills to the south-east. At 9 a.m., down on this plain, the humid heat felt suffocating.

Approaching Eshowe on its hilltop, numerous gracious residences affirm white Natal's legendary wealth. By the roadside, a high narrow ugly sign shows the borough's coat of arms, upheld by a Zulu warrior and a British redcoat, and welcomes visitors in three languages. (There is an affinity between the public monuments and state-sponsored décor of South Africa's apartheid regime and Eastern Europe's Communist regimes.) The warrior and the redcoat remind us that Eshowe grew out of a permanent garrison stationed here after the Anglo-Zulu War. In 1881 my hostess's great-grandfather, Alfred Adam, opened his Camp Store and became Eshowe's pioneer entrepreneur. Rapidly the store expanded and remained in the family until 1983 when it was sold to the OK supermarket chain. However, Jenny still owns 'a few farms'.

By 10 a.m. I had found Jenny's split-level, open-plan house, designed by an architect brother-in-law, shaded by mature trees, overlooking colourful rockeries. In the cool stone-flagged kitchen I drank pot after pot of sweat-replacing tea while we considered 'the future'. In Eshowe, despite continuing political violence, it looks secure enough. Industry flourishes and the average income of its 10,000 or so whites, Indians and Coloureds is well above the provincial average. (Black incomes were not mentioned.) No one disputes this town's claim to be 'the Flower of Natal' and its 'tourist potential' is obvious at a glance. Most people do not share my objection to a subtropical climate and Eshowe has the unique advantage of being built *around* the ancient, indigenous Dlinza Forest. We drove through this nature reserve on the way to the Zululand Historical Museum.

Today (Sunday) the museum is closed but Jenny, most fittingly, is the curator. The building itself is an exhibit: Fort Nongqai, built in 1883 to house the first Zululand Native Police, Sir Melmoth Osborn's personal guard. We spent all afternoon within those sturdy whitewashed walls. Among the more conspicuous exhibits is a wheelchair made for King Mpande and presented to him as a sweetener by the Norwegian Lutheran Bishop Schreuder. In 1859 the King duly invited the Norwegians to open a mission station, Eshowe's first white settlement. Twenty years later the ten-week Siege of Eshowe confined Colonel Pearson and his troops to the area around the kwaMondi Mission Station.

Tomorrow I descend to Mtunzini to spend a night in the Tradewinds Hotel as guest of the owner, Alan Veitch, chairman of the Mtunzini Publicity Association. I have also been invited to stay with Albert van Jaarsveld, son of Professor F. A. van Jaarsveld, he who once was tarred and feathered by the AWB. Albert lectures at the University of Zululand (UZ) and, though we talked only briefly at Ondini, I recognized a kindred spirit.

Mtunzini, 17 October

Nothing less than Albert's invitation could have lured me to this 'delightful protected coastal resort offering a wide array of leisurely [*sic*] activities'. The houses are so spaced out that Mtunzini seems like a well-tended forested park in which a privileged few live behind high hedges of variegated shrubs. In the near distance sparkles the Indian Ocean, beyond lagoons and mangrove swamps and a plantation of rare raffia palms. The supermarket and bottle-store beside the hotel are inconspicuous – a rare attribute of commercial premises in South Africa – as are the police station and prison, the library and municipal offices. Mtunzini's tranquillity is remarkable – there is no through-road – and its property prices are among the highest in South Africa. The only industry is an unobtrusive newish prawn-farm where I watched a Filipino 'trainer' showing Zulu youths how to separate baby fish from the almost invisible baby prawns caught in a nearby lagoon. Most residents are retired tycoons, or men with top jobs in Richard's Bay some twenty miles up the coast. This is South Africa's 'biggest industrial growth point'; its population has recently increased tenfold – to 35,000 – and its harbour boasts of being 'the world's largest coal export facility'.

I arrived at 8.15, after a pre-dawn start to avoid the coastal heat, and found that Alan had planned my day: a visit to the raffia palm plantation and a motor-tour of the new Conservation Park run by the Natal Parks Board on territory for many years used as 'a recreation area'. The conservation officer who drove me around – a young Afrikaner woman – didn't share my concern at the fact that speedboats are still allowed on certain stretches of the lagoon and have driven away all the crocs and much of the birdlife. Also, four-wheel-drive vehicles still have access to some beaches where turtles lay their eggs. It seems the Parks Board is reluctant to anger whites by completely banning their 'recreations'.

The Tradewinds' cosy bar is also Mtunzini's 'village pub' where the regulars' dogs are greeted by name. At sunset Alan introduced me to half a dozen 'regulars' including Edward, a plump Richard's Bay managing director untroubled by the new South Africa. 'The ANC aren't fools, they've accepted socialism never works. So I say let's forgive and forget, it's their future behaviour counts. I've the same admiration for Thatcher and Mandela – shrewd leaders, both. People grumble about affirmative action but that's only a short-term problem, while enough blacks are being educated and trained. I always hated apartheid – *we* didn't need it, it was the Afrikaners needed it.'

Then an 'irregular' replaced Edward beside me, a tall Afrikaner wearing a long blond ponytail and a shaggy beard, quite a usual combination among hardliners. Having ordered his brandy and Coke he borrowed my cigarette-lighter without acknowledging my presence, then made a thing of counting his change. 'Have to watch you fellows,' he shouted to Luke, the barman. 'Half of you can't count and the other half cheat.' (Luke is a handsome young Zulu: tall, slender, intelligent, his English fluent.)

I turned to stare at this abomination – was he drunk? No, it didn't seem so. Again he addressed Luke, while sprawling across the bar. 'Why are you fellows so fuckin' lazy? Why don't you get off your fat arses and do some work? Why should we do all the work and pay all the taxes? Can't you answer? Can't you speak English for fuck's sake?'

By now Alan and Edward had gone. I looked at my fellow-drinkers – was no one going to intervene? Then I looked at Luke. He appeared to be unruffled, he was half-sitting on his high stool considering the Afrikaner with a slight pitying smile. I caught his eye and the smile became a wide reassuring grin. 'Don't worry,' he said. 'Some people have problems – especially now.'

The Afrikaner seemed to notice me for the first time. 'Hey! You fancy this guy? Wanna be his sugar-mummy?'

I picked up my beer and moved to the far end of the bar where elderly Mrs Holroyd, much bejewelled, patted my hand. 'Take no notice, dear – Afrikaners are like that! *Crude*, I call it.'

Ponytail was still baiting Luke. 'But,' I said, 'shouldn't someone be taking notice? By any standards this is intolerable.'

Mrs Holroyd chuckled. 'My dear, you're in South Africa! Our Luke doesn't mind – you can see he doesn't mind. He's a darling boy!'

The same, 18 October

In 1960 the University of Zululand (uz) was founded as a 'bush college' at the foot of the gentle green Ngoye Hills, then a remote undeveloped area served by a dirt track. uz has since become a startlingly 'contemporary' agglomeration of ostentatious buildings a mere fifteen minutes' drive, on the N2 toll road, from Richard's Bay. There black graduates are now in great demand but, Albert explained, uz lacks adequate equipment, texts, teachers. Its generous private-sector funding is insufficiently monitored. In the early 1980s a Vice-Chancellor visited Britain, was dazzled by the new library at some red-brick university and insisted on having a copy. The result cost R16 *billion* and is the academic equivalent of Buthelezi's Legislative Assembly. Since its opening in 1987 its shelves have remained three-quarters bare. The uz's Bureau for Development and Public Relations notes that: 'If instructional quality is to be maintained, a minimum of 750,000 more volumes must be added to the current collection. Private funding will be needed to augment library holdings...'

Walking to the arts department, Albert and I had to negotiate high stacks of building materials – jerry-building requires much remedial work – and the groups of students toing and froing, in an unpurposeful way, ignored us. At present, whites in general and Albert in particular are not too popular; Albert's problem is his non-pc insistence on maintaining standards.

On this campus you can hear, with the psychic ear, the clash of cultures. For most of these youngsters there are no links between their family and university lives. Many come from bookless homes; very likely one or both parents are illiterate; a degree is seen as an economic rather than an intellectual benefit. The minority who thrive on exposure to Western academe can eventually compete with the best in their field anywhere in the world. For the rest there is only more mental confusion, more spiritual fracturing, while they are being introduced to a 'free market' South Africa that will in practice continue to downgrade 'African-ness' while being fulsome about black culture on appropriate occasions. Yet without this pseudo-academic processing there can be no affirmative action above the manual-worker level – or so I'm often told.

This year uz has 1,107 staff, academic and otherwise. Fifteen years ago the academics were more than 80 per cent white, mainly Afrikaners; now they are 51 per cent black. Of the 6,608 registered students (one-quarter Zulu) some 75 per cent qualify for 'private sector' scholarships and most – handicapped by poor schooling – take a year or two longer than average to graduate. At present the annual fee, including board and lodging, is R12,256 (approximately £2,450) and by October of last year (1993) student debts totalled R17 million. This has become a major problem for what are now known as 'the historically black universities'. Their previous tendency was to make allowances, not to insist on 'fees first, tuition after'. However, in the new South Africa most universities are using debt collectors and withholding exam results and degrees until fees have been paid.

In May 1993 the appointment of Professor R. M. Dlamini as Rector and Vice-Chancellor of UZ was seen as 'undemocratic' and provoked three weeks of demos and boycotts. A self-selected advisory committee of graduates, staff and students drew up a shortlist of more suitable – in their view – candidates. When this was ignored the students demanded the postponement of exams to allow them to make up for time lost during the boycotts. And when the Senate refused a postponement much university property was trashed (the in-word for vandalized) and most students boycotted the exams.

Last year the South African Students' Congress (SASCO) announced that it was organizing 'a national campaign for the transformation of all universities', black, white or Coloured. The present Councils, it argued, must be replaced by 'credible transformation forums, a quota system for admissions to ensure that universities were representative of South African society and an end to the exclusion of students on financial grounds'. This campaign is understandable; until recently the Broederbond ran all black universities and many of the staff were dumb Afrikaners who could never have held down a job in a white university. However, SASCO's transformation forums are likely to toss students from the frying-pan of Broederbond domination into the fire of black community pressures – coming from people with no comprehension of academic traditions, standards, requirements.

On our way back to Mtunzini we called on Walter in his handsome rambling home, built a century ago when the family cane-plantation was established and surrounded by indigenous trees. Here blue-headed lizards scamper across the lawn, weaver-birds create their usual impression of rush-hour frenzy and campus tensions seem very far away.

Formerly Walter was a journalist based in Jo'burg; six years ago he inherited the family farm – 180 hectares. (Is 'farm' the right word here? Cane cultivation requires no annual ploughing and sowing; having been cut, the canes simply grow again like grass, given adequate rain.) Locally Walter is seen as a softie who pays his workers above-average wages: R10.50 a day during the eight-month year, but at certain seasons this can go up to R24, including overtime and piecework. Many cane-cutters come from Lesotho, Swaziland, Zimbabwe, Mozambique – even Zambia – and cane-farmers ask no questions about their papers; local blacks do not rush to work for less than £2 a day. Walter thinks it unlikely that a cost-effective machine will ever be invented to cut cane on Natal's precipitous slopes. Long after the rest of South Africa's commercial farming has been mechanized, cane-cutting remains labour-intensive.

This year, because of the drought, no sugar was exported and over 100,000 tons had to be imported. Yet the industry is adapting fast to the new South Africa. It has set up a fund to provide loans (repayable within six years) to 15,000 blacks and Indians, for whom 30,000 hectares of new canefields will be made available. Walter's neighbours are not unanimously in favour of this project, minimal though it is. 'But,' said he, 'they'll soon adjust, they'll soon realize such sharing actually increases their own security. Now 100,000 or so of their fellow-citizens – including the families – will have less reason to feel resentful. Those fellow-citizens do have land rights and they know it. That's what rattles some whites – *most* white farmers. In the end everyone happily accepted blacks having voting rights but *land* rights are something else.'

Albert's large self-designed house, on the western edge of Mtunzini, overlooks from a height the raffia plantation and the low blue hills beyond. When his friend Ronnie had joined us we took our beers up to the flat roof and leaned on the parapet as the sun declined into a mass of rose-gold cloud. By chance I mentioned Stoffberg and found that Albert, having come upon numerous long-neglected documents, wrote his thesis on the white settlement of that area. Contrary to 'official' history, the Boers did forcibly dispossess the Ndebele who had been inhabiting the region for generations. The invaders were openly supported by Swazi chiefs, for their own domestic political reasons, and furtively supported by the British as part of their 'secure Natal' strategy.

Albert is among the half-dozen genuinely non-racist whites I have met in South Africa – is it a coincidence that most have been Afrikaner? Looking ahead, he takes everyone's needs and fears into account, sympathetically yet detachedly. The future, he believes, cannot thrive on a pretence that the past is irrelevant, to be disregarded as one disregards a nightmare at breakfast time. He said, 'No South African of any colour can wipe their personal slate clean and claim, "All is well now, we're going to work together in harmony for a prosperous future." Each of us has to look bravely at what is written on our own slate and not try to wipe it off before coming to terms with it.'

Eshowe, 19 October

At 4.45 a.m. I crept out of Albert's house by the back door, feeling deservedly below par after beers beyond counting and only four hours' sleep. But an early start was essential: the N1 from the Mtunzini turn-off to Gingindlovu is dangerously narrow for the amount of two-way industrial traffic spawned by Richard's

Bay. Incidentally, this stretch of road was last year listed as among the three most hazardous, for white travellers, in all of South Africa.

A full moon was setting above the long line of hills to the west – a huge disc of molten gold. There was no darkness; as the moon slid below the colourless bulk of the hills a red glow spread upwards from the Indian Ocean.

On 2 April 1879, at the opening of the Anglo-Zulu War, the village of Gingindlovu was burned out by the invading British troops – who inevitably referred to this battle site as 'Gin, Gin I love you!' Here begins the long climb to Eshowe during which, for the first time in South Africa, I was the target of an act of aggression – albeit a minor one. Several youths threw large stones at me and one blemished Chris's crossbar; had it struck my head I would have graded the incident *not* minor. I pedalled on without any change of pace, ignoring the youths; an apparent attempt to 'escape' might have stimulated them to pursue a frightened Whitey.

Having passed yet another monument to men who fell 'For Queen and Country, in the Conquest of Zululand', I was between steep cane-covered slopes, crossed by vermilion pathways, the separating kloofs full of tangled vegetation. Dismounting to walk the severest gradient, I marvelled at the endurance of the British troops who marched up these hills in the sweltering midsummer humidity to relieve besieged Eshowe. Their uniforms were brutally unsuitable: thick, tightly buttoned red jackets, thick white trousers, heavy boots and ridiculous shakos – cylindrical stovepipe hats, peaked and plumed. Worst of all was the stock, a high stiff leather collar; all were cut to one size and alterations forbidden, whatever the length of a man's neck. These were described as 'implements of torture' – many sweating necks were completely skinned. Sometimes the men's loads could be left in camp or transported by wagon but too often this was not practical. On the ascent to Eshowe each man carried his musket, bayonet, leather ammunition pouch, a small barrel of drinking water, a large square knapsack for personal possessions and a greatcoat which was the maddest item of all. How much more of the world could Britain have conquered with sensibly dressed soldiers?

By 8.45 I was in the basement of Zululand Tyres, having Chris's brakes fixed – never have I known a bicycle suffer from so many ailments. Then to Michelle's home in a new 'mixed' suburb where the back gardens run down to Dogs' Delight, a muddy stream at the bottom of a long grassy slope. On the opposite forested slope, monkeys bend the tree tops.

This afternoon I walked to the Teacher Training College (TTC), Michelle's workplace, where a staff braai was to conclude a stressful meeting about the latest crisis. (In the new South Africa, on the educational scene, people seem to move from crisis to crisis with little routine activity in between.) The college is now being overwhelmed by demands for admission that ignore all financial and physical constraints. A new residential block has recently been built and is visible from the road, therefore extra space is assumed to be available. But it isn't. Already 230 students have been admitted though there are adequate (more or less) resources for only 180. At first 'crisis' seemed too strong a word for this situation. Then I heard about the Registrar of Nongoma TTC: since my visit he has been shot dead for refusing to admit 200 more students than his college could accommodate. And last month, in Mokopane College of Education, a youth was killed in a fierce battle between student teachers and a crowd of young men whose applications had been rejected. Soon after, SAPS had to rescue these same students when Mokopane residents stormed the campus, accusing them of having deprived 'locals' of their 'rightful' places.

Thousands of youngsters with a desperate longing for third-level education see a teaching qualification as a substitute for a degree though they may have no interest in teaching. Some 20 per cent of newly qualified teachers never enter a classroom – or want to – yet at present one-third of black teachers are un-qualified.

The extremist Azanian Students' Movement (ASM) is now threatening white teachers in black schools: 'If necessary we will use physical force to remove those who won't resign to make way for unemployed black teachers.' But would the parents or pupils like to see white teachers replaced by blacks? Most certainly they would not.

The correcting of skewed perceptions about university degrees needs to begin *now* in primary schools. In Europe no one feels obliged to pretend that all citizens are equal, intellectually, but one of apartheid's after-effects is a reluctance to point out that most blacks, like most whites, are not university material. (Unless they go to some American college where they can get a degree in Floral Arrangement or Rabbit Breeding.) A nervous subservience to PC muzzles those who should be making that statement, loudly and clearly. Yes, everyone should have access to equally good schooling. Then comes the time when demanding exams, honestly marked, determine who goes on to university.

As all this was being discussed a small shiver went through me – while clouds of braai smoke drifted over the green lawn and through the branches of the hazily blue jacarandas and people fetched beer from ice-boxes in vehicle boots. Below the calm surface of white Eshowe I sensed tensions not acknowledged – perhaps not even inwardly recognized since tensions forming part of daily life are often dealt with by being ignored. A group such as the ASM may be dismissed as 'extremist' but everyone knows they could be dangerous. Small shivers are allowable in a country where violence does not shock enough, and cheap guns proliferate, and the police cannot be trusted.

Acknowledged tensions have their sources within the college. Last term a young man was expelled for attempting to rape a fellow-student at knife-point.

He is now taking the black principal to court for infringing his right to education; and he doesn't lack supporters, among both his contemporaries and the black staff. There is, as one white lecturer dryly remarked, 'an incomplete awareness of the need for discipline'.

Another flashpoint concerns the right of pregnant students to continue studying; several have been intimidated off campus because the spectacle of a big-bellied woman is 'indecent'. (What echo of missionary influence do we have here?) The white staff unanimously uphold this right. Most blacks – staff and male students – insist the women must leave: permanently if unmarried, until after their delivery if married. No one suggests penalizing unmarried fathers though a few staff members and many students are boastful about their illegitimate progeny.

During our braai the race groups – numerically about equal – rarely merged.

The same, 20 October

While breakfasting outside, watching the monkeys do likewise, Michelle and I debated the inherent conflict between a Bill of Rights guaranteeing equality for all and a Constitution guaranteeing respect for customary law, which permits polygamy. A multicultural society cannot have it both ways; something has to be sacrificed. Hardline traditionalists argue that the Bill of Rights is a new-fangled Western concept (true enough) and its adoption by GNU a surrender to cultural imperialism. Others point out how recent, and not yet complete, is the West's acceptance of gender equality – so why should all South Africans be expected to accept it instantly at the stroke of a legislative pen?

Like other optimistic liberals I've met, Michelle believes the ANC's passionate long-term commitment to women's rights will prevail. Legal equality must be a cornerstone of the new state, even if at present it makes no impression in some areas. By publicly upholding the ideal, GNU will gradually erode the traditionalists. And Constitutional lawyers will have the power to identify equality as a 'sovereign' value – of extraordinary, immeasurable importance (emotional as well as legal) in this post-apartheid society. They could then require customary family law to be reviewed and made compatible with gender equality, a consummation devoutly to be wished.

The whitening of South Africa – the Western lifestyle long since outwardly adopted or aspired to by the majority – is real enough to make this country seem unlike anywhere else in Africa. Yet its superficiality often disconcerts. This morning, when I talked to three classes of trainee teachers, they asked many apparently naive questions – reminders that apartheid denied most blacks any opportunity to comprehend the whites' world as a whole, apart from participating in it as consumers of fast food, fashion and popular entertainment.

After lunch I visited Saul, a 34-year-old Ndebele maths teacher, in his empty classroom. It was empty because the students had taken off to organize a demo. Much of the present turmoil in the historically black universities can be traced back, in Saul's view, to the white staffs' failure ever to become involved in student life and concerns: 'Those Afrikaners didn't have to exert themselves in their Broederbond sinecures.' A criticism often heard, from academics both black and white.

Saul graduated from UZ with distinction, then declined a bursary to do postgraduate work in Germany. 'We could see the new South Africa coming and our kids most urgently need good maths teachers. Last year, only 30 per cent of blacks took maths for matric.'

Saul grew up in a northern Transvaal village, the nearest school an hour's walk away on a veld path. His father worked in the Messina mine, his mother 'did women's work and trained six kids how to behave. Back from school we'd our chores to do, depending on age and strength. This stereotype of lazy kaffirs – how can people be lazy who have to build and maintain their own homes, grow and cook their own food, collect fuel and fetch water, tend animals far away in the bush? But the hard work didn't matter, we had so much love and stability. We kids loved each other and our mother most of all. And she loved us, worked seven days a week for us – but was she strict! The punishments came hard and fast when we deserved them. That's what's missing now, respect for elders and for authority – and I know it's the same overseas, I've read about it. Except here among the poor it's gone to extremes. The township kids know no discipline with working mothers away all day – or away all the time, living in a backyard, seeing their kids maybe once a month. What's the future for babies being born into that sort of social chaos? And what sort of role models is the new South Africa giving youngsters? "Miss South Africa"! Is that the best we can offer them? Did you see her on TV at Sun City draped over the bonnet of her BMW wearing a gown costing six months of a miner's wages! Then we got her "social caring", visiting handicapped kids and opening bush-clinics – like she was a princess! That's messing our kids' minds up even more, making her the "success-ful black" to be imitated.'

Saul is chip-free, completely at ease with himself as an Ndebele. He said, 'There's nothing wrong with tribalism, though now it's used like a dirty word. I'm proud to think of myself as an Ndebele, I don't want to lose my traditions in a big stew of people called "South Africans", I like to keep my own flavour. But politically I support our new united Republic and want to work for it – that's why I wouldn't go to Germany.'

Reconciliation, as preached by President Mandela, Saul described as 'a necessary game of "Let's pretend" – for this generation it can only be a pretence.' The general lack of black vengefulness he attributed less to *ubuntu* –

while acknowledging its contribution – than to an apartheid-generated sense of impotence and dependence. His analysis of what apartheid has done to both blacks and whites was devastating; even at this stage of my journey, some of his words moved me almost to tears. We became so soul-matey that at sunset we found ourselves locked in and Saul had to climb through a lavatory window to find the askari with the key.

Melmoth, 21 October

Today I paid the price for yesterday's injudicious over-taxing of The Arm. When an elderly woman, unable to lift a heavy load from ground to head, sought my assistance I hesitated – then did my best because a refusal to help could be misconstrued. As a result, cycling uphill was impossible this morning and it took me five hours to cover the thirty miles back to Melmoth where I'm staying with Pat and Barry Schmidt. Pat lectures at Eshowe's TTC, Barry is a farmer whose great-grandfather was for fifty years a colonial administrator in Natal, both are relaxed about the new South Africa. Their small bungalow – high on a steep hill – is in a state of mild disrepair and agreeable untidiness and is *book-filled*. (In South Africa a matter for italics, as I've noted previously.) The cat is also an intellectual; he helps himself to milk, from a narrow jug on the tea-tray, by skilfully inserting a paw, soaking it – then delicately withdrawing it.

Babanango, 22 October

A cool, windless, overcast morning: ideal weather for my long tough climb onto the Babanango plateau, first seen from afar as I arrived in Ulundi. At times, from the edge of the plateau, I was overlooking that vast expanse of broken terrain across which King Cetshwayo's impis – all 20,000 of them – moved silently and swiftly towards the British encampment at Isandlwana. How would it feel, I asked myself, to cycle through South Africa unhaunted by the past? One would be much more responsive to the beauty of the landscape, in a region like this, if not tormented by a vision of all those commercially forested hills being grazed by Zulu herds. Yet no country is now as it was a century or two ago; everywhere time remoulds.

Babanango surely merits an entry in the *Guinness Book of Records* for possessing the world's tiniest public library: – some ten feet by six, built entirely of corrugated iron and standing alone and forlorn in the middle of a large field. It opens, I was told, 'not often'.

Babanango occupies a slight hollow on the plateau and retains the character of a frontier settlement: a few stores, an agricultural machinery depot, a police station and Stan's Pub Hotel. At one of these stores King

Solomon ka Dinuzulu (1892–1933) bought the material for his first wife's wedding gown. (Her name was Christina, she was the first of many.) Since the end of the seventeenth century this district has been a sacred place, the main burial site for chiefs of the Zulu Royal House; it is still of profound significance to the Zulu people.

For the past fortnight I've been hearing about Stan's Pub – 'The most famous pub in South Africa! Don't miss it! It's something else!' Indeed it is. Flimsy bras and frilly panties, lewdly inscribed, are draped over the bottles behind the bar. On the counter, rubber monkeys copulate at the touch of a button. When cigarettes are lit from within a monk's mouth, his penis pops pinkly out from the folds of his black robe – and so on. This is locker-room humour of the more ingenious sort but I'm of the wrong sex and perhaps the wrong generation to appreciate it fully. Alas! the legendary Stan was away in Durban for the weekend but his son Jeremy welcomed me warmly – the drums had told him I was on the way.

Isandlwana, 23/24 October

Yesterday it rained all day with a gloomy gentleness that might have made me feel homesick were I prone to that disease. Therefore six long letters are ready for posting in Pietermaritzburg.

This morning the dawn air was deliciously chilly – energizing. At road level banks of pale grey cloud shifted and paused, merged and separated, on their drifting way across Babanango's bleak, wide, moorlike uplands. The sunrise fused these into a thick frustrating fog, obscuring the splendid lonely expanses lying far below on my right. As the descent began the sky turned milky blue and the dispersing clouds revealed hills all around – close-packed, their flanks green-gold, their rock-crests silver.

A small sign pointed left to Isandlwana, invisible from the main road. A rough track climbs the intervening ridge, skirting a spread-out colony of shacks – and then I was overlooking the battlefield, still a few miles away. Isandlwana has been so often sketched and photographed that to gaze upon the original is like first seeing some famous building – the Taj Mahal, the Kremlin, St Peter's. 'Isandlwana' means 'cow's stomach' in Zulu. To my non-cattle-obsessed eyes this solitary outcrop of rock, some 250 feet high and perhaps 300 yards long, more closely resembles a colossal boot. It dominates the surrounding flatness, a red-brown plain encircled in the near distance by those long low ridges which concealed Cetshwayo's impis until it was too late...

Soon Isandlwana village came into view at the western edge of the plain, a traditional village inhabited by Zulus whose ancestors have been living here since long before 1879. Barry Marshall had arranged for me to stay with its only white residents, the site's guardians. Leaving Chris in the Taylors' little bungalow I continued on foot to the battlefield.

There are malevolent plans to 'develop' this tourist attraction but as yet it remains undefiled. Sitting high on a boulder-strewn ridge, facing Isandlwana, I compared a photograph taken in May 1879 with the scene before me. Only one change is discernible: the abandoned British Army wagons then dotting the plain have been replaced by many little mounds of whitewashed stones marking nameless British graves, and by a few inconspicuous regimental monuments honouring the victims of (directly) Cetshwayo's impis and (indirectly) an individual's blundering. Even without human intervention most landscapes change over time: trees fall or take root, collapsing banks alter river courses, landslides reshape the contours of mountains. But here the harsh aridity of the terrain resists change.

On 22 January 1879 20,000 warriors, armed with assegais, took the invading British by surprise and killed 858 whites, including 52 officers, and 471 of their black allies (mostly Natal 'natives'). The Zulu losses were hard to calculate but certainly exceeded a thousand; before being overwhelmed, the redcoats had used their last bullet. Isandlwana brought down Disraeli's government. So many casualties (including 52 *officers*!) could not be tolerated.

The main monument, of mottled red-brown marble, matches the local soil. It bears a quintessentially Victorian inscription, making the best of a bad job.

ISANDLWANA
Not Theirs To Save The Day
But Where They Stood,
Falling To Dye The Earth
With Brave Men's Blood
For England's Sake And Duty
– Be Their Name Sacred
Among Us – Neither
Praise Nor Blame
Add To Their Epitaph –
But Let It Be Simple As That Which
Marked Thermopylae.
Tell It In England Those
That Pass Us By,
Here, Faithful To Their Charge,
Her Soldiers Lie.

What did they know of Thermopylae, those wretched troopers who were – most of them – soldiers not for England's sake but for the sake of the Queen's shilling? 'Neither praise nor blame ...' But the only person to blame was not killed. The Commander-in-Chief, Lieutenant-General Lord Chelmsford – described by General Sir Garnet Wolseley as 'that poor noodle' – was away on an irrelevant skirmish of his own from which he returned to Isandlwana in a bad mood because his 'bag' was 'only' eighty Zulus killed. The 1,379 corpses awaiting him had died as a result of his own myopic arrogance.

For the bereaved families, was it comforting to be told their sons, brothers, husbands had been 'faithful to their charge'? Perhaps it was. In our own day this kind of conditioning continues, this cynical romanticizing of war – 'to dye the earth with brave men's blood' and so on. Although the language has been altered to suit changing sensibilities, the technique is the same when leaders deem it expedient to make 'our boys' look like heroes. Yet the same boys, if jobless, frustrated and socially disruptive, are referred to by the same leaders as 'young thugs'.

Slowly I climbed Isandlwana – the hot sun was tempered by a strong cool breeze – and from the highest point watched a line of head-loaded women following the old wagon-trail to another village of round thatched huts. Strangely, Isandlwana is now a tranquil place. Some benign exorcist has banished all traces of violence, terror and hatred, leaving only a melancholy spirit hovering over the silent plain – a neutral spirit, mourning for all.

16

Below the Drakensberg

Dundee − Pietermaritzburg − Ladysmith

Tradition has it that on the way northward to fight the Zulus the young Abraham Cronje
marked this area [the area of present Dundee] 'Mielietuin' as a place where he would
settle once the danger of Zulu attacks had been reckoned with. The district made a
marked impression on him as a field of mielies, the first he had seen since leaving
the Cape, had been cultivated by the natives living there. This convinced him
that the ground was suitable for farming. Descendants of this pioneer are farming
here to this day.

Inscription in the Talana Historical Museum, Dundee

Dundee, Natal, 25 October 1994

South of Isandlwana a narrow road climbs around drab bare hills, then crosses
parched grassland where nothing grazes and deep red erosion gullies have
wounded the earth. Here is extreme impoverishment, ecological and social.
The only moving figures were women carrying water up precipitous paths.
Always, in these rural communities, one sees far fewer males than females.

Under Chief Minister Buthelezi the little town of Nqutu − once a colonial
outpost, now the region's trading and administrative centre − acquired imposing
red-brick local-government offices, all now embraced by razor wire. Nqutu is
not *muzungu*-friendly and I didn't linger.

Soon a line of green willows appeared ahead, marking the course of the
Buffalo River, the frontier of the old Colony of Natal. Here Malonjeni dominates the landscape, a towering angular mountain. As the road climbed again I
noticed a few faded farm signs − Longueval, Oelville, Beaucamp, Bapume − the
only remaining traces of the British ex-servicemen settled here in 1920. Three
years previously the British government had bought vast tracts of land throughout the Union for leasing on easy terms to Soldier Settlers. But unfortunately
Whitehall − forgetful of 1820 − didn't bother to ask why it was so easy to
purchase these undeveloped, underpopulated areas. Soon all the settlers' hard
work had been defeated by scarce water, poor soil, rough tracks and an abrupt
fall in the prices of cattle and maize. By the mid-1930s they were working at
whatever town jobs they could find to support young families. Now tall grasses,
coarse and dry, grow between thorn trees on their abandoned farms.

At noon I arrived here feeling heat-exhausted despite the altitude – 3,750 feet. I fear the rest of this journey will be an endurance test.

Dundee looks emphatically English and not long ago was prosperous. Now it feels subdued and disheartened. Business is slack since its coal mines expired and most of its factories were closed – by sanctions, say the white natives. In a few formerly 'white' suburbs Indians and Coloureds occupy tree-shaded bungalows, their ample gardens rarely maintained as in the old days. Some houses on the previously exclusive Victoria Road have been taken over by black families and are beginning to look ramshackle. Dundee's population now consists of 1,000 Coloureds, 3,000 Indians, 5,500 whites and 18,500 blacks. The new South Africa sometimes concedes that townships have names and in Dundee's centre a signpost points to 'Sibongile: 2 km'.

I found the Sibongile residents welcoming and chatty. Their township is tension-free, they assured me, because there are no local ANC supporters – or infiltrators – to disturb the peace. Here 'Buthelezi Rules OK'. Several people described King Zwelithini as 'a greedy traitor'. At present he is rumoured to be hiding in disguise in Mozambique; allegedly his minders discovered an IFP plot to kill him and choose a replacement as malleable as he once was, pre-GNU. (One teacher said, 'This is right policy. Zulus were always democratic, if we didn't like a king we killed him and made another one.') The ease with which rumours can be used to destabilize, especially in rural areas, is frightening.

The same, 26 October

I arrived in Dundee five days too late to celebrate an anniversary. On 20 October 1899 the first battle of the second Anglo-Boer War was fought on and around Talana Hill, overlooking the town, where now stands one of South Africa's finest museums. This occupies twenty acres and nine of its buildings pre-date 1899 – as does the bluegum plantation that served as cover for the British forces and now shades British graves. Above them flutter the Vierkleur, the Union Jack, the flag of apartheid South Africa and the flag of liberated South Africa – 'reconciliation' written in bright colours against a deep blue sky.

For the British, Talana foreshadowed woes to come. Their Commander-in-Chief, Major-General Sir W. Penn Symons, foolishly left himself exposed to Boer sharpshooters against his staff's advice. When shot in the stomach he gallantly insisted on remounting and riding out of sight of his men before collapsing; four days later he died. After the Boers had abandoned the crest of the hill, some of the 69th Battery mistook the 60th for the enemy and opened fire from the plain below. Soon the ground was strewn with the victims of what would now be oddly described as 'friendly fire'. Near the crest, Colonel Gunning of the 60th risked standing upright to yell to the artillery – 'Stop that firing!' At once he was shot through the heart. Captain Connor of the Dublin Fusiliers was shot through the stomach and shrapnel blew away both of Lieutenant Hambro's legs. As Captain Nugent of the 60th plaintively remarked next day, 'It seemed so hard, after escaping the Boers, to be killed by our own people.' Later, the twelve gun crews ordered to rout the enemy held their fire when a swirling mist caused them to mistake the retreating Boers – wearing capes – for the 18th Hussars. Therefore the Boers did not have to retreat far. They went on to occupy Dundee for seven months and renamed it Meyersdorp, in honour of the leader of that victorious Boer commando.

Tugela Ferry, kwaZulu, 27 October

At sunrise I was crossing the Biggarsberg, a bush-covered spur of the Drakensberg, hilly rather than mountainous. The sky was overcast, the air as yet cool, the wide brown landscape empty. This was the route taken by the retreating British who stealthily pulled out of Dundee at 10 p.m. on 22 October, a rainy pitch-dark night. They had to leave behind a two months' supply of food and stores and many badly wounded officers and men, including the dying Penn Symons.

At 8.15, where the uninhabited terrain levelled out, Chris's back tyre suddenly went flat. There was no traffic but I walked on cheerfully; one has to be cheerful about punctures when too incompetent to mend them. Maybe someone could help in the hamlet of Helpmekaar, a few miles on. When a SAPS van slowly overtook me, the plump young woman driver staring, I accepted her rescue offer. Ellen is a police captain's wife, stationed in Helpmekaar, a kindly communicative Afrikaner.

During the Anglo-Zulu War Helpmekaar became a household word in Britain as the headquarters of Lord Chelmsford's doomed army. Ellen pointed out the neat little cemetery where lie twenty-four British victims of that war and sundry minor skirmishes. Four nearby koppies are crowned by the ruins of British forts. Chelmsford chose this site, perched on the highest and windiest point of the Biggarsberg, because cold nights lessened the risk of horse sickness. And, presumably, of human sickness – but men were less important, being easier to replace. Helpmekaar has a present population of thirty-five, of whom seven (policemen and their families) are white. The hotel and post office ceased to function in the 1970s; the small store opens only occasionally; the stone-walled police-station compound contains a courtroom, magistrate's office, revenue office – all now obsolete.

While a 'boy' cured Chris, Ellen served me with coffee and boerebiskuite in the ex-courtroom, complete with dock and jury-box. She agreed that kwaZulu's poverty is very shocking – then checked herself and said, 'But it's not as bad as it looks. Plenty of money comes in from the mines. All the men like to move to the mines.' *Like* to . . . ?

The long, long descent to the Tugela valley took me through a cruel region where no amount of rain could relieve the aridity. Here is pure shale, on which thornbushes and cacti sustain a few bony goats and even bonier donkeys, needed to transport water. There are few traditional Zulu huts; most dwellings are the meanest of shacks. And, significantly, the local children beg. Those children, hopefully running towards the passing white, harrowed me. They are not 'professionals', like so many children in Black Africa where mindless expats distribute 'candies' as they tour rural areas. Here the feeling is quite different. Small boys and girls looked *ashamed* while desperately whispering, 'Give money, one rand, I hunger!' Beyond dispute they hunger; all the visual evidence is there. And I did give money, contrary to my usual practice. But donations from emotionally upset whites are not the answer to their problem. Perhaps South Africa does need a genuine revolution. Perhaps you can't make a justice omelette without breaking corporate eggs.

In this desolate corner of kwaZulu, maidens still walk proudly bare-breasted. And matrons wear enormous flat hats – like satellite dishes – and knee-length sleeveless tunics tied in a particular way to accentuate their prodigiously ample bosoms. A royal-blue cloak and a scarlet apron complete the ensemble – the cloak pinned to one shoulder, giving an air of casual elegance. These are *bhinca*, defiant 'heathens' who have steadfastly resisted missionary blandishments. They are not fond of whites and even without a Dundee forewarning I would have intuited their allergy to cameras.

Over the final stage of this descent the road cuts deeply through a ridge, then overlooks a long narrow gorge on the right, running down to meet the Tugela valley. By 11.30, at river-level, the humid heat was intolerable.

Tugela Ferry's 400-bed Church of Scotland Mission Hospital, serving the whole ex-'homeland' area between Dundee and Greytown, comes as a shock. An architectural conceit of the 1990s, its plate-glass façade, high metal pillars and aimless curves and angles belie the three-quarters-empty medicine cupboards within. Near the steel gate (high, wide, the security exceptionally strict) stands a severe little church of dark grey stone with a red-tiled roof – and beside it floats the blue cloud of a jacaranda tree in full bloom, its subtropical gaiety contrasting with the imported dourness. Here I was seeking a Dr Wilson, to whom I had an introduction from an Eshowe friend, but he has moved to Nqutu. Another doctor, Graham, invited me to stay in his roomy bungalow, one of several built for the medical staff when this hospital was established in 1932. In the 1970s it was taken over by the State, then grandly rebuilt to the Chief Minister's taste in 1991.

At noon a brief spectacular thunderstorm with torrential rain reduced the sultriness. Astonishingly, no trace of that rain remained when I went shopping two hours later.

On either side of Tugela Ferry's main (and only) street – the half-mile of motor road between hospital and bridge – hawkers display their seasonally limited range of fruits and vegetables: oranges, apples, pumpkins, onions, tomatoes and giant heads of dark green cabbage. The more prosperous women sit under jolly striped beach umbrellas, the haggling is vigorous and prolonged. A brand new red-brick post office is not much used in this region of mass-illiteracy. There is also a smallish Khonzi Nkosi supermarket, a biggish bottle-store and a filling station for passing traffic and the few beat-up local vehicles. One enterprising mother, with an eye on that passing traffic, has dressed her sturdy 13-month-old son in traditional attire – a four-inch cattle tail skirt – and charges R2 per photo. When I had collaborated in this exploitation of Zulu culture the infant was encouraged to stretch out his pudgy hand for payment. A tourist tout in the making... The rare smiles bestowed on Whitey came from elderly folk; younger generations viewed the eccentric pedestrian impassively.

A rough path on the Tugela's left bank took me past a score of small weatherbeaten bungalows, shaded by fig and mango trees. In this 'suburb' live the local *kholwas*, members of Zululand's long-established class of moderately affluent blacks. A century ago their forefathers became loyal adherents of the many mission stations then operating and applied themselves to studying not only the Bible but 'civilized' ways: how to dress, eat and behave (at least outwardly) like Europeans. Polygamy posed a problem but most missions compromised, allowing the wives to receive Holy Communion – since each had only one husband – while the polygamist himself was debarred from the sacrament. In the 1920s the *kholwa* leaders accepted racial segregation for reasons of expediency and this brought them relative prosperity.

Chief Buthelezi's current follies and erratic whims may be partly explained by the culturally mixed soil in which he is rooted, as nephew of King Soloman ka Dinuzulu who ruled after a fashion from 1913 to 1933. Soloman shared many of King Goodwill's weaknesses but was much more intelligent, before pickling his brain in alcohol. As a young man he founded the first Inkatha, then invented a new 'royal culture' by grafting the missionaries' version of 'civilization' onto Zulu aristocratic traditions. His numerous *bhinca* wives and their countless children were brought for baptism to an Anglican outstation at Mahashini, near Nongoma, and there a kindergarten-cum-prep-school was set up for the Zulu élite. Soloman's sister, Magogo, was the first teacher. She married Chief Matole Buthelezi and their son, Mangosuthu Gatsha, received his primary education at Mahashini, only returning to the main Buthelezi homestead, kwaPhindangene, as an adolescent. By then he (who fifty years later would form a pre-election alliance with the white right wing) had thoroughly absorbed the *kholwa* philosophy, an unwholesome blend of Christian piety and cynical pragmatism that demanded no real loyalty to any tradition. It did, however, reinforce his anti-Communist paranoia; the Inkatha leadership has always been in the McCarthy league of anti-Communists.

Tugela's ferry has long since been replaced by a blot on the landscape, a rusty metal bridge. From here the wide slow river can be seen for miles in both directions, between banks sometimes low and sandy, sometimes high and bushy. Tomorrow's road to Greytown can also be seen, curving up and up, then disappearing into a muddle of rounded mountains.

Graham and his physiotherapist wife – both from the Eastern Cape – have lived here for ten years without learning Zulu. Their home is untainted by alcohol and they deplore the ANC's determination to legalize homosexuality and abortion.

At sunset Graham invited me to accompany him on a disconcerting mission. In a Land Rover we drove six miles up the Greytown road to fetch from his hut a 38-year-old AIDS patient. Two weeks ago Mr N— 'absconded' from the hospital's TB ward because he wishes to die at home. He is no longer TB-infectious, having responded to treatment. (His wife, though HIV-positive, as yet shows no AIDS symptoms.) All efforts to persuade him to return to hospital have failed; therefore Graham, moved by Mrs N—'s pleas, made a plan. Earlier today he and Audrey, the hospital AIDS counsellor, gave Mr N—a sedative injection. Now they were returning – he would imagine this to be another kind painkilling visit – to drug him so heavily that he could be kidnapped.

Near the pass we turned onto a mountainside; here was no track, only a footpath. The vehicle was left amidst huge boulders and misshapen cacti and by torchlight we found the isolated hut, mud-walled and loosely thatched. A candle was lit only when we arrived; artificial illumination is a luxury many South Africans cannot afford. Mr N— lay groaning on the one narrow bed, his wife's rolled-up mat stood in a corner. Over the bed a few spare garments hung from a roof-beam. Three children, aged 2, 4 and 5, were sound asleep on a mat under a blanket; the 2-year-old is HIV-positive.

I held the torch while Graham made much of examining Mr N— and Audrey talked to his wife – a beautiful young woman, I noticed later, when two lantern-bearing men arrived. The patient's eyes glowed with gratitude at the prospect of another sleep-inducing jab. Although at the last stages of emaciation, and too weak to sit up unsupported, Graham believed he could still summon the strength to fight for his liberty should he come to in the vehicle. As the first injection was being prepared the children slept on while Audrey and Mrs N— continued to

laugh and joke. None of the emotions we would show in comparable circumstances came to the surface.

Some twenty minutes later, when the second injection had taken effect, two
neighbours lifted Mr N— off his bed, carried him to the Land Rover and heaved
him onto the back seat.

Back on the road, Graham remarked that if Mr N— continues to respond to
his TB treatment he may have 'a little more of life'. But does he, at this stage, want
a little more? Audrey seemed to sense my distress; I shrank from the image of this
dying man coming to in an alien and hated hospital ward – vast and white-walled
and brilliantly lit – and finding himself again at the mercy of authoritarian
strangers equipped with terrifying gadgets. I was grateful for Audrey's assurance
that she would be there when he awoke and would give him all the comfort she
could. 'And for his wife this is kinder,' she added.

In response to Graham's comment that the AIDS rate is soaring in kwaZulu/
Natal – so far the worst-hit province – I mentioned the many girls I had met
elsewhere in Africa who had been forced into prostitution by poverty.

'I wonder,' said Graham, 'if anyone in our district is *so* poor?' His tone implied
doubt. But when he directed this query to Audrey she replied, 'Yes, doctor, we
have such people.'

'In the village?' asked Graham.

'Yes, in the village several – and one in the hospital.'

'In the *hospital*? A patient?'

'No, doctor – one of the staff.'

'But she has a wage!' protested Graham.

'Yes, doctor – a very small wage. And no one else in her family can find any
job.'

Graham lapsed into a shocked silence as we drove through the village where
our headlights picked out a few of the local 'sex-workers' sitting on the bottle-
store steps.

Greytown, 28 October

Today heat-dodging was no problem. I arrived here at noon too wet and cold to
open the panniers before thawing my hands under a hot tap. Once over the high
pass above Tugela Ferry, visibility was down to thirty yards (I measured it) and
for three hours a gale drove fine, stinging, ice-cold rain into my face. Yet only
half of me felt frustrated, so needed is this rain.

I thought often of Mr N—. Everyone's ignoring his wish to die at home is
quite shocking by our standards. But other standards have to be taken into
account. His wife's wish for him to die in hospital is bound up with a complex
set of traditional taboos. A death in that hut might have required it to be burned

down and the replacement of even the most primitive dwelling costs something. Also, expensive ceremonies might have been obligatory. Numerous extra stresses would have been imposed on that young – and doomed – widow. Not to mention the strains, both physical and emotional, of nursing an AIDS patient in such cramped quarters, so far from water, surrounded by small children.

This aptly named little town (where, in April, I was advised not to linger) boasts two enormous hotels, now under one management – though this 'management' is not very evident. The corridor outside my first-floor room is seriously flooded, as rain pours through a sagging patch of ceiling.

A farm near Greytown, 29 October

The rain continued until noon, when it was too late – too hot – to set out on the forty-five-mile ride to Pietermaritzburg.

In the ladies bar my only companion was Greg, a middle-aged English-speaking maize-farmer: short, round, ruddy and hospitable. 'Stay with us tonight,' he urged. 'Lizzie, the wife, she'll be thrilled to meet an overseas visitor – scarce around here now!'

Greg's thousands of fertile hectares lie some two miles west of Greytown. A long private road leads to a mansion-bungalow overlooking a sloping acre of garden. In fact Lizzie was far from thrilled to meet me; seen through white Natalian eyes, I am not at present socially acceptable. But then Greg revealed my profession and you could almost hear the click as Lizzie 'made allowances'.

A surly-looking maid wheeled in the tea-trolley: cucumber sandwiches, hot buttered scones, a jam sandwich, plum cake.

Greg helped himself to two cucumber sandwiches and said, 'You know our problem? The ANC won the propaganda war – hoodwinked people overseas.'

Lizzie poured the tea daintily and tried to be liberal. 'But Mandela learned a lot on Robben Island. The tax-payers educated him.'

When the maid brought a jug of hot water nobody thanked her.

'I still have hope,' said Lizzie, cutting the jam sandwich triangularly. 'Buthelezi could save Natal, here the story isn't finished. Our Zulus will never accept a Xhosa dictatorship.'

Two neighbouring couples came to supper and we sat on the stoep being served with spicy Indian titbits and a wide choice of drinks. The sunset was flamboyant, a virtuoso performance of swiftly shifting colours – crimson and gold, purple and orange, then silver-grey and lemon and salmon pink. All flaring and fading and blending over an open landscape of maize-fields, extending to those blue hills (navy blue, now) that I crossed en route from Tugela Ferry. That was the best part of the evening.

Pietermaritzburg, 30 October

This is the first city on my route since leaving Jo'burg six weeks ago and even the Sunday traffic seemed quite scary – especially the kombi taxis. When I took refuge from a prolonged deluge in Tommy's brothel/hotel, free accommodation was again offered. But business is brisk on the Sabbath (day of rest/lust) so no room will be available for overnight guests until 8 p.m. The black prostitutes queue in the foyer while their clients – fifty–fifty black and Indian – drink at the bar awaiting an empty room to be hired by the half-hour. Despite this province's incidence of AIDS my charming Hindu host has no scruples about running a brothel devoid even of AIDS-information posters – never mind bedside condoms.

Next door is one of Pietermaritzburg's many mosques from where, as I write, comes the sound of little boys shrilly chanting the Koran; the mosque school functions on a Sunday to avoid clashing with secular studies. By now this city feels like a home-from-home; I have an expanding circle of good friends and am recognized by the Indian in the newspaper shop, the Zulu hawkers on Commercial Road, the Coloured bar-girl in the 'English' pub, the Afrikaner couple who run my breakfast café – the only one open at 6 a.m.

The same, 31 October

As I queued for breakfast a score of blacks, wearing heavy sweaters or donkey jackets against the 'cold' early air, were enjoying litres of beer at the end of their factory nightshift. Other workers called in to buy curried eggs, fish-cakes, sandwiches and cooldrinks for their lunchtime breaks. This café's seating is sadistic; long metal tables and benches are bolted to the floor, leaving customers (all but the slimmest) squeezed against the tables' sharp edges.

I was about to fetch a second polystyrene mug of tea when the invasion happened. Two railway-station kombi taxis stopped outside and more than forty young men, wearing new khaki uniforms or worn jungle fatigues, swarmed into the café. Each had a large canvas kitbag slung over his shoulder, all were aggressively unruly. They shouted their demands for beer and food, pushing the orderly queue aside, unnerving the regulars and causing the elderly owners to go pale while serving them fast and po-faced. Several walked across the tables, their boots clanging on the metal – at which point I saw the usefulness of having immobile furniture. Their paying technique prevented the Afrikaners from checking on whether or not they had received the correct amount – but they weren't going to argue. This was, in effect, a raid on the café by MK soldiers who – together with some 6,000 of their comrades – yesterday went AWOL from various military bases.

When the ANC suspended 'the armed struggle' in 1990, the MK 'terrorists' overnight became a 'non-statutory army'. South Africa was then in the uncomfortable position of having two armies, each conditioned to regard the other as The Enemy.

In February 1993 the ANC rashly volunteered to disband the MK before the elections, by way of soothing white fears that they would react to a defeat at the polls like Savimbi in Angola. Then the dangers inherent in disbandment emerged. Some 12,000 Comrades were still in training camps abroad – mainly in Uganda (8,000) and Tanzania (4,000) – and it would have done nothing for the nation's stability had those returnees been unloosed in the townships.

Not only idealists went into exile. A small minority were young criminals. A much bigger minority (some say the majority) saw exile as an escape from relentless security-force harassment and/or from extreme poverty. In the camps their basic daily needs were provided for, however sparsely. Now thousands are home in liberated South Africa – many unskilled, many with young dependent families. They are homeless, jobless, hungry and angry, feeling surplus to the requirements of GNU. For most, absorption into the new South African National Defence Force (SANDF) is their only hope of earning an honest living. But they need more help than they have been getting from the ANC to come to terms with the notion of serving in a restructured SANDF in which blacks who accept the discipline of a conventional army will be (officially) welcome. Even among its most loyal supporters, many criticize the ANC's handling of this admittedly formidable problem.

Later in 1993, Mr Thabo Mbeki proposed a post-election union of the SADF and the MK in the new SANDF. This plan became part of the pre-election compromise, despite Buthelezi's opposition, but numerous impediments to the union have brought about the present AWOL crisis. Recently President Mandela gave in to demands that he should visit the Wallmannstal military base near Pretoria to listen to MK grievances, many of which are horribly real: racist insults, bureaucrats deliberately slowing assimilation, unsuitable food, overcrowded living quarters. This insistence on direct communication with Madiba is significant – and partly his own fault. The MK have no shred of respect for the present Minister of Defence, Joe Modise, their previous C-in-C, whose record as a military leader in exile doesn't bear scrutiny (but needs it) and whose inclusion in the Cabinet is a scandal. Last June he made a bad smell by trying to muzzle the WM&G through a court order. He wished to prevent the publication of information received from the Directorate of Covert Collection (DCC) whose sleuths had exposed certain senior MK leaders who spied for the Nat government while in exile. The SANDF also threatened to prosecute any DCC member who identified those men, claiming that 'not only would they be severely compromised in their current capacities, but the exposure of military secrets would amount to a contravention of the Official Secrets

Act'. Many were alarmed by this ominous overlapping of the old South Africa and the new.

The same, 7 November

The past week has been hectic: many reunions with white and Indian friends, then a quick dash to Jo'burg (up by kombi taxi, down by night train) to apply for a Mozambican visa. As Rachel is now suffering from bilharzia I plan to visit her again, 17–25 November.

Medmar, Natal, 8 November

Today's weather was no mere challenge but a serious threat. At 5.30 I began a nine-mile marathon up continuously severe gradients through Pietermaritzburg's richest suburbs – each garden like a medium-sized botanical park. By 6.30 the heat was debilitating. By 9.30 a roaring scorching gale had sprung up and was against me. By 10.30 it seemed I was sickening for something; I felt dizzy, nauseous, headachy. At 11 I gave up and for the next five hours lay under a giant bluegum, the sweat flowing non-stop as I read Edward Said's 1993 Reith Lectures. Meanwhile, that strange scorching gale never abated for a moment. At 4 p.m. I struggled on, too enfeebled to cycle though the road was level. It took me almost three hours to walk the next six miles and I reflected that if this is typical Natal summer weather I won't get much further. But just now the TV news reassured me; today's was the highest temperature recorded locally since December 1968 – 41.2°C. And humidity 'reached the danger level of 105'. Small wonder I still feel a bit odd. Tomorrow must be a rest day.

The same, 9 November

Medmar ('South Africa's most popular spot for inland watersports') must be unendurable at weekends but now the restaurant is closed and the hundreds of chalets overlooking the dam are empty. This dam makes up for a lot: miles and miles of clear deep water, surrounded by a nature reserve – the only enjoyable swimming South Africa has offered me. At sunset I observed another chalet being occupied and half an hour later Tina and Trudie arrived on my stoep, bearing beers. They had noticed my name in the register, they had read some of my books...

Tina comes from the northern Transvaal and fifteen years in Natal have not blurred her accent. She and Trudie – recently widowed, about my own age – are old friends. Trudie needs to talk about her husband, a Pietermaritzburg surgeon already known to me by repute. She said, 'He was so happy to be a citizen of

President Mandela's South Africa! Only last year he retired and started voluntary work – there was so much for him to do...' At one stage her husband attracted the attention of BOSS by organizing illegal (mixed-race) meetings in their home. After a year under surveillance, he was arrested at three o'clock one morning and detained for a week. After that 'he ceased to be active'; state terrorism silenced all but the single-minded. Said Trudie, 'Our four children were small at the time and Jeremy had to put them first. Not an easy choice but I supported him. And that's how it went, for most of us.' Looking back to the years when my own daughter was small and dependent, I knew that that is how it would have gone for me, too.

Tina and Trudie first met when Tina was still a student and both were working for the Progressive Party.

'You've been to the northern Transvaal?' asked Tina. 'OK, so you know my parents' type. Most of our "conversions" happen at university but mine was earlier, after I saw my father sjamboking a maid. Why? Because she kept her small daughter with her for one night – the child was sick. Then, aged 11, I saw blacks are people just like us. When I got angry my father said he'd sjambok me if I didn't shut up. He meant it so I did shut up. But he'd lost me. We couldn't communicate after that. Same with my mother and brother – I was an outcast, a traitor. But now, after the election, we've had our own family miracle – we're communicating again.'

I was baffled. 'How could the elections "convert" such extremists?'

Trudie intervened. 'They're not afraid now. Those they've sjamboked over the years haven't united to murder them and seize their farms. So they can relax and accept their liberal offspring – not that many up there will have such a thing. Actually most Afrikaners are more adaptable than we are. They still have this pioneering instinct – what took Tina's ancestors from the Kei to the Limpopo. They thrive on challenges and the new South Africa is another sort of challenge. We're different, we had a Great Power behind us. The Voortrekkers and the boertrekkers were on their own.'

Tina had a less flattering (more realistic?) explanation for the Afrikaners' adaptability. President Mandela is their legitimately elected leader and GNU is the creation, in part, of Mr de Klerk and his team of negotiators; it has not been imposed on whites by black violence. And so the Afrikaners, long habituated to submitting meekly to the Unholy Trinity, are now equally submissive to their new legitimate authority. Even the militant right wing in its multitude of polysyllabic manifestations – those fanatics so noisily belligerent before the elections – have been seen to lack what it takes to defy the State by Law Established. Previously they could – as during their invasion of the Trade Centre in June '93 – rely on support from within the security services. Deprived of that support, they count for nothing.

Before we parted, Tina handed me a newspaper and pointed to a brief paragraph. 'Read it and heed it!' said she. I read:

Criminals, apparently foiled by sophisticated car security devices, have taken to hijacking bicycles. A 16-year-old boy cycling home at 6 p.m. on Monday was threatened by a man with a knife and forced to hand over his bicycle. A 26-year-old woman was cycling home at 5 p.m. on Tuesday when she was stabbed in the arm and robbed of her bicycle as well as a pistol she was carrying in a back-pack. A passer-by saw the attack and chased and caught the assailant. Said Warrant-Officer Andy Pieke of the saps, 'This just illustrates that no one is safe, even if you are on a bike. It's worrying.'

Kamberg, 10 November

My heat-allergy is prompting earlier and earlier starts – 4.30 this morning when there was only a hint of non-darkness to the east. As the sun rose, a bridge took our quiet little road across the N3 – the Durban–Jo'burg motorway – and I looked pityingly down at the noisy stinking rush of vehicles. Then the landscape became astonishingly English: gentle hills, stands of oak, pine, gums and poplars, herds of stout glossy Herefords browsing in small green fields around handsome thatched or red-tiled homesteads.

At Rosetta – in atmosphere a village, in status a town – Mr Naidoo, an Indian merchant, tried to persuade me to avoid Kamberg in kwaZulu. 'At this moment in time there's too much anti-white anger. It's not politics, don't get me wrong. It's cattle-rustling. Kamberg's near the Lesotho border and there's big trouble. Our police have been killing Sotho rustlers, chasing them in choppers and shooting them. You won't see that in the papers but it's true.'

Here I turned towards the Drakensberg and soon could see the 10,500-foot Vergelegen peak in the far distance – southern Africa's highest mountain, just over the Lesotho border. A cooling west wind helped me across a series of high ridges above uninhabited expanses – the grasslands golden, the rocks and cliffs streaked red and silver, the light crystal clear, the sky azure, the massive wall of the Drakensberg blue-grey.

Back in kwaZulu, the tarred road was replaced by a track so rough that I had to walk the final five miles, between steep ochre stony mountains scattered with wattle-groves. Beyond, in a wide valley, sprawls a large Zulu village. By 'homeland' standards this area looks prosperous; the local river is fed from the Berg and green fields soothe the eye.

While pushing Chris through the hilly village centre, I recalled Mr Naidoo's warning. Unfriendly remarks were shouted in Zulu (their unfriendliness deducible from the shouters' expressions) and there was unease in the air. The new school at the far end of the village is not the standard red-brick model but single-storey, painted white and green. Here I tried my usual 'research' ruse, a request

for drinking-water which normally leads to fraternization. But Kamberg's taciturn principal, having provided water, brusquely sent me on my way. Is this
unwelcoming atmosphere really linked to the current 'cattle war' or does it have
deeper roots? When I questioned the amiable Afrikaner woman who booked me
into my Kamberg National Park rondavel she was evasive, feigning surprise that
I had sensed something amiss – it's her job to make tourists feel secure.

Today I'm the only tourist in this glorious place. A dozen one-room huts,
scattered over grassy slopes at the base of the Berg, face a long high ridge on the
far side of the river. Only bird-calls break the deep mountain silence – this
afternoon was an orgy of bird-watching – and the young warden couple live so
far away they might not exist. There is, however, one snag: visitors are expected
to bring their own food. Fred, standing by to cook it in the kitchen-hut, was
touchingly concerned about my lack of sustenance.

Fred is a classic Zulu – tall, well proportioned, dark-skinned, with wide-set
clear eyes, a high forehead, shapely hands. As we sat under a milkwood tree he
brooded over his big problem. Aged 26, with seven younger siblings, he cannot
afford to marry because the lobola (bride price) is eleven cattle at R1,000 per
head. 'If my father could pay school fees I would be a lawyer – or maybe fly
planes. Here my wage for one month is R900 and I must give to my family. My
father has no work since an accident in the mine. Tips I get, maybe R300 in a
month, and those rands I keep. But how many months to save R11,000? I must
be an old, old man when I can have a wife!'

Lobola, in traditional African societies, has several advantages – especially for
the wife. But now it has one sinister disadvantage: by delaying marriages it
speeds the spread of AIDS. Unsurprisingly, Fred had never heard of the virus and
my spiel left him looking incredulous.

When I casually mentioned cattle-rustling Fred, too, was evasive. 'Those
Sothos, they are bad people. They make too much trouble for us. They are
cruel people. And dirty, with too much diseases and no schooling. Now I go to
my home and you will be safe here because no one comes into this park at night.'

Writing outside at sunset, I paused to watch the presiding mountains change
colour – and, it seemed, texture, their fluted grey cliffs becoming walls draped in
royal-blue velvet. Now I'm in my well-lit rondavel; everywhere there must be
electricity for whites. Even for this one white the generator was switched on,
while a few miles away thousands are now lighting candles or little oil lamps or
making do with firelight.

Estcourt, 11 November

Soon after dawn a thin silvery vapour briefly surrounded me, one of those fairy-
tale mists through which trees loom like graceful ghosts. Then, near the top of a

precipitous slope, I suddenly emerged into sunlight and below, on my left, lay slender lines of white cloud between long ridges, partially wooded – with the Berg towering above, sharply etched against a clear blue sky.

Forty of today's fifty miles were on an erosion-ravaged track. In a wide golden valley many thatched huts lined the far bank of a shallow river, rich in birdlife. Another climb, between bushy mountains or bare windy downs, led to a high pass where I nut-munched before jolting down and down, around the flanks of naked red hills – only to climb again, very steeply, towards an enormous rural slum covering several mountainsides.

Here a young man wearing school-uniform begged me to 'lend' him Chris 'for ten minutes only'. His three schoolgirl companions rounded on him angrily and warned me, 'It's a bad boy!' As I walked on with the girls their school principal overtook us and invited me to meet his *kholwa* family, living in a neat bungalow wallpapered with poster portraits of Buthelezi.

The descent to Estcourt – soon visible, very far below on the plain – was one long freewheel (on tar) through a grossly overpopulated rural slum. All morning I had met only one vehicle, a bread van, but here the heavy taxi traffic unnerved me as drivers swung around blind bends in the middle of the narrow road.

Estcourt seems a pleasant enough biggish town with several factories around the edges and a large gloomy hotel on the main street. But I didn't explore: the afternoon temperature was 32.4°C.

Colenso, 12 November

Between Medmar and Rosetta, and again today between Estcourt and Colenso, I have enjoyed a new sport: racing goods trains. The drivers enter into the spirit of the thing, cheering loudly if I overtake them, as I usually do on level ground.

The second Anglo-Boer War is half-forgotten throughout much of South Africa, but not hereabouts. Numerous signposts point to significant sites; binoculars reveal the remains of stone sangars on every other hill; the harsh landscape is scattered with military graves and monuments commemorating 'fallen heroes'. Colenso now is not much bigger than it was in 1899. Here, at 4.30 a.m. on Friday 15 December 1899, the biggest British army to march into battle for half a century (since Alma) advanced towards the Tugela: 14,000 infantry, 2,700 cavalry and 44 heavy guns. General Sir Redvers Buller had also recruited a thousand blacks to cope with his 400 teams of oxen.

At 5.20, when the naval guns began to bombard the koppies beyond the river, there was no response from Louis Botha's 4,500 commandos. During the next hour the gunners inexplicably advanced beyond the protection of the infantry. Then the Irish Brigade heard an unfamiliar sound, soon to become disastrously familiar: the roar of Mauser rifle fire. When a third of the gunners had been wounded or killed the rest very sensibly gave up, losing ten guns – a fact naturally not publicized in Britain at the time. As Thomas Pakenham has noted (he is travelling in a pannier side-pocket), 'the advance of the guns indeed followed one of the great traditions of the British army: courage matched only by stupidity'.

The simple spade, described by Thomas Pakenham as 'the Boers' secret weapon', brought victory at Colenso. Fierce Mauser fire, from hidden and unsuspected trenches concealed amidst the high grass of the veld, made the British imagine they were facing at least 20,000 men. And Major-General Fitzroy Hart, Commander of the Irish Brigade, didn't help by adhering to old-fashioned military thinking – despite the enemy being innovative and agile guerrillas operating in mountainous Natal.

My planned battlefield stroll never happened; today, as on that memorable 15 December, a heatwave struck this region. By 11 a.m. the temperature was 102°F in the shade of Colenso's museum, a tiny stone cottage built in 1879 to house the tollkeeper of the nearby Bulwer Bridge. Subsequently Dr R. E. Stevenson, the military historian, set it up as a museum but few now visit his labour of love. The key lives in the next-door police station where it took a Zulu lieutenant ten minutes to find it at the back of a drawer, under sheaves of yellowing files.

Two instructive hours later I found a Poor White family sitting on the police-station steps: an elderly man, his daughter and her husband – who had a nasty gash on his forehead, the congealed blood attracting flies which he seemed too tired to combat. All were shabbily dressed, severely sunburned, dehydrated, emotionally distressed. The young couple left the talking to Dad. He told me the lieutenant had gone in search of a free lift to Pietermaritzburg, where a relative might be able to find them jobs. Last night they came from Pretoria by train – had only enough money to get to Colenso – spent the day by the roadside trying to hitch a lift – had kept R10 for food but were mugged, hence that gash. Dad is a panel-beater, his daughter and son-in-law used to pick up odd jobs in fast-food outlets and supermarkets. 'But now all those jobs go to blacks,' said Dad – speaking without bitterness, simply stating a fact.

Several young blacks had gathered around and were listening attentively. One youth took out his cigarettes and gave the packet to Dad. 'Keep it,' he said. 'Keep them all.'

On my return from the nearest food-shop three black women were converging on the trio with a loaf of bread, a large bag of oranges and a mega-bottle of Coke. Then a fourth arrived with a bowl of warm water and began gently to clean the gash.

Soon the lieutenant returned, looking triumphant. Tomorrow an Indian trader's truck will take the trio to Pietermaritzburg and they can spend tonight in the police station.

Standing on Bulwer Bridge I could hear thunder distantly growling away to the north. South of the bridge the wide brown Tugela flowed slow and deep between low grassy banks under a milky blue sky. A few hundred yards downstream it curved west, creating that fatal loop into which Major-General Hart led 4,000 men – who then were trapped on a strip of ground scarcely a thousand yards wide, with the river on three sides and many hidden Boer trenches directly opposite on the far bank. The British were lucky to lose only 143 killed, 755 wounded, 240 missing presumed dead. Or did those last prudently run away, having realized they were being led by an idiot?

Crossing to the other side of this narrow bridge, I caught my breath. Towers of inky clouds stood immobile over Grobelaar's Mountain and Mount Hlangwane while beneath them stretched a wide band of rosiness – and the river, reflecting that strange radiance, shone mushroom pink between dark green, densely bushy banks. Then without warning a gale banished the day's torpid stillness, pulling a curtain of rain across the scene. As I sprinted back to the hotel – everyone in sight was sprinting somewhere – a premature twilight fell, thunder crashed continuously overhead, blue sheet lightning danced above the veld and the first huge raindrops splashed me.

Here the barman is an alarmingly thin Afrikaner youth with a pallid spotty face, pale blue eyes, a crew-cut and what I have come to think of as an AWB expression. He ignored my greeting, didn't trouble to open my Castle, then resumed reading something under the counter. When he was summoned to the black bar I peered at his reading matter, a glossy *Guns & Other Weapons* periodical costing R8.50.

Soon another customer arrived, sodden after his short dash from the car park. He stared at me and exclaimed, 'You're a woman! Seeing you this morning I thought you were a *man!*' While buying a crate of beer he invited me home.

Kowie is thirtyish, short, blond, moustached, slightly overweight and very mixed-up. Lisa, his heavily pregnant Messina-born bride, seems half-afraid of him. They live in a neat new bungalow crammed with the sort of potted plants that are perfectly real but look plastic.

I noticed Lisa's face tightening as Kowie embarked on reminiscences about his army days when South Africa was running covert operations in Angola and Mozambique. His eyes shone as he recalled jungle warfare. 'Hey, man – there's a real thrill! Stalking and killing when you know it's them or you, it's the best sport!' For half an hour he continued, the details becoming gorier and gorier. Yet he wasn't drunk – or only drunk with the memories of those good old days. When he left to answer the telephone Lisa looked at me and blurted out, 'I don't like this talk, it scares me.'

I tried to reassure her. 'It's better that he talks, if all that was hidden away you might have a problem.'

Many men returned from South Africa's 'secret wars' irreparably trauma-tized, utterly unable to cope with their memories. I know the following story to be true. A young officer led his platoon into an Angolan village, shot all the men – none was armed – then asked his co what he was to do about the women and children. The order came back: 'Kill them.' So he and his men did kill them. (Those barbarities were designed to terrorize the population into refusing to support the MPLA – Popular Movement for the Liberation of Angola – and the ANC.) On returning home this officer resumed his academic career, married a suitable young woman, seemed a happy, normal citizen. Then the first baby arrived, was brought home from hospital, cried . . . At that sound the father went berserk and attempted to kill both mother and child. He has been in a psychia-tric ward ever since. His mother later found the diary in which he had recorded his military experiences, a risky thing to do given the SADF's 'security' regulations. Demobbed soldiers were programmed to tell no one where they had been or what doing. But this wretched young man had written: 'If I can't express myself now I shall go mad.'

Ladysmith, 13 November

Early this morning, not far from Colenso, a car overtook me, then stopped. A young man got out, lean and suntanned, wearing sharply creased khaki shorts and a trim bush-shirt. He looked worried. 'Excuse me,' said he politely, 'but I think you should have a lift, we can easily fit the bike in.'

I thanked him and explained that I cycle by choice. A pause followed. Then, 'You know there's lots of blacks around here?'

'Well of course, this is South Africa – the majority of the population is black.'

The young man looked nonplussed, as though that demographic fact had never before occurred to him. He frowned and said, 'But they're *dangerous* around here, there's a big new squatter camp over that hill.' He pointed. 'They've moved in, settled on the veld without permission, and they don't like whites.'

'I'm sure they don't – but probably I'll be safe. Please don't worry.'

My thwarted knight shrugged, got into his car – then leaned out and asked, 'You have a gun?' When I shook my head he shouted, 'You're *mad*!' and slammed the door.

Where our road ran level along the crest of a grassy ridge, dotted with a few kraals, I saw an Indian standing inside the wire fence. He was surveying a wrecked kombi lying some thirty yards off the road. As I waved a greeting he beckoned me: would I please hold the barbed strands apart? He had torn his jacket getting in and didn't want to tear it again. He was in a vile temper. 'See that vehicle? Crashed late last night, now stripped – a skeleton!'

I looked. The kombi was indeed stripped: wheels gone, windows and doors gone, seats gone, engine gone.

'Gutted!' said the Indian. 'Even to the steering wheel, would you believe it! Now I'm supposed to salvage it but what's the point? In twenty minutes they strip a crash, that's what they live off on this road – and they *cause* crashes. They've taken over here, if this is the new South Africa I don't want it! I'm a tax-payer, I pay for the council to wire-fence their squatter camps to keep their cattle off the road, then they steal the wire. This is the third crash this week, all cattle collisions. Seven were killed last night, of their own people. But do they care? They'd kill their mothers for a bottle of beer!'

The next ridge-top overlooked the squatter camp; it occupies slopes that were grassy before the migrants' cattle arrived. These people have fled from the political violence of northern kwaZulu and are without any resources. Given their desperate poverty, it is quite possible that had I stopped to talk Chris would have been hijacked. Why do so many who are not desperately poor fail to realize how people must react to that condition? Naturally the squatters steal wire fencing and strip crashed vehicles. So would I, so would the young white man, so would the Indian, if we and our families were starving.

Surveying this wildly beautiful terrain through the eyes of General Sir Red-vers Buller's scouts, I could see – and feel, as I pushed Chris up a near-vertical gradient – why the Siege of Ladysmith lasted 118 days. The British had a ten-to-one advantage in artillery and a four-to-one advantage in men but given this sort of country hundreds of nimble guerrillas could outwit thousands of regular soldiers.

Ladysmith was the main British military depot in Natal, to which Brigadier-General Yule's column had retreated from Dundee. On 30 October 1899 the British attacked Pepworth Hill, a nearby enemy position. But when four hours of Boer shelling had broken the troops' nerve regimental discipline collapsed and the survivors straggled back to Ladysmith in disorganized, demoralized groups. This was 'one of the gloomiest days in the history of the British army' and the defeat shattered General White, a weak man – indecisive, unimaginative, inflexible in his planning. However, he did take full responsibility for the disaster – he could hardly have done otherwise, it was entirely his fault. Repeatedly he had rejected his staff officers' advice, as British generals were wont to do in those days, and now he blundered yet again, hesitating too long before deciding to withdraw from Ladysmith. By 2 November it was too late. The four-month siege had begun. Trapped within the little town were 13,745 European soldiers and 5,400 civilians, including Indian camp-followers and black servants.

As so often during this war, confusion was compounded by the scarcity – or cutting – of telegraph lines. On 15 December the besieged British could hear Buller's guns during the Battle of Colenso, yet three days later White's staff knew few of the details about that débâcle. Around Ladysmith, communication was mainly by heliograph (rather public), absent-minded carrier pigeons and oil lamps for which oil was not always available. Also, on overcast nights, naval searchlights brought up from the coast on railway trucks were capable of flashing Morse messages onto clouds and these could be read as far as sixty miles away. Another sort of communication problem arose out of the deep-rooted antagonism between General White, besieged in Ladysmith, and General Buller of the relieving force.

On my left as I approached Ladysmith was Hart's Hill where the Irish Brigade were slain by the hundred. Other hundreds, grievously wounded, had to be abandoned to a slow death on these steep rocky slopes. The Inniskillings alone lost 27 per cent of their men and 72 per cent of their officers – prompting Queen Victoria, as she read her war telegrams, to exclaim, 'My brave Irish!'

By noon I was back on the Breedts' lawn, celebrating my reunion with Sheila and Andy. 'The English are an odd lot,' reflected Andy. 'Towards the end of our siege they had to eat some of their cavalry horses – and the cavalry officers were furious!'

The same, 14 November

Sans panniers (therefore feeling as though cycling on the moon) I set off at dawn for Spion Kop – Dutch for 'Lookout Hill'. From here, in 1840, northern Natal's fertile miles were first seen by the Voortrekkers – the prize they had struggled so hard to reach. But soon it was to be snatched by the 'imperialists', inspiring the more stubbornly independent Boers to trek on into the Transvaal.

Ten miles from Ladysmith I turned onto the old wagon-track along which rode the 17-year-old Deneys Reitz, son of the ex-President of the Orange Free State, on the morning of 24 January 1900. His leave had been cut short two days before when Pappa ordered him back to Natal to join his commando – fifty men from Pretoria – in their efforts to repulse Buller's latest attack, expected soon. Deneys provided his own horse and rifle and biltong, as did every commando. These were true amateurs, receiving no pay or uniform or rations, no pensions if wounded, no decorations for gallantry. Deneys's journal gives the most detailed account, from the Boer side, of the improbable events on and around Spion Kop on 24/25 January 1900.

From several koppies near Ladysmith British observers could see part of the battle and they rejoiced as the Boers withdrew. But next morning their disappointment and bafflement were acute. Why were the Boers' white tents blossoming again on that flat summit? What could have happened?

What happened defies belief. The British troops, though already exhausted and disheartened by this gruelling campaign, here displayed extraordinary – by any standards – courage and stamina. After a seven-hour climb to the summit, and an eleven-hour battle in midsummer heat, they won Spion Kop. Then, after dark, their commanding officers got in a muddle and imagined that the Boers, who had already retreated, were in a strong surrounding position. Therefore this vital 'key to open the door to Ladysmith' was abandoned during the night – to the incredulous joy of the Boers, whose favourite adjective for the 'Khakis' (*kopschuw*: 'bone-headed') now seemed fully justified. The Khakis had lost some 1,500 men: 243 killed, over 1,000 seriously wounded, the rest captured.

The old wagon-track climbs gradually through uninhabited green-brown veld (more brown than green this year) to the base of Spion Kop. From there it was a long steep push to a level saddle between the two crests – the fact that there are two took the British by surprise and gave the Boers a considerable advantage. I rested beside the Boers' memorial, a simple stone obelisk inscribed with 335 names. The several British memorials are scattered about a sloping plateau near a long mass-grave marked by whitewashed stones. Here I remembered the hundreds of wounded left bleeding and groaning among their comrades' corpses. All night they lay where I now stood; when the Indian stretcher-bearers arrived on the following afternoon many had died.

In its austere way Spion Kop is very beautiful; were it not a graveyard, it would certainly be a popular picnic spot. Since leaving the road I had seen no one, the air was still, the light filtered through gauzy cloud, the silence unbroken even by bird-calls. A bank of shifting vapour concealed Ladysmith but in every other direction I could see for many miles over an incoherence of sombrely shaded mountains and valleys. And almost directly below – some 1,500 feet below – stretched a newish dam, a glistening sheet of silver. Here Buller's troops crossed the Tugela by pontoon bridge.

For hours I wandered to and fro, Thomas Pakenham in hand. Several locals had advised: 'Don't go alone to Spion Kop, it's too creepy!' Haunted this *slagveld* may well be, yet I felt no unease while crisscrossing its silent acres or standing on the edge of the precipice near Aloe Knoll, gazing down the sheer cliff, swathed in cassia, mimosa thorn and aloes. The British assault was impeded by this tangled, thorny vegetation, by loose scree and stones, by house-sized boulders. And a temperature in the high nineties caused quite a few Khakis to collapse.

At noon the clouds lowered and thickened and on the way back I was soaked by icy driving rain, the sort of rain that on the night of 25/26 January 1900 added to the misery of the needless British retreat to Buller's headquarters behind Mount Alice.

This afternoon Andy took me to visit his friends Barry and Wendy, bibliomaniac octogenarians for whom the two Anglo-Boer Wars are a hobby – but no, 'hobby' is too frivolous. This couple's home has been taken over by related volumes in numerous languages and the various battles and sieges, studied in minute detail, are a non-boring obsession – easily understood. Its David and Goliath aspect gives the Anglo-Boer conflict an unusual human interest. And locals who enjoy arguing about strategy and tactics, and how and where So-and-So went wrong, have a plenitude of printed and photographic material at their disposal and some battlefields on their doorstep – in Andy's case, literally on his doorstep.

Barry presented me with a magnificently bound copy of *Three Years' War* by Christian Rudolph de Wet, one of a limited edition of 1,000 copies. This trophy – both too precious and too heavy to be transported by bicycle – must be posted home. Reading a few chapters tonight, I noted de Wet's 1902 comment:

> This I will say, that whatever his own people have to say to his discredit, Sir Redvers Buller had to operate against stronger positions than any other English General in South Africa.

Tomorrow I leave Chris in the Breedts' garage and take off to visit Rachel for a week in post-elections Mozambique. This is no extravagance; the Jo'burg–Maputo second-class return rail ticket costs £16.

Happenings behind my Back

On 17 November, while I was en route to Maputo an historic event took place. On that Thursday morning President Mandela signed onto the South African statute books the Land Rights Restitution Act, Act No. 22 of 1994 – eighty-one years and five months after the passing of the Natives Land Act, Act No. 27 of 1913, which, in Sol Plaatje's words, 'made the South African native not actually a slave, but a pariah in the land of his birth'.

The Restitution Act looks like the brightest star in GNU's legislative constellation. Yet in practice its efficacy will depend on numerous factors bristling with question marks. However, it does provide a morally and intellectually sound basis for immediate action on behalf of a minority of poor blacks. Prudently, President Mandela described it as 'a real effort to ensure that those people who were deprived of their land in the course of apartheid are given back their property'.

Derek Hanekom, the ANC's Afrikaner Minister for Land Affairs, has already worked wonders, winning the trust of both rich recalcitrant Boers and destitute impatient peasants. But Land Rights should be dealt with by members of the judiciary and the Restitution Act establishes a Land Claims Court and a Commission on the Restitution of Land Rights. Whenever possible, the Commissioners will settle claims; their failures will be referred to the Court. For three years from 2 December 1994 claims may be submitted, dating back to 19 June 1913. Henceforth, communities who return to invade land which they regard as their own, without reference to the Commission, will be regarded as illegal squatters.

This Act is designed both to 'bring hope and justice to the victims of racially discriminatory laws' and to reassure white farmers. Luckily, most disputed land is still state-owned. But some has been sold and where claims involve this private land the Constitution provides for the payment of full compensation, even to those who must be served an expropriation order. The President foresees such cases being 'relatively rare'.

It is much too late simply to 'give South Africa back' to the (indigenous) South Africans. All along my way, since first crossing the Limpopo, I have noticed how seldom land ownership is discussed, even in circles eloquent about the many other national problems. Time sets its seal on events and that seal, however outrageous the circumstances of its setting, cannot be broken generations later without initiating another cycle of injustice. My own reservations about the new South Africa are partly rooted in this need to accept the ultimate 'white supremacy' – white ownership of most of the fertile land, the crucial supremacy in Africa.

On my return to Jo'burg, on 26 November, I lunched with a senior SACP official (let's call him John) who knows President Mandela well and loves him dearly – regards him as a father-figure rather than an idol. Sadly he observed, 'Now everyone can see Madiba's a natural capitalist, willing to protect all vested interests – nobody needs to twist his arm.'

(How does an interest look without its vest? Is it then called 'disinterest'?)

John and I agreed that South Africa's most malevolent vested interest is Armscor, a vicious component of the old militaristic regime. John had brought a file of relevant documents, morbidly fascinating.

Pre-elections, the naive assumed that a Mandela-led government would withdraw from arms trading and divert Armscor's massive subsidies to the RDP. As no external enemy threatens, and South Africa has no expansionist ambitions, the SANDF's future role will be domestic: catching illegal immigrants on the border, providing emergency and security services – duties not requiring the back-up of a sophisticated arms industry. And yet, President Mandela opened the 1994 Dexsa Defence Exhibition in Jo'burg.

Then, as reported in *The Star* on 22 November, Defence Minister Joe Modise told a 'defence equipment co-operation seminar' that 'the defence industry, which employs tens of thousands of people and brings in billions of rands in foreign exchange, is one of the key ingredients for peace in South Africa and on the African continent as a whole. The countries of sub-Saharan Africa have so far this year alone spent about US$1.3 billion on equipment not standardized with that of their neighbours and which would cost a lot to maintain and upgrade. Many smaller countries do not have knowledgeable buyers and are therefore being exploited. Co-operation on the continent could ensure that better value for money is obtained by larger orders and the use of the expertise of an organisation like Armscor.' It seems Mr Modise imagines Armscor would not exploit smaller countries – which puts him in a minority of one.

The newly appointed Defence Secretary, Lieutenant-General Pierre Steyn, also addressed the assembled senior government and military officers from such countries as Gabon, Tanzania, Zambia and Zimbabwe. 'South Africa is ready', he announced, 'to challenge weapons manufacturers in the US and Europe if they attempt to prevent this country from selling armaments on the open market and particularly in Africa. Our weapons sales drives will spread South African influence across Africa.'

Reading as I ate, I almost choked. US$1.3 billion in less than a year! I have cycled through three of the above-mentioned countries and failed to get water from many defunct standpipes. I have visited rural clinics serving thousands of people yet lacking even an aspirin. I have listened to a despairing doctor in a 500-bed hospital equipped with three hypodermic needles. Arms trading and Third World poverty are so closely linked that no government can cope with the latter while the former continues.

'Isn't it odd,' said John, 'that that's never emphasized at all those grand "macro-summits" about hunger and homelessness and disease?'

Related to that silence is the arms traders' abuse of language, designed to exclude from view all who are, in various ways, their helpless victims. The very phrase 'defence industry' is tendentious. In South Africa's case, could Mr Modise specify defence against whom or what? Little striped men from Jupiter? Less tendentious, because clearly absurd, is his claim that the 'defence' industry is 'one of the key ingredients for peace...' Tell that to the people of Rwanda; in October 1992 their government bought from South Africa US$4 million-worth of automatic rifles, grenade launchers, machine-guns and ammunition. Or to the people of Iraq. In July 1994 a Palestinian sued Nimrod, Armscor's international marketing subsidiary, for unpaid commission – and papers presented to the Pretoria Supreme Court revealed that South Africa had sold US$4.5 billion-worth of armaments to Saddam Hussein.

Yes, the arms industry employs hundreds of thousands of First World workers – in Britain, for instance, one-tenth of the manufacturing workforce, since the UK 'enjoys' some 20 per cent of the global arms market.

'Jobs for whites, destitution for the rest,' said John. 'In our so-called defence sector, not many blacks are employed by Armscor, Denel and the private companies.'

Denel – a parastatal arms manufacturer, offspring of former Armscor subsidiaries – claims to be 'the armourer of the Persian Gulf', quoting as proof a recent artillery sale to Oman worth US$120 million.

'In September '93,' said John, 'after the "defence" budget was cut, Armscor lost R172 million of tax-payers' money in cancellations and contracts costs. They'd been forewarned about the cuts but their forward-planners didn't allow for them. And over the years they've lost billions of rands through myopia, muddle and ignorance – and mixing with too many cosmopolitan crooks smarter than the home-grown variety!'

The ANC's pre-election policy document stated: 'The standards of responsible global citizenship and the requirements of South Africa's wider foreign policy goals will have priority over considerations of the armaments industry within the South African economy.' 'Not a model of lucidity,' commented John, 'but it did give us some hope. Now it seems GNU has no foreign policy – only arms salesmen.' We wondered then precisely what pressures have been applied to persuade the ANC to abandon 'responsible global citizenship' – and to whom have they been applied? The immoral argument, 'If we don't do it someone else will', could also be used to justify government-run drug-smuggling, child-prostitution, financial scams. Now some ANC politicians are talking nonsense about 'regulating' the arms industry, making it 'more accountable and transparent', restructuring Armscor, sacking its 'Total Onslaught' unconvertibles – and so on. But no armaments industry anywhere can be regulated, by anyone. It can only be dismantled. And in South Africa, as John pointed out, that process need involve no waste of human and material resources. Always the arms industry has been able to monopolize the best and the brightest of scientists and technicians, and to afford the choicest manufacturing equipment, leaving the civilian sector seriously short of such assets. Post-dismantlement, there would be no lack of opportunities for the brightest and the best in non-lethal industries.

The arms industry has become so powerful – its tentacles wrapped around the whole world – and so corrupting for those engaged in it, *because* it is indifferent to all laws or embargoes, national or international, and uninhibited about removing individuals who get in the way. Armscor has gagged many employees and associates. Some were sacked and smeared, some hastily emigrated. John's file held a list of recent deaths. In January 1988 the Armscor Director of Finance, Helmie Snyman, was shot through the head in Pretoria and his safe emptied of all files and tapes relating to Armscor's secret foreign procurements.

'Suicide!' said the police, very promptly.

'Murdered to silence him!' said the Snyman family.

In 1991 the dismembered body of the international sales director of Thor Chemicals, Alan Kidger, was found in the boot of his car. A few weeks later the managing director of Wacker Chemicals, John Scott, was found gassed in his car; nearby his wife and two children had been stabbed to death. Immediately the police announced that he had murdered his family before killing himself. Much later they admitted that his death was linked to the trade in 'red mercury', a mysterious substance much sought after by arms manufacturers. Since then the deaths of three other men – Don Lange, Dirk Stoffberg, Wynand van Wyk – have been associated by the police with the 'red mercury' trade. In July 1994 Tielman de Waal, Armscor's executive general manager, denied ever having had dealings with Lange, Kidger or van Wyk. Two months later it was proved that he had done at least one major deal with Lange – illegal, of course, or it would have been unnecessary to deny it.

Closing his file, John said, 'And this is the industry some fatuous politicians imagine they can "regulate"!'

*

My Mozambican week was overshadowed by Rachel's bilharzia. It has proved resistant to the biltricide treatment and her debilitated condition reactivated my maternal instinct (long dormant: she will soon be 26). So instead of enjoying peaceful post-elections Maputo I was most of the time engaged, with Andrew's invaluable support, in persuading the patient to be sensible and fly immediately to London.

17

To Griqualand East

Willow Grange – Underberg – Kokstad

Typical of both the old and the new set-ups in South Africa is our indigenous philistinism
– 'good taste' and even better intentions, sentimentalism, anti-intellectualism and
'commitment', mutual moral balls-squeezing and political correctness.
Breyten Breytenbach (1994)

Willow Grange, Natal, 29 November 1994

When I rejoined Chris two days ago Ladysmith's afternoon temperature was 38°C in the shade. Next morning I set off for Winterton at 4 a.m. to stay with Sheila's parents, whose warm-heartedness and lively conversation made memorable my sixty-third birthday. Having left Zimbabwe, Liz and Francis built themselves an enchanting home thirty miles from Ladysmith, an L-shaped, whitewashed cottage – ecologically sound, no luxuries – with thick stone walls and a steeply pitched thatched roof. At 7 a.m. I found both hard at work in the garden. They are almost self-sufficient in food and Francis produces the finest home-brewed beer I have ever tasted. On this subject I can speak with some authority, being a home-brewer myself.

This morning a bumpy twenty-mile short cut took me through low, desolate mountains onto the R74 near Estcourt. By 10 a.m. heat-stroke threatened. Soon after turning onto the Willow Grange road, I collapsed under a tree and lay on the rock-hard ground sympathetically remembering Private Frederick Tucker. In his *Boer War Diary* he wrote, on 5 December 1899, 'We marched to Willow Grange, a distance of ten miles. I find the marching very hard as it is very dusty and hot, and the country is very hilly. I wish I had my body in a pool and my head in a public house.'

Incidentally, Private Tucker was appalled to discover that the Boer government was being lavishly supplied by a British armaments firm, Ely of London, with explosive .303 dum-dum bullets – the use of which had been formally forbidden during this war. So what's new!

Now Willow Grange consists of little more than an agreeable hotel in the form of heat-resistant rondavels scattered over grassland high above a trickling river. In the bar a local farmer complained, 'We've no law and order left! In Estcourt last week, on the main street in the middle of the day, they stole a crate of eggs from my very hands – 600 eggs, big money. And nobody made a move to help me – they call it "affirmative shopping"! We all notice farmworkers stealing now like never before. With me, they know they've only to ask and they get what they need. But they seem to *want* to steal, to prove something. In Mandela's democracy they feel free to help themselves to my property – they feel *liberated*!'

Loteni, kwaZulu, 30 November

Soon, at this rate, 'today' will be starting yesterday; by 3.45 a.m. I was pedalling slowly by starlight up a long, long hill with the street lights of Estcourt visible far below like luminous silver powder spilled on the blackness. Then came level miles overlooking undulating uplands shrouded in a thin cold mist. But the rising sun warmed me on the exhilaratingly fast descent to Mooi River – where begins another tough climb.

An hour later, having turned south, I saw something freakishly unlikely. Although this is summer, the whole distant escarpment of the Berg was gently gleaming – snow-mantled. And all day a strong cool wind refreshed me, while the sky resembled a lake of half-mixed paints – high white thin cloud forming swirling streaks against the deep blue.

Beyond the Loteni signpost the tar continued for some fifteen miles through the ranches of the rich, uninhabited green hills where cattle and zebra – bred for their pelts – grazed together. Then I was on a kwaZulu track that became rougher and steeper as the mountains became wilder and higher and grander, hiding the Berg. For some thirty miles this territory – where I saw neither man nor beast – is securely fenced; it has recently been bought by a Dutch developer 'with plans for the area'.

This was a special day: traffic-free, offering silence and solitude amidst soaring silver escarpments, deep bushy valleys, red rocky ridges and line after line of dusky-blue mountains piled against the horizon. A two-and-a-half-hour walk took me to the pass – from where I continued to walk. Freewheeling would have meant not daring to take my eyes off the track and I wanted to use them otherwise. Close by on the right rose a sheer grassy boulder-studded mountain, miles long and crowned with columns of grey rock, smooth and stout and regular as the pillars of a Romanesque cathedral. Below, on my left, stretched a confusion of bare brown hills and narrow jungly ravines. And ahead, as we lost height, a profound chasm came into view with another mighty mountain wall beyond, its vegetation dense and olive green. Here, pink and yellow flowering creepers draped the cliffs above the track.

A corner of Loteni appeared then. I had been warned that it has no shop but this is no longer true; on the edge stands a new breeze-block store behind a high wire-mesh fence. Ken, the welcoming owner, moved last year from Estcourt's township. 'I couldn't take the violence any more. I've three small kids and I want them to grow up. Here schooling is bad but survival is more important than education. All these changes have done nothing for us Zulu. We never had killing so bad before they let Mandela out.' He told his beautiful wide-eyed 8-year-old daughter to bring a chair for 'Madam' and offered me a Coke. 'Sorry, no beer – alcohol makes more trouble, I won't sell it.' Neither does he sell milk. 'It's too expensive, no one here has money like that.' We agreed there is something very wrong with a country where milk costs twice as much as Coca-Cola.

Explained Ken, 'We've no police station but there's a Stock Theft Unit, you'll see it near the bridge. They'll be happy to give you accommodation. They've a lonesome life here.'

Descending to river-level, I again felt the central sadness of the white traveller in South Africa. You must stay in your place – with the only resident whites.

The Stock Theft Unit, balanced on a couple of narrow ledges above a dry river-bed, consists of two concrete rows of monastically furnished rooms for the eight black policemen and a fine bungalow for the captain's family. Half a dozen sturdy ponies graze nearby, the steeds on which stock thieves are pursued through the many passes leading into Lesotho. In this area – Danie explained, as we sat drinking wine in the kitchen while Nellie cooked supper – thefts are mostly black from black. Many cattle fall over precipices while being driven fast by night up treacherous paths; they die slowly, while scores of vultures gather. Sometimes a police helicopter is summoned by radio and on one such occasion, a few months ago, an armed Sotho was shot dead and two others were arrested. When both received 'ridiculously short sentences' the enraged Loteni Zulus abused Danie for not having shot them, also. 'They couldn't understand our reasoning. The unarmed thieves weren't threatening to kill us. Sometimes we can feel very discouraged. Seems we can't ever get it right, operating between two worlds – white and black, with such different mindsets.'

Last month a local was caught in possession of thirty stolen sheep – hidden in an isolated hut, released at night to graze. He claimed to have found them straying – he was only looking after them while seeking their owner – he grazed them by night because by day he was working and had nobody to shepherd them. This implausible story was accepted in court and he got off, there being no witnesses to the theft. 'Or if there were,' added Danie, 'they'd been intimidated. We're blamed for being lazy and corrupt and stupid, but when we're energetic and honest and smart it doesn't take us far. More often than not we're outwitted. A European system of justice only works if everyone accepts European standards. If people think nothing of murdering witnesses to a small crime like stock theft – well, what do you do?' Then Danie quoted his German missionary uncle, who for thirty-five years harvested souls in Tanzania. 'He knew the blacks

– surely he knew them, after so many years! And he always said, "When a black opens his mouth he lies. When he shuts it he stops lying." With them silence is an admission of guilt.'

Danie, aged 30, did his military service in the Caprivi Strip. 'But as a teaching officer, no fighting – and that suited me, teaching basic literacy and arithmetic to young men. Really I was doing propaganda, the idea behind the schooling. "Democracy is good! Communism is bad!" That could sound funny to you, us preaching democracy. But then we believed in our mission.'

Danie concedes that in the past the police were often 'too tough'. But he resents the new ethical code being imposed on SAPS by the Bill of Rights and questions its relevance to 'ordinary life the way we have to live it in this country'.

Nellie is of 1820s stock, Danie a German-Afrikaner who for two years served in Pietermaritzburg's Internal Stability Unit, a section of the old SAP notorious for exacerbating instability wherever they intervened.

'We didn't deserve our bad reputation,' asserted Danie. 'By the time we arrived on a scene it was all out of hand – usually a case of "attack or be attacked". But the psychology was bad, we were left too long hanging about waiting. Standing by, ready for instant action, all hyped up – and maybe nothing happening and nothing happening . . . So you got to be longing for trouble and set off with too much aggro inside. That could lead to over-reaction, once I nearly shot a kid for no reason. That scared me and I talked to the colonel, said maybe we should have shorter stand-by periods. But he only stamped on me. It's not kosher for lieutenants to advise colonels!'

Now affirmative action is angering the SAPS's white component – officers' exams have been 'made easier'. (I can't believe they were ever very difficult.)

Nellie, a public-health-nurse-cum-midwife, works in three local clinics – near the border, to which many desperate Sothos ride on their ponies for four days in search of free treatment. 'It's illegal to give it but how can I turn them away? Some bring poorly babies – usually malnutrition, no specific disease, just like with the Zulus. If the babies haven't gained weight in a month I know their milk ration was divided amongst other hungry kids. All that makes tension for me with our own people. Zulus hate Sothos and it's not just around stock theft. Zulus hate Sothos, period.'

As elsewhere, injections are the locals' preferred – because undetectable by husbands – form of contraceptive. Nellie finds that interest in family planning varies from district to district. Here the women – and even some of the men – are quite 'advanced', despite the prevailing poverty. 'But generally,' said Nellie, 'it's true the birth rate goes down as incomes go up.'

Nellie's horror stories echoed those I have heard from medical workers all over rural South Africa. Mothers who kill small babies by giving adult-dose emetics, grannies who treat their grandchildren's internal parasites with Jeyes Fluid, adolescent surrogate mothers who conceal toddlers' broken bones until a limb has to be amputated – and phoney sangomas who make a fortune on AIDS 'cures'. AIDS-testing is not available (too expensive) but a soaring TB rate tells the story. However, more and more genuine sangomas are sharing with 'Western' health-workers their knowledge of effective herbal medicines and are keen to learn which symptoms indicate that a patient *must* go to hospital.

One of Danie's black colleagues has eight children – four illegitimate, for each of whom he regularly pays maintenance at R120 a month. This means he must take on extra jobs and/or demand higher bribes. In rural areas fathers rarely deny paternity, being bound by custom to acknowledge it – and anyway being proud of their procreative prowess. For this reason many women now choose not to wed; maintenance money from various fathers can amount to much more than one husband's wage. In Edendale township near Pietermaritzburg I met one such mother, a prosperous 47-year-old hawker whose twelve children ranged in age from 30 to 3. Eight fathers were involved and she had only recently heard of AIDS. Nellie recalled the case of a 15-year-old schoolgirl and her school principal in a neighbouring settlement; when rape was followed by pregnancy, the parents refused to charge the rapist lest he might lose his job and be unable to pay maintenance.

Underberg, 1 December

On today's sensationally rough track it took me six hours to cover twenty-five miles: very beautiful, very hilly, very hot miles. By 5.30 the sun was up in a cloudless sky and, ominously, there was no wind.

Everyone was friendly in the few large settlements en route but no one spoke English. Small boys herded fat goats, youths herded thin cattle. On the lower slopes of steep mountains stand groups of substantial round or oblong huts, securely thatched and brightly painted – lime green, pale pink, dark blue. These are still called 'kraals' though no longer wattle-fenced to protect livestock from four-legged predators. Some, however, have new anti-rustler fences reinforced by packs of hunting-dogs.

I visited a new school (seven teachers: 580 pupils) – of course tin-roofed, wired for electricity though the nearest supply point is thirty miles away and with elaborate plumbing though there is little hope of piped water in the foreseeable future. The statutory wayside board lists the Durban architect firm, the electrical engineering consultants, the construction company, the accountants... Will the Reconstruction and Development Programme boffins make any effort to persuade blacks that their South Africa does not have to ape the whites' South Africa? All the skills and materials are locally available to build a school more suited to this region's climate at a fraction of the cost, leaving millions over for the training and adequate payment of teachers. Or is it too late to restore the blacks' pride in doing things their own way?

According to a Zulu TTC lecturer who befriended me in Pietermaritzburg, the only teachers who may safely be appointed to rural schools in this province are IFP-approved locals, at best semi-qualified. These resent fully qualified outsiders who show up their own incompetence and try to teach pupils something about how democracies are supposed to work.

That same friend enlightened me about the sudden puzzling disappearance throughout kwaZulu of *The Sowetan*, the blacks' admirably objective English-language newspaper. Because it often criticizes Buthelezi it has been banned – not officially, but following the murders of three foolhardy newsagents who ignored 'warnings' it went off the market. No other paper so strongly condemns Buthelezi's links with the Far Right. The IFP has leaders like Walter Felgate (formerly RTZ's African Affairs adviser) and Peter Miller (kwaZulu/Natal's MEC for Housing and Local Government) and Senator Phillip Powell (ex-SAP).

When heat-stroke threatened at 10.15 no shade was available – not a tree, not a bush, not even a boulder. On either side shimmered bare rocky slopes or bare stony veld. As an enemy the sun is very frightening and panic soon sets in. On reaching the tarred road near Himeville, an exclusive holiday-home village, I felt too dizzy to pedal and dragged Chris along a grass verge in the blessed shade of pine trees, then freewheeled the last lap to Underberg. In the hotel my arrival after dark in July '93 was remembered. This year a new defiant example of racist 'wit' hangs behind the bar: 'Small black man wanted as mud-flap. Must be flexible and willing to travel.' Automatically I ordered a Castle but felt too queasy to drink it. After a warm bath I lay shivering on the bed for two hours and even now I want to drink only water.

Kokstad, 2 December

A strong cool tailwind helped me to cover sixty-five miles by 1 p.m. despite three hailstorms from which I sheltered under my space-blanket. Small hailstones are said to be much better for the land than torrential rain but these were not small; they tore several holes in my 'tent'.

Kokstad has a Cape flavour, architecturally, and in atmosphere recalls Matatiele. When this region formed part of the old Cape Province, these little towns were Griqualand East's dozy 'white' market centres. Only in 1976, on the setting up of the Transkei 'homeland', did Griqualand East – being commercial farmland – become part of Natal. Then the departure of white merchants from 'black' territory transformed both Kokstad and Matatiele into bustling trading centres, attracting Xhosa customers from all over the northern Transkei.

Tomorrow will be a rest day. Last June Fay Rennie called on me in Ireland – we have mutual friends – and offered hospitality on her farm fifteen miles from Kokstad, near the Transkei border. In 1883 the Rennie family purchased 4,600 acres from an English-speaker named Woolridge who had probably bought the land from Griquas. Fay's grandfather-in-law then entered the history books by importing South Africa's first herd of Hereford cattle.

By 1860 the Griquas had sold all their land in Griqualand West to the Orange Free State, having for decades been the victims of both British and Boer expansionism. The British then gave them a conscience-salving present of this area, known as Niemandsland (no man's land). Before accepting the gift Adam Kok, the Griqua leader, sent a delegation to inspect it – in summer, when the treeless pastures were green and all the streams full. Joyfully the Griquas moved, only to discover that in winter their cattle and sheep could not survive here. Soon most of them had sold their farms to whites and settled in Kokstad. In fact this region was not a no man's land. The winter cold, at 5,000 feet, deterred permanent settlement but generations of Xhosa had used it for summer grazing.

Palmiet Farm, 3 December

This is a magical region, of extraordinary beauty and with a 'Secret Garden' feeling. To the traveller it seems (but it isn't) outside the turbulence of South Africa in transition.

Beyond Kokstad I left the Matatiele road to follow an old wagon-track into the hills. It was a fresh bright morning, the air pure, the sunrise quietly glorious, painting delicate tints above tawny rocky slopes and silent expanses of pasture-land that should now be green but this year remain cinnamon-brown. Yet the several dams are quite full and the numerous pedigree herds thriving; white capital and know-how soon transformed Niemandsland into profitable ranching country. When the first Rennies settled, how long did it take them to drive their ox-wagons to the nearest store? But the family would then have been largely self-sufficient, needing only an occasional excursion to embryonic Kokstad.

Palmiet's short private road leads past groups of thatched workers' huts set amidst tall pines. Then the original homestead appears, built in 1884 of mud and stone, long and solid and now used as a barn. Its successor was built in 1925: a stately mansion-bungalow with long corridors, high ceilings, a wide stoep, a brick patio. Here live Michael and Jeanette, Fay's son and daughter-in-law, surrounded by handsome mahogany furniture and the portraits of not-always-handsome ancestors. Fay herself occupies an elegant dower-bungalow overlooking the lake-like dam, its shores home to flocks of Egyptian geese, yellow-bill duck, blacksmith plover and spoonbills. Above the water rises a steep grassy hill, planted a century ago with oaks, poplars, deodars, bluegums. Griqualand East, explained Fay, lacked indigenous trees.

In such a confusing country, where paradoxes cover the political landscape like weeds, one can come to feel quite guilty about failing to maintain a reasonable level of optimism. This seems to put one, superficially, on the side of those who undervalue the comparatively peaceful transition and ignore its positive implications. I therefore needed this Palmiet interlude; to Fay I could confess my scepticism about the majority's present capacity to function as citizens of a democracy.

Why is it so often assumed that African countries are capable of compressing into a few years what in Europe took several centuries? To try quickly to transform apartheid-maimed South Africa into a Western-style democracy is a brave but rash undertaking. Those who scoff at the notion of blacks ever being able to run a parliamentary democracy, or efficiently manage Africa's most industrialized economy, may well have a point. But their latter argument is not at present being tested. Behind the elaborate GNU façade, blacks are not being allowed even to try to manage South Africa's economy for the benefit of the majority.

Fay told me a sad but not unusual story about a neighbour who found his Zulu farm-school teacher inflating attendance figures so that she could claim more rations under GNU's supplementary feeding scheme for poor children. She then sold the surplus – not her first offence but the most serious. (Why doesn't GNU compel farmers to raise workers' wages so that their children don't need supplementary feeding?) When the neighbour heard of a white teacher interested in the job, he requested the Department of Education to sanction her appointment. Almost immediately the intimidation started – threats against his life, threats to torch his home and the school. Although both parents and pupils pleaded for a white teacher, the Zulu kept her job. Said Fay, 'It's very disturbing when professional people think they can do what they like and issue death threats to anyone who has the temerity to gainsay them. And will the next generation of teachers be any better, given the lack of professional ethics by now built into the system?'

As we walked the land in the cool of the evening – wattle plantations on one side, serenely ruminating Herefords on the other – Fay passed on the latest joke: 'There's no point in moving Parliament to Pretoria as there will soon be nothing to move!' Theft within Cape Town's Parliament buildings has become a major problem; even the press-corps offices have had to acquire security gates. Computers, fax machines, mobile phones, typewriters – 'Whitey's goodies, let's help ourselves!'

Having for long been a federalist, Fay is now 'beginning to question whether, at this stage of our political development, devolution of important powers to the provinces is feasible'. Whatever the arguments against 'centralism', my innate frugality revolts against the running of *nine* provincial governments – all lusting after governmental status symbols – for a population two-thirds that of France. Eventually this structure may collapse under the weight of its own efficiency. Or it may not – with every year that passes the vested interests at provincial level will become more entrenched.

The same, 4 December

At sunrise I rambled among the huts beneath the pines, being greeted with big smiles by the workers and their numerous relatives. Each family receives a monthly mealie ration, a weekly meat ration and a generous daily milk ration. On special occasions – hatching, matching or dispatching – Michael provides an ox to be solemnly slaughtered and merrily consumed. At present the Palmiet hamlet accommodates fifty-four, of whom twelve are workers. Given the changing economic situation – higher taxes, fewer subsidies, uncertainty about future prices – it is doubtful if this feudal community can survive. A year ago there were seventy-two in residence, then Michael had to insist on some returning whence they came. During the worst period of township violence (1990–93) more and more young cousins, nephews, nieces – and some not so young – retreated to their areas of origin, to farms like Palmiet with a 'caring' reputation.

Today Michael pointed out, as others have done, that low agricultural wages are not as unjust as they sound because the value of free accommodation, food, medical care and schooling (such as it is) increases annually. But a system so open to abuse must go, and the 'agrivillage' option is now under consideration in Natal, involving higher wages and no perks. Families could build their own homes on their own plots, buy their own supplies from black-owned shops, avail of subsidized water and electricity, send their children to state schools, and generally live as citizens rather than serfs.

At Palmiet one is prompted to consider the rights of the whites – by observation, not by anything anyone says. When Charles Rennie bought this farm he was only doing his best for his family. He was willing to invest all he had in improving the land and to work hard to earn an honest living, like his son and grandson and great-grandson Michael. Other settlers may have come by their thousands of hectares more bloodily but they too worked hard. All those pioneers were ingenious and dogged, making profitable the sort of land from which the blacks, for lack of water, could never have drawn the same wealth. Granted cheap labour formed the cornerstone of white prosperity but in those days that was how the cookie crumbled all over the white-conquered world. And how it still crumbles, in too many places. Incomes in rich countries are now growing three times faster than in poor countries. GATT stands for Greater Anguish Throughout the Third World.

This afternoon, as we bird-watched, Fay commented, 'Many whites know the only solution to escalating crime lies in the upliftment of the disadvantaged – meaning higher taxation for us. But then attitudes harden when we see vast sums being squandered on gravy train excesses – or disappearing unaccountably. And it worries me how Ramaphosa tried to deflect accusations against certain prominent figures. He claimed the whistle-blowers were trying to divide the ANC – which must close ranks when leaders are accused of corruption.'

Even more worrying is GNU's foreign policy (or lack of same) being largely determined by the size of certain governmental donations – from Indonesia, Algeria, Taiwan and etc. – to the ANC's coffers.

Michael joined us then, a most engaging young man but with great sadness, and some anger, behind his eyes. This I had noticed before Fay told me the reason. A year ago, in November 1993, the Rennies' nearest neighbour – James Baxter, aged 32, one of Michael's closest friends – was murdered while on a routine milk-delivery run into the Transkei. A Zulu stopped his bakkie and shot him at point-blank range. He died instantly, leaving a widow and three small children. Months later an 'outsider' was arrested and charged; rumours abound regarding his origins and history but no one will give evidence against him.

The Baxters, like the Rennies, had long been respected as caring employers and James was an apolitical, hard-working cattle-rancher – which job demands more year-round exertion from white farmers than cane or maize growing. (Michael must dip his thousand cattle every three or four weeks in the summer. Young stock are dosed quarterly, their elders annually.)

While Fay was telling me this dreadful story in her gentle voice, I could hear the Baxter children's distant laughter as they splashed in the mini-pool; the older two are the same age as Michael's son and daughter and most afternoons they come here to play.

Such ruthless and apparently aimless killings, and the much more numerous killings of blacks by whites – what must these crimes do to race relations within the hearts and minds of the bereaved? Suddenly my appreciation of the miracle that is the new South Africa was revived. There can be little forgetting but there has been much forgiving. Mainly, it has to be said, on the black side.

18

Where Chaos Rules OK

Mount Ayliff – Umtata – Aliwal North

Paycheck embezzlement in the Transkei health department was so entrenched the
new government has had to tender an outside contractor to manage the payroll.
Phantom teachers at phantom schools were paid very real salaries. The Transkei
government defrauded itself in a bizarre scam where it charged itself illegally high
interest through its own bank.

Mark Gevisser (1996)

Mount Ayliff, Transkei, 5 December 1994

The little-used Kokstad–Palmiet track continues south over the mountains to
join the N2 near Mount Ayliff. By dawn I was on the edge of the Niemandsland
plateau with mountains close by on three sides – at first darkly bulky against a
colourless sky, then all their gullies and rock-walls and irregular crests defined
and made to glow as the light strengthened. I paused, leaning on Chris, to
watch. A long belt of saffron cloud suddenly flushed pink; moments later half the
sky was aflame and the western escarpments reflected that redness and in the
deep valley below a rosy effulgence replaced shadows.

Very slowly I freewheeled down, twice stopping to rest my wrists and bird-
watch. High dove-grey cloud defended me from the sun, plants and herbs
unknown gave off strange pungent scents. This was a long, long descent through
rugged bushy mountains, the terrain too precipitous for habitation, cultivation
or even grazing. Sweat began to flow as the cloud dispersed and on emerging
into a narrow populated valley I thought again of James Baxter. Here he was
killed.

This village extends for miles. Hundreds of round thatched huts, and scores of
tin-roofed shacks, overlook a rain-deprived river trickling between huge smooth
boulders. The women and girls fetching this filthy water in plastic basins and
buckets seemed half-scared when I greeted them. Each *umzi* (group of huts)
stands in an ample garden. On long level strips of riverside land pairs of young
men were ploughing – one leaning on the clumsy home-made wooden plough,
the other cracking a long whip and, at each turning point, chanting stylized
commands to teams of two or four magnificent oxen. Comparing their way of

life to the turmoil of the townships – predatory SDUS, frustrated Young Lions, disillusioned MKS – I thought, 'How lucky they are!'

Several older men were encouraging one or two oxen to drag odd wheelless carts – wide platforms of wood – along the bumpy track. They, too, looked somewhat apprehensive when greeted. But various friendly youths, fascinated by the mama on the bike, tried to engage me in conversation. As their mangled English was incomprehensible we settled for sign-language and to try to clarify things I unfolded my map. They, however, had never before seen a map, and were illiterate, so clarification foundered.

A reassuring calm pervades this self-sufficient village in its tucked-away valley. One senses it has retained a purposefulness unknown – impossible – in those rural slums dependent on the earnings of migrant menfolk.

At the valley's end the track swings right to ascend the arid flanks of rock-strewn mountains. Below me – farther and farther below – the wattle-lined river wound through a ravine where something lay dead or dying; vultures were gathering from all directions, gliding over the crests of the hills, their wing-movements not discernible – which gave them a macabre sort of dignity.

I stopped to eat a Fay-provided brunch below a solitary slim summit of naked grey rock – aloof and severe, towering above wide slopes offering meagre grazing to many moving dots: sheep and goats. Then a young man appeared, climbing up the nearby hillside followed by two hunting-dogs. Seeing me, he froze. Then cautiously he advanced, half-smiling – but lost his nerve, sprinted across the track and disappeared around a corner. Here was an ironic reversal of roles: in South Africa white women are supposed to be afraid of black men.

Beyond the pass the road undulated for miles between steep scrubby ridges, then coiled down and down, the temperature rising as we lost height. Arriving abruptly on the N2 motorway I got a double voltage of culture-shock – incessant speeding traffic and littered verges resembling an extended municipal rubbish tip. The noon heat was menacing and the garbage-stink revolting over the next few miles to the edge of Mount Ayliff.

In the small café of a large petrol station I drank two litres of amasi in ten minutes. Dissolute-looking youths and ragged little boys gathered around the doorway to stare at me unsmilingly. On the far side of this squalid little town, well away from the N2, stands an L-shaped colonial-era hotel. In its securely fenced garden blossom-laden shrubs seem to spout from the smooth green lawn like fountains of colour – red, purple, orange. Two sagging single beds furnish my room which became an intolerable furnace during the afternoon; its tin roof is also the ceiling.

In the grotty supermarket a surly security officer swooped on me to remove my plastic bag, holding precious objects never left in hotel rooms. I stifled my protest, realizing I was about to be racist – a white expecting *not* to be treated as a potential shoplifter. Having emptied the bag I handed it over. The officer scowled. 'Think I'm a thief? Think all blacks steal?' I looked at him helplessly, too heat-addled to come up with a soothing reply. He turned away, making some remark in Xhosa that caused great merriment among the checkout queue.

Remembering Mount Fletcher, I had been eager to revisit the Transkei. But Mount Ayliff is different. In the hotel bar – carpeted with cigarette ends, bottle tops, crisp packets – the atmosphere was not welcoming. At 3 p.m. a dozen or so scruffy men and women, already half-drunk, greeted me by demanding beers all round. When I claimed to be short of cash one elderly man lurched to the counter and appropriated my half-full bottle of Castle. Then a younger man moved to the stool beside me. 'Let's share!' said he, and took a swig from my glass. Retrieving it, I withdrew to the stoep, the preserve of the élite, where well-dressed youngish men, some with stylish briefcases between their feet, occupied a long bench. When I sat on the end my reception was cool. However, several spoke English – ungrammatical but graphic – and soon I was making progress. Two MK returnees from Uganda, very angry young men, were not at all interested in 'amalgamation' with the SANDF. If things don't quickly change, they foretold, the growling Young Lions will show their claws. 'People says justice comes but we can't see it. Where has they hid it? We know! It's hid for them and their white friends! We listen about "economic empowerment" for blacks. For what blacks? For them who make deals with white friends!' And so on...

As we talked, one of those instant-gales sprang up. Under a black sky I hastened to my room as the storm broke with a ground-shaking crash of thunder and a fusillade of hail – sharp chunks of ice – on the rusty tin roof. Then, for forty minutes, torrential rain poured through countless holes onto both beds.

Surprisingly, dinner was excellent: perfectly cooked rice, tender roast chicken cleverly herbed, runner beans, grated raw carrot, and an onion and tomato salad. I had the large, shabby, high-ceilinged dining room to myself until the waitress said, 'You are lonely' and pulled out a chair and sat beside me.

This handsome young woman ran away from a violent husband in Umtata. 'He has a good job with government and we lived nicely in a big bungalow. But after four years of it I couldn't take any more of the drinking and beating. He wouldn't let me go so I gave the kids to my mother – he didn't care about them. Then I left in the night and found work here. Now I've a good man, a policeman but kind. And next June' – she beamed – 'I'll have another baby.' Her expression hardened when I brought up the new South Africa. 'Nothing has changed,' she said. 'We wait for change, after we'll praise.'

Mount Frere, 6 December

I packed by candlelight; the hotel generator is switched off at 11 p.m. Because of the Transkei's topography I must endure motorway traffic all the way to Umtata and, despite a dramatically mountainous landscape, today's thirty miles were penitential. Where the gradients permitted, formless settlements covered every slope and valley floor. By 7 a.m. it was hot, by 8 much too hot, by 9 dangerously hot yet again. Then a long freewheel took me down to the Keneka river, a mere dribble in a wide bed. Ahead the road could be seen soaring upwards, for miles, around heat-radiating mountains.

Dismounting to drink, I noticed an unusual scene on the far side of the road. A white woman had just stopped a black motorist and was negotiating a lift for a well-dressed Coloured girl. When the car had driven on the woman noticed me and beckoned. 'Where are you going?' she shouted. 'It's too hot, be careful! Would you like tea? Come, you need to rest.'

I crossed the road and Cinder introduced herself: 'I was christened Cinderella but that's too long.' A plump effervescent young woman, she was avidly curious. 'Tell me your story, come and have tea with my friend Liz.'

As Cinder led me along a dusty track to a tumbledown bungalow I realized that she is in fact Coloured, though more fair-skinned than I am. The new black crinkly hair around her ears belied the rest – straightened, dyed auburn, pulled tightly back into a ponytail. Moreover, her purely European features are contra-dicted by distinctively African buttocks – also to be observed among certain Afrikaner women whose ancestors mated democratically. (The longer one spends in South Africa the more sensitive one becomes to these physiological nuances; not a desirable sensitivity, but inevitable.) Sadly, Cinder likes to present herself as white: there was much talk about her Irish mother, and growing up on a big farm, and her wonderful father who was related to the Duke of Kent... Well, I know nothing of the Dukes of Kent and I daresay it's possible that one contributed to the Cape's gene pool.

Behind Liz's bungalow, once a white farmer's home, decrepit outbuildings are now used by a black dealer in second-hand (or fifth-hand) cars. He and his family live in two-thirds of the dwelling; Liz, her daughter and two fatherless grandchildren occupy the rest. A fawn hunting-dog bitch, about to pup, lay panting in the shade of the stoep and languidly wagged a welcome as we approached. Liz breeds hunting-dogs, selling the pups at three months for R150 each. Later, she proudly showed me two nursing bitches in an outhouse, each with a litter of nine. These dogs are still used to hunt buck – for meat – in remote mountain areas; a pack of six or seven can bring down and kill their prey without assistance. Care is taken to keep the breed pure and recently there has been talk of applying to Crufts for recognition.

Liz is Cape Coloured and proud of it. Olive-skinned, with a shaggy head of African hair, she has a keen intelligence, a sardonic sense of humour and (like many educated Coloureds) the sort of English accent white English-speakers strive for but rarely attain. Why is such a woman living in poverty in the back of beyond? Although uninhibited when trawling for political or religious views, I can never bring myself to ask the more personal questions.

As we drank tea at a rickety table in the small kitchen a baby was being bathed in a stone sink and two cauldrons of dog food were simmering on the gas stove – lucky dogs, their lunch smelled delicious.

'If you breed you must feed,' said Liz. 'You wouldn't credit how much suckling bitches eat. I never keep accounts, my daughter says if I did I'd find I make nothing. But it's my hobby, I love those bitches and their pups, I dread the selling days . . . But they all go to people who value them. And blacks treat dogs well, even in poor families they get fair shares.'

Soon Cinder looked at her watch and jumped up; the shoe shop she manages in Mount Frere should already have been opened. Giving me a spontaneous hug she asked, 'Can you stay with us tonight? Please! My husband works in Kokstad, coming home only weekends. But I'll ring him and he'll be back this evening to meet you. He *enjoys* foreigners!'

While recycling our tea bags Liz remarked, 'I'm sorry for Cinder, she can't be happy with herself. Often I feel apartheid harmed some of us more than the blacks. In the old days her husband passed for white. She didn't – because of her hair. And no way would their son have. He's a gorgeous little boy, you'll meet him this evening, takes after an uncle in features though not quite so dark-skinned. I'm sorry for him, too. How will he ever sort out his identity, brought up by two pretend-white parents?'

I went on my way with refilled water bottles and my dripping bathing-togs (this was Liz's idea) tied around my head, protecting my neck. I shall never forget those six miles – mostly walking, though that incline should have been cycleable. Within fifteen minutes the sodden togs were bone-dry.

I was gulping amasi in the shoe shop when news came of a ghastly crash in Kokstad. Six 10-year-old pupils, on their way home from a school outing, were killed this morning when their minibus collided with a truck.

'It's those drunkards!' exclaimed Cinder. 'Even early morning they're drunk, all night they're drinking with their mates in the cabs, next day they're not fit to wheel a barrow!'

'But we don't yet know,' I protested, 'which vehicle caused the accident.'

'I know!' said Cinder. 'A drunken black caused it – a nice white teacher drove that minibus, a real gentleman, I've met him.'

Then another violent storm temporarily reduced the humidity. Within moments the steep street had become a river and when ragged blacks scuttled into the shop Cinder said, 'Watch them! Move around so they can see you're watching – if anything's stolen, I pay! A few years ago I wouldn't have them inside my door, now they've no respect for anyone.'

After the storm I explored Mount Frere, not a time-consuming exercise. These ex-'homeland' towns have a war-zone air of places abruptly abandoned to 'aliens'; thirty years ago they must have looked just like the Eastern Cape's neat, moribund dorps. Their deterioration provides much-used ammunition for whites intent on shooting down the new South Africa. Few acknowledge that the bizarre and tragic circumstances surrounding 'relocation' were not conducive to an orderly transfer of administrative power. Mount Frere's war-zone flavour is strengthened by the blackened shell of a fine town hall, in the Cape Dutch style; it was torched by the ANC (some say the PAC) during the last phase of the Struggle.

Mount Frere is built high on the side of a mountain, overlooking an array of lower hills. Many shops are 'old colonial', some arcaded. Recent developments include a bank, a car showroom, a glitzy-shoddy shopping-mall, all owned by a local black tycoon. He drives a Jaguar and his wife drives a Mercedes and their only child, a daughter, is married to a burgeoning Durban tycoon and drives a BMW. These curiously precise motor-breed details were provided by Cinder, who extolled this man's kindness and friendliness. But several blacks with whom I talked condemned him as 'no better than the whites, he does nothing for his own people, only exploits'.

Socially Mount Frere is a great improvement on Mount Ayliff. Apart from a few groups of young men who regarded me with open antagonism, most people were cheerful and chatty – though their good humour was not linked to optimism about the future. One high-school teacher forcefully expressed what others indicated more obliquely. 'We're all fucked up,' said he. 'And we'll be that way for years and years. Let me tell you something, lady – our new provincial government doesn't want us! They'd give us away – to the Free State, to Natal, to anyone fool enough to take us. You think Lebowa is bad, or Venda or Bop? Hey man – sure they're bad but not like us! You know what is anarchy? OK, so you know what we've got. At school I tell the kids, "It's over to you, you must make a new Transkei, we can't, we're all fucked up, if we're not corrupt we're intimidated." I want those kids to get politically aware but not so's to think politics is all about yourself getting rich quick. Now that's all they know about politics. Voter education, it's not enough. Why won't the ANC send good trainers to our schools to teach kids about having a conscience? I'm a religious man, I tell kids the Lord will help them make a new Transkei if they have new attitudes. Right? I go to no church, but inside myself I trust the Lord Jesus. If you live here you gotta trust in something that's someplace else or you'd give up. Maybe you think all Xhosas believe in Madiba to save us? Wrong! We love him but we don't believe he'll solve our problems. Sure, some do – but not me, I'm not stupid, right?'

Anarchy indeed! By now everything in this former 'homeland' has collapsed: health care, education, the police service, water supplies, garbage collection, the postal service, local administration at every level. And the latest Human Sciences Research Council report reckons 85 per cent of households in the Transkei and the Ciskei are living in poverty.

Five years ago Cinder and Grant moved to Sophiatown, some two miles away, where the 'kind' tycoon has jerry-built a dozen bungalows and two-storey villas. Their neighbours, occupying villas, are doctors from Ghana and Kenya attached to the government hospital. ('Very stand-offish,' commented Cinder, 'like our Indians.') A dirt road leads to Sophiatown, winding between maize-fields and patches of brown grassland where small boys herd goats and cattle and several fine horses belonging to the Kenyan.

The Ficks' five-roomed bungalow, brightly furnished from the tycoon's emporium, has a fitted bathroom and two flush lavatories but as yet nothing with which to flush them. Outside the back door stands a circular rain-depend-ent water tank, ten feet high; when it runs dry Detta must carry buckets from a muddy dam more than two miles away. Detta, the maid, is one of a family of twelve from a Pietermaritzburg township; she left school after Standard Six but speaks adequate English. I winced when Cinder, showing me around, made a point of inspecting her room in her presence: 'You have to watch them, see they sweep under the bed and so on.' These houses, built by a black in the 1980s, follow the traditional white plan and the servants' quarters are in outhouses: two tiny rooms with concrete floors.

To supplement their wages the Ficks keep hens – over 200, huddled in a dark, cramped smelly shack – and sell pullets and eggs door-to-door. A black youth, the 'poultry manager', was loudly reprimanded for some minor misdemeanour; it seems Cinder fancies this is the way to impress me – by treating servants as she doubtless imagines all white women treat them.

Soon Grant arrived: a jovial vulgarian, unsure how to relate to me and veering throughout the evening from impertinence to subservience. Conversa-tion was impeded by pop music blaring from an enormous tape-deck; simulta-neously, the TV was on full volume for Victor's entertainment. Victor, the 'gorgeous' 3-year-old, is half-spoiled, half-bullied – as are two adolescent hunting-dogs. Cherry and Sharon complete the household – Cinder's orphaned nieces, aged 18 and 20.

Grant – fleshy and florid, with deep-set grey-green eyes – sat combing his blond curls over the dining table. Then, clutching a tumbler of brandy and Coke (half and half) he turned to me. 'Those blacks, they only look civilized on the surface. They wanted to govern – OK, now they've the chance but those new MPs won't work at it. While they're paid like Oppenheimer! If I don't get to the depot on time every morning I'm fired, like *that*!' He punched his left palm with his right fist. 'Why should they be able to choose to work or not?' He leaned forward and helped himself to two of my mini-cigars, putting one behind an ear.

Then Sharon brought a large tin basin of hot water to the table for hand-washing before eating. Cherry followed with a grubby towel. Both girls are charming, good-looking and obviously Coloured. Cherry – heavily pregnant – spent most of the evening studying articles on baby-care in tattered women's magazines. She has been deserted by the father ('He was only a casual boy-friend') but this is no source of tension. The baby will be joyfully welcomed – 'Though it would be easier if I could find a job,' said Cherry. Neither sister can find work; this morning Sharon was the hitch-hiker going to Kokstad for an interview with a supermarket manager. She returned disappointed. 'These days only blacks get jobs,' said Cinder sourly.

Umtata, 7 December

As I set off in starless darkness every Sophiatown dog went berserk and the figures of several nervous householders appeared on stoeps, shining torches in our direction. I enjoyed the long pre-traffic climb out of Mount Frere, the air cool, the vast depths of the valley on my left only revealed as the road curved away from it at sunrise. The Transkei is superbly unpredictable. That climb led not to a pass but to the first of a series of high, broad ridges – all overpopulated. Probably many of the children seen here have been left with granny by young single mothers struggling for survival in urban townships where caring for a baby would be impossible. Not that these rural children have much to look forward to; some thin little faces are old – hunger-lined – some kwashiorkor bellies are grossly swollen.

In recent years the incidence of rural child-abuse has increased ominously – a very 'unAfrican' crime but normal devotion to children cannot always withstand the multiple unnatural stresses of 'homeland' life. These communities have neither land to sustain them physically nor the structures of traditional family life to sustain them spiritually and emotionally. In theory, the Bantustans were to have been self-supporting, the women farming and rearing the next generation of miners (born in September: December is the holiday month) while the men earned cash. But now three-quarters of the workforce are jobless; since 1982, the number employed in gold or coal mines has gone down by 76 per cent to about 2,500.

The Transkei's estimated population is 3.5 million – 94 per cent classified as 'rural', without access to water that would be considered 'safe' in white areas or adequate sanitation. This morning my nose confirmed that last lack. For millennia, in villages, people have been devising hygienic alternatives to a sewerage system but in overcrowded rural slums this is not feasible.

A long descent to a dry river-bed – then again up and up – then a long descent to a petrol station at a junction where I stopped for amasi. Here friendly truck drivers sympathized with mama's poverty and offered lifts. After one more brief climb the final twenty miles were downhill: the longest continuous freewheel in my fifty-three years of cycling. Between Mount Frere and here I saw not one green leaf or blade of green grass – as if the Transkei didn't have troubles enough, without a drought. When I reached Umtata soon after noon the temperature was 38°C in the shade.

The Transkei's 'capital' is a large straggling town, its commercial centre replete with the usual range of prestige skyscrapers. There is a baffling plethora of hotels: the Imperial, the Royal, the Savoy, the Protea, the Transkei, the Holiday Inn and the stately 1890s Grosvenor, which I had been advised is now the cheapest. Long and two-storeyed, painted mustard-yellow with white lacy wrought-iron balconies, it faces the brash expanse of a new Total petrol station.

I was approaching the Grosvenor when distant anger became audible. Then two young men raced towards me, pursued by a dozen others who brought their quarry to the ground almost beside me. As they crowded around the young men I hastily dragged Chris onto the pavement. The pair screamed in terror, their screams curiously like women's cries. Some of the nearby pedestrians hurried away, while groups of excited youths sprinted to the scene and urged on the attackers – one armed with a long metal rod, three wielding sjamboks. When a police van appeared, slowly driving down the centre of Owen Street, I felt a huge relief. But the two officers simply glanced at the fracas, accelerated and were gone. The screaming ceased before the attackers stood back, sweat streaming down their faces. I braced myself to see two corpses but the victims had survived, were evidently meant to survive. They lay writhing with pain, pouring blood. One of the sjambok-wielders, noticing me, stepped closer and grinned and said, 'See how we do it in Umtata? Here we don't like car-thieves!' As he spoke, four of the youths who had been revelling in the violence went to pick up the victims, stopped a passing taxi and hauled them aboard. Then a red Toyota bakkie pulled up and the smiling driver leaned out to address the attackers in Xhosa. Their spokesman turned to me and shouted, 'Lady, you listening? This guy thanks us – right? He don't want to lose his bakkie!'

As I moved on, a stout well-dressed woman trotted to overtake me. Breathlessly she said, 'Madam, excuse me – this is bad, what you have seen. This is kangaroo court punishment. Those boys – I saw it – they only fiddled with the bakkie doors. Sort of aimless – laughing, not looking like car-thieves, looking silly. This gives you a bad impression of Umtata. And you're right. We have only disorder here, no respect for laws, no justice, much fear. I want to say to you not every person is bad here. Many of us want change, hope for it, pray for it.' She paused, glanced up at me, asked, 'Why are you here with this bicycle?' When I explained she looked blank, then silently shook hands and crossed the street to enter a café.

My R50 ground-floor room – sans TV, radio and telephone, amenities I rarely use and resent paying for – is very small and very hot. The Grosvenor now has several long-term inmates, young foreign NGO workers helping (or not, as the case may be) to pull the Transkei out of its Slough of Despond. The Americans are falsely hearty with their black colleagues; the Germans show symptoms of frayed nerves ('These people, they don't know about *time!*'); the Scandinavians seem bemused but resolutely tolerant; the Dutch wear rose-tinted spectacles (they have only recently arrived) and are extremely polite to everyone. I don't envy this contingent; Umtata's population is notoriously ambiguous in its attitude to whites. And foreign whites, intent on 'straightening things out', must be anathema to the élite who for so long have had everything their own way. Not to mention their dependent followers, the 90,000 civil servants now arguing that GNU's 'no job losses' guarantee to the old South Africa's Afrikaner employees should also apply to them.

Umtata has several large banks, as befits a 'capital' where so many billions of tax-payers' rands have been swilling around for eighteen years. I went as usual to the First National Bank – said to be Barclays' associate company in the days when British customers were sensitive about apartheid. The tennis-court-sized floor was thronged, the numerous long queues resembling an army awaiting marching orders. It took me two hours and twenty minutes to complete a transaction that takes four or five minutes in any little dorp bank. Here the transaction is subdivided and I had to stand in three separate queues, always starting from the back. In one section, at this the busiest time of day, six out of ten tellers were absent: in the other section three out of four. Those on duty were farcically incompetent, vaguely messing about with photocopiers and computers and customers' bank-books and ID-books and chequebooks, repeatedly getting something wrong and having to do it all over again. Corruption may not be entirely to blame for those missing billions referred to in a recent report by the Auditor General. I surveyed the silent, docile crowd with astonishment; they seemed to regard this outrageous situation as normal.

'Where are all the other tellers?' I asked the pinstriped young man in front of me.

He looked puzzled, then said, 'They must take it in turns to rest.'

I felt myself becoming acidly Eurocentric. 'To *rest*? But these are their *working* hours!'

The young man gestured dismissively. 'Here is Umtata, we have other working habits.' And pointedly he turned away.

A middle-aged woman in the adjacent queue touched my arm and half-whispered, 'You are right, we should complain. But here we have given up complaining so nothing is properly conducted. And you are thinking we seem like fools – am I right?'

I smiled. 'Wrong! I am thinking you seem like victims!'

In the Protea Hotel bar I paid R8 instead of R3 for a Castle: my fee, as it were, for the privilege of observing Umtata's élite in relaxation mode. The bar sported a novel floor-covering widely advertised in South Africa: 'Genuine Oriental Carpets, Guaranteed Made in Britain.' A cut-glass chandelier glittered above animated groups sitting in low red-plush armchairs around glass-topped tables with gilded bow legs. The women's clothes showed taste as well as money; they had purple lips and nails, loud laughs, gold earrings and bracelets, fingers laden with bulky zirconia rings. The men wore dark suits, flamboyant ties, pointed shoes and Rolex watches; some played compulsively with lap-top computers. Everyone was drinking 'shorts' and nibbling cocktail snacks. Sitting alone at the bar, I briefly considered trying to ingratiate myself with this ruling class. But I am improperly attired, my arrival had drawn glances of incredulous disdain.

I was about to seek a more congenial area of operations when Nkane appeared, a 'smart-casual' young man who shyly responded to my smile and sat on the next stool but one. He is a 25-year-old UCT student (chemical engineering) from the nearby village of Centuri, now on vacation and finding his domestic scene hard to take after the bright lights of Cape Town. 'That's why I come in here, life feels too poor in the village – and today too hot, with so much *dust*!'

Two beers later Nkane allowed himself to grieve over his close friend, a Fort Hare University student, who died last week. He was an *abakhweta*, which had to be translated for me. It means a Xhosa undergoing initiation to manhood through circumcision, following a period of isolation – with fellow-initiates – in the bush. Nkane's friend was one of four local *abakhweta* who have died within the past six weeks.

'It's part of our confusion now,' said Nkane. 'We are educated not to drink dirty water but the *abakhweta*, during their alone time, have only very dirty water to drink. My friend, he tried not to drink and in this terrible heat got kidney failure and died. The same with the others. It's not possible to have your new ideas about health and our old ideas. If my friend drank dirty water he would be here with me today. Maybe he would have some small problem with his stomach but he would be alive. In my village everyone drinks dirty water. There is no other water. But this year, because of the drought, the only water for the *abakhweta* was *very* muddy – with a smell. So the well-educated wouldn't drink it. All who died were university students. The uneducated drank and were safe.'

Nkane is alarmingly thin and his dry little cough, he admitted, keeps him awake 'half the night'. Last term he had pneumonia twice. Yes, he knows all about AIDS and since the elections condoms have been distributed free at UCT. But, 'You forget all you know when you're young and meet a beautiful girl. That's natural. AIDS education can't make people behave against nature. And I never heard of AIDS seven, eight years ago when I needed many girls.'

Nkane knew that I knew he was dying.

This evening's meal in the Grosvenor restaurant was singularly repulsive. Very tough, dry roast 'lamb', grey greasy potatoes – the grease indicating a thwarted intention to roast them – and slimy red and green heaps that proved on investigation to be carrots and beans boiled to destruction. It is unprecedented for me to walk away from a meal costing good money but I did walk away from this, feeling queasy. Was the heat partly responsible? One slow-motion ceiling-fan in a large dining room does nothing to help when the temperature is nearing 40°C. Even now, at 9.30 p.m., it remains so hot that I must write with a towel under my forearm to protect the paper.

The same, 8 December

At 5 a.m. it was walkabout time. I roused the nightwatchman, sleeping on a black horsehair couch in Reception with his woolly cap pulled over his face. Blearily he released me into the humid dawn air, then woke up some more and called after me, 'Madam, take care! We have bad men everywhere!'

I didn't have to walk far; the Grosvenor forms part of old Umtata. In 1877 the Anglicans established a mission station here and five years later the town was founded. In the 1990s the Anglican cathedral, dark grey and stern, seems to have strayed far from home. The nearby town hall (1907) speaks of confounded imperial certainties and the formally laid out Town Hall Gardens, now smothered in litter, have fine wrought-iron gates, a memorial to Major Sir Henry G. Elliot, Chief Magistrate from 1877 to 1902. Elliot was a benevolent despot so appreciated by the 'natives' that they collected over £1,000 – then a vast sum – and presented it to him on his retirement. With it he endowed 'native' wards in Umtata's hospital, which provided a much better service then than now.

Around the next corner stands Umtata's architectural *pièce de résistance*, the Bunga Hall, its classical façade designed to remind the 'natives' – or so legend has it – that democracy came from Greece. Once it served as a pretend parliament where the territory's twenty-seven British magistrates met annually with the Xhosa chiefs to discuss regional affairs for sixteen days. The chiefs' collective opinions/advice/requests were then conveyed by the Minister for Native Affairs to the Parliament in Cape Town. Soon the Bunga Hall may be used again by the chiefs (the *amakhosi*, now known as 'Traditional Leaders') if they get their way in negotiations with GNU. The Congress of Traditional Leaders of South Africa (Contralesa, founded in the late 1980s, backed by Winnie Mandela) is agitating for the establishment of Houses of Traditional Leaders in six of the nine provinces.

In June '93 I discussed with an ANC Big Man the awkward fact that the chiefs' claims and the claims of a democracy are irreconcilable. No amount of constitutional juggling, however deft, can give equal legitimacy to their standards, methods and attitudes and a Western-style Bill of Rights. I suggested then, 'The new government will be calling the bluff of the white right-wingers – why not let it be seen that you are dealing even-handedly with anti-democratic elements on both sides?'

'Speaking personally,' said the Big Man, 'I completely agree with you. *But...*'

The intervening eighteen months have taught me a lot about those 'buts'. They are legion. For instance, if your Bill of Rights guarantees 'freedom of religion', how can you reduce chiefs to the status of ordinary citizens when their role, in the lives of millions, is intertwined with certain African religious beliefs that have survived – by courtesy of a super-fudge – alongside conversion to various brands of Christianity? In theory it should be possible to respect the *amakhosi*'s ceremonial religious role while depriving them of all political power. But not in practice, not in a context where those two exercises of power are seen as indivisible.

Most senior ANC leaders and activists have little time for the *amakhosi*. They want to get on with the job of transforming their country into a modern state untrammelled by witchcraft, sexism and too much fuss about the ancestors. But they know, though it is not PC to say so aloud, that they are in a minority. Urbanized township dwellers may have shed their loyalty to individual chiefs yet much respect remains for old customs – and much fear of the consequences of disregarding them. In the new squatter camps migrants from ex-homeland' areas on the whole remain loyal to their chiefs, a more comprehensible source of authority than MPs elected to a puzzling parliament. Recently the *amakhosi* have provoked unrest in several rural districts and, through Contralesa, have formally threatened to spread that unrest should the need, as they perceive it, arise. Chief Buthelezi asserts, 'There can be no peace in Africa unless tribes are allowed to uphold their traditions and culture.' A plausible enough argument: elsewhere in Africa I have met many who favour a return to customary law – having suffered so much, since independence, from the failure of imported systems. But this country doesn't quite fit in with the rest of Africa.

By way of controlling 'native territories', the British saw to it that the chiefs and their headmen lieutenants prospered. Confident of white support, many chiefs then bullied their followers unmercifully – which abuse of power has to some extent weakened their present position. But not enough to make it safe for GNU to defy them. The Constitution therefore protects chiefly stipends, an ad hoc manoeuvre that has left impoverished provincial governments committed to paying out many millions annually – to Zulu chiefs (not members of Contralesa) as well as the rest. (The five Transkei Paramount Chiefs will each receive £58,000 p.a.) In return, these *amakhosi* hold an occasional *imbizo*, a jolly get-together with their followers during which an ox is slaughtered and eaten and much beer imbibed. Work of any description is not on the *imbizo* agenda and villagers pay for the party. In reaction to this constitutional concession, new MPs may be heard indignantly complaining that they earn 'only' R154,000 per annum (£30,800). Some also argue that such generosity to the *amakhosi* is sending the wrong message to all South Africa's citizens: 'If you've got a problem, buy your way out.'

Last evening I rang my four Umtata contacts: an ANC community leader, a school principal, a woman lawyer and Mr Ngozwana – described to me by our mutual friend as 'a returnee with a difference!' The community leader was in jail and the teacher in hospital but Mrs Mngomyana, the lawyer, invited me to her home this evening and Mr Ngozwana came to the Grosvenor this morning.

A remarkable man, Mr Ngozwana: tall and lean and grey-haired, wearing a vividly patterned shirt à la Madiba and green cotton slacks and leather sandals. In 1992 he returned from a twenty-six-year exile in Moscow, Lusaka, London. We settled down in the pleasant wood-panelled lounge, furnished with worn leather armchairs and long stinkwood coffee tables. The Grosvenor is barless; drinks are brought to guests (only) by slow-moving Xhosa waitresses. Mr Ngozwana ordered tea – 'In Moscow I became an alcoholic, too much tension and vodka, a bad combination. In Lusaka I became a teetotaller.' We had the lounge to ourselves and it is a TV-free zone. I like the Grosvenor, despite its chef.

Mr Ngozwana, I already knew, is a scion of one of the Transkei's chiefly houses but exile has modified his traditional allegiances. He believes any attempt to power-share at local level with the *amakhosi* must lead to disaster.

Since the elections, this province has been plagued by rivalry between SANCO, Contralesa and the Eastern Cape government. ('The battle is for power and money – nothing original!') In July a bloody confrontation followed the taking over by SANCO members of the *amakhosi* office near Herschel. Soon after, another squad of SANCO thugs kidnapped a headman in the Nqamakwe district and interrogated him ('you know that usually means "tortured"?') for twelve hours. His wife and children were then intimidated out of the area. In September Chief Zamodla Ndamase was badly beaten up and a fortnight ago two headmen shot dead two SANCO members. (SANCO, formed during the 'make South Africa ungovernable' campaign, has in some areas become a grievous embarrassment to the ANC.)

'After returning I lived in Katlehong for a few months,' said Mr Ngozwana. 'I like to find things out for myself, not just reading reports. But this South Africa of '92, down on the ground – it was not the country I left. We have paid a terrible price for success. I don't want to exaggerate, most of our people remain sound. But the baddies – yoh-yoh, they are *very* bad! And powerful. People who can kill their neighbours casually, like swatting a fly, are very powerful. They don't have to be many to dominate. Some say our biggest problem is education. I disagree. Our biggest problem is lawlessness. A democracy can't work without respect-worthy laws and a population that knows the State will enforce them. Now we do have respectworthy laws but no matching police force.' He paused before adding, 'I'm just an observer in my old age, resting in my own place and watching. In exile I studied and worked for liberation. But I'm not sure I was working for *this*.' (He studied comparative religion at London University – 'I thought that might be useful for understanding my own country. Here religious beliefs are very relevant, in all sorts of indirect ways.')

Mr Ngozwana peered into his empty teapot, said 'Excuse me' and went to find a waitress. Ten minutes later he returned. 'They were in the basement, playing with their boyfriends. It's only a harmless aspect of lawlessness.' Then he asked rhetorically, 'Have I been too negative? Actually by nature I'm positive. I believe our new South Africa can work. You know, I like the English language – its nuances. *Can* work doesn't mean *will* work. It can work if we don't try to dodge the challenges. The Struggle wasn't only about overthrowing apartheid. We were struggling *for* something, we had ideals. Now we must avoid making do with a modification of white supremacy. We've taken on a sick, psychotic society – my wife says I was an idiot to stay in Katlehong. She says it unbalanced me and she could be right. *Seeing* the necklacing and so many other cruelties . . . *Smelling* the roasting bodies – alive bodies roasting, necklacing wasn't a quick death. And children enjoying the spectacle, thinking it was fun . . . Then I did almost lose faith in our future, watching children laughing and clapping and dancing around the victims. Was I overreacting? Could you *over*react to such a thing?'

In response I told Mr Ngozwana about the English badger-baiting cult – men enjoying the reality and later on gathering to watch, over and over again, videos of that same sickening scene. And I told him about a new 'fashion' among some depraved Irish children; light a bonfire, find a cat with a litter, throw the kittens into the flames and watch the mother burn to death as she tries to rescue her young. Granted, badgers and cats are not human beings. But, given the town-ships' political/emotional ambience, those badger-baiters and cat-roasters would surely regard a necklacing as entertainment.

Mr Ngozwana shuddered. 'That's even sicker – coming from within them-selves, nothing to do with ambience.'

We fell silent for a little, then talked of cheerful things. Like the considerable achievements of Kader Asmal as Minister for Water and Forestry and of Derek Hanekom as Minister for Land Affairs. And the fact that certain cabinet ministers, who wish to remain anonymous, donate all their salaries to self-help township projects. 'This secretiveness I can understand and admire,' said Mr Ngozwana, 'but it's a mistake. Our people need to know some of their leaders boycott the gravy train.'

At sunset I crossed the narrow, winding Mthatha river, brown and sluggish but lined with pale green gracefully drooping willows – their greenness a refreshment, here and now. Cascades of litter pour down the high banks and bright wild flowers peep out from under a cloak of tins, cartons, takeaway boxes and plastic bags and bottles.

Uphill from the Mthatha, some of Umtata's middle class (the less wealthy) live in colonial bungalows, almost all well maintained. I found Somikazi Mngomyana playing with her 4-year-old son on a vine-draped stoep. Somikazi is a young widow – 'Three years ago my husband was killed in mysterious circumstances.' She lives with Nona, her unmarried doctor sister, and Freddy, a rather dour businessman brother whose wife speaks no English and therefore didn't join us. Sitting on the lamplit stoep, surrounded by hot darkness, we could see Umtata's street lights twinkling dimly between the shrubs – until suddenly they went out. 'Here we don't even pretend to be First World,' observed Freddy.

Nona's attractive oval face – dainty, almost childlike under a high mass of hair – looked haggard with exhaustion. She admitted to being 'stressed out' and Somikazi explained, 'The Transkei's doctor–people ratio is 1 to 30,000.'

'That wouldn't matter,' said Nona, 'if we could function. We can't *do* anything in our hospital. For a week past we've had no supplies because we owe suppliers more than quarter of a million rands. As we speak, people are dying from neglect in intensive care. We've no working phones or X-ray machines, no ambulances. We've patients with typhoid, meningitis, hepatitis-B all stuffed into the same ward and the ceiling falling down on their beds. Our nurses, paid half-nothing, often use their own money on aspirin to try to save babies with fevers. Three years ago the Blood Transfusion Service gave up taking donations here – so much was HIV-positive. But still the Education Department wouldn't help us set up AIDS education in schools.'

'But now,' said Freddy, 'the holiday season is coming. We'll have thousands driving through, whites who might have an accident in the Transkei. So the *army* is being sent to our hospitals with reliable drugs and trained staff – "emergency relief" they call it. And they want us to believe this is a new South Africa! Who are they trying to kid?'

Dinner was served by a gargantuan maid who had to turn sideways to get through the kitchen doorway. She was very excited to meet me because her taxi-driver son had noticed the cycling mama near Mount Ayliff. 'Hey, it is too dangerous! May our loving Lord Jesus protect you!'

As we helped ourselves to mashed potatoes ('because you're Irish') and mildly curried beef, Nona admitted – 'To be honest, I'm on the edge of quitting this place.'

'Me too,' said Somikazi. 'And let them get on with their mob law and stock theft and police-force mutinies.'

Since 1990 stock theft has been a well-organized trade here, as in parts of the Transvaal. Certain wealthy chiefs, their names known to all, employ armed gangs to steal villagers' cattle. These are bought by whites who truck them to the PWV for sale to hostel dwellers. A percentage of the profits go to the police who terrorize any villagers rash enough to seek justice through official channels. Hence the popular support for mob justice. Last year more than one hundred men, mostly stock-theft suspects, were sentenced to death by 'people's courts'. 'And this year we've had even more executions,' said Somikazi.

Nona, I noticed, was eating little. Suddenly she turned to me and asked, 'Are we being too impatient? Our first democratic government, it doesn't have a magic wand.'

'But maybe,' I said, 'it needs to feel the pressure of an impatient public. Maybe South Africa's blacks have been too patient for too long.'

The same, 9 December

Today's weather forecast included a health warning so I took off at dawn, by taxi, for Madiba's birthplace – Qunu, twenty miles to the south. In the over-crowded kombi many heads turned as we passed Umtata's latest development, opened three days ago. Shell Ultra City is conspicuous from afar on the flat fawn veld, its garish lettering and consumerist glitter seeming to taunt the locals' destitution.

Soon the University of Transkei appeared below road-level – another visual horror, perpetrated in 1976, and another academic disaster. But the threadbare young man beside me pointed it out with pride.

As we crossed undulating grassless pasture bony donkeys laden with jerry-cans and women carrying buckets on their heads were walking slowly home in knee-high clouds of dust. The young man smiled at me and said, 'Next year we will have piped water, clean and coming from taps!'

Qunu is no longer a traditional village but one of a series of straggling settlements. The driver dropped me off opposite Madiba's private retirement home, a red-brick bungalow built in 1992, standing alone on the veld. The casual passer-by wouldn't give it a second glance; it resembles the homes of countless middle-income whites. Nothing indicates its owner's identity – until, as you approach, two policemen emerge from a gateway in the eight-foot brick wall. Agreeable policemen, pleased to have this break in the monotony of guarding an empty house – 'Sometimes Madiba comes here to rest but he has little resting in his life.' Proudly they told me the Eastern Cape government has plans to put Qunu on the tourist map 'as part of an "In the Footsteps of the President" initiative'. Then they allowed me to wander around the paved forecourt and little garden where a few adolescent shrubs struggle against the drought. If I wanted to take photographs, that would be R5 per shot...

Strolling across the veld, I was moved to think of Nelson Rolihlala Mandela, who could have built his home in any of South Africa's famed beauty spots, wanting to end where he began – his only neighbours the 'surplus' people of Qunu.

When I turned towards the nearest settlement, one of the policemen pursued me. 'Not to walk here!' he ordered. 'Is not safe, please go home.' He escorted me to the roadside and said, 'We wait, I get you safe taxi.'

Moments later, as I signalled an approaching kombi, he caught my hand and lowered it. 'This one not good, wait more, be patient.'

'Why are you so worried?' I asked.

'Too much crime,' came the succinct reply. But I intuited something more; traces of pre-election-type tension linger around Umtata. A year ago five APLA activists were shot dead here when the SADF raided their local base and Whitey is rarely smiled upon.

Back in Umtata, even the locals were wilting; by noon the temperature was 42°C and the streets were deserted. Near the taxi terminus I noticed an inscription in black letters two feet high on a white wall: KILL A WHITE A DAY VIVA PAC APLA. Someone had tried to erase 'WHITE' but it remained legible. This wall happens to be the gable-end of a handsome old building in which the Tourist Board has its office. Presenting myself there, I suggested that it might be a good idea, in the interests of tourism, thoroughly to obliterate this whole exhortation. Point not taken.

The four youngish women staffing this office seemed to regard me as a tiresome distraction from whatever they do when unbothered by tourists – which is 99 per cent of the time. Under pressure one woman grumpily rummaged through a drawer to find a glossy brochure promoting the Wild Coast, one of South Africa's most famous natural glories – soon to be despoiled by a motorway, if the provincial government's dreams come true. Then I was more or less dismissed – the door held open for me to leave.

Across the road I fared even worse in the two-roomed cobwebby Transkei National Museum. The curator exuded hostility and sat smoking in his office with his feet on the desk ignoring all my questions as I viewed waxwork figures displaying tribal beadwork and headdresses. Recently this museum has been hastily rearranged to emphasize, through newspaper cuttings and photographs, the historic Eastern Cape/ANC links. Sepia studio photographs showed the earliest generation of academically successful Xhosa dressed as Victorian gentlemen, precisely placed between classical pillars – their demeanour grave and elderly, even when captions recorded their youth. Several clergymen – standing or sitting stiffly, looking awed by their own achievement – reverently rested long-fingered hands on large bibles.

The Xhosa were the first tribe to be baptized and mission-educated in bulk. When Madiba was born in 1918 the only way forward, for intelligent ambitious young blacks, was along the road of white thinking. This led to the 1955 Freedom Charter, a document inspired by Western values imbibed at the mission schools and universities. The ANC-led Struggle was never black versus white. It was a crusade to establish a European-style democracy.

In the Department of Health, visibly overstaffed, my queries about the Transkei's six AIDS-prevention organizations provoked angry rudeness. (Do these organizations really exist? I find it hard to believe in them.) In the Department of Agriculture sullen silences followed my queries about the scandal-stained Qamata and Ncora Irrigation Schemes, supposedly 'valuable community-development projects'. I then withdrew to the National Library of the Transkei; most of its stock was donated in times past by homebound colonial officials. The five dozy pseudo-librarians stared at me as though I were a spectre and during my hours of browsing nobody else entered the building. However, in 1994 one must make allowances; these sinecure jobs are doomed and the Transkei's (un)civil servants know it. One can't fairly blame them, as individuals, for their present idle lifestyle. They, too, were 'surplus people', left with no choice but to become parasites on a puppet government.

Engcobo, 10 December

At 4 a.m. many blanketed bodies lay on Umtata's pavements. Some were hawkers, their boxed goods piled between themselves and the wall; daily taxi fares home would devour their profits. Others were beggars, of whom an uncommon number, mostly male, congregate around Umtata. Last evening an SACP leader told me why. During the NUM-led strikes of the 1980s, Transkeians were renowned for their militancy. After the 1987 strike the AAC referred to them contemptuously as 'Mandela's children' and leaned on the Chamber of Mines to reduce recruitment from here and hire more Zulus. (Zulu peasants, conditioned to obey chiefs meekly, are much less politically aware than Xhosas.) As some 90 per cent of employed Transkeians were on contract to the mines, their 'homeland' rulers panicked and ran an expensive anti-union propaganda campaign. Also delegations hastened from Umtata to Jo'burg to beg the Chamber not to limit recruitment. But limited it was and now 'Mandela's children' are suffering the consequences.

Today was cloudy and cool, with quite heavy traffic on my main-ish road to the Free State. For fifty miles I was never out of sight of shacks. From one, a ragged old man hurried to the road as I pedalled slowly uphill and offered me R1.50 – 'Mama, buy some food, you are hungry!' Small herds of dejected-looking cattle pulled at the short wiry brown grass; one could see little puffs of dust as they uprooted clumps. Every roadside bus-shelter has been vandalized, roofs and seats removed. And each bears an inscription in red or green letters three feet high: APLA KILLS WHITES or HIT THEM HARD APLA or BEST SETTLER DEAD SETTLER. How quickly some things have changed! According to yesterday's paper, the PAC/APLA leadership 'sees no further need for violence' and has launched a campaign to recruit white members.

At noon I crossed a red rocky mountain, then sped down and around green forested slopes marking a new 'climate zone'. Once Engcobo was a busy commercial and administrative centre, the seat of a magistrate, the social centre for rich white farmers. Now it is forlorn: the colonnaded shops unpainted, the main street potholed, the gutters rubbish-blocked, the Royal Hotel closed, the jobless conspicuous – scores of young people hanging about, apathetic and malnourished, wearing those often incongruous second-hand garments imported from the First World and sold throughout Africa. But here, unusually, many older women wear what is known as 'traditional dress' – in fact a missionary-imposed fashion, long skirts and high-collared bodices. The only genuinely traditional item is a piled headdress, like a small blanket worn turban-wise.

On the edge of the town, down a rough track, the Ulundi Motel looks onto a small field where cattle and ponies graze. In lieu of electricity and plumbing a candle in a beer-bottle lights my room and a ewer and basin are provided – prettily painted with bouquets of violets and made in Nottingham, England. Sometimes I wish inanimate objects could tell their stories. The outdoor Ladies and Gents have WCs where the w stands ready in a bucket – always immediately refilled by a bouncy young maid who giggles whenever she sees me.

Having locked Chris to my bed I wandered through dense indigenous forest, lively with unfamiliar birdlife, then crossed a stream and climbed for miles to fertile uplands – maize-fields and well-watered pastures. Three formerly white homesteads now house several families each – judging by the juvenile population – and are in a sad state of disrepair. Where the track petered out I was on the edge of a deep ravine, its vegetation lush, with a range of sheer green-cloaked mountains beyond. 'Relocation' also punished whites; the farmers moved from here must have felt like Adam and Eve turned out of Paradise.

Engcobo's colonial suburbs, shaded by 'settler trees' – magnificent limes and horse-chestnuts – are now slum-like. The middle class enjoy a small new suburb of identical, brightly painted, neat little houses on a wooded slope. Here I met Bongiwe Ngumbela (most Transkeians choose to use their African names) and was mistaken for an NGO rep. Could I donate funding to complete the nursery school? Bongiwe is one of three teachers coping with eighty-five 3-to-6-year-olds (fee: R50 per annum) in what used to be the white primary school catering for thirty children. She led me across wasteland where cattle grazed and goats tore strips of bark from sycamore saplings. The half-built school has three classrooms, a teachers' common room, a row of lavatories, a 'lie-down room for tired little ones' – all roofless. In the four years since Umtata's funding was cut off, vigorous weeds have cracked walls and floors.

Bongiwe lives in two minuscule rooms – an outbuilding previously used by the white school's caretaker. She is soon to do her finals for a University of South Africa (UNISA) arts degree. Pumping a Primus stove to make coffee she said, 'I want to be properly qualified, not to get a good city job but to give our kids here the best start. They must have nursery education to prepare for a European curriculum. I don't agree about making the curriculum more Afro-centric – that's crazy, our kids must compete with whites.'

Then Bongiwe showed off her bedroom; a double bed, draped in a frilly rose-pink nylon counterpane, took up most of the floor space. Opposite hung a portrait photograph of a Xhosa Adonis. 'My fiancé,' smiled Bongiwe. 'But he has a lobola problem. He's a teacher too, poorly paid. And our families are old-fashioned, there must be lobola. In cities modern young couples can make their own arrangements.'

It began to rain as I returned to the hotel, the sort of gentle, persistent rain that gladdens farmers' hearts. I found the dingy, sparsely furnished bar surprisingly crowded; local ANC members had assembled to discuss their future relationship with the reformed non-violent PAC and how best to defeat stock thieves.

Barkly Pass, 11 December

The day before yesterday, in Umtata, I had to endure 42°C in the shade. This morning, as I climbed for an hour from Engcobo, I had to endure a thick freezing fog. Where the road at last levelled out I could only try to imagine what must lie on either side of this high saddle; yet again, South Africa's fickle climate was discriminating against me.

During the descent, heavy cold rain replaced the fog. Beyond a shallow valley on my left rose overgrazed hills, deeply grooved by cattle-tracks. Broken gates marked the entrances to formerly white farms but now this area – a buffer-zone between the Transkei and the old Cape Province – is unpeopled. At the junction with a wider, smoother road the sky cleared; freewheeling down to Elliot I soon thawed and dried out.

At Elliot begins the thirteen-mile ascent to Barkly Pass's solitary hotel. Here are harsh angular mountains, streaked red and ochre, all loose slabs and boulders and dramatic escarpments bristling with scrub. Ahead rose sharp peaks, but halfway up these disappeared as pale clouds rolled towards me. Moments later it was snowing. 'This,' I thought, 'is unreal.' However, those fine white particles were so real that I arrived here wearing an icy helmet.

Having rethawed in my bath, I joined two young off-duty police officers sitting by a cheery log fire in the bar. Astonishingly, the English-speaker remembered seeing me last year on the road from Elliot to Maclear.

His Afrikaner companion is quitting the force next week to start work with a Bloemfontein car-dealer. 'It's my wife,' he explained defensively. 'Barring Natal, political violence is over. But the criminals are running wild, we've had 203 officers murdered since January. My wife can't take it, every time I leave the house she looks like crying – and now there's a baby on the way...'

Aliwal North, 12 December

My cycle tours of South Africa seem destined to end abruptly. Actually this one could have ended bloodily; I was lucky today.

At dawn, Barkly Pass wore a thin white mantle and small untidy clouds drifted between the jagged rock peaks. Soon a steady gale-force wind was behind me, the sort that propels you *uphill*. On the traffic-free road to New England, through an almost unpopulated region, the colours and contours were ever-changing in brilliant sunshine and each turning revealed something unexpected – an isolated misshapen mountain, an awesome chasm directly below the verge, a distant range of symmetrical serrated peaks like silver battlements along the horizon.

From this plateau the descent is very long and very steep. Then comes the Free State's flatness: a semi-desert landscape, its thornbushes, cacti and aloes quivering in the heat. Despite the gale, the temperature here was menacing. As we passed the '16 km' marker (ten miles from Aliwal North), I calculated that we had covered exactly 100 miles in eleven and a quarter hours.

Moments later Chris's back tyre burst. Had this happened on the descent, at a speed of some 35 m.p.h., I would now be in an intensive-care unit – or perhaps a coffin. Contemplating my good fortune I plodded on, feeling heat-sick. I had resolved to seek succour in a farmhouse, should one appear, when an elderly Boer who spoke no English offered a lift in his bakkie and dropped me outside the Balmoral Hotel.

A shocking fact then emerged. In Aliwal North on the Sabbath there is no source of beer. The Drankwinkels and the hotel bar remain closed all day. Despair threatened – but I held it at bay. Even in Aliwal North there must surely be a corner where the local dominees are defied.

I bathed and changed, then walked three miles to the golf club – well sign-posted, as golf clubs usually are. Ominously, no cars were parked nearby and the only person visible greeted me with a scowl. He was the nastiest sort of Afrikaner and when nasty they're very nasty. No one plays golf on the Sabbath nor does the club bar open. And even if it did, he added venomously, I couldn't use it. It is 'Members Only' and for security reasons this is a strict rule . . . It seems Aliwal North has not yet arrived in the new South Africa.

By my count, seven denominations cater for the spiritual needs of this pious dorp and the place only came to life at 5.50 p.m. when Sabbath-smart families piled into their cars and zoomed off in seven different directions.

I ended up drinking tea with geriatric Irish nuns well to the right of ET. It seems blacks are lesser beings, though redeemable if turned into Catholics cast in the Irish mould – or what was the Irish mould sixty years ago, when these ladies left home.

Just now I have sadly come to a sensible decision: to sell Chris here instead of in Bloemfontein. For one thing, a new tyre would cost R65. For another, in this heat the 140 miles to Bloemfontein, via Wepenet, would be an endurance test rather than a pleasure. Yet I know I'll feel desolately incomplete tomorrow. For three months, over 2,140 miles, Chris and I have been a team.

19

What's Wrong with Bloemfontein?

Bloemfontein – Botshebelo

The year is 1846. The city of Bloemfontein is founded. Between 1848 and 1899 farmers of the Orange Free State are continually at war with the Basutos or the British.
Henry Gibbs, Twilight in South Africa *(1949)*

Bloemfontein, 15 December 1994

Albert van Jaarsveld gave me an introduction to Sue and Maurice and on arrival I discovered that Maurice and Margaret are also old friends. (The white population of South Africa is little more than the population of Ireland, where every other stranger you meet knows someone who knows your cousin/brother-in-law/grandmother/aunt-by-marriage.) Maurice is an English-speaker, Sue a Cape Afrikaner. They have two lovable teenage daughters and three lovable dogs and seem very positive, though not at all starry-eyed, about the new South Africa. For many years both have been in close touch, through their work, with a cross-section of black society and they have made me wonder if perhaps I am too sceptical an observer, too anxious about the hazards ahead and not sufficiently appreciative of what has already been achieved.

During the past three days I have become quite fond of Bloemfontein – ringed by flat-topped koppies, small enough for everywhere to be accessible on foot, the traffic light by urban standards, the atmosphere agreeably laid-back, the natives of all pigmentations friendly. Yet the mere mention of this city makes most South Africans groan and say, 'D'you *really* want to go there?'

This prejudice is not unfounded. Bloemfontein is (was?) the Vatican of the DRC, where until quite recently dancing was forbidden on the Sabbath and no such thing as a ladies bar existed because women were supposed not to drink. However, despite its ultra-conservative past Bloemfontein – and the Free State in general – is now being acclaimed as a model of adaptability to the new South Africa.

In this provincial legislature, twenty-four of the thirty elected representatives are ANC, including two Afrikaners. Four Nat men, and a man and woman from the right-wing Freedom Front, make up the opposition. During the legislature's first session, the Freedom Front leader thanked Premier Patrick Lekota in

English for so often using Afrikaans in his public speeches. (The Free State's Hansard records are to be kept in Sesotho, Afrikaans and English. Members are also free to debate in Tswana, Zulu and Xhosa.) Among these supposedly hardline 'Staters' their black premier's organizational abilities are much praised, as are his quick intelligence, warm heart and sense of fair play.

Some say Bloemfontein was South Africa's most beautiful city before the developers got at it. In 1986 the controversial Sand du Plessis Theatre was completed at a cost of R60 million – 'one of the most modern theatres in the world', claims the Tourist Board. Anywhere its soaring shiny vulgarity would be repellent. Here, at the very heart of gracious, dignified, mellow Bloemfontein, it is unforgivable. Not far away looms the Provincial Administration's twenty-six-storey Swart building. 'The pride of the Free State', say the tourist folk. An affront to the Ionic columns of the nearby Raadzaal, say I.

Even in Bloemfontein, most employers seem to be taking affirmative action seriously, if only because the new South Africa doesn't leave them much choice. During the past few months I have found myself dealing more and more often – on trains, in hotels and banks, at supermarket checkouts – with ill-trained blacks whose hasty hiring or promotion, and minimal English, can lead to countless trivial but tiresome errors, misunderstandings and delays. Whereupon the average white exclaims, 'I told you so!' Affirmative action is often the first change to affect individuals personally and, as it gains momentum, it is testing white acceptance of the new regime. The sharing of scarce jobs calls for a much more strenuous feat of adjustment than constitutional change, however cataclysmic.

Bewilderingly, a fragment of Bophuthatswana was to be found thirty-two miles east of Bloemfontein, despite this being Sotho country. Botshebelo is South Africa's second largest township (after Soweto) with a guesstimated population of 250,000. In 1979, 38,000 Thaba'Nchu Sothos were forced to settle on a godforsaken expanse of semi-desert at the foot of low bare hills. Soon after, they were joined by more and more labour tenants – evicted from their homes as mechanization rendered them 'surplus' – and by countless thousands from 'deproclaimed townships'. (The language of apartheid had a flavour all its own.)

At dawn yesterday I set off on a day-trip to Botshebelo, walking to the city centre's chaotic taxi terminus where three kindly men found me a Botshebelo minibus – battered but not overcrowded. This year I notice SAPS daring to be strict about overloading and random checks are common, with on-the-spot fines. Pre-elections, any such police intervention would have been likely to start a riot; now it is resented but accepted.

Directly behind me sat a male figure of indeterminate age, a small man lacking a left arm, his right hand distorted and burned, his face like a mask in a horror film – the nose missing, the left eye a blind bloody mess, the skin shiny pink and taut, the forehead smashed in, the teeth few and decayed in a twisted, permanently open mouth.

'A mining accident,' explained Vax, the young man beside me. After the minimum of hospital treatment this pitiable ruin was dispatched to Botshebelo to become his family's responsibility. The mining bosses, Vax believed, would have preferred him to die; they don't like victims in his condition being on view to the public.

Vax offered to introduce me to his uncle, Ngoako, an ANC community leader. 'He talk fine English and give you big information.' In the Free State blacks speak Afrikaans rather than English, perhaps as their third or fourth language. Most blacks are linguistically gifted (one notices this throughout Africa) and often speak several complex languages fluently. No wonder they regard my monolingual status as a sort of congenital handicap – which indeed it is.

Botshebelo is short of everything except space; the land being valueless, its seventeen 'sections' cover a vast area. As we turned off the main road, Vax pointed out the Botshebelo Stadium, recently made famous when the Housing Minister, Joe Slovo, held a Housing Summit here – drawing 800 bankers, senior civil servants and construction-industry tycoons to where they could not avoid seeing and smelling the magnitude of the problem they were conferring about. This original strategy (a typical Slovo ploy) raised Botshebelo's morale, making people feel their desperate state had at least been recognized. It also shattered many of the delegates, who hitherto had conferred only in conference centres and seen townships only on their TV screens. And it led to the setting up of a provincial housing bank which will lend to those whose monthly earnings are below R1,500.

An industrial estate of 136 small factories at first sight looked hopeful. But most are closed – and by now vandalized. 'My uncle will explain,' said Vax.

The taxi delivered everyone to his/her exact destination, which meant our driving to nine of the seventeen sections, and during this tour I stayed on board. Botshebelo's few posh homes are breeze-block shoe-boxes, their tin roofs weighted with stones and tyres; the low hills to the north give scant protection from the frequent gales that drive dust into every crevice. Many live in tiny mud huts, crudely built, or (some 60 per cent) in 'informal residences' – one room, constructed of scraps of scavenged materials. Electricity is available in some sections but rarely affordable. The scarcity of litter is owing to an ANC anti-litter campaign which in this loyal-to-Madiba township has worked miracles. Ninety-five per cent of families must use the bucket sewage system and we passed two 'sanitation' tractors lurching along the rutted tracks, their trailers piled with black plastic buckets. Only three sections have a domestic water supply; the rest depend on one standpipe per street and since mid-November many of those have been dry. All the basic services deteriorated after the setting up of Botshebelo's Transitional Local Council (TLC) and 'the old guard' within the Provincial Administration are suspected of trying to sabotage it.

My tour ended at a startlingly grand taxi terminus where labelled stands for the various services are sheltered by a high curved blue metal roof. Opposite, across a brick-paved plaza, rises a shopping-mall extravaganza – its incongruity painful. In the mid-'80s Pretoria diagnosed Botshebelo as a well-organized ANC flashpoint. The reaction was to try to placate the destitute by providing a veneer of 'white' affluence – like giving an expensive toy to a baby dying of malnutrition.

Outside the shopping-mall entrance hawkers spread their wares on the ground, or on trestles made of beer-crates. Inside, the shops are either poorly stocked or closed. And the would-be American trendiness of this concourse is decisively diminished by a sangoma's display – laid out on a tarpaulin – of traditional cures and spellbinding (literally) artefacts. Here are bundles of many varieties of tree bark, dried venom sacs from mambas green and black, powders made from crushed stones of various hues, bunches of leaves and herbs tied with bands woven from multicoloured cattle-tail hairs, monkey skulls, crocodile eyes, teeth and feet, porcupine quills stuck in strangely shaped roots, and the paws, tails, penises and obscure internal organs of other unidentifiable creatures. The youngish sangoma wears a white headband, a leopard-skin scarf and a long triple necklace of nuts. He ignored me, which seemed to confirm his authenticity; fake sangomas target tourists. Most blacks still value traditional healers' remedies, sometimes in conjunction with Western cures, and business was brisk around this rent-free space. Later, Ngoako told me no one (black or white) would have the temerity to demand rent from a genuine sangoma. When whites who jeer at black superstitions are themselves tested – when they have to do business with a sangoma – many suddenly become subdued if not actually conciliatory.

I was to wait for Ngoako in a café/bar kiosk beside the taxi terminus. Beer-drinkers stood at the front, resting their bottles on the little counter; at 7.30 a.m. three taxi drivers were enjoying large Castles. Tea-drinkers sit at the back around the one small table; on joining them my milkless tea was served in a chipped enamel mug – the only mug. A ragged elder followed me but had to wait until I had finished. He wanted sugar in his tea but was told that would be extra. He took a stale hunk of bread from his pocket and softened it in the sugarless tea.

Ngoako is a vigorous confident 40-year-old, tall for a Sotho. On arrival he mopped his glistening face with a sleeve of his Berkeley University T-shirt and said, 'Welcome, mama! My nephew says travelling is your job – you can organize some bus tours through Botshebelo for foreigners? Like Soweto has –

or are we not entertaining enough? Not enough crime and publicity? Come, mama, come to my house.' And he led me away by the hand.

A taxi drove us (for free) down the central strip of narrow tarred road to a street of concrete cubes where two other ANC officers (they used to be called activists) awaited me. Moses is a COSATU organizer, Charlie a redundant miner now working as an unpaid 'empowerment officer'. Under the tin roof one felt one's lungs being scorched at each breath. I looked out to see if there was any nearby shade, not under a roof. There wasn't. Blue fertilizer bags papered the living-room walls and a certificate over the doorway told me that Ngoako is a qualified car mechanic.

Ngoako translated Moses's explanation for all those empty factories. 'When government subsidies stopped the Taiwanese left. They were lured with a big package of incentives, with a monthly subsidy of R120 for each worker! That skewed things like crazy – overmanning, people paid R60 a month and the Taiwanese keeping the rest. With 75 per cent unemployed, people will settle for any wage. This country's economy depends on that fact. It was a crazy thing about apartheid, the State would pay anything to keep races separate. For us to go to work in Bloemfontein, they spent over R80 million on daily transport subsidies – instead of on housing for the same workers *in* Bloemfontein!'

In theory Botshebelo's TLC is controlled by the ANC/SACP alliance. 'But,' said Ngoako, 'we can't really control it, we've no assets and no trained staff. Our place never had municipal structures like other townships. In the '80s the state tried so hard to force a puppet council on us. But we resisted, even when the army came in to give us hell under the State of Emergency. We're united here, you never heard of Botshebelo shootings and stabbings and house-burnings and necklacing like on the Rand. But we're determined, we're not going to be messed around by small white officials. It's the mean little boere puppies working out here make all the difficulties. Their seniors in Bloemfontein work well with our new government.'

Ironically, there is much to be said for a lack of diversity in Archbishop Tutu's 'rainbow nation'. Botshebelo's Sothos, though so recently uprooted from different places in different circumstances, have been able to form a stable community cemented by loyalty to the ANC/SACP alliance. (The SACP's local membership, over 10,000, makes Botshebelo's branch the biggest in the country.) Had some of the 'relocated' been Inkatha-controlled Zulus, the Third Force could have created bloody mayhem here as elsewhere.

However this enviable stability is now, according to Ngoako, itself making problems. Another 'relocation' has been suggested, to new housing forming a suburb of Bloemfontein, but to everyone's amazement the residents are reluctant to move; they want their decent houses and urban amenities in Botshebelo.

How, then, can the two communities be 'married', to give birth to a uniform tax base? Somehow the Botshebelo folk must be convinced that this would be greatly to their advantage.

At 10.30 a TLC meeting required Ngoako's presence. 'Go see our hospital,' he urged. 'Come back after and tell me what you think.'

Half an hour later I could see the two-storeyed hospital, brightly spreadeagled on the drab veld, all freshly painted red and green including its curved metal roofs – these evidently the architectural flavour of the '80s in Botshebelo. Despite the midday heat several bucket-bearing women were converging on the imposing pillared and arched entrance – their nearest water-source. Morning and evening, hundreds queue at the borehole within the hospital grounds.

Like Aliwal North's golf club, Botshebelo's hospital has not yet arrived in the new South Africa and Afrikanerdom's manic bureaucracy still rules. Many true stories circulate about the tangled skein of trivial regulations co-existing through-out the public service with every sort of chicanery and crookery. Where else could you find a Public Service Staff Code specifying job applicants' maximum and minimum weights, depending on heights? This is bureaucracy fallen over the cliff into dementia.

In a bullet-proof office beside the hospital gate lounged a long-armed, low-browed security officer who seemed to have missed out on several evolutionary stages. He ordered me to wait but declined to explain why. Then the women with their buckets began to pass through the narrow pedestrian entrance and he moved from behind his desk to stand silently in the doorway. The women walked by with downcast eyes, each dropping a coin into a nearby flower-tub. The guard glanced around the immediate vicinity, saw no one else in sight and quickly pocketed the coins. Who said Botshebelo residents pay no service charges?

Fifteen minutes later a senior sister arrived, short and dumpy and smiling. She beckoned me into a curtained-off corner – where else would an elderly woman visitor to a public hospital have to undergo a body-search? 'It is the rule,' said Sister pleasantly, while checking my person in intimate ways – as though 'the rule' were a magic spell that could render normal any aberration. She then led me – firmly grasping my elbow – to a large bare reception area within the central building, not unlike a Pollsmoor waiting room. And there I sat for half an hour under the eye of another armed guard of a certain type – small blond moustache, thin mouth, fat belly, tattooed forearms. Sister had explained, 'The hospital secretary must see you.'

There was something eerily impersonal about the hospital secretary – bony, dour, grey-haired, with colourless dead-fish eyes. Perhaps a lifetime dominated by the Public Service Staff Code vitiates a man's humanity. Methodically he scrutinized my passport, health certificates, publisher's letter. Next he entered various details in a ledger and requested me to sign the page. Then a male nurse attendant who spoke no English (coincidence or not?) was summoned to show me around. He was a Sotho; here all the nurses and servants are black, apart from an Indian cook. And all the security officers, admin. staff and most of the doctors are Afrikaners.

Jacob led me into every corner of the building, including electronically locked store-rooms; the fraudulent procurement of pharmaceutical goods within the public-health system, and theft from hospitals, is estimated to be costing some R500 million a year. In one store – its door wide open – a solitary nurse was unpacking crates of infant formula, each tin proclaiming in English: MOTHER'S MILK IS BEST. This scene seemed to negate the purpose of those electronic locks.

Various departments, in their separate buildings, are linked by long, tunnel-like tiled corridors. I fumed inwardly at this waste of money and the conse-quence soon becomes apparent. Unlike the average black hospital, Botshebelo's is underused, with numerous empty beds and some empty wards in which cheerfully chatting nurses were relaxing. Only the outpatients' department was as busy as one would expect. Even the paediatric ward had empty cots, from which I did not deduce that the average Botshebelo child is robust. A young woman doctor, avoiding my eye, gave one explanation: 'This is a forwarding hospital, we send the most serious cases elsewhere. And of course we also have clinics in the different sections.' Later, Ngoako's explanations were different. 'They spent so much on the buildings there's nothing over to staff and run it properly. And for most of our people even the low fees charged are too high.' A familiar Third World story: Pretoria's toleration of corruption aligned the white supremacists' administration with those of Moi in Kenya, Mugabe in Zim-babwe, Mobuto in Zaire.

In a children's ward a nurse was bathing a 3-month-old baby, handling this miserable mite with great tenderness and looking at him with love. His emacia-tion was so extreme he hardly seemed human. 'What's the diagnosis?' I asked. The nurse sighed and said, 'His mother smokes, it is not good for pregnant women to smoke.'

I felt a sort of despair then, so well does this reply illustrate the vulnerability of the uneducated to unexplained slogans.

Jacob handed me over to Dr Pretorius: tall, handsome, welcoming. We sat in his office and he described himself as 'a new South African, a Free State liberal!' Throughout the Free State, he assured me, Boers and blacks got on well for nearly two centuries before Grand Apartheid.

Dr Pretorius – a keen traveller, uninterested in conventional tourism – is planning a motoring safari with his family from Bloemfontein to Mombasa.

'What puzzles me is – how do you get to know the ordinary people of a country, especially in Africa?'

When I had given a few helpful hints Dr Pretorius shook his head in bewilderment. 'It's different for you from Europe, I can see that. Never could I live with blacks – eating, sleeping, bathing in their homes. For me this would be impossible psychologically – or emotionally, or whatever.'

'But is this more class than race? Could you live in a white slum? Would you accept a black colleague's invitation to stay in his home?'

Dr Pretorius laughed. 'You're trying to let me off the hook – yes? But the answer is I could stay in a white slum – I wouldn't want to, I hope I never have to, but I could. And no, I would not accept an invitation from a black colleague to *stay* in his home. It will be different for my kids, after integrated schooling. It makes me happy to think of all our people being at ease with one another in the future. I could send my kids to mainly white private schools but I don't want to. I've nothing against desegregation. But if you're brought up one way you can't buy a new mindset at the age of 42!'

After lunch in the staff canteen Dr Pretorius escorted me to the entrance where we said goodbye under a gigantic hoarding. It announces that another R8 million is soon to be spent on an extension to Botshebelo's hospital and my expression must have been easily read. Dr Pretorius said soothingly, 'Don't worry, it's likely our new Premier will put a stop to that. If he doesn't he'll have a revolution in Botshebelo. The people here are mostly illiterate but they're not stupid.'

Back in Bloemfontein, I heard that the Transkei Deputy Commissioner of Police has been assassinated, shot fifteen times outside his Umtata home. His wounded wife is recovering. Lieutenant-General Mdluli Wheedon Mbulawa was the man held mainly responsible for the boiling discontent within the lower ranks of his force. The weapon used was an R4, a police rifle.

Tomorrow is the last Day of the Vow; from next year 16 December will be a truly national holiday, South Africa's Day of Reconciliation. It is a measure of President Mandela's sensitivity that in 1994, the year of *uhuru*, Afrikaners have not had their very special day cancelled – which may be why most people (right-wingers apart) are already calling it by its new name. As usual, the main commemoration will be at the Voortrekker Monument where a short service within the building is to replace the customary open-air mass-rally harangued by fanatics. Not more than 1,500 are expected tomorrow; twenty years ago you could have added a nought to that.

Near a Voortrekker cemetery outside Brandfort, thirty-five miles north of here, ET is staging his own AWB commemoration and Sue has volunteered to drive me to this terminal event.

The same, 16 December

All the way to Brandfort the veld lies bare and pallid and sun-scourged: you can almost hear it pleading for rain. A few low koppies break the flatness, thorn-bushes try to be green but are dusted grey. Once the whiff of a decomposing cow, drought-killed, penetrated the car.

Brandfort is that isolated little dorp to which Winnie Mandela was banished in 1977 – banished but not subdued. She had to live in a three-roomed shack, without water or electricity, in the township Phathakahle (meaning 'handle with care'). From there she emerged daily, wearing flowing African robes, to sweep regally through the dorp breaking every possible apartheid law while giving drab little Brandfort a glimpse of how to dress stylishly and live flamboyantly. No plebeian brandy and Coke for this lady: the Drankwinkel's sales of Cinzano and champagne rocketed. The dour volk were pole-axed; never had they imagined that a black could behave as though she owned their town. Meanwhile, behind the scenes, something astonishing was happening. Winnie had found a good friend of the most unlikely lineage: Adèle de Waal, a direct descendant of the Voortrekker leader and martyr, Piet Retief, killed by Dingane in 1838. Adèle's husband Piet, being the only lawyer in Brandfort (the sort of place that has only one of everything), had no option but to handle Mrs Mandela's affairs and her rapid integration with the de Waal family – her frequent visits to their home – could be disguised as 'legal consultations'. This closeness to the 'enemy' was to have momentous consequences. It so happened that Kobie Coetsee and Piet de Waal were life-long friends and it was de Waal who first suggested to Coetsee (Minister for Justice, Police and Prisons) that the time had come to open negotiations with his most famous prisoner, Nelson Mandela.

Sue fell silent as we drove up Voortrekker Street – long and straight, no one in sight, most shops shut. The AWB 'trek' could be seen ahead, the width of its ox-wagon blocking oncoming traffic, and I was eager to follow the last bakkie. But suddenly Sue freaked out. She could not bring herself to seem to be supporting ET; plainly this was something as visceral as Dr Pretorius's inhibition about living with blacks. 'Let's park in the shade,' she said, 'and follow when they've reached the cemetery. It's the processing with them that shows allegiance. Being an onlooker is different.' I appreciated then how noble had been her offer to drive me here.

We bought cooldrinks before parking under a jacaranda; even in hardline Brandfort the new South Africa emboldened Indian store-keepers to trade on what used to be a Christian-National 'Sabbath'. Our vantage point afforded an unexpectedly good view of the procession. Having turned off the road, it was very slowly crossing the veld, led by seven oxen drawing a wagon-load of maidens wearing Voortrekker dress. ET followed on his famous black horse and behind him rode some thirty young men. The bakkies brought up the rear, rather spoiling the nineteenth-century effect. As we watched this forlorn gesture of loyalty to times past – to a mythology no longer sustaining – I was suddenly unaccountably touched. To me there was a pathos about those oxen and those horsemen moving through the thornbush in the shimmering heat – now visible, now hidden – seeming as insubstantial as ghosts, as irrelevant as last year's calendar, as sad as the death of any cherished illusion. When I said as much to Sue she stared at me with horrified incredulity. 'But,' she protested, 'they're being loyal to a hateful ideology!'

'Yes, of course,' I said – and remembered my reaction to the Voortrekker Monument. Then I added lamely, 'I just get a bit sentimental about the Voortrekkers – in one way they're kindred spirits.'

'*I'm* an Afrikaner,' retorted Sue, 'but they're not *my* kindred spirits!'

We drove on then, parked at a pointed distance from the bakkies and went first to admire the magnificent oxen, red with touches of white – a classic well-matched span. (Though one short: the eighth fell ill last night.) No self-respecting Boer would be seen driving grey or all-white oxen; only black and white or red and white were lekker. (How, we wondered, did those bovine fashions originally come about?) As Sue pointed out, 'drive' is the wrong word because no reins are used. Every well-trained ox knows its name, and a span (from eight to sixteen beasts) is directed verbally and with whip cracks – or a light flick on the flanks if an ox now and then eases off. (During the Great Trek, extreme cruelty had to be involved in forcing oxen through pathless territory, over high mountains; but the Boers were being equally cruel to themselves.) Each ox has its own permanent place in a span; the strongest pair lead, yoked to a single shaft. These seven were complacent creatures, well aware of being special, accepting respectful caresses as their due. Very few spans of working oxen remain in South Africa.

The oxen owners – two brothers – were tall, big-boned, sun-tanned. Both their rough-hewn features and their aloof, humourless expressions – eyes ever watchful – marked them as thoroughbred descendants of Boer War commandos. Now their breed, Boers who have let the twentieth century pass them by, is almost extinct. Their expressions softened when I stroked the oxen and asked permission to photograph them. The Boers' affinity with their cattle once forged a strong link between Xhosas and trekboers. Some say the modern Afrikaners' devotion to their motor vehicles is a degenerate mutation of that affinity.

Then I went on – Sue lingering in the background – to introduce myself to ET's steed, a docile gelding of some eighteen hands who after a brief conversation allowed me to examine his teeth; he is advanced in years though AWB publicity presents him as young and mettlesome. His two teenaged Tswana attendants were hugely amused by my dental inspection. I asked them, 'How is it, working for Mr Terre' Blanche?' Both laughed and one replied, 'He is *kind* man.' And I daresay he is kind to his black servants, just as Mr Paisley sees to the welfare of his Roman Catholic constituents.

Tentatively Sue and I moved closer to the little crowd – tentatively because of ET's inclination to turn on outsiders and inflame his followers against them. But today was different, this *is* a new South Africa.

No more than 200 had assembled, including children. The horsemen remained in their saddles, hock-deep in tawny grass, mostly mounted on glossy chestnuts, many displaying a Vierkleur saddle-cloth. Beyond them rose a long flat-topped ridge, mauve and trembling in the cruel heat. The maidens clustered under a thorn tree, slim and solemn-faced in their ankle-length white gowns and nun-like bonnets. Hymn-singing was in progress: hauntingly beautiful hymns, devoutly sung, their cadences muted by the immensity of the empty veld, harsh and parched under its molten sky. Then came a prayer and every adult head was bowed. The age of the little gathering struck me; I doubt if anyone was over 35. Then I was struck by the scarcity of guns; a year ago every male would have been weapons-laden, here I counted only ten revolvers. (Leaving aside the bodyguards' – one official SAPS, the other unofficial AWB.) This was very much a family occasion; there were as many women as men, some with toddlers perched on their shoulders, others with babies in slings. And, essentially, it was a religious occasion. One knew that these were simple, frightened, rigid people: too rigid to cope with the new South Africa and here seeking a reassurance that wasn't on offer.

When the khaki-clad ET began his harangue I studied him through my binoculars. He looks older than his fifty years and has spectacularly lost weight. Conveniently, Sue is a professional translator so I received the core of his message as he spoke. His demands were irrational and futile but he was also implicitly conceding defeat, addressing a black as his President, begging for clemency from a black on behalf of the AWB's numerous convicted psychopathic murderers. He roared, 'Release our prisoners before Christmas! President Mandela, send the political prisoners home. They are not criminals! Not me, not the President, or anyone else can stop retaliation if my people are not set free. If this government really wants peace, if they want to bury the past, let the soldiers go home. We will always remember this day, we will remember it as a Sunday, I will have nothing to do with Reconciliation Day . . . '

And so on, tediously, while the horses began to stamp and toss restlessly and the babies began to whimper and the toddlers to stray through the thornbushes. But the rage was counterfeit, the bluffing pathetic. ET was ranting without fire, without conviction, without rousing the crowd's emotions. He knows and they sense that an era has ended.

20

Christmas in Khayelitsha

I fear a hideous human harvest in the children who have grown up with
this limitless violence around them.
Shaun Johnson (1986)

Last May, my Khayelitsha friends invited me back for Christmas and at Cape
Town railway station, on 20 December, I noticed two potent symbols of the new
South Africa – both stern and practical. Now each platform entrance has metal
barriers and turnstiles, electronically operated, to thwart those still disinclined to
co-operate with the State by paying train fares. And outside the station I found
Strand Street blocked by barrels of concrete. Once this street was a noisy
whirlpool of passengers eddying around untidily parked rows of taxis, the
questioning shouts of passengers and the answering shouts of drivers' assistants
drowning each other out. Now a splendid new taxi terminus, enormous and
orderly, stands on the station deck. Here are ample queuing spaces, equipped
with litter bins, for each marked destination – all sheltered under high arched
roofs. The several men on those roofs at first puzzled me – they looked like
sentries but wore no uniforms. In fact these are monitors appointed by the
Western Cape Traffic Department and various Taxi Associations – a novel
collaboration – to prevent the overloading of vehicles and to intervene should
trouble arise. Much trouble arose two months ago when the terminus was
opened and drivers were forbidden to use Strand Street. In a shoot-out involving
AK-47s and 9mm pistols ten people – mostly innocent bystanders – were
seriously injured.

Early on 23 December I walked from my friends' house in Observatory to
Mowbray. But taxis to Khayelitsha are no longer leaving from there – not
since two men were killed, and four critically injured, in another recent shoot-
out. Khayelitsha passengers must now start from Guguletu township, a roundabout and more expensive route.

Guguletu's vivaciously chaotic taxi terminus – an uneven expanse of wasteland – becomes a series of lakes after rain and is plagued by dust-devils when the
famous Peninsular winds blow. Savoury smells, sizzling sounds and plumes of

blue smoke mark a row of improvised braai-stands offering offal hamburgers – or boerewors for the comparatively wealthy. In the Khayelitsha group (no queues here) I stood beside an elderly man wearing a homburg hat and, despite the balmy midsummer air, a tweed overcoat much too long and too wide. He looked at me with some concern. 'Lady, are you lost? Give care to your nice bag' – a small scruffy knapsack – 'Here is too criminal, even more than before...' I was often to hear that complaint during the next few days. Last year I could safely leave my camera in Blossom's shack: not so now.

Mrs Galela joined us, her three enchanting small children wearing their Sunday best – off to visit Granny in Khayelitsha. For twenty years she has been 'the domestic' of a Constantia family, leaving Guguletu at 5.30 every morning and getting back at 7.30 every evening – except Thursdays, her half-day. 'They are very rich people,' she said, and paused for a moment before adding, 'But poor in spirit.' On those words her voice trembled and I turned to see her eyes glistening. Annually she had received a Christmas bonus but this year it was withheld. 'Madam says now whites must pay extra taxes to Mandela – R700 extra a month, she says.' Mrs Galela dabbed her eyes. 'The money – it's not the money upsets me though I counted on it for the kids' gifts. It's the unkindness I feel in my soul. Hey, it's hard! After twenty years and never once did I let her down!'

This route severely tests one's nerve. It is, in effect, a taxi racetrack. At one point we swerved sickeningly as a Coloured-driven SAPS van overtook us and hooted very loudly on drawing level. Our driver roared unrepeatable things relating to the police officer's private parts.

'He wanted us to crash,' said Mr Homburg grimly.

My spirits rose as we approached Khayelitsha's familiar graffitied periphery walls, with their drifts of litter piled against them. The vandalized school buildings have now acquired Coca-Cola-sponsored name-hoardings and outside the day hospital where it all began I asked to be set down.

It is untrue that nothing has changed for the poor. Electricity has come to Khayelitsha. The leaking sewage pipes have been mended and some of the main tracks roughly tarred. Near the hospital, within an old shipping container, are six public telephones guarded by two young men – who must now be described as ex-Comrades, the days of Madiba-approved militancy being over. Also (a seasonal change) the midsummer crop of maize is growing dense and green in many tiny gardens.

Five boys in their early teens were the first to notice my return. 'Comrade Noxolo!' they yelled, then bounded towards me giving the V-sign, their eyes bright and their smiles wide. None speaks English but they knew where I was going. While escorting me to Blossom's new shack they loudly chanted, 'Viva President Mandela Viva! Viva ANC Viva! Viva Comrade Noxolo Viva!' Our progress was slowed by friends young and old dispensing hugs, kisses and invitations.

I was greeted by Blossom's sister Beauty, now aged 17 and even more beautiful. For Blossom, the new South Africa has speedily delivered the goods; she is working in a white-owned Cape Town hairdressing salon which had rejected her for this job before the elections. As she collects a 50 per cent commission (R42.50) on each perm, and averages two perms a day during a six-day week, she is on the way to becoming a Khayelitsha woman of substance. Hence her new five-roomed shack shared with only seven others. And she hopes soon to be able to move closer to Cape Town; now she must be up at 5.30 a.m. and rarely gets home before 8 p.m.

Already several families have moved from 'my corner'. Affirmative action allows some skilled people to get comparatively well-paid work and this gives a trickle of jobs to others not lucky enough to have found steady employment – joiners, cobblers, seamstresses. Khayelitsha is far from being transformed, economically. Yet there are changes, scattered like the first shoots of spring wheat on winter-brown ploughland. Granted, some are more apparent than real, like the forest of electricity poles. At a cost of R48 every shack can be connected and have a card-operated meter installed; but this does not mean being able to afford cards. In many shacks bulbs now hang from ceilings but at sunset oil-lamps are lit. Electric cookers may stand in corners, the ovens serving as cupboards, but most suppers are still cooked on oil-stoves or outside fires. Various electrical appliances have been 'found' and are displayed like trophies: kettles, irons, toasters, hair-dryers – even a few fridges, also useful as cupboards. However, the fact that such appliances can be used, whenever enough rands are available, is in itself morale-boosting. And some spaza shops (now stocking a wider range of goods) offer iced beer, cooldrinks and fresh milk from giant fridges cunningly donated by Coca-Cola. Also, space in those fridges may be rented at so many cents a day for storing a hunk of meat or a bag of vegetables.

To celebrate my return Beauty put a saucepan of water on that super-de-luxe oil stove which last year was my farewell present. Now, through abuse, it is smoking almost as eye-searingly as its paint-tin predecessor. Lucretia hurried in, beaming, to show me her month-old son. She and Tony – a free man since February, cleared of all those false charges – are now married. And Tony has found a job with a Cape Town firm who previously employed only Coloured truck drivers. 'That's why,' said Lucretia gloomily, 'most Coloureds will vote again for the Nats in our local elections.'

Beauty then suggested going into Mitchells Plain to shop; Blossom had left a list of goodies – tins and packets of rubbish foods – she would like Comrade Noxolo to provide. (Was this the same Blossom who, in June '93, would not allow me to buy a loaf of bread when she and all her family were permanently hungry?) We braved the Christmas rush in Shoprite where Beauty developed her own cravings and loaded our trolley with fizzy drinks of hectic hue and breakfast cereals with gimmicks attached and squidgy cakes smelling of synthetic flavourings.

That was only the start: within fifteen minutes of Blossom's getting home she was begging me to buy her a gold necklace seen in an Adderley Street jewellers – 'I particularly fancy it.' Several other friends were equally insistent on obtaining full value from my return, though usually rather less blatant about it. At first, this altered attitude upset me, seeming almost a betrayal of our earlier friendships. Yet it is an aspect of the new reality that must be accepted. In June '93, my moral support was valued. Eighteen months later the political Struggle is over and emotionally the victorious blacks have no further need for a sympathetic white ally. Instead, they feel the time has come to use me in their economic struggle. They have generously contributed to the reconciliation process and now there is a balance to be redressed: reparations are due.

Apart from 25 December being a national holiday, life goes on much as usual in Khayelitsha during the Christmas season – undecorated, unmolested by Santas, with little present-giving and no recognizable festive feasts. A vague sense of occasion seeps out from Cape Town's world of rich fun-seekers, but in many corners of the shanty city Christmas is all about visiting prisoners.

During the Struggle – especially during its last phase – the line between 'political' and 'criminal' offences became uncomfortably blurred and a grey area continues to discolour the new South Africa's ethical map. Who, now, should be granted amnesty? Many arbitrary decisions have been made – but Thabo and Molefi have not been among the lucky ones. They remain in Blandvlei prison, serving thirteen and fourteen years respectively for killing police officers (to which they admit) and possessing bombs (which they deny).

Since the elections the ANC has given up paying for prison visits to convicts who claim to be 'political'. This has left Nosingile (Thabo's sister) and Kaizer (Molefi's brother) with a problem. The high-security Blandvlei prison is near Worcester, eighty miles away, and the round trip costs R40. As both families are centless, neither prisoner has had a visit since March. Therefore it was decided that on Christmas Eve Comrade Noxolo should accompany Nosingile and Kaizer to Blandvlei.

Nosingile suffers from bad-diet obesity and is a rather grumpy young woman – but who could blame her. At 7.30 we went to rouse Kaizer who shares with two adult brothers a one-roomed driftwood shack, some six feet by eight and seven feet high. This is one of a colony of such 'garden-sheds', without lavatories or water, standing in deep, loose sand on the far side of the motor road from

Blossom's Site. Kaizer speaks no English; a shy, timid young man, he has the defeated expression of one who knows he has been sentenced to life at the bottom of the pile.

First we had a long wait for a taxi to Belleville, standing on the malodorously garbage-strewn verge near Kaizer's shack. In dreary Belleville we bought 'comforts', then had another wearisome wait for a taxi to Worcester.

Nosingile and Kaizer had never before done this trip (previously, other relatives visited) and both were aghast to discover that from the junction where the taxi dropped us there is a nine-mile walk; in the days of ANC-subsidized visits a chartered taxi would have driven all the way. On this little-used link road my malnourished and unexercised companions could not keep pace with Comrade Noxolo – almost old enough to be their grandmother. By the time we arrived both were in real distress, close to collapse.

Blandvlei's setting, like Pollsmoor's, is more appropriate to a luxury hotel than a maximum-security jail. One approaches through unfenced, pleasantly landscaped grounds, neatly mown and shrub-filled. Groves of pine, willow, acacia surround the car park. The complex of one-storey brick buildings has variegated flower-beds below each barred window and its two twelve-foot-high steel-mesh fences look no more daunting than any police station's. Prowling Alsatians guard the double corridor of open space around the cells. There are no escapees.

Less agreeable than the environment is the staff, Afrikaner and Coloured warders who treated my companions with unveiled contempt and sneeringly asked me why I'd forgotten my black sash. Here most convicts are Coloured; as the only visitors for black prisoners, we were made to wait longer than was fair.

The car-park scene fascinated me. Around a score of large expensive vehicles the atmosphere was festive; this might have been a Bank Holiday crowd gathered at some beauty-spot. Picnic baskets were opened, tapes of favourite pop groups competed disharmoniously, older children noisily played hide and seek amidst the trees, toddlers tried out their new toys, Daddies drank furtively inside their vehicles (alcohol is forbidden within the precincts), Grannies sat on camp-chairs dandling babies and Mummies rummaged in ice-boxes for cool-drinks. One can scarcely ask, 'What's he in for?' but I did feel intensely curious, observing these prosperous and conventional family groups. Were they visiting political prisoners? Or drug dealers? Or fraudsters?

Thabo, sentenced last year, was allowed only a twenty-minute visit and in his wing the security arrangements duplicated those in Pollsmoor's remand section. Molefi, entitled to 'good-behaviour' concessions after five years, could enjoy an 'open' forty-minute visit. He joined us in a long room, many-windowed with cheerful primrose walls, where coarse grey blankets had been spread on rows of hard benches for the visitors' comfort. Here prisoners can embrace their relatives and cuddle their small children, a four-day-old baby the smallest. His father wept for joy and sadness on taking the little bundle into his arms.

Most prisoners had made gifts for their families in the workshops, some quite beautiful. Model ships (one with Union Jack sails!), churches and castles, meticulously finished sets of dolls'-house furniture, carved animals and birds, miniature guitars and drums, tins painted with intricate designs and so turned into gay flowerpots holding cuttings from the prison garden. Everyone except the warders looked relaxed – perhaps a stiff-upper-lip display? How, I wondered, did they feel?

As we returned to the motor road at 3 p.m. Nosingile announced that neither she nor Kaizer could walk another step. I then tried thumbing, while sheets of rain were driven across the nearby Blandvlei Lake by a sudden gale and the temperature dropped dramatically. This must have been shift-changing time; within twenty minutes seven men, each alone in his car, drove past us. But none would stop for blacks and a poor white. Two shouted angrily at us and there was something close to hatred on those faces.

We returned to the car park, soaked and shivering, but every vehicle had come packed with family and friends. Then I noticed one ancient Ford saloon about to drive off with only an elderly couple in front and desperately I begged for a lift to the junction. The burly fair-skinned husband had African features and crinkly brown hair. 'Where is your car?' he demanded. 'How did you get here? Why are you with those people? You must ask my wife for permission.' His wife was a small sour shrivelled woman who looked Indian and offered all sorts of excuses for not taking us. In disgust I walked away. But then a young Muslim man – we had talked earlier – intervened and after an overheated argument in Afrikaans we were taken aboard. Mr Burly asked how much we had paid the taxi and said, 'You can come as far as Belleville for twice that price.'

Nosingile and Kaizer slept soundly during the journey, their heads resting on my shoulders.

South Africa's prison conditions are notoriously inhumane yet both Thabo and Molefi look better dressed and fed and much fitter than many of their comrades in Khayelitsha. Observing Kaizer and Molefi together, it occurred to me that Molefi enjoys a sort of freedom denied to his brother. True, Kaizer has freedom of movement, though that is limited by Khayelitsha's isolation. Molefi, on the other hand, is free of the relentless stress of wondering where the next meal and garment will come from – and his living quarters cannot be more cramped than his brother's. Also, he has access to facilities way beyond Kaizer's reach: like a bathroom and a workshop. At the very bottom of the pile, isn't 'freedom' an abstraction?

We got back to find Beauty weaving false hair through a customer's springy fuzz. False nylon hair, straight and black, is the 'in' thing – even among girl toddlers, many of whom wear silly-looking false top-knots. Blossom has passed on her expertise to Beauty and a huge hoarding nailed to the fence outside their shack offers a selection of twenty-five coiffures costing up to R200. This affirms faith in the future; so far no customer has gone beyond the R20 range. However, painting that board gave several hours' work to a sign-artist.

Christmas Day is Pollsmoor Day. Would I like to accompany Nosingile, Tessie and Sarah to visit imprisoned Comrades? In Sarah's case an imprisoned husband and their sons Tammie and Ollie, aged 8 and 6, were of the party. On our way to the motor road Tessie suggested dropping into a crowded shebeen where everyone was drinking milk-stout. After a round of Castles, Nosingile urged Comrade Noxolo to provide a six-pack for the journey. Meekly Comrade Noxolo obliged. We then took a taxi to Site B railway station and from there another to Wynberg.

That six-pack was not needed. In the second taxi a young man sitting with my companions – a total stranger to us all – opened a full litre bottle of Scotch (genuine, an airport duty-free bottle) and insisted on sharing it. Seeing Tammie and Ollie gulping the neat spirit as though it were Coke I frantically yelled, 'Don't! Stop! It's not for children!' But above the sinister beat of a heavy-metal tape people were laughing and shouting – 'Merry Christmas to *you*! Merry Christmas to *me*! Merry Christmas to *us*!' My repeated pleas went unheard or unheeded and in the packed kombi I could take no action.

Even on Christmas Day breakfast doesn't feature in 'my corner' and that Scotch was hitting empty stomachs. At Wynberg the young man stumbled away, having flung his empty bottle against a shop wall, just missing the window. Sarah had to be lifted out, then fell to the ground still shouting 'Merry Christmas to *us*!' Nosingile and Tessie were swaying and giggling and trying to sing 'Silent Night'. At that moment Ollie collapsed, unconscious – as his brother threw up. Those boys had lowered a perilous amount of whisky and Ollie is a frail scrap. I feared for his life and thought wildly of sending for an ambulance. But how? And from Wynberg, on Christmas Day, for a black child – forget it! Luckily we had stopped beside a boerewors stall. Seizing a handful of salt, I thrust it down Ollie's throat and held him up by the ankles – half-aware as I did so that a small crowd was gathering. An uneasily muttering crowd, wondering why the hell this white woman should be so maltreating a black child... Then the lad vomited – pungently, the alcohol fumes plain to be smelled. Instantly the crowd understood and laughed and dispersed.

I sat on the edge of the pavement with Ollie across my lap; he was breathing fast and too shaken to stand. I felt quite shaken myself. Tammie sat beside me, sobbing, with his head between his knees. Their mother now lay asleep in the gutter. Nosingile and Tessie were leaning against a wall, propping each other up and hiccupping. Our taxi had moved off to its departure point, away on the far side of the railway bridge; otherwise I would have organized an immediate return to base – because how could I possibly get this lot to Pollsmoor? When another taxi arrived from Site B it almost ran over Sarah before disgorging a large party of Pollsmoor visitors – led (Praise the Lord!) by Lucretia and Tony.

Soon twenty of us were aboard a fifteen-seat kombi, Sarah still stupefied, Tessie and Nosingile laughing uproariously and begging every man to kiss them. But suddenly they switched to an angry mood and began to abuse Coloureds in general; happily none was present. Then, as suddenly, they fell asleep and had to be half-carried into the prison's thronged waiting hall. While the boys curled up together on a bench, our three adult casualties were laid on the floor in a corner – attracting contemptuous glances from prim-looking Coloured ladies. Sarah woke for long enough to vomit, then again became comatose. Lucretia hastily mopped up with one of her baby's nappies and said cheerfully, 'They have time to get better, at Christmas we must wait long hours.'

She was right; we had a four-hour wait. Extra Christmas visits are not allowed but most families save up their visits for this occasion. The midday heat was stifling and the air opaque with cigarette smoke, despite an open door leading to a shadeless concrete yard. Every male – and a few of the more daring young black women – seemed to be chain-smoking. Beside me sat a 14-year-old Xhosa lad who informed me as he lit up, 'This Rothman is what sportsmen choose all over the world.' Now who could have told him *that*?

Some two-thirds of those present were Coloured, their younger offspring quaintly decked out in sailor-suits or frilly flounced frocks and be-ribboned bonnets. Beside the expensive junk-food shop the queue never shortened; on every wall conspicuous notices warned that only prison-bought food may be presented to the inmates. Even as Christmas treats, homemade foods are verboten. Around us litter was piling up fast and teams of small boys irritated their elders by kicking cooldrinks cans around the floor.

Lucretia introduced me to her friend Mpho – of the Georgina calibre, an articulate, fiery young woman who grew up in Crossroads and whose revolutionary zeal has been deflected, post-Struggle, into AIDS-prevention campaigning. Until recently she was a Khayelitsha community AIDS worker but she lost her job when an NGO, the National Progressive Primary Health Care Network (NPPHCN), was forced to sack half its staff for lack of funds. This meant the closure of most of the region's AIDS projects – in Khayelitsha, Namaqualand, the Karoo, the Boland, all areas without any State-sponsored programmes.

Said Mpho, 'The big frustration is we're no way as infected yet as kwaZulu/Natal and the PWV. Here we've a chance to stop it – we should be working overtime, not sacked! Now what can I do? I've three small kids' – she pointed to them, being entertained by Grandad. 'And I've a husband in jail for five years for "possession" – how can I work without pay? I can only do a little, in spare time, at weekends.'

The three Scotch victims were by now sitting up, looking cross-eyed and silently combating dehydration with a giant bottle of Coke provided by kind Tony.

This proved to be another 'open' visit for well-behaved prisoners. While Sarah and her husband sat holding hands I found myself delegated to talk to Luyunda and Prosper, 19-year-olds whose relatives all live in the Transkei. Likeable lads they are, with cheerful open faces – sentenced last December to ten and twelve years, respectively, for 'possession'. As 15-year-olds they came together from their village, joined the ANC Youth League, moved around the fringes of small-time Mandrax dealing, eventually were accepted as members of an SDU and soon after were arrested. A hope that soon some amnesty will include them underpins their stoicism. They seem to feel no resentment towards the Western Cape ANC leadership for having encouraged the keeping of weapons, then abandoned many of those charged with that offence. If released now they would show the police where other guns are hidden and co-operate with them in every way, as directed by Madiba. Or so they said . . . Both assured me that all they want is to find jobs and live peacefully with maybe a little mandrax-dealing on the side. They seem to see no harm in that commercial activity but admitted it could be dangerous – less because of police activity than because of Coloured gangs resenting blacks getting onto the scene. These youngsters do not strike one as 'baddies' but they are without a moral compass. If they fail to find steady jobs, one can easily imagine them becoming professional criminals. As easily, one can imagine them becoming like Tony, a happily married, happily employed ex-prisoner, a respectable citizen of the new South Africa.

Back at No. 7164, Blossom and Beauty had borrowed extra oil stoves and were cooking Christmas dinner: a pot of rice, stewed chicken and beef, mashed butternut and boiled potatoes, a salad of raw cabbage and grated carrot with mayonnaise. Never have I seen such a meal in Khayelitsha. It was being prepared for eleven children, aged 8 to 14 – all members of Blossom's extended family for whom, as an earner, she now feels some responsibility. The food was tipped into one enormous tin basin and served on the coffee table in the centre of the living-room floor. Nobody sat down, the whole group crowded around the basin, jostling for position, and at once the six boys snatched all the chunks of meat leaving not so much as a chicken wing for the girls. There is an urgency about the ingestion of food when one is really hungry that has nothing to do with greed. This was a race – who could eat fastest, get most – and with twenty-two hands and eleven plastic spoons it took less than six frantic minutes to empty the basin. Then there was a fight – a real fight, not horseplay – between two of the older boys for a bone with scraps of gristle attached.

Aki had invited Georgina and me to eat Shoprite Christmas cake and drink rooibos tea; her black Church forbids not only alcohol but ordinary tea and coffee – 'unnatural stimulants'. This year the portable TV, squatting amidst the Taiwanese china menagerie, is usable and never switched off. 'I don't care for all this American nonsense,' said Aki a trifle defensively. 'But the girls love it and it keeps them out of mischief.' Her three daughters now have secure jobs. 'For the educated, affirmative action is working well,' she acknowledged.

A freelance photographer arrived then; Aki always sends a Christmas Day family-group picture to the Transkei. It took me a few moments to recognize Phineas, my first Khayelitsha friend, who by now has found a replacement for his broken camera. An NGO which sponsors individual enterprise enabled him to take a photography course and he has recently sold three pictures to Cape Town newspapers.

Many of the poorest Khayelitsha residents have never seen the sea, close as it is. So I had invited eight adults (all, except Georgina, the mothers of small children) to spend 26 December on Muizenberg beach, setting off at 9 a.m. in a chartered taxi. But then mysterious difficulties arose, to do with *which* taxi . . .

Three argumentative hours later, a non-taxi arrived to collect us, an awesomely decrepit little van driven by a small slim young SANCO leader appropriately if improbably named Golden Sands Msiza ('Call me Goldie'). 'We can't all fit in,' was my first not unreasonable reaction. But I should have known better. Africans, when spatially challenged, defy reason. The positioning of seventeen bodies within that van took time, then jerkily we were on our way, Georgina and I squeezed beside Goldie with a pair of toddlers apiece on our laps.

'This is illegal,' said Goldie cheerfully. 'But at holiday seasons the boere don't notice.'

Georgina, true to form, snorted scornfully. 'At every season the boere make trouble!'

I have had my share of the Peninsula's midwinter gales, now I was to experience the midsummer variety. During our three-hour wait a strong wind had blown up – and on the coast road it reached Force 9. Slowly we drove through a blinding sandstorm. Despite all the windows being closed, fine grains quickly penetrated this antique vehicle, turning black faces fawn. The toddlers rubbed their eyes and wailed. On our left raged the sea, its beaches deserted. I realized then that my 'treat' was doomed.

Muizenberg is overdeveloped, the most popular beach on False Bay, aggressively dominated by a solitary skyscraper – wide as well as high, visible for miles in every direction, desecrating the mighty mountain immediately behind it. Once this was 'white territory'. Now, as the only beach accessible by public transport, it is almost entirely taken over by blacks on national holidays when most whites (and the better-off Coloureds) go elsewhere. On such occasions Muizenberg is supposed to be an alcohol-free zone but many overcome this little local difficulty by arriving equipped with mega-bottles of Coke pre-laced with brandy. Takeaways abound, drug dealers lurk within the public lavatories and the brightly painted pavilion houses a fast-food restaurant reeking of overused cooking oil. Normally I would do a long detour to avoid Muizenberg.

Goldie decanted us in a car park, slightly sheltered from the gale by the surrounding buildings, and promised to collect us at 5.30. When we ventured beachwards, struggling against the wind, stinging sand flayed us and all the children began to sob and had to be picked up and enfolded in maternal garments. Hastily we retreated towards the pavilion, via a raised concrete walkway thronged with jolly young blacks.

We were halfway across when a piercing scream – a scream of pure terror – attracted general attention. It came from a lower walkway and looking down I saw, directly below me, a young Coloured woman who had been thrown to the ground. She was lying with her legs wide apart being kicked all over – but especially in the genitals – by three black youths. What happened next will haunt me for a long time. On our level everyone crowded to the railings and cheered on the youths. Everyone. Including my companions, with their excited little children standing on tiptoe to see what was happening. Mob hysteria – a mad relish for violence – had taken over within seconds. One could feel it charging the atmosphere, dreadfully uniting this throng.

I stood staring down, doubly paralysed – by the barbarity itself and by the mass reaction to it. I have no doubt that my companions would have enjoyed witnessing the death of the young woman. This was a stage worse than enjoying the necklacing of someone perceived as a 'sell-out'. This was enjoying vicious brutality as sheer entertainment. The world seemed to have gone off its axis. Light-heartedly we had left Khayelitsha to have fun by the seaside and now evil had engulfed us.

Murder would almost certainly have been done but for the intervention, within moments, of two shouting Coloured police officers waving cocked guns. The attackers fled, the police pursued them and two Coloured youths picked up the young woman – by then unconscious – and carried her away. What was it all about? No one seemed to know or care. Once the visible violence ceased, the atmosphere reverted to normal. As suddenly as it had flared up, the blood-lust died down. We went on our way, everyone except me chatting and laughing – in party mood again.

Georgina took my arm and said, 'Don't be upset. This is how we are. You like to be with black people so you take it how it comes – right?'

Faintly I smiled and said, 'Right!'

While my companions consumed stacks of fast foods I longed for a very stiff drink. Then I asked myself if I had been overreacting? That relish for violence – is 'evil' too strong a word? Is 'degenerate' nearer the mark? Or 'desensitized'? Many young blacks were raised amidst extreme violence, both government-inflicted and internecine, in communities vulnerable to every sort of manipulation and intimidation. Or was I now trying to excuse the inexcusable? I asked Georgina would it have been different were the victim black. 'Yes,' she replied, 'because she was Coloured there was a reason for it.' Then my friend looked away and I could see her reprimanding herself. She is an honest person and brave enough to confront her own confusions. Looking back at me she said, 'That's bad – and I could be wrong, maybe we just like any sort of excitement – that kind of excitement ... It's bad, I know it's bad. But always you get a buzz from it. I can't explain it, it's like an addiction, like brandy or mandrax.'

I said no more. There was no more to be said.

Goldie was late. For half an hour we sat waiting for him; luckily the gale had calmed to a strong wind. Overhead the sky was clear but sinuous clouds were hurrying along the mountains, moulding themselves to the shapes of the crests – sunset clouds, pale gold above ink-blue slopes. Then I thought I was seeing an exotic bird, floating between two high ridges in the near distance. In fact it was a large solitary piece of litter, rising and falling, doing a solo ballet in the erratic air currents. Sometimes it almost touched the ground, then again soared very high, then swooped this way and that, all the time changing shape – from rippling snake to crescent moon to straight line to triangular sail. Never before have I seen beauty in a piece of litter.

My last day in Khayelitsha was spent with the 'Gang of Four': Aki, Muriel, Pius and Sam, my middle-aged ANC community leader friends. They are uneasy about the future. Not only the younger generation in Khayelitsha feel alienated from – almost rejected by – their new government. This has nothing to do, emphasized Pius, with 'unreasonable expectations'. It is much more complicated, a hurtful awareness of a gulf having opened up between the ruling élite and the millions whose courageous opposition to the old regime enabled black politicians to gain power and suddenly become conspicuously rich. The Struggle, as Sam pointed out, was unifying. From world-famous Nelson Mandela to the anonymous 12-year-old revolutionaries in every township, all were in it together. At that time the foot-soldiers never foresaw – how could they? – that Liberation would split the ranks, leaving them still hungry though equal before the law.

While blacks and whites got together to form a new controlling class, apparently for their own mutual benefit...

But the bitterest humiliation/disillusion, at the end of the generation-long Struggle, has to do with being suddenly uninvolved, unimportant, without a role. This is a cruel paradox, as Aki noted. In theory the vote gets every citizen politically involved. Yet it was the Struggle, rather than the exercising of the franchise, that gave the blacks a feeling of shared responsibility for their country's future.

On 9 May 1994, having watched the first all-inclusive South African Parliament assembling, I wrote in my journal: 'This is indeed a Government of National Unity – heroes and villains, the honest and the dishonest, the brilliant and the dim-witted, idealists and schemers, rabid racists and fervent liberals, all on their way to vote unanimously for a black President...' My mood was uncritical, sentimental; the momentousness of the occasion – the victory of Good over Evil, Freedom replacing Apartheid – blotted out all other considerations.

Eight months later, Pius commented that expediency had to dictate who got the top jobs. There were too many waiting to torpedo the new ship of State unless they were up on the bridge. So of course there are bad guys (black, white, Indian, Coloured) holding some of those jobs, in Cabinet and elsewhere – their misdeeds common knowledge. Aki argued that this makes the new ship of State seem leaky. If the first 'free and fair' elections could not produce an entirely respectworthy crew, why should people be expected to see democracy as the begetter of honest government?

To cheer everyone up (including myself) I pointed out that *uhuru* has brought about one hugely significant change: future wrongdoers will lead much less comfortable lives with the sword of exposure hanging over their heads. This country is healthily thirsty for freedom of information and freedom of speech, liberties abhorred and outlawed by the old regime. Nowadays bureaucratic inefficiency is exposed. Educational chaos is exposed. Racial discrimination is exposed. Diplomatic ineptitude is exposed. Political cupidity is exposed. Regularly dirty linen is washed openly on the riverside of public opinion. It is even possible for new South Africans to sniff the dirtiest linen of all, still hidden in the laundry basket awaiting the attention of the Truth and Reconciliation Commission.

Florida, 5 January 1995

Tonight I fly home – not, this time, consoled by the thought of a fixed return date. Yet away in the future there must be a return, so numerous and well loved are my South African friends, not all of whom can be persuaded to visit me in

Ireland. Moreover, I have become inexplicably attached to this crazy country – to use a favourite South African adjective.

Often my experiences here have been emotionally gruelling – some verging on the traumatic – but strong bonds are forged in high emotional temperatures. And there is an addictive quality about South Africa's pattern of paradoxes, its patchwork quilt of mass-produced prejudices and disarming unpredictabilities. Within this liberated Republic co-exist genuine political idealism and silly political posturing, fractured 'Struggle' alliances and new enthusiastic black/ white collaborations, pride in the 'peaceful transition' and panic about the soaring crime rate, comic-opera dissensions and numerous rumours of sinister conspiracies, reverence for reconciliation and lethal feuding, concessions to expediency and campaigns against those concessions, fine words contradicted by devious deeds, throbbing open wounds and ingenious healing compromises, paranoid suspicions and touching trust, wary cynicism and a determination to 'make the new South Africa work'.

Will it work? Despite my well-founded doubts about this unique experiment, I do have hope (hope rather than faith) that eventually justice will prevail – though the mechanism whereby it could do so at present remains invisible. It would be good to return in, say, five years' time and discover that my doubts were not, after all, well-founded. Sometimes it is exhilarating to be proved wrong.

Glossary

AAC Anglo American Corporation

amakhanda Zulu military quarters

amakhosi chiefs

amasi fermented milk

ANC African National Congress

APLA Azanian People's Liberation Army

ASM Azanian Students' Movement

AWB Afrikaner Weerstandsbeweging

Azapo Azanian People's Organization

baas boss

baasskap white tyranny over blacks

bakkie small pick-up van

BC Black Consciousness

BCMA Black Consciousness Movement of Azania

biltong strips of salted and dried meat

bittereinder Boer commando who fought to the end of the Anglo-Boer War

Black Sash anti-apartheid white women's organization (usually middle-class, middle-aged, English-speaking women) founded in 1955 and famous for its members' courage

boere (derogatory) police, specifically security police, and prison warders

boerebiskuite substantial homemade biscuits

boerewors large sausages

Bop the ex-'homeland' of Bophuthatswana

BOSS Bureau of State Security

boy (derogatory) male servant of any age

braaivleis (braai) barbecue

brakbos heathery plant with tiny dark blue flower

Broederbond an Afrikaner Masonic-type semi-secret society founded in 1918, powerful in the setting up of apartheid

bywoner tenant farmer

Codesa Convention for a Democratic South Africa

Contralesa Congress of Traditional Leaders of South Africa

coolie (derogatory) a South African of Indian descent

coon   (derogatory) a Cape Coloured person
COSAS   Congress of South African Students
COSATU   Council of South African Trade Unions
CP   Conservative Party
dagga   cannabis
dassies   rock-rabbits
DCC   Directorate of Covert Collection
DEIC   Dutch East India Company
dominee   Dutch Reformed Church minister
donga   ditch
dorp   village or small town
DP   Democratic Party
DRC   Dutch Reformed Church
ET   Eugene Terre' Blanche (AWB leader)
FNB   First National Bank
FW   Frederik Willem de Klerk (NP leader)
fynbos   indigenous heather-like scrub
GNU   Government of National Unity
IEC   Independent Electoral Commission
IFP   Inkatha Freedom Party
IMF   International Monetary Fund
impi   Zulu footsoldiers
impimpi   spies or informers
indaba   formal collection
ISU   Internal Stability Unit (of SAP)
jolling   enjoying a jolly social occasion
kaffir   (derogatory) a black person
kaffirboetie   'nigger-lover'
kombi   minibus
kraal   African homestead, traditionally with cattle-protecting fence
KZP   kwaZulu Police
ladies bar   whites' bar
lekker   good, nice, approved of
LMS   London Missionary Society
lobola   bride price
mealie/mealie-meal   maize
meerkat   ground squirrel
mense   white people, who are 'human'
MI   Military Intelligence
MK   Umkhonto weSizwe (pre-election armed wing of ANC)
MPLA   Popular Movement for the Liberation of Angola

munts (derogatory) blacks

muti traditional medicines or magical concoctions

muzungu white person

Nats the National Party, which established Grand Apartheid

NCRC National Children's Rights Committee

NEON National Elections Observer Network

NGO Non-Governmental Organization

nooi polite form for addressing a woman or sweetheart; servile form for addressing a white woman

NP National Party

NUM National Union of Miners

Numsa National Union of Metal Workers of South Africa

Nusas National Union of South African Students

Obs Observatory, a district of Cape Town

ouma grandma

oupa grandpa

PAC Pan-Africanist Congress, founded in 1959 by those who rejected the Freedom Charter's non-racist ideology

pap thick mealie porridge

public bar blacks' bar

PWV Pretoria-Witwatersrand-Vereeniging (region around Johannesburg, renamed Gauteng after the elections of 1994)

RDP Reconstruction and Development Programme

rondavel round thatched hut

RTZ Rio Tinto Zinc

SAAF South African Air Force

SAAU South African Agricultural Union

SABC South African Broadcasting Corporation

SACC South African Council of Churches

SACP South African Communist Party

SADF South African Defence Force (changed to SANDF on 27 April 1994)

SANCO South African National Civic Organization

SANDF South African National Defence Force

sangoma traditional healer

SAP South African Police (changed to SAPS on 27 April 1994)

SAPPI South African Paper and Pulp Industries

SAPS South African Police Service

SASCO South African Students' Congress

SDU Self-Defence Unit

skepsels non-white people, who are 'creatures'

slagveld battlefield

snoek   South African barracuda

SOMAFCO   the Solomon Mahlangu Freedom College, established by the ANC at Mazimbu in Tanzania

stoep   verandah

swart gevaar   'black peril'

TEC   Transitional Executive Council

TLC   Transitional Local Council

tokoloshe   malevolent spirit who appears in the form of a hairy dwarf

township   residential area to which blacks were consigned under apartheid laws, always at some distance from white areas

toyi-toyi   dance performed in mass demonstrations and to celebrate victory

trekboer   nomadic stock-farmer who gradually migrated north from the Cape during the eighteenth century

Tripartite Alliance   alliance between the African National Congress (ANC), the South African Communist Party (SACP) and the Congress of South African Trade Unions (COSATU)

tsotsi   township hooligan

TTC   Teacher Training College

tuinhuis   a farmer's town house

ubuntu   African view of the individual in relation to the community, with emphasis on the greater importance of the community

UCT   University of Cape Town

UDF   United Democratic Front

uitlander   foreigner

umzi   group of huts

Unisa   University of South Africa

USAID   US Aid for International Development

UWC   University of the Western Cape

UZ   University of Zululand

Vaalies   (mildly derogatory) white inhabitants of the Transvaal

Vierkleur   four-coloured flag of the old Transvaal Republic

volkstaat   independent homeland for Afrikaners

Voortrekker   participant in the Boers' Great Trek of 1838 from the Cape Colony to Natal and the Transvaal

WHO   World Health Organization

WM&G   *Weekly Mail & Guardian*

Young Lions   members of the ANC Youth League and other youngsters previously involved in the Struggle to 'make South Africa ungovernable' and win liberation

ZCC   Zionist Christian Church

Select Bibliography

Alexander, Neville, *Some Are More Equal than Others* (Buchu Books: 1993)

Amato, Rob, *Understanding the New Constitution* (Struik: 1994)

Attwell, Michael, *South Africa: Background to the Crisis* (Sidgwick & Jackson: 1986)

Barber, James, & Barratt, John, *South Africa's Foreign Policy* (CUP: 1990)

Borstelmann, Thomas, *Apartheid's Reluctant Uncle: The USA and South Africa in the Early Cold War* (OUP: 1993)

Bot, Monica, *The Blackboard Debate* (South Africa Institute of Race Relations: 1990)

Breytenbach, Breyten, *Return to Paradise* (Faber & Faber: 1993)

Brotz, Howard, *The Politics of South Africa: Democracy and Racial Diversity* (OUP: 1977)

Bryce, James, *Impressions of South Africa* (Macmillan: 1900)

Burman, Sandra (ed.), *Growing Up in a Divided Society* (Northwestern University Press: 1986)

Cawthra, Gavin, *Policing South Africa* (Zed Books: 1993)

Christie, Pam, *Open Schools* (Ravan Press: 1990)

Cope, Nicholas, *To Bind the Nation: Soloman kaDinuzulu* (University of Natal Press: 1993)

Davids, Achmat, *The Mosques of Bo-Kaap* (South African Institute of Arabic and Islamic Research: 1980)

Davids, Achmat, & da Costa, Yusuf, *Pages from Cape Muslim History* (Shuter & Shooter: 1994)

Dean, Elizabeth; Hartmann, Paul; Katzen, May, *History in Black and White* (Unesco: 1983)

Davis, Stephen M., *Apartheid's Rebels: Inside South Africa's Hidden War* (Yale University Press: 1987)

de Klerk, W. A., *The Puritans in Africa* (Penguin: 1976)

Desmond, Cosmas, *The Discarded People* (Penguin: 1971)

de Villiers, Marq, *White Tribe Dreaming* (Viking: 1988)

de Wet, Christiaan Rudolph, *Three Years' War* (Charles Scribners: 1902)

Doyle, Arthur Conan, *The Great Boer War* (Nelson: 1900)

Duff Gordon, Lady, *Letters from the Cape: 1861-6* (Humphrey Milford: 1921)

Emden, Paul H., *Randlords* (Hodder & Stoughton: 1935)

Fugard, Athol, *Notebooks 1960/1977* (Faber & Faber: 1983)

Gibbs, Henry, *Twilight in South Africa* (Jarrolds: 1950)

Goldstuck, Arthur, *Ink in the Porridge: Urban Legends of the South African Elections* (Penguin: 1994)

Gordimer, Nadine, *The Essential Gesture* (Jonathan Cape: 1988)

Graham Botha, C., *Social Life in the Cape Colony During the Eighteenth Century* (Struik: 1970)

Harrison, David, *The White Tribe of Africa* (BBC: 1981)

Hattersley, Alan F., *Portrait of a Colony* (CUP: 1940)

Hockly, H. E., *The Story of the British Settlers of 1810 in South Africa* (Juta: 1957)

Hofmeyr, Isabel, *'We Spend Our Years as a Tale that is Told'* (Witwatersrand University Press: 1993)

Hofmeyr, Jan H., *South Africa* (Ernest Benn: 1931)

Horowitz, Donald L., *A Democratic South Africa?* (OUP: 1991)

James, Wilmot G., *Our Precious Metal* (Indiana University Press: 1992)

Johnson, K. W., *How Long Will South Africa Survive?* (Macmillan: 1977)

Johnson, Shaun, *Strange Days Indeed* (Bantam: 1993)

Kane-Berman, John, *South Africa's Silent Revolt* (Institute of Race Relations, 1990)

Laband, John, & Thompson, Paul, *Kingdom and Colony at War* (University of Natal Press, 1990)

Laband, John, *King Cetshwayo kaMpande* (Shuter & Shooter: 1980)

—— *Fight Us in the Open* (Shuter & Shooter: 1985)

—— *The Battle of Ulundi* (Shuter & Shooter: 1988)

Leach, Graham, *The Afrikaners: Their Last Great Trek* (Macmillan: 1989)

Lelyveld, Joseph, *Move Your Shadow* (Michael Joseph: 1986)

Levine, June, *Inside Apartheid* (Contemporary Books: 1988)

Lewin, Hugh, *Bandiet: Seven Years in a South African Prison* (David Philip: 1981)

Lukhele, Andrew Khehla, *Stokvels in South Africa* (Amagi Books: 1990)

Malan, Rian, *My Traitor's Heart* (Bodley Head: 1990)

Mall, Thami, *Chris Hani: The Sun that Set before Dawn* (Sached Books: 1993)

McKendrick, Brian, & Hoffmann, Wilma (eds), *People and Violence in South Africa* (OUP: 1990)

Molebatsi, Caesar, *A Flame for Justice* (Lion Paperbacks: 1991)

Morris, James, *South African Winter* (Faber & Faber: 1958)

Morton, H. V., *In Search of South Africa* (Methuen: 1948)

Mostert, Noel, *Frontiers* (Jonathan Cape: 1992)

Motlhabi, Mokgethi, *Towards a New South Africa* (Skotaville: 1992)

Ndebele, Njabulo S., *Rediscovery of the Ordinary* (COSAW: 1991)

Oden, Rertil, & Othman, Haroub (eds), *Regional Co-operation in Southern Africa: A Post-Apartheid Perspective* (Institute of African Studies, Uppsala: 1989)

Pakenham, Thomas, *The Boer War* (Cardinal: 1991)

Palmer, Eve, *The Plains of Camdeboo* (Collins: 1966)

Pampallis, John, *Foundations of the New South Africa* (Maskew Miller Longman: 1991)

Peires, J. B., *The Dead Will Arise* (Ravan Press: 1989)

Perham, Margery, *African Apprenticeship* (Faber & Faber: 1974)

Preller, Gustav S., *Day Dawn in South Africa* (Wallachs: 1938)

Reed, Daniel, *Beloved Country: South Africa's Silent Wars* (BBC: 1994)

Rex, John (ed.), *Apartheid and Social Research* (Unesco: 1981)

Roberts, Brian, *Cecil Rhodes* (Hamish Hamilton: 1987)

Schire, Robert, *Adapt or Die: The End of White Politics in South Africa* (Ford Foundation: 1991)

Smith, Ken, *The Changing Past* (Southern Books: 1988)

Smuts, J. C., *Freedom* (Alexander Maclehose: 1934)

Sparks, Allister, *The Mind of South Africa* (Heinemann: 1990)

—— *Tomorrow is Another Country* (Struik: 1994)

Suzman, Helen, *In No Uncertain Terms* (Sinclair-Stevenson: 1993)

Todd, Pamela, & Fordham, David (eds), *Private Tucker's Boer War Diary* (Elm Tree Books: 1980)

Tomaselli, Keyan & Ruth, *John Muller Narrating the Crisis: Hegemony and the South African Press* (Richard Lyon: 1987)

Troup, Freda, *In Face of Fear* (Faber & Faber: 1950)

—— *South Africa: An Historical Introduction* (Eyre Methuen: 1972)

Uhlig, Mark A. (ed.), *Apartheid in Crisis* (Penguin: 1986)

van der Post, Laurens, & Taylor, Jane, *Testament to the Bushmen* (Viking: 1984)

van der Post, Laurens, *Venture to the Interior* (Hogarth Press: 1952)

—— *The Dark Eye in Africa* (Hogarth Press: 1955)

—— *A Mantis Carol* (Hogarth Press: 1975)

van Wyk, At, *The Birth of a New Afrikaner* (Human & Rousseau: 1991)

van Zyl Slabbert, F., *The System and the Struggle* (Jonathan Ball: 1989)

Venter, Al J., *Coloured: A Profile of Two Million South Africans* (Human & Rousseau: 1974)

Walker, Eric A., *The Great Trek* (A&C Black: 1948)

Wells, A. W., *South Africa* (Dent: 1939)

Winter, Gordon, *Inside BOSS: South Africa's Secret Police* (Penguin: 1981)

Round Table on Apartheid (Unesco: 1979)

Changing Fortunes: War, Diplomacy and Economics in Southern Africa (Ford Foundation: 1992)

South Africa: Inside Guides (APA Publications: 1992)

Annual Race Relations Survey for 1991/92, 1992/93, 1993/94, 1994/95 (South African Institute for Race Relations)

Index

Abdullah Kadi Abdus Salaan, Imam, 124
Abe (of Messina township), 12–15
Adam, Alfred (of Eshowe, *fl.* 1881), 316
affirmative action, 176, 251, 274, 360, 374, 391;
  for educated/skilled, 39, 403, 410
African National Congress, *see* ANC
Afrikaanse Studentebond Congress, 122
Afrikaans language, 74, 113, 122, 124–5
Afrikaners, xii, 286–7; adaptability, 48, 341;
  aggression, 11–12, 298–9, 318–19; ANC
  members, 390; and blacks, 22, 73, 264, 286–7,
  290, 318–19, 341; Cape, 31, 131; Coloureds'
  cultural bonds, 122, 125, 131; conformity, 12,
  48, 103–4; English language, 106, 114, 124,
  286, 292; and English-speakers, 23–4, 75, 76,
  112; hospitality, 72; humourless, 43–4, 77,
  187, 400; inbreeding, 18; laagerism, 48, 75–6,
  302; liberal, 131, 168, 172; moderate, 75, 78,
  167–8; in new South Africa 261, 264, 274,
  286–7, 288, 341; non-racist, 321; non-white
  genes, 122; north Transvaal, 11–12, 31, 43–4,
  117, 341; stoic majority, 264; as a tribe, 23,
  75–6; *see also* AWB; Boers; DRC
Agricultural Unions, 81–2, 86–7
AIDS, 335–7, 343; education, 9, 36, 228, 378, 385,
  408–9; ignorance about, 20, 30, 47, 150, 204,
  228, 338, 378, 382; related diseases, 36, 170,
  204, 361; scares, 190–1, 195–6
Aki (of Khayelitsha), 410, 412–13
Albanus (of Duiwelskloof), 22
Albany (of Khayelitsha), 137–8, 150, 155–7, 161
Alexandra township, 12, 15, 61
Alf and Muriel (Rhodesians, of Jo'burg), 87–9
Algeria, 366
Aliwal North, 388–9
Alt, Jennifer, 57, 63, 69, 212, 218, 219
amakhosi, see chiefs
ANC (African National Congress): chanting, 162,
  158, 159, 161, 162; and chiefs, 380; and
  Coloureds, 170, 208, 250; corruption
  charges, 366; effects of victory, 283, 412–13;
  ex-prisoners, 165–6; and IFC, 65, 68, 217, 220,
  232–3, 236, 248, 308, 314; Mandela holds
  together, 252; and MK, 51, 155, 339;
  non-assassination policy, 149; non-black
  members, 170, 208, 390; and PAC, 55, 56, 140,
  147, 161, 201, 387; political education, 67–8,
  146; –SACP/COSATU alliance, 51, 66; Soviet

support, 67, 68; in townships, 134, 135, 392,
  393–5; training camps abroad, 9, 67, 339;
  uncontrolled elements, 118, 236; Western
  democratic values, 385; white attitudes to, 116,
  118; and white authorities, 60, 61, 67, 68–9;
  Women's League, 158, 162, 232; and women's
  rights, 295, 324; Youth League, 53, 57, 59, 67,
  118, 243, (and PAC), 55, 140, (rallies), 144–6,
  157–62, (SDUS), 61, 70; *see also* boycotts;
  stayaways; *and individual leaders*
Andrew (Rachel Murphy's partner), 272, 274,
  356
Andries (Bloemhof sheep-farmer), 84, 85
Anglican Church, 209, 279–80, 378
Anglo-Boer Wars, 71, 74–5, 94, 112, 260, 357;
  campaigns, 331–2, 344–5, 348–51; experts
  on, 220, 350–1
Anglo-Zulu War, 190, 227–8, 311–12, 316, 322,
  332; Isandlwana, 311, 312, 326, 327–9
Angola, xii, 9, 67, 114, 154, 237, 346–7
Ann (UCT lecturer), 173
anthems, national, 241
Antonia (of Khayelitsha), 141–2
Anyberg, 178
apartheid, xiv–xv, 30, 74–5, 76, 166, 326; and
  Coloureds, 122, 128; DM's experience of,
  14–15, 197–8; limited effect of repeal, xv, 14,
  27, 29, 48, 155, 289
APLA (Azanian People's Liberation Army), 12,
  384, 386; violence, 29, 118, 145n, 184, 206
Arabs, Venda intermarriage with, 20
arms trade, 353–5, 357
Asbestos Mountain, 92
asbestosis, 33, 34, 35
Asmal, Kader, 137, 255, 382
Assembly of God, 34
Athlone, 257
Atomic Energy Board, South African, 55
Audrey (Tugela Ferry AIDS counsellor), 335–6
AWB (Afrikaner Weerstandsbeweging), 73, 74–5,
  85, 86; Day of Action against, 167–8;
  Day of the Vow, 397, 398–400; disrupt
  negotiations, 166–7; DM's encounters, 46–8,
  69, 73, 74–5; pre-election period, 217, 230,
  237, 246; and SADF/SAP, 52–3, 86, 166–7; and
  van Jaarsveld, 265; Waluz in, 69; *see also* Terre'
  Blanche, Eugene
Azanian People's Liberation Army, *see* APLA